OUTLINES

OF

UNIVERSAL HISTORY,

FROM THE

CREATION OF THE WORLD

TO

THE PRESENT TIME.

TRANSLATED FROM THE GERMAN OF

DR. GEORGE WEBER,

PROFESSOR AND DIRECTOR OF THE HIGH SCHOOL OF HEIDELBERG,

BY

DR. M. BEHR,

PROFESSOR OF GERMAN LITERATURE IN WINCHESTER COLLEGE.

REVISED AND CORRECTED, WITH THE ADDITION

OF

A HISTORY OF THE UNITED STATES OF AMERICA,

BY

FRANCIS BOWEN, A. M.,

ALFORD PROFESSOR OF NATURAL RELIGION, MORAL PHILOSOPHY
AND CIVIL POLITY, IN HARVARD COLLEGE

FOURTEENTH EDITION.

BOSTON:
HICKLING, SWAN AND BREWER.
CLEVELAND:
INGHAM AND BRAGG.
1859.

Entered according to act of Congress, in the year 1853,

By Jenks, Hickling, and Swan,

In the Clerk's Office of the District Court of the District of Massachusetts

PREFACE.

The Translator of this work makes the following extract from the Author's preface to the German edition.

"Believing that a Guide to History can answer its object only when it awakens the interest of the pupil, stimulates his desire for information, and excites his zeal for inquiry, I have everywhere arrayed the historical material in a narrative form, and have endeavored to give clearness, consistency, and animation to that form. My effort has been so to bring together the events of the world's history in their more prominent aspects and decisive moments, that the reader may obtain a clear idea of them; that the important facts may be exhibited together with their causes and consequences, and thus be more strongly impressed upon the imagination, and consequently upon the memory; and that the course of the narrative may not be disturbed or broken by interpolations or remarks which might require a further explanation. Instead of following the usual course of compendiums, textbooks, and outlines, by heaping up a mass of materials in the smallest possible space, and thus forming a kind of skeleton register of the events of history, I have rather endeavored to limit my materials, giving place only to the most important and influential, and arranging these in historical succession. . . . . Mere historical events, with names and dates, are not easily retained by the memory, and do not possess any instructive or educative power. It is only when the historical fact is presented in combination with other objects, so that the imagination and thinking faculty are both employed upon it, that it permanently impresses itself upon the mind of youth."

The Translator justly adds, that "the book is written throughout in the spirit of orthodox Protestantism, and is entirely untinctured with the neology and infidelity at this time so prevalent in Germany."

Believing that the method here explained is the right one, and that the scheme is, in the main, carried out with fidelity and spirit, I have subjected the work to a thorough revision, in the hope of making it still more suitable for use as a textbook of instruction in American colleges and schools. Errors of the press and the pen had been multiplied by the translation and republication of the book in England; and the translation itself, though generally correct and elegant, was sometimes obscure and inadequate. Accuracy being an essential qualification of a school-book, every paragraph in these Outlines has been laboriously examined, and almost every name and date tested by reference to trustworthy sources of information. It would be rash to assert that it is now free from blemish; but it is certain that hundreds of small errors have been weeded out by this scrutinizing process. If any remain, it is hoped that they may be discovered and removed in a subsequent edition. A few notes have been added, sometimes to explain, and sometimes to qualify, statements in the text.

One very important defect was to be supplied before Dr. Weber's work could be considered worthy of republication in America. Except an imperfect sketch of the Revolutionary war, contained in four or five pages, the history of this country was entirely omitted. The gap thus left might have been cheaply filled by transcription and a judicious use of the scissors; but as the book would then have lacked unity of execution, I preferred to write out anew a sketch of the history of the United States, from the period of the first settlements at Jamestown and Plymouth, down to the peace of

1815. The addition thus made is considerable, as it occupies nearly one hundred pages, thus enlarging the bulk of the original about one fifth. It consists of three parts; — 1. a brief history of the Colonization of North America (pp. 291 — 314); 2. a sketch of the French and Indian wars during the first sixty years of the eighteenth century, followed by a history of the War of Independence and the formation of the Federal Constitution (pp. 342 - 388); and, 3. a summary of political events from 1789 to 1815 (pp. 468 — 491). In preparing these historical sketches, I have sedulously endeavored to follow Dr. Weber's original conception of his work, by passing lightly over all the details, and grouping together the leading events with a view to their causes and consequences. Only in this manner is it possible to preserve the interest of a continuous narrative, a proper distribution of light and shade, and a correct appreciation of personages and events, in a mere compend of history. The pages that are burdened with details are wearisome to read and difficult to remember. A compend of history must be a true compend, and not merely a complete history viewed through the wrong end of a telescope. The general plan, therefore, upon which these Outlines of History have been prepared, I am convinced, is a good one; time and use will bring to light the defects in its execution.

THE AMERICAN EDITOR.

CAMBRIDGE, February, 1853.

CONTENTS.

FIRST BOOK.

HISTORY OF THE ANCIENT WORLD.

INTRODUCTION, pp. 1—4.

A. THE EASTERN RACES, pp. 5—23.

B. HISTORY OF GREECE, pp. 23—67.

I. GREECE BEFORE THE PERSIAN WAR, pp. 26—38.

II. THE FLOURISHING PERIOD OF GREECE, p. 39.

III. THE MACEDONIAN PERIOD, p. 56.

THE ALEXANDRIAN PERIOD, p. 62.

C. THE HISTORY OF ROME, p. 68.

I. ROME UNDER THE GOVERNMENT OF KINGS AND PATRICIANS, p. 69.

II. ROME'S HEROIC PERIOD, p. 78.

II. THE MIGRATION OF NATIONS, pp. 117—125.

III. MOHAMMED AND THE ARABIANS, pp. 125—128.

B. THE MIDDLE AGE.

I. THE PERIOD OF THE CARLOVINGI, pp. 129—133.

II. NORMANS AND DANES, p. 133.

III. THE SUPREMACY OF THE GERMANO-ROMAN EMPIRE, p. 135.

IV. THE ASCENDANCY OF THE CHURCH IN THE TIME OF THE CRUSADES, p. 140.

V DECAY OF CHIVALRY AND CORRUPTION OF THE CHURCH, p. 163.

VI. HISTORY OF THE REMAINING EUROPEAN STATES DURING THE MIDDLE AGE, p. 176.

THIRD BOOK.

THE MODERN EPOCH.

I. THE FORERUNNERS OF THE MODERN EPOCH, p. 202.

II. THE TIME OF THE REFORMATION, p. 208.

III. THE SEVENTEENTH CENTURY, p. 256.

IV. THE COLONIZATION OF NORTH AMERICA, p. 291.

[A. D. 1606—1732.]

V. THE EIGHTEENTH CENTURY, p. 314.

VI. THE PROGRESS OF THE NEW WORLD.

FOURTH BOOK.

THE LATEST PERIOD.

D. DISSOLUTION OF THE FRENCH EMPIRE, AND ESTABLISHMENT OF A FRESH SYSTEM, p. 459.

E. THE UNITED STATES OF AMERICA, p. 468.

F. THE PEOPLE AND STATES OF EUROPE FROM THE HOLY ALLIANCE TO THE PRESENT TIME, p. 491.

BOOK FIRST.

HISTORY OF THE ANCIENT WORLD.

INTRODUCTION.

I. THE FIRST RACE OF MEN.

§ 1. After God in the beginning had created the heavens and the earth, had adorned the heavens with the sun, moon, and stars, had clothed the earth with plants, and animated it with living animals; he made man in his own image, the crown of creation, and designed him by the gifts of speech and reason for the ruler of the world. The first pair came forth pure and spotless from the hands of their Creator, and lived in childlike innocence in their native dwelling-place, Paradise, until seduced by the tempter, the serpent, they ate of the forbidden tree of knowledge, and, by this violation of the commands of God, lost their unconscious innocence and the possession of their first dwelling-place.

After this, they and their posterity were obliged to spend their lives in labor and trouble, and to eat their bread in the sweat of their face. Evil passions and desires were awakened, and disturbed the peace of society; the violent impulses of a savage and unrestrained nature plunged the later generations deeper and deeper into the disorders of vice and crime, till at length a great flood, called the deluge, destroyed the whole race, with the exception of Noah and his descendants, from the face of the earth. Noah's posterity, however, increased again so rapidly, that the later generations, descended from his three sons, Shem, Ham, and Japheth, were compelled to spread themselves abroad over the neighboring countries, on account of their home being no longer large enough to contain them. It then entered into their minds to erect the Tower of Babel, "whose top was to reach unto heaven,"* and to be a perpetual memorial to them. God frustrated this presumptuous attempt by confusing their language, and by this diversity of speech brought about their

* Gen. xi. 4.

separation. They dispersed themselves to all the four quarters of the earth, and colonized the three oldest divisions of the globe, Asia, Africa, and Europe, forming themselves into different peoples and nations, according to the varieties of their language.

II. THE MANNER OF LIVING AMONG THE EARLIEST RACES.

§ 2. Men chose different occupations and manners of living, according to the diversities in their places of residence. The inhabitants of steppes and deserts, interspersed only here and there with fruitful pasture grounds, chose the life of shepherds, and roved as wandering tribes from place to place, with their tents and herds. These are called nomads (wanderers), and their principal occupation is the breeding of cattle. Those who settled upon favorably situated parts of the sea-coast soon discovered, with increasing population and development, the advantages of their position. They practised navigation and commerce, and sought after wealth and comfort, and, in furtherance of these objects, were incited to lay out towns and erect elegant dwelling-houses; whilst the inhabitants of inhospitable shores supported a joyless existence by means of fisheries. Those who lived on plains devoted themselves to agriculture and the arts of peace; whilst the rude and hardy mountaineer gave himself up to the chase, and, urged on by a violent impulse for freedom, sought his delight in wars and battles.

By the taming of wild cattle, man procured for himself at an early period those indispensable assistants of labor, domesticated animals.

A mighty instrument in the civilization of the human race was commerce, and the intercourse among different nations that sprang out of it. Those who lived on fruitful plains, or on the banks of suitable rivers, carried on an inland trade; the dwellers on the shores, on the contrary, a coasting trade. At first, men exchanged one article for another (barter), and it was not till a later period that it occurred to them to fix a certain value upon the precious metals, and to employ coined money as an artificial and more convenient means of exchange. The inhabitants of towns addicted themselves to trade and inventions, and cultivated arts and sciences for the enriching and embellishment of life and the development of the human understanding.

III. FORMS OF GOVERNMENT. DISTINCTION OF CASTES.

§ 3. With the process of time, nations were divided into the civilized and uncivilized, according as the development of their intellectual powers was furthered by talents and commerce, or cramped by dulness and isolation. Uncivilized nations are either wild hordes, under the command of a chief who possesses uncontrolled power over life and death, or wandering nomadic tribes, guided by a leader, who, as father of the family, exercises the functions of prince, judge, and high priest. Neither these nomadic races with their patriarchal government, nor the wild hordes that dwell in the unknown deserts of Africa (Negroes), in the steppes and lofty mountain ranges of Asia, or in the primeval forests of America, find any place in history. This concerns itself only with those civilized nations, who, from similarity of manners and for mutual convenience, have united themselves in peaceful intercourse and fellowship.

States are divided into republican and monarchical, according to the form of their government or constitution. A state is called a monarchy, when a single person stands at the head and manages its affairs. This single person is called Emperor, or King, Duke, or Prince, according to the extent of his dominions. The term, Free State, or Republic, is given to that form of government in which the supreme power is placed in the hands of an elective body, composed of numerous members. The republican form of government is sometimes aristocratic, that is, when only a few families, distinguished by birth or wealth, govern the community; sometimes democratic, when the whole body of the people make the laws and select the responsible officers of government.

The most ancient states were simple and uniform in their forms of government, and possessed for the most part that great hinderance to freedom, the system of castes. By this is to be understood, a strict separation of men according to their states and callings, which descended in unalterable succession from father to son; by which means, all interchange of conditions, or passing from one state to another, was rendered impracticable. The priests, who alone possessed a knowledge of the religious customs and institutions, and who bequeathed their knowledge to their descendants, constituted the first caste. The second caste comprehended the soldiers, who were afterwards successful in raising themselves to an equality with the priestly condition. These two castes divided the government between them. The third caste were the cultivators of the soil. The fourth, the artisans. If shepherds constituted a distinct caste, they were the lowest and most despised. The institution of castes was preserved for the longest time, and in the greatest purity, in India and Egypt.

IV. THE RELIGION OF THE HEATHEN WORLD.

§ 4. As men dispersed themselves over the earth, the original belief in the one true God (Monotheism) was lost, and people fell into the worship of many deities (Polytheism), adoring the visible works of creation, more particularly the sun and the stars of heaven, instead of their Creator, or else reverencing the operative powers of nature as divine beings. The faith in a single divinity was preserved among the Jewish people alone, in the worship of their hereditary God, Jehovah. The religions of all other nations, diversified as they may be, are included under the term Paganism. Instead of regarding the Supreme Being, the Creator and Preserver of the universe, as a Spirit, and worshipping him in spirit and in truth, the ancient nations gave him the figure of a man, deified his different powers and attributes, and then represented them under the greatest variety of forms. Idols were fashioned from stone and metal, wood and clay; temples and altars were erected, and sacrifices offered to them; partly to appease their wrath, and partly to obtain their favor. The sacrifices varied in character with the civilization of the people who offered them. The Greeks and Romans instituted joyous festivals to their gods, in which the fruits that were presented, and the animals that were slain, from the modest gift of a firstling of the flock to the solemn sacrifice ot a hundred oxen, (hécatomb), were socially consumed; whilst savage tribes slaughtered human beings upon their altars, for the purpose of appeasing by blood the wrath of hostile powers, for such they considered their divinities to be. The Phœnician and Syrian tribes actually placed their own children in the arms of a red-hot idol, Moloch. If, at first, the image of the idol was only a visible symbol of a spiritual conception, or of an invisible power, this higher meaning was lost in the progress of time, in the minds of most nations, and they came at length to pay worship to the lifeless image itself. The priests alone were acquainted with any deeper meaning, but refused to share it with the people; they reserved it under the veil of esotéric (secret) doctrine, as the peculiar appanage of their own class. With the same object, they invented legends, stories, and fables about the gods whom they worshipped, clothed these in poetical forms, and thus gave origin to mythology, or the science of the gods. In these stories, the actions and histories of the different deities, and the relations of men in regard to them, are described, not in clear and intelligible language, but veiled in enigmatical allusions, allegorical histories, and figurative forms of expression. The greater the amount of creative imagination and religious impulse possessed by a nation, the richer is its mythology. If these legends of the gods served to excite the people to superstition, the solemn worship in the sacred spaces of the temple, with its mysterious ceremonies and symbolical usages, was no less calculated to maintain in them a feeling of veneration and religious awe; and, for the purpose of establishing a belief in the presence of God, and his interference in human affairs, more firmly, sacred places and temples of note were provided with oracles, from which the credulous multitude might gain information of the future, in obscure, and oftentimes ambiguous, language. In this way, the mind of man was led away from Divine Truth, and ensnared in lifeless ceremonies; the simple relations and inward tendency of the creature to the Creator were disturbed and torn asunder; the priesthood ruled the people by the might of superstition, and acquired wealth, honor, and power for themselves.

A. THE EASTERN RACES.

I. THE ASIATICS.

§ 5. Asia, called from its situation the Eastern land, was the cradle of the human race. The situation of Paradise must be sought for in the attractive neighborhood of the Himaláya mountains, the tops of which lose themselves in the clouds. In the East arose those great nations and cities whence other lands have derived a part of their civil institutions, their religion, and their culture, and which have consequently received the name of centres of civilization. In the East, the land of the camel, "the ship of the desert," first originated the splendid inland traffic called the caravan trade, which exercised so important an influence on the progress of human culture. For the purpose of more easily undergoing the difficulties and perils of lengthened journeys through regions but little known, and thickly inhabited by predatory tribes, the Eastern merchants assembled themselves in companies, and escorted their wares, packed upon camels, from one place to another, in large, and frequently armed, bands. These commercial journeys were the occasion for building towns and places for traffic, and for the erection of storehouses and caravansaries. They brought about intercourse between the inhabitants of distant places, and were the means of communicating not only the productions, but also the religious institutions and the social policy, of one land to another. Temples and oracles of celebrity frequently served for markets and warehouses. It was in the East that nearly all the varieties of religion took their origin, and gained their perfect development; not only the belief in one God, which prevailed among the Jews, and which afterwards reappeared with renewed strength and purity in Christianity, but the pagan worship of idols, in all its multiplied varieties, with its priestly power, its sacrifices, and its ceremonial worship. For upon every thing that concerns the relation of the creature to its Maker, the people of the East have thought most deeply and zealously, and have attained results at which no other nations have arrived.

The forms of Eastern governments and constitutions were less numerous than the religions. Among the nomadic races, the heads of the tribes ruled with patriarchal authority; in countries where the distinction of castes prevailed, the privileged classes were priests and soldiers. from both arose, in the course of time, the unlimited kingly power, (despotism), which gave to the ruler the uncontrolled sovereignty of the nomadic chief, and the religious sanctity of the priestly king. In this manner, the kingly authority gradually grew to such a height in the East, that the possessor shared a respect almost equal to that which was paid the Divinity. In relation to the ruler, all the officers of state were regarded as slaves and menials, without either personal rights or property The king disposed at will of the lives and possessions of his subjects ; he gave or took away at his pleasure ; and no one dared to appear in his presence, except with his body prostrated on the ground. He lived like a god, in the midst of pleasure and enjoyment, surrounded by slaves, who complied with his wishes, executed his commands, and submitted themselves to his pleasures ; and he was encircled by all the riches and possessions, by all the pomp and magnificence, of the earth. Such governments as these, in which law and human rights go for nothing, where despotism and slavery are alone to be met with, possess no vital energy and no capability of permanent civilization ; and for this reason, all oriental states have become the prey of foreign conquerors, and their early civilization has either been destroyed, or prevented from making farther advances.

By original disposition, the Orientals are more inclined to contemplative ease and enjoyment than to active exertion ; hence it has come to pass, that the Eastern nations have never attained to freedom or spontaneous activity, but have either silently submitted themselves to their native rulers, or groaned under the yoke of foreign oppressors.

By dint of their intellectual capacity, they quickly attained to a certain grade of civilization, but afterwards gave themselves up to an unenterprising pursuit of pleasure, until they gradually sunk into sloth and effeminacy. This effeminacy was further promoted by the practice of polygamy, a custom peculiar to the East, which is subversive of the family affections, and of the domestic purity and morality which are their attendants.

As regards the art of the Orientals, the gigantic designs of their buildings, and their incredible patience and perseverance in erecting and completing them, are most worthy of admiration ; but their architecture never displays the symmetry, the harmonious beauty, or the adaptation of means to ends, which characterize the architecture of a free people. The productions of their arts and industry afford evidence rather of manual dexterity, attained by long practice, and rendered inalienable by the tyranny of castes and guilds, than of inventive genius or active handicraft. Slavery hung like a leaden weight on every outward manifestation of life in the East.

II. THE CHINESE.

§ 6. As the progress of the human race has in general followed the course of the sun, it will be most advisable to commence its history with the tribes of the extreme East. In the vast empire of China has lived, since the earliest period, a race of Mongolian origin, which has preserved unchanged for ages the same culture and the same institutions. Every thing is there regulated by hereditary laws and customs, and freedom is entirely banished. This want of progressive development is occasioned partly by the tenacious character of the people, which induces them to cling fast to the customary and traditionary modes of living; partly by the empire being cut off, by mountains, seas, and the lofty and extensive wall of China, from all intercourse with foreign nations, and from all strangers being strictly prohibited from entering the kingdom; and is partly produced by political institutions. The emperor, who is possessed of absolute power, and regarded with almost religious veneration, and the numerous and privileged aristocratic class (mandarins), alike compel the slavish and despised people to a strict observance of their traditionary customs and usages, and deprive them of every thing new. As the Chinese are thus prevented from profiting by the experience of foreign nations, they remain inferior to other people in civilization; though they have been acquainted from the earliest ages with gunpowder, the art of printing, and the mariner's compass. Notwithstanding they have long been celebrated for their skill in the manufacture of silk, and in the preparation of porcelain, writing materials, carved work, and similar productions, their industry cannot be compared with the commercial activity and diligence in the arts of the cultivated states of the West. The object of their education is not such a development of the intellectual powers as would lead to the cultivation of the whole of the human faculties, but rather the teaching of that which their predecessors have known and practised before them. This education, this mode of life, and form of government, render the Chinese weak and cowardly; they entertain, nevertheless, the highest opinion of their own excellence, and regard all other nations with lofty contempt. Their language is so clumsy and difficult, that it requires several years to learn even to read it. The Chinese pay great respect to Confucius (Hong-fu-tse) as the founder of their religion.

B. C. 550.

III. THE INDIANS.

§ 7. To the south of the snow-covered heights of the lofty Himaláya, extends a fertile and prosperous region, blessed with a healthy and varying climate, and rich in productions of the most diversified character. In this land, watered by the Indus, the Ganges, and other large rivers, lived, ages ago, a remarkable people, called Hindoos, or Indians, whose former greatness is still attested by numerous buildings, ruins of towns and temples, surprising memorials in inscriptions on stone, and innumerable historical recollections.

The Indians are descended from the Aryans, who at one time undertook an expedition from their native highlands, and subjected the less powerful aborigines of India. They soon changed their native nomadic customs for the system of castes, which they adopted in its severest form.

The most important caste were the priests, a wealthy, honorable, and privileged class, who were called Brahmans, or Brahmins. This caste was considered sacred and inviolable; they could not be subjected to corporal punishment for any crime, they were exempt from taxation, formed the chief council of the king, and filled all offices. Next to the Brahmins came the warriors, who, in return for their pay and certain privileges, were responsible for the security and defence of the kingdom. As, however, the frequent necessity for waging war or encountering enemies was precluded by the remote situation of the country and the peaceful character of its inhabitants, these soldiers soon became slothful and degenerate, and thus rendered it easy for the priests to retain their political ascendancy. The kings belonged to the caste of soldiers. The farmers and artisans were heavily impressed with imposts, and held their land only in fee.* The Pariahs, from whom the Gipsies are said to be descended, are the dark-colored descendants of the wild aborigines, and are regarded by the other Indians as the refuse of mankind, and treated with the deepest contempt. "They do not venture to dwell in the towns, cities, or villages, or even in their neighborhood; every thing they touch is looked upon as unclean, and it is pollution even to have seen them." Any intermixture of castes, by means of marriage, was severely prohibited. Persons who were guilty of an infringement of this law, were cast out of society, and exposed to contempt. This rigorous division into castes, which the priests laid down as a divine ordinance, checked the progress of civilization, and was the occasion that it never passed beyond a certain point, and then lapsed into a state of repose and stagnation.

RELIGION, LITERATURE, ART.

§ 8. The Indians reverenced in Brahma a divine first principle, which appears under three forms, as Creator, Preserver, and Destroyer; and besides him, a crowd of spirits and inferior divinities. The central point of their religion is the doctrine of the transmigration of the soul (metempsychosis). According to this doctrine, the human soul is only joined to earthly bodies for the purposes of punishment, and its aim and effort are to again unite itself with the Divine Spirit of the universe. The Indian, therefore, regards existence in this world as a time of trial and punishment, which can only be abridged by a holy life, by prayer and sacrifice, by penance and purification. If man neglects this, and sinks himself still deeper into vice by departure from God, his soul after death will be joined to the body of a different and inferior animal, and will have to commence its wanderings afresh. On the other hand, the souls of the wise, of heroes and penitents, enter upon their upward path through shin-

* The phraseology here is ambiguous and not strictly correct. The actual cultivators of the soil had only a right of occupancy, not of ownership. *Am. Ed.*

ing stars, and are finally united with the spiritual first principle whence they proceeded. This doctrine was interpreted by the Brahmins to signify that man could attain the end of his being only by the uninterrupted contemplation of divine things, and by abstraction from earthly concerns. They placed, therefore, a higher value upon silent meditation and abstraction, than upon an active life; withdrew from the inferior castes, and believed, that, by acts of penance and self-inflicted tortures, by alms-giving and acts of outward holiness, and by the strict observance of innumerable laws, rules, and precepts, they brought themselves into closer union with the Deity. Since it followed from the doctrine of transmigration, that the souls of men might inhabit the bodies of animals, the Brahmins dared not kill or injure anything endowed with life, or eat any flesh unless it had been offered in sacrifice.

The Indians possessed sensibility and a creative imagination. This is particularly apparent in their copious literature. Many of their works and poems, the whole of which are composed in the sacred and now obsolete Sanscrit language, and are intimately related to their religion and theology, are already three thousand years old. The most important works are the four books of the Vedas, which are held in the most profound respect, as the sources of the Brahminical religion. They contain religious hymns and prayers, directions respecting sacrificial offerings, and moral precepts and proverbs. Next to the Vedas, the code of Menu is held in the greatest estimation. Besides these, the Indians possess a great multitude of poetical works of all descriptions, distinguished by highly figurative language, as well as deep sensibility and religious feeling. Many of these works were brought to Europe by the English who conquered the country, and were afterwards translated by learned men into German and other European languages. Indian art, as well as literature, is intimately connected with religion. More particularly worthy of remark are the rock-hewn temples and grottos, of which the most celebrated are to be found at Ellora in the middle of Lower India, at Salsette near Bombay, and at the island of Elephanta in the bay of Bombay. In these places, we meet with temples, grottos, dwelling-houses, and passages, covered with images and inscriptions hewn one above another in the rock, and extending for miles. These grottos contain an incredible quantity of works artistically and elaborately executed, which must have required the labor of many thousand hands for numberless ages, and the greatest patience and perseverance for their completion.

The abundance of the productions of nature and art, pearls, precious stones, ivory, spice, frankincense, and silks, made India, from an early period, the great centre and emporium of the maritime and caravan trade; but it also proved a lure to foreign invaders. Disunited and dismembered, as well by the system of castes as by their political institutions, and enervated and stupefied by their want of freedom, the Indians fell an easy prey to their warlike enemies.

IV. BABYLONIANS AND ASSYRIANS.

§ 9. The fertile regions watered by the Euphrátes and Tigris, and the grassy uplands of Mesopotámia, were formerly inhabited by Semitic tribes, including the Babylonians and Assyrians.

Nimrod, B. C. 2100.

Nimrod, "a mighty hunter before the Lord," is named as the founder of the Babylonian empire, and its chief city Babylon. This city was built in form of a square, and washed by the waters of the Euphrátes, which flowed through it.

Ninus, B. C. 2000.

A hundred years later, Ninus is said to have built the great city of Níneveh, on the banks of the Tigris, and to have subjected the Babylonians to his rule. The wife and successor of Ninus, the legendary Semíramis, is described as

Semiramis.

an heroic and victorious woman, who carried her conquests as far as India, embellished Babylon with magnificent works, (the hanging gardens, raised upon terraces,) and provided her land with skilfully constructed roads, canals, and buildings of every description. Beneath the rule of her incapable and effeminate successors, the Assyrian empire fell gradually into decay, till at length the warlike governor of the Medes rose against the unworthy sovereign, took possession of Níneveh, and

Sardanapalus. B. C. 888.

reduced the last king, Sardanapálus, who was notorious for his luxury, intemperance, and voluptuousness, to such straits, that he burnt himself in his palace, together with his wives and treasures. Nevertheless, in the following century, a few warlike sovereigns,

Salmanasser, B. C. 730. Sanherib, B. C. 720.

(among whom were Salmanásser and Sanherib, who were distinguished by their deeds and fortunes in Palestine,) were successful in again restoring the Assyrian empire, and increasing it by fresh conquests. But the new Assyrian monarchy was, like the old, but of short duration.

Nineveh destroyed, B. C. 605.

A hundred and twenty-five years after the reign of Salmanásser, Níneveh was taken and destroyed by the Medes and Chaldéans, and the victors divided the land among themselves. Babylon fell to the lot of the Chaldéans. Antiquities and works of art are still dug from the ground where Níneveh once stood.

§ 10. From this period, the Chaldéans or Babylonians possessed the ascendancy, particularly during the reign of the warlike and powerful

Nebuchadnezzar, B. C. 600.

Nebuchadnezzar, who laid Judah under tribute. But the splendor of Babylon soon passed away. A generation later, the Medes were the dominant race, and after them came the Persians. Babylon was provided with wonderful architectural works by the Chaldees. A broad and lofty wall surrounded the whole city, which is said to have had a circumference of nearly sixty miles. The two imperial palaces on the banks of the Euphrátes, the square and lofty temple of Baal, the god of the sun, which was magnificently adorned with statues and ornaments of gold, and served the purposes of an observatory, were, together with the hanging gardens, the most remarkable objects

In building, the Chaldéans made use of burnt bricks. Their water buildings, bridges, canals, dams, dikes, and so forth, were the most remarkable of their works. The worship of the heavenly bodies led the Babylonian priests (who were more especially called Chaldéans) to make astronomical observations; they reckoned the course of the sun, and divided the year: but as they mingled astrological speculations with their science, they fell into errors, and wandered about the world at a later period as diviners, interpreters of dreams, and magicians. We are also indebted to the Chaldéans for the divisions of weights and measures, and for the elements of geometry and medicine. The fertility of the land, and their extensive commerce, brought wealth and its necessary attendants, splendor and luxury. The Babylonians were, in consequence, not less celebrated for their luxurious productions, their fine linen, their sumptuous carpets, &c., than they were renowned and infamous for their sensuality, their luxury, and their voluptuousness. Masses of ruins, and heaps of rubbish, and a few monuments with inscriptions, mark the spot where once stood the world-renowned Babylon.

V. THE EGYPTIANS.

§ 11. The Greeks called Egypt a gift of the Nile; for it is from the regular annual overflow of the river, occasioned by rains in the high lands of Abyssinia, the waters of which are drawn off by all sorts of means, canals, dams, and cisterns, that the land preserves its remarkable fertility. The valley of the Nile was divided, even at a remote period, into three parts. First, Upper Egypt, where the vast and striking ruins of Thebes, with their gigantic fragments of statues and columns, their colossal sphinxes, (lions with women's heads), the tombs of kings hewn in the bare rock, the subterranean catacombs, and the colossal statue of Memnon, which is reported to have uttered musical sounds at the rising of the sun, yet testify to the former splendor and magnificence of the priestly city. Secondly, Middle Egypt, with its capital, Memphis, the vicinity of which is also distinguished by the magnificent remains of an historical antiquity. Among these are the ruins of the Labyrinth, a building consisting of a number of intricate passages communicating with each other, and the group of pyramids, which to this day are gazed upon with amazement, as the miracles of architectural science. These pyramids are built of hard freestone, rise from a square base, and terminate at an immense height, in a point, or small flat surface; they appear to have served as the sepulchral memorials of kings. Thirdly, Lower Egypt, with its ancient metropolis, Heliópolis, which was, however, afterwards eclipsed by Alexándria, and the historically remarkable places, Sáis, Naúcratis, &c. Two branches of the Nile inclose Lower Egypt, and, together with the sea, give it the triangular form whence it derives its name, Delta.

§ 12. Egypt possessed, at an inconceivably early period, numberless towns and villages, and a high amount of civilization. Arts, sciences, and civil professions were cherished there, so that the Nile-land has always been regarded as the mysterious cradle of human culture; but the system of castes checked free development and continuous improvement. Every thing subserved a gloomy religion and a powerful priesthood, who held the people in terror and superstition. The doctrine, that, after the death of man, the soul could not enter into her everlasting repose unless the body were preserved, occasioned the singular custom of embalming the corpses of the departed to preserve them from decay, and of treasuring them up, in the shape of mummies, in shaft-like passages and mortuary chambers. Through this belief, the priests, who, as judges of the dead, possessed the power of giving up the bodies of the sinful to corruption, and by this means occasioning the transmigration of their souls into the bodies of animals, obtained immense authority. The religion of the Egyptians consisted partly in the worship of the heavenly bodies, but also bore relation to the Nile and the natural qualities of the country. Their principal deities were Osíris, Serápis, and Isis; but as, besides these gods, the animals sacred to them were objects of veneration, the Egyptian religion gradually degenerated into the most monstrous animal worship. This degeneracy became apparent in their art. At first, the statues of their gods were represented with the human figure, although in stiff attitudes and in stern and solemn repose; but they appeared, at a later period, with the heads of beasts, and soon after, under an exclusively animal form. Notwithstanding the magnificence of their architectural productions, and the vast technical skill and dexterity in sculpture and mechanical appliances which they display, the Egyptians have produced but little in literature or the sciences; and even this little was locked up from the people in the mysterious hieroglyphical writing, which was understood by the priests alone. There were three kinds of these hieroglyphics, which are met with on the writing-rolls which the Egyptians prepared out of an aquatic plant called papyrus, and on the obelisks,—pointed, four-cornered columns, hewn from a single block of granite, and erected before the porticos of the temples.

Egypt was already an object of wonder and curiosity, in the time of the Romans; and such she remains, even to the present day. The fact is attested by the eleven obelisks and the innumerable Egyptian carvings in the hardest stone, at present in Rome, and by the multitude of mummies, ancient utensils, trinkets and ornaments, rolls of papyrus, and so forth, that are to be met with in all the museums and cabinets of natural history in Europe. But much as we may admire the patience of the Egyptians, and their skill and dexterity in the practice of their arts, we are everywhere struck with a want of free development, creative industry, and personal freedom. The curse of the caste-system lay upon every external manifestation of life, whilst superstition and religious oppression gave a gloomy coloring to existence, and disturbed every cheerful and pleasurable feeling.

§ 13. So long as the priestly class possessed the government and elected the king, the "hundred-gated" Thebes may have remained the principal city; but when the Egyptians were subjected to hostile attacks from neighboring nations, and the military caste attained in consequence to greater importance, Memphis appears to have been chosen as the metropolis of Middle Egypt. Warlike sovereigns were about this time successful in raising the military caste to an equality with the priestly, so that they divided their privileges between them, and were both subjected to the kingly power. Sesóstris, who reduced the Ethiopians to tribute, and who is said to have reigned over a considerable portion of Asia and Africa, is particularly mentioned as one of these victorious monarchs. After him, Mœris and Chéops are the most renowned kingly names. The first, on account of the lake which he constructed, and which was named after him, and which appears to have served the purpose of regulating the inundations of the Nile; the second, as the builder of the largest of the pyramids, which is 450 French feet in height, and on which 100,000 men are said to have been employed for 40 years. The lives and actions of these ancient kings are shrouded in darkness. The gloom begins to disappear about the middle of the seventh century, when the royal house of Sáis, in Lower Egypt, assumed the sovereignty, in the person of Psamméticus. For the purpose of weakening the power of the priests, Psamméticus entered into alliance with the Greeks, and received Greek soldiers and colonists into Egypt. Disgusted at this proceeding, 240,000 Egyptians migrated into Nubia, and there founded a state of their own. Among the successors of Psamméticus, Necho, the founder of the Egyptian naval and maritime power, and the warlike Amásis, are particularly to be mentioned. The son of the latter, Psammenítus, lost both kingdom and victory to the Persians, in the bloody battle of Pelúsium (Suez). The Persians afterwards reigned over Egypt for a period of 200 years. But the Egyptians did not unite themselves with their conquerors; they retained their own manners, institutions, and religious customs, together with their aversion to every thing foreign.

Sesóstris, B. C. 1500.

Mœris and Chéops, 1080.

Necho, B. C. 600.

VI. THE PHŒNICIANS

§ 14. On the narrow strip of coast between the Mediterranean and Lebanon, dwelt the maritime and commercial people of Phœnicia, in many populous towns, among which Tyre and Sidon were the most remarkable. The Phœnicians, an active and energetic race, would not subject themselves to the restraints imposed by the caste-system. On the contrary, every city, with the territory adjacent to it, constituted an inde pendent commonwealth, at the head of which stood an hereditary sovereign, whose power, however, was greatly restricted by the priests and nobles. Collectively they formed a league of towns, of which, at first Sidon, and afterwards Tyre, was the chief. Intellectual activity and diligence in business led this people to many discoveries; among them were glass, the art of dyeing purple, and of writing by means of letters. They were also distinguished by their skill in casting metals, weaving, architecture, and various other matters. Sidonian garments, Tyrian purple, Phœnician glass, and articles of ivory, gold, and other metals, were precious and coveted wares in all antiquity. The favorable situation of their country made them sailors, and the cedars of Lebanon supplied the materials for ship-building. Not only did the Phœnicians navigate the coasts and islands of the Mediterranean in their splendid ships, for the purpose of trafficking both in their own productions and in those of the distant East, spices, frankincense, oil, wine, corn, and slaves, but they even ventured beyond the Pillars of Hercules, (Straits of Gibraltar), purchased tin from the inhabitants of the British Isles, and amber from the people of the Baltic, and undertook venturous expeditions to India (Ophir) and the southern parts of Arabia. They are even said to have doubled the Cape of Good Hope, in a voyage of three years' duration, undertaken at the instigation of Necho, King of Egypt. They established colonies on Crete and Cyprus, at Sicily and Sardinia, in the south of Spain (Tartessus and Gades, now called Cadiz), and in northern Africa. The commercial city, Carthage, founded there by the Tyrians, under the conduct of Queen Dido, soon eclipsed the renown of the mother country. The Phœnicians paid less attention than the other Oriental nations to the cultivation of religion. Their worship of Moloch was accompanied with frightful human sacrifices, that of Baal with obscene rites.

B. C. 880.

§ 15. In their contests with the warlike nations of Asia, the Phœnicians displayed both courage and patriotism. When the Assyrian Salmanásser subjected Phœnicia to his sceptre, and compelled the inhabitants to pay tribute, the Tyrians built New Tyre upon a neighboring island, and defended it with success, for five years, against the superior power of the enemy. The merchant fleet of Tyre soon again ruled the sea. Even the Babylonian Nebuchadnezzar, who had subdued the mainland of Phœnicia, and had transplanted the inhabitants of Old Tyre, along with the Jews, into the interior of his kingdom, was unable to shake the courage of the New Tyrians. But these repeated attacks seem to have broken their power; for when, shortly after, the Persians subjected the countries of western Asia, Tyre also lost its freedom and independence. Phœnicia became a Persian province. In the middle of the fourth century, the oppression of the foreign governor produced a rebellion, a

B. C. 750.

B. C. 590.

B. C. 350.

the head of which stood Sidon. It was unsuccessful. Sidon fell into the hands of the Persian king; and when this prince gave orders for the execution of the principal citizens, the inhabitants themselves set fire to the town, and consumed themselves and their treasures. Tyre existed some time longer; but when Alexander the Macedonian overthrew the Persian empire, and Tyre, proud of its former glory, ventured to oppose the conqueror, it was taken and destroyed after a seven B. C. 332. months' siege. It never recovered from this stroke; and its trade and maritime power were transferred to Alexandria.

VII. THE PEOPLE OF ISRAEL.

§ 16. Whilst the whole world was sunk into idolatry, a people of shepherds, of Semitic origin, dwelling in Mesopotamia, preserved the original Abraham, belief in a single God. Abram (Abraham), one of the B. C. 2000. ancestors of this nomadic race, left his native pastures at the command of Jehovah, and settled himself, with his cattle, his men-servants and maidens, and his brother's son, Lot, in "the promised land" Cánaan (Palestine), where they continued their pastoral life, and received from the inhabitants the name of the "Strangers from the other side" (Hebrews). Isaac, who was born to Abraham by Sarah at an advanced period of life, continued the race; whilst Ishmael, Abraham's son by his concubine Hagar, is regarded as the progenitor of the Arabs. Isaac took to wife Rebekah, one of his own relatives acknowledging the true faith, who brought him two sons, Esau and Jacob. By the cunning of his mother, Jacob, the younger son, contrary to the usage that had hitherto obtained, was declared to be the chief of his race, but could only gain pos- Jacob. session of his inheritance after a long period of probation. B. C. 1836. Jacob had twelve sons; but as he distinguished Joseph, the gift of his beloved Rachel, by his peculiar affection, the others, moved Joseph, by envy, entertained the purpose of getting rid of their B. C. 1750. brother, and sold him to some travelling merchants, who took him with them into Egypt. As Joseph held fast his integrity, God rewarded him with prosperity and wisdom. By his skill in the interpretation of dreams, he obtained the favor of the Egyptian king, and arrived at high dignity and honors. He saved the land from famine, and by this means attained such credit, that he was permitted to invite his father and brethren into Egypt, and to bestow upon them the fertile pasture-lands of Goshen. The Hebrews were generally called Israelites, from Jacob's surname of Israel.

§ 17. At first, the Israelites were prosperous in the rich meadows of Goshen. But when Joseph was dead, and fresh rulers, who knew nothing of his services, assumed the government, dislike to strangers, and contempt for the pastoral state, incited the Egyptians to cruelty and severity against the foreigners. They commenced by imposing severe socage duties upon them; and when it was found that, despite this oppression, they increased so rapidly that the Egyptians at length became alarmed at their superior numbers, Pháraoh gave commandment to drown all their newly-born male children in the Nile.

Moses, B. C. 1500. Moses would have experienced this fate, had not the daughter of Pháraoh, who chanced to be walking on the banks of the river just as he was about to be drowned, taken pity on the infant, and saved him. Moses came to the Egyptian court, where he was carefully brought up, and instructed in all wisdom. The slaughter of an Egyptian, whom he saw misusing one of the Israelites, compelled him, when he was forty years old, to fly to the deserts of Arabia. It was here that he was inspired with the lofty purpose of becoming the deliverer of his people from their Egyptian bondage. At first, Pháraoh refused to let the Israelites depart; but after terror and distress had been spread over the land by the ten plagues which were sent upon it, he at length consented to the retreat required by Moses and his brother Aaron. The attempt to bring them back again by force, after their passage over the Red Sea, was attended with the destruction of the pursuers.

§ 18. For a period of forty years, Moses led a discontented people, who were often pining for the fleshpots of Egypt, wandering in the desert, for the purpose of strengthening their bodies, restoring virtue and a love of freedom to their minds, and of rearing up a young and hardy race, who should possess strength and courage for the conquest of the promised land. It was during this period that the Ten Commandments, and other laws relative to the religion and policy of the Israelites, were delivered to Moses on Mount Sinai. These laws were preserved in the ark of the covenant, the most sacred of tabernacles. Their interpreters were the high priests, to whose office Aaron and his posterity were appointed. By their side stood the Levites, as sacrificing priests, teachers, lawyers, and physicians. According to the system of Moses, Jehovah himself was king and ruler; it was in his name that the elders of the tribes conducted the temporal government, whilst the chief priest and Levites superintended the affairs of religion. Sacrifices and feasts (those of the Passover, Pentecost, and Tabernacles) formed the pleasant bond between Jehovah and the "chosen" people. In the sabbath-year, the lands were left untilled, and that which grew spontaneously was given up to the poor. In every fiftieth year (year of Jubilee), lands that had been alienated were returned to their original possessors, that property might not be too unequally divided. Moses determined upon agriculture in preference to the pastoral life, as the principal occupation of his people.

§ 19. It was not permitted to the great lawgiver to lead his people into the promised land. He gazed from the top of Mount Nebo on the

Joshua, B. C. 1450. beautiful plains of the Jordan, and then departed from among the living, after having chosen Joshua as his successor, and exhorted the assembled people to hold fast upon the God of their fathers, and to root out the Canaanites. Scarcely, however, had the people, under the command of the valiant Joshua, conquered the Amorites and the other tribes, than they gave up war, and demanded the distribution of the vanquished lands. This distribution took place by lot (in accordance with the regulation of Moses) among the twelve sons of Jacob, in such a way that Ephraim and Manasseh succeeded to equal shares; while, on the other hand, the descendants of Levi had no distinct inheritance, and received only a few towns and a tenth part of the productions of the earth. Reuben, Gad, and half Manasseh, chose the pasture-land on the east of Jordan; the others settled on the western side of the river.

§ 20. But many powerful tribes, as the Ammonites and Philistines, were still left unsubdued, and disturbed the Israelites in the enjoyment of their possessions. Bloody and destructive wars induced a rude and barbarous condition of society; and the Israelites not unfrequently forgot the living God, who had brought them out of bondage, and fell into the practice of idolatry, until misfortunes and defeats again brought them back to a better understanding. At these times, men of heroic courage would arise, defeat the enemy in victorious fields, and restore the ancient manners and the faith of their ancestors. These men are called Judges, in the sacred writings. . . . The most renowned among them are Gideon,
Samuel, Jephthah, Samson the strong, and the heroic Deborah. But
B. C. 1150. the high priest Samuel, a pious and patriotically disposed man, was the first who was successful in reuniting the ancient ties which bound the people of Israel to their God, and in restoring to the laws of Moses their former ascendancy. He overthrew the Philistines, and founded the schools whence proceeded those inspired oracles of the people, distinguished in the Bible by the name of Prophets.

§ 21. The sons of Samuel did not walk in the steps of their father, but perverted the right. At this period, the Israelites, in imitation of the surrounding nations, desired a king, who, as perpetual chief, might lead them forth to battle and victory. It was in vain that the gray-headed high priest sought to dissuade them from this request, whilst he portrayed in the strongest colors the misery and oppression that awaited them under a kingly rule. The Israelites persisted in their intention, and Samuel
Saul, anointed Saul, of the tribe of Benjamin, to be king. Saul
B. C. 1095. was a man of majestic person, brave, experienced in military affairs, and successful in the field; ut as he placed his trust in his army, and did not hold fast the commandments of Jehovah, he was rejected, and Samuel anointed the shepherd lad, David, of the tribe of Judah. Saul at this time was attacked with a spirit of melancholy, which nothing but the harp of David could alleviate. But envy of the renown acquired by David in the wars against the Philistines, and a secret presentiment of

the destiny that awaited him, urged Saul to hate and persecute the young shepherd; Saul's son, Jonathan, on the other hand, was devoted to him with true affection. David, nevertheless, in the midst of dangers and distresses, escaped the attempts of his enemy; and at length, when Saul, after having sustained a defeat, threw himself in despair upon his sword, David was gradually recognized as king by the whole of the tribes.

David, B. C. 1050.

§ 22. The reign of David is the glorious period of Jewish history. By means of successful wars, he enlarged his kingdom to the South and East; he made the Syrian town, Damascus, his footstool, and broke forever the power of the Philistines; he conquered Jerusalem, the chief city of the Jebusites, together with the strong fortress Zion, and selected it for a residence, and the central point of a solemn religious worship; and with this view, commanded the ark of the covenant to be brought thither. David was also a great poet, as is abundantly shown by his admirable religious hymns (Psalms); and despite many grievous transgressions, he still remained the "man after God's own heart," since by sorrow and repentance he always regained the forgiveness of Jehovah. The end of his reign was disturbed by the rebellion of his beloved son, Absalom, who was led astray by evil counsellors. The wise Solomon completed the work of his father. As David had been great in war, so his son was illustrious in the arts of peace. He adorned his capital with splendid buildings, and erected on the hill of Moríah, by the aid of Tyrian artists and masons, the magnificent temple which bore his own name, and which, on account of the richness of its gilding and ornaments, was the object of universal admiration. But Solomon departed in many things from the laws of Moses. He traded with the neighboring nations, and thereby acquired incalculable wealth, which stimulated his love of luxury, pleasure, and magnificence; he took to himself wives from a foreign people, permitted them the exercise of their idolatrous worship, and even took part in it himself. His lofty mind and admired wisdom did not secure him from folly. His love of magnificence and extravagance was the occasion of oppressive taxes; and even during his own life, an insurrection broke out under the guidance of Jeroböam. This was indeed suppressed, and the originator compelled to take flight; but when Solomon's son, Rehoböam, pursued the same course his father had taken, and repelled with threats the prayers of the people for relief, many of the tribes fell from him, and chose Jeroböam for king. Judah and Benjamin alone remained faithful to the legitimate royal race.

Solomon, B. C. 1000.

Jeroboam.

Rehoboam, B. C. 975.

§ 23. From this division there arose two states of unequal magnitude, the kingdom of Israel, or Ephraim, formed of ten of the tribes, with its capitals, Shechem and Samaria, and the kingdom of Judah, consisting of two tribes, with its chief city, Jerusalem. As Jerusalem preserved the ark of the covenant, and was in consequence regarded by the Levites and many pious Israelites as the true chief city, Jeroboam set up the worship of idols in the southern and northern parts of his kingdom, a sin which was shared by the whole of his successors. One of the most impious among these was Ahab, whose wife, Jezebel, a Tyrian, introduced the blasphemous Phœnician worship of Baal, and raged violently against those who would not do him homage. By means of her daughter, Athaliah, who was married to a king of Judah, the same worship was introduced into Judah, and favored by the court. The consequences were, intense hatred and contention, and at length, civil wars between the two kingdoms, by which they were mutually weakened; they then entered into alliances with other nations. The voices of the prophets, who boldly foretold the destruction of the state if the worship of Jehovah were thrust aside for the worship of idols, died away unheeded. When the land was threatened by the Babylonians and Assyrians, Isáiah referred to the coming Messiah as the only Savior; and Jeremiah lived to see that destruction of the state, concerning which he had in vain warned the blinded people.

§ 24. The Ephraimitic kingdom of Israel was first subjected to tribute by the Assyrians. But when the king, Hoshea, entered into an alliance with the Egyptians for the purpose of escaping from this impost, the Assyrian king marched an army into the land, subdued Samaria, and led away the king, with the greater portion of his subjects, into
B. C. 722. the Assyrian captivity. Foreigners entered into the land, and the intermixture of these with the remaining Israelites gave rise to the Samaritans. Judah survived 130 years longer. After the fall of Israel, it became tributary to Assyria. But when this nation went to war with Egypt, the king of Judah sided with the latter, and refused the tribute to the Assyrians. The Assyrian king, Sanherib, (Sennachérib,) came up against Jerusalem and laid siege to it. But Judah's hour was not yet come, whilst the pious Hezekiah sat upon the throne. The host of the Assyrians was almost entirely destroyed in a single night, and Sanherib (Sennachérib) retreated from the land in horror. It was to the victorious Nebuchadnezzar of Babylon, that it was first allotted to make an end of the nation polluted with new idolatries. He took
B. C. 600. Jerusalem, plundered the temple, carried away the king and the chief inhabitants into the interior of his dominions, and oppressed with a heavy hand those whom he suffered to remain. This induced the last king, Zedekiah, to try once more the chances of war; but he
B. C. 588. met with little success. Nebuchadnezzar burnt the city and temple, slaughtered the citizens, and at length carried away the deluded king and the greater part of his people into the seventy years' Babylonian captivity. In their necessity, the Jews again sought the God of their fathers, and found grace in his sight. One of the prisoners, the prophet

Daniel, arrived at high honors, and alleviated the fate of his brethren.
B. C. 538. After some years, Babylon was conquered by the Persians, upon which Cyrus suffered the Jews to return to their homes. Only a small portion returned at first, under the conduct of Zerúbbabel; these commenced the rebuilding of the temple. But as they avoided all intercourse with the Samaritans, this people, moved by hatred, endeavored in every possible way to disturb their purpose. They procured a prohibition of the building, which was already commenced,
B. C. 515. and which, in consequence, was not completed till the reign of Daríus. During the reign of Artaxerxes in Persia, fresh
B. C. 460. troops, led by Ezra and Nehemiah, returned to their homes, rebuilt the city, and reëstablished the laws of Moses. They had been taught by suffering, that salvation and deliverance were only to be found in a steadfast adherence to the faith of their ancestors; and from this time forth, they were more careful in shunning idolatry, and all contact with idolatrous nations.

VIII. MEDES AND PERSIANS.

§ 25. Media and Persia, two countries where savage and occasionally attractive mountainous regions alternate with rich pasture grounds and fertile arable lands, were formerly inhabited by tribes who drew their origin from the ancient Zend races dwelling farther to the eastward. They possessed a remarkable religion, which was founded by the ancient sage, Zoroáster, and had been delineated by him in the sacred books of the Zend-Avesta. According to this system, there are two first principles; a spirit of light, Ormuzd, and an evil spirit of darkness, Ahriman. Both of these have armies of similar spirits under them, and are to wage perpetual war with each other till the end of the world, when the spirit of light will become victorious; upon this, the evil spirit is to disappear, and the human race to be rendered happy. This doctrine was represented by a powerful hierarchy of priests, the Magi, in a solemn religious ceremonial. The god of light was worshipped under the form of the sun and of fire, the spirit of darkness was propitiated by sacrifices and prayers.

§ 26. The Medes remained for a long time under the dominion of foreign nations; at length, they roused their courage and fought valiantly for their freedom. But a few warlike kings soon after succeeded in suppressing the newly-acquired liberties of the people, and in establishing a military despotism. They at the same time subdued some of the neighboring people, and among others, the cognate tribe of the Persians. But their
Astyages, rule was but of short duration; Astýages, the last of the Me-
B. C. 575. dian kings, had a vision, which the diviners interpreted to signify, that the son of his daughter should, at some time, rule over Media and western Asia. Alarmed at this, he gave his daughter in mar

riage to a petty prince of the subjected tribe of Persians, and when she brought forth a son named Cyrus, he commanded him to be put to death in the obscurity of a remote forest. Cyrus only escaped the fate designed for him, through the compassion of the shepherd to whom the execution of the murder was intrusted. He was brought up as the son of the shepherd, but whilst yet a youth, gave such evidence in his pastimes of an innate spirit of command, as led to his being brought before the king and recognized. Astýages, pacified by the diviners, now allowed Cyrus to be brought up in a manner suitable to his rank, and sent him back, when he had arrived at maturity, to his parents in Persia. It was here that the project of freeing his brave but subjected countrymen from the yoke of the Medes, and leading them forth to victory and conquest, first arose in his mind. His mighty spirit and commanding person compelled the Persians to admiration and obedience. He marched against the Medes; Astýages, betrayed and overcome, relinquished the throne to his successful grandson, who now became the founder of an empire that embraced almost all the civilized nations of Asia.

Cyrus, B. C. 560.

Crœsus.

§ 27. At this time, King Crœsus, who possessed such enormous wealth that his name is become proverbial, reigned in Sardis, the principal city of Lydia. Cyrus declared war against him. Crœsus, deceived by an ambiguous oracle, passed over the boundary stream of the Halys to attack the Persians, but suffered a defeat, and was obliged to fly in haste to his capital. Cyrus pursued him, took Sardis, and commanded the captured king to be cast into the flames. Crœsus already sat bound upon the funeral pile, when his recollection of Solon, the wise man of Athens, saved him from destruction. Solon had once visited Sardis, and been hospitably entertained by the king. Proud of his prosperity, Crœsus had the sage led through his treasure-chambers, and displayed before him the whole of his riches. He then asked him who it was that he considered to be the happiest of mortals, nothing doubting that Solon would name Crœsus. The sage, however, mentioned a few persons, who, after leading a virtuous life, had met with a becoming death: when Crœsus again asked him whether he did not look upon himself as a happy man, Solon made the significant reply, "that no man could be considered happy before death." These words occurred at this moment to the captive king, and he exclaimed bitterly, "Oh! Solon, Solon!" The exclamation awakened the curiosity of Cyrus; he had the story related to him, and struck by the truth of the words of Solon, set Crœsus at liberty, held him in high estimation, and consulted him in all his undertakings.

§ 28. With the same good-fortune did Cyrus overthrow the empire of Babylon. As the Babylonians, in full security of the impregnability of their city, were celebrating a festival, and their luxurious king, Nabonnédus, (Belshazzar), was contemptuously defiling the sacred vessels of

the Jews, the Persians penetrated into the town by an arm of the Euphrates, the waters of which they had drained off, killed the king, and subdued the country. By this conquest, Syria, Palestine,
B. C. 538. and Phœnicia also fell under the dominion of the Persians, and the captive Jews received permission to return to their country.

Soon after this, Cyrus undertook an expedition against the Masságetæ, a wild nomadic race, living near the borders of the Caspian Sea. He was successful at first, by means of a military stratagem, and destroyed many of the enemy, among them a son of their queen, Thómy̆ris. But shortly after this, he and a great part of his army fell into the hands of the Masságetæ; and the queen, thirsting for revenge, cast the severed head of the mighty Persian king, with an expression of contempt, into a vessel filled with blood.

Cámbyses, B. C. 529. § 29. Camby̆ses, the victorious and tyrannical son of Cyrus, enlarged the Persian empire by the conquest of Egypt. The fate of the dwellers on the Nile was frightful. The unfortunate king, Psammenítus, after witnessing the oppression of his subjects,
B. C. 521. and the dishonor of his family, was put to a violent death; the Egyptian temples and sanctuaries were profaned, the treasures plundered, and the inhabitants abused. But the Persians also encountered a heavy doom. Two armies, that Camby̆ses despatched for the conquest of the priestly state of Ammónium, found their graves in the sandy deserts of Libya. This state had its central point in the temple and oracle of the ram-horned Jupiter-Ammon, in the oasis of Siwah, and was, like Thebes, a colony of the original pontifical state, Méroë, which had once subsisted in Nubia, in the midst of a savage negro population. Camby̆ses died after a violent reign of seven years, in consequence of an injury he accidentally inflicted on himself with his own sword. The Egyptians ascribed his sudden death to the vengeance of the gods for the slaughter of the sacred ox, Apis.

Darius Hystaspes, B. C. 521. § 30. Some time after this, seven illustrious Persians agreed together, that they would ride in the direction of the rising sun, and that the man whose horse neighed first should be made king. In this manner, Daríus, the son of Hystáspes, and the son-in-law of Cyrus, gained the throne, which he occupied, not without renown, for the space of thirty-six years. He divided the kingdom into satrapies, regulated the imposts, and conducted great wars. But his arms were not always successful. When he invaded the nomadic tribes, called Scythians, dwelling on the steppes of the lower Danube, this people retreated with their tents and herds, and surrendered their naked fields to the enemy, who were soon reduced by want to the brink of destruction; and when at length attacked by the Scythians, were compelled to make a most disastrous retreat over the Danube.

§ 31. The simple manners and military virtue of the Persians soon degenerated. The magnificence of the court, where crowds of officials and priestly counsellors, of servants and guards, battened on the prosperity of the country, destroyed the well-being of the provinces. The royal table was furnished with dishes and liquors of the rarest quality, brought from the most distant regions. A harem of ostentatious and intriguing women, who frequently had the revenues of whole towns and provinces allotted to them to defray the expenses of their trinkets and wardrobes, increased this luxury and profuseness. The court moved with the seasons. The winter was passed in the genial climate of Babylon; the spring in Susa; the summer in the cool Ecbátana. Numerous gardens arranged for the production of fruit, and inclosures where wild animals were preserved, contributed to the more refined pleasures of the Persian monarchs when on their travels. The governors of the provinces imitated the luxury and extravagance of the royal court, to the detriment of their lands, which were protected neither by laws nor the regular administration of justice from arbitrary and despotic authority. For the rest, the vast empire of Persia was but a conglomeration of heterogeneous elements, where the most diversified manners, institutions, and nationalities were approximated to each other without internal union without strength, and without support.

B. HISTORY OF GREECE.

I. GEOGRAPHICAL SURVEY.—*a.* THE GREEK CONTINENT.

§ 32. Greece is the southern portion of a large half-insular piece of land, which appears broad and unbroken in its northern part, narrow, irregular, and perforated by bays and inlets on its southern coast. It is traversed by numerous ranges of mountains, and consists of rocky and hilly tracts, which divide the country into a multitude of small, secluded, and isolated regions, and favor the production of numerous and separate states. Greece is divided into—Northern Greece, Central Greece, and Peloponnésus. Northern Greece consists of the rude mountain region of Epírus and Thessaly. Between these two lands extends, from north to south, the wild and rugged mountain range of Pindus, the summit of which is almost always covered with snow. Thessaly, with its fruitful plains and luxuriant pasture grounds, admirably fitted for the breeding of horses, is inclosed by another branch of the same range. The vale of Tempe, near Olympus, the hill of the gods, was celebrated in antiquity for its natural beauties. Among the cities may be mentioned Laríssa, on the Penéus, and Pharsálus, with its battle-field. The southern range of hills is called Œta. Between the foot of these mountains and the bay, is a narrow defile, that forms the only natural communication between Thessaly and central Greece. This is the celebrated pass of Thermópylæ. Central Greece, or Hellas, traversed by branches of the Œtian range, is divided into eight small and independent states. The most important among them are, Attica, a hilly country, rich in olives, figs, and honey, with its chief city, Athens, its seaport, Piræ'us, and the battle-field of Márathon. Opposite Athens lie the two islands, Ægína and Sálamis; the first renowned for its early cultivation, its trade and navigation; the latter, for the naval engagement during the Persian war. Bœótia, a fertile corn-producing country, with its seven-gated capital, Thebes; the heroic Platæ'a, and the renowned battle-fields of Leuctra and Chæronéa. Phocis, with the hills of Hélicon and Parnássus, renowned as the seats of the Muses. At the foot of the latter, in a spot that was looked upon as the centre of the earth, lay the sacred temple city of Delphi, with its celebrated oracle, and numerous magnificent buildings.

Peloponnésus (at present Moréa) is connected with Central Greece by the isthmus of Corinth. This peninsula is surrounded on four of its sides by the sea, and is an entirely mountainous country. In its centre is situated the rude region of Arcádia, with its beautiful valleys and fertile pastures inhabited by a hardy race of shepherds. Mantinéa, and the Megalópolis founded by Epaminondas, are among the most celebrated of its towns. In the north of the peninsula, on the shores of the Corinthian gulf, lies Acháia, with its twelve cities, which were united together in the third century by the celebrated Acháian league. Sícyon, and the rich and art-loving Corinth, were also joined in this confederation. To the East was Árgolis, a rocky region abounding in bays and creeks, with its chief city, Argos; Mycénæ, the ancient royal seat of Agamemnon and Tirynthus, in the neighborhood of which were to be found the remains of gigantic buildings (Cyclopean walls). To the south lay the rugged Lacónia, or Lacedæmónia, with the mountain of Táygetus, and a few fertile plains in the valley of the Eurótas; near this was the renowned city of Sparta, with about 60,000 inhabitants. Westward from Lacedæ'mon extended to the sea-coast the fruitful region of Messénia, with the fortress Ithóme, and the maritime city Pylos: northward from this lay Elis, the territory of which was regarded as sacred, and, in consequence, was never visited with war, together with the city and plain of Olympia, rendered famous by the Olympian games.

b. THE GREEK ISLANDS.

§ 33. To the east and west of Greece lay a multitude of large and small islands, which are of the greatest importance in Greek history. They were almost all remarkable for their fertility in wine, oil, fruits, and similar productions; carried on an extensive trade, and possessed even at an early period a high amount of civilization. The most remark able among them are, on the west, Corcýra, (at present Corfu), renowned even in the earliest ages for its wealth and culture, and where, at a later period, the Corinthians founded a colony; and the stony Íthaca, the dwelling-place of Ulysses. In the southern sea, the large island of Crete, which in the time of Homer, numbered a hundred cities, but which was dreaded and infamous on account of its piracy; Cyprus and Cythéra, celebrated for the worship of Venus; and Rhodes, renowned for the casting of metals, and for its statue of the god of the sun (Colossus), seventy cubits in height. But the sea the most rich in large and small islands is the Ægéan on the east, which for this reason has given its name — Archipelago — to every sea abounding in islands. Off the eastern coast of Greece, and only divided from it by the narrow channel Eurípus, lies the long and fertile island Eubœ'a (Négropont), with the maritime and commercial cities Erétria and Chalcis. Farther eastward, we meet with Lemnos, Thasos, Imbros, and Samothráce, the anciently renowned localities of mysterious religious customs. The group of islands lying nearest the east coast of Peloponnésus, are called Cýclades, because they lie in a circle (Cyclos). Among them are Delos, the sacred birthplace of Apollo and Diána; Paros, celebrated for its marble; and Naxos, for its wine. Eastward from these we encounter a number of scattered islands, the Spórades. The most important, both on account of their size and fertility, and the wealth and civilization of their inhabitants, are the islands lying off the coast of Asia Minor, — Lesbos, with its flourishing town Mityléne, Chios, Samos, Cos, and others. Lastly, the rocky island of Patmos, celebrated as the residence of the Evangelist, St. John.

II. RELIGION OF THE GREEKS.

§ 34. Nowhere did the heathen worship of idols assume a more cheerful aspect than among the Greeks, a great part of whose mythology was afterwards adopted by the Romans and incorporated with their own religious system. According to the religious views taken by the Greeks, the world was originally a rude and formless mass (chaos), from which the heaven and earth separated themselves as independent divinities. The earth, after this, produced beings of superhuman stature and strength, the Titans, who were possessed of the supreme authority, until a more spiritual race arose, who gathered themselves around the king of heaven, Zeus, or Jupiter, deprived them of their power, overcame the giants and Titans who attempted to storm the skies, and buried them in the abysses of the earth. After the unruly forces of nature and the power of the elements had been thus subdued, Zeus erected his throne upon Olympus, whilst Pluto governed the gloomy regions of the subterranean world, (Hades, Tártarus, Orcus), and Poséidon (Neptune), with his trident, ruled the sea. Hera or Juno, the queen of heaven, the virgin Pallas Athéne (Minerva), armed with helm and shield, the protectress of the liberal arts, and of all intellectual employment, Apollo, the glorious god of light, and some others, were the objects of similar veneration. Besides these, woods and mountains, fields and meadows, rivers and lakes, were inhabited by an innumerable multitude of divine beings, — nymphs, nereids, tritons, sirens who with their magic songs allured men to destruction, and many others that frequently interfered in human affairs. An heroic race, that derived its origin from Zeus, was the connecting link between gods and men; whilst the interval between men and the animal tribes was filled up by an inferior race of fauns and satyrs, who united together human and bestial qualities. Human life and this world of divinities were supposed to be most intimately related with each other. From the moment of his birth, a guardian spirit (genius, demon) stood by the side of every man for his whole life, and exercised an influence upon his resolutions and actions, without however interfering with the freedom of his will. The household hearth was the residence of sacred domestic and family deities (Lares, Penátes), who preserved the dwelling from evil; and every important event of life was under the guardianship of a separate divinity. In opposition to the Christian view, which looks upon the life of this world as a state of probation, and of transition to a higher form of existence, the joyous Greeks referred all their pleasures to the earthly life, and looked upon the shadowy existence of the subterranean world as but its melancholy continuation. They nevertheless believed in rewards and punishments, and in a state of immortal existence. The departed were brought by Hermes (Mercury), the conductor of the dead, before the three judges of the lower world, and, according to their decision, they were either sent to the residence of the righteous (Elysium, the happy islands), or to the place of condemnation (Tártarus). Many sacrifices were offered on the graves by the survivors to the souls or shadows (manes) of the departed. This free and beautiful system of mythology is displayed in the most perfect productions of Greek art and poetry.

I. GREECE BEFORE THE PERSIAN WAR.

I. THE TIME OF THE TROJAN WAR.

§ 35. The Pelasgi are believed to have been the most ancient inhabitants of Greece. They were an agricultural and peaceful people, with a religion that was founded upon the veneration of nature, and in which the earth-mother Deméter (Ceres), the wine-producer Dionýsus (Bacchus), and the oracle-giving nature-god, Zeus of Dodóna in Epírus, were the divinities that enjoyed the greatest reverence. This religion of nature, together with the remains of a primeval architecture, towns and royal cities, and especially the imperishable Cyclopean walls in Peloponnésus, which are built of huge stones fitted together without cement, leads to the opinion that the Pelasgi bore a resemblance, in their culture and religious institutions, to the people of the East; and that, consequently, intercourse must have existed at an early period between Greece, Asia, and Egypt. This view receives corroboration from the legends respecting oriental colonists, who settled in Greece and diffused the seeds of civilization at an inconceivably remote period. In the same way, Cecrops the Egyptian came to Attica, the Phœnician Cadmus to Bœótia, the Phrygian Pelops to the peninsula, named after him, Peloponnésus.

§ 36. The Pelasgi were either driven out or subjugated by the warlike Hellénes, who gradually subjected the whole of Greece to their power. These Hellénes are divided into three tribes: the Dorians, in Peloponnésus; the Ionians, in Attica and the islands; and the Æólians, in Bœótia and the other states. They distinguished themselves at an early period by great warlike achievements, and by founding cities and foreign colonies. It is in the poetical legends of the twelve labors of Hercules, of the voyage of the Athenian hero Theseus to the sea-ruling Crete, and of the daring Argonautic expedition, that the first traces of historical facts are preserved, distorted and obscured, as they may be, by a mass of fables. The Thessalian Jason, with the most renowned heroes of his time, (Hercules, Theseus, Castor and Pollux from Lacedæ'mon and the Thracian musician Orpheus), undertook the Argonautic expedition, in the ship Argo, to the distant land of Colchis, on the east coast of the Black Sea, for the purpose of obtaining the golden fleece, which, as the legend reported, Phryxus, the son of the Thessalian king, had years before suspended there, and which was watched over by a sleepless dragon. This Phryxus and his sister Helle had a wicked step-mother, who entertained designs against the lives of the two children. Their departed mother, Néphele, the goddess of clouds, appeared to her two children, and presented them with a wonderful ram, which conveyed them across the sea; Helle, however, fell off, and was drowned at the spot which has received from her the name of the Hellespont. Phryxus reached the land and sacrificed the ram. Jason and his companions reached Colchis after a difficult voyage, completed their undertaking by the aid of the sorceress Medéa, daughter of the king of the country, and returned home with their spoil. But the Argonauts had many wonderful adventures and perils to encounter on their return through the ocean and the mysterious river Erídanus, which formed the materials of many a poetical legend. The early commercial intercourse between the Eólic race and the inhabitants of the distant Asiatic coast, appears to be symbolized by this history of the Argonautic expedition.

§ 37. The greatest event of the Greek heroic age is the celebrated Trojan war. In Ilium, or Troy, on the north-west coast of
B. C. 1184. Asia Minor, reigned King Príamus over a rich and cultivated people. His youngest son, Paris, carried off Helen, wife of the Lacedæmonian king, Meneláus, who had hospitably received him. The injured husband summoned the princes of Greece to undertake an expedition to revenge the affront. This expedition shortly after took place under the command of Agamemnon of Mycénæ, brother of Meneláus, and with the assistance of the most renowned warriors of Greece. Achilles and his friend Patróclus from Thessaly, the subtle Ulysses from Ithaca, Diomédès from Argos, the sage Nestor from Pylos, Ajax, and many others were among the number. The army, having embarked in a vast fleet, sailed for the Asiatic coast from the seaport town of Aulis, where Agamemnon had devoted his daughter as a sacrifice to Diana. They found, however, the Trojans, especially Hector, son of Priam, and Ænéas, such valiant opponents, that it was only after a ten years' struggle that the city was at length taken and destroyed, by an artifice of Ulysses (a wooden horse filled with armed men). Priam and most of his subjects fell either in battle or at the destruction of the city; the rest were carried away as slaves. But the victors also suffered many misfortunes. Achílles, Patróclus, and many others found an early grave in Ilium. Agamemnon, after a troublesome voyage home, was murdered at the instigation of his faithless wife Clytemnestra; and Ulysses, tossed by tempests, wandered for ten years to inhospitable shores, over islands and seas, before it was permitted him again to see his faithful wife Penélope and his son Telémachus, and to purge his house of the audacious suitors who were contending for the hand of his spouse, and who in the mean while were feasting themselves upon his property.

§ 38. Homer.—The Trojan war is of more importance to poetry and art than to history, since the combats of the heroes, and their adventures and wanderings on their return home, formed two legendary cycles, from which the materials of heroic or epic poetry have usually been selected. The first and greatest poet, who has employed these legends in the construction of an immortal work, was Homer, who, according to tradition, was a blind singer, whose life was so obscure that, even in ancient times, seven cities contended for the honor of having given him birth. The two great heroic poems, that pass under his name, are the Iliad, in which the battles that took place before Troy in the last year of the siege are described, and the Odyssea, in which are sung the fate and adventures of Ulysses and his companions, on and around Sicily in the western sea. Even a mock heroic poem, Batrachomyomáchia, in which the combats of frogs and mice are described in the same manner as those of the Grecian and Trojan heroes, has been attributed to him. But as, at that time, the art of writing was unknown in Greece,* these poems were at first circulated from mouth to mouth, and portions of them were committed to memory and recited by wandering singers (Rhapsodists). Even at a later period, when they had been collected and reduced to writing, they were still impressed upon the memory of young people, and employed as a means of exciting patriotism, religion, and a feeling for the beautiful. As Homer was the chief of a school of poets in Asia Minor, who, under the name of Homérides, continued for some centuries to compose poetry in a similar spirit to their master, so Hésiod, about a hundred years later, became the founder of an Æólic school of poetry, that flourished more especially in Bœótia. We still possess an epic poem of Hésiod on the origin and fate of the Grecian deities (Theógony), and a didactic poem, the "Works and Days." The hexameter measure derived from Homer was, from this time, made use of in epic poetry.

§ 39. Shortly after the Trojan war, great disturbances and political revolutions took place in Greece. New races of men drove the old ones from the possessions they had hitherto occupied; these, in their turn, attacked other tribes, till at length the weaker resolved to expatriate themselves, and to found transmarine colonies. The most important in its consequences of these emigrations, was that undertaken

B. C. 1104.

by the Dórians to Peloponnésus, under the conduct of the descendants of Hercules (hence called the return of the Heraclídæ). This event entirely changed the fate of Peloponnésus, by giving the command of the peninsula to the hardy mountaineers of Dóris, instead of the Ionic population that had hitherto possessed it. The Dórians gradually subdued Árgolis, Lacónia, Messénia, Sícyon, Corinth, and Mégaris beyond the isthmus. They even made an irruption into Attica, and

B. C. 1068.

threatened Athens, but were compelled to a retreat by Codrus, the Athenian king, offering his life in sacrifice for his country. An oracle had declared that victory would incline to the side of those whose king should fall. When the Dórians heard this, they gave the strictest commands that no injury should be done to Codrus. But this king, disguising himself as a peasant, commenced a quarrel before the gates with the outposts, and was killed without being recognized. The Dórians, despairing of victory, immediately retreated from Athens.

The old inhabitants of Peloponnésus experienced a triple fate. The boldest and strongest quitted their country, and established the Ionian colonies on the western shores of Asia Minor, and the islands of Chios, Lesbos, Samos, &c. These colonies, by the fruitfulness of their soil, their navigation, their trade, and their diligence in business, soon attained a

* This is too sweeping an assertion. The art of writing was certainly practised in Egypt long before Homer's day; and the Greeks could hardly have been ignorant of it, though the Homeric poems may not have been reduced to writing for a century or two after they were composed. *Am. Ed.*

degree of prosperity and civilization that far surpassed that of the mother country. Those that remained behind either submitted freely to the Dórians, in which case they were compelled to pay tribute, and were excluded from all participation in the government, but were permitted to retain their possessions, or they were subdued with weapons in their hands, by force of arms; in the latter case, they were reduced to the condition of serfs or slaves. The first class were called Periæ'ci, or Lacedæmonians, to distinguish them from the Doric Spartans; the second class were styled Helots.

§ 40. Colonies.—In process of time, the Ionian colonies united themselves into a confederacy, consisting of twelve commonwealths, among which Milétus, Éphesus with the celebrated temple of Diana, and Smyrna, were the most powerful. The affairs of the union were debated in a temple on the promontory of Mýcale. The twelve colonial towns of the Æólians to the north of Ionia, and the six Dórian towns on the south, possessed similar arrangements. Among the latter, the town of Halicarnassus, the birthplace of the historian Heródotus, is the most remarkable. The island of Rhodes also belonged to the latter union. The shores of the Hellespont (Dardanelles), of the Propontis (sea of Marmóra), of the Pontus Euxínus (Black Sea), were covered in a similar manner with Greek colonies. The most important were Byzántium (Constantinople), Sinópe, Cérasus (the native land of cherries), and Trapézus. Flourishing colonies were also to be found on the coasts of Thrace and Macedónia; viz. Abdéra, Amphípŏlis, Olýnthus, &c. In Lower Italy, the number of Greek colonial towns was so great, that the inhabitants of the interior spoke Greek, and the whole country was known by the name of Great Greece. The most celebrated of these towns were Tarentum, the wealthy and luxurious Sýbaris, and the ancient Cumæ, the parent city of Naples. The greater part of the beautiful island of Sicily was in possession of the Greeks, who founded numerous opulent cities there, but none of which, in point of size, power, and civilization, could compare with Syracuse. On the north coast of Africa, Cyréne rivalled Carthage in wealth and commerce; and in South Gaul, Massilia was a model of civil order, and a seminary of cultivation to the rude population in its neighborhood. All these towns carried on a flourishing trade in the productions of art and the produce of the soil. Their vicinities were covered with beautiful buildings, and adorned for miles with villas and summer-houses. They exercised a salutary influence on the manners and culture of the natives, but degenerated in course of time, when wealth and refinement introduced luxury, sensuality, and effeminacy. The colonial cities occupied the position of blood relations to the mother state, but were entirely free and independent. They retained the manners and religious customs of the parent city, and honored it with filial piety; but they entered into no dependent relations with it, like the colonies of the Romans, or those of modern times.

II. THE PERIOD OF THE WISE MEN AND LAWGIVERS.

a. GENERAL VIEW.

§ 41. Greece never formed a united state, but was separated into a number of independent communities, among which the most powerful exercised from time to time a predominant influence. Sparta, Athens, and Thebes, ruled for the most part. But language, manners, and religious institutions united the different tribes into a single nation. They called themselves Hellénes,—all other people they included under the general term of barbarians. The Greeks, a people full of talent, and eminently capable of civilization, arrived at a degree of culture that has never since been equalled. Love of freedom, and a masculine energy, led them to establish a number of independent republics, to which, at first, they attached themselves with enthusiastic patriotism, and in defence of which they poured forth their heart's blood, till the rage of faction had choked the more generous feelings. Activity and diligence produced general prosperity, and a beautiful land under a sky of unvarying brightness, with a healthy and happy climate, engendered cheerfulness of mind, and made existence a pleasure. Simplicity of life lessened the number of the wants, and the frugal use of what a fruitful soil and a happily situated country produced with but little labor, banished the cares and anxieties of life, and permitted every one to enjoy the pleasures afforded by poetry, art, and the sciences.

§ 42. Certain institutions and establishments connected with religion were common to all the Greek races. The first among these was the ancient Amphictyonic Council, a court of arbitration to which twelve states sent their deputies, and the office of which was to defend the national sanctuary at Delphi, and to prevent the wars that broke out between single states from becoming too cruel and destructive. It was also the defender of the Delphic oracle, with its rich temple. In all important undertakings, the Delphic Apollo was consulted; the response was given by the inspired priestess, Pythia, from her golden tripod, in obscure, and frequently ambiguous and enigmatical expressions. The temple of Delphi possessed extensive territories, and rich treasures in gifts and offerings. The celebration of numerous games, as the Pythian (at Delphi), the Isthmian, Némean, &c., was a third bond to connect together the various states and families of Greece. None of these games, however, were so renowned as the Olympic, which, from the time 776 B. C., were celebrated every fourth year, in the plain of Olympia, in Elis. They principally consisted in running, boxing, wrestling, throwing the discus or spear, and in chariot racing; and the crown of olive branches, that was presented to the victor, was regarded as an enviable distinction that rendered illustrious, not the receiver only, but his whole family and his native dwelling-place. The works of artists, poets, and literary men were also objects of attention. There is even a tradition that Heródotus, the father of history, read the first book of his works at these games, and by so doing excited the emulation of Thucýdides, the greatest of historical writers. The temple of the Olympian Jupiter, and the colossal sitting statue of this deity, which was overlaid with ivory and gold, were among the most splendid examples of Greek art. Pindar, of Thebes, the great lyric poet, celebrated the victors in these games in his immortal odes.

b. LYCURGUS THE SPARTAN LAWGIVER.

§ 43. The manners of the Dórians gradually degenerated in their new possessions; the affairs of the state fell into disorder, and an unwarlike spirit threatened to diffuse itself. To remedy these evils, Lycúrgus, a patriotic Spartan of royal descent, determined to give his native city the preëminence over the other states, by restoring and establishing the ancient institutions of the Dórians. With this purpose, he visited the island of Crete, which was at this time celebrated for its excellent laws; made himself acquainted with the systems that prevailed there, and, on his return, gave the Spartans the remarkable constitution, of which the following are the chief outlines: —

B. C. 884.

a. INSTITUTIONS OF STATE. — The whole power of government was in the hands of the Dórians, who, without engaging in any other occupation, devoted themselves entirely to the exercise of arms, the conduct of war, and the affairs of the state. In the assemblies of the people, they elected the senators, or council of ancients, whose duty it was to conduct the government and protect the laws; and the five Éphori, who at first superintended the regulations of the city, but who afterwards obtained the greatest power of control over the public life and actions of those who were in office, and by this means gained such an authority for themselves, that even kings were subject to their tribunal. The senate consisted of twenty-eight members, of at least sixty years of age; the presidency of this assembly devolved upon the two kings of Sparta, who were chosen from the race of the Heraclídæ, and whose office was consequently hereditary. At home, they possessed more honor than power; but in war, they were always the leaders, and had an unlimited command. The fundamental principle of the whole constitution was the equality of property. In furtherance of this, the whole lands of Lacónia were divided in such a way, that each of the 9,000 Spartan families received an equal portion. These estates were indivisible, and descended to the eldest born by the law of primogeniture. The 30,000 families of Periœ'ci were in a similar manner provided with lands of less extent, whilst the Helots were left uncared for, and were obliged, in their capacity of serfs, or day-laborers, to till the ground of the Dórians, and to deliver a certain proportion of the productions of the soil, in corn, wine, oil, and similar matters, to the Spartan magazines.

b. MODE OF LIFE.—The rights of the Dórian depended less upon his birth than upon his education; this, therefore, was entirely undertaken by the state. Weak and deformed children were cast into a gulf immediately upon their birth; the vigorous were removed from their parents at the age of six years, and educated in public. The great object of this education was to produce bodily hardihood; the gymnastic exercises of the palæstra were, for this reason, one of its most important branches. But the understanding was also cultivated, and the Spartan was not less celebrated for his craft and shrewdness, than for the terse brevity of his speech, which was afterwards distinguished by the term "laconic." The feelings and imagination were alone neglected, and consequently, science and poetry were neither esteemed nor cultivated in Sparta. Doric art was merely distinguished by vast strength; not, like the Ionic, by grace and beauty. The male part of the population were divided, according to their ages, into companies, who dined together at public meals, (syssitia), fifteen usually sitting at one table. These meals were extremely temperate and simple, and were furnished from the supplies of the Helots. The so-called black broth and a vessel of wine were the chief features of the entertainment. The kings sat at the heads of their tables, and received a double portion. Luxury and effeminacy were by all means to be avoided; for this reason, the houses were rude and devoid of convenience; no instrument but the axe was permitted to be employed in their construction. Money was banished in ordinary intercourse, to the end that no one should possess the means of procuring unnecessary pleasures; and that the Spartans should not learn and accustom themselves to these pleasures, they were not permitted to travel into foreign countries, nor were strangers allowed to make a long residence in Sparta. The chase, and the exercise of arms were the chief employments of those who were grown up; the cultivation of the ground was left to the Helots; trade and business to the Periœ′ci. The whole life of the Spartan was a preparation for war. In the city, he lived as though he were in the camp, and the time of war was his time of joy and rejoicing. The Spartans marched into the field with purple mantles and long hair, and adorned themselves before battle as if for a festival. The strength of the army lay in the heavy-armed infantry (hoplítes), which consisted of numerous divisions, and which was, in consequence, enabled to execute without confusion many movements and evolutions. The Spartan never retreated from his ranks; he conquered or died in his place. Strict obedience, and subordination of the young to their elders, was the soul of the military education and discipline in Sparta, which was the true temple of honor of the age.

§ 44. After these laws had been confirmed by the oracle of Delphi, Lycurgus caused the Spartans to take an oath that they would never alter any thing contained in them, till he came back from the journey he

was about to undertake. Upon this, he is said to have gone to Crete, and there to have died. The consequences of the laws of Lycurgus soon became apparent. Not only did the hardy Spartans overcome the kin-
B. C. 743. dred race of the Messenians in two lengthened wars, but
B. C. 724. they soon established their power over the whole Peloponnésus. The Messenians were reduced to pay tribute in the first of these wars, after their citadel, Ithóme, had been destroyed, and their hero, Aristodémus, had slain himself on the grave of his daughter whom he had sacrificed. The tyranny of the Spartans in a short time
B. C. 687. provoked the Messeniáns to a second war. In this, they at first obtained some advantages, by the heroic deeds of the brave and cunning Aristómenes; but the Spartans, inflamed by the war-songs of the Athenian poet, Tyrtæus, finally proved the victors. A part of the Messenians quitted their country, and founded Messína in the island of Sicily: those who remained were led into slavery, and condemned to the miserable fate of the Helots.

c. SOLON, THE LAWGIVER OF THE ATHENIANS, B. C. 600.

§ 45. Whilst the Spartans, a race of steady and inflexible character, held fast for centuries the laws of Lycurgus, the lively and fickle Athenians introduced among themselves every possible form of government. After the glorious death of Codrus, (§ 39) the Athenians
B. C. 1068. declared that no one was worthy to be his successor, and abolished the monarchy. Some one of the nobles (eupatridæ), chosen for life to the office of archon, received the supreme power. At first, the family of Codrus had the preference in this election; but as the government with time assumed more and more the form of an aristocratic republic, the office of archon was thrown open to the whole body of
B. C. 752. nobles, and the period of its existence reduced to ten years.
B. C. 682. For the purpose of admitting a greater number to this honor, they at length adopted the expedient of electing nine archons every year, who were to superintend the government, the affairs of religion, military matters, legislation, and the administration of justice. The nobles now held the power in their own hands, and excluded the people (demos) from all share in the government, or in the administration of the laws. They alone gave judgment, because they only were acquainted with the unwritten and traditionary statutes; in this way, arbitrary decisions, partiality, and injustice, were of no unfrequent occurrence. This induced the citizens, in the assemblies of the people, to insist upon the framing of written laws. The nobles for a long time refused to accede to the demands of the people; but when at length they found that further resistance was impossible, they determined upon a different method of
Draco, oppressing the commons. They commissioned one of their
B. C. 624. own number, Draco, surnamed the Cruel, to draw up a code

of laws. These proved so severe, that they were said to be written in blood. Every offence was punished with death. By this means, the nobles hoped again to reduce the discontented people to their former state of dependence. Desperate struggles followed, and contention and party spirit rose to such a height, that the state was reduced to the verge of destruction. At this juncture, Solon, one of the seven wise men, and greatly esteemed both as a poet and a friend of the people, proved the savior of his country. He gave the state a new and republican form of government, in which the principal authority was vested in the assemblies of the people. These assemblies made the laws, named the judges and officers of state, and elected the council of the four hundred; that the nobility, however, might not be deprived of the whole of their power, he secured to them certain privileges: they alone could fill the office of archon, or sit in the high court of the Areopagus, which Solon had established to preserve the laws, the government, and public morals. This court consisted of the most respected citizens; it superintended the education of youth, and kept an eye upon the lives of the burghers, to the end that morality and discipline might be preserved, and an honorable and industrious course of life be maintained; and that luxury, riot, and extravagance in dress, might be banished. Solon, at the same time, relieved the necessities of the people by the so-called remission of burdens, by which the poorer citizens were freed from a portion of their debts, and restored to the unfettered enjoyment of their mortgaged estates. After Solon had completed these measures, he caused the Athenians to swear that they would make no alterations in them for the space of ten years: he then set forth on his travels to Asia and Egypt, in the course of which he held the before-mentioned conversation (§ 27) with Crœsus at Sardis.

d. THE TYRANTS.

§ 46. All the Grecian states had at first been governed by kings, who, as high priests, judges, and leaders of the army, exercised a patriarchal power. But the rich and distinguished class, who had hitherto stood by the side of the king as his councillors, gradually attained the upper hand, and seized the first favorable opportunity of ridding themselves of the monarch, and of establishing an aristocratic republic, in which they exercised the supreme power. This institution became, in time, extremely oppressive to the people. But as the nobles were in the exclusive possession of arms, and of the practice of war, it was no easy matter to deprive them of the government. This took place for the first time, when an ambitious noble separated himself from his order, and placed himself at the head of the people. But the rule of the aristocracy was not at once succeeded by a democratic government; on the contrary, the leaders of the people (demagogues) seized in most of the states upon the supreme power. They were distinguished by the name of "tyrants;" by which term, however, we are not always to understand a violent and arbitrary ruler, but merely one who unites in his own person all the functions of government, in a state that had previously been a republic. Many of these tyrants possessed great talents for their office, and ruled with splendid success. For the purpose of giving employment to the people to whom they were indebted for their rise, they erected magnificent buildings; their wealth gave them the means of attracting artists and poets, whilst their splendid courts contributed to the magnificence of the cities. But the government of the tyrants was not of long duration. The nobles neglected no means to effect their overthrow; and in this they were supported by the Spartans, who were everywhere favorable to aristocratic institutions. Their sons, who had grown up in the enjoyment of power, frequently forgot the consideration they owed to the people, and hastened their own destruction by cruelty and despotism.

Periander, B. C. 600.

§ 47. The most celebrated of the tyrants were Periander of Corinth, Polýcrates of Samos, and Pisístratus of Athens. The first two are well known by poetical legends. Periander's friend, the singer Aríon, once wished to return to Corinth by ship, from Lower Italy. The sailors, who were greedy after the treasures he had acquired in Tarentum, made attempts upon his life. When every hope of deliverance had vanished, Aríon sang, and played some notes upon his harp, and then leaped into the waves. The dolphins, who had followed the ship, bore the singer to the shore. He hastened to Periander, at Corinth, who easily discovered and punished the offenders. Not less celebrated is the story of the ring of Polýcrates. The rich and powerful ruler of Samos was successful in every thing he undertook. At one time, when the king of Egypt was paying him a visit, messenger after messenger came to announce some fortunate event. Psammétichus appeared thoughtful, and warned his friend of the instability of fortune and the envy of the gods, and advised him to inflict some vexation upon himself to appease the irritated divinities. Upon this, Polýcrates cast a costly and exquisitely wrought ring, upon which he placed a great value, from the roof of his house into the sea. But the gods despised the gift. On the following day, some fishermen brought a large fish to the palace, and, as the servants were preparing it for the table, they discovered the ring in its entrails. They presented it with joy to the tyrant; but Psammétichus saw in this the omen of approaching misfortune, and took a melancholy leave. Shortly after, Polýcrates was taken prisoner by the Persians, and crucified.

Polycrates, B. C. 550.

Pisistratus, B. C. 560.

The most celebrated of all the tyrants was Pisístratus, of Athens, who succeeded, even during the lifetime of Solon, in grasping the sole power. He contrived by dint of cunning, having first wounded himself, and then giving out that his life had been attempted, to procure a body-guard, and to obtain possession of the citadel. His enemies were indeed twice successful in banishing him from the city; but he again returned, succeeded in establishing himself in the government, and bequeathed it at his death to his two sons, Híppias and Hippárchus.

B. C. 527. Pisístratus, and, at first, his son Híppias, ruled with much glory. Agriculture, trade, and commerce received a great impulse. The poems of Homer, that had hitherto only been delivered orally by the wandering singers (rhapsodists), were now reduced to writing, and by this means preserved to posterity. Artists of every kind found in them liberal patrons. Athens was embellished with temples and public buildings, and the lyric poet, Anácreon, was a resident at Híppias's court. But when Hippárchus, who was a man devoted to riot and the pleasures of the senses, had been killed at the panathenaic festival, by two Athenians, Harmódius and Aristogíton, in revenge of some injury they had suffered from him, Híppias gave free scope to his violent disposition. By his severity and cruelty, he alienated the affections of the popular party, and by this means prepared the way for his own expulsion. He took refuge with the Persian king, Daríus, and encouraged him in his design of making war upon the Athenians. Shortly after his departure, the democratic republic was established in Athens.

THE SEVEN WISE MEN. — PYTHAGORAS.

§ 48. Periander of Corinth, and Solon of Athens, were numbered among the seven wise men; of the remainder, Thales of Milétus, the founder of the Ionic school of philosophy, was the most renowned. Their principles and practical rules of life were embodied in short mottoes, as "Know thyself," "Avoid excess," "Consider the end," "Be watchful for opportunities," and numerous others.

One of the most distinguished men of this period, who did not however call himself a wise man (sophos), but only a lover of wisdom (philosophos), was Pythágoras of Samos, the founder of the sect of the Pythagoreans, which had many adherents in Crotóna and other towns of Lower Italy, and enjoyed great respect. The members of his sect led a life of temperance and severe morality, had their meals and exercises in common, and were devoted with the greatest veneration to their master. They practised themselves in mathematics, geometry, and music; for Pythágoras is known as the inventor of the theorem, which is named after him, the Pythagorean.

e. LYRIC POETRY.

§ 49. A cheerful mode of life prevailed at the courts of the tyrants, where singers and poets were welcome guests. The severe heroic poetry

4

was not suited to the pleasures and amusements that were there principally sought after, and its place was in consequence supplied by a lighter and less prolix kind, which was distinguished by the term lyric, because it was intended to be sung to the lute (lyra). All lyric poetry, therefore, originally consisted in cheerful songs, which exhorted to the enjoyment of life on account of the shortness of its duration, and were filled with the praises of love and wine, because they drove away care and trouble. In this style, Anácreon of Teos, in Iónia, who passed his life at different courts, and died in his eighty-fifth year,
B. C. 474. was the most celebrated; and for this reason, this kind of song is called Anacreontic.

If the shortness of life, and the transitory character of every thing earthly, gave occasion to Anácreon to exhort to the enjoyment of existence, there were not wanting others to whom these considerations were a source of melancholy and sorrow, and who poured forth their complaints over the instability and uncertainty of human happiness. This style was called the "elegíac," and was usually composed in a measure consisting of hexameters and pentameters united (disticha). The best known elegiac poets are Mimnérmus of Cólophon, and Simónides of Ceos. Those lyrical compositions that are distinguished by a more lofty feeling, and in which the poet sings with enthusiasm or passion of some sublime object, are called "odes." Sappho, of Lesbos, a poetess celebrated
B. C. 600. for her amatory songs, and her voluntary death, distinguished herself in this style of composition. But the Theban, Pindar, was the first who gave to the ode its full perfection. At a later period, the term "lyric" was applied to all the shorter specimens of poetry, even though they were not fitted to be sung to music. Thus satire, the object of which is to punish the vices and failings of men by ridicule, and by this means to bring about their instruction and improvement, is called "lyric poetry."

B. C. 700. Archílochos, of Paros, the discoverer of iambics, is named
B. C. 600. as the first satiric poet; at whose side, Alcæ'us of Mityléne, the freedom-inspired opponent of the tyrants, occupies no unworthy place. In like manner, the short stories where animals are introduced acting and speaking (fables), and the object of which is the inculcation of some useful maxim or rule of life, are distinguished by the same term. Æsop, a Phrygian slave, whose history is involved in obscurity, and disfigured by many fabulous stories, acquired a great renown in this sort of composition

II. THE FLOURISHING PERIOD OF GREECE.

I. THE PERSIAN WAR.

§ 50. The Greek colonial cities, on the coasts of Asia Minor, had been brought by Cyrus under the Persian dominion. Accustomed to freedom, they bore this foreign yoke with the greatest reluctance ; but were unable to free themselves from it, because the principal Greeks, who were appointed by the Persians to the office of prince, or tyrant, of the different towns, and who were consequently devoted to the court of Susa, knew well how to keep their countrymen in subjection. One of the most powerful of these was Histiæ'us, prince of Milétus. He had accompanied Daríus in his expedition against the Scythians, (§ 30), and had received, together with some other Greeks, the charge of guarding the bridges that had been thrown over the Danube. When the news of the disasters of the Persians became known, Miltíades, the Athenian, advised that these bridges should be destroyed, and the king and his whole army given up to destruction. But Histiæ'us opposed this project, and was afterwards rewarded by being invited to the Persian capital, and passing his life there in splendor and luxury. But no pleasures could extinguish his longing after his native country ; and when he found that he was so much mistrusted as not to be permitted to depart, he secretly instigated his relative, Aristágoras of Milétus, to stir up the discontented Greeks to rebellion, hoping by this means to gain an opportunity of returning. In a short time, Milétus and the other Greek towns were in arms. Sparta, and the other states of the mother country, were applied to for assistance ; but Athens only, who was afraid that Daríus might again restore Híppias, who was residing at his court, and the small town of Erétria, in Eubœ'a, sent a few ships. At first, the insurrection appeared successful. The Greeks took and burnt Sardis, the chief city of Asia Minor, upon which the revolt spread over the whole of Ionia. But fortune soon changed Divisions among themselves, and the superior force of the enemy, occasioned the loss of a maritime engagement, and the capture and destruction of Milétus. Many of the Milesians were led into slavery;
B. C. 494. Aristágoras fled to the Thracians, where he met with his death ; Histiæ'us was taken prisoner and crucified. Ionia again fell under the dominion of the Persians, and Daríus vowed a bloody vengeance against the Athenians and Erétrians, for the assistance they had afforded the rebels.

§ 51. Mardónius, the son-in-law of Daríus, sailed with a fleet and army along the coast of Thrace, towards Greece, whilst the Persian heralds demanded earth and water, the symbols of submission from the whole of the Greek cities. But the fleet was driven against the promontory of Athos by a storm, and the Thracians destroyed a part of the land force, so that Mardónius was compelled to lead back the remains of his army into Asia, without effecting his purpose. It fared no better with the heralds. Ægína, and the greater number of the islands indeed, presented the earth and water; but when they made the same demands at Athens and Sparta, they were put to death by the inhabitants, in defiance of all the laws of nations. Daríus, enraged at this insult, despatched a second fleet, under the command of Datis and Artaphérnes. They sailed through the Archipelago, and reduced the islands of the Cýclades to submission, and afterwards landed at Eubœ'a. Erétria, after a gallant resistance, fell by treachery into the hands of the enemy, who razed the city to the ground, and sent away the inhabitants into Asia. The Persians marched through the island, burning and destroying; and at length, under the command of Híppias, landed on the coast of Attica, and encamped on the plain of Márathon. The Athenians sent in haste to the Spartans for assistance; but these not appearing at the proper time, in consequence of an ancient law of their religion, which forbade them to march to battle before a full moon, the Athenians, under the command of ten leaders, advanced upon the enemy. The most esteemed among these leaders was Miltíades, who had formerly served in the Persian army, and was thoroughly acquainted with its qualities and tactics. By his direction, 10,000 Athenians, and 1,000 Platæ'ans, attacked the army of Persians, of ten times their number, in a place unfavorable for cavalry, and gave them a complete overthrow in the battle of Márathon. The victors gained a rich booty, and placed the fetters they discovered, and which were intended for themselves, on the bodies of their enemies. Great was the renown acquired by the Athenians, who here for the first time proved that they were worthy of the democratic freedom they had lately introduced among themselves; and centuries later, patriotic orators would excite the enthusiasm of the people, by calling to their remembrance the victory of Márathon. Híppias was one of the slain.

B. C. 490.

§ 52. Miltíades, the savior of Greece, did not long enjoy his honors. He persuaded the Athenians to equip a fleet for the purpose of subduing the islands of the Ægéan Sea, which had submitted to the Persians. But when the attempt upon the island of Paros miscarried, the people condemned him to pay the cost of the expedition, and to be cast into prison till the debt should be discharged. The sentence was carried into execution, and Miltíades died in prison of his wounds. Cimon, his son, paid the debt, and conferred an honorable burial upon his father.

At that time, there lived in Athens two men of remarkable character, Aristídes, surnamed the Just, and Themístocles. Both sought to render their country illustrious, but by different methods. Aristídes would make use of no means that were not strictly just and honorable, nor consent to any measure that excited the scruples of his conscience. Themístocles was less scrupulous: he would regard nothing but the greatness and advantage of his native city, and not unfrequently had recourse to artifice and deceit. Shrewder and more talented than his rival, Themístocles soon won a greater share of the popular esteem; and to free himself from a hinderance to his plans, he urged the banishment of the more honest Aristídes by ostracism.*

By this means, Themístocles became the sole leader of the Athenian republic, and he exerted the whole of his influence to obtain an increase of the fleet; for it was only by this means that the Athenians could attain a superiority to the other states. A declaration of the Delphic oracle, that the safety of Athens depended upon its "wooden walls," was of great service to him in the execution of this project.

§ 53. Daríus died in the midst of vast preparations for a fresh invasion of Greece. But his successor, Xerxes, a man puffed up with pride and arrogance, pursued his father's designs of vengeance, and carried on his preparations on such a scale, that he collected an army of a million and a half of men, and more than 1,200 triremes and 3,000 smaller vessels. But this immense crowd of people of all nations and tongues, with habits and weapons of the most diversified character, and accustomed each to its own method of warfare, was rather a hinderance than an assistance to the enterprise. When Xerxes had completed his preparations, and with wonderful good fortune had quelled a revolt that broke out in Egypt, (a circumstance that contributed not a little to swell his confidence), he ordered his troops, with an enormous crowd of sutlers, beasts of burden, wagons, and dogs of chase, to defile for seven days and nights across the Hellespont, on two bridges of boats, and then to march through Thrace and Macedonia towards Thessaly, whilst his fleet coasted along the shore to supply the army with whatever it needed. To prevent his ships being wrecked on the promontory of Athos, as in the first expedition, Xerxes separated the mountain from the mainland, by cutting a canal. Thessaly submitted without a blow. Bœótia, and a few of the smaller states, pusillanimously yielded earth and water; and the threatening foe still marched on. At this juncture, Greece showed what union, courage, and patriotism are capable of effecting. The greater number of the states united in a confederacy, and placed themselves under the guidance of Sparta.

* Ostracism was an arrangement by which any citizen who was so superior to his fellows in power, influence, authority, or other qualities, as to endanger the civic equality, or the democratic constitution of the state, might be banished for a term (usually ten) of years.

The term was derived from the Greek word for the shell (ostracon) on which the name of the accused citizen was written. — *Trans.*

It was in July, just at the time of the celebration of the Olympic games, that Xerxes arrived at the narrow pass of Ther-
B. C. 480. mópylæ, which Leónidas had occupied with three hundred Spartans and a few thousands of the allies. It was in vain that the Persian king attempted for several days to force a passage; thousands of his troops fell beneath the swords of the brave Greeks; even the 10,000 Immortals, as they were called, the flower of the Persian army, were compelled to yield to the Spartan valor. At length, a traitorous Greek conducted a part of the Persians by a footpath over the summit of the mountain Œta, who attacked the rear of the Greeks. Upon receiving intelligence of this, Leónidas dismissed the troops of the allies. He himself, with his 300 Spartans, and about 700 of the citizens of Thespia, who united themselves to him, devoted themselves to an heroic death for their country. Surrounded on all sides, they fought like lions, till, overpowered by numbers, and wearied with slaughter and contest, they sunk to the earth. Leónidas and his heroic band lived long in song, and a monument pointed out to the traveller the spot where they fell. The Persians now subjected Bœótia without opposition, pursued their devastating course into Attica, and reduced Athens to ashes. The old warriors who defended the Acropolis were slaughtered. The citizens who were fit to bear arms were serving in the fleet. The women and children, together with their effects, had been sent, by the advice of Themístocles, to Ægina, Sálamis, and Trazœ ne.

§ 54. Themístocles now became the saviour of Greece. The united fleet of the Greeks had sailed from the promontory of Artemísium, where it had been for some days successfully engaged, into the Sarónic gulf, whither it was followed by the Persians. It was here that Themístocles, by his prudence, rendered abortive the ruinous design of the Spartan admiral, Eurybíădes, of removing the Peloponnesian fleet from Sálamis, and deciding the battle at the isthmus of Corinth, by craftily provoking the Persian king to a sudden attack in the narrow channel, where the enemy's fleet was embarrassed by its own magnitude. Thus originated the sea-fight of Sálamis, in which the Greeks obtained a complete
B. C. 480. victory. Xerxes gazed in despair from a neighboring eminence on the destruction of his fleet, and then commenced a hasty retreat, with a portion of his army, through Thessaly, Mácedon, and Thrace, during which he lost some thousands of his soldiers from cold, hunger, and fatigue.

§ 55. Xerxes on his retreat left 300,000 of his best troops behind him in Thessaly. These marched again into Attica, in the following spring, and compelled the Athenians, who had returned home, once more to disperse themselves. But the Greeks, under the conduct of the Spartan Pausánias, assisted by the Athenian general, Aristídes, obtained so signal a victory in the great battle of Platæ'a, over a force of three times their number, that only 40,000 of the Persians saved themselves across the Hellespont. The remainder, with their leader, were slain, either in battle, in the storming of their camp, or in the flight. The booty was enormous. On the same day, the Persians suffered a decisive defeat at the promontory of Mўcăle, in Asia Minor, from the Greeks on board the fleet. In this case, also, a Spartan was the leader; but it was the Athenians and Milesians who bore off the prize of valor. The fleet and camp of the enemy were taken and destroyed. The slaughter among the broken and flying crowd was frightful. Valor triumphed over strength, and the truth, that patriotism and love of freedom can bear away the victory from superior numbers, received a splendid confirmation in the glorious triumph of the Greeks over the Persians. Ten years afterwards, the double victory of Cimon on the river Eurўmĕdon, over the fleet and army of the Persians, brought the war to a temporary conclusion. A peace concluded soon after the death of Cimon freed all the Greek cities in Asia Minor from the Persian yoke.

B. C. 469.

THE SUPREMACY OF ATHENS, AND THE AGE OF PERICLES.

§ 56. After the battle of Platæ'a, the war was principally carried on at sea. As the Spartans possessed but few ships, the command had gradually fallen into the hands of the Athenians, who, moreover, during the whole war, had displayed the greatest courage and magnanimity. The supremacy of the Athenians was also forwarded by the treachery of the Spartan general Pausánias. Pausánias, at the taking of Byzantium, had made prisoners of some illustrious Persians. He sent these without any ransom to Xerxes, with the message, that "He would assist him in subduing the Greeks, if Xerxes would give him his daughter in marriage, and make him governor of Peloponnésus." When the Persian king acceded to these terms, the vain and ambitious man became so insolent, as entirely to neglect the Spartan laws and manner of living; he clothed himself in costly garments, maintained a luxurious table, and was waited on and accompanied by a band of Persian guards. At the same time, he rendered the Lacedæmónian rule universally odious by his imperious behavior. The Spartans, when made acquainted with this conduct, recalled their faithless general; but their authority in maritime affairs was already so much weakened, that they voluntarily renounced the command. Pausánias, even in Sparta, kept up a private correspondence with the king of Persia. But this treachery being exposed by means of a slave, he perished of hunger in a temple in which he had taken refuge.

§ 57. Whilst Pausánias was thus weakening the power of his native city, the three Athenian generals, by their various capacities and talents, were instrumental in raising that of their own. Themístocles, by dint of wisdom and cunning, succeeded in getting Athens surrounded by a

strong wall, and in founding the admirable harbor of Pïræ'us, which Cimon and Péricles afterwards connected with Athens, by means of a ong double wall. By this undertaking, Themístocles incurred the implacable hate of the Spartans, who were very averse to the fortification of Athens, and who, for this reason, attempted at a later period to implicate him in the treachery of Pausánias. This happened at a time when his enemies in Athens had succeeded in getting the ambitious man
B. C. 471. banished by ostracism, for a term of ten years. Persecuted in this way, the great general fled, in the midst of innumerable dangers, to Asia, where he was honorably received by the Persian king, and had the revenues of three cities of Asia Minor allotted to him for his support. But when the king wanted his assistance in the subjection of Greece, he is said to have swallowed poison rather than prove a traitor to his country.

As Themístocles by prudence, so Aristídes by justice, aided the interests of his native city. The perfect confidence that was placed in his character and opinions, induced the islands and maritime cities to enter into alliance with the Athenians, and to pledge themselves to a supply of ships and money for the continuation of the war. The treasury of the confederacy, which was established in Delos for this purpose, was intrusted to the management of Aristídes, and the command of the united fleet was also given to an Athenian. The supply of ships soon became burdensome to the smaller states, and they were glad to compromise for their delivery, by the payment of an additional sum of money. This gave the Athenians the opportunity they so much wished for, of increasing their fleet, of subjecting the smaller maritime states, and treating them as tributary vassals. Aristídes died so poor, that the state was obliged to defray the expenses of his burial, and to provide for the establishing of his children.

§ 58. Cimon, the son of Miltíades, and Péricles, were not less instrumental in the aggrandizement of Athens. The first rendered many services to his country by successful expeditions at sea, and gained the people by his affability and generosity. He enlarged the territory of Athens, and employed his vast wealth in the embellishment of the city, where he established the beautiful gardens called the Academy.

During his time, Sparta was visited by a fearful earthquake. The greater part of the principal city was destroyed, and, to increase the calamity, the Helots and Messénians seized their arms for
B. C. 465. the purpose of regaining their freedom. In their distress, the Spartans turned to Athens for assistance, and by the influence of Cimon, an army was despatched to their aid. But the suspicious Spartans sent it back again, a proceeding which so offended the Athenians, that they banished Cimon by the ostracism; and when the Messénians,

after a contest of ten years, were compelled to surrender their citadel, Ithóme, they gave up the seaport town, Naupactus, to them for a residence. Cimon died, much respected, in Cyprus, B. C. 449.

Péricles, a soldier and statesman, distinguished by great talents, cultivation, and eloquence, exercised during his life such an influence on the state and people of Athens, that the years of his rule were distinguished as "the age of Péricles." This period includes the time when Athens had attained its highest point of refinement at home, and possessed the greatest power abroad. Péricles adorned Athens by the erection of temples and magnificent buildings; he encouraged the arts and sciences, he invited men of genius, and in particular the great artist, Phídias, to his hospitable home. He gave to every one the means and opportunity of educating and distinguishing himself, and produced by these means a taste for art, literature, and poetry, even among the lowest classes of the people. Though descended from a rich and illustrious family, he was nevertheless a man of the people, and devoted to democratic principles. He procured a law, by which every Athenian citizen who sat in judgment, or was present at an assembly of the people, or served in the fleet or army, was entitled to a stipend. He distributed large alms to the necessitous, he instituted magnificent festivals, plays, and processions, for the gratification of the sight-loving people. By his exertions, the Athenian state attained such an exalted state of cultivation, that the citizens were almost all equally well fitted to fill offices or discharge business; so that the regulation, that the greater part of the public offices should be filled by lot, was attended with less inconvenience at Athens, than such arrangement would have produced at any other place. At the same time, Athens, by means of Péricles, attained the greatest renown abroad. Her ships ruled over the Ægéan sea, and compelled the islanders to pay tribute, by which means enormous sums of money flowed into her treasury. The statue of Minerva was covered with a robe of solid gold; the Athenian armies engaged in successful conflicts with the Thebans and
B. C. 447. Spartans, till the unfortunate battle of Coronéa put an end to their military glory. After this engagement, in which the Athenians were either killed or taken prisoners, Péricles was obliged to save Athens from the destruction by which it was threatened, by concluding the peace, named after him "the peace of Péricles."

THE PELOPONNESIAN WAR, B. C. 431–404.

§ 59. The peace of Péricles was of short duration. The prosperity of the Athenians filled the Spartans with envy and malevolence; and the insolence and severity with which they treated their subjected allies, more particularly the inhabitants of Ægína, who had only submitted after a long struggle, excited hatred and disgust. In a short time, two armed and hostile powers stood opposed to each other: the Athenian confederation, which included most of the islands and maritime towns, and which was favored by the democratic party in all the states, and the chief strength of which lay in its fleet; and the Peloponnésian alliance, with Sparta at its head, to which the Dóric and the greater part of the Æólian states (Bœótia and others) attached themselves, and which reposed its confidence on a gallant army. The Spartans declined for a long time to commence hostilities. But when the Corinthians complained that Athens had violated the peace by assisting the island of Corcȳra in its war against the mother country, Corinth, and had laid siege to the Corinthian colony, Potidæ'a, in Mácedon, the Peloponnésian war, which, for a period of twenty-seven years, ravaged Greece in the most frightful manner, at length broke out.

§ 60. As soon as war was declared, a Spartan army marched into Attica, and devastated the country. Upon this, Péricles summoned the inhabitants of the country into the town, fitted out a fleet, and, landing on the coast of Peloponnésus, commenced reprisals. These were continued for some time, till at length a plague broke out in Athens, in consequence of the overcrowded state of the city, swept away many thousands of the inhabitants, and finally carried Péricles himself to the grave, after he had witnessed the death of his two sons. The death of this great man was a heavy loss to Athens: for now a crowd of selfish demagogues, and among them, Cleon, a tanner, obtained great influence, seduced the people by flattery, and strove to prolong the war. Weakened by their own divisions, the Athenians were compelled to look on, whilst the Platæ'ans, their most faithful allies, were subdued, after an heroic struggle, by the Lacedæmónians and Bœótians: Platæ'a itself was levelled with the earth, the citizens who were capable of bearing arms were put to the sword, and their wives and children led into slavery.

B. C. 429.

B. C. 425.

The Athenian general, Demósthenes, shortly after succeeded in gaining possession of the Messenian town of Pylos, whence he harassed the Spartan territories with devastating inroads. It was in vain that the Spartans endeavored to drive him from his posi tion; their attacks were repulsed, and more than four hundred heavy-armed Spartan troops were shut up in the barren island of Sphactéria, where they were reduced to great extremities. They only obtained the means of subsistence by the desperate landing effected by some Helots, to whom the Spartans had promised freedom if they were successful in the attempt. At last, to escape starvation, they were compelled to surrender themselves to Cleon, who had arrived with reinforcements. This success inflamed the insolence of the democratic leader. He fancied himself a hero, and obtained the command of an army that was intended to subdue the Spartan general, Brásĭdas, in Thrace. But Cleon suffered a defeat before the city of Amphípŏlis, and was afterwards killed in the flight; whereupon

B. C. 421. the opposite party gained the upper hand in Athens, and concluded the peace of Nícias. In the mean time, a desperate struggle was going on between the aristocratic and democratic factions, in the greater number of the Greek cities; but nowhere was the strife more sanguinary than in the island of Corcy̆ra, where the most illustrious families were completely destroyed. By the help of the Athenians, the democrats got their adversaries in their power, shut them up in a building, and killed them by casting down stones upon their heads. Where the Spartans gained the upper hand, the aristocratic party became predominant, and punished their enemies by death and banishment; if the Athenians prevailed, the democrats assumed the direction of affairs, and treated their opponents with similar severity.

§ 61. The conclusion of peace separated the Spartans and Corinthians. The latter, in consequence, united themselves with Argos, Elis, and Mantinéa in Arcádia, for the purpose of depriving the Spartans of their superiority (hegemony) in Peloponnésus. In this attempt, they received the assistance of Alcibíades, who was then about thirty years old, and sister's son to Péricles, and who here displayed for the first time his address and powers of persuasion. Alcibíades was endowed with the greatest advantages both of mind and person. He was rich, handsome, accomplished, and a most admirable orator; so that he was exactly fitted to supply the place of Péricles, had he only possessed more stability and prudence. The war, which the Spartans now had to sustain with the Corinthians and allies, would have been fatal to their authority, had not fortune
B. C. 418. declared for the Lacedæmónian arms in the battle of Mantinéa.

§ 62. Not long afterwards, the Athenians despatched the finest fleet
B. C. 415. and the most admirable army that had ever sailed from the Piræ'us, to Sicily, under the command of Alcibíades, Nícias, and Lámachus, for the purpose of attacking the Dórian city, Syracuse. This undertaking failed. Alcibíades, during his absence, was accused by his enemies of many crimes against religion and the government, and was in consequence hastily recalled by the Athenian magistrates. Thirsting for vengeance, he fled to Sparta, and endeavored to stir up that state to make war upon Athens. The brave Lámachus fell in the siege of Syracuse; the Athenian fleet was destroyed in the harbor; and when Nícias attempted to escape by land with the remains of the army to a friendly city, he was attacked during a night march, and, after a bloody fight, taken prisoner with the whole of his troops. Those who did not fall in the engagement, were employed as slaves in the stone-quarries. The valiant generals, Nícias and Demósthenes, died in the market-place by the hands of the executioner.

§ 63. Dark reports conveyed to Athens the first news of this dreadful blow; when the frightful intelligence was confirmed, there was scarcely a family that had not occasion to mourn. The Athenian allies fell off and joined the Lacedæmónians; the Spartans renewed the war by sea and land, and were assisted by the Persian governor of Asia Minor. Within the city, the aristocratic party were attempting to overturn the constitution, and entered secretly into a traitorous alliance with the Spartans. Athens nevertheless defended herself for eight years against the superior force of the enemy, and was victor in two important engagements at sea. But no exertions could restore the crippled state to its former greatness. It was in vain that the Athenians recalled Alcibíades, gave him the command of the fleet and army, and cast the column, on which his crimes were inscribed, into the sea; — even he could not bring back its ancient glories to the Athenian navy. A few months after he had entered Athens amidst the exulting shouts of the populace, he was again deprived of his command, because his lieutenant in his absence had lost a sea-fight near Éphesus.

§ 64. About this time, the Spartans gained an excellent leader in the artful and adventurous Lysander, who obtained the favor of the new governor of Asia Minor, Cyrus the younger, for the purpose of increasing the Lacedæmónian fleet by the assistance of the Persians. This Lysander took advantage of the carelessness of the Athenian commanders, who had suffered their men to go on shore, by making an unexpected attack upon their ships at the Goat's River (Ægos-pótamos), on the Hellespont, and capturing the whole of them, except nine. The power of Athens was now vanished. After Lysander had reduced to submission the islands and towns that were friendly to the Athenians, he blockaded Athens itself by land and sea, and the overcrowded city was soon reduced by hunger to surrender. The long walls and fortifications were pulled down to the sound of flutes; the ships, with the exception of twelve, delivered to the Spartans, and all fugitives and outlaws recalled. Lysander then annulled the democratic constitution, and placed the government in the hands of thirty illustrious Athenians, who were the allies of Sparta. These aristocrats, distinguished by the name of the Thirty Tyrants, with the clever but violent Critias at their head, breathed nothing but death and banishment against the democratic party. But this reign of terror was but of short duration. Thrasybúlus, a patriotic man, collected around him the fugitives and those who had been banished, and marched upon Athens. Critias was slain in battle; the rest fell by treachery into the hands of the conqueror, who put them to death, reëstablished the democratic constitution, and, by the assurance that the past should be forgotten and forgiven, succeeded in again restoring tranquillity and order.

B. C. 405.

B. C. 404.

4. SOCRATES.

§ 65. During the Peloponnésian war, the morals of the Athenians had deteriorated, and honesty and civil virtue came to be less esteemed than wit and intelligence. This state of things was in a great degree brought about by the sophists, — false teachers, who paraded a factitious kind of wisdom founded upon fallacies and sophisms, and who presumed, by oratorical arts and tricks of disputation, to put lies in the place of truth, and to convert truth into error. They enticed to themselves wealthy young men, and for great rewards instructed them in these arts, by which means domestic and public life were poisoned in their very sources. At this juncture arose Sócrates, an Athenian citizen, who unmasked these sophistical mountebanks, and awakened the sentiments of religion, justice, and virtue in the bosoms of his pupils. Sócrates taught his practical philosophy, the end of which was "Know thyself," not in elaborate discourses from the lecturer's chair, but by questions and answers in the public streets, under the open sky, or in the workshops of mechanics. The sophists were reduced to silence by his clear intellect, his simple and upright life, and his moral worth; whilst the richest and most talented young men united themselves to him. This exasperated the vain and greedy sophists, and they accused him of seducing the youth, and introducing false gods. Sócrates, in a simple defence, disproved before the judges the truth of this accusation. But instead, as was then the custom, of imploring his acquittal with prayers and lamentations, he concluded his discourse by asserting that he was entitled to be received into the number of those illustrious men, who, on account of their services to the commonwealth, were maintained at the public expense. This offended the judges, and Sócrates was condemned to death by a small majority. It was in vain that his friends, particularly the rich citizen Crito, urged him to fly; he rejected their counsels, and in the midst of elevating discourses on the immortal nature of the soul, (Plato's Phædo), he drank the cup of poison, and died with the cheerfulness and composure of mind of a philosopher. He has left nothing in writing: but his illustrious disciple, Plato, has placed his own philosophy in the mouth of Sócrates. This Plato was so distinguished as a writer and thinker that he was named the "Divine," as well on account of his splendid and exalted ideas and poetical images, as of the perfect art of representation which is displayed by his works, written in the form of dialogues. Next to him, Xénophon the Athenian, at once a soldier and a writer, was the most distinguished of the disciples of Sócrates. He has made the world acquainted with the life and doctrines of his master, in the philosophical work, entitled "Memorabília of Sócrates."

5. THE RETREAT OF THE TEN THOUSAND. B. C. 400.

§ 66. Xénophon's most admirable historical work is the "Anábăsis," or the description of the campaign of the younger Cyrus in Persia, and of the retreat of the Greek troops under the command of Xénophon himself. After its contest with Greece, the Persian empire had grown gradually weaker. The governors ruled the provinces in an arbitrary manner, and excited insurrections by their oppression. The court was swayed by selfish and effeminate men and intriguing women, who practised the most frightful crimes, gave themselves up to every lust and excess, and perplexed the affairs of the kingdom by their contests for the crown. It was under these circumstances, that the younger Cyrus, governor of Asia Minor, entertained the project of depriving his elder brother, Artaxerxes, of the crown. He assembled a considerable army of mercenaries, the flower of which was composed of Spartan and other Greek troops, and marched with them into Persia. A battle was fought in the plain of Cunáxa, a few miles from Babylon, in which the Greeks indeed proved victorious, but Cyrus fell by the hand of his brother. The Greeks were summoned to surrender, and when they refused, the Persians invited Cleárchus and the other captains to an interview, in which they were treacherously murdered. The Athenian, Xénophon, then placed himself at the head of the helpless host, and led them, under the most incredible hardships, through Armenia to the Black Sea, and thence to Byzantium. Without any knowledge of the land or of the language, without guides on whom they could depend, they were compelled to climb pathless mountains, to wade through rivers, to march through inhospitable and snow-covered deserts, pursued by the Persians, and attacked by the inhabitants. When they caught the first glimpse of the Black Sea from an eminence, they fell upon their knees and saluted it with a shout of joy, as the termination of their miseries.

6. THE TIME OF AGESILAUS AND EPAMINONDAS.

§ 67. Sparta, by the Peloponnésian war, had become the first power in Greece. She abused her authority, however, by tyrannizing over the other states, and by this means brought upon herself the hatred of her allies, in the same way that Athens had formerly done. Her inhabitants had long degenerated from the simplicity and severity of manners enjoined by Lycurgus. Foreign wars had brought riches, these produced avarice and love of pleasure, and from these again proceeded a host of vices. Kings and generals suffered themselves to be bought by sums of money, and disgraced themselves by corruption. A few families acquired enormous wealth and possessions, and plunged into luxury and intemperance, whilst the poorer classes starved. Even the powerful king, Agesiláus, a strenuous advocate for the old Spartan virtue and simplicity, was unable to restrain these vices.

The other states had also long equally degenerated from the virtues and patriotism of an earlier period. Their citizens disaccustomed themselves from the use of arms, and relinquished the practice of war to hired mer cenaries; and when king Agesiláus declared war against the crumbling empire of Persia, and penetrated with his victorious banners into Asia Minor, the Athenians, Corinthians, Bœótians, and some others, were so forgetful of their honor and national feelings, that they suffered themselves to be persuaded by the Persian monarch to take the field against Sparta; so that Agesiláus was compelled to retreat, and to turn his arms, in the so-called Corinthian war, against the Greeks themselves. Disunion, enervation, and jealousy at length produced such an indifference to national honor, that the Greek states rivalled each other to secure the favor of Persia, and consented to the shameful peace of Antálcidas, by which the west coast of Asia Minor was given up to the Persians, and in consequence lost forever to liberty and Greece.

B. C. 387.

§ 68. The peace of Antálcidas contained the farther condition, that all the Grecian states should be free. The Spartans, who were appointed the guardians and executors of the treaty, took this opportunity to dissolve all alliances between the states, and to increase their own power. But their arrogance was soon punished. The Greek town Olýnthus, in Macedonia, had united several neighboring cities in a confederation, over which, as the principal city, it exercised authority. The Spartans objected to this, as contrary to the conditions of the peace of Antálcidas, and on the Olýnthians refusing to dissolve the confederacy, marched an army into the country, besieged their town, and compelled them to submission. During the march through Bœótia, the Spartan general allowed himself to be persuaded by the aristocratic party in Thebes to invest the town and overturn the democratic constitution, The undertaking was successful. The chiefs of the popular party were either executed, banished, or imprisoned; the aristocrats seized upon the government, and, confident of the support of the Spartans, ruled with insolence and violence.

§ 69. But the hour of retribution was approaching. The banished democrats united themselves in Athens, whence they commenced a correspondence with their friends in Thebes. At their instigation, they in a short time returned in secret, in the disguise of clowns, assembled themselves in the house of one of the party, and, issuing forth at midnight, fell upon the aristocrats who were collected together at a luxurious repast. After these had been despatched, they summoned the citizens to liberty, reëstablished the democratical government, and forced the Spartan garrison to retreat from the citadel. This occasioned a war between the Thebans and Lacedæmónians. The commonwealth of Thebes was at that time conducted by two men, who joined patriotism and virtue to courage and military talents, and who were united together by the bonds of friendship,— Epaminóndas and Pelópidas. They united their efforts in the attempt to elevate their country. Epaminóndas introduced a new

system of tactics, "the oblique order of battle," and Pelópidas was the originator of the sacred band, which, composed of a number of youths united together by friendship, and inspired by a love of honor and freedom, offered a successful resistance to the Spartans. At first, the Athenians sided with the Thebans, and by means of their generals, Iphícrates, Chábrias, and Timótheus, did much mischief to the Lacedæmónians, both by sea and land. But when Thebes subjected the lesser cities of Bœótia to its authority, and destroyed Platæ'a, a town that was on friendly terms with Athens, the old jealousy again awoke, Athens concluded a peace with Sparta, and when the Thebans refused to accede to its conditions, the Lacedæmónian troops again marched into
B. C. 371. their territory, but suffered so terrible a defeat from Epaminóndas and Pelópidas, in the battle of Leuctra, that Sparta never recovered from its effects. For the first time, the Lacedæmónian troops fled from the field of battle, so that the old Spartan law, which declared fugitives to be infamous, could not be put in force.

§ 70. Epaminóndas shortly after marched into Peloponnésus, and approached the unwalled capital of Lacónia, that for five centuries had never seen an enemy in its neighborhood. But the preparations for defence made by the old king, Agesiláus, and the determined attitude assumed by the Spartans, whose wives and children prepared to aid in the struggle, preserved it from attack. But Epaminóndas expiated an old act of injustice. He called the Messénians to liberty, and restored to the exiles who returned from abroad the land of their fathers, with the newly-built town of Messéne. Some years later, Epaminóndas again appeared in Peloponnésus. The Spartans and their allies, under the command of Agesiláus, presented themselves, and fought
B. C. 362. with him the battle of Mantinéa. In this battle, the Thebans indeed proved victorious, but conquest was dearly bought by the death of Epaminóndas. A javelin had pierced his breast, but it was not till he heard that the enemy were defeated, that he allowed the weapon to be withdrawn, and breathed forth his heroic spirit. Two years before, the brave Pelópidas had lost his life in Thessaly, and in the following year, at the age of eighty, died Agesiláus, after witnessing Sparta's highest glory and her deepest fall. Epaminóndas was magnanimous, experienced in war, and as just, unselfish, and poor as Aristídes himself; the loftiness of his aims, and the sense of his own personal worth, elevated him above avarice and the pursuit of pleasure, and the single cloak which he possessed was a greater ornament to him than any wealth could have been. His death was followed by a general flagging in the energies of the Greeks.

7. THE MOST FLOURISHING PERIOD OF GREECE IN LITERATURE AND THE ARTS.

§ 71. Whilst the Greeks were destroying their own power and disturbing the public tranquillity by their internal contests, literature and the plastic arts attained their highest perfection. Dramatic poetry, that in its origin had been connected with the festivals of the wine-god, Dionýsus, was raised to a wonderful height by the three great poets, Sóphocles, Eurípides, and Æ'schylus. The lives of these three men, who were the perfecters of the serious drama (tragedy), may be connected with the battle of Sálamis, since Æ'schylus, who was then in his forty-fifth year, fought in the ranks of the combatants; Sóphocles, at fifteen, took a part in the chorus of youths in the festival held after the battle for the celebration of the victory, and Eurípides was born on the day of the engagement. In the seven pieces of Æ'schylus, (the Prométheus vinctus, Persæ, Agamemnon, &c.), we may recognize the great period of the Persian war, when the souls of the Greeks were inspired by a noble enthusiasm for freedom and their fatherland. His compositions, which breathe a reverence for the gods, a respect for ancient institutions, and the self-consciousness of a lofty mind, are occasionally rendered obscure by the bold flight of the ideas, and the solemn energy of the language.

In the tragedies of Sóphocles, of which also seven are preserved (Antígone, Œ'dipus, Electra, &c.), we see the age of Péricles, with its cultivation and intellectual sociality; and hence these compositions remain unapproachable models of beauty and harmonious perfection of style. Eurípides, of whom we possess nineteen pieces (Medéa, Hécuba, Iphigenía, &c.), belongs to a less energetic period. He prefers to linger amidst scenes of justice, in which the Athenians took especial delight; he makes abundant use of the artfully-constructed speeches, sentences, and common-places then in vogue among philosophers, and seeks to affect his auditors by scenes of sorrow and distress. He replaces the creative power and genuine feeling of his predecessors, by sensibility and elegant and polished language. Eurípides's contemporary, Aristóphanes, brought comedy to perfection. His pieces, in which he contrasts the vices of his own age with the virtues of an earlier period, were often rendered more effective by living characters, who were introduced by name, and portrayed so accurately, that it was impossible to mistake them. Thus, in his "Frogs," and in another of his pieces, he ridiculed Eurípides and his flat and lachrymose tragedies; in his "Clouds," he held up to derision the sophists (under the name of Sócrates*) who attempted to undermine

* This is an ingenious plea to save Aristophanes from the serious charge of intending to ridicule, and hold up to public contempt, the greatest and purest character of his age, and indeed of all antiquity. But the excuse cannot be maintained; there can be no doubt that the satirist, who was as licentious as he was witty, actually intended to injure the reputation of Socrates, whom for the time he much disliked. *Am. Ed.*

the faith of the people; and he was even bold enough to attack the powerful Cleon, and the selfish demagogues, in his "Knights."

The chorus, which was a feature peculiar to the Greek drama, uttered in impassioned and lyrical poetry the sentiments and reflections of the audience upon what was going on upon the stage. The splendid theatres which were everywhere erected, and which were magnificent specimens of architecture, contributed not a little to the elevation of the dramatic art. A rich citizen could find no better way to the favor of the people than exhibiting a dramatic performance at his own expense.

§ 72. It was at this same period that the prose literature of the Greeks rose to its highest point of cultivation. In the dialogues of Plato, (§ 65,) the lofty thoughts of a rich and creative mind are clothed in the finest language, and presented in the most attractive form. Heródotus, of Halicarnássus, is looked upon as the father of history. He described the contests of the Greeks and Persians in simple and copious language, but occasionally introduced portions of the earlier history of the oriental and Greek tribes, so that his account contains a great deal that is fabulous, which he copied from the narrations of the priests. During his extensive travels, he made himself acquainted by personal observation with most of the countries of which he relates the history. His work was written for the people, and therefore its language is simple and cordial. He shows how the love of freedom, the discipline, and the moderation of the Greeks, bore off the victory from the servility, the disorderly masses, and the pomp of the Asiatics. The historical works of Heródotus kindled the emulation of the patriotic Athenian, Thucýdides. He had been banished at the time of the battle of Amphípolis, (§ 60), and devoted the years of his absence to the composition of his "History of the Peloponnésian war." His "thought-weighted" language, and the profundity of his reflections, render this work unintelligible, except to the learned. The history of Thucýdides ends with the twenty-first year of the Peloponnésian war.

Plato, B. C. 429-348.

Herodotus, B. C. 450.

Thucydides, B. C. 430.

Xénophon, his continuator, takes up the historical thread where Thucýdides relinquished it. He is distinguished by the clearness, ease, and beauty of his style, but is far inferior to Thucýdides in depth and historical accuracy. Although an Athenian, Xénophon respects and praises the Spartans, especially their king, Agesiláus, of whose life he had also written a description. For this reason, his Greek history is composed with a conscious partiality; the illustrious Thebans, Pelópidas and Epaminóndas in particular, are thrown entirely into the shade. His history concludes with the battle of Mantinæ'a. Another work of Xénophon's was a history of the elder Cyrus (Cyropædía), a sort of romance, in which he displays the founder of the Persian empire as the model of a regent.

Xenophon, B. C. 400.

§ 73. Rhetoric, also, about this time, rose in Athens to its highest point of perfection. If eloquence had originally been a gift of nature, an inborn talent, it began, after the Peloponnésian war, to be treated as an art, and rules and theories were established respecting it. Schools of oratory were opened, where the Athenian youth who wished to devote themselves to public life, or to the affairs of government or the law, received instruction. For in a democratic republic like Athens, he alone could hope to exert himself with success, who was capable of speaking well. Among the ten Athenian orators who have left written discourses behind them, B. C. 436—338. Isócrates takes a high rank, both on account of the artistic skill and perfection of style displayed by his discourses, and more particularly, from the great success of his oratorical school. Isæus, Demosthenes, B. C. 385—322. a pupil of Isócrates, was the instructor of Demósthenes, who, from his youth upwards, kept his purpose so steadily before his eyes that he made incredible efforts to overcome his natural impediments, so that he might render himself an orator. No one possessed to an equal degree with himself the gift of exciting, enchaining, and inspiring his auditors. Animation of delivery, alternations from severity to ridicule, bitter outbursts, and happy turns of expression, all served him as weapons. The most remarkable of his productions are the twelve political orations against Philip of Macedon (Philíppics), in which he endeavors to excite the Athenians to make war upon this enterprising monarch, who was at that time meditating the subjection of Greece. The rival of Demósthenes was Æ'schines, an orator like himself, who sided with the king of Macedon and his party. When the Athenian senate awarded a golden crown to Demósthenes, Æ'schines attempted, in a brilliant speech, to procure a revocation of the vote by calling in question the merits of him to whom the crown had been presented. This gave Demósthenes the opportunity of so overwhelming his opponent, in his incomparable oration " de Coróna," that Æ'schinès was sentenced to punishment, and experienced so much annoyance, that he betook himself to Rhodes, where he established a school of oratory.

§ 74. The most flourishing period of the fine arts, under which term are included architecture, sculpture, and painting, was from the time of Péricles to the death of Alexander. The feeling for art that was inherent in the Greeks, was the chief cause of this perfection. Grecian architecture was particularly distinguished by symmetry and harmony, so that every building formed a beautiful whole. The principal feature in a Greek edifice are the pillars, which are divided into three orders by the differences in their capitals. The plain and massive Doric, the slender Ionic with its voluted capital, and the highly-decorated Corinthian. They were particularly employed in the entrances of the temples, and in halls and porticos. The dwelling-houses of the ancients were small and insignificant, so that their architectural skill could only be displayed in their public buildings, temples, theatres, senate-houses, monuments, &c.

The art of sculpture was carried to its highest perfection by the Greeks, and the masterpieces of antiquity that have been preserved to us are even now regarded as unapproachable examples of beauty. Amongst the artists, the next in celebrity to Phídias (§ 58) are Scopas of Paros, Praxíteles of Athens, and Lysíppus of Sícyon. Since the best way of showing respect to a celebrated or deserving man, in Greece, was to erect his statue, or set up his bust or "hermes" (bust placed on a pedestal), artists everywhere found employment and encouragement. Every city made it a point of honor to possess a multitude of statues in its streets and public places. The splendid physical conformation of the Greeks, which was disfigured by no ugly habiliments, and the opportunity, afforded by the exercises of the gymnasium, of seeing the naked figure in every variety of attitude, tended materially to the perfection of the art of sculpture. The statue of the Belvidere Apollo, the group of the Laócoon, and innumerable figures and works in bas-relief, afford splendid evidence of the high artistic capabilities of the Greeks.

In painting, the names of Parrhásius, Zeuxis, and Apélles are particularly celebrated. We possess no specimen of ancient painting except the figures on the Grecian vases of burnt earth, and a few pictures on the walls of old buildings. Music, dancing, and the histrionic art were also cultivated by the Greeks with enthusiasm.

III. THE MACEDONIAN PERIOD.

1. PHILIP OF MACEDON, B. C. 361–336.

§ 75. Northward from Greece lies the rude and mountainous tract of Macedónia, the inhabitants of which were not looked upon as belonging to the Hellénes, though they had adopted the military system and many institutions of the Greeks. They were a military race, delighting in war and the chase, and in chivalrous exercises and entertainments. A year after the death of Epaminóndas, Philip assumed the government of this people. He was a man who united the shrewdness and dexterity of a statesman, the talents of a general, and the generosity and magnanimity of a prince. He both loved and respected the cultivation, and the artists and poets, of Greece, but held fast, nevertheless, to the manners of his own people, and even shared the disposition to intemperance indulged in by his nobles. He possessed a well-appointed and efficient army, which was rendered particularly formidable by a newly-invented order of battle, called the phalanx.

§ 76. Philip's great aim was the subjugation of the disunited Greek states. The sacred war afforded him the wished for opportunity for this purpose. The Thebans wanted to reduce the neighboring state, Phocis, under their own dominion, and had cited the inhabitants before the council of Amphíctyons, on a charge of having taken possession of, and brought into cultivation, some of the lands belonging to the temple of Delphi. The council inflicted a heavy fine upon the Phócians, and upon their refusing to pay it, they were placed under a ban, and the Thebans were directed to carry the punishment into execution. Upon this, the Phócians took possession of the temple of Delphi, and employed the treasures deposited there in hiring an army of mercenaries, by whose assistance they succeeded in defending themselves for ten years against all the attacks of their enemies. The Thebans addressed themselves to Philip for assistance. Philip yielded to their request, first subjected the Thessalians, and then penetrated by the pass of Thermópylæ into Phocis. After a gallant resistance, the Phócians were compelled to submit. They were thrust out of the council of the Amphíctyons, as a people accursed, and Philip was admitted in their place; their cities were razed to the ground, some of the inhabitants quitted their country, others were carried into slavery, and those that remained were compelled to pay tribute.

§ 77. Previous to this, Philip had taken possession of the Greek colonial cities, Amphípolis in Thrace, and Potidæ'a in Macedónia, and founded the strong town of Philíppi in the neighborhood of the former, in a region abounding in gold mines; after this, he had subjected the haughty city Olýnthus, and punished it severely in its possessions and liberties. But it was only by the breaking out of a second sacred war, that he was enabled to attain his object. The Lócrians were now accused in the same way the Phócians had formerly been, of having appropriated and brought under cultivation a portion of the lands belonging to the temple of Delphi; and for this crime, they were visited with a heavy fine by the council of Amphíctyons. As this fine was not paid, the Amphíctyons, at the suggestion of the orator, Æ'schines, who, in his capacity of Athenian deputy, was present at their council, commuted the punishment of the Lócrians. The Macedónian king, Philip, hastened southward with his army, but instead of subduing the Lócrians, he seized and fortified the importantly situated town of Elatéa. This arbitrary proceeding roused the Athenians from their indifference, and induced them to give a hearing to the exhortations of Demósthenes. The orator himself arranged an alliance with the Thebans, and effected the equipment of a considerable army. But these troops, collected together in haste, and placed under the command of incompetent leaders, were unable to sustain the shock of the Macedónian phalanx. Despite the valor of the sacred band of the Thebans, who fell to a man on the field, Philip gained the battle of Chæronéa, which put an end forever

B. C. 338. to the liberties of Greece. Demósthenes pronounced the funeral oration over the bodies of those who had fallen, and Isócrates, who was then nearly a hundred years old, put himself to death rather than survive the liberties of his country. For the rest, Philip treated the Greeks with kindness and affability, to accustom them more readily to the Macedónian yoke. He cherished the purpose of attacking the crumbling empire of Persia, at the head of the united states of Greece, and summoned an assembly of the whole nation at Corinth, to make the necessary preparations. He was already named generalissimo of the forces, with unlimited powers, and every state was directed to furnish him with its contingent of troops, when he was killed, from motives of private vengeance, by one of his body guard, at the nuptials of his daughter Ægæ, in Macedónia.

2. ALEXANDER THE GREAT.

§ 78. After the death of Philip, the Macedónian throne was ascended by his son Alexander, then in his twentieth year; a high-spirited prince, and susceptible of all that is great and honorable. He was brought up and instructed in the culture of the Greeks by Áristotle, the great philosopher, thinker, and inquirer; and in consequence, remained through his whole life a friend and admirer of the Grecian art and literature. As soon as Alexander had established himself upon the throne, he was acknowledged by the Greeks as the successor of his father in the office of generalissimo against the Persians. Before, however, he could undertake the campaign to Asia Minor, he had to sustain a severe encounter with some wild tribes, who had made an irruption into Macedónia. A false report of his death was suddenly spread abroad in Greece, and filled the Greeks with the hope of again regaining their independence. The Thebans killed a part of the Macedónian garrison in their citadel, and the Athenians and Peloponnésians made preparations for war. But Alexander came upon them with the rapidity of lightning, Thebes was taken, its walls and houses levelled with the ground, and the inhabitants reduced to slavery. Only the temple and the house of the poet Pindar were spared. The rest of the Greeks were terrified, and the victor, who soon repented of his severity, forgave them.

§ 79. It was in the spring of the year 334 B. C., that Alexander commenced his expedition against the Persians, with a small but valiant army, commanded by admirable officers, Clitus, Parménio, Ptolemæ'us, and Antígŏnus. The army arrived at the Hellespont by the same path that Xerxes had taken, but in the contrary direction. At the passage, Alexander was the first who sprang upon the Asiatic continent, where, upon the plain of Troy, he instituted solemn games and sacrifices in honor of the ancient heroes who had fallen there. Achílles was his model; for this reason, he always carried the compositions of Homer

B. C. 334. about with him. Shortly after, the battle at the stream Granícus took place, where Alexander carried off the victory from the far superior force of the Persians. His courage and chivalrous spirit here plunged him into imminent hazard of his life, from which he was only rescued by the timely assistance of his general, Clitus. The conquest of Asia Minor was the consequence of this victory. The Greek cities submitted themselves voluntarily, and hailed with joyful enthusiasm the kingly hero who had sprung from their own race. In the city of Górdium, there existed a very ancient royal chariot, with a knot twisted in the most intricate manner, respecting which an oracle had declared, that whoever should unfasten this knot should gain the empire of Asia. Alexander accomplished the prophecy by cutting the Gordian knot with his sword. After this, he crossed by perilous marches the Cilician mountains, where he got a dangerous illness by bathing in the cold waters of the Cydnus, from which he was only restored by the skill of the Greek physician, Philíppus, and his own confidence in human virtue.

§ 80. Daríus Codománnus himself now opposed him with a much stronger force, but suffered a complete overthrow in the battle of the Issus. This unfortunate king, who was worthy of a better fate, fled with the remains of his army into the interior of his dominions, whilst Alexander prepared to attack Phœnícia and Palestine, so as not to leave these lands unsubdued in his rear. The booty, after the battle of the Issus, was immense; and the number of the prisoners, amongst whom were the mother, wife, and daughter of Daríus, who, contrary to the customs of antiquity, were generously treated by the conqueror, not at all inferior.

§ 81. Palestine and Phœnícia submitted without resistance; but Tyre, confident in the strength of its position, rejected the summons to surrender with defiance. Upon this, Alexander undertook the celebrated siege of Tyre, which lasted seven months. He commanded a mole, with towers, to be erected from the main land to the island on which the city was built; and from this mole his soldiers attempted the conquest of the town by machines for casting stones, and by every means that art could supply, whilst his ships blockaded the place by sea. But the Tyrians defeated his attempts by ingenious methods of defence, and maintained a desperate resistance. For this, Tyre had to make a heavy B. C. 332. expiation when it was at length taken. Those of the inhabitants who had not escaped or perished in the siege, were reduced to slavery, and the city itself was levelled to the ground. For the purpose of directing the commerce of the world into a different channel, Alexander, after he had conquered Egypt, built Alexandria on an arm of the Nile, and this city soon became the central point of trade and civilization. From Egypt he marched to the widely-renowned temple of Jupiter Ammon in the oasis of Sivah, where the priests declared him to be the son of Jupiter, a distinction that gained him no little respect in the eyes of the superstitious orientals.

§ 82. After Alexander had established a new government in Egypt, he marched against Daríus, who, in the mean time, had collected a large army. He crossed the Euphrátes and Tigris, and with a
B. C. 331. force only the twentieth part of that of the enemy, he defeated the enormous host of the Persians which had been assembled together from all the East in the plains of Babylon, in the battle of Arbéla and Gaugaméla. The conquest of Babylon, and the capture of the two ancient capitals, Susa and Persépŏlis, with an enormous treasure, were the fruits of this splendid victory. Daríus fled from Ecbátăna, the beautiful summer residence of the Persian kings, to the mountainous region of Bactria, where he received his death from the hand of his treacherous governor, Bessus. Alexander shed tears over the fate of his unfortunate rival, and caused his murderer, who had assumed the title of king, but who was soon overcome and taken prisoner by the Macedónians, to be crucified in conformity with the Persian custom.

§ 83. The enterprising conqueror succeeded, by dint of a daring march across the snow-covered Indian Caúcasus, during which his soldiers narrowly escaped perishing by hunger and fatigue, in making himself master of the mountain region to the south-east of the Caspian Sea, and rendering it approachable by the roads he caused to be constructed. His lofty spirit was not entirely absorbed by scenes of war and conquest, but could attend to the civilization of the savage inhabitants. Four newly-erected towns, named after him, Alexandria, became the centre of the caravan trade, and diffused the Greek cultivation among the farthest nations of the East. At the storming of a strong fortress, he took prisoner the beautiful princess, Roxána, "the Pearl of the East," and made her his wife.

§ 84. Although the Macedónians repeatedly expressed their discontent at their leader's unbounded love of conquest, Alexander nevertheless proceeded onwards, to subjugate the lands on the banks of the Indus. But the warlike inhabitants of northern India, urged on by their priests, offered him a far more vigorous resistance than the dastardly subjects of the Persian king. Alexander's life was exposed more than once to the greatest peril in the storming of their strong-holds. The quarrels of the native princes facilitated the conquest of the Land of the Five Rivers (Punjaub) by the Macedónians. Some of them leagued themselves with Alexander against Porus, the most powerful of these princes on the farther side of the Hydáspes (Dschelum). The passage of this river in the face of the enemy, and the action that followed, in which the gallant Porus was wounded and taken prisoner, are among the greatest military achievements of antiquity. Two new cities, Bucéphăla (so named in honor of Alexander's charger, Bucéphalus), and Nicæ'a (city of Victory), were to diffuse Grecian civilization among these lands also. Alexander continued his course by difficult marches, still farther east ward, to Hýphăsis, and was already making preparations to add the rich lands of the Ganges to his dominions, when the murmurs of the Macedónians became so loud that he was compelled, though with inward reluctance, to retreat. Twelve stone altars on the banks of the river mark the eastern termination of his conquests. After restoring their lands to Porus and the other Indian princes under Macedónian supremacy, he sailed down the Indus to discover another way of returning.

This undertaking proved most fatal. In two months, he lost three fourths of his army in the frightful deserts of Gedrósia. The heroic warriors, who had bidden defiance to sword and lance in so many battles, fell victims in the barren and waterless desert to want and fatigue, to the miseries of the climate, the fervid sun, the heated sand, and the nightly frosts. Alexander magnanimously shared all the dangers and difficulties with the meanest of his troops, and rewarded those who escaped with entertainments and presents; by this means, the feasting became as excessive as the previous want.

§ 85. Upon his return, Alexander dismissed his veteran soldiers to their homes, after having laden them with presents; inflicted punishments upon the faithless governors and officers, who, during his absence, had committed acts of violence and oppression, and then devoted himself zealously to the plan of assimilating the conquered people with their victors, and uniting them together in one nation possessed of the arts and cultivation of Greece. He treated the Persians with kindness, for the purpose of attaching them to his person and his rule. He surrounded himself with a court after the fashion of their kings, assumed the royal habit and diadem, and employed Persian guards and attendants. He encouraged marriages between his generals and soldiers and the maidens of the country, by presents, and he himself espoused one of the daughters of Daríus. By this conduct, Alexander offended the Macedónians and Greeks, who wished to rule over the conquered people. Already, during the Indian campaign, the soldiers had displayed their discontent and ill humor in dissatisfied murmurs. This induced Alexander to have Philótas, the playfellow of his youth, and who was now the head of the malcontents, stoned by the army, and to put to death his aged father Parménio, who had remained behind in Media.

Alexander had at first imitated the customs of the Persian monarchs for the purpose of conciliating the conquered people; but he soon began to take delight in this oriental magnificence. His court at Babylon, which he intended to make the seat of the government of his empire, shone with the highest splendor; riotous feasts and banquets crowded upon each other, and in the intoxication of sensual indulgence, he committed deeds that afterwards cost him bitter repentance. On his march to the Indus, he had slain his deserving general, Clitus, who saved his life at the Granícus, but who afterwards excited his anger by some sarcastic

speeches as they were drinking. His heart was corrupted by flatterers, who thrust his honest and well-meaning advisers from his side. The intemperate indulgence in strong wines undermined his health, and brought him to an early grave. One of the last acts of the hero was instituting magnificent funeral solemnities in honor of his prematurely departed friend, Hephæ'stion. His grief for this friend of his youth had not yet passed away, when an illness carried him to the grave in the midst
B. C. 323. of fresh schemes of conquest, and before he had determined upon a successor. When he was asked to whom he left his kingdom, he is said to have replied, "To the worthiest." His dead body was brought from Babylon to Alexandria, and there interred.

---

3. THE ALEXANDRIAN PERIOD.

a. ALEXANDER'S SUCCESSORS.

§ 86. As Alexander left no heir behind him who was capable of assuming the government, — only a brother, who was imbecile, and two children who were minors, — his empire fell to pieces as rapidly as it had been constructed. After many fierce and bloody wars, in which the house of Alexander was totally destroyed, his generals succeeded in grasping separate portions of his territories, and erecting them into independent kingdoms. At first, Perdíccas, to whom Alexander had given his signet ring, received the greatest respect, and took upon
B. C. 321. himself the office of regent. But when he made war upon Ptolemy, the governor of Egypt, he was killed by his own soldiers; whereupon Antígŏnus assumed the chief power. Antígŏnus
B. C. 316. made himself master of the treasury in Susa, and hired such a number of mercenary troops, that he was enabled to bid defiance to the rest of the generals, and compel them to acknowledge him as commander and regent of the empire. As he allowed it, however, to be pretty plainly seen that he aimed at nothing less than the sovereignty of the whole of the Alexandrian dominions, the other generals, Seléucus of Syria, Ptolemy of Egypt, and Cassander of Macedon, leagued themselves together against him and his son Demetrius, who afterwards obtained the surname of Poliorcétes (Taker of Cities). From this originated a long contest, that was carried on at the same time both in Greece and Asia, with various success, and which was only terminated by the great battle of Ipsus, in Asia Minor, where the hero Antígŏnus, who was then eighty years old, lost his life, and his son Demetrius was obliged to fly. After many partitions and interchanges, Alexander's

empire (a few smaller states excepted) was finally divided into the three following kingdoms: —

I. Macedonia and Greece.
II. The Syrian empire of the Seleúcidæ.
III. Egypt under the Ptolemies.

b. GREECE'S LAST STRUGGLE. THE ACHAIAN LEAGUE.

§ 87. From the time of the battle of Chæronéa, Greece had remained under the government or influence of the Macedónian kings, and all attempts made by individual states to shake off this yoke had proved ineffectual. Thus the attempt of the brave Spartan king, Agis II., who, B. C. 330. with 5000 of his followers, died the death of heroes in the bloody field of Megalópolis, was productive of no result. The contests between the aristocratic and democratic parties still continued in Athens during the Macedónian period. When the aristocrats, with the noble Phócion at their head, obtained the government by the aid of the Macedónians, many of the popular party, and among others, Demósthenes, the vehement opposer of the royal house of Macedon, B. C. 322. quitted the city. Threatened with being given up, the great orator fled to a temple of Neptune, where he destroyed himself by poison, to save himself from falling into the hands of his enemies. Some years afterwards, the democrats again gained the upper hand, when they compelled Phócion, in his turn, to drink the cup of poison. From this time, party violence diminished in Athens, but the love of freedom, patriotism, and civic virtue decayed with it. Effeminacy and the pursuit of pleasure choked the nobler feelings, and although the arts and sciences still continued to flourish, and Athens still remained the centre of civilization, the greatness of the people was gone forever. The citizens disgraced themselves by servility and flattery, particularly at the time when the two Demetrii, Phaléreus and Poliorcétes, were resident in their city, and destroyed all morality by their sensuality and debauchery.

§ 88. About the middle of the third century, Greece made a final B. C. 250. effort in the Acháian league, to which Arátus of Sícyon gave such power and consequence, especially after the strong city of Corinth had placed itself at the head of the confederation, that he was enabled to assume the supreme power over Peloponnésus, and even over the whole of Greece. This excited the jealousy of Sparta, where, just at that time, two high-spirited kings, Agis III. and Cleómenes, were endeavoring to restore the ancient strength and military virtue. For since the Spartans had decided that one person might become the proprietor of numerous estates, the whole of the land had gradually got into the possession of a few rich families, who governed the state by choosing the éphori from among themselves. The remainder of the citi-

zens possessed neither rights nor property, and were in debt to the rich. The two kings sought to remedy these evils by abolishing the office of the éphori, by destroying the bonds of the debtors, and by reëstablishing the laws and customs of Lycurgus. But Agis was dethroned and cruelly murdered by his enemies; and Cleómenes, who by dint of resolution succeeded in carrying his objects in Sparta, and then endeavored to compel the rest of the Peloponnésian states to acknowledge the Spartan supremacy, was defeated in the battle of Sellásia in Laconia
B. C. 221. by the Acháian league, supported by the Macedonians, and found himself compelled to fly to Alexandria; where he and his faithful followers, after being baffled in attempting an insurrection, perished by their own daggers. In the same year in which Cleómenes met with his death, Sparta was subdued by the valiant Philopœ'men (who had been chosen head of the Achaian league after Arátus), and compelled a short time after to join the league and abolish entirely the laws of Lycurgus. Philopœ'men afterwards fell into the hands of his enemies, during a war with the Messenians, and was obliged to drink the cup of poison. After the death of this "last of the Greeks," the power of the Acháian league declined, so that the Romans were enabled to take possession of the whole country without any great effort.

c. THE PTOLEMIES AND SELEUCIDÆ.

§ 89. Seleúcus and Ptólemy were the most fortunate of Alexander's successors. The former, after many wars which were attended with important results, succeeded in reducing all the countries between the Hellespont and the Indus, and founding the Syrian empire of the Seleúcidæ. He built the magnificent city of Antioch on the Orontes, and Seleúcia on the Tigris. By means of these cities, and forty others, erected by himself and his successors, the Greek language and culture became more and more predominant in the East; and from this period, Asia Minor, Syria, and Egypt, were the chief seats of civilization and commerce. But this condition of extreme refinement afforded little matter for rejoicing. The enormous wealth that flowed into these states produced luxury, effeminacy, and sensuality; indolence enervated the people, and produced a servile spirit, which displayed itself by the most abject adulation of oppressive rulers. Sanguinary crimes, the empire of women and favorites, universal reprobation and corruption of morals, are the prominent features in the history of the Seleúcidæ, of whom Antíochus III., surnamed the Great, is the best known, as well by his expedition into India, as from his unfortunate contest with the Romans. Under monarchs so weak and abandoned as these, it was no difficult matter for enterprising men to establish small independent states. The most celebrated of these were the kingdom of Pérgamus in Asia Minor, and that of the Parthians on the north-east of the Euphrátes.

The Egyptians under the Ptolemies were in a similar position. The three first kings established a large naval and military force, by means of which they enlarged their empire on all sides. Trade and commerce produced wealth; the science of government and taxation was brought to a high degree of perfection. Alexandria became the seat of the commerce of the world, and the centre of Greek art, literature, and civilization; the world-renowned museum, with its extensive library and residences for poets and men of learning, was connected with the royal palace. But the men who were the producers of all this prosperity were, like the royal family itself, aliens — Greeks and Jews. The glory of the Ptolemáic dynasty was of short duration, for the civilization of Alexandria had no root among the people. It was an exotic plant that embellished the surface, but left the soil unchanged. The court of Alexandria was not less distinguished by cruelty, debauchery, and corruption of morals, than by its splendor, wealth, and refinement.

d. THE JEWS UNDER THE MACCABEES.

§ 90. Judæ'a was for a long time an object of contention between the Seleúcidæ and the Ptolemies. The latter were the first to take possession of the land and to render it tributary; but they suffered the old institutions to remain, and allowed the high priest, with the council of seventy (Sánhedrim), to manage the affairs of religion and the internal government. Many of the Jews settled in Alexandria, where they acquired wealth and power, but gradually lost the language, manners, and religion of their own country, or mingled them with those of the Greeks.
B. C. 284. The translation of the Hebrew text of the Bible into Greek, which was executed at the instigation of the second of the Ptolemies, by seventy-two Alexandrian Jews (hence called the Séptuagint), was afterwards extremely serviceable to the propagation of Christianity.

Judæ'a was subjected to the Seleúcidæ by the Syrian king Antíochus III. (the Great), and grievously oppressed with taxes. His second successor, Antíochus Epíphănes, plundered the temple in Jerusalem of its treasures, and even entertained the purpose of destroying the Jewish institutions and the worship of Jehovah, and substituting the Greek idolatry in its place. To this project the Jews offered an obstinate resistance, and by this means drew a severe persecution on themselves. When this persecution was carried beyond all endurable limits, the people rose in desperation against their oppressors, and under the command of the
B. C. 142. high priest, Mattathías, and his five heroic sons (Máccabees), encountered the Syrians with courage and success. The eldest son, Judas Maccabæ'us, enforced a peace, which granted the
B. C. 135. reëstablishment of the Jewish worship. His brother Simon freed Judæ'a from the Syrian yoke, and reigned wisely and

righteously as prince and high priest. Under his successors, the limits of the kingdom were enlarged, and the Idumæ'ans (Edomites) induced to accept the Jewish law. But internal dissensions, and the hatred of sects, soon again impaired the strength of the people. The Pharisees, who held firmly to the prophets and the law of Moses, attributed great merit to the accurate observance of trifling precepts and outward ceremonies, and fell by this means into hypocrisy and false righteousness; the Sadducees were less severe in their interpretation of the Mosaic laws, and attempted to bring them into accordance with the morals, doctrine, and way of thinking of the Greeks; the Essénes lived together in brotherhoods, who had all their possessions in common, and served God by acts of penance and works of charity. The weakness produced by the mutual hostility of these sects at length brought the Jewish race under the dominion of the Romans. The last of the Máccabees was slain by Herod the Idumæ'an, who thereupon ascended the throne of David by the assistance of the Romans, and ruled over Judæ'a as tributary king (Tetrarch). For the purpose of conciliating the Jews, who hated him as a foreigner, he enlarged and beautified the temple of Solomon; but towards the end of his reign, suspicion caused him to degenerate into a bloodthirsty tyrant, who even attempted the life of that Jesus of Nazareth who was sent into the world to redeem the lost race of man.

C. THE STATE OF CIVILIZATION DURING THE ALEXANDRIAN PERIOD.

§ 91. By the conquests of Alexander and his successors, the Grecian arts and refinements were diffused over the greatest part of the old world, and a high amount of civilization in consequence produced. The great increase of commerce and intercourse among all nations was favorable to the spread of this civilization. But the inward strength was weakened by the outward diffusion. Nothing worthy of notice was produced in poetry, except the Idyls, in which Theócritus the Sicilian (B. C. 280.) describes a pastoral life full of innocence and simplicity, and a few dramatic compositions which are now lost. History and oratory were far behind the splendid examples of an earlier period. Learning, and the practical sciences, which are based on experience and inquiry, attained, on the other hand, to a great degree of perfection. Learned critics and grammarians arranged and illustrated the works of the older Greek writers; natural history and mathematics, geography and astronomy, of which the elements alone had previously existed, were now greatly advanced. (Euclid, B. C. 280.) Euclid, a contemporary of the first Ptólemy, composed a text-book of geometry that was employed in education for centuries; (Archimedes, B. C. 212.) Archimédes of Syracuse gained imperishable renown by his discoveries in mechanical and physical science; and the art of medicine, that had been first established on a scientific basis by Hippócrates, was considerably extended by the Alexandrian physicians. But philosophy was the subject that received the greatest attention. As Paganism in its corruption afforded no rest to the soul, and no support in life, men sought for refuge in the pursuit of wisdom. The precepts of the philosophers of an earlier period were expanded and applied to the regulation of life. In this way arose the schools of philosophy, some of which reposed on the doctrines of Plato and Áristotle, and others were originated by the disciples of Sócrates and other wise men. The Stoics and the Epicuréans became the most distinguished of these philosophical sects. Sócrates had especially taught, that happiness was the end of existence. His scholar Antísthĕnes believed that the surest way of attaining this happiness was to renounce all pleasures, and taught that moderation, abstinence, and a freedom from wants, were the highest objects of human exertion. His disciple Dióĝĕnes carried these doctrines to the greatest excess: he lived in a tub, deprived himself voluntarily of property and all the pleasures of life, and by this "heroism of abstinence," excited the admiration of the great Alexander. This school was called the Cynic, from the place in which Antísthĕnes taught; and in allusion to this, Dióĝĕnes received the surname of kuōn (hound), because the wretched and joyless life he led seemed fitter for a dog than a human being. This doctrine in a more noble form constitutes the basis of the Stoic philosophy, which was taught by Zeno, a contemporary of Alexander, in the porticoes (stoa) of Athens. According to his teaching, man only attains felicity by bearing with invincible indifference all the changes and chances of life,—joy and grief, misfortune or happiness: this is his duty the rather, that every thing is determined on beforehand by an eternal natural necessity or fate. In opposition to this view, another disciple of Sócrates, Aristíppus of Cyréne, maintained the enjoyment of life as his chief principle, and taught the art of wisely mingling together sensual and intellectual pleasures. This art of enjoyment was erected by one of his scholars, Epicúrus, into a system that numbered many adherents. Whilst, however, Epicúrus made happiness to consist in a freedom from all painful and distressing emotions, his followers overstepped the bounds of moderation, placed luxury and the gratification of the appetites as the ends of existence, and rendered Epicurism the philosophy of effeminacy and excess.

Diogenes.

Zeno.

Aristippus.

C. HISTORY OF ROME.

THE RACES AND INSTITUTIONS OF ANCIENT ITALY.

§ 92. The beautiful peninsula which is bounded on the north by the Alps, surrounded on the east, west, and south by the Mediterranean, and traversed throughout its whole length by the Appenines, was formerly inhabited by numerous races of men of different origin. Upper Italy, on either bank of the Po (Padus), was the dwelling-place of the Gallic race, who were divided into many tribes and states, and possessed numerous cities, both in the fertile plains and on the sea-coast. Central Italy was inhabited by many small tribes, a part of which had dwelt in the land from time immemorial, and might be looked upon as the aborigines of the country; whilst others had wandered thither from abroad. To the latter class belonged the remarkable family of the Etruscans, to the former the sturdy race of the Sabélli, who were again divided into numerous warlike and freedom-loving tribes, among whom the Sámnītes, the Sábīnes, and the Æqui, were the most distinguished. The Latins, a powerful rustic tribe on the south of the Tiber, were a mixed race, composed of natives and immigrants, to which, after the conquest of Troy, a Trojan race, under the conduct of Ænéas, is said to have united itself. The coast of Lower Italy was covered with Greek colonies; the inland parts were the seat of warlike tribes of Sabélline origin, Sámnītes, Campánians, Lucáni. Campánia, with its vineyards and cornfields, is one of the most beautiful and fertile spots on the globe, and was chosen accordingly by the Romans for the erection of their magnificent villas. Of all these races, that of the Etruscans is the most worthy of remark. They formed a confederation of twelve independent cities, of which Cære, Tarquínii, and Perusia, in the neighborhood of the Trasiménian lake, Clúsium, and Veii, are the best known. The separate cities were governed by an aristocratic priesthood. These nobles (Lúcumos) elected the head of the confederation, the insignia of whose office were an ivory chair, a purple mantle, and axes inclosed in bundles of rods (fasces), such as were afterwards borne before the Roman consuls. The Etruscans were a religious people, and paid great observance to predictions derived from the sacrifice of animals (auspices), and the flight of birds (auguries). They were proficient in the art of founding, and in working earth and metals, and their skill in architecture is attested by the existing remains of gigantic walls, and the ruins of temples, dykes, roads, &c. The innumerable vessels of clay and cinerary urns (Etruscan vases), ornamented with paintings, which are dug out of the earth, are evidence of the diligence of the Etruscans in arts and manufactures.

But the oppressive power of the aristocracy, which proved destructive to the freedom and energy of the middle and lower classes, was the occasion of the early decay and extinction of the arts of culture among the people. The Sábīnes, Sámnītes, and other tribes of Sabélline origin, led a simple and temperate life in open or only slightly-fortified towns. They loved the pastoral life, agriculture, and war, and looked upon their freedom as their greatest blessing. From time to time, they celebrated a sacred spring, during which the newly-born cattle were offered in sacrifice; and the children who came into the world in the course of the year, left their country as colonists, on arriving at the age of twenty.

The Latins dwelt in thirty cities, which were united together in a confederation, of which Alba Longa was the head. Agriculture and civil freedom flourished among them; their religion was founded upon the worship of nature, and bore a relation to the cultivation of the soil. The seed-god Saturn, and his spouse Ops (the abundance flowing from the earth), were among their deities. The venerable goddess Vesta, whose sacred and perpetual fire was watched by twelve virgins (Vestals), was also one of the native deities of the Latins. The representatives of the union held their meetings in a wood on the Albanian hill.

I. ROME UNDER THE GOVERNMENT OF KINGS AND PATRICIANS.

I. ROME UNDER THE KINGS.

§ 93. We are told by an old legend, that king Numitor of Alba Longa, a successor of the Trojan Ænéas, (§ 37), was deprived of his crown by his brother Amúlius, and his daughter Rhæa Silvia placed among the sacred virgins of Vesta, that she might remain unmarried and without offspring. But when she bore the twins Rómulus and Remus, to the god Mars, her cruel uncle commanded the children to be exposed on the banks of the Tiber, where, however, they were discovered and brought up by shepherds. Informed by an accident of the mystery of their birth and the fate of their grandfather, they restored the throne of Alba Longa to Numitor, and then founded Rome on the Pálatine hill, on the left bank of the Tiber. The rising walls of the city are said to have been stained by the blood of Remus, who was slain in a quarrel, by his brother.

B. C. 753.

Romulus, B. C. 730.

§ 94. When the little town was built, Rómulus attracted inhabitants, by declaring it a place of refuge for fugitives. But as the fugitives had no wives, and the neighboring people hesitated to give them their daughters in marriage, Rómulus arranged some military games, and invited the neighbors as spectators. At a given signal, every Roman seized upon a Sábine virgin, and carried her off into the city. This outrage gave rise to a war between the Sábines and the new colony. The two armies were already opposed to each other, when the abducted virgins rushed between the combatants, and put an end to the strife, by declaring that they would share the fate of the Romans. A treaty was arranged, in consequence of which the Sábines, who dwelt on the Cápitoline hill, agreed to unite themselves in a single community with the Latins, who lived on the Pálatine, and the Etruscans, who inhabited the Cælian hill: it was decided further, that the Sábine king, Titus Tátius, should share the government with Rómulus; and that a Latin and a Sábine should be elected alternately from the senate to the office of king. Rómulus disappeared from the earth in an unknown manner, and received divine honors under the name of Quirínus. The citizens from this time bore the name of Quirítes, conjointly with that of Romans.

Numa Pompílius, B. C. 700.

§ 95. The warlike Rómulus was succeeded by the wise Sabine, Numa Pompílius, who reduced the rising state to order by his laws and religious institutions, and improved and civilized the inhabitants. He built temples, and established a form of religious worship, increased the number of priests, and made regulations respecting sacrifices and divinations. He dedicated a temple at the entrance of the forum to Janus Bifrons, the god who presides over the beginning of every thing, both in time and space: the doors of this temple were open in time of war, and closed during peace. As the Greeks confirmed their laws by the means of oracles, so Numa maintained that he had derived his system of religion from conversations with the nymph Egéria, who had a wood sacred to her on the south of Rome.

B. C. 650. B. C. 625.

§ 96. The two following kings, Tullus Hostílius the Latin, and Ancus Mártius the Sabine, enlarged the territory of the little state by successful wars; so that four other hills were added to the three before mentioned, and gradually supplied with inhabitants. For this reason, Rome is called the seven-hilled city. Under Tullus Hostílius the Romans engaged in a war with Alba Longa. Just as the armies were about to engage, it was agreed to decide the fate of the two cities by a combat between three brothers, the Horátii and the Curiátii, chosen from each of the parties. Two of the champions of the Romans had already fallen, when the victory was decided in their favor by the cunning and bravery of the third, and the possession of Alba Longa fell at once into their hands. The city was destroyed, and the inhabitants transplanted to Rome. The same fortune happened to many other cities in the neighborhood, during the reign of Ancus Mártius. The conquered citizens settled in Rome, where they received houses and small estates, but were not admitted to the privileges of the elder citizens. The latter from this time, were called "patricians," the new-comers bore the name of "plebeians." Ancus Mártius founded the sea-port of Ostia, at the mouth of the Tiber.

§ 97. The last three kings, Tarquínius Priscus, Servius Tullius, and Tarquínius Supérbus, belonged to the Etruscan race, as is evident from the buildings they erected, and the Etruscan institutions they introduced

B. C. 600. into Rome. The elder Tarquin laid the foundation of the vast structure of the Capitol, which was completed by his son Tarquínius Supérbus, in accordance with his father's design. It consisted of a citadel and a magnificent temple. He constructed, in addition, the enormous cloácæ (sewers), built of freestone, for the draining of the city, the Circus Máximus, and the Forum.

After the murder of Tarquin by the sons of his predecessor, his son-

B. C. 550. in-law Servius Tullius ascended the throne. He originated two measures that were followed by important consequences. First, he divided the plebeians in the city and its vicinity into thirty tribes, with their own overseers and assemblies; he then divided the entire population of the state, according to their property, into five classes, and these again into hundreds, in order to facilitate the collection of imposts and the arrangement of military service. By these means, the rich obtained greater privileges, coupled however with the condition of serving as heavy-armed troops without pay, and at their own expense. A sixth class, which included the proletaries (persons without property), were exempt from taxes and military service, but were also excluded from all political rights. By these measures, Servius Tullius brought upon himself the hate of the patricians, and was in consequence murdered by his son-in-law, Tarquínius Supérbus, with their assistance.

B. C. 533. § 98. Tarquínius Supérbus enlarged the boundaries of the state by successful wars with the Latins, whom he united in

B. C. 509. a confederacy under the direction of Rome; he completed the Capitol, and ordered the collection of ancient oracles, called the Sibylline books, to be preserved there; he founded the first colony in the neighboring country of the Volscians, for the purpose of extending the power of Rome. But despite all these services, he rendered himself odious to the patrician party by attempting to extend the limited kingly authority. His acts of violence against the senate and the patricians, and the severe imposts and soccage duties with which he visited the plebeians, produced general discontent, which finally burst into rebellion when it became known in Rome that the outrage which one of the king's sons had offered to the virtuous Lucretia had driven her to self-destruction. Two relatives of the royal house, Lucius Tarquínius Collatínus, the husband of Lucretia, and Junius Brutus, were the leaders of the insurrection. Upon receiving information of what was taking place, the king, who was just then occupied in the siege of the ancient seaport of Árdĕa, hastened to Rome with his army, for the purpose of suppressing the tumult; but he found the gates closed against him, and being deposed from the throne by a vote of the popular assembly, and finding himself deserted by his army, he and his sons were obliged to retire into banishment.

---

2. ROME AS A REPUBLIC UNDER THE PATRICIANS.

a. HORATIUS COCLES. THE TRIBUNES. CORIOLANUS.

§ 99. After the banishment of the royal family, the supreme power in Rome fell into the hands of the senate. They confirmed the laws that were passed in the assemblies of the people, and proposed the officers that it was the province of the commons to elect. Instead of a king, two consuls were chosen every year, who ruled the state, superintended the administration of justice, and, in time of war, led the army to the field. The patricians alone could be chosen to these or any other offices.

The young republic had severe conflicts to sustain both within and from without. Under the first consuls, a number of young Romans of patrician family entered into a conspiracy, for the purpose of bringing back the banished royal family. When this was discovered, the inflexible Brutus punished the offenders, among whom were two of his own sons, with death. From without, the Romans were threatened with the most imminent danger, by the Etruscan king Porsénna, to whom Tarquin had applied for help, and who had taken possession of the hill Janículum, on the right bank of the Tiber. The Romans were repulsed in an attempt to drive him from this position, and were only saved by the valor of Horátius Cocles, who defended the wooden bridge that crossed the river. After the Romans had secured themselves and destroyed the bridge, Cocles sprang into the stream, armed and weaponed as he was, and swam safely to the opposite shore. Another Roman, Mútius Scæ′vola, penetrated into the Etruscan camp for the purpose of killing the king. He made a mistake, however, and stabbed the royal secretary. When Porsénna, upon this, endeavored by threats to terrify him into a confession, Mútius, to show that he feared neither pain nor death, laid his right hand in the midst of a fire that was burning on an altar. It was from this circumstance that he received the name of Scæ′vola (left hand). Astonished at such a proof of courage and patriotism, Porsénna made a peace with the Romans, and withdrew his forces. The Romans were however obliged to relinquish a third part of their lands, and to give hostages. The Véians also, and the confederation of the Latins, took the field in support of the Tarquins. Brutus, the founder of the republic, and Aruns Tar quinius, encountered in the battle, and fell by the hands of each other. It was in the war against the Latins that the Romans for the first time appointed a dictator, an officer who was superior to the consuls, and who possessed unlimited power both in the city and the field. It was only in times of the greatest distress and danger that such a dictator was appointed, and he relinquished his extraordinary office as soon as the necessity for it ceased to exist.

§ 100. When Tarquin found that all the attempts to regain possession of his throne had miscarried, he retired to Cumæ, in Lower Italy, where he died. B. C. 495. The patricians now governed the state, and oppressed the plebeians by their severe laws of debtor and creditor. They (the plebeians) were obliged to pay ground-rent for their small properties, to perform military service without pay, and to provide their own arms and accoutrements. When they were engaged in war, their lands were left untilled at home: bad harvests brought poverty, and for the sake of escaping from the temporary pressure, they incurred debts with the wealthy patricians. If the plebeian failed in paying the large interest (10 or 12 per cent.) the moment it became due, his person and estate were seized upon by his creditor, he was reduced to the condition of a serf, and his family were left to starve. When this state of things became intolerable, and there was no law to protect the unfortunate debtor against his merciless creditor, B. C. 494. the plebeians resolved upon quitting Rome, and building a new town upon the sacred hill, about a league and a half from the city. The patricians sent Menénius Agríppa after them, to induce them to return. He explained to them the disadvantages that were likely to arise from their dissensions, by relating the fable of the quarrel between the stomach and the limbs, and the danger the whole body was reduced to in consequence, and promised them a redress of their grievances. The plebeians allowed themselves to be persuaded, and obtained on their return at first five, and afterwards ten, tribunes. These were accounted sacred and inviolable whilst they were in office: they possessed the power of placing their veto upon any resolution of the senate or decree of the consuls, which appeared injurious to the interests of the people; and if this was not sufficient, they could prevent the levies of troops and the collection of taxes.

Shortly after this, a famine broke out in Rome; and when at last ships arrived from Sicily with corn, the haughty patrician, Marcius Coriolánus, proposed that none should be yielded to the people till they had consented to the dismissal of their tribunes. Upon this the people, in their assembly, passed a sentence of banishment upon Coriolánus. B. C. 490. and compelled him to fly. Thirsting for vengeance, he betook himself to the Volscians, and persuaded them to make an inroad under his command upon the Roman territories. They had already penetrated in their destructive course to within five miles of Rome, when their general was prevailed upon to retreat by the united prayers of his wife and mother. Coriolánus is said to have fallen a victim to the rage of the Volscians, who nevertheless retained possession of the towns they had conquered.

b. THE FABII. CINCINNATUS. THE DECEMVIRS.

§ 101. Rome was so weakened by the dissensions between the different classes, that her foreign foes were able to possess themselves of one provincial town after another, and gradually to diminish her territory. The plebeians, whose arms were to win the battle, had little pleasure in shedding their blood to increase the wealth and power of their oppressors; they even willingly allowed themselves to be defeated, when they were under the command of one of the rigorous patricians. Such an event took place in a war against the people of Véii, when one of the Fabii was general. The disgrace was so severely felt by the high-spirited family of Fabius, that they deserted their own party, and making common cause with the plebeians, proceeded together to attack the Véians, but were all ensnared in an ambuscade, and died like heroes. One only, who had not arrived at years of maturity, survived the destruction of his race. Whilst the Véians were attacking the Roman territory on the north, the Volsci and Æqui made inroads no less destructive on the south. The latter of these tribes, whose possessions extended as far as Prænéste, but a few miles from Rome, once attacked the Romans at mount Álgidus, with such success, that the latter were

B. C. 458.

surrounded in their camp, and must have been taken prisoners if Cincinnátus had not come to their rescue. When the senate were informed of the danger the army was in, they appointed the patrician Cincinnátus dictator. Cincinnátus was so reduced in his circumstances by misfortunes, that he possessed nothing but a small estate on the right bank of the Tiber, which he was tilling with his own hands, when the summons of the senate was brought to him. He at once quitted the plough, hastened to the place of danger with the Roman youth that assembled themselves about him, and surrounded the Æqui in the night. When these, awakened in the following morning by a great shout, saw the situation they were in, they were compelled to surrender themselves prisoners of war, and, after giving up their arms, to pass under a yoke formed of three spears.

§ 102. The plebeians waged a hot contest with the patricians for an equality of rights. They demanded, above all, an agrarian law, a written code, and a share of the public offices.

The Roman state was in possession of large tracts of land, which were not the exclusive property of any one, but the use of which had been granted to the patricians, upon condition that a tenth part of the produce should be paid to the state. This common land (*ager publicus*) the patricians looked upon as their own, had it cultivated by their clients, and mutually overlooked each other's remissness when the stipulated duty did not find its way to the treasury. The plebeians demanded from time to time an agrarian law, by which a portion of these common lands should be surrendered to them. But as often as the application was made, it was encountered by a most decided resistance. The consul Sp. Cassius, who moved the first agrarian law, was thrown from the Tarpéian rock of the capitol, and the place where his house had stood remained empty and desolate.

§ 103. The administration of the law was exclusively in the hands of the patricians, who gave judgment and pronounced decisions according to custom and unwritten traditionary rules, and were thus frequently guilty of arbitrariness and partiality. The plebeians, to escape from these evils, demanded a fixed and written code, but experienced a violent resistance from the patricians. After many stormy debates, the tribunes of the people were at last successful in having envoys sent to Græcia Magna and Athens, to examine the laws, and to select those that should appear suitable. When these envoys returned, both parties agreed that all the officers of government (consuls, tribunes, &c.) should give up their places; and that ten patricians should be appointed with absolute power, and commissioned to draw up fresh laws. At first, the new officers, who, from their number, were called "decémvirs," performed the task committed to them in an exemplary manner, and at the end of the year, their laws gave so much satisfaction to the assembly of the people, that the decemvirate was allowed to continue another year, for the completion of its work. But now the ten patricians abused their authority by violent and arbitrary measures; they proceeded against their plebeian opponents by fine, imprisonment, banishment, and the axe of the executioner; when a war broke out with the Æqui and Volscians, they put to death an ancient plebeian hero in the field; and continued themselves in office by their own power, after the second year had passed, and the compilation of the laws of the Twelve Tables had been completed. The general discontent was fanned into revolt by a licentious outrage of Appius Claudius, the most illustrious of the decémvirs. This man had conceived a passion for the beautiful Virginia, daughter of one of the plebeian leaders, and the betrothed of another. In order to gain possession of her, he instructed one of his adherents to declare the maiden to be one of his runaway slaves, and to claim her as his property before the judgment-seat of the decémvirs. Appius Claudius heard the claim in the forum, in the presence of a great multitude of the people; but scarcely had he, by his decision, put Virginia into the power of the appellant, when her father hastened to the spot and plunged a knife into her heart. The plebeians now seized upon the Aventine

B. C. 452.

hill, and insisted with threats upon the expulsion of the decémvirs and the restoration of the old system. They obtained both: Appius Claudius destroyed himself in prison, another of the decémvirs was executed, and the rest expiated their crimes by perpetual exile. The laws of the Twelve Tables, however, remained in operation, and became the basis of the Roman code.

§ 104. Shortly after this, the plebeians succeeded in having it enacted, that the two classes might contract lawful marriages with each other, without the children of such unions forfeiting any of the privileges of their class; and they at length proceeded to claim a participation in the consulate. But this demand was resisted by the patricians with their whole strength; and when, at last, the plebeians prevented the raising of levies for military service, they declared that they would rather have no more consuls than agree to the admission of the plebeians to the office. At length it was arranged, that three or four military tribunes, with the authority of consuls, should be chosen every year from both classes, as leaders of the army and chief magistrates. This arrangement lasted nearly eighty years. But it occasionally happened that the patrician party gained the upper hand, and then consuls would be again elected for a few years, or the office of military tribune would remain unfilled. To make amends for their loss, the patricians instituted the office of censors. These, two in number, had the keeping of the lists in which every Roman was entered, according to his property, as senator, knight, or citizen; they superintended the building of temples, streets, and bridges, and exercised a censorial supervision, by virtue of which they might deprive men of vicious lives of the privileges of their class. The office of military tribune with consular power was abolished by the Licinian laws. (§ 107.)

B. C. 444.

B. C. 442.

c. THE TAKING OF ROME BY THE GAULS (B. C. 389), AND THE LAWS OF LICINIUS STOLO (B. C. 366).

§ 105. Whilst these struggles were going on within the city, the Roman army was successfully engaged against the enemy. Since the regulation that the citizens should receive pay during war, the troops could continue longer in the field. After extending their territories on the south, they turned their whole force against the Etruscans, and, under the command of Camillus, subdued, after a siege of ten years, the hostile city of Veii, the inhabitants of which were either killed or reduced to slavery. The haughty general, who had drawn upon himself the hatred of the plebeians by his splendid triumph and unequal distribution of the booty, withdrew voluntarily into exile when summoned by the tribunes of the people to answer for his conduct, and by this means deprived the state of his aid at the very moment it was most required.

B. C. 396.

§ 106. For it was about this time that the Gauls, in the neighborhood of the Po, crossed the Apennines and laid siege to the Etruscan city of Clúsium. The inhabitants turned for assistance to the Romans, who, however, contented themselves with sending an embassy to effect a reconciliation. When this failed of success, the ambassadors took part in the contest, and killed one of the leaders of the Gallic army. This outrage upon the rights of nations inflamed the anger of the Gauls. They left Clúsium, advanced by rapid marches upon Rome, and gave the force sent to oppose them so complete an overthrow at the river Allia, that only a few fugitives saved themselves across the Tiber in Veii; and the day of the battle was ever after distinguished by a black mark in the Roman Calendar, and observed as a time of fasting and prayer. Rome itself, after being deserted by the women and children, fell without resistance into the hands of the enemy. The Gauls burnt the empty city to the ground, slaughtered about eighty old men in the forum, who were desirous of devoting themselves as expiatory sacrifices, and then laid siege to the Capitol, whither those who were capable of bearing arms had withdrawn themselves. The garrison, however, under the command of the heroic Marcus Manlius, making a gallant resistance, and the ranks of the Gauls being thinned by sickness and hunger, a treaty was entered into, after the siege had continued seven months, by which the Gauls consented to withdraw themselves upon being paid a ransom of a thousand pounds weight of gold. It is well known how their insolent leader, Brennus, increased the stipulated amount by the weight of his sword, which he cast into the scale. The story of the banished Camíllus pursuing the retreating enemy with a troop of fugitive Romans, and again recovering the spoil from them, is doubted, and may be attributed, not without reason, to Roman vanity.

§ 107. After the retreat of the enemy, the Romans were so dispirited that they had not courage to rebuild their city, but wished to settle themselves in the empty town of Veii. It was only with difficulty that the patricians prevented the execution of this project, and that no similar purpose might again be entertained, the houses in Veii were given up to the people to be pulled down. Scarcely had Rome been hastily rebuilt with narrow and crooked streets, and small dwelling-houses, when the patricians again asserted the whole of their claims, and in particular revived the ancient laws of debtor and creditor in all their ancient severity. The preserver of the capitol, M. Manlius (Capitolínus), took the part of the oppressed and impoverished plebeians; but incurred the enmity of those of his own order to such an extent by doing so, that, under the frivolous pretext that he was attempting to gain the kingly power, he was condemned to death, and thereupon cast from the Tarpéian rock, his house levelled with the ground, and his memory declared
B. C. 383. infamous. But this severity against the friend of the people roused the plebeians from their apathy. Two bold and able tribunes,

Licínius Stolo and Sextius Lateranus, proposed the following laws:— 1. Consuls shall be again chosen, but one of them shall always be a plebeian. 2. No citizen shall hold more than 500 jugera of public land in lease; the remainder shall be distributed in small portions, among the plebeians as their own property. 3. The interest already paid upon debts shall be deducted from the capital sum, and the residue shall be paid in the course of three years.

These proposals were resisted to the utmost by the patricians, for the space of ten years; but all their efforts proved unavailing against the firmness of the tribunes, who prevented the election of officers and the military levies. The proposals became laws, and the privileges of the patricians received a severe shock. It is true that they still retained exclusive possession of the priesthood and certain other dignities; but in the course of a few decades, the plebeians were admitted to these offices also, so that a perfect equality between the two classes shortly followed. This civil concord, to which Camíllus a short time before his death dedicated a temple, brought with it a period of civic virtue and heroic greatness.

II. ROME'S HEROIC PERIOD.

1. THE TIME OF THE WAR WITH THE SAMNITES, AND THE BATTLES WITH PYRRHUS.

§ 108. After the Romans had exercised their military prowess in some successful engagements with the wandering hordes of the Gauls, they attempted to subdue the neighboring tribes. Among these the warlike and freedom-loving Sámnītes, who dwelt amidst the lofty ridges of the Apennines, gave them the greatest trouble, and they were forced to carry on the war against them, almost without intermission, for more than seventy years. The inhabitants of Capua and the Campánian plain, who were unable to withstand the hostile attacks of the warlike Sámnītes, and who turned to the Romans for assistance, were the occasion of the war. At first, the Romans refused them assistance; but the Capuans having recognized their authority, and placed themselves entirely under their protection, they marched into the field and defeated the enemy with great courage, at Cumæ, near Mount Gaurus.

B. C. 342. § 109. Shortly after this, the Romans found themselves menaced with a war by the Latins, who had hitherto been their allies. These were no longer disposed to recognize Rome as the head of the confederation, but required a share in the senate, the consulate, and all offices. Upon this, the Romans, who were not inclined to yield to these demands, concluded a hasty peace and alliance with the B. C. 340. Sámnītes, that they might turn their arms against the nearer enemy. When the army was at the foot of Vesuvius, the consul Manlius Torquátus forbade any skirmishing. In defiance of this command, his valiant son engaged one of the enemy in single combat, and slew him, but was condemned to death for disobedience by his inflexible B. C. 338. father. The battle of Vesuvius was determined in favor of the Romans by the patriotism of the plebeian consul, Decius Mus, who, having had himself devoted to death by a priest, enveloped himself in a white robe, and, mounting on horseback, plunged among the thickest of the enemy; whereupon the Latins, together with their neighbors, the Volsci, Æqui, and Hérnici, submitted themselves, and were received, with different privileges, as the allies of the Romans. In this capacity, they were obliged to perform military service in the Roman army.

§ 110. The success of the Romans awakened the jealousy of the Sámnītes. B. C. 325. Quarrels respecting boundaries led to a renewal of hostilities, in which the Romans at first had the advantage, till the imprudent advance of the consuls, Vetúrius and Posthúmius, into the Caudine passes, brought the army into such a desperate position, that it was obliged to surrender to the hostile general, Pontius, who had surrounded it on every side, and after giving up its weapons, to pass ignominiously under the yoke. The senate, however, with an unworthy equivocation, declared the treaty that their generals had concluded in their necessity with Pontius to be invalid, and delivered up the consuls, at their own request, in chains to the Sámnītes. The generals who succeeded them, especially the vigorous Papírius Cursor and Fabius Máximus, strained every nerve to wipe away the disgrace; and their endeavors were crowned with such success, that, after a few years, the Sámnītes, being no longer able to resist the attacks of the Romans, were obliged to look around them for assistance. They united themselves with the Umbrians, the Gauls, and Etruscans, who were also threatened by Rome's love of conquest; and, for the sake of being closer to their new allies, B. C. 295. they quitted their own country and marched into Umbria. But the battle of Sentínum, which was decided in favor of the Romans by the self-oblation of the younger Decius Mus, destroyed the last hopes of the allies. Their great general, Pontius, fell shortly afterwards into the hands of the Romans, and was put to a violent death. It was in vain that the sacred band of the Sámnītes once more tried their strength and their swords against the Romans; Curius Dentátus gave them a second overthrow, in which the Samnite youth, the pride of the nation, moistened the field of battle with their blood. The Sámnītes B. C. 290. and their confederates, the Umbrians, Etruscans, and the Senónian Gauls, were compelled to acknowledge the supremacy of Rome, and to serve as allies in her army.

§ 111. During the war with the Sámnītes, the rich, effeminate, and cowardly Tarentines had behaved in an equivocal manner, and insulted a Roman ambassador. Scarcely therefore had the Romans completely mastered their enemies, than they turned their arms against Lower Italy. Hereupon, the Tarentines called the warlike Pyrrhus, king of Epírus, to their assistance, who eagerly seized this opportunity for conquest and military renown, and embarked with his forces for Italy. Pyrrhus was victorious in two engagements, partly from the admirable
B. C. 281. disposition he made of his army, and partly by means of his elephants, an animal with which the Romans were unacquainted; and the senate seemed not unwilling to conclude a disadvantageous peace with the conqueror, who was marching upon Rome. But the blind Appius Claudius opposed this design, and induced the assembly to reply, that no proposals for peace could be entertained till Pyrrhus had quitted Italy. The admiration of the king, who had hitherto only been acquainted with the degenerate manners of the Greeks, was not less excited by the wisdom and dignified demeanor of the senate, and the civic virtues, honesty, and simplicity of the Roman generals, Fabrícius and Curius Dentátus, than by the heroism, the bravery, and the warlike skill of the legions.

A short time after, Pyrrhus was called into Sicily by the Syracusans, to assist them against the Carthaginians. A love of adventure and conquest induced him to accept the invitation; but he failed in his plan of making himself master of the beautiful island, and was compelled by the Sicilian Greeks to return. He again marched towards Tarentum, but suffered such a defeat at Maleventum (afterwards called
B. C. 275. Beneventum), from Curius Dentátus, that he found himself obliged to make a hasty retreat. Pyrrhus fell, a few years afterwards, before Argos, a city of Peloponnésus; and about the same
B. C. 272. time, the Tarentines lost their fleet, and a portion of their treasures of art, and were made tributaries by the Romans. The fall of Tarentum was followed by the subjugation of the whole of Lower Italy, in the course of which the Greek states were treated with peculiar severity.

---

2. THE TIME OF THE PUNIC WARS.

a. THE FIRST PUNIC WAR. (B. C. 263 – 241.)

§ 112. Many centuries before, some Phœnician emigrants had founded the trading city of Carthage, on the north coast of Africa (§ 14), which soon attained to power and opulence by the skill and enterprising spirit of its inhabitants. The Carthaginians carried on an extensive traffic with all the lands on the coast of the Mediterranean, established tributary

colonial cities in Sicily and the south of Spain, and acquired such wealth, that they laid out the land in the vicinity of their own city after the manner of a garden, and embellished it with innumerable magnificent villas. But civic freedom, mental cultivation, and nobility of mind were possessions foreign to the Carthaginians. The government was in the hands of a purse-proud aristocracy, art and literature were little esteemed, their religious system was so barbarous as to permit the sacrifice of human victims, and their cunning and falsehood so notorious, that the "Punic faith" was proverbial.* Long was the contest between the Carthaginians and Syracusans, for the possession of the island of Sicily. At the time that the gallant adventurer Agáthocles had raised himself from the humble condition of a potter to the empire of Syracuse, this contest was carried on with such changes of fortune,
B. C. 317. that Syracuse was besieged by the Carthaginians, and Carthage by the army of Agáthocles, at the same time. The latter made himself master of the north coast of Africa, and assumed the title of king. But a change soon took place: his army was destroyed, and he himself obliged to fly secretly to Syracuse, where his vital powers were so wasted by a poison that was administered to him, that the hoary tyrant consented to his own death by fire. His death gave rise to a state of lawless violence in Sicily, owing to his Campanian soldiers (Mámer-
B. C. 289. tīnes) having seized upon the town of Messína on their way home, slaughtered or driven away the male part of the inhabitants, and then filled the island with robbery and devastation. In this distress, the Syracusans elected the valiant Híero for their king. He marched, in conjunction with the Carthaginians, against the Mámertīnes, defeated them, and laid siege to their city Messína. The Mámertīnes were shortly reduced to such extremities that they applied to the Romans for assistance.

§ 113. The Romans did not long hesitate to enter into a defensive alliance with the rapacious Mámertīnes, and to gain by this means an opportunity of subjecting the rich and beautiful island, although they saw plainly that the jealous Carthaginians, who were already in possession of the citadel of Messína, would oppose them with all their strength. A Roman army shortly after succeeded in driving back the disunited enemy from the walls of the city, in bringing Híero into an alliance with Rome, and depriving the Carthaginians of the important town of Agrigéntum. Upon this, the Romans built a fleet after the model of a shipwrecked Punic vessel, and won the first naval engagement, by means
B. C. 261. of the consul Duíllius, at Mylæ, near the Lipárian islands. Encouraged by this success, they now determined to deprive the Cartha-

* It should be remembered, however, especially in reference to this charge of bad faith, that most of our knowledge of the Carthaginians is derived from their ancient and inveterate enemies, the Romans. *Am. Ed.*

ginians of their supremacy at sea, and passed over to Africa with a fleet and a large army, under the command of the heroic consul Régulus. Régulus gradually approached, conquering and devastating, to the gates of Carthage. The terrified Carthaginians sued for peace, but when they found the conditions offered them by the haughty conqueror too severe, they prepared for resistance, increased the number of their mercenary troops, and committed the conduct of the defence to an experienced general, the Spartan Xantíppus. This leader gave the Romans so severe a defeat at the seaport town of Tunes, that only 2,000 of their splendid army escaped; the others were either killed or made prisoners of war, together with the consul Régulus.

§ 114. This blow was followed by a succession of misfortunes: two fleets were destroyed by tempests, so that, for some years, the Romans renounced all thoughts of success by sea; on land, they only ventured upon trifling engagements, from fear of the elephants, of which they themselves never made use, though the battle at Tunes had been decided by them. In a few years, however, they recovered themselves; they made a successful sally from Panórmus (Palermo), drove
B. C. 250. back the Carthaginians, and took possession of all their elephants. Hereupon the Carthaginians sent Régulus to Rome to negotiate an exchange of prisoners, after they had obtained from him an oath, that, if not successful, he would return to captivity. Régulus advised the senate not to consent to the exchange, on the ground that it would be disadvantageous to their country; and then, true to his oath, returned to Carthage. Upon this, the Carthaginians were greatly enraged, and put Régulus to death in a most barbarous manner.

Victory remained for some years dubious. At length, the admirable Carthaginian general, Hamilcar Barcas, made himself master of the citadel Eryx, and overlooked from a lofty rock all the movements of the Romans. But this was only possible so long as there was no Roman fleet to prevent the communication with the sea. As soon as 200 ships had been fitted out at Rome, by private contributions, and by employing the treasures in the temples, and the consul Lutátius Cátulus
B. C. 242. had defeated the enemy's fleet at the Ægátian islands, the Carthaginians were compelled to consent to a peace, in which they renounced their claims upon Sicily, and promised to pay a large sum to defray the expenses of the war.

b. THE SECOND PUNIC WAR. (B. C. 218 – 202.)

§ 115. Whilst the Carthaginians, after the peace, were engaged for three years in a frightful war with their rebellious mercenaries, the Romans were enlarging their territory in every direction.
B. C. 238. They transformed Sicily into the first Roman province; took possession of Córsica and Sardínia after a severe struggle with the semi

barbarous inhabitants; and wrested the island of Corcýra (Corfu) and a few maritime towns from the piratical Illyrians. But the hardest conflict they had to sustain was with the Cisalpine Gauls, who, supported by their brethren in the Alps, had made a destructive inroad upon Etruria. After the Romans had overthrown their brave, but badly-armed enemies, in two bloody engagements, the fertile regions on either side of the Po were erected into a Roman province, under the name of Gállia Cisalpína, and connected with Rome by two military roads.

B. C. 222.

§ 116. In the mean while, the Carthaginians, at first under the command of the brave Hamilcar Barcas, and after his death under that of the prudent Hásdrubal, extended their conquests into the richly metalliferous region of South Spain, and established an admirable military station in New Carthage (Carthagéna). This aroused the fear and envy of the Romans, and induced them to enter into a defensive alliance with the Greek colony of Sagúntum, on the eastern coast of Spain. Hásdrubal soon died, and his place was supplied by Hamilcar's son, Hannibal, who was then twenty-five years of age, and who joined the courage and military talents of his father to the prudence of his predecessor, and who, whilst yet a boy, had sworn eternal hatred against the Romans upon the paternal altar. Eager to measure himself against the Romans, he laid siege to the confederate town of Sagúntum. It was in vain that the Roman envoys warned him to desist; he referred them to the Carthaginian senate, but in the mean while pressed the town so closely, that he took it in eight months. The most resolute of the inhabitants collected their goods together in the market-place, set them on fire, and threw themselves into the flames; the others died by the sword of the enemy, or beneath the ruins of their houses. Sagúntum was reduced to a heap of rubbish. The Roman embassy, when too late, declared war in Carthage.

§ 117. It was in the spring of the year 218 B. C. that Hannibal crossed the Ebro, subjected the tribes in that neighborhood; and then, with an army of 60,000 men, and thirty-seven elephants, penetrated across the Pyrenees into Gaul, whilst his brother Hásdrubal, with an equal number of troops, held Spain in subjection. After Hannibal had forced a passage through South Gaul and over the Rhone, he commenced his ever-memorable passage of the Alps (probably by the way of Mount Cenis.) In the midst of perpetual contests with the savage inhabitants, the soldiers climbed over lofty mountains covered with snow and ice, without road and without shelter, — over precipices and gulfs. Nearly half the troops and the whole of the beasts of burden were destroyed. But these losses were soon replaced, when, after a march of fourteen days, Hannibal arrived in Upper Italy. For no sooner was the consul Cornelius Scipio defeated and severely wounded, in an affair of cavalry on the Ticínus, and

his fellow-consul, the imprudent Semprónius, completely routed at the rashly-undertaken battle of the Trébia, than the Cisalpine Gauls joined Hannibal's standard. After a short rest in Ligúria, he
B. C. 217. crossed the rugged Apennines, a most toilsome march, (in the course of which he lost an eye from inflammation), and continued his devastating course into Etrúria. The consul Flamínius encountered him at the Lake Trasiménus, but by his inconsiderate rashness sustained a total defeat, in which he himself lost his life, and his soldiers were either killed or drowned in the waters of the lake. The road to Rome was now open to the victor; but he determined upon marching into Apúlia, for the purpose of inducing the inhabitants of Lower Italy to revolt.

§ 118. It was at this time, that a man opposed himself to the Carthaginian general, who, by his prudence and circumspection, occasioned him many difficulties, — the dictator Fabius Máximus, the Delayer. He avoided an open engagement, but followed the hostile army foot by foot, and turned every unfortunate movement to his own advantage. He reduced it to such a perilous position in Campánia, by taking possession of the mountain heights, that Hannibal was only able to save himself by an artifice, — driving oxen, with bundles of lighted brushwood tied to their horns, up the hill, by which means he deceived the enemy. But the discontent of the imprudent people at this lingering mode of warfare, induced the consul Teréntius Varro, in the following year, again to hazard an engagement, against the advice of his colleague, Paulus Æmílius. Hereupon followed the dreadful defeat of the
B. C. 216. Romans at Cannæ, where the number of the slain was so great, that Hannibal is said to have sent three bushels of rings to Carthage, which were stripped from the hands of the Roman knights. The high-minded Paulus Æmílius was found among the slain. The day of the battle of Cannæ, like that of the defeat at the Állia, (§ 105,) was marked in the Roman calendar as a time of prayer and fasting. The immovable senate, however, preserved its courage and composure; all who fled at Cannæ were declared infamous, and expelled from the army.

§ 119. Hannibal did not consider it advisable to advance at once upon Rome with his shattered forces, but established his winter quarters in the rich and luxurious city of Cápua. But it was here that his rugged warriors were rendered effeminate and lost their love of war. The Romans, on the other hand, made new preparations with extraordinary rapidity, so that, in the spring, they were able to send fresh troops into the field, whilst in the mean time Hannibal's army had received no reinforcements from Carthage. Two successful engagements
B. C. 215. restored the courage of the Romans, and put them in a position to chastise the towns of Sicily and Lower Italy, which after the battle of Cannæ, had revolted to Hannibal. Marcellus went over to

Sicily and laid siege to Syracuse; which defended itself with so much B. C. 214. courage and success, by the aid of the ingenious mathematician and philosopher, Archimédes, that it was only by the B. C. 212. greatest efforts, and after a siege of three years, that Marcellus could make himself master of the place. The revenge of the Romans was fearful: the soldiers plundered and slaughtered; Archimédes was slain at his studies, the finest works of art were sent to Rome, and the glory of Syracuse was gone forever. Cápua experienced a similar fate. The place was closely besieged by two Roman legions; the terrified inhabitants implored the assistance of Hannibal, who advanced upon Rome, in the hope that the Romans would hasten to the relief of their capital, and relinquish the siege. But one legion, in con- B. C. 211. junction with a few other troops, was sufficient to compel Hannibal to retreat, and the Cápuans, reduced by hunger, were obliged to surrender to the other. Twenty-seven senators died by their own hands, and fifty-three by the axe of the executioner; the citizens were reduced to slavery, and their property bestowed upon foreign colonists. The treasures of Cápua were sent to Rome, all her privileges were destroyed, and from henceforth the city was governed by a Roman prefect. Two years later, Tarentum fell again into the hands of the Romans. Fabius Máximus reduced the inhabitants to slavery, and took possession of the treasures, but suffered the statues of the "Angry Gods" to remain. Fear soon brought all the revolted states back to the Romans, and Hannibal's position, without money, without reinforcements, and without supplies, became every day more precarious.

§ 120. Spain was now Hannibal's only hope, since he was deserted by his ungrateful country. It was there, that Hannibal's brother, Hásdrubal, after having opposed the Romans for a long time with success, was at length reduced to such straits by the young and high-spirited Cornelius Scipio, that he was unable to remain in the country any longer, and consequently resolved upon uniting himself with his brother, who had summoned him into Italy. Following Hannibal's passage across the Alps, he marched into Upper Italy, and then directed his course B. C. 208. towards the coast of the Adriatic Sea, with the purpose of joining his brother, who was encamped in Lower Italy, opposite the consul Claudius Nero. But the daring resolution of this consul to effect a secret junction with his colleague, Livius Salinátor, by a rapid march upon Umbria, led to the death of Hásdrubal and the destruc- B. C. 207. tion of his army, at the river Metáurus, before Hannibal had received notice of his approach. In the bloody head of Hásdrubal, which the consul, on his return, threw into the enemy's camp, the dispirited general recognized the "fearful fate of Carthage."

§ 121. It was in misfortune that Hannibal displayed the real greatness of his military talents. Without help from without, and without allies

8

in Italy, he still maintained himself, with the remains of his army, for some years, in the extreme south, against the superior force of the enemy. But when the victorious Scipio returned, after the subjugation of Spain, passed over from Sicily into Africa, with some fugitives and volunteers, and, setting fire in the neighborhood of Utica to
B. C. 204. the enemy's camp, which consisted of tents made of straw and reeds, attacked them during the confusion, Hannibal was recalled to defend his country. Sorrowful and angry he quitted the land of his renown. It was in vain that he endeavored, during a conference, to persuade his opponent to conclude a treaty, by representing the instability of fortune. Scipio would not listen to the proposal; where-
B. C. 202. upon the battle of Zama followed, and ended in the defeat of the Carthaginians. Hannibal himself now advised a peace, hard as the conditions were. The Carthaginians were obliged to take an oath never to commence war without the consent of the Romans, they were compelled to renounce their claims upon Spain, to give up their ships of war, and to pledge themselves to pay an enormous sum to defray the expenses of the contest. After burning the Carthaginian fleet, and investing Masiníssa, a friend of the Romans, with the kingdom of Numidia, Scipio, (afterwards called Africánus), returned to Rome, where a splendid triumph awaited him. Hannibal, on the other hand, was obliged, a short time after, to leave his home, a persecuted refugee, and carried his hatred of the Romans to the court of the Syrian king, Antíochus.

c. MACEDONIA CONQUERED; CORINTH AND CARTHAGE DESTROYED.

§ 122. About this time, King Philip II. reigned over Macedónia and a part of Greece. He had entered into an alliance with Hannibal, and made war on the Romans and their confederates in Greece and Asia Minor. It was for this reason that the Romans now turned their arms against him. They sent their general, Flaminínus, a clever man, and one who took an interest in Greek art and literature, into Greece; he summoned the states to freedom, and then gave the Macedónians an overthrow at the Dogsheads (Cynoscéphalæ) a range of hills in
B. C. 197. Thessaly. By this, Philip saw himself compelled to a peace, by which he acknowledged the independence of Greece, gave up his fleet and a great sum of money, and renounced the right of making war on his own account. To gratify the vanity of the Greeks, the subtle Flaminínus caused the deliverance of Greece from the Macedónian yoke to be proclaimed with magnificent ceremonies at the Isthmian games. But it was soon evident that the Romans were quite as eager to assume the government of Greece as ever the Macedónians had been. It was for this reason that many of the Greek tribes, and in particular the warlike Ætólians, who had united themselves in a confederation

similar to that of the Acháians, applied to the Syrian king, Antíochus III. for aid, (§ 90). Antíochus, at whose court Hannibal was living, yielded to the demand; but instead of joining Philip II. and attacking the Romans with united forces, he squandered his time idly in feasting and luxury, and gave offence to the Macedónian king; whilst the Romans marched rapidly into Thessaly, and after storming the pass of Thermópylæ under Porcius Cato, compelled the Syrian king to retreat into Asia. But he was immediately followed thither by a Roman army, under the command of Cornelius Scipio, with his brother Africánus at his side, for counsellor.

A murderous engagement took place at Magnésia, near mount Sípy̆lus, which terminated to the disadvantage of Antíochus, who was compelled to purchase a peace by the cession of Western Asia, this side of the Taurus, and by the payment of an enormous sum for the expenses of the war. The rapacious Ætólians were also subdued and punished in their purses and their treasures of art.

Hannibal, threatened with being delivered up to the Romans, fled to Prusias, king of Bithy̆nia; but when this prince could no longer venture to defend him, he swallowed poison on a lonely hill, to escape

B. C. 183. falling into the hands of his mortal enemies. At the same time, his great antagonist, Scipio, died at his estate in Lower Italy, far away from Rome, whence he had been driven by the malice of his enemies. To make this year thoroughly fatal, Philopœ'men was also compelled to drink the cup of poison (§ 88).

§ 123. Perseus, the wicked son of Philip II., made his way to the Macedónian throne by crimes, inasmuch as he provoked the suspicious father to murder his younger son Demetrius, a noble prince, and well disposed to the Romans. Perseus was scarcely in possession of his crown, before his hatred to the Romans induced him to begin a new war. His enormous wealth enabled him to make vast preparations, but avarice and perverse measures soon occasioned his fall. After the victory obtained by the expert tactician and accomplished man,

B. C. 168. Paulus Æmílius, at Pydna, Perseus fell into the power of the Romans, was led in triumph, together with his treasures and his captive children and friends, through the streets of the mistress of the world; and shortly after, ended his life in solitary confinement. Macedónia was divided into four provinces, and placed under a republican form of government; 1000 noble Acháians, among whom was the great historical writer, Poly̆bius, were conveyed to Rome as hostages, on the plea of a secret understanding with Perseus. Twenty years later, a pretended son of Perseus raised the standard of rebellion. This gave the Romans the wished-for opportunity of converting Macedónia

B. C. 148. into a Roman province, after the subjection of the impostor by Metellus. Metellus had not yet quitted the conquered territory, when the Acháian league also took up arms to rid themselves of Rome's oppressive authority. Metellus overthrew the Acháians who marched against him in two engagements; but was obliged to leave the termination of the war to his rude successor, Múmmius, who stormed Corinth, and burnt it to the ground. The inhabitants were either slain or reduced to slavery, the treasures of art destroyed or sent to Rome, and Greece was converted into a Roman province, under the name of Acháia. The prosperity of the once flourishing states disappeared beneath the pressure of Roman taxation, and every spark of the patriotism and love of liberty of a former age was extinguished. The Spartans continued their rude trade of war as mercenaries, whilst the Athenians sought a subsistence among the Romans, as artists and men of learning, as players and dancers, as poets and *beaux esprits;* but they were treated with little respect.

B. C. 146.

§ 124. In the mean while, Carthage had again recovered a portion of her prosperity. This reawakened the envy of the Romans, and gave emphasis to Cato's expression, "that Carthage must be destroyed." Masiníssa, king of Numidia, relying upon Roman protection, enlarged his own territories at the expense of those of the Carthaginians; and at last, irritated them so much by perpetual quarrels about boundaries, that they took up arms to defend their own possessions. This was looked upon in Rome as an infringement of the peace, and occasioned a declaration of war. The Carthaginians implored indulgence, and delivered up, at the demand of the Romans, first, 300 respectable hostages, and afterwards, their ships and weapons. But when this was followed by a decree that Carthage should be burnt to the ground, and a new city erected farther from the coast, the inhabitants determined rather to perish beneath the ruins of their houses than submit to such a disgrace. A spirit of courage and patriotism took possession of all sexes and conditions. The town presented the appearance of a camp; the temples were converted into smithies for forging arms, and every thing was made subservient to the lofty purpose of saving the state. Even the veteran legions of Rome were unable to withstand such enthusiasm as this. They were repeatedly repulsed and reduced to a precarious condition, until the younger Scipio, the able son of Paulus Æmilius, who had been adopted into the family of Scipio during childhood, was appointed to the consulate before the lawful age, with dictatorial power. After a most desperate resistance, and a murderous conflict for six days in the streets, it was he who at length succeeded in reducing the city, after it had suffered all the extremities of famine. The rage of the soldiers, and a conflagration that lasted for seventeen days, converted Carthage, the once proud mistress of the Mediterranean, into a heap of ruins; 50,000 inhabitants, whom the sword had spared, were carried into slavery by the conqueror, who from this time bore the name of the younger Africánus. The territory of Carthage was turned into a Roman province, called Africa, and the rebuilding of the city denounced with a curse.

d. THE MANNERS AND CULTURE OF THE ROMANS.

§ 125. The acquaintance of the Romans with Greece was attended with the most important consequences to their civilization, manners, and mode of living. The works of Greek art and literature that had been taken from the conquered towns, produced, in the more susceptible part of the nation, a taste for cultivation, and awakened a fresh class of feelings. A powerful party, at the head of which stood the Scipios, Marcellus, Flaminínus, and many others, patronized the Greek philosophy, poetry, and art; cherished and supported the learned men, philosophers, and poets, of that nation; and sought to transport the spirit and language of the conquered people to Rome, together with their works of art. Under the protection of the Scipios, Roman poets wrote verses in imitation of their Greek prototypes. This was the case with their writers of comedy, Plautus and Terence, the latter of whom is said to have been assisted in his compositions by the younger Scipio and his friend Lælius. Since, however, the minds of the Romans were directed entirely to the practical, to the conduct of war, the government of the state, and the administration of justice, intellectual culture never could attain to the same height among them as with the Greeks: the people found more pleasure in spectacles addressed to the senses, rough gladiatorial combats, and the contests of wild animals, than in the productions of the mind.

But literature and the arts were not the only things that were borrowed; elegance and refinement in the arrangement of dwellings, luxury and extravagance in meals and dress, politeness and suavity in social intercourse, sensual enjoyments and luxurious pleasures, were copied by the Romans from the Greeks and Orientals. The victors inherited the vices and excesses of the conquered people, along with their wealth and civilization. An opposite party, with Porcius Cato at its head, earnestly combated the new system that threatened to destroy the ancient manners, discipline, simplicity, moderation, and hardihood. The severity with which this remarkable man, in his office of censor, opposed the new direction of things, has made his name proverbial. By his aid, the Greek philosophers were banished from Rome; the schools of oratory closed; the dissolute festivals of Bacchus, and other religious customs derived from abroad, interdicted; the Scipios punished as corrupters of morals; and laws proclaimed against luxury and excess. For the purpose of counteracting the influence of the new literature, he himself wrote works upon agriculture, the basis of Rome's former greatness, and upon the people of ancient Italy, whose simplicity and purity of morals he wished to contrast with the commencing degeneracy of his time. But the example of Cato, who learned Greek in his old age, shows that the rigid attachment to the ancient and traditional invariably gives way before new efforts at progress.

III. ROME'S DEGENERACY.

1. NUMANTIA, TIBERIUS, AND CAIUS GRACCHUS.

§ 126. In proportion as the Roman territory increased in extent, the heroism, the civic virtues, and the patriotic feelings on which Rome's greatness had been built, disappeared. Fresh aristocratic families were formed from the rich and the illustrious, who, like the patricians of old, monopolized all honors and offices. They sought perpetually for new wars, the conduct of which was given to them alone, for the purpose of increasing, by victories and triumphs, the renown they had inherited from their ancestors; and the provinces were exhausted to the end that they might give themselves up to all kinds of pleasure and enjoyment, without lessening the wealth on which the power and splendor of their families were founded. As proconsuls and proprætors, they conducted the government and the administration of justice in the conquered provinces, with a host of writers and subordinates, and kept their own interest more in view than the welfare of the governed. The wealthy members of the knightly class undertook, as farmers-general of the revenue, for a certain sum they paid into the exchequer, to collect all taxes, imposts, and tolls, and then sought, by the most shameless exactions practised by their toll-collectors, receivers, and under-farmers, to indemnify themselves for their outlay by an enormous profit. What the officials and revenue-farmers left, was appropriated by a tribe of hungry merchants and usurers, so that a few decades sufficed to ruin the prosperity of a Roman colony. It is very true, that there existed a law which gave the abused provincials the right of impeaching their oppressors on the expiration of their term of office; but as the judges all belonged to the same wealthy and noble families, the criminal generally escaped free, or was fined in a small amount, for the sake of appearances.

Single provinces would occasionally attempt to shake off this oppressive yoke, and to regain their freedom by dint of arms. The first example of such a revolt was given by the inhabitants of the Pyrenean peninsula, and above all others, by the heroic race of Spain, whose chief city was Numántia. For five years, they set all the efforts of the Romans at defiance, and extorted a treaty of peace and an acknowledgment of their independence, from a consul whom they had inclosed in the hollows of their mountains. But the senate did not confirm the treaty, and behaved as they had done in the affair of the Caudinian passes (§ 110). It was only when the younger Scipio, the conqueror of Carthage, put himself at the head of the army, and restored the abandoned energy and discipline of the camp, that Numántia, after a desperate defence, was compelled by hunger to surrender. The citizens escaped from the insults of the victors, by heroically killing themselves. Scipio destroyed the empty town, the ruins of which still look admonishingly down upon posterity, a memorial of a magnanimous struggle for freedom.

B. C. 135.

§ 127. The new family aristocracy not only filled all the offices, and excluded men of inferior birth from posts of honor, but they also possessed the whole of the arable land, inasmuch as they again claimed an exclusive right to the common lands, and got the smaller farms into their hands by purchase, usury, chicanery, and sometimes even by violence. By these means, the greatest inequality of property was produced. The class of free husbandmen, upon which the ancient strength, honesty, and military virtue of Rome was established, disappeared entirely; whilst the nobles got possession of immense estates, which they had cultivated by hosts of slaves, who had been made prisoners in war. Numbers of impoverished tenants, who had been driven from their houses and farms by hard-hearted landlords, wandered through the land, a picture of misery and distress.

In the midst of this state of things, the noble tribune of the people Tiberius Gracchus, (son of Cornelia, daughter of the great Scipio Africánus,) presented himself as the defender of oppressed poverty, by proposing a renewal of the agrarian law of Licínius Stolo (§ 107), which enacted that no one should possess more than 500 acres of the public land, and that the remainder should be distributed to necessitous families in small lots, as their own propety. Upon this, the nobles raised a dreadful storm, and prevailed upon another tribune to oppose the measure. According to the Roman code, no proposal could become law unless all the ten tribunes were unanimous. It was owing to this, that Gracchus allowed himself to be seduced into the illegal course of getting his refractory colleague deposed by the people, and thus violating the sanctity of the tribunitial office. This afforded his adversaries ground for the suspicion that Gracchus was meditating the overthrow of the constitution, for the purpose of assuming the kingly authority. He lost the favor of the misguided people, and was killed in the Capitol, together with 300 of his adherents, during a new election of tribunes. The people discovered their delusion when it was too late, and erected a statue in honor of their high-spirited champion.

B. C. 133.

§ 128. This result did not deter the younger and more able brother, Cáius Gracchus, ten years afterwards, from agitating anew for the agrarian law, and, in connection with it, for a corn

B. C. 123.

law, (by which deliveries of corn were to be made to the poorer citizens for a moderate price), and other popular measures. His great eloquence and his philanthropic exertions gained him a powerful party among the lower class of the people, whose immediate distress he sought to alleviate by the making of roads and public works. But when, at the instigation of his impetuous friend, Fulvius Flaccus, he proposed that the right of Roman citizenship should be extended to the allies, the nobles became alarmed and tried to destroy him. A dreadful combat took place at one of the popular assemblies between the aristocratic party, with the consul Opímius at their head, and the adherents of Gracchus and Fulvius. The latter were defeated: Fulvius, with 3,000 of his companions, was killed, and their bodies thrown into the Tiber. Gracchus fled into a wood on the other side of the river, and commanded a slave B. C. 121. to thrust a sword into his bosom. Their laws and institutions were annulled, and their adherents punished with death, imprisonment, and banishment. The aristocracy were now, more than ever, the rulers of the republic.

---

2. THE TIMES OF MARIUS AND SYLLA.

THE JUGURTHINE WAR. B. C. 112–106.

§ 129. The aristocrats disgraced their government by avarice and corruption, and renounced all sentiments of honor and justice. Jugurtha, the grandson of Masiníssa of Numidia, a cunning and ambitious man, and experienced in war, trusting to the depravity of morals and the corruption prevalent in Rome, put to death the two sons of his uncle, who had been made co-heirs with himself, seized upon their states, which had been conferred upon them by the Romans, and succeeded, by dint of bribing the most influential senators, in retaining possession of his plunder, and heaping crime upon crime with impunity. When at length the senate were compelled, by the indignation of the people, to send an army into Africa, the Numidian king actually succeeded in producing such enervation and looseness of discipline among the troops, by bribery and seduction, that they were defeated at the first attack, and obliged to pass under the yoke. This disgrace produced the greatest exasperation in Rome, so that the senate were compelled to adopt more stringent measures, in order to appease the discontent of the people, and conciliate the outraged sentiment of justice, by the punishment of the offender. They accordingly despatched the upright Metellus, with fresh troops B. C. 109. into Africa. Metellus restored the discipline of the army, and brought back the military renown of the Romans by successful engagements and conquests. But the people were so embittered against the aristocracy, that they resolved to deprive them of the government by any means. For this purpose, they required an intrepid leader; and the aspiring and ambitious C. Marius presented himself, a man of obscure condition, who was at that time serving as lieutenant in the army of Metellus, and who joined courage, the talents of a general, and rude military virtue, to rough manners, hatred of the nobles, and contempt for their cultivation and refinement. Disgusted at the aristocratic haughtiness of B. C. 107. his commander, Marius returned to Rome, where he was chosen consul by the popular party, and intrusted with the conduct of the Jugurthine war. Jugurtha, with all his cunning and inventive genius, was unable long to withstand the energetic Marius and his army, now hardened by severe discipline. He was conquered, and fled to the faithless Bocchus, king of Mauritánia; but was delivered up by him to the shrewd and dexterous quæstor Cornelius Sylla, and led in triumph to Rome, where he was starved to death in prison.

§ 130. Cimbri and Teutones. — Marius had not yet concluded the Jugurthine war, when the Cimbri and Teútones appeared on the borders of the Roman empire. They were a northern people, of Germanic origin, and gigantic stature and strength, who had left their country with their wives, children, and all their property, to seek for a new habitation. They were clad in iron coats of mail and the skins of beasts; they bore shields the height of a man, with long swords and heavy maces. They B. C. 113. first defeated the Romans in a bloody battle in Noricum, passed through Rhætia, devastating and plundering, and, within four years, cut to pieces five consular armies on the banks of the Rhone and the lake of Geneva. Marius, whom the Romans, against the law, had elected five successive times to the consulate, came forward as deliverer. With his army, hardened by the labors of digging and hewing, B. C. 102. he defeated the Teútones in a bloody engagement at Aquæ Sextiæ, (Aix in Provence), in South Gaul. In the mean time, the Cimbri, in a separate body, had penetrated through the Tyrol and the valley of the Ádige, into Upper Italy; but when there, had carelessly given themselves up to the pleasures afforded by the rich country, till they suffered a similar frightful overthrow on the plains near Vercéllæ, from Marius, who had joined forces with his colleague Lutátius Cátulus. The courage of these Germans, who killed themselves and their children, to prevent their being reduced to slavery, made the Romans tremble.

B. C. 100. § 131. The social war. — A sixth consulate rewarded Marius, the savior of Italy, the pride and hope of the popular party. By his assistance, this party again gained the superiority, which induced the aristocracy to array themselves around Cornelius Sylla, a politic and ambitious man, and versed in war, who united in himself the cultivation and love of art of the nobles, with their vices and excesses.

From this time, two powerful parties, the democrats under Marius, and the aristocrats under Sylla, stood opposed in arms to each other. The former endeavored to strengthen their ranks by attracting thither the allies, and for this purpose held out to them the prospect of the Roman citizenship. When this was not conceded, the disappointed party took up arms for the purpose of freeing themselves from Rome, or of compelling the cession of the refused privileges. This occasioned the B. C. 90-88. perilous Social war. All the tribes of Sabellian origin, the warlike Sámnītes and Marsians at their head, renounced allegiance to the Romans, formed an Italian confederation, and declared Corfínium, which was also called Itálica, chief city of the new alliance. Veteran armies marched into the field. In Rome, the people put on mourning, armed the manumitted slaves, and conferred the privileges of Roman citizenship upon the Latins, Etruscans, and Umbrians, who had remained faithful, to prevent their joining with the others. The Romans were successful, after many changes of fortune and many bloody engagements, in gradually mastering their opponents. But the ferment was still so dangerous, that they thought it advisable to prevent a fresh insurrection, by conferring the rights of citizenship upon the whole of the allies. They nevertheless restricted the elective rights of the new citizens.

§ 132. THE FIRST WAR AGAINST MITHRIDATES.—The allies were scarcely appeased, before the Romans were threatened from the East, by an enemy as sagacious as he was bold,—Mithridátes, king of the Pontus, on the Black Sea. Like Hannibal, an enemy of the Romans, this warlike prince, who was a good linguist, endeavored to unite the Grecian and Asiatic states in a vast confederacy, and to free them from the Roman dominion. By his orders, all the Roman subjects (togati) in Western Asia, 80,000 in number, were put to death in one frightful day of slaughter. At the same time, he seized upon some countries in alliance with the Romans, and sent an army into Greece to protect Athens, Bœótia, and other states that had joined him. Hereupon the Roman senate gave the command against Mithridátes to B. C. 88. Sylla, who had distinguished himself in the social war, and been rewarded by the consulate. But Marius envied his opponent this Asiatic campaign, and procured a resolution of the people by which he himself was appointed to conduct the Mithridatic war. Sylla, who was with his army in Lower Italy, now marched upon Rome, had Marius and eleven of his confederates outlawed as traitors to their country, and adopted proper measures for the preservation of peace. He nevertheless behaved with moderation, that he might be able to commence the campaign against Mithridátes as soon as possible. Marius, after multitudinous dangers and adventures, escaped over the marshes of Mintúrnæ into Africa.

§ 133. THE FIRST CIVIL WAR.—Sylla now passed over into Greece, stormed Athens, that expiated its revolt by a frightful effusion of blood, seized upon the treasures in the temple of Delphi, and overthrew the generals of the king of Pontus in two engagements. He then marched through Macedonia and Thracia into Asia Minor, and compelled Mithridátes to a peace, by which Rome not only recovered her dominion over the whole of Western Asia, but was indemnified for the expenses of the war by the payment of a large sum of money, and the cession of the Pontic fleet. The revolted towns and districts were severely punished in their property.

B. C. 87.

In the mean time, Marius had returned from the ruins of Carthage again into Italy; and surrounding himself with a band of desperate men, had marched to the gates of Rome in conjunction with the democratic leaders, Cinna and Sertórius. The city, weakened by famine and dissension, was compelled to surrender; upon which, Marius gave free course to his thirst for vengeance. Troops of rude soldiers marched, plundering and slaughtering, through the streets of the capital; the heads of the aristocratic party, including the most renowned and respected senators and consuls, were murdered, their houses plundered and destroyed, their estates confiscated, and their dead bodies given to the dogs and the fowls of the air. After this gratification of his vengeance, Marius had himself chosen consul for the seventh time, but died about two weeks after, from the effects of excitement and a dissolute life.

B. C. 86.

§ 134. In the year 83 B. C., Sylla landed in Italy after the termination of the first Mithridatic war, and marched, with the support of the aristocracy, upon Rome. In Lower Italy, he defeated the democratic consuls in numerous engagements, drove the younger Marius to self-destruction in the strong city of Prænéste, by the close siege he laid to the place, and in a murderous battle before the gates of Rome, annihilated the Marian party and the rebellious Sámnītes, 8,000 of whom he slaughtered before the eyes of the trembling senate. The civil war had already cost the lives of 100,000 men, when Sylla (surnamed the Fortunate), for the purpose of completing his triumph, made public his proscriptions, upon which were written the names of the Marian party who were to be killed and plundered. Hereupon all the ties of blood, of friendship, of dependence and piety, were torn asunder: sons were armed against their parents, and slaves against their masters; informations were rewarded; terror and corruption of morals were everywhere prevalent. Upon this Sylla, who was named dictator for an indefinite period, proclaimed the Cornelian law, by which the whole power of the government fell into the hands of the aristocracy, and the influence of the tribunes was destroyed. After the conclusion of these arrangements, Sylla retired to his estate, where he shortly after died of a frightful distemper.

B. C. 78.

3. THE TIMES OF CNÆUS POMPEY, AND M. TULLIUS CICERO.

§ 135. Sylla's death did not bring back repose to the disturbed state. The outlawed and persecuted Marians assembled themselves around the brave and upright democratic leader, Sertórius, and fought against the Roman armies in Spain with fortune and success. It was not until Sertórius had been assassinated by his envious associates, that Pompey, who, whilst yet a youth, had joined himself to Sylla, and was now regarded as the head of the aristocratic party, succeeded in overpowering
B. C. 73. the rebels. His mild and placable character, and his courteous and popular bearing, rendered him an admirable mediator between contending factions.

§ 136. When Pompey returned to Italy from Spain, he encountered a new enemy — the rebellious slaves. Seventy gladiators had
B. C. 72. fled, in Cápua, from the scourge of their task-masters, broken open the slave prisons in Lower Italy, and exhorted the inmates to fight for their liberties. Their numbers soon increased to 70,000. The valiant Thracian, Spártăcus, was at their head. Their intention at first was to return to their homes; but after they had overthrown two Roman armies that opposed their passage, they entertained the hope of destroying the Roman power, and revenging themselves for the injuries they had received. The danger of the Romans was great. But dissension and want of military discipline produced a division among the
B. C. 71. slaves, and led to uncombined movements, so that the consul, M. Crassus, succeeded in subduing their ill-armed bands in detail. After the bloody fight on the banks of the Sílărus, in which Spártăcus fell after an heroic contest, the remainder marched into Upper Italy, where they were utterly destroyed by Pompey.

§ 137. Pompey rendered his name even more illustrious in Asia,
B. C. 67. where he brought the war against the pirates, and the second
B. C. 74-65. Mithridatic war, to a conclusion, than in the expedition against the slaves. In the sterile mountain regions on the south of Asia Minor, lived a daring race of freebooters, who disturbed the whole Mediterranean by piracy, visited the coasts and islands with plunder and desolation, dragged off noble Romans as prisoners, for the purpose of exacting a heavy ransom, and interrupted trade and commerce. Hereupon, Pompey was invested with the most unlimited dictatorial power over all seas, coasts, and islands. With a splendidly-equipped fleet and army, he cleared in three months the whole Mediterranean from the pirates, subdued the towns and fortresses in their own country, and settled many of the inhabitants in the newly-built town, Pompeiópolis.

§ 138. In the mean time, Mithridátes, encouraged by Rome's internal disturbances, had begun a fresh war. Lucullus was besieging the rich island town of Cýzicus, and Mithridátes attempted to relieve it; but

Lucúllus fell upon him and gave him such an overthrow that he retreated in haste to his kingdom of Pontus; and when this also fell a prey to the victor, he sought aid and protection from his son-in-law, Tigránes, king of Armenia. But Lucúllus defeated the enormous host of the
B. C. 69.
Armenian king in the neighborhood of his capital, Tigranocérta, and was already making preparations for overthrowing the whole empire, and extending the Roman dominions as far as Parthia, when the legions refused obedience to their general. Upon this, Lucúllus retired to his wealth and his pleasure-gardens, and Pompey united the command of the Armenio-Pontic army to his other dignities. He con-
B. C. 66.
quered Mithridátes, who had assembled fresh forces, in a night engagement on the Euphrátes, reduced the Armenian king to homage and submission, and then put an end to the rule of the Seleúcidæ in Syria. Mithridátes, deprived of the greater part of his territories, and despairing of a successful issue, destroyed himself. After Pompey, at his own pleasure, had disposed of the conquered lands in Asia, in such a way that the Roman empire was enlarged by three provinces, and some of the more distant lands had been ceded to tributary kings, he returned to Rome, where he held a public entry of two days, and filled the treasury with enormous wealth.

§ 139. A short time before this, M. Tullius Cicero, Pompey's friend and the companion of his thoughts, had acquired the honorable title of father of his country. Cicero, born in a provincial town, and of citizen parents, had so distinguished himself by his talents, his industry, and his irreproachable life, that although ignoble (novus homo) he obtained the consulate. He had devoted himself in Athens and Rhodes with such zeal and success to the sciences of the Greeks, and especially to eloquence and philosophy, that he might be compared, both as a statesman and an orator, to Demósthenes, and had composed profound works on rhetoric and philosophy. Though vain, boastful, and weak, he possessed civic virtue, patriotism, and a strong sense of justice.

During his consulate, Catiline, a man of noble family, but disgraced by an infamous life, and loaded with debts, formed a conspiracy with certain other Romans of desperate fortunes, the objects of which were, to murder the consuls, to set fire to the city, to overthrow the constitution, and in the confusion to seize upon the government by the aid of the soldiers of Sylla and the populace. But the vigilant consul Cicero had baffled this atrocious project. By his orations against Catiline, he unmasked the dissembling villain in the senate, and compelled him to fly into Etrúria, where he met with his death in a courageous defence against the consular army. His confederates were put to a violent death in prison.

4. THE TIMES OF JULIUS CÆSAR.

§ 140. THE TRIUMVIRATE.—Sylla's fortune excited ambitious men to imitate it. Every one sought to be first, and to rule the state at his pleasure. But whilst Pompey, who was now in possession of almost kingly authority, was reposing upon the laurels of his renown, in the full enjoyment of his happiness and prosperity, he was gradually overtaken by his great competitor, Julius Cæsar. This man united talents of the most varied character, so that he was not less distinguished as a writer and orator, than as a general and soldier. His liberality gained him the favor of the people, and his ambition urged him to great deeds. To make himself a match for the old republican party, at the head of which stood the eccentric M. Porcius Cato, Cæsar formed an alliance with

B. C. 60. Pompey and Crassus, called the triumvirate (league of three men), in which they pledged themselves to assist each other. From this time, these three men ruled the state without troubling themselves farther about the senate. In a short time, Cæsar had the govern-

B. C. 58. ment of Gaul, in which he had a long war to conduct, transferred to himself. That he might not be disturbed in his undertakings, he renewed the triumvirate in a meeting that was held at Lucca. By this means, the government of Gaul was continued to him for five years. Pompey received Spain as his province, but governed it by means of his legates, whilst he himself exercised a dictatorial power in Rome. Crassus, the richest man in Rome, to gratify his avarice, chose Syria with its riches; but was overthrown by the Parthians in the plains of Mesopotámia, and killed in the flight. His more valiant son, and almost the whole of the army, died on the field of battle. The Roman ensigns fell into the hands of the enemy.

B. C. 58-50. § 141. CÆSAR'S WARS IN GAUL.—The Celts, a people divided into many states and tribes, were the ancient inhabitants of Gaul (France) and Helvetia (Switzerland). The southern part of this Gaul had already become a Roman province (hence Provence), when the Helvétii embraced the project of leaving their sterile mountains, and settling themselves in its south-western portion. The Romans would not permit this, and Cæsar in consequence marched into Gaul. He overthrew the Helvétii in a battle, compelled them to return to their burnt villages and desolated country, and reduced them to pay tribute. He then subdued the German leader, Ariovístus, who by means of his hardy troops had severely oppressed the Séquani and Ædui, who were dwelling in eastern Gaul, and obliged him to return again to his trans-Rhenish country. After Cæsar had subdued the Belgæ and other Gaulish tribes, he twice crossed the Rhine for the purpose of terrifying the warlike inhabitants of the rude and woody Germany, and preventing their hostile attacks upon Gaul. It is to this undertaking that we owe the first short

description of Germany, in Cæsar's commentaries on the Gallic war. But the Roman general never thought of making permanent conquests, either in Germany, or Britain on the coasts of which he twice landed. After a few engagements with the skin-clad inhabitants of the British islands, he sailed back again for the purpose of completely subjecting the Gauls. For this restless and fickle people were perpetually revolting and taking up arms, when Cæsar was employed in another quarter. It was not till he had put down the last general insurrection, at
B. C. 52. Alésia, in Burgundy, that he succeeded in reducing the whole country as far as the Rhine, and converting it into a province of the Roman empire.

B. C. 49-48. § 142. THE SECOND CIVIL WAR. — In the mean while, the rage of party had grown in Rome to the greatest excess, and murder and plunder were matters of daily occurrence. This induced the senate and the old republicans to attach themselves entirely to Pompey, and to place the consulate at his disposal. Pompey employed this vast power to depress Cæsar, of whose military renown he had become jealous. At his instigation, an order was sent to Cæsar from the senate, at the termination of the war in Gaul, to lay down his command and to quit his army. Two tribunes of the people (Cúrio and Antónius) who opposed this resolution, and demanded that Pompey should also give up his power, were driven out of the city; they fled to Cæsar's camp, and summoned him to step forward as the defender of the outraged privileges of the people.

B. C. 49. After a little hesitation, Cæsar crossed the boundary stream of the Rúbicon, and advanced upon Rome. Pompey, aroused when it was too late from his indolence and careless security, did not venture to await his approach in the city: he hastened to Brundúsium with a few troops and a great train of senators and nobles; and when the victor approached that place, he escaped across the Ionian Sea into Epírus. Cæsar did not pursue him, but fell back upon Rome, where he took possession of the treasury, and then proceeded to Spain. Here he compelled the army of Pompey to a capitulation, the result of which was, that the generals and officers were allowed to depart, and the greater part of the common soldiers joined the victor. When Cæsar on his return, after a close siege, had reduced Massília, a town that wished to remain neutral, and punished it severely in its possessions and liberties, he again marched to Rome, had himself appointed dictator and consul for the following year, and adopted many serviceable measures. He then passed over the Iónian Sea, for the purpose of making head against
B. C. 48. Pompey. The decisive battle of Pharsálus, in the plains of Thessaly, was soon fought, in which Cæsar's veteran troops gained a splendid victory over an army of double their numbers. Pompey, with a few faithful followers, fled to Asia Minor and thence to Egypt,

where, instead of a hospitable reception, he met his death by assassination. Ptólemy, in the hope of obtaining the favor of Cæsar, ordered the conquered Pompey to be killed on his landing at Pelúsium, and his dead body to be cast unburied upon the shore.

§ 143. Cæsar's triumphs.— Shortly after, Cæsar arrived in Italy. He shed tears of compassion over Pompey's death, and refused the instigator of the murder his promised reward. For when he was chosen umpire between Ptólemy and his beautiful sister Cleopátra, in a dispute concerning the throne, he decided in favor of the latter, and by this means got involved in a war with the king and the people of Egypt, that retained him for nine months in Alexandria, and reduced him to great peril. It was only when fresh troops had arrived, and Ptólemy had been drowned after an unsuccessful engagement on the Nile, that he could place the government in the hands of Cleopátra (by whose charms he had been enchained), and proceed to fresh conquests. The rapid victory that he gained by the terror of his name over the son of Mithridátes has been rendered immortal by the memorable letter that announced the event: "I came, saw, conquered" (*Veni, vidi, vici*). After a short delay in Rome, he passed over into Africa, where the friends of republican government and the adherents of Pompey had collected a vast army. Here Cæsar gained the bloody battle of Thapsus, where the hopes of the republicans were destroyed. Thousands fell in the field; many of the survivors perished by their own hands, and among them, the high-spirited Cato the younger, who put himself to death in Utica with calm composure. A magnificent triumph of four days awaited the victor on his return to Rome, which he, however, soon quitted, for the purpose of attacking the last of his enemies, who had assembled themselves around the sons of Pompey. The last remnants of the friends of Pompey and the republic were destroyed in the frightful battle near Munda, where they fought with the courage of desperation. One of the sons was killed in the flight, and the survivor followed the life of a pirate, till he fell by the hand of an assassin.

B. C. 46.

B. C. 45.

§ 144. Cæsar's death.— Cæsar now returned, as chief and ruler of the Roman empire, to the capital, where he was saluted as "Father of the country," and elected dictator for life. He sought to win the soldiers and people by liberality, and the nobles by offices: he encouraged trade and agriculture, embellished the city with temples, theatres, and public places, improved the calendar, and forwarded all kinds of good and useful projects; but his evident attempts to gain the title and dignity of king induced some fanatical friends of liberty to engage in a conspiracy. His friend and flatterer, Marc Antony, offered him the kingly diadem during a feast; and despite the feigned distaste with which Cæsar rejected it, his secret satisfaction was discernible. At the head of

the conspiracy stood the high-minded enthusiast for liberty, M. Junius Brutus, the friend of Cæsar, and the severe republican, Caius Cassius. In despite of every warning, Cæsar held a meeting of the senate on the ides of March, in the hall of Pompey. It was here
B. C. 44. that, with the exclamation, "*Et tu Brute!*" he fell, pierced by twenty-three daggers, at the feet of the statue of his former opponent.

5. THE LAST YEARS OF THE REPUBLIC.

§ 145. It was soon apparent that the idea of freedom only existed among a few men of cultivated minds, but was quenched in the hearts of the populace. The first enthusiasm for the newly-acquired freedom was soon changed into hatred and invectives against the murderers of the dictator, when Marc Antony, in an artful speech at the funeral of Cæsar, extolled his merits and services, and ordered presents of money to be distributed among the poor. The senate, on the other hand, were for the most part favorable to the conspirators, and conferred upon some of them the government of provinces; and when Antony attempted to take possession of one of these provinces by force, Cicero obtained, by his Philippic Orations, that the senate declared him an enemy of the country. The senate, at the same time, gave offence to Octávius, the grandson of Cæsar's sister, who was then nineteen years of age, and who, as heir of his uncle's name, (Cæsar Octaviánus, afterwards Augustus), had all the old soldiers on his side. Octavius, in consequence, raised the standard of Cæsar's vengeance, and formed a second triumvi-
B. C. 43. rate with Antony and Lépidus, on a little island of the river Reno, near Bologna. New proscriptions took place, which proved particularly fatal to the knightly and senatorial ranks. The most deserving and illustrious men fell beneath the blows of assassins, the dearest relations of blood, of friendship, and of piety were torn asunder. Among the victims of Antony was Cicero, who was killed during an attempt at flight. His head and his right hand were placed upon the rostrum.

§ 146. After the possessors of power in Italy had satiated their vengeance, they marched against the republicans, who had established their camp in Macedonia, under the command of Brutus and Cassius. It was here, in the plains of Philippi, that a decisive double
B. C. 42. engagement took place, in which Cassius was obliged to yield to Antony, whilst Brutus repulsed the legions of Octávius. But when Cassius, deceived by false intelligence, had over-hastily fallen upon his own sword, and the triumvirs, twenty days afterwards, renewed the fight with united forces, Brutus, "the last of the Romans," was forced to succumb, and fell, like Cassius, upon his own sword. His wife, Portia (Cato's daughter), destroyed herself with live coals, and many champions of liberty died by their own hands; so that Philippi became the grave of the republic. Henceforth, the contest was no longer for free-

dom, but for empire. The victors divided the Roman territory between them; Antony chose the east, Octávius the west; the feeble Lépidus, who at first received the province of Africa, but who never possessed much influence, was soon robbed of his share.

§ 147. But whilst the luxurious Antony was leading a voluptuous life at Cleopátra's court in Alexandria, the shrewd Augustus and his high-spirited admiral, Agrippa, were winning the affections of the Roman people by liberal donations and diversions, rewarding the soldiers by a distribution of lands, and keeping up the discipline of the fleet and army. At length, when Antony lavished Roman blood and Roman honor in an unsuccessful campaign against the Parthians, married Cleopátra, and gave the provinces of Rome to her son, the senate, at the instigation of Octávius, deprived him of all his honors, and declared war against Cleopátra. East and west stood opposed in arms. But the sea-fight of Áctium, despite the superiority of the Egyptians, was decided in favor of Octávius. Antony and Cleopátra fled. But when the victor approached the gates of Alexandria, the former fell on his sword, and Cleopátra, finding that her charms produced no impression on the new potentate, destroyed herself by the poison of an asp. Egypt became the first province of the ROMAN EMPIRE.

B. C. 31.

B. C. 30.

IV. THE ROMAN EMPIRE.

1. THE TIMES OF CÆSAR OCTAVIANUS AUGUSTUS.

Augustus, from 30 B. C. to A. D. 14.

§ 148. The bloody civil war had swept away all the men of ability and patriotism; and the crowd that was left demanded nothing but food and entertainment, and forgot freedom and civil virtue in the enjoyment of the moment. This rendered it easy to the dexterous Augustus to change the Roman republic into a monarchy; but he yielded so far to the prejudices of the Romans, as not to assume the title of king, or master, and to retain the republican names and forms, with the appellation of Cæsar, whilst he gradually got all the offices and privileges of the senate and people placed in his own hands, and had them renewed from time to time. He united a profound understanding and talents for government, with clemency, temperance, and constancy; and as he was a master in the art of dissimulation, and knew how to turn the failings of men to advantage, he gained his ends more surely than his greater uncle, Cæsar. It was under Augustus that the Roman empire possessed the greatest power abroad, and the highest cultivation at home. It extended from the Atlantic Ocean to the Euphrátes, and from the Danube and Rhine to the Atlas and falls of the Nile; art and literature flourished to such a degree, that the reign of Augustus was called the golden age. Vast military roads, provided with milestones, connected the twenty-five provinces with Rome, and facilitated intercourse; magnificent aqueducts and canals attested the enterprising spirit of the Roman people; Rome itself was adorned with temples, theatres, and baths, and so much changed, that Augustus was able to say that he found Rome brick, and left it marble. The temple which Agrippa consecrated to all the gods (the Pantheon), is still one of the greatest ornaments of the eternal city. Augustus and his friend Mæcénas, Póllio, and others, were the favorers of art and literature, and the patrons of poets and authors. The first public library was founded on the Palatine hill; the citizens, who now no longer marched to the wars, and who had relinquished the conduct of state affairs to Cæsar and his ministers, employed their leisure in reading and writing, left actions for words, and performing for thinking; it was by this means that polished manners soon prevailed among all classes.

§ 149. Roman literature. — Virgil, Horace, and Ovid claim the first place among the poets that adorned the Augustan age. The first composed the Ænéid, an heroic poem on the model of Homer (§ 38), pastoral poetry, and a didactic poem on agriculture; Horace, to whom his patron Mæcénas presented a small Sabine farm, wrote odes, satires, and humorous epistles, in which he exhibits his cheerful views of life in a witty and engaging manner; Ovid, the clever writer of mythological stories (Metamorphoses), was banished by Augustus to the rude shores of the Black Sea, whence he wrote letters of complaint to his distant home.

Among historians, the most celebrated are Sallust, who, in his account of the wars against Jugurtha and Catiline, gives a true but frightful picture of the corrupt times; and Titus Livius, the tutor of the grand-nephew of Augustus, who wrote a complete history of Rome, in 142 books; of which only thirty-five are preserved. We possess a biography of distinguished men, by his contemporary, Cornélius Nepos. The Romans took the Greeks for their models in art and literature, but fell far short of their masters.

2. THE STRUGGLES OF THE GERMANS FOR LIBERTY.

§ 150. About the time that the Saviour of the world was brought forth in lowliness and humility in Bethlehem, in the land of Judæ'a, to bring the joyful news of salvation to the lost race of man, the Germans were engaged in a severe struggle with the Romans for the preservation of their liberties and national customs. Drusus, the brave step-son of Augustus, was the first Roman who made any conquests on the right bank of the Rhine. He undertook many successful campaigns against the tribes in alliance with the Suevi, between the Rhine and the Elbe,

and attempted to secure the land by intrenchments and fortifications. Being killed in the flower of his years, by a fall from his horse during his return home, his brother Tibérius completed the conquest of western Germany, rather by dint of skilfully-conducted negotiations with the disunited Germans, than by force of arms; whereupon the country between the Rhine and the Weser was erected into a Roman province. Foreign customs, language, and laws already threatened to destroy German nationality; German soldiers already fought in the ranks of the Romans, and prided themselves on foreign marks of distinction; when the insolence and indiscretion of the governor, Quintilius Varus, aroused the slumbering patriotism of the people. Several tribes united themselves in a confederacy, under the guidance of Hermann (Armínius), the valiant prince of the Cherúsci, for the purpose of throwing off the foreign yoke. It was in vain that Segéstus, whose daughter Thusnelda had been carried off and married by Hermann, against the consent of her father, warned the careless governor. Varus marched with three legions and several auxiliaries, through the Teutoburger forest, for the purpose of quelling an insurrection that had been purposely raised; but suffered such a defeat from the Germans under Hermann's command, that the defiles of the wood were covered far and wide with the
A. D. 9. corpses of the Romans. The eagles were lost, and Varus died by his own hands. Augustus, when he heard the news, exclaimed in despair, "Varus, give me back my legions!"

§ 151. Upon the death of Augustus, in his 76th year, at
A. D. 14. Nola, in Lower Italy, Germánicus, the valiant son of Drusus, again crossed the Rhine, ravaged the lands of the Catti (Hesse), buried the bleaching remains of the Romans in the Teutoburger forest, and carried off into captivity Thusnelda, the high-spirited wife of Hermann, whom her treacherous father had given up to the enemy. But although he defeated the Cherusci and their allies in two engagements, and at the same time pressed Germany closely by sea, the Roman dominion was never firmly or permanently established on the right bank of the Rhine. Storms destroyed the fleet, and a pathless country and the swords of the Germans brought the army to the brink of destruction; and when at length Germánicus, (to whose noble wife, Agrippína, the town of Cologne owes its prosperity), was recalled by his jealous uncle, Tibérius, and shortly after, met with his death by poison in Syria, the Germans were no longer disturbed by the ambition of the Romans. But the Lower German confederation of the Cherusci now turned its arms against the Upper German confederation of the Marcomanni, at the head of which stood Marbódius. This gave the Romans an opportunity of embroiling Germany from the south. Marbódius fell into the power of the Romans, who kept him for eighteen years at Ravenna, as their pensioner; Hermann was killed by envious friends. His deeds survived

in song, and our own age has erected a colossal statue, on the Teuthill at Detmold, in joyful commemoration of the deliverer of Germany.

TACITUS ON THE MANNERS AND CUSTOMS OF THE GERMANS.

§ 152. About 100 years after Augustus, the great historian Tácitus, after having portrayed the events of the Roman empire in his History and Annals, embraced the resolution of describing the manners and customs of the German tribes, and presenting them as models to his degenerate countrymen. Although the work remained a mere sketch, it is tc this resolution that we are indebted for the first accurate information respecting this region. We learn from it, that Germany was inhabited by numerous independent tribes, sometimes united and sometimes at war with each other, who were perpetually changing their places of residence in obedience to an innate wandering impulse.

War and the chase were their chief employments; they built neither towns nor strong-holds; their huts and farms were scattered about in the midst of their grounds; a peaceful life behind stone walls agreed neither with their love of liberty nor their passion for war. They united purity of morals, hospitality, good faith, and honesty, respect for women, and reverence for the marriage tie, to the external advantages of lofty stature, beauty of person, strength, and courage. The only vices attributed to them are a disposition to drunkenness and gambling.

3. THE CÆSARS OF THE AUGUSTAN RACE.

§ 153. Domestic misfortunes disturbed the happiness of Augustus. The promising sons, who sprung from the marriage of his daughter Julia with Agrippa, died in their youth; Julia herself occasioned her father such distress by her profligate life that at length he banished her. By the intrigues of the ambitious Livia, the emperor's third wife, the empire descended to Tibérius, the adopted step-son of Augustus. The clemency at first displayed by this hypocritical prince soon gave way to his natural malevolence, particularly when his crafty and vicious favorite, Sejánus, assisted him in establishing a military despotism. He advised him to unite the prætorian body-guard in a permanent camp before Rome. Here they soon became the oppressors of the people, raised and dethroned emperors, and introduced a military despotism. The assemblies of the people were no longer held, and the dastardly senate sank into a mere tool of the despot. The frightful court which took cognizance of cases of high treason, was a means of destroying every man of ability, inasmuch as it inflicted the punishment of death, and imposed fines, not only for actions, but even for words and thoughts. Pensioned spies undermined all faith and trust among the people, and destroyed every spark of freedom by terror. The misanthropical Tibérius, tortured by fear and the reproaches of his conscience,

Tiberius, A. D. 14 — 37.

passed the last years of his life in the island of Cápreæ (Capri), in Lower Italy, where he abandoned himself to luxury and the most infamous pleasures, whilst Sejánus was practising every vice in Rome. When the latter at length attempted to possess himself of the throne, the emperor sent an order to the senate to put him to death. Tibérius, sick and advanced in years, perished by a violent death on his estate in Lower Italy. During his reign, a dreadful earthquake destroyed many of the richest and most beautiful cities in Asia Minor.

Caligula, A. D. 37-41. § 154. His successor, Caius Calígula, the unworthy son of the noble Germánicus and the high-minded Agrippína, was a blood-thirsty tyrant, who took delight in signing sentences of death and having them executed; a frantic spendthrift, who lavished money in buildings without a purpose; an insolent boaster, who caused divine honors to be paid to himself, and celebrated magnificent triumphs over the Germans and Britons, whom he scarcely ever saw; and a glutton, by whose riotous table enormous sums were swallowed up. The Prætorians at length killed the crazy tyrant, and raised his uncle, the imbecile Claudius, to the throne. (Claudius, A. D. 41-54.) This emperor was led by women and favorites; the latter especially the freedmen Narcissus and Pallas, were in possession of all the offices, and enriched themselves at the expense of the people, whilst his wife Messalína yielded herself up to every lust, and trampled morality and decency under foot. At length, the emperor commanded her to be put to death, and married his ambitious and profligate niece Agrippína, who, however, soon got rid of her weak and uxorious husband by poison, for the purpose of raising the depraved Claudius Nero, her son by a former marriage, to the throne.

Nero, A. D. 54-68. § 155. The clemency which Nero displayed in the commencement of his reign, soon gave place to the most exquisite cruelty. He, who once, when he had to sign an order for an execution, wished that he could not write, now not only persecuted, put to death, and confiscated the property of every man who displayed the virtues of a citizen or the mind of a Roman, but exercised his tyranny at the expense of his nearest relations. His step-brother, Britannicus, died by poison from the imperial table; his mother was first sunk at sea in a ship, and when she succeeded in saving herself, was put to death by assassins despatched for the purpose; his virtuous wife, Octávia, the daughter of Claudius, found a violent death in an overheated bath. A conspiracy, in which the republican poet Lucan (whose heroic poem Pharsalia still breathes the old Roman spirit) was implicated, was made use of by the emperor to destroy not only Lucan, but his uncle Séneca, the Stoic philosopher, who had been Nero's own preceptor. Séneca opened his own veins. Nero, at the instigation of his courtiers and mistress (Poppæ'a Sabína), perpetrated the most shameful follies and crimes. Spectacles and riotous processions, in which the emperor himself, disguised as a singer and harp-player, took a share along with the companions of his pleasures, luxurious feasts and banquets, and extravagances of every description, consumed the revenues of the state. The despot, in the plenitude of his insolence and wickedness, ordered Rome to be set on fire,* that he might sing the destruction of Troy from the battlements of his palace. To divert the hatred of his subjects from himself, he afterwards attributed the crime to the Christians, who were subjected, in consequence, to the most frightful persecutions. The rebuilding of the city, and Nero's "Golden House," on the Palatine hill, increased the oppression, till at length, repeated enormities induced the Spanish legion to revolt. As the troops under the command of Galba approached the capital, Nero fled to a country house, where he caused himself to be stabbed by one of his freedmen.

§ 156. The house of Augustus became extinct with Nero. Galba was his successor. But as the avaricious old man would not gratify the rapacity of the Prætorians, they proclaimed Otho emperor, and put Galba and the successor he had appointed to death. At the same time, Vitellius raised his standard on the Rhine, marched with his legions into Italy, and defeated the army of his opponent on the banks of the Po. Otho, and several of his adherents, died by their own hands. Vitellius was a mere glutton, who found pleasure in nothing but luxurious banquets. Accordingly, when Vespásian, whom the Syrian legions had proclaimed emperor, approached the gates of Rome, Vitellius was killed by a troop of rude soldiers, and his body dragged with hooks into the Tiber.

Galba, Otho, Vitellius, A. D. 68–70.

4. THE FLAVII AND ANTONINES.

Vespasian, A. D. 70–79.

§ 157. Vespásian, the first in the succession of good emperors, restored the discipline of the army and the Prætorians by severe measures, improved the administration of justice after abolishing the court of high treason, and by economy and good management succeeded in replenishing the treasury. At the same time, he embellished the city by building the Temple of Peace and the Amphitheatre, the gigantic remains of which (Coliséum) still excite the admiration of travellers, and enlarged the boundaries of the empire by the conquest of Judæ'a and Britain.

§ 158. The tyranny of the Roman governor who ruled over the land of Judæ'a had at last driven the people to rebellion. They fought with the courage of despair against the advancing legions, but were forced to yield to Roman superiority and take refuge in their capital, where they

* This is an exaggerated account of Nero's guilt. It is not probable that he was the author of the conflagration, and Tacitus says there was no authority but a vague rumor among the populace for the story, that Nero showed his indifference or exultation at the event by playing and singing while the flames still raged. *Am. Ed.*

were now besieged by Vespásian's son, Titus. Thousands were soon carried off by famine and pestilence in the over-crowded city. It was in vain that the compassionate general made offers of pardon: rage and fanaticism urged the Jews to a desperate resistance. They defended themselves in their temple with an utter contempt for death, till that magnificent structure was destroyed by fire on the taking of the city, and death raged in every shape among the conquered. The
A. D. 70. complete destruction of Jerusalem then took place. Among the prisoners, who followed the triumphal car of the conqueror, was Joséphus, the Jewish historian of this war. The triumphal arch of Titus in Rome displays, to this day, representations of the sacred vessels of the Jews that were at this time conveyed to the metropolis of the world. Those who were left behind were exposed to grievous oppression under the Roman yoke. But when a heathen colony, fifty years after the destruction of the city, was transplanted by the emperor Adrian to the sacred soil of Jerusalem, (which from this time was called Ælia Capitolína), and a temple erected to Jupiter on the eminence once occupied by Solomon's temple to Jehovah, the Jews, deceived by a false Messiah, took up arms once more to prevent this outrage. After a
A. D. 122–125. murderous war of three years' duration, in which upwards of half a million of the natives were slaughtered, the Jews submitted to the military skill of the Romans. The survivors left the country in crowds, the land resembled a desert, and the Jewish state was at an end. Since then, the Jews have been scattered abroad over the whole earth, but without mingling with other people, and faithful to their own customs, religion, and superstitions.

§ 159. It was during the reign of Vespásian, that the high-spirited Agrícŏla, father-in-law to the historian Tácitus, by whom his life has been written, subdued Britain as far as the highlands of Caledonia (Scotland), and introduced the Roman language, manners, and institutions. Britain remained subject to the Romans for nearly four hundred years. The warlike energy of the people was destroyed by civilization, so that they were afterwards as little able to resist the attacks of the rude Caledonians (Picts and Scots) as the wall erected by Adrian proved a defence against their inroads.

Titus, A. D. 79–81. § 160. The simple and energetic Vespásian was succeeded by his son Titus, who cast off the failings and crimes of his youth when he ascended the throne, and became so admirable a prince that he was justly called "the delight of mankind." It was during his reign that a frightful eruption of Mount Vesuvius destroyed the towns of Herculáneum, Pompéii, and Stabiæ. The inquisitive natural philosopher, the elder Pliny, lost his life by the vapor produced by this eruption, as we learn from two letters, written by his nephew, Pliny the younger, the friend and encomiast of the emperor Trajan, to the historian Tácitus.

The exhumation of these buried towns, which was begun about a hundred years ago, more especially that of Pompéii, has been of the utmost importance to the knowledge of antiquity and to the artistic taste of our own day.

§ 161. The noble Titus was unfortunately followed by his brother, the

Domitian, A. D. 81-96.

cruel Domítian, a gloomy and misanthropical tyrant, who took pleasure in nothing but the contests of wild beasts and gladiatorial combats. When he was at length murdered at the instigation of his wicked wife, the throne was taken possession of by Nerva, an old senator.

Nerva, A. D. 96-98.

Nerva adopted the energetic Spaniard, Trajan, who, by his government at home, and his victories abroad, deserved the surname of the best, and the glory of the greatest, of the Cæsars.

Trajan, A. D. 98-117.

He provided for the proper administration of justice, facilitated trade and commerce by making new roads and harbors (Cívita Vécchia), and embellished Rome with public buildings, temples, and a new forum, in which he ordered the beautiful column of Trajan to be erected. He at the same time reduced the turbulent Dacians on the Danube, and established the province of Dacia (Wallachia and Transylvania), which was soon peopled by Roman settlers, on the northern bank of the river. In the east, he made war on the Parthians, conquered Babylon, Seleúcia, and other cities, and converted Armenia and Mesopotámia into Roman provinces. The country between the sources of the Danube and the Upper Rhine, (Black Forest), was surrendered to settlers from Gaul and Germany, and was afterwards protected from hostile attacks by a ditch fortified with stakes. It was called Decumátian land, and the ruins of numerous towns, and the antiquities that are dug up there, show that it must have shared in the civilization of its conquerors.

§ 162. Trajan's relative and successor, Ælius Adriánus (Hadrian) was more intent upon defending than enlarging the bounds of his empire, and found greater pleasure in art and literature than in war.

Hadrian, A. D. 117-138.

He was a man of great cultivation of mind, but vain, and open to flattery. His eagerness for knowledge, and love of art, induced him to take journeys of many years' duration, both into the East, where he lingered in Greece, Asia, and Egypt, and into the West, where he visited Gaul, Spain, Britain, and the Rhine-land. Among the many writers, artists, and interpreters who surrounded the brilliant court of Hadrian, the most distinguished was the Greek Plutarch, the author of numerous writings. His biographies, in which he compares together the Greek and Roman statesmen and generals, are especially calculated to excite admiration for the heroic deeds of antiquity. Hadrian's love of art is borne witness to more particularly, by the ruins of his villa at Tívoli; his magnificent mausoleum, now the castle of St. Angelo at Rome; and innumerable remains of sculpture and building.

Antoninus Pius, A. D. 138-161. § 163. Hadrian's adopted son, the simple and benevolent Antonínus Pius, was an ornament of the throne. He avoided war that he might devote all his care to the arts of peace. Marcus Aurelius, A. D. 161-180. His successor, Marcus Aurélius Antonínus, the philosopher, was as much distinguished in war as in peace. He conquered the Marcomanni on the frozen Danube, and drove back over the frontiers, after a long war, the German tribes who were their confederates. He died at Vindobóna (Vienna), during a campaign. Marcus Aurélius was a man of simple and hardy habits, who, when on the throne, remained true to his stoic virtue and severity of morals (§ 91). He promoted civilization and useful institutions, and the collection of reflections, which he composed and dedicated to himself, bears witness to his noble principles and efforts.

§ 164. Cultivation and morals. — During this period, the highest civilization prevailed in the Roman empire, along with the greatest depravity of morals. Arts and sciences were encouraged in the courts of the Cæsars and the palaces of the wealthy, and were shared in by persons of all conditions. Trades and commerce flourished, and prosperity and refinement were visible in the populous cities and elegant dwelling-houses; establishments for education sprang up in Rome and the more considerable provincial towns. The ruins of buildings, military roads, and bridges that we admire even at this day, not only in Italy, but in many provincial towns (Trèves, Nîmes), the statues, sarcophagi, and altars with bas-reliefs and inscriptions, the vases of clay and bronze of elegant forms that are dug out of the earth, all bear testimony to the cultivation and feeling for art existing among the people in the times of the Cæsars. But this refinement was but a superficial polish; morality, nobility of soul, and strength of character, were held in no estimation. The people, no longer invigorated by war, or the labors of the field, sank into luxury and effeminacy; they sought their gratification in the barbarous sports of the amphitheatre, gladiatorial combats, and the contests of wild beasts, and gave themselves up to a relaxing enjoyment of the luxurious baths, with which the city was amply provided by the emperors, for the purpose of withdrawing the citizens from the consideration of graver matters. It is in vain, that Persius angrily shakes the scourge of his stern satire over the degenerate race, and endeavors to bring back the ancient vigor, simplicity, and morality; — it is in vain, that the witty Júvenal unveils in his sportive satire the frightful depths of crime and wickedness, and lashes his degenerate contemporaries; it is in vain, that the waggish Greek, Lucian, in his witty and satirical writings, jests at all the existing conditions of life and religion, for the purpose of destroying what is old, and thereby making room for something new and better; — human counsel came too late; nothing but a higher power could save the perishing world; the help had already appeared, but the blinded Romans did not recognize it, because it came not in the pomp of authority, but in the garment of humility.

5. ROME UNDER MILITARY GOVERNMENT.

Commodus, A. D. 180–192.

§ 165. Rome's downward course commences with Cómmodus, the unworthy son of Aurélius. He was a barbarous tyrant, who delighted in nothing but the combats of gladiators and wild beasts, and who distressed the people in every way, till at length he was put to death by those around him.

Pertinax, A. D. 193.

Pértinax, his valiant successor, had a similar fate. After his death, the insolence of the prætorians rose to such a height, that they put up the crown to the highest bidder.

Septimius Severus, A. D. 193–211.

Septímius Sevérus first restrained their insolence by his inexorable severity, and reëstablished the imperial power. He was a rude soldier, and enlarged the empire by his conquests in the East, where he took Mesopotámia from the Parthians; and he secured Britain by new defences against the turbulent Picts and Scots. But he deprived the senate of their last remains of power, and placed his whole reliance on the army, so that he was the actual establisher of the military government.

Caracalla, A. D. 211–217.

§ 166. The death of Septímius Sevérus at Ebórăcum (York) in Britain, placed his cruel son, Caracálla, on the throne, who, true to his father's teaching, honored the soldiery, but treated other men with contempt. He killed his brother, Geta, in the arms of his mother, and then put his preceptor, the great jurist Papínian, to death, for refusing to justify the fratricide. For the purpose of augmenting the revenue, he gave the right of Roman citizenship to all the free-born men in the empire. After the murder of this profligate tyrant by his own soldiers, in a campaign against the Parthians, his relative, Heliogabálus, a priest of the Syrian sun-god, succeeded to the throne.

Heliogabalus, A. D. 218–222.

Heliogabálus was a weak and cruel epicure, who, by the introduction of the sensual worship of Baal from Syria, destroyed the last remnants of the ancient Roman discipline and morality. The prætorians at length put the effeminate debauchee to death, and raised his cousin, Alexander Sevérus, to the throne.

Alexander Severus, A. D. 222–235.

Sevérus was a man of respectable character, who adopted many excellent measures, and listened to the advice of his sagacious mother; but his powers were inferior to the conduct of such difficult affairs of state. The prætorians killed the great jurist, Ulpian, before his eyes, with impunity; and on the eastern boundary, Ardshir (Artaxerxes) overthrew the Parthian government, and established the new Persian empire of the Sassánidæ, who soon pursued their conquests into the Roman territory.

§ 167. The death of the emperor and his mother, by an insurrection of the soldiers at Mayence, reduced the empire to such confusion, that twelve emperors were raised and dethroned within the space of twenty years. Philip the Arab, who, like Alexander Sevérus, was a friend to

Philip the Arab, A. D. 243-249.

the Christians, sought to signalize his reign by a magnificent celebration of the thousandth anniversary of Rome. His

Decius, A. D. 249-251.

successor, Decius, persecuted the Christians, but found an early death in battle against the Goths, a German tribe who had established themselves on the Lower Danube, and made predatory excursions thence, both by land and sea, into the Roman territory. After his death, the empire seemed on the point of dissolution. The generals in the different provinces caused themselves to be proclaimed

Gallienus, A. D. 259-268.

emperors, so that the historians of the period, during which Galliénus reigned in Rome, and his father, Valérian, was pining in captivity in Persia, call this the age of the thirty tyrants. In the mean time, the empire was attacked on the east by the New Persians, under the command of the valiant Sapor, whilst the German tribes threatened the other quarters.

§ 168. At this juncture, Aurélian, a man imbued with the old Roman

Aurelianus, A. D. 270-275.

courage and military discipline, was the restorer of the empire. He subdued the rebellious generals, and marched against the kingdom of Palmyréne, which Odenátus had founded on an oasis in Syria, and which was governed, after his death, by his beautiful and heroic wife, Zenóbia. Palmýra, the capital city, rich in arts, philosophy, and commerce, was taken and destroyed, and Zenóbia led in triumph to Rome. Her preceptor and adviser, the gallant philosopher Longínus, died a violent death. At first, a follower of the new Platonists, who joined the Oriental profundity, superstition, and belief in miracles, to the doctrines of Plato, and put the inactive contemplation of the East in place of the practical intelligence of ancient Rome, Longínus had afterwards relinquished this obscure wisdom. The ruins of Palmýra yet enchain the admiration of the traveller. Aurélian again restored the boundary of the Danube on the north, gave up the province on the farther side of the river to the enemy, and transplanted the inhabitants to the right bank. Lest his capital should be endangered by any sudden attack, he surrounded Rome with a wall.

§ 169. After Aurélian had been killed by his soldiers, and his suc-

Tacitus, A. D. 275-276.

cessor, Tácitus (a descendant of the historian), had perished in an expedition against the Goths, the courageous and up-

Probus, A. D. 276-282.

right Probus was raised to the throne. He enlarged and completed the boundary wall (Devil's Wall), from the Bavarian Danube to the Taunus, and secured it by means of troops; he planted vineyards on the Rhine and in Hungary, and reformed the affairs of the army. After Probus also had been killed by his troops, and his

successor, Carus, had fallen in an expedition against the Persians, either
Carus, A. D. 282-284. by a stroke of lightning or the hand of an assassin, the throne was assumed by the sagacious Dioclétian.

§ 170. Dioclétian increased the imperial power, and lowered the dig-
Diocletian, A. D. 284-305. nity of the senate; he projected a division of the empire, for the purpose of more easily resisting the enemy. He himself, with the title of Augustus, governed the Eastern region, together with Thrace, whilst his assistant in the empire (Cæsar), Galérius, was at the head of the Illyrian provinces; in the same manner, Maxímian, under the title of Augustus, ruled over Italy, Africa, and the islands; and his son-in-law, Constantius (Chlorus), governed the western provinces, Spain, Gaul, and Britain. For twenty years, Dioclétian governed the empire with vigor and dexterity, and restored its former strength and stability. But when he allowed himself to be seduced into commanding a bloody persecution against the Christians, he disturbed the evening of a most active life, and stained his name and government with an indelible mark of infamy. The sword of persecution was still raging among the confessors of the crucified Jesus, when Dioclétian abdicated his throne, to pass his remaining years in rural retirement at Salóna, in Dalmátia, and to forget the bustle of the world in the arrangement of his palace and gardens.

§ 171. The abdication of Dioclétian was followed by a period of confusion and sanguinary civil wars, which was only put an end to, when Constantínus, the brave and wise son of Constantius, assumed the government of the West, and marched into the field against Maxímian's hard-hearted son, Maxéntius. Constantine, who had been won over to Christianity by his mother, Hélĕna, erected the banner of the cross
A. D. 312. (lábarum), overthrew the cruel Maxéntius at the Milvian Bridge, and took possession of Rome, after his opponent had been drowned in the waters of the Tiber. After this period, Cónstantine ruled over the West, whilst his brother-in-law, Licínius, govered the East. But the ambition of Cónstantine soon occasioned another war, in which Licínius lost his kingdom and, at last, his life. It was thus that Cónstan-
A. D. 325. tine became sole governor of the Roman empire, and showed favor to the Christians. But that the doctrines of Jesus had little effect upon his mind, is shown by the cruelty with which he caused whole troops of his captured enemies to be thrown to wild beasts, by the severity he displayed in the execution of his wife and his noble son, Crispus, and by the love of vengeance and want of truth displayed in his character.

BOOK SECOND.

MIGRATION OF NATIONS AND THE MIDDLE AGE.

A. MIGRATION OF NATIONS AND ESTABLISHMENT OF MONOTHEISM.

I. THE TRIUMPH OF CHRISTIANITY OVER PAGANISM.

1. THE CHRISTIAN CHURCH OF THE FIRST CENTURY.

§ 172. The Romans were very tolerant of the heathen forms of religion amongst other nations, as is apparent at once from the fact, that they adopted not only the mythology of the Greeks, but also, by degrees, the theology of the East, of the Chaldéans, Persians, Egyptians, and Syrians. But as Christianity forbade any combination with Paganism, the Christians carefully avoided all participation in the feasts and religious rites of the heathen, and kept themselves separate even in the daily intercourse of life; thus the hatred of the people and the mistrust of their rulers were roused, and heavy persecutions arose against them. Ten persecutions of Christians are recorded from the days of Nero, when Peter and Paul are said to have met their death, to the first decennium of the fourth century, when Dioclétian and Galérius drove the confessors of the crucified Saviour, by rack and axe, to the altar of sacrifice, burnt down the churches, and gave the Holy Scriptures to the flames. Even the noble-minded Marcus Aurélius thought it his duty to break by force the stubbornness of the supposed fanatics; and the short reign of Decius has become memorable for one of the most violent persecutions of the Christians. But the *holy joy* with which the martyrs, bearing witness by their blood, endured torture and death, multiplied the number of believers, so that the blood of martyrs is justly called "the seed of the Church." The objects of persecution concealed themselves in subterraneous passages (the Catacombs), near the graves of those they loved, and in caves and mountain clefts. Oppression heightened their trust in God; and the number of apostate believers who delivered up the Bible to be burned, or offered incense before the statue of the emperor, was small when compared with the number of those who stood firm in their faith. During the years of persecution, Christianity continued to spread, by the indwelling force of truth, and favorable circumstances from without, to all quarters of the heavens, so that, as early as the third century, before Cónstantine raised it to a state religion, it overstepped the bounds of the Roman empire.

2. CONSTANTINE THE GREAT AND JULIAN THE APOSTATE.

§ 173. Cónstantine, as sole emperor, transferred his residence to Byzantium, which from this time forward was called Constantinople. He fortified the city, which was favorably situated, with walls and towers, and embellished it most magnificently with palaces and churches, race-grounds, and works of art. He then abolished the antiquated constitution of the Roman empire; vested all power in the imperial throne; surrounded himself with a brilliant court of chamberlains, ministers, officials, and servants; and established a galling system of taxation. The better to conduct the management of his vast empire, he divided it into four prefectures or lieutenancies: the East, to which Thrace and Egypt were assigned; Illýricum with Greece; Italy with Africa; the West (containing Gaul, Spain, Britain). Each of these he divided into a greater or less number of districts (dioceses), and these again into states (provinces). The last years of his life Cónstantine devoted principally to religious and ecclesiastical matters; but he deferred the rite of baptism which cleanseth from sin, till shortly before his death. He founded many churches, and endowed them with landed estates. He granted to the clergy an immunity from taxes, and other privileges, and allowed legacies to the Church. From this time forward, the constitution of the Christian Church took a new shape; whereas before, the Elders and Bishops were chosen from the whole Church-community, and the principle of brotherly equality amongst all Christians was held in honor, now, the priesthood (clergy) separated from the people (laity), and introduced degrees of rank, so that the Bishops of the principal cities were placed over the remaining Bishops as metropolitans, and these again had the superintendence of the priests in their immediate neighborhood. At the same time, the Church services, which before consisted only in singing, prayer, and reading the Bible, and concluded with the love-feasts, were made more solemn by the aid of music and other arts.

§ 174. Arianism. — Augustine. — Fathers of the Church. — The doctrine (dogma), also, of Christianity did not long remain in its original simplicity and purity, when many learned men made it the subject of their inquiry and meditation. The first point which they investigated was the relation of Christ to God, and the mysterious junction of His divine and human natures. On this question, vehement contentions arose as early as the time of Constantine, between the Alexandrian ecclesiastics, Arius and Athanasius, the first of whom maintained that Christ, the Son of God, was inferior to God the Father, and dependent on Him; while the latter laid down the doctrine of the Trinity in Unity, through the principle that God the Son was of the same substance with God the Father. The first general Church Council (Œcumenical Synod), which Constantine convened at Nice, declared the opinion of Athanasius to be the true (orthodox) faith of the Church; but the German nations, the Goths, Vandals, Longobards, to whom Christianity had been brought by Arian missionaries, continued in Arianism for another century, and were therefore excommunicated and driven out as heretics from the Catholic (universal) Church. An equally important dispute arose in the fifth century, about original sin and predestination, since Augustine, Bishop of north Africa, laid down the principle that the nature of man, through Adam's fall, has become unable to do good by its own strength; that this strength is produced only by the grace of God in one portion of mankind, while the other remains abandoned to ruin; so that one man may be from the beginning appointed (predestinated) to salvation, another to condemnation. These harsh doctrines were disputed by Pelágius, a monk residing in Africa, and the principle maintained, that man can, by the strength of his own free will, do good, and become a partaker of salvation. — The Christian writers of the first five or six centuries were called Fathers of the Church. Their works are the more important, because on them depend the traditional doctrines of the Catholic Church. The nearer, therefore, they stand to the time of the Apostles, the greater is their authority, as we assume that the disciples of Jesus made many oral communications to their contemporaries, which are not found in the apostolic writings, but might well be known from the works of the Fathers. They wrote partly in Greek and partly in Latin.

Constantius, A. D. 357 - 360. § 175. Of Constantine's three vicious sons, who, according to their father's will, divided the empire, Constantius, after long years of bloody struggles, obtained the sole sovereignty. As he was himself busied in Asia, he sent his cousin, Julian, to Gaul, to protect the frontiers of the empire against the Germanic nations. A. D. 357. Julian besieged the Allemánni in Strasburgh, twice passed the Rhine, repulsed the Franks in the Netherlands, and restored the ancient renown of the Roman arms. A. D. 360. Proclaimed emperor by his soldiers in his favorite city, Paris, Julian marched against Constántius, and a civil war would have ensued, had not the latter died just at this crisis. Julian, A. D. 361 - 363. Julian now without hinderance entered the imperial castle in Constantinople, as sovereign of the vast empire. He immediately removed all the superfluous officers of the court, reduced the imperial household, and in his dress and mode of living studied the greatest simplicity; he provided for the impartial administration of justice, and restored discipline and military virtue in the army.

Strongly as he worked by these means on an indolent generation, yet his zeal to revive paganism hindered the success of his efforts. The constraint which he endured in his youth under Christian masters had produced in him an aversion to the Gospel; whilst his lively imagination and his love for Plato's philosophy (§ 65, 72), and for the literature and poetry of antiquity, made him a most enthusiastic admirer of paganism. For this reason he was branded by Christian writers with the title of Apostate. Nevertheless, he was too just and too wise to inflict bloody persecutions on the Christians. He contented himself with removing them from his presence, and from public and professional offices, opposing their opinions in writings, and reëstablishing the heathen worship, with its feasts and sacrifices. He himself sometimes offered solemn hecatombs of 100 bulls to the god of the sun. Having, however, with the heroism of old Rome, undertaken an adventurous campaign against the New Persians, he pressed forward victorious over the Euphrátes and Tigris; but being entrapped into an inaccessible mountainous district, and compelled to commence a difficult retreat, he was wounded mortally

Jovian, A. D. 363-364.

by an arrow, and his schemes brought to nought. His successor Jóvian, in a dishonorable peace, restored the conquered territory, and made Christianity again the dominant religion.

Valens, A. D. 364-378.

After his death, the empire was divided, the Arian Valens ruling over the East, whilst his brother, the rude and warlike Valentínian I., governed the West.

Valentinian, A. D. 364-375.

II. THE MIGRATION OF NATIONS.

1. THEODOSIUS THE GREAT.

§ 176. When Valens was ruling the East, the Huns, a wild, hideous, well-mounted nomad people, came from the steppes of Central Asia to Europe. They overthrew the Alâni and the brave East Goths (whose gray-haired king, Hérmanrich, devoted himself to death), and they then fell upon the West Goths. But this people having been already converted to Arian Christianity by Bishop Ulfilas, obtained permission from Valens to cross the Danube, with their wives and children, and to occupy new abodes. Through the venality of the Roman officers, the West Goths, contrary to agreement, remained in possession of their arms; and as, from the severity and avarice of the governor, they soon fell into the greatest distress from hunger, they seized the accustomed sword, stormed the city of Marcianópolis, and carried robbery and desolation through the land. Valens marched hastily against the enemy; but in the murderous battle of Adrianóple he lost the victory, and his life, during the flight, in a burning hut. The victors now roved through the defenceless land with unrestrained fury, as far as the Julian Alps, and menaced even the frontiers of Italy. Then was the brave Spaniard Theodósius chosen sovereign of the East. He terminated the Gothic war, by settling one part of the enemy in the southern Danubian provinces, and enlisting another part as soldiers in the Roman armies. After many contests and military exploits, Theodósius, henceforth called the Great, at length obtained the sovereignty of the West also, and so united, for the last time, the whole world-wide Roman empire under one sceptre. He was a powerful, but passionate prince; and on one occasion, in Thessaloníca, he put to death 7,000 citizens, because they had slain his governor. For this, the Church's penance was inflicted on him by the undaunted bishop, Ambrose, of Milan, — a punishment which he willingly underwent. Theodósius was a zealous champion of the Catholic faith. He denounced and persecuted Arianism, interdicted the use of sacrifices and divinations, and permitted the heathen temples to be plundered and destroyed. Now was extinguished the sacred fire of Vesta — the oracles and sibyls were silent — and the pagan pantheism yielded to the faith in the crucified Saviour. At his death, Theodósius made over the East, with Illýria, to his son, Arcadius, who was eighteen years old, by whose side stood the Gaul, Rufínus; while Honórius, then in his eleventh year, under the guidance of the politic and warlike Vandal, Stílicho, was to be lord of the West. From this time forward the empire remained divided.

2. WEST GOTHS. — BURGUNDIANS. — VANDALS.

§ 177. Alaric, king of the West Goths, invaded the provinces of the Eastern empire immediately after the death of Theodosius. He marched, murdering and plundering, through Thessaly, Central Greece, and Peloponnésus, and trod under foot the remains of Greek civilization, until, being surrounded by Stílicho's forces, he was compelled to retreat. Envy of Stílicho now led Eutrópius, the successor of Rufínus, to induce Alaric to invade the Western empire. He accordingly fell upon Upper Italy, pursued his devastating course up the banks of the Po, but suffered so much loss in two undecisive battles against Stílicho, that he retreated upon Illýria, to wait for a more favorable opportunity. This enemy of the empire had scarcely been repulsed, before vast hordes of Vandals, Alani, Burgundians, Suevi, &c., burst into Italy, under the command of duke Radagaísus, destroyed the towns and villages, and filled every place with cruel slaughter and desolation. But these also were overcome near Florence, by the military skill of Stílicho. Their leaders were killed; thousands fell beneath the swords of the victors, or perished by hunger and disease; others entered into the Roman service. The remains of their army threw themselves into Gaul.

A. D. 396.

A. D. 403.

A. D. 406.

where, after repeated acts of devastation, the Burgundians settled on the Rhine and the Jura, and founded the kingdom of Burgundy, which extended from the Mediterranean to the Vosges. The Vandals and Suevi, on the other hand, crossed the Pýrenees, and won dwelling-places for themselves by the sword, in Spain and Portugal, which they however gave up again twenty years afterwards, and crossed over into Africa with the Vandal king, Génseric.

§ 178. The brave Stílicho, in his necessity, had entered into a friendly alliance with Álaric, and consented to pay him a yearly tribute. His enemies founded an accusation of high treason upon this, and procured his execution at Ravénna. Hereupon, Álaric, enraged at the withdrawal of the tribute, and appealed to by Stílicho's adherents for protection, marched into Italy, laid siege to Rome, and compelled the terrified inhabitants to purchase the clemency of the conqueror with gold, silver, and costly apparel. But when the court at Ravenna disdainfully rejected Álaric's proposals of peace, the Gothic prince again appeared before the walls of the former mistress of the world, stormed it at length A. D. 410. during the night, and surrendered it to be plundered for three days by his army. The hero died shortly after, in the flower of his age, in Lower Italy. There is a legend that declares that his coffin and treasures were buried in the bed of the stream Busénto, which had been diverted from its course for the purpose. His brother-in-law, Adolf, concluded a treaty with Honórius, by virtue of which the West Goths marched into Southern Gaul. It was here that they founded A. D. 412. the kingdom of the West Goths, which at first extended from the Garónne to the Ebro, and had Tolosa (Toulouse) for its principal city. When, however, the Vandals, some years later, went into Africa, the West Goths gradually conquered the whole of Spain; but, on the other hand, were compelled to relinquish the territory between the Pýrenees and the Garónne to the Franks.

Valentinian III., A. D. 425 -455. § 179. Valentínian III., followed Honórius with Æ'tius at his side, for general and influential minister. The governor of northern Africa, Bonifácius, lived in enmity with this Æ'tius; and being afraid of his anger, he rebelled, and summoned the Vandals, under their bold and crafty king, Génseric, out of Spain, to his assistance. It is true, that, upon their arrival, he repented of this rash act, and opposed them with his forces. But the warlike Vandals overcame him, and, in defiance of the court of Ravénna, made themselves masters of northern Africa, where they established the empire of the Vandals, with its capital, Carthage, conquered Sicily and the Baleáric islands, and rendered themselves formidable to all islands and lands near the coast by their piracies. The kingdom of the Vandals existed for a hundred years in north Africa. Génseric died in 477.

3. ATTILA, KING OF THE HUNS (A. D. 450.)

§ 180. About the middle of the fifth century, Áttila, surnamed the Scourge of God, left his wooden residence on the banks of the Theiss, in Hungary, for the purpose of conquering the western empire of Rome by the sword. More than half a million savage warriors, partly Huns and partly Germans, who were their subjects or allies, marched through Austria, Bavaria, and Alemánnia, to the Rhine, where they annihilated the royal house of Burgundy in Worms, destroyed the Roman towns, and then carried slaughter and desolation into Gaul. It was here that the valiant Æ'tius, with an army composed of Romans, Burgundians, West

A. D. 451. Goths, and Franks, succeeded, in the Catalaúnian plains (Chalons on the Marne), in setting a limit to Áttíla's victorious course. 162,000 dead bodies, and among them that of Theodoric, the brave king of the West Goths, covered the field of battle. From his camp, fortified with wagons, the Hun bade defiance to the attacks of the

A. D. 452. enemy, and then retreated into Hungary (Pannónia), with the purpose of invading Italy in the following year. Aquiléia was destroyed; Milan, Pavia, Veróna, and Padua taken by storm; and the fertile banks of the Po turned into a desert. The unfortunate inhabitants of Aquiléia sought for refuge on the rocks and sand-islands of the lagunes, and thus laid the foundation of Venice. Áttila was already on his march towards Rome, where he was induced by the prayers of the Roman bishop, Leo I., to conclude a peace with Valentínian, and to retreat. Áttila's sudden death, either by hæmorrhage, or the vengeance of his Burgundian bride, checked the progress of the Hunnish empire. The Ostrogoths, the Gépidæ, and the Longobards obtained their independence after a severe struggle, whilst the remains of the nomadic Huns were lost in the rich pastoral steppes of southern Russia.

4. DESTRUCTION OF THE WESTERN ROMAN EMPIRE.

§ 181. The Roman power was now rapidly approaching to its fall. Valentínian with his own hand killed Æ'tius, the last support of the empire. Shortly after, the luxurious emperor lost his own life by Petrónius Máximus, whose wife he had corrupted. Petrónius, raised to be Valentínian's successor, aspired to the hand of the imperial widow, which induced the latter to summon the Vandals against the murderer of her husband. Génseric landed at Ostia, took Rome, and subjected the city for fourteen days to plunder, during which time the works of art were ruthlessly mutilated (Vandalism). Laden with plunder and prisoners (the empress and her two daughters among the number), the Vandals returned to the coast of Africa, where they resumed their piratical employments with more audacity than before. After some time, the Sueve, Rícimer, a bold, crafty, but blood-stained man, acquired such power, that to the day of his death, he managed the crown and empire at his pleasure, without even assuming the imperial title. Three years after Rícimer's death, the ambitious general, Orestes, invested his son, Rómulus Augústulus, with the powerless crown. Upon this, the German troops in the pay of the Romans demanded a third part of the lands of Italy; and when this was not granted, the valiant Odoácer commanded the captive Orestes to be put to death, and, by assuming the title of King of Italy, put an end to the Western empire of Rome. Odoácer bestowed a yearly pension, and a residence in Lower Italy, upon the inoffensive Rómulus Augústulus.

A. D. 476.

5. THEODORIC THE OSTROGOTH (A. D. 500).

§ 182. Odoácer had reigned, not without renown, for twelve years, when Theódoric, king of the Ostrogoths, with the consent of the Byzantine emperor, marched from the Danube upon Italy. He was followed by 200,000 men fit for war, with their wives, children, and goods. Odoácer was unable to resist this force. Overcome by Theódoric near Veróna, he concealed himself behind the walls of Ravenna; and it was only after a gallant defence of three years that he at length surrendered upon honorable conditions. But he was killed not long after, by the Goths, at a riotous banquet. From this time, the empire of the Ostrogoths, which extended from the southern point of Italy to the Danube, was governed wisely and justly by Theódoric, from Ravenna. He paid respect to the ancient laws and institutions, employed the original inhabitants of the country in trade, agriculture, and commerce, and committed war and the use of arms to the Goths. Even literature and civilization rejoiced in his protection; and learned Romans, like the historian Cassiodórus, were advanced to the highest offices of the state. Theódoric's authority was so great abroad, that contending kings brought their differences to his judgment seat. It was only a short time previous to his death, that he was rendered cruel by suspicion, and commanded the worthy senator Boéthius, and his father-in-law, Sýmmachus, to be executed, because they were suspected of having invited the Byzantine court to expel the Goths. It was in prison that Boéthius wrote his celebrated work, the "Consolations of Philosophy."

6. CLOVIS, KING OF THE FRANKS AND THE MEROVINGIANS.

§ 183. The Franks, a tribe of German origin, had marched from their hereditary possessions on the Lower Rhine to the Meuse and the Sambre. From this place, their warlike king, Clovis, led them forth to war and plunder. After he had conquered and put to death the last Roman governor, Syágrius, in Soissons, and made himself master of the country between the Seine and the Loire, he advanced against the Alemánni, who were in possession of an extensive kingdom

A. D. 486.

on both banks of the Rhine. He defeated them in the great battle of
Zülpich (between Bonn and Aix), and subjected their
A. D. 496. country on the Moselle and the Lahn. In the heat of the battle, Clovis had sworn, that if the doubtful combat should terminate in his favor, he would embrace the faith of his Christian wife; and in the same year, he, with 3,000 nobles of his train, received baptism in the waters of the Rhine. But Christianity produced no emotions of
pity in his savage heart. After he had extended the Frank
A. D. 507. empire to the Rhone on the east, and to the Garónne on the south, he attempted to secure the whole territory to himself and his posterity, by putting to death the chiefs of all the Frank tribes.

§ 184. The wickedness of the father was inherited by his four sons, who, after Clovis's death, divided the Frank empire between them; the eldest received the eastern kingdom, Austrásia, with the capital, Metz; the three younger sons shared the western territory, Neustria, and Burgundy, which was connected with it. But the empire was again from time to time united. The history of the kingly house of the Merovingians displays a frightful picture of human depravity. The murders of brothers and relatives, bloody civil wars, and the explosion of unbridled passions, fill its annals. The savage enormities of the two queens, Brunhilda and Fredigonda, are particularly dreadful. These horrors at length destroyed all the power of the race of Clovis, so that they are distinguished in history as sluggish kings, whilst the steward of the royal possessions (mayor of the palace) gradually obtained possession of all the powers of government. A visit to the yearly assemblies of the people (Marzfelder), upon a carriage drawn by four oxen, was at last the only occupation of the imbecile Merovingians. At first, each of the three kingdoms had its own mayor, until the brave and shrewd Pepin of Heristal succeeded in uniting the mayoralties of Neustria and Burgundy with that of Austrásia, and making them hereditary in his own family. From this time, Pepin's descendants, who were called dukes of Francónia, possessed the regal power, whilst the Merovingians were kings in nothing but the name.

7. THE ANGLO-SAXONS.

§ 185. About the middle of the fifth century, the Roman army left Britain, which it was unable any longer to retain. The inhabitants, who were too weak to resist the attacks of the wild Picts and Scots (§ 159, 168), sought assistance from the Angles and Saxons of the Lower Elbe. These obeyed the summons; but after they had repulsed the enemy, they turned their swords against the Britons themselves, and, after a fearful contest, subdued their country, which was henceforth called England (Angle-land). The greater number of the Celtic inhabitants perished by the sword; those who were able took refuge in Gaul (Bretagne). It

was only in the mountainous districts of Wales and Cornwall that the Celts asserted their independence and national peculiarities, till as late as the thirteenth century. The rest of the kingdom fell into the power of the Anglo-Saxons, who established there seven small monarchies. These existed in a separate state, in the midst of perpetual contests, till
A. D. 827. the ninth century, when Egbert united the seven kingdoms (Heptarchy), and assumed the title of King of England. The paganism of Britain had yielded to Christianity as early as the seventh century, when the Benedictine monk, Augustine, with a crowd of missionaries, landed in Kent, led the king and his nobles to baptism, and founded the seat of the archbishopric of Canterbury.

8. THE BYZANTINE EMPIRE AND THE LONGOBARDS.

§ 186. The Byzantine empire displays a melancholy picture of moral depravity. A court filled with oriental luxury and magnificence, where women and favorites raise and dethrone weak or vicious emperors by crimes or intrigues; an insolent body-guard, who carried on the same audacious game with the crown that the prætorians had formerly done; and a fickle population, who took pleasure in nothing but questions of religious controversy, and the rude sports of the race-course (hippódromus). In these race-courses, two great parties, who mortally hated and persecuted each other, distinguished themselves, according to the colors of the chariot drivers, into the Blue and the Green. It was under
Justinian, these circumstances, that Justinian, a man of low origin,
A. D. 527-565. ascended the throne, where he completed several great undertakings. He subdued the Green party, that had raised an insurrection against him, and closed the race-course for two years; he ordered the code of laws, known by the name of Corpus Juris and Pandects, to be prepared by his minister, Tribónian; he procured silk-worms from China by an artifice, and transplanted the manufacture of silk into Europe; he built the church of St. Sophia in Constantinople, and he persecuted the heathens and Arians.

§ 187. Both the Vandals and Goths had made a profession of Arianism. Hence Justínian embraced the project of visiting them with war, and, by the conquest of their lands, of restoring his empire to the same extent it had possessed under Constantine. Belisárius, the great hero of his time, subdued in a few months the kingdom of the Vandals, which was already disturbed by a religious war, and carried the last king, Gélimer, a prisoner to Constantinople. About this time, Theó-
A. D. 534. doric's noble daughter, Amalasunta, was murdered by her dastardly husband. Hereupon Justínian assumed the part of her avenger, and sent Belisárius to Italy. Belisárius took Rome, and defended it with military skill and heroic courage for a twelvemonth
A. D. 537. against the Gothic king, Vitiges. The Goths, filled with

amazement at the courage of Belisárius, offered him the sovereign authority, and delivered up to him the chief city, Ravenna. He took possession of it in the name of the emperor, but did not, nevertheless, escape the envy and calumny of the Byzantine courtiers. He was recalled in the midst of a course of victories, to defend the eastern frontier against the Persians. After his departure, the Goths, according to the German custom, raised the valiant Totila upon a shield, and saluted him as king. Totila soon reconquered the whole of Italy. Belisárius again made his appearance, but, being slenderly supplied with money and troops by the suspicious emperor, with all his courage he could effect but little. Justínian angrily summoned him back, and punished him with his displeasure. He is said, when a blind old man, to have supported his life by begging alms. His successor was Narses, a dexterous courtier, but a hero like Belisárius. Narses gained a victory at Tagina, near the ancient Sentínum (§ 110), where Totila and the bravest of his warriors died in the field. It was in vain that the remainder of the Goths raised the valiant Tejas upon the royal shield; he also, after many bloody encounters, fell at the head of his nobles, near the ancient Cumæ; and it was only a small band who sought an unknown dwelling-place upon the farther side of the Alps.

A. D. 540.

A. D. 554.

§ 188. Henceforth, Narses, as the emperor's lieutenant, governed the conquered country from Ravenna. But when Justínian died, and his successor deprived Narses of his office, he called the Longobards out of Pannónia (Hungary), a short time before his death. These advanced to the neighborhood of the Po, which received from them the name of Lombardy, under the warlike Alboin. Pavia was taken by assault after a siege of three years, and erected into the capital of the Lombard kingdom. Alboin died by the bloody vengeance of his wife, the beautiful Rosamunda. He had killed her father, the king of the Gépidæ, some years before in battle, and, in accordance with the German custom, had had his skull fashioned into a goblet. He once compelled his daughter, during a festival, to drink from this cup, a proceeding that so enraged her that she procured his assassination. The rude Longobards treated the natives with violence, and deprived them of the greater part of their possessions. But the fruitful fields were soon brought to a splendid state of cultivation by the sturdy arms of German laborers. A powerful nobility of dukes and counts stood at the head of this nation, who elected their kings in the assemblies of the people (Maifelder). The Longobard kingdom remained independent for two centuries.

§ 189. The glory that Justínian had shed upon the Byzantine empire, was soon obscured by the depravity of the court. Wicked princes ascended the blood-stained throne in the midst of the most revolting horrors; deprivation of the eyes, mutilation of the nose and ears, were things of daily occurrence in this God-forsaken court. With all this, Constantinople remained, through the whole of the middle ages, the seat of learning and refinement, and the Byzantine history confirms a fact derived from experience, that external civilization and a refined manner of living are frequently conjoined with barbarousness of mind and depravity of morals. The affairs of the Church always excited the greatest interest at Constantinople. When the increasing veneration for images and relics threatened to establish a new form of idolatry, inasmuch as the ignorant people worshipped the images themselves, Leo the Isaurian issued a command to remove them altogether from the churches. This gave rise to a storm that shook throne and empire for more than a century. Two parties, the image worshippers (Iconoduli) and the image breakers (Iconoclasts) stood in hostile opposition to each other. Leo's energetic son, Constantine Copronymus, followed his father's example. He had the worship of images condemned by a council of the Church, and punished the refractory by death and banishment. His son also, Leo IV., belongs to the number of iconoclastic emperors. But after his sudden death, his wife, Iréne, abrogated the former resolutions by a new council, and restored to the churches their ornaments of images. This violent woman put out the eyes of her own son from motives of ambition, and was meditating a union with Charlemagne, when she was hurled from the throne by a conspiracy. She died in misery at Lesbos. A later attempt to remove images from the churches, undertaken by Leo the Armenian and his successors, was less violent, and was interrupted by the empress Theodóra. Shortly after, a new imperial house ascended the throne, in the person of Basilius the Macedónian, which ruled with little interruption for 200 years, and restored some strength to the empire. In the West, the decrees against images were not recognized.

Leo the Isaurian, A. D. 717-741.

Constantine Copronymus, A. D. 741-775.

Leo IV., A. D. 775-780.

Irene, A. D. 800.

Leo the Armenian, A. D. 813-820.

A. D. 867.

II. MOHAMMED AND THE ARABIANS.

§ 190. On the south-western coast of the peninsula of Arabia, which, on account of its great fertility in coffee, frankincense, cinnamon, and other spices, is called Arabia Felix, lived for ages, in proud independence, a people capable of civilization. Their religion was a rude paganism; a black stone in the Caaba at Mecca served as the national palladium, the care of which belonged to the Koreishites. They were rendered rich by an extensive commerce, and took pleasure in mental cultivation

and poetry. It was in the midst of this people that Mohámmed was
Mohammed, born, towards the end of the sixth century, from the re-
A. D. 571–632. spected priestly race of the Koreishites. During his youth, he made journeys with the caravans into foreign lands in the capacity of merchant, and thus became convinced that the religion of the Jews and Christians must be preferable to the idolatrous worship of the Arabs. As soon, therefore, as he had acquired an independent position by his marriage with a rich widow, he withdrew from the bustle of the world, to the recesses of his own bosom, and sought how he might elevate his countrymen from their degradation. The expectation entertained by the Jews of a Messiah, the promise of Christ to send a Comforter to those who loved him, who should guide them into all truth, wrought upon his ardent imagination, and excited within him the conviction, that he must be the person of whom the world stood in need. His epileptic fits favored the pretence that he held communion with angels, and was the subject of divine inspiration.

§ 191. In his fortieth year, Mohámmed came forth with his doctrine, "There is but one God, and Mohámmed is his prophet." But with the exception of his wife, his father-in-law Abu Bekir, his son-in-law Ali, and a few of his friends and relations, no one at first believed in his mission; nay, he was even compelled, by a menacing tumult, to fly from Mecca to Medína. (The Mohámmedans reckon their years
16th July, 622. from this event, which is called Hejira.) He here found adherents with whom he undertook expeditions, and at length, after some victorious encounters, he forced his return to Mecca. In Medína he composed a part of the sentences of which the holy book of the Koran consists. Mecca soon acknowledged him as a prophet, and his doctrine, called Islam, was soon predominant all over Arabia. He combined in it the fundamental doctrines of Judáism and Christianity, with maxims that were adapted to the East. He commanded frequent ablutions and prayers, circumcision, fasts, almsgiving, and pilgrimages to Mecca, forbade the use of wine and swine's flesh, and sanctioned polygamy. A chief commandment of the Koran was, to diffuse Islam by every means, and to compel the nations to receive it by fire and sword. Those who fell bravely in battle were promised a paradise of sensual enjoyments. The prophet died in the eleventh year of the Hejira. Mecca, where he was born, and Medína, the place where his grave is situated, are regarded as sacred cities of pilgrimage. Mohámmed united gravity and dignity in his carriage and bearing; he was benevolent, simple in his manner of living, and not devoid of domestic virtues.

§ 192. Ali, the husband of the favorite daughter of the prophet, hoped
Abu Bekir, to become Mohámmed's successor (Khalif). But Mohám-
A. D. 632–634. med's intriguing wife, Ayesha, procured the election of her

father Abu Bekir, who was succeeded by the simple and energetic Omar.
Omar, A. D. 634-644. Under this man, the Arabs, inspired by their new faith, carried their victorious swords beyond the limits of Arabia. Palestine and Syria were conquered, and Mohammed's warriors marched into the Christian cities of Antioch, Damascus, and Jerusalem. Kaled, "the sword of God," and the crafty Amru conducted the valiant bands.
A. D. 634. Persia was subjected, after a succession of bloody engagements. The last king, Yesdejird fled (as once Daríus before Alexander), with the sacred fire in his hand, to the mountainous highlands, where he perished by the hands of an assassin. The Arabs now pursued their victorious course through the eastern highlands, and carried the doctrines of Mohammed to the Upper Indus. The Persian fire-worship fell before the Koran, and henceforth, Islam was the ruling religion of the East. The new cities of Basra, Cufa, and Bagdad, on the Tigris, soon became the centres of trade, and the seats of oriental luxury
A. D. 640. and magnificence. Shortly after this, Amru marched from Syria into Egypt, took Alexandria, (by which means the remains of the great library are said to have perished), (§ 125,) burnt Memphis, (in the neighborhood of which the chief city, Cairo, took its origin from the camp of the general,) and thrust aside the Gospel by the Koran.

§ 193. Omar shortly after fell by the dagger of a Persian slave, and
Othman, A. D. 644-656. Othman, the collector and arranger of the Koran, succeeded to the Khalifate. But Othman was also assassinated; and when Ali at length ascended the sacred chair that had long been his right, the family of the Ommiades rose against him and excited a civil war, in which Ali and his whole house perished, and the Khalifate was
A. D. 660. taken possession of by the Ommiades, who established their residence in the beautiful Damascus. The Arabians prosecuted their conquests under the Ommiades both by land and water. Cyprus, Rhodes, Asia Minor, all felt the edge of their swords; the capital of the Byzantine empire had to sustain seven attacks and sieges, and was
A. D. 668-675. only saved by the newly-discovered Greek fire. The north coast of Africa was subdued at the same time, and the Christian religion and civilization there destroyed in the course of a lengthened war. The Arabians also gained a firm footing in Sicily, whence they made predatory excursions upon the coasts of Italy.

§ 194. It happened about the beginning of the eighth century of the Christian era, that the West Goth, Roderick, deprived Witiza of the Spanish throne. Hereupon, the sons of the banished man called the Arabs out of Africa to revenge him. Tarik, the Arabian general, crossed the straits of the sea, founded the town of Gibraltar (Gebel al Tarik), and
A. D. 712. overthrew the West Goths at the battle of Xeres de la Frontera, where Roderick and the flower of his chivalry were slain in

the field. The Arabians overran the whole of Spain, as far as the rocky Asturias, in a rapid course of victories. The Saracens crossed the Pyrenees, conquered the south of France as far as the Rhone, and threatened France and Christianity with destruction; when Charles Martel, the mayor of the palace and son of Pepin of Heristal (§ 184), overthrew them between Tours and Poitiers, in a battle that lasted seven days, and com-
A. D. 732. pelled them to fall back upon Spain. Charles Martel was thus the savior of Christian Germany in the West.

§ 195. Twenty years after Charles Martel's victory, the dynasty of the Ommiades was overthrown by the Abbassides, and their family
A. D. 750 destroyed. Abderahman alone escaped. He fled to Africa, whence he was invited into Spain. He there conquered the Abbasside governor, and was proclaimed Caliph at Cordova. Spain was prosperous under its Mahometan rulers, and the arts and sciences were greatly cultivated. But after the race of the Ommiades became ex-
A. D. 1030 tinct, the Moorish power in Spain was broken up into a number of small states, that gradually yielded before the Christians of the North. The latter had enlarged their territories by successful wars from their head-quarters, the Asturias, so that, with time, three kingdoms had been established, Castile, Aragon, and Portugal, each of which existed independently of the other, and waged furious contests with the Arabs of the South. These wars produced a spirit of chivalry, religious zeal, and freedom among the Christian Spaniards. The deeds of these God-inspired warriors, particularly those of the great
A. D. 1099. Cid Campeadór, were handed down to posterity in heroic songs (Romances), and kept alive the courage and chivalrous spirit of the Spanish nobility. Civic freedom was at the same time flourishing in the cities. The victory gained by the united Christian force at Tolosa, in the Sierra Morena, broke forever the power of the Arabians.

§ 196. The arts and sciences flourished in all the countries inhabited by the Arabs, as well as in Spain. Mosques, palaces, and gardens, were to be met with in every Arabian town. Industry and commerce brought wealth,—the source of refinement, but, at the same time, of the love of splendor and effeminacy. Architecture, music (the system of notes), and decorative painting (arabesques), flourished in all the chief Arabian towns. The sciences were taught at Cordova, Cairo, Bagdad, Salerno, and many other cities; more particularly, grammar, philosophy, mathematics, (the Arabian ciphers, algebra), astronomy, and astrology, natural philosophy, (chemistry), and medicine. The Arabians translated the writings of the Greeks, especially those of Aristotle and Euclid, and cultivated the art of poetry. The literature and civilization of this people had the greatest influence upon the development of the Christian middle age.

B. THE MIDDLE AGE.

I. THE PERIOD OF THE CARLOVINGI.

1. PEPIN THE LITTLE (A. D. 752–768); CHARLEMAGNE (A. D. 768–814.)

§ 197. The Austrasian duke, Pepin of Heristal, and his son Charles Martel, had gained the confidence of the nation by their warlike deeds, and the favor of the priests by their zeal in the propagation of Christianity. Both parties were instrumental in raising Pepin the Little, the son of Charles Martel, to the throne of the Franks. For when the assembly of the nation deposed the last imbecile representative of the Merovingians (Childeric III.), and proclaimed the chief steward, Pepin, king, the pope confirmed the election, in the hope of finding in the Frank ruler a support against the Longobards and the iconoclastic emperor of Byzantium. In return for the royal consecration, which was first performed by Boniface, and afterwards by Pope Stephen himself, Pepin endowed the Roman chair with the portion of coast on the Adriatic Sea, southwards from Ravenna. This was the foundation of the temporal power of the pope.

This Boniface (properly Winfried) was one of those active English missionaries, who, under the protection of the first Carlovingian monarchs, proclaimed the doctrine of a crucified Redeemer to the rude inhabitants of Germany. He preached the Gospel in Hesse, (where he built the abbey of Fulda), founded bishoprics and colleges for education among the Thuringians, Franks, and Bavarians, and displayed such zeal that he obtained the name of the "apostle of the Germans." Having been appointed archbishop of Mayence, he undertook in his old age another mission to the heathen Finlanders, among whom he met with a violent death. All the bishoprics and colleges established by Boniface were closely united with the Roman see; and as these efforts were favored by the Carlovingian monarchs, the pope, about the year 800, came to be looked upon as the head of the Church in Franconia.

§ 198. Pepin reigned for sixteen years with vigor and renown over the Frank empire, which extended far into South and Central Germany, and
A. D. 768. which, at his death, he divided between his two sons, Charles and Carloman. About three years afterwards, Carloman died,
A. D. 771. and Charlemagne (Charles the Great) was declared sole ruler of the Franks, by the voice of the estates of the Empire. He conducted many wars, and advanced Christian cultivation and civil order. For the purpose of securing the boundaries of his kingdom and extending

Christianity, he made war for thirty-one years on the Saxon confederation, which was formed by various pagan tribes on the Weser and Elbe.

A. D. 772. Charles took the fortress of Eresburg, on the south of the Teutoburger forest, destroyed the national palladium — the statue of Arminius, and compelled the Saxons to a peace. He next proceeded against the Longobard king, Desidérius, in obedience to the summons of Pope Adrian. With an army collected together near Geneva, he crossed the St. Bernard, stormed the passes of the Alps, and conquered Pavia. Desidérius ended his days in a cloister. Charles

A. D. 774. erected the Lombard throne in Milan, united Upper Italy to the kingdom of the Franks, and confirmed the gifts made by Pepin to the pope.

§ 199. During the absence of Charles, the Saxons had expelled the Frank garrisons and reëstablished their ancient boundaries. Charles

A. D. 777. again marched into their country, subdued them, and compelled the chiefs of the tribes to submit at Paderborn. Their warlike duke, Witikind, alone, fled to the Danes and refused to confirm the treaty. In the two following years, Charles fought against the Moors in Spain, took Pampelona and Saragossa, and united the whole country, as far as the Ebro, to his own kingdom, as a Spanish province. But during his return, his rear, under the command of Roland, suffered a defeat in the valley of Roncesválles, in which the bravest champions of the Franks were destroyed. Roland's battle at Roncesválles was a favorite theme with the poets of the middle ages. The Saxons took advantage of his absence to make a fresh insurrection, and pursued their devastating course as far as the Rhine. Charles hastened to the spot, gave them repeated overthrows, and subdued their land afresh. But when he attempted to employ them as militia against the Slavonic tribes in the East, they fell upon the Frank troops who were marching with them, at the Suntal (between Hanover and Hameln), and slew them. This demanded vengeance. The Frank emperor marched through the land, plundering and destroying, and then held a court of judgment at Verden on the Aller. 4,500 prisoners expiated with their blood the crime of their brethren. Upon this, hostilities were resumed with fresh violence. But the battle on the Hase, which terminated to the disadvantage of the Saxons, put an end to the war. Witikind and the other chiefs took an oath of fealty and military service, and allowed themselves to be baptized. The people followed their example. Eight bishoprics (Osnabruck, Minden, Verden, Bremen, Paderborn, Munster, Halberstadt, Hildersheim,) provided for the maintenance and extension of Christianity among the Saxons. Another insurrection, however, was occasioned a few years afterwards, by the oppressive *arrière-ban*,* and the unwonted

* The summons to all the tenants, even those of secondary rank, to quit their occupations, and follow the king to the wars. *Am. Ed.*

payment of tithes to the Church, which resulted in 10,000 Saxon families being carried away from their homes, and colonies of Franks being established in their place. To oppose the Slavonic tribes to the east of the Elbe, Charles founded the Margraviate* of Brandenburg.

A. D. 788. § 200. Shortly after, Thassilo, duke of Bavaria, attempted to render himself independent of the Frank power, by the assistance of the Avars who lived to the east. He was overpowered, and expiated his breach of faith by perpetual confinement within the walls of the cloisters of Fulda. Bavaria was hereupon incorporated with the Frank empire, and Charles established the Eastern Margraviate as a check upon the wild Avars. When Charlemagne had reduced all the lands from the Ebro and the Appenines to the Eider, and from the Atlantic Ocean to the Raab and the Elbe, he repaired to Rome at the conclusion of the century. It was here that, during the festival of Christmas, he was invested with the crown of the Roman empire, in the church of St. Peter, by Leo III., whom he had defended against a mob of insurgents. It was hoped, that by this means, western Christendom might be formed into a single body, of which the Pope was to become the spiritual, and Charles the secular head. It was at this time that the long-existing variance between the Western (Roman Catholic), and the Eastern (Greek Catholic) churches, terminated in a complete separation.

§ 201. The domestic policy of Charlemagne was not less fertile of results than the foreign. 1. He improved the government and the administration of justice by abolishing the office of duke, dividing the whole kingdom into provinces, and appointing counts and deputies for the conduct of the affairs of justice, and clerks of the treasury for the management of the crown lands and the collection of imposts. The laws were confirmed by the popular assemblies (maifelder), in which every freeman had a share. 2. He promoted the cultivation of the land, and the education of the people. Agriculture and the breeding of cattle were encouraged, farms and villages sprang up, and barren heaths were converted into arable fields. He founded conventual schools and cathedrals, had the works of the ancient Roman writers transcribed, and formed a collection of old German heroic ballads. Learned men, like the British monk, Alcuin, and the historian Eginhard, from the Odenwald, had ample reason to congratulate themselves on his encouragement and support. 3. He favored the clergy and the church. It was by his means that the former obtained their tithes and vast gifts and legacies; church music was improved, missionaries supported, and churches and monasteries erected. Ingelheim on the Rhine, and Aix, were Charles's favorite places of residence. He lies buried in the latter town.

* A Margrave (Marquis) was a Count of the frontier, the frontier being called the **Mark** (March). *Am. Ed.*

2. DISSOLUTION OF THE FRANK EMPIRE.

Louis the Debonnaire, A. D. 814–840. § 202. The son of Charlemagne, Louis the Debonnaire (the Gentle), was better fitted for the repose of a cloister than for the government of a warlike nation. A too hasty division of his kingdom among his three sons, Lothaire, Pepin, and Louis, was the occasion of much sorrow to himself, and confusion to the empire. For when, at a later period, he proposed an alteration in favor of his fourth son, Charles (the Bald), the fruit of a second marriage, the elder sons took up arms against their father. A. D. 833. Louis, faithlessly deserted by his vassals on "the field of lies," near Strasburg, and betrayed to his own sons, was compelled by Lothaire to do penance in the church, and to abdicate his throne; and was afterwards shut up for some time in a cloister. It is true that Louis procured his father's reinstatement; but when the weak emperor, after the death of Pepin, by a new division of the kingdom, deprived Louis of Germany, in favor of his brothers, Lothaire and Charles, Louis raised his standard against him. This broke the old emperor's heart. Full of sorrow, he ended his days on a small island of the Rhine, A. D. 840. near Ingelheim. The hostile brothers now turned their arms against each other. A bloody civil war depopulated the country, so that at last, after a battle of three days' duration, at Fontenaille in Burgundy, the Frank nobility refused to obey the *arrière-ban*, and by this means brought about the treaty of partition of Verdun. A. D. 843. By virtue of this treaty, Lothaire received the imperial dignity, together with Italy, Burgundy, and Lorraine; Charles the Bald, western Franconia (France); and Louis the German, the lands on the right bank of the Rhine, — Spire, Worms, and Mayence.

§ 203. This division was followed by a time of great confusion, during which, Europe was severely harassed, on the south by the Arabs; on the east, by the Slavi; and on the north and west, by the Normans. To oppose these predatory inroads, the Carlovingian monarchs, who were all men of weak and narrow minds, were obliged to restore the ducal office in the different provinces, and to sanction the hereditary authority of the Margraves, so that, in a short time, all the power fell into the hands of the nobles. By the rapid deaths of most of the posterity of Louis the Debonnaire, nearly the whole of the empire of Charlemagne devolved upon Charles the Fat, a prince weak and indolent, and simple almost to imbecility. Charles the Fat, A. D. 876–887. Incapable of resisting the valiant Normans, he purchased a disgraceful peace from them. This proceeding so exasperated the German princes, that they decreed his deposition, at Tribur on the Rhine, and elected his nephew, the brave Arnulf, as his successor. Arnulf, A. D. 887–898. Arnulf governed with vigor. He overthrew the Normans at Louvain, and called in the aid of the wild Magyars, or Hungarians, from the Ural, a people expert in horsemanship and archery, and who were now, under their valiant captain, Arpad, occupying the plains on the Danube (named after them Hungary), against the Slavi and Avars. The Avars were either subjected or compelled to retreat. But the strangers (the Hungarians), soon became a more dreadful scourge to Germany than either the Slavi or the Avars. They made their predatory inroads and exacted a yearly tribute, even under Louis the Child, the youthful son of Arnulf, who died in the flower of his age, after a glorious campaign in Italy. This still continued, when, after the early death of this last of the Carlovingian race, the German nobles, among whom the dukes of Saxony, Franconia, Lorraine, Swabia, and Bavaria were preëminent for power, met together and elected Duke Conrad of Franconia, emperor. Germany thus became an elective empire.

Conrad I. A. D. 911-919.

§ 204. The rule of the Carlovingians survived longest in France, but it possessed neither strength nor dignity. Under Charles the Simple, who had ascended the French throne after the deposition and subsequent death of Charles the Fat, the dukes and counts rendered themselves entirely independent, and one of the most powerful among them, Hugh of Paris, kept the imbecile king in strict confinement. France, on the other hand, was delivered from the devastating forays of the Normans, by Charles admitting duke Rollo into the province named after them, Normandy, upon condition that he and his followers would suffer themselves to be baptized, and recognize the king as their suzerain (feudal sovereign). The Normans, a people readily susceptible of civilization, soon acquired the language, manners, and customs of the Franks. Charles the Simple was followed by two other kings of the Carlovingian race; but their power was at last so limited that they possessed nothing but the town of Laon, with the surrounding country; every thing else had fallen into the hands of the insolent nobility. After the death of the childless Louis V., Hugh Capet, son and heir of Hugh of Paris, assumed the title of king, and put to death in prison Louis's uncle, Charles of Lorraine, who attempted to assert his right to the throne by force of arms.

Charles the Simple, A. D. 898-929.

Hugh Capet, A. D. 987-996.

II. NORMANS AND DANES.

§ 205. The inhabitants of the Scandinavian peninsula belong to the German race, and share with it the violent passion for liberty, love of action, and disposition to wander, as well as language, religion, and manners. Divided into numerous tribes, they undertook vast expeditions to all quarters, and trusted their lives and property on the stormy waves in their light rowing vessels. Under the name of Normans, they ravaged the coasts of the North Sea, sailed up the mouths of rivers in their small ships, and returned laden with booty to their homes; as Danes, they were feared by the English, from whom they exacted a heavy tribute (Danegeld). The remote island of Iceland was discovered and peopled by Norwegians, who founded a flourishing republic there, with the religion, language, laws, and institutions of the mother country; and Norman Varangians* were invited as rulers by the Slavonic inhabitants of the shores of the Gulfs of Finland and Bothnia. Ruric, the warlike prince of the Russians and of the Varangian race, accepted the invitation, established himself in Novogorod, and became the progenitor of a race that ruled over Russia till the end of the sixteenth century, but adopted the manners and language of the aborigines. Greenland was discovered and peopled from Iceland. Even America is said to have been known to the Normans. The Normans loved war, the chase, and the exercise of arms; agriculture and the breeding of cattle they left to the Slavi. Good faith was their most prominent virtue, and a love of poetry the solitary tender feeling indulged by these rude men. The singers (scalds) celebrated the illustrious deeds of their forefathers in melancholy songs and legends. The most celebrated collection of such sacred and heroic songs is called the Edda.

Alfred the Great, A. D. 871-901.

§ 206. England, under the weak successors of Egbert (§ 185), suffered the most severely from the Danes. They plundered the coasts and the shores of the rivers, and destroyed the Christian churches. Even Alfred the Great was thrust from his throne by them for a short time, until he contrived, by dint of cunning, courage, and watchfulness, to put an end to their inroads. Crowds of them, who had been converted to Christianity, were permitted to settle in Northumberland. After this, Alfred devoted himself to the internal improvement of his people. Like Charlemagne, he divided his land into communities and districts, and placed counts and aldermen over them to conduct the affairs of justice; he founded schools and churches, made a collection of the Anglo-Saxon heroic ballads, and translated the writings of Boëthius (§ 182). But when the Anglo-Saxon population, under his successors, slaughtered several thousands of the Danes in Northumberland (the Danish vespers), Sweyn the Fortunate, king of Denmark and Norway, recommenced the predatory incursions with such success, that his son, Canute the Great, united the English crown to the Danish and Norwegian. He governed justly and wisely. After his death, and that of his son Hardicanute, Edward the Confessor, a descendant of the ancient royal family, ascended the throne. He had resided a long

Canute the Great, A. D. 1014-1035.

Edward the Confessor, A.D. 1041-1066.

* The name *Varangians* signifies Corsairs, or Pirates. *Am. Ed.*

time in Normandy, and imbibed a preference for French Norman customs. It was for this reason, that, during his reign, he encouraged foreigners to the prejudice of the natives, and appointed William, Duke of Normandy, heir to his crown, in the event of his death without issue. This was resisted by the nation, who elected the chivalrous Harold to be king. But by the battle of Hastings, in which Harold and the flower of the Anglo-Saxon nobility fell on the field, William the Conqueror was made master of England, where he proceeded with great severity to establish a new condition of things. He endowed his Norman knights with the estates of the Anglo-Saxon landlords, introduced the French language and the Norman law, and presented the richest benefices of the Church to his friends.

A. D. 1066.

§ 207. A short time before, Robert Guiscard, a Norman noble, had made himself master, by his courage and cunning, of the greater part of Lower Italy. He called himself Duke of Apulia and Calabria, and acknowledged the pope as his feudal superior. His heroic son, Bohemond, increased this territory by further conquests. But Robert's family soon became extinct, upon which his brother's son, Roger II., united Sicily with Lower Italy, obtained from the pope the title of king, and established the kingdom of Naples and Sicily. For fifty-six years, these rich and beautiful lands remained in the possession of Roger and his descendants; they then passed to the house of Hohenstaufen.

A. D. 1060. A. D. 1072. Roger II., A. D. 1130-1154.

III. THE SUPREMACY OF THE GERMANO-ROMAN EMPIRE.

1. THE HOUSE OF SAXONY (919-1024).

§ 208. The violence of the nobles, and the destructive inroads of the Hungarians, had reduced Germany to a wild and lawless state. The first freely elected emperor, Conrad of Franconia (§ 203), endeavored to correct these evils by harshness and severity, and ordered the insubordinate Count Erchanger and Berthold von Allemanien to be beheaded as examples. But as he saw that his family did not possess sufficient political influence, he favored the advancement of his powerful rival, Henry I. (the Fowler), of Saxony. This energetic prince enlarged the boundaries of the empire on the north, where he established the march (frontier) of Schleswig against the Danes; on the west, where he again won back Lorraine to the empire; and on the east, where the march of Meissen was intended to keep the Slavi in check. He purchased a nine years' truce from the Magyars, and employed the time in the improvement of the

Henry the Fowler, A. D. 919-936.

army, and in erecting strong fortresses. By the building of these citadels, which grew up with time into towns, Henry became the originator of the burgher class, and earned the name of the Founder of Cities. Relying on these preparations, he refused the Hungarians, at the termination of the truce, the tribute that had hitherto been paid; and when
A. D. 933. they undertook an expedition for the purpose of revenging themselves, he gave them a severe defeat at the battle of Merseburg.

Otho the Great, A. D. 936–973. § 209. Otho I. the Great, trod in the steps of his father. He sought, like him, to preserve the peace of the empire by conferring dukedoms and bishoprics on his friends and relatives; he also enlarged the bounds of his territories, and diffused Christianity; and when the Hungarians again renewed their inroads upon Germany, this valiant prince defeated them with such slaughter in the Lechfeld
A. D. 973. near Augsburg, that only a few out of the vast multitude escaped; from this time, there was an end of their depredations. Christianity, which, towards the end of the century, in the reign of the Magyar king, Stephen the Pious, the lawgiver and regulator of the country, penetrated even into Hungary, produced gentler manners and a more peaceable disposition. Otho's attainment of the imperial dig-
A. D. 962. nity was an occurrence pregnant with results for Germany, which, from this time, remained part of "the holy Roman empire of the German nation." By his marriage with Adelheid, queen of Burgundy and Upper Italy, who had appealed to him for protection against the attempts of Berenger of Ivrea, Otho gained the kingdom of Italy, and was invested in Milan with the Lombard crown. Hereupon he proceeded to Rome, obtained the imperial Roman crown, established the protectorship of the German emperor over the papal chair, and exacted an oath from the Romans, that they would never acknowledge a pope without the knowledge and consent of himself or his successors. This protectorship the popes were afterwards unwilling to allow to be valid.

Otho II., A. D. 973–983. § 210. The ten years of Otho II.'s reign were filled with contests with the turbulent nobility in Germany and Italy; with the French, who wished to get possession of Lorraine; and with the Greeks in Lower Italy, where he laid claim to the Byzantine possessions, as the dowry of his wife Theophania. Being overcome near Bassantello, he fell into the hands of the enemy, from whom he only
Otho III., A. D. 983–1002. escaped by his skill in swimming. His son, Otho III., was superior to most of his contemporaries in cultivation and learned acquirements, in which he had been instructed by the celebrated Gerbert, under the guidance of his mother Theophania, and his grandmother Adelheid, so that he was called the Imperial Prodigy; but he was wanting in the vigor necessary to the ruler of a rude and warlike

people. His love for Greek and Italian refinement induced him to entertain the notion of making Rome the metropolis of his kingdom; but all his plans were thwarted by his early death.

§ 211. After many struggles, Henry II. of Bavaria, a relative of the Othos, succeeded him in the empire. His love for the church and the clergy, which he displayed more particularly in founding the cathedral and bishopric of Bamberg, procured him the surname of Saint. When this cathedral was consecrated by the pope in person, it was from his hands that the emperor received the signs of his imperial power, the sceptre and the golden apple; and although, during his Roman expeditions, he exercised the right of protectorship over the holy city, yet the ceremonies practised on the occasion afforded a pretext to succeeding popes to represent the imperial throne as their fief. Under Henry II. and the military bustle of the following age, the civilization that had flourished in Magdeburg, Halle, Bremen, and Bardewick, during the reign of the Othos, and under the influence of the foreign empress and Otho II.'s sisters, was again extinguished. The mathematical science of Gerbert, who was versed in Greek and Arabian learning, and who was raised to the papal chair, A. D. 999, under the title of Sylvester II., the Latin poetry of Khoswitha and others, found little encouragement; nevertheless, the colleges founded by the Othos still preserved the germs of civilization.

2. THE HOUSE OF FRANCONIA.

§ 212. Conrad II. was more bent upon enlarging his kingdom and
Conrad II. obtaining knightly renown, than upon governing in peace.
A. D. After he had been invested with the iron crown of the Lom-
1024-1039. bards in Milan, and the imperial diadem in Rome, he added to his dominions the kingdom of Burgundy on the Rhone and the Jura. This involved him in many quarrels, both with the Burgundian nobles and bishops, who looked upon themselves as independent princes; and with his son-in-law, Ernest of Swabia, who asserted a more valid claim to the empire, and raised the standard of rebellion in the south of Germany, in conjunction with his friend Welf. Both were subdued after a long struggle, and the deeds and fate of the chivalrous duke Ernest supplied the materials for poetry and popular legends. Conrad and his successor lie buried in the cathedral of Spire, of which magnificent struc-
Henry III. ture the former was the commencer. Conrad's son, Henry
A. D. III., was a man of great power, under whose reign Germany
1039-1056. attained its greatest limits; even Bohemia, Poland, and Hungary acknowledged the supremacy of the Germano-Roman emperor. For the purpose of suppressing the insolence of the turbulent nobles of the kingdom, he entertained the project of founding an absolute, imperial, here-

ditary monarchy, and either of abolishing the office of duke in Germany, or making it entirely dependent upon the emperor. In the same manner, he took advantage of a division in the church to depose the three contending popes, and to raise the German bishops in succession to the papal chair. He attempted to elevate the imperial power above the princes of Germany, as well as over the court of Rome. He enforced respect throughout his whole kingdom for the "peace of God," according to which, no weapons might be used between the evening of Wednesday and Monday morning; an arrangement which, in that iron time, was the only means of preserving a vestige of order. He also preserved himself unspotted from the crime of simony, *i. e.*, disposing of the property or dignities of the church for money or worldly considerations.

§ 213. Henry III.'s son was the highly-gifted but misled Henry IV., who, from the age of five years, was under the tutelage of his judicious mother, till the ambitious Hanno, archbishop of Cologne, succeeded in getting the young emperor into his power. The severe method of education employed by this prelate disgusted Henry, who was only the more pleased with the magnificent Bishop Adelbert, of Bremen, who snatched him from the hands of Hanno, and made himself agreeable to the young prince by flattery, and the gratification of his sensual inclinations. The emperor established his residence at Goslar, for the purpose of chastising the Saxons, among whom, Henry's rival, Otho of Nordheim, had many adherents. He here established a riotous court; oppressed and maltreated both the nobles and people; and, in the insolence of youth, disturbed, with his companions, the security of the neighboring country. The Saxon nobility at length took up arms under the conduct of Otho; the fortresses were taken, the strong citadel of Harzburg destroyed, and the emperor compelled to take flight. This proved the commencement of a destructive war, which was terminated to the disadvantage of the Saxons, by the superior talents of Henry, and his victory on the Unstruth. This finally induced them to call in the pope as umpire.

A. D. 1075.

§ 214. The chair of Rome was at that time occupied by Gregory VII., a prelate of resolute will and decided temper, who cherished the purpose of rendering the church independent of the secular authority, and of exalting the papacy above the power of the emperor, and that of every other temporal prince. With this object, he had induced his predecessors to withdraw the election of pope from the hands of the Roman people, and to transfer it to the newly-created college of cardinals. After his elevation, he turned his attention to the purifying of the church; he accordingly issued a strict prohibition against all simony, deposed and banished the bishops who had obtained their offices by purchase, and forbade lay investiture (appointment to church offices by a temporal prince); and, for the purpose of binding the clergy more closely to the church, he

passed a law which enforced a rigid observance of celibacy by all persons of the priestly condition. The appeal to his arbitration by the Saxons came very opportunely to the daring priest after these arrangements; it served to confirm the principle that the pope, as Christ's vicegerent, was superior to all temporal rulers, and that emperors, kings, and princes, were consequently his vassals. He summoned Henry IV. before his judgment seat. Instead of obeying the summons, the emperor obtained a resolution from a council of the church assembled at Worms, which declared the pope to be deposed, and this resolution he forwarded to Gregory with a contemptuous letter. Upon this, Gregory excommunicated Henry and his adherents, and deposed him from the throne. This happened at a time when Henry's conduct towards the Saxons, and his matrimonial quarrel with his virtuous wife, from whom he attempted to get himself separated by the archbishop of Mayence, created universal dissatisfaction. He soon found himself forsaken by his people, and the princes who assembled at Tribur announced to him his deposition, unless he were released from the excommunication within a year. Upon this,
A. D. 1077. Henry hastened across the Alps, in the midst of a severe winter, to the pope, who was residing at the castle Canossa; but it was not until after waiting three days barefoot, and in the dress of a penitent, in the court of the castle, that he was admitted to an audience. After this humiliation, the excommunication was withdrawn.

§ 215. During Henry's absence, his enemies had raised Rudolf, duke of Swabia, to the imperial throne. A civil war broke out in consequence, in which Henry remained the victor. Rudolf, having lost a hand in the battle of the Elster, died shortly afterwards, upon which Henry undertook an expedition to revenge himself upon Gregory, who,
A. D. 1081. deceived by false intelligence respecting the victory, had renewed the excommunication. He left the finishing of the war in Germany to his son-in-law, Frederick of Hohenstaufen, whom he had created duke of Swabia, and then marched with his army over the Alps. A council of the church, assembled by him at Brixen, deposed
A. D. 1083. Gregory and elected Clement III., from whom Henry immediately received the crown. It is true, that Gregory still maintained himself for some time in the castle of St. Angelo, under the protection of Robert Guiscard (§ 208), with whom he had entered into an alliance; but the dreadful excesses of the Normans produced so much exasperation among the Romans, that the pope thought it most advisable
A. D. 1084. to take refuge in Salerno, where he died in the following year. But Henry's troubles were not yet at an end. Two rival emperors arose in Germany, and in Italy the successor of Gregory created him a crowd of enemies, and renewed the sentence of excommunication. At length, his own misguided children rose against him. Conrad was disowned by him, and died in disgrace; but in a short time

after, Henry, who was already crowned, drew the sword against his father, took him prisoner, and when he escaped from confinement, continued the war against him so long, that Henry IV., bowed down by misery and misfortune, ended his days at Liege. But even now he was not at rest. For five years, his dead body remained unburied in an unconsecrated chapel at Spire, before it was allowed to be interred in the imperial sepulchre.

Henry V. A. D. 1106 - 1125.

§ 216. As long as Henry V. continued the disgraceful contest with his father, so long he remained the friend of the pope. But scarcely was he in exclusive possession of the imperial dignity, before he quarrelled with his ally on the subject of investiture. He seized upon the pope and cardinals, and succeeded, despite the thunders of excommunication by which he was assailed, in effecting a fair compromise of the subject of dispute, by means of the concordat of Worms. It was arranged by this contract, that the bishops and abbots should be freely elected and installed in their offices by the pope, but that they should be endowed with their temporalities and privileges by the king with his sceptre.

Lothaire the Saxon, A. D. 1125 - 1137.

The severity with which Henry had humbled the insolent princes of the empire, prevented them from raising to the throne the nearest relative of the house of Franconia, Frederick of Hohenstaufen, upon Henry's death without children. They elected Lothaire the Saxon, the heir of Otho of Nordheim, but produced a fatal division by this step. For when the brothers of the Hohenstaufen family refused to do homage to the new emperor, Lothaire united himself with Henry the Proud of Bavaria, of the house of Welf, by giving him his daughter in marriage, and increasing the vast possessions of this family by the dukedom of Saxony. The Hohenstaufens were unable to resist such superior power, and they were compelled to acknowledge Lothaire emperor, and to accompany him in his Italian campaign.

IV. THE ASCENDENCY OF THE CHURCH IN THE TIME OF THE CRUSADES.

1. THE CRUSADES.

§ 217. Ever since the fourth century, it had been a prevalent custom to undertake a pilgrimage to Jerusalem, for the health of the soul and the expiation of a sinful life, and to pray at what was believed to be the site of the sepulchre of Christ, and where, in consequence, the Empress

Helĕna had erected a church. These pilgrimages became more numerous as the Christian faith acquired more influence over the minds of men. As long as the mercantile Arabians retained possession of the land, the pilgrims came and went without molestation; but when Syria and Palestine were conquered by the Seljookian Turks, the native Christians, as well as the pilgrims, were exposed to severe oppression. They were compelled to pay a heavy tax, and were frequently robbed, maltreated, and killed. At this juncture, a pilgrim, Peter of Amiens, who was returning from Jerusalem, presented himself before Pope Urban II., described the sufferings of the Christians in the East, and received the charge of wandering through town and country, and preparing the minds of men for the great enterprise of recovering the Holy Land from the hands of the infidels. Wonderful was the agitation produced in all lands by the descriptions of the eloquent and meagre-visaged pilgrim. A. D. 1095. When the pope, in consequence, held an assembly at Clermont, in the south of France, at which several bishops and nobles, and a numberless crowd of people of all conditions were present, called upon the West to arm itself against the East, and concluded his passionate address by an exhortation to every one, "To deny himself and take up his cross, that he might win Christ," the shout, "It is the will of God," pealed from every throat, and thousands fell on their knees, and demanded to be at once admitted among the number of the sacred warriors. They attached a red cross to the right shoulder, from which the new brotherhood received the name of crusaders. Complete remission of sins, and an everlasting reward in heaven were promised to them. This was the commencement of the first crusade, 1096 — 1099.

§ 218. A mighty enthusiasm took possession of all minds; no sex, age, or condition would be left behind. Many were too impatient to wait for the preparations of the princes; a disorderly and half-armed crowd, A. D. 1096. under the direction of Peter of Amiens, and a French knight, Walter the Penniless, marched through Germany towards Hungary, on their way to Constantinople. When they were denied the necessaries of life in Bulgaria, they stormed Belgrade, and filled the country with robbery and murder. Hereupon the inhabitants rose upon them, and slaughtered them by thousands. The remnant reached Constantinople with their leaders, but were nearly all destroyed in Asia Minor by the Seljooks. The disorderly crowd, which, after a bloody persecution of the Jews, marched out of the Rhenish towns, Strasburg, Worms, Mayence, &c., under the conduct of the priest, Gottschalk, and the count Emico of Leiningen, fared no better.

§ 219. A hundred thousand men had already perished, when the high-spirited Godfrey of Bouillon, duke of Lorraine, marched towards Constantinople by the same path, with his brothers and a vast host of well-appointed knights, whilst Hugh of Vermandois, the brother of the French king, and the Norman prince, Bohemond of Lower Italy, with his chivalrous nephew, Tancred, departed by sea to the same destination. After they had promised the Byzantine emperor, Alexius Comnenus, the restoration of all the Greek towns that had formerly belonged to the Eastern empire, they were transported into Asia. A review took place in a plain near Nicæa, and the army was found to consist of 100,000 cavalry, and 300,000 foot, fit for battle. The most celebrated of the leaders, besides those already named, were Robert of Normandy, son of William the Conqueror (§ 207); Stephen of Blois, who numbered as many castles as there are days in the year; the rich and powerful Count Raymond of Toulouse, and others. The siege and capture of Nicæa was the first important deed of arms achieved by the crusaders. From this point, their march proceeded southwards through the dominions of the sultan of Iconium. The Seljooks suffered a defeat in the battle of Dorylæum. But the Christian army was roon reduced to the greatest straits by the want of the necessaries of life, so that many returned home, and others, separating themselves from the main body, established independent governments among the pagans. In this way, Baldwin, Godfrey's brother, established himself in Edessa, on the Euphrates. At length, the host reached the beautiful territory of Antioch. But the siege of this strong and amply-provided city presented so many difficulties to the unpractised knights, that that it was only after an investment of nine months that they obtained possession of it, by a stratagem of the crafty Bohemond, who contrived that a door should be treacherously left open to him. The punishment inflicted by the Christians on the conquered city was frightful. But they had scarcely held possession of it for three days before the Seljook sultan of Mosul made his appearance, and inclosed the place with an innumerable army. The crusaders were in a short time so reduced by famine, that their destruction appeared inevitable. From this perilous position they were rescued by a holy lance, that was found in the church of St. Peter in Antioch, and the discovery of which produced such enthusiasm amongst them, that, sallying out of the city, they put to flight a very superior army of the besiegers, and opened for themselves the road to Jerusalem. The faith in the genuineness of the lance soon however disappeared, when the priest who had discovered it died from the consequences of the divine ordeal to which he was subjected.

A. D. 1097.

§ 220. The army now compelled the contending princes to a rapid march. When they arrived, about the time of Pentecost, at the heights above Ramla and Emmaus, whence Jerusalem first becomes visible, they fell upon their knees in an ecstasy of devotion, shed tears of joy, and glorified God with psalms of thanksgiving. But the conquest of this strong city was a difficult undertaking for an army of pilgrims, wearied with travel, and unprovided with the necessary

A. D. 1099.

engines. The want of water, and the burning heat, proved more destructive than the arrows of the enemy. But the newly-aroused enthusiasm triumphed over all obstacles. Having endured a siege of thirty-
15th July, A. D. 1099. nine days, Jerusalem was at length taken by the crusaders after a two days' storm, accompanied by the shouts, "It is the will of God," "God helps us." The fate of the vanquished was frightful. The steps of the mosques were washed by the blood of 10,000 slaughtered Saracens; the Jews were burnt in their synagogue; neither age nor sex was spared, the streets were filled with corpses, blood, and mutilated limbs. It was only after the thirst for revenge and plunder had been slaked, that Christian humility again resumed its empire over the mind, and the same men who, a short time before, had been raging like ravenous beasts, might now be seen, with bare feet and uncovered heads, marching with songs of praise to the Church of the Holy Sepulchre, to thank God with fervent devotion for the success vouchsafed to their enterprise.

§ 221. The next step was to elect a king of Jerusalem. The choice fell upon the pious and valiant Godfrey of Bouillon, who refused, however, to wear a kingly diadem on the spot where the Saviour of the world had bled beneath a crown of thorns. He rejected the outward symbols of power, and called himself the Defender of the Holy Sepulchre. The new kingdom of Jerusalem was arranged according to the principles of the western feudal system (§ 241). Godfrey, moreover, won the glorious
August, A. D. 1099. victory at Ascalon, over the army of the Egyptian sultan, but died during the following year, from the effects of the climate and his extreme exertions. His brother, Baldwin, succeeded to the government, and assumed the title of king.

§ 222. The kingdom of Jerusalem had severe encounters to sustain with the infidels. When reinforcements no longer arrived from the West, the situation of the Christians became extremely precarious, especially after the powerful sultan of Mosul had taken and destroyed Edessa,
A. D. 1145. and threatened their borders from the East. At this juncture, St. Bernard, abbot of Clairvaux, in Burgundy, aroused
A. D. 1149. afresh the slumbering zeal for religion, and was the originator of the SECOND CRUSADE. The authority of this pious man was so great, that Louis VII. of France yielded obedience to his exhortations, and even Conrad III. was unable to resist the fiery eloquence with which he addressed him in the cathedral of Spire. Conrad assumed the cross, and marched with a stately army through Constantinople into Asia Minor. But here he was decoyed by the artifice of the Greek generals into a waterless desert, where the crusaders were suddenly attacked by innumerable squadrons of Turkish cavalry, who gave them so signal an overthrow, that scarcely a tenth part escaped with Conrad into Constantinople. The French army that marched along the coast fared no better.

The greater number of the pilgrims perished either by the sword of the enemy, or by hunger and fatigue. The shattered forces of the two kings at length reached Jerusalem, but were unable to perform any action of importance, so that the position of the Christian kingdom became from day to day more difficult, especially as, shortly after their retreat, the magnanimous and valiant Curd, Saladin, made himself master of Egypt, and united in a short time all the lands between Cairo and Aleppo under his sceptre. The kingdom of Jerusalem was soon in distress. Saladin granted a truce; but when this was violated by a Christian knight, who had audaciously interrupted the passage of Saladin's mother, robbed her of her treasures, and slaughtered her attendants, the sultan took the field with his army. The battle of Tiberias was decided against
A. D. 1187. the Christians. King Guy of Lusignan and many of his nobles were taken prisoners; Joppa, Sidon, Acre, and many other towns fell into the hands of the conqueror, and at length, Jerusalem was also taken. The crosses were torn down, and the furniture of the churches destroyed, but the inhabitants were treated with forbearance. Saladin, far superior in virtue to his Christian adversaries, did not stain his triumph with cruelty.

§ 223. The news of the taking of Jerusalem occasioned the utmost alarm throughout the whole West, and gave rise to the
A. D. 1189. THIRD CRUSADE. From the southernmost point of Italy
A. D. 1192. to the rude mountains of Scandinavia, armed bands streamed towards the Holy Land. Those who remained behind paid a tax (Saladin's tenth). The three most powerful monarchs of the West, Frederick Barbarossa of Germany, Philip Augustus II. of France, and Richard Cœur de Lion (Lion-heart) of England, assumed the cross. The Emperor Frederick, with a well-appointed army, took the way by land to Asia Minor, defeated the sultan of Iconium in a furious battle near the walls of his chief city, and displayed prudence, courage, and resolution in the whole undertaking. But when the old hero attempted, with the boldness of youth, to cross the rapid mountain stream of the Saleph, into the south of Asia Minor, he was carried away by the torrent. His dead body was dragged on shore near Seleucia. Some of the knights returned home, and others followed the second son of the emperor, Frederick of Swabia, to Palestine, where they took part in the siege of Acre. The kings of France and England, who had taken the sea voyage by Sicily, met shortly after, before this town. Their united efforts were crowned by the fall of Acre, where Richard distinguished himself as much by his severity, pride, and cruelty, as by his valor and heroism. The German banner, that duke Leopold of Austria had first planted on the battlements, was torn down and trampled under foot by the commands of Richard; and when the stipulated ransom for the captive Saracens was not paid at the appointed moment, he ordered 3500 of these unfortunates to be

put to the sword. Richard's name was the terror of the East. But despite all his strength and bravery, he was unable to take Jerusalem. Quarrels between Richard and Philip Augustus, (who returned home after the capture of Acre), and dissensions among the crusaders, checked the enterprise. After the conclusion of a treaty, by which the sea-coast from Tyre to Joppa, and undisturbed access to the holy places, were assured to the Christians, Richard also turned homewards. Having been cast by a storm on the coast of Italy, he attempted to pursue his journey through Germany, but was seized near Vienna, and given up to the avaricious emperor Henry VI., who shut him up in the castle of Trifels, and only released him on the payment of a heavy ransom.

A. D. 1202. § 224. The FOURTH CRUSADE had a termination alto-
A. D. 1204. gether peculiar. The knights of France and Italy assembled together at Venice, in the beginning of the thirteenth century, under Baldwin of Flanders, for the purpose of getting themselves conveyed to the Holy Land. Whilst here, the Byzantine prince, Alexius, whose father, Isaac Angelus, had been deprived of the throne, rendered blind, and shut up in prison by his own brother, presented himself before them, and implored their assistance against the usurper. Alexius prevailed upon the crusaders, by the promise of vast rewards. They sailed for Constantinople under the command of the blind doge, Dandolo of Venice, who was then in his ninetieth year, took the city, and placed Alexius and his father on the throne. But when they insolently demanded the fulfilment of the promises made to them, the populace excited an insurrection, during which Alexius was killed, and his father died of fright, whilst the leader of the tumult was raised to the government. Upon this, the Franks stormed Constantinople, plundered the churches, palaces, and dwelling-houses, destroyed the noblest works of art and antiquity, and filled the whole city with terror and outrage. They flung the emperor from a pillar, and then divided the Byzantine kingdom. The newly-established Latin empire, with its chief city, Constantinople, fell to the share of the heroic Baldwin; the Venetians appropriated the lands on the coast and several islands of the Ægean Sea, and gained possession of the whole trade of the East; the count of Montferrat received Macedonia and Greece, under the title of the kingdom of Thessaloníca; Villehardouin, the describer of this transaction, became duke of Acháia; Athens and other Greek towns were shared among the Frank nobles. As before, in Jerusalem, so here, the feudal monarchy was established under the western forms, by which means the greater part of the old population was reduced to the condition of serfdom. But the new empire had no solid foundation nor any long continuance. It preserved itself with diffi-
A. D. 1261. culty for half a century, by aid from the West, against its numerous enemies; the greater part of it then returned to

Michael Palæólogus, a descendant of the ancient imperial family, who had established an independent government in Nicæa.

§ 225. This crusade, however, was without results as far as Jerusalem was concerned; and as the Latin kingdom also drew away the strength from the Holy Land, the latter soon fell into distress. The separate bands, that, without leaders and without system, from time to time ventured upon this hazardous undertaking, brought as little assistance to the closely pressed kingdom, as did the fanatical enthusiasm that impelled crowds of children to assume the cross. Nearly

A. D. 1213. 20,000 children left their paternal homes for the purpose of reaching the holy sepulchre, but either perished by hunger and exhaustion, or were sold for slaves by rapacious merchants and pirates. The expedition to Egypt, undertaken by Andrew of Hungary and other princes, was also unproductive of any permanent result. With such examples before him, the excommunicated emperor, Frederick II., undertook the FIFTH CRUSADE, at a time when the sultan of Egypt

A. D. 1228. was engaged in a war with the governor of Damascus, respecting the possession of Syria and Palestine. But the pope was indignant with the excommunicated man, and forbade all Christian warriors to support his undertaking; and when Frederick nevertheless succeeded, by dexterously availing himself of circumstances, in bringing the sultan to a treaty, by which Jerusalem, Bethlehem, and Nazareth,

A. D. 1229. together with their territories and the whole of the sea-coast between Joppa and Sidon, were ceded to the Christians, the pope fulminated an excommunication against the city and the holy sepulchre, so that Frederick II. was obliged to place the crown of Jerusalem on his own head, without either a mass or the consecration of the Church. Hated and betrayed by the Christian knights and priests in Jerusalem, Frederick, with shattered health, retired from the Holy Land. Fourteen years afterwards, the Carismians, a savage Eastern race, poured themselves into Palestine, carrying death and destruction in their train. They took Jerusalem, destroyed the holy sepulchre, and tore the bones of the kings from their graves. The flower of the Christian chivalry fell at Gaza beneath their blows. Acre and a few other towns on

A. D. 1244. the coast were all that remained to the Christians.

§ 226. Upon receipt of this intelligence, Louis IX. (the Saint), of France, with many of his nobles, took the cross and sailed by Cyprus to Egypt. The strong frontier town of Damietta fell into the hands of the Franks, but when they proceeded up the Nile to attack Cairo, the army was inclosed between the canals and an arm of the river, whilst the fleet was destroyed by the Greek fire. After the king's brother and the bravest knights had fallen, Louis and the remainder of the army were taken prisoners, and he was compelled to ransom himself and a portion of his followers by the payment of a large sum of money and the surrender of

the conquered towns. In the mean while, the government of Egypt had fallen into the hands of the warlike Mamelukes, the former slaves of the
A. D. 1270. Curds. Sixteen years after his return, Louis again undertook another crusade, which, however, he first directed against the piratical Saracens at Tunis in northern Africa, partly to compel them to pay tribute, and partly with a hope of introducing Christianity amongst them. He had already laid siege to their principal city, when the unusual heat produced an infectious disease, which hurried the king himself and many of his warriors into the grave. The French leaders concluded a hasty treaty with the Saracens, and returned home. The feeble remains of the kingdom of Jerusalem were more and more threatened by the warlike Mamelukes. When Antioch fell into their hands, and Acre or Ptolemais was stormed after an heroic defence, the Frank
A. D. 1291. Christians that were still alive voluntarily retired from Syria, that for the last two hundred years had been drenched by the blood of so many millions.

§ 227. The consequences of the Crusades were of vast importance to the progress of the European races. — 1. Cultivation of mind was forwarded by them, inasmuch as an acquaintance with foreign lands and nations enlarged the hitherto contracted sphere of human knowledge, gave men an insight into the sciences and arts of other people, and enlightened their minds with regard to the world and human relations. — 2. They ennobled the knightly class, by furnishing a more elevated aim to their efforts, and gave occasion for the establishment of fresh orders, who presented a model of chivalry, and were supposed to combine all the knightly virtues. Of these orders, those which most distinguished themselves were the knights of St. John (Hospitallers), the Templars, and the Teutonic knights. They combined the spirit of the knight and the monk; for in addition to the three conventual vows of chastity, poverty, and obedience, they joined a fourth, — war to the infidels and protection to pilgrims.

a.) The order of St. John was divided into three classes: serving brothers, who were devoted to the care of sick pilgrims; priests, who ministered to the affairs of religion; and knights, who fought with the infidels and escorted pilgrims. After the loss of the Holy Land, they obtained the island of Rhodes, and when they were compelled, after a
A. D. 1522. most desperate resistance, to relinquish this to the Ottomans, the island of Malta was presented to them by the emperor Charles V. — *b.*) The Templars acquired vast wealth by donations and legacies. After the loss of their possessions in Palestine, the greater number of their members returned to France, where they gave themselves up to infidelity and a life of voluptuousness, which finally occasioned the dissolution of their order (§ 256). The order of Teutonic knights is less renowned for its deeds in Palestine than for its services in the civilization of the countries on the shores of the Baltic. Summoned

to defend the germs of Christianity against the heathen Prussians on the banks of the Vistula, the Order, after many bloody encounters, succeeded in converting the people between the Vistula and the Niemen to Christianity, and introducing the German manners, language, and cultivation. The cities of Culm, Thorn, Elbing, Konigsburg, and others, arose under the influence of the active traders of Bremen and Lubeck. Bishoprics and churches were founded; the woods were cleared and converted into arable land; German industry and German civilization produced a complete transformation; but the ancient freedom of the people was destroyed. The knights of the Order (who, since 1309, had had their residence in Marienburg,) conducted the government, and the peasantry sank into the condition of serfs.

About the time of the first crusade, the Mohammedan prophet, Hassan, formed the fanatical sect of the Assassins, who dwelt in the ancient Parthia and the mountainous heights of Syria, and were remarkable for the entire renunciation of their own wills. They obeyed the commands of their chief, "the old man of the mountain," with the blindest devotion, executed with subtelty and courage every murderous deed that was intrusted to them, made a jest of the torture when seized, and were the terror of both Turks and Christians.

§ 228.—3. The Crusades gave rise to a free peasantry, inasmuch as, by means of them, many serfs attained their liberty, and raised and extended the power and importance of the burgher class and of the towns; whilst a nearer acquaintance with foreign lands and foreign productions gave an impulse to trade, developed commerce, and produced prosperity. 4. They increased the power and the authority of the clergy, multiplied the riches of the church, (the clergy and the monasteries got possession of vast estates during the Crusades, either by legacies and donations, or by purchase), and exalted the zeal for religion into a gloomy fanaticism. The latter quality was frightfully displayed in the persecution of the Waldenses and Albigenses, a religious sect who were desirous of restoring the apostolical simplicity of the church and clergy. Provence and Languedoc in the south of France, where, under a beautiful and serene sky, a prosperous race of burghers had developed their free institutions, where the cheerful Provençal poetry of the Troubadours had indulged its petulant and satirical humor at the expense of priests and bishops, was the residence of these Albigenses (so called from the city Alby).

A. D. 1205. Against these men and their protector, Raimond VI. of Toulouse, Innocent III. ordered the cross to be preached by the Cistercian monks. Hereupon, bands of savage warriors, with some fanatical monks bearing the cross before them, marched into the blooming land, destroyed the rich cities, towns, and villages, slaughtered the innocent with the guilty, lighted up the flames of death, and filled the whole country with murder, plunder, and desolation. Raimond for a long time resisted his enemies; but when Louis VIII., excited by an ignoble cupidity for extending his possessions, undertook the war against the heretics, the count submitted, and concluded a peace by which he surrendered the greater part of his territories to France. But a desolating war of twenty years had destroyed the beautiful culture of the south of France, turned the land into a wilderness, and silenced forever the cheerful song of the Troubadour. A few years afterwards, the gallant peasant republic of the Stedingers was visited in a similar manner by a war of extermination, at the instance of the bishops of Bremen and Ratzburg.

2. THE HOHENSTAUFENS (A. D. 1138–1254).

§ 229. Upon the death of the emperor Lothaire (§ 216), on his return from Italy, his son-in-law, Henry the Proud, believed himself to possess the nearest claims to the throne. But the great power of the house of Welf, who held Bavaria and Saxony, and whose possessions extended from the Mediterranean to the Baltic, together with the arrogance of the haughty duke, induced many of the princes, assembled at the imperial diet at Coblentz, to elect Conrad of Hohenstaufen. But Henry hesitated to recognize the election, and refused the required homage. Upon this, Conrad pronounced the ban of the empire against him, and declared the forfeiture of both his dukedoms. This occasioned a renewal of hostilities between the houses of Hohenstaufen and Welf, and a desolating civil war. It was at the siege of Weinsberg, an hereditary possession of the Welfs, that the war cries, "Hurrah for Welf!" "Hurrah for Waibling!"* which gave rise to the party names, Welfs and Waiblings (Italicè, Guelfs and Ghibellines), were first heard. The citadel was obliged to surrender to the emperor, but the garrison was preserved by the wit and fidelity of the women. The war continued till the death of Henry the Proud. It was only when his son, Henry the Lion, received back his paternal inheritance and the two dukedoms of Bavaria and Saxony, that a complete reconciliation was, for a time, effected.

Conrad III., A. D. 1138–1152.

A. D. 1142.

Conrad was a brave and good man; but his war against the Welfs, and the second crusade in which he engaged, prevented his being of any great service to Germany. A short time before his death, he exerted his influence with the princes to procure the election of his high-spirited and energetic nephew, Frederick Barbarossa (Red-beard), who was esteemed the flower of chivalry, and with whose qualities Conrad had made acquaintance during the crusade. This great emperor, Frederick I., gave

* Waibling was the name of one of the hereditary possessions of the Hohenstaufens. Guelphs and Ghibellines were the names of the two great political parties that divided Italy and Germany during the Middle Ages, the former adhering to the Pope, the latter to the Emperor. *Am. Ed.*

peace and order to the empire within, and respect and security without. The genius for government displayed by this powerful man, who combined severity with justice, awakened everywhere respect and obedience.

Frederick Barbarossa, A. D. 1152-1190.

§ 230. Frederick found the hardest conflict in Italy, to which country he made six expeditions. The Lombard towns, and the haughty Milan in particular, entertained the project of erecting their territories into small republics. Inspired by patriotism and a love of freedom, they formed an effective burgher militia, and attempted to rid themselves of the imperial authority. This refractory spirit displayed itself even during Frederick's first campaign, when, in accordance with a long-established custom, he held a review of his troops in the plains near Piacenza, and required the princes and cities of Upper Italy to do him homage. He could not, indeed, at this time, coerce the powerful Milan, but he sought to terrify her by the destruction of some smaller towns, before he had himself invested with the Lombard crown in Pavia, and with the imperial crown in Rome. He only obtained the latter by giving up Arnold of Brescia. This remarkable man wished to bring back the church to its apostolic simplicity. In furtherance of this project, he denounced the worldly possessions and the arrogance of the clergy, and affirmed that the temporal authority of the head of the Church was an infringement on the Holy Scriptures. Inflamed by these discourses, the Romans renounced their obedience to the pope, and set up a republic in imitation of the ancient government. But when the bold preacher of this reformation was delivered up to the pope and burnt before the gates of the city, the courage of the Romans was subdued. They consented to abolish the new institutions, and again submitted to the power of the pope.

§ 231. After Frederick's departure, the Milanese persisted in their defiance, and destroyed several cities that adhered to the emperor (for example, Lodi). Upon this, Frederick undertook a second expedition, had his sovereign rights (regalia) determined by jurists according to the code of Justinian (§ 186), and when Milan refused to submit to the decision, uttered the ban against the refractory city. A fierce war was at length decided in favor of the emperor. Milan was obliged to surrender, after a siege of three years and a half. After the carriage (carroccio) that supported the chief banner of the city had been broken to pieces, and the citizens had humbled themselves before the conqueror, the walls and houses were levelled with the earth, and the inhabitants were compelled to settle themselves in four widely-separated points of their territory. Terrified at this result, the remainder of the Lombard towns submitted themselves, and received the imperial legate (podesta) within their walls. A short time after, Frederick engaged in a violent quarrel with the obstinate pope, Alexander III. The angry priest fulminated an excommunication against the emperor,

A. D. 1158.

and united himself with the Lombard cities, which were exasperated with the tyranny of the imperial legate. Under the guidance of the pope, a confederation of Lombard cities was rapidly formed, which was joined by Milan, which had again recovered itself, and by almost all the city communities of Upper Italy. The confederation built the strong city of Alexandria, which was named after the pope, in defiance of the emperor, and defended itself with courage and success against all the attacks of Frederick; so that the latter, having lost many of his soldiers by the summer fever, and being busied with the affairs of Germany, was obliged to leave Italy for a long time undisturbed.

§ 232. At length, Frederick again crossed the Alps with a vast army, but was detained so long by the siege of Alexandria, that he feared to lose all the fruits of his campaign, and resolved, against the advice of his friends, upon hazarding a battle. But Henry the Lion deserted the emperor in the hour of danger; he refused his assistance, though Frederick implored it at his feet at the lake of Como; and thus brought about the defeat of the Germans at the battle of Legnano, where the Milanese,
A. D. 1176. united together for the defence of the car which bore the ensign (the legion of death), performed prodigies of valor. The emperor himself was missing for some days. But so great was the respect for Frederick's heroism, that the pope and Lombard confederation willingly accepted his proffer of peace. At a meeting in Venice, a truce of six years, which proved the foundation of the peace of Constance, was arranged between the belligerent parties. Alexander was acknowledged as the lawful head of the church, Frederick was released from the anathema, and the confederate towns were required to do homage, and admit the emperor's rights as sovereign. Imperial legates were to fill the chief offices of justice, and the imperial troops were to be supported by the towns during their marches through them. Before Frederick quitted Italy, he married his eldest son, Henry, to Constantia, the heiress of the Norman kingdom in Naples and Sicily.

§ 233. Henry the Lion was much alarmed when the news of Frederick's reconciliation with the pope became known in Germany. He had extended his rule over the Slavonic tribes in Pomerania and Mecklenburg; had made war upon the Frislanders on the Baltic, and the peasant republic of the Ditmarsens, in Holstein; and had got possession of a large kingdom. He had established mines in the Harz mountains; he had founded cities and bishopricks (Lubeck, Munich, Ratzburg), and attracted settlers from the Netherlands. But his ambition and acts of violence against princes and clergy were not less known than his great feats in war, so that the brazen lion that he erected before the citadel of his chief city, Brunswick, might be regarded as an emblem of his rapacity, as well as of his strength. The complaints, accordingly, that arose on all sides against Henry, upon the emperor's return, gave the latter the opportunity he so much wished for, of summoning him before the supreme court of the empire, and upon his neglect of the repeated

A. D. 1179. summons, of pronouncing against him the ban of the empire, and depriving him of his two dukedoms, Bavaria and Saxony. The former devolved to the Wittelsbachs, who were devoted to the Hohenstaufens, and who afterwards received the palatinate of the Rhine; and Saxony was shared between Bernhard of Anhalt, son of Albert the Bear, and the neighboring bishops and princes. But the Lion could only be subdued after a destructive war. For two years he withstood all his enemies. It was not until Frederick himself took the field against him, that he humbled himself before his great adversary, prostrated himself at his feet at Erfurt, and retired into three years' banishment in England. He nevertheless retained for himself and family his hereditary possessions of Brunswick and Luneburg. After Frederick had subdued all his enemies, he undertook the third crusade, that he might finish his heroic course in the same manner that he had commenced it. From this expedition he never returned; he found his death in the distant East. But he lives still in the legends of his people, in which the restoration of the ancient strength and greatness of the German empire is connected with his return.

Henry VI., A. D. 1190-1197. § 234. Frederick's son, Henry VI., was an avaricious and cruel prince, who resided more in Italy than in Germany. After the death of the last Norman king, he wished to take possession of Naples and Sicily, the inheritance of his wife, Constantia. But the nobility, who were afraid of Henry's ambition and avarice, opposed this project, and attempted to place one of the native nobles, the brave Tancred, on the throne. It was not until Henry had equipped fresh armaments with the ransom of the English king (§ 223), that he succeeded, with the assistance of the crusaders of Northern Germany and Thuringia, whom he enticed by a promise of a free passage to Lower Italy, in subduing his enemies, and in getting possession of Naples and Palermo. The revenge of the angry ruler was frightful. The prisons were filled with nobles and bishops, some of whom were deprived of their eyes and impaled, while others were burnt, or buried alive in the earth. The plunder was conveyed by heavily-laden pack-horses to the Hohenstaufen castles. Henry died suddenly a few years afterwards, at the age of thirty-two, leaving behind him a son of two years of age, who was intrusted to the guardianship of the highly-accomplished pope, Innocent III. The adherents of the Hohenstaufens elected Philip of Swabia, brother of Henry VI., to be emperor, whilst the Welf faction proclaimed Otho IV., second son of Henry the Lion: the former was acknowledged in the south, the latter in the north. The consequence of this division was a ten years' war, during which the greatest lawlessness and violence prevailed, and such devastations were committed, that sixteen cathedrals and 350 parishes with churches were burnt to the ground. Even after Philip had been murdered at Bamberg, from motives of private revenge, A. D. 1208. by the hasty palgrave, Otho of Wittelsbach, peace did not return for any length of time. For now a quarrel broke out between the emperor Otho IV. and pope Innocent III.

§ 235. Innocent III., a politic prince, endowed with unusual talents for government, gave the papacy its highest power by establishing the principle, that the church was superior to the state, and its spiritual head superior to any temporal ruler; so that all the princes of the world were bound to consider the pope as their liege lord and arbiter. He at the same time laid the foundation of an ecclesiastical state, by getting all previous donations confirmed by Otho, and inducing him to renounce all the imperial feudal rights over Rome and the central provinces of Italy. A. D. 1210. But when the emperor at length attempted to set some limits to the ambition of the pontiff, the latter excommunicated him, and sent the young Frederick into Germany, to stir up afresh the war between the Guelfs and the Ghibellines. The Ghibelline party gladly united themselves to the handsome and promising youth, so that A. D. 1215. Frederick II. of Hohenstaufen was universally acknowledged emperor, even before Otho IV.'s death. Otho IV. died at Brunswick, in the year 1218. But a powerful opponent of the head of Frederick II., A. D. 1218–1250. the church arose in the freethinking Frederick II., who had been educated in the wisdom of the Arabians, and who entertained a favorable feeling towards the professors of Islam, and the Oriental mode of life; so that his reign presents a continual contest between the imperial power and the papacy. Frederick's position, as king of Upper and Lower Italy, threatened no less danger to the temporal power of the pope, than his sceptical turn of mind to the authority of the church. It was for this reason, that Innocent and his successors labored to separate the government of Naples and Sicily from the imperial office.

§ 236. As Frederick for a long time refused to undertake the promised crusade (§ 225), he was first excommunicated by Gregory IX., and when he proceeded to the Holy Land in the following year, without being released from the curse, the pope became more angry than ever, and not only paralyzed all the emperor's undertakings in Palestine, but commanded his territories in Lower Italy to be attacked by soldiers, who were distinguished by the badge of the keys of St. Peter. This hastened Frederick's return. He repulsed the papist troops, and approached the frontiers of the ecclesiastical territories, upon which Gregory consented to a peace, and the removal of the excommunication. After this, Frederick devoted his whole attention to the internal well-being of his kingdom. He restrained the increasing feuds and depredations of the knights in Germany; he gave the inhabitants of Lower Italy a new code of laws; he encouraged trade, industry, and poetry. But when he attempted to compel the inhabitants of the Lombard towns to fulfil the conditions of the peace of Constance (§ 232), and to discharge the regalian rights that pertained to him as emperor, a furious war broke out. Frederick, in conjunction with the Ghibellines, under the inhuman tyrant Ezzelino, in Verona, and supported by his trusty Saracens, whom he had settled in Lower Italy, overcame the united army of the Lombards, and reduced most of the towns to submission. But when he pursued his conquest with severity, threatened the Milanese with a fate similar to that which they had experienced from Frederick Barbarossa (§ 231), and presented his natural son, the brave and handsome Enzio, with the kingdom of Sardinia, the aged prince of the church again renewed his excommunication, joined the Lombards, and attempted to raise up enemies on every side against the emperor, whom he accused of infidelity and contempt for religion. Frederick retorted these accusations in some violent written replies, and repaid invective with invective; but the church carried off the victory.

A. D. 1241. § 237. When Gregory IX., at the age of nearly a hundred years, at length sunk into the grave, Frederick's position seemed to become more favorable. But the pope's successor, the resolute Innocent IV., trod the same path. For the purpose of being free from restraint, he left Italy, and called a solemn council of the church, at Lyons. Without listening to Frederick's defence, Innocent here renewed the sentence of excommunication against the emperor in the severest form. He denounced him as a blasphemer of God, a secret Mohammedan, and an enemy of the church; declared him to have forfeited his kingdom, released all his subjects from their oath of allegiance, and threatened his adherents with the ban of the church. Upon this, the war broke out afresh in every country. The popish party succeeded in Germany in carrying the election of a rival emperor, Henry Raspe, of Thuringia; and when, after the unfortunate engagement at Ulm, against Frederick's son Conrad, Henry died powerless and forsaken in the castle of Wartburg, the young count, William of Holland, allowed himself to be persuaded to assume the title of emperor. But the imperial towns and most of the secular princes sided with Conrad.

A. D. 1246.

§ 238. In the mean time, the war between Guelfs and Ghibellines raged furiously in Italy. The fiery temperament of the revengeful southerns occasioned deeds of unheard-of atrocity; family was arrayed against family, city against city; neither age nor condition refrained from the combat. Ezzelino, the leader of the Ghibelline nobility, perpetrated the most monstrous cruelties in his attacks upon the Guelf cities, till at length he met with the punishment he deserved in the prison of Milan.

Frederick for a long time maintained his lofty attitude; the number of his foes only increased his courage. But when his son, Enzio, fell into the hands of the Bolognese, who kept the fair-haired king for twenty years in confinement; when his chancellor, Peter of Vinea, suffered himself to be gained by the opposite party, and then, either from fear or remorse, deprived himself of life in prison, — his heart at length broke. He died in his fifty-sixth year, in the arms of his best beloved son, Manfred, in Lower Italy. Frederick II. united great cultivation of mind and aptitude for science and poetry, with courage, heroism, and beauty of person. Surrounded by pomp, luxury, and pleasures of all descriptions, he had every pretension to happiness, had not his sceptical spirit resisted the church, and had he only learnt to moderate his desires and bridle his passions.

§ 239. Upon the news of Frederick's death, Innocent IV. returned in triumph to Rome. He declared Naples and Sicily to be lapsed fiefs of the chair of St. Peter, and excommunicated Conrad IV. and Manfred, who wished to take possession of their paternal inheritance. Conrad soon sank into an early grave; but his chivalrous half-brother, Manfred, defended Lower Italy with his German and Saracen troops with such courage and success, that the greater part of the towns tendered their allegiance, and the Guelfic troops were obliged to retreat into the ecclesiastical states. Distress at this hastened the death of Innocent IV. His successor, Urban IV., pursued however the same path. Determined to deprive the Hohenstaufens of Naples and Sicily at any price, he offered this beautiful kingdom, as a papal fief, to the energetic but despotic Charles of Anjou, brother of the French king, Louis IX., under condition that he should conquer it by Guelfic assistance and with French troops, and should pay a yearly tribute to the Roman court. Manfred valiantly resisted his insolent rival. But when the battle of Bene-
A. D. 1260. ventum was decided against him by Italian treachery, he plunged into the thickest of the enemy, and died the death of a hero. A simple grave, to which every soldier contributed a stone, inclosed his remains.

§ 240. After the battle of Beneventum, the power of the Ghibellines was broken; Naples and Sicily fell into the hands of the stern victor, who made the unfortunate land feel all the miseries of conquest. The adherents of the Hohenstaufens were punished with death, imprisonment, and banishment; their possessions were divided among the French and Guelfic soldiers. Upon this, the oppressed people called Conrad IV.'s youngest son, Conradine, from Germany into Italy. Conradine, in whose bosom dwelt the lofty spirit and heroic courage of his ancestors, left his home for the purpose of again conquering the inheritance of the Hohenstaufens, with the assistance of his youthful friend, Frederick of Baden, and a few faithful adherents. Received with rejoicing by the Ghibellines, he marched victoriously through Upper and Middle Italy, put the pope to flight, and crossed the frontiers of Naples. The battle at Scurcola terminated in his favor; but his over-hasty advance threw the victory into the hands of the enemy, who were watching in ambuscade. His troops were either killed or dispersed; he himself, betrayed into the hands of his rival, Charles of Anjou, was beheaded at Naples, along with his bosom friend, Frederick. Thus sank the last scion of a glorious race of heroes, robbed of his honor, into an early grave.

A. D. 1268.

The still remaining members of the house of Hohenstaufen also experienced a cruel fate. King Enzio died in prison in Bologna. (§ 236). The ruthless Charles allowed the sons of Manfred to pine in prison till they died; and Margaret, the daughter of Frederick II., was ill-treated and threatened with death by her husband, Albert of Thuringia, called the Uncourteous, so that she fled by night from the castle of Wartburg. In her agony at her separation from her two sons, she bit one of them in the cheek whilst embracing him, so that he retained the mark and the surname of "the Bitten."

After Conradine's death, Charles proceeded with cruelty and severity against all his adherents. Upon this, John of Procida, a Ghibelline, who had been deprived of his property, swore vengeance against the tyrant. By his influence, all the French were killed by the Sicilians, on the so-called Sicilian vespers, and the island was given up to Manfred's valiant son-in-law, Peter of Aragon, by whose assistance, the inhabitants successfully repelled all the attacks of Charles, and established an independent kingdom. Peter's second son, Frederick, was the first king of Sicily.

A. D. 1282.

3. GENERAL VIEW OF THE MIDDLE AGES.

§ 241. The institutions which existed during the middle ages originated from a mingling together of Roman and Germanic customs and laws, and were based upon the greater or less amount of personal freedom or the want of it. These intricate relations are included under the general term of "feudal system." After the conquest of the depopulated Roman provinces, the land was generally divided into three portions: the king took one; another he divided among his companions in the war, as their free property (allodial), under the condition of military service; the third was left to the original inhabitants, upon the payment of a tax. But for the purpose of binding the freemen more closely to the throne, the king granted portions of his own lands to a part of them for life. This was called a fief; the giver was the liege lord, the receiver was called liegeman, or vassal. In the same way, rich freemen enfeoffed those who were less wealthy with portions of their estates, and even of their fiefs (sub-infeudation), and thus obtained liegemen or vassals of their own. Bishops and abbots also gave fiefs to knights, subject to the condition of defending the convent and supplying the required contingent of troops to the *arrière-ban*. These relations, founded upon

Feudal system.

mutual good faith, constituted a chain that bound the men of the middle ages in a variety of ways, and proved a grievous hinderance to the freedom of person and property. The vassals of the crown or empire gradually obtained possession of their fiefs as hereditary estates, and by this means became so powerful, that they opposed the king as his equals; the rich proprietors deprived the less wealthy of their lands, so that, in their capacity of free landlords (barons), they belonged to the class of nobles, whilst the freeholders of small estates were degraded to the condition of dependents, and cultivated their former possessions as hereditary tenants. The number of serfs, who were looked upon as belonging to the land, and surrendered as slaves without rights to the arbitrary will of their masters, was still very great. All who were in the position of dependents or serfs, were under certain obligations to the land-owner, either to pay tithes on their produce of fruit, wine, or cattle, or contributions of money upon stated occasions, or to perform unpaid labor (soccage duties). These taxes and duties, under the name of "feudal burdens," became more numerous and oppressive with time.

§ 242. In the middle ages, society may be said to have been composed of three classes, — warriors, teachers, and producers: —

1. The warrior class embraced the nobility and the knights with their vassals and followers. The rank of knight depended upon being descended from a knightly family, and the knightly education as page or squire, during which, the spurs were to be earned by some feat of arms, before the candidate could be received into the fellowship by the *accolade*. The great end of knighthood was war, sometimes for the purpose of displaying strength or acquiring honor; sometimes, to defend religion and its ministers, the church and the clergy; and sometimes, to protect women, as the weaker sex. That respect for women, which is the peculiar distinction of the German character, produced the devotion to the fair sex and the services of gallantry which were the soul of the chivalry and poetry of the middle ages. Knightly games or tournaments, in which the prize was presented to the victor by a maiden of noble condition, served to preserve and invigorate the spirit of chivalry; and that no unqualified person might surreptitiously introduce himself under cover of his armor, coats of arms were introduced as symbols of names and families.

§ 243. — 2. The teacher class included the whole of the clergy; not only the manifold grades of the priesthood, but also the monks. In exclusive possession of the learning of the time, and invested with the power of deciding the salvation of men's souls, the clergy acquired vast authority over the ignorant and superstitious people of the middle ages. The head of the church, the pope, assumed the command over all temporal princes and kingdoms, and regarded the imperial crown as his fief; the superior clergy, besides their ecclesiastical dignities, were frequently in possession of the most influential offices of the state; and

Hierarchy.

the greater number of the archbishoprics, bishoprics, and abbacies gradually acquired great possessions, so as to be raised to an equality with principalities. Magnificent cathedrals, adorned with all the productions of art, gave evidence of the greatness of the episcopal residences. A luxurious life in splendidly-ornamented houses seemed the chief privilege of the superior clergy. The episcopal power, which at first was very considerable, was perpetually curtailed by the Roman Consistory. The investiture of bishops, which had originally been in the hands of the prince, was gradually claimed as the exclusive privilege of the Roman court; the spiritual jurisdiction of the rural bishops was more and more abridged, whilst the papal court of judicature in Rome decided all important questions before its own tribunal, and withdrew many cloisters and abbeys from the episcopal authority, and placed them under its own immediate jurisdiction. Vast sums were obliged to be paid for all appointments, decisions, and dispensations, by which means much money poured into Rome. For the purpose of keeping a watchful eye upon the affairs of the whole church, and managing every thing from Rome, papal legates were constantly traversing the different kingdoms. By these means, the papal power became unlimited, and the higher it rose, the less did any one dare to raise his voice against it. Every opposer of the existing ecclesiastical institutions was regarded as an enemy of the church, and the audacious offenders were threatened with the most fearful punishments of the church in their triple gradation,— *excommunication*, which affected only the individual; the *interdict*, which was pronounced over whole countries, and forbade the exercise of every religious and ecclesiastical function; and a *crusade*, with the inquisition, by which whole provinces were given up to utter destruction. This power of the papacy was especially promoted, first, by the spurious Isidorian decretals, a collection of ecclesiastical laws and decisions, which, professedly belonging to the first four centuries, were in reality, most of them, produced in the ninth, and which give the whole legislative and judiciary authority of the Church to the pope; secondly, by the rapid increase of the monks, of the ecclesiastical orders, and of convents; thirdly, by the learned men of the middle ages, called schoolmen.

Monachism.

§ 244. Monachism took its rise in the East, where a solitary and contemplative life, devoted to the consideration of divine subjects, had always been considered more meritorious than active exertion. This calling was gradually adopted by so many, that, at the end of the third century, the Egyptian Antonius who had cast away his vast possessions and chosen the desert for his residence, collected together the hitherto dispersed anchorites (monachi) into fenced places (monasteria, cœnobia, claustra, cloisters), that they might live together in fellowship, and his disciple, Pachomius, gave the brotherhood a rule. Monachism soon extended to the West. In the sixth century, Benedict of Nursia established the first monastery on Mount Casino, in Lower Italy, and became by this means the founder of the widely-spread order of Benedictines, which rapidly extended itself among all nations, and built many convents. These monasteries, erected for the most part in beautiful and remote situations, and the inhabitants of which were obliged to take the three vows of chastity (celibacy), personal poverty, and obedience, proved, in those days of lawlessness and barbarism, a blessing to mankind. They converted heaths and forests into flourishing farms; they afforded a place of refuge (asylum) to the persecuted and oppressed; they ennobled the rude minds of men by the preaching of the Gospel; they planted the seeds of morality and civilization in the bosoms of the young by their schools for education; and they preserved the remains of ancient literature and philosophy from utter destruction. Many of the Benedictine monasteries were the nurseries of education, the arts, and the sciences, as St. Gallen, Fulda, Reichenau, and Corvey (in Westphalia), and many others. When the Benedictine order became relaxed, the monastery of Clugny, in Burgundy, separated itself from them in the tenth century, and introduced a more rigid discipline. In the twelfth century, the monks of Clugny numbered upwards of 2000 cloisters. But this order, also, soon proved insufficient to satisfy the strong demands of the middle age against the allurements of sin and the seductions of the flesh; so that, at the end of the eleventh century, the Cistercians, and a few decades later, the order of Premonstrants, sprang up; the former in Burgundy (Citeaux), the latter in a woody country near Laon (Premontré). The order of Carthusians, founded about the year 1084, which commenced with a cloister of anchorites (Carthusia, Chartreuse) in a rugged valley near Grenoble, was the most austere in its practice. A life of solitude and silence in a cell, a spare and meagre diet, a penitential garment of hair, flagellations, and the rigid practice of devotional exercises, were duties imposed upon every member of this fraternity.

Franciscans and Dominicans.

§ 245. The establishment of the so-called mendicant orders, in the thirteenth century, was remarkably productive of results. Francis of Assisi (A. D. 1226), the son of a rich merchant, renounced all his possessions, clothed himself in rags, and wandered through the world, begging and preaching repentance. His fiery zeal procured him disciples, who, like himself, renounced their worldly possessions, fasted, prayed, tore their backs with scourges, and supplied their slender wants from voluntary alms and donations. The order of Franciscans, or Minorites, founded by him, spread themselves rapidly through all countries. Contemporaneously with the Franciscans, who in process of time divided into numerous branches, arose the order of Dominicans, or preaching monks, founded by an illustrious and learned Spaniard, Dominicus, and whose dearest objects were the maintenance of the predominant faith in its purity, and the extinction of heretical opinions. The conversion of the Albigenses (§ 228), among whom their founder had resided for a considerable time, was the first attempt of the order, the members of which took a vow of entire poverty, and endeavored to win heaven by austerity and the practice of a rigid devotion. It was for these reasons that the court of inquisition, with its frightful examinations, dungeons, and tortures, was committed to them. The mendicant orders were the most powerful support of the pope, by whom they were consequently endowed with the greatest privileges, and withdrawn from the jurisdiction of the bishops. The Franciscans possessed the hearts of the people, with whose joys and sorrows they sympathized, and were principally occupied in the cure of souls: the Dominicans devoted themselves to the sciences, gradually filled the chairs of the universities, and numbered many of the greatest teachers of the Church among their members.

§ 246.—3. To the productive class belonged the inhabitants of the towns and country who were engaged in the occupations of peace. The peasantry, who were for the most part in a condition of serfdom, and took no share in public life, were at first exclusively understood by this title. But when the number of the towns was increased by the efforts of the emperors of the Saxon and Hohenstaufen lines, and many of the inhabitants of the country settled in them, the third class divided itself into citizens and peasants, and obtained various privileges and liberties. These towns were distinguished as imperial towns, which were under the immediate control of the emperor, and represented in the imperial diet; and provincial towns, which belonged to the territory of a prince. The former were the most ancient, as well as the richest and most powerful, and it was in them that the town policy of the middle ages was developed. The inhabitants originally consisted, as in ancient Rome, of free patrician families, and a tributary and dependent class employed in trade and agriculture, who, as tenants and inferior burghers, possessed no share in the privileges of the citizens. It was from the former that the mayor was chosen. After a time, the inferior burghers succeeded in gaining the ascendency over the patrician families. With this object, the artificers formed themselves into guilds and corporations, by which means a public spirit was awakened, and the inferior class of citizens rendered more powerful. These guilds, whose strength consisted in the stout arms of their members, soon attained such power, that they not only everywhere obtained the rights of citizenship, and a share in the government of the city, but, in very many towns, the rule of the patricians was thrust aside by the power of the guilds. The guilds marched into the field with their own banners, under the conduct of the guild-master, and defended their liberties without, as they had known how to gain and maintain them within.

§ 247. The literature of the middle ages was of a threefold character:—

1. Writings on religion and the Church; the most important of which

were composed by the schoolmen and the mystics. By schoolmen are to be understood those philosophical writers who made the doctrines and dogmas of the Church the objects of their speculation and inquiry. In doing this, they employed the rules of the Aristotelian dialectics, and invented a number of formulas and scholastic terms (terminologies), and descended at length to trifling subtleties and frivolous definitions and demonstrations. The schoolmen produced works in which we hardly know whether most to admire the acuteness displayed in the divisions of the subject, and in the development and connection of the conclusions, or the diligence, the learning, and the wonderful power of application. In the thirteenth century, scholasticism attained its highest perfection in the persons of the Dominican, Thomas Aquinas, and the Franciscan, Duns Scotus; so that, from this period, the scholastics were all divided into Thomists and Scotists. Men of warm feelings and sensitive natures were not content with the dry logic of these schoolmen; they opposed therefore a religion of feeling, of poetry, and of imagination, to the Christianity built upon philosophical rules and forms of reasoning. This was first done by St. Bernard of Clairvaux (§ 222), and by the noble Bonaventura (A. D. 1274); but in the most comprehensive way, by the mystics. These latter imitated the necessitous life of Christ, and sought to overcome the wickedness of the world by the castigation of the body and the mortification of the fleshly appetites, and strove to effect a spiritual union between themselves and God. Mysticism has had a powerful influence both upon life and literature; and although the inculcation of meekness and self-humiliation paralyzed active exertion, and a life devoted to the emotions and sentiments occasionally produced fanaticism, yet its influence upon a race which was sunk in barbarism and stupidity was, on the whole, beneficial. The "Imitation of the Life of Christ," by the Dominican monk, John Tauler of Strasburg, and the "Book of Everlasting Wisdom," of Henry Suso of Constance, were held in great esteem. The brethren of the Common Life, to whom belonged Thomas à Kempis (A. D. 1471), the writer of the widely-circulated devotional work, called the "Imitation of Christ," which has been translated into all languages, were the most active among the mystics.

Schoolmen.

Mystics.

§ 248.—2. Not only theological and philosophical studies were, and remained, in the hands of the clergy, but also mathematical and natural science, and the writing of history. The Greeks and Arabians exercised the greatest influence in extending and perfecting the material sciences. It was from the Arabian schools that the western clergy drew the greater part of their admired wisdom. Albertus Magnus, a widely-travelled and much esteemed teacher, possessed such a knowledge of physics, chemistry, and similar subjects, that he was generally regarded as a sorcerer. Among the composers of Latin chronicles and annals, William of Tyrus, the historian of the Crusades and the Holy Land, took the first place in France; and Otho of Freisingen, the half-brother of the emperor, Conrad III., in Germany. By the side of these learned historical compositions, there were already, at the time of the crusades, in Italy, France, and Spain, historical descriptions of particular periods and events, in the vernacular tongues, which, although less trustworthy than the former, are more interesting to read, and of more importance to the history of civilization. Among these may be mentioned the History of the Fourth Crusade, by Villehardouin (§ 224), Joinville's History and Chronicle of St. Louis; and, before all, Froissart's History and Chronicle of his own Times (A. D. 1329–1400).

§ 249.—3. Whilst learned literature was cultivated by the priests exclusively, the art of poetry passed at an early period into the hands of the knights, chiefly because love (*minne*), and devotion to the ladies,—feelings, to which the clergy, on account of their condition, dared not devote themselves, were the soul and essence of the latter. The poetry of the middle ages was alike, both as to its form and subject-matter, in all the nations of Europe. This was partly occasioned by the great intercourse that took place among people during the crusades, which facilitated the interchange of legends and poems, and partly by the great diffusion and general intelligibility of the Romance language. In France, Italy, Spain, and, to a certain extent, in England, languages were then spoken which bore a strong resemblance to each other, so that the literary productions of one country could be understood without difficulty in the rest. The middle-age poetry was divided into three kinds, according to the subject;—Heroic poems and heroic ballads (Epopee, Romance), where the deeds of knights, battles, adventures, and love affairs—the indispensable element of romantic poetry—formed the materials; sonnets, in which the poet expressed his feelings, emotions, or thoughts, in melodious verses; and religious poetry, in which the outpourings of devotion and religious enthusiasm, the praises of God and the Virgin, or the pious actions and histories of the saints, formed the subject. The epic poems dealt with certain cycles of legends, partly derived from the ancient world, as the Alexandriad of the priest Lamprecht, and partly from the Christian period, as the romance of Charlemagne and his Paladins (for example, the lay of Roland, by the priest Conrad), and the British king Arthur and his Round Table, with which the Welsh legend of the Grale was afterwards connected. To the latter cycle of romance belong two of the greatest epics of the middle age, the Percival of Wolfram of Eschenbach (A. D. 1200), and the Tristan and Isolde of Gottfried of Strasburg. But the glory of German heroic poetry is the Niebelungenlied, the materials of which are derived from the migrations of nations. The lyric poets, that in Germany were called "minnesanger," and in France, "troubadours," made the tender emotions of the heart, or the feelings of love, the subject of their poems; or they lashed depravity of morals and the corruptions of the clergy in satirical compositions, called Sirventes. In Germany, the most celebrated of the minnesangers was Walter Vogelweide, who lived at the court of Hermann of Thuringia. At that time, the castle of Wartburg, near Eisenach, in Thuringia, was the place of assembly for the greatest and most renowned singers. But Italy could display the greatest poet of the middle ages. After the stern Ghibelline, Dante of Florence (A. D. 1321), had moulded the poetical language of Italy in his great epic poem, "The Divine Comedy," Petrarch (A. D. 1374) brought it to the highest perfection of harmony in his Odes to Laura, while his contemporary, Boccaccio, became the creator of Italian prose by his tales and novels (Decameron). Dante's sublime poem, which consists of three parts, Hell, Purgatory, and Paradise, contains the whole wisdom of the middle ages, the whole treasure of the then acquired science, so that it was said with truth, that heaven and earth had each put a hand to Dante's poem. Petrarch's other works are written in Latin. He, as well as Boccaccio, was mainly instrumental in the restoration of the ancient literature and civilization.

V. DECAY OF CHIVALRY AND CORRUPTION OF THE CHURCH.

1. THE INTERREGNUM (1250—1273).

§ 250. The period after the death of Frederick II. was a momentous one for Germany. The imperial title was borne by foreign princes without power or influence, whilst at home a state of disorder and lawlessness prevailed, in which the strong alone could obtain justice. After William of Holland (§ 237) had fallen in battle against the brave Frislanders, the archbishop of Cologne turned the election to the wealthy Richard of Cornwall, brother of the English king, whilst the archbishop of Treves and his party adorned Alfonso X. the Wise, of Castile, with the title of emperor. The former sailed repeatedly up the Rhine laden with treasures, to satisfy the avarice of the princes who had elected him; the latter never visited the kingdom to the government of which he had been invited. The princes and bishops employed this interregnum in enlarging their territories, and possessing themselves of privileges, whilst the knights and vassals abused their strength by waylaying and plundering. They led a wild and predatory life in their castles, which, as the ruins yet show, were built upon the banks of navigable streams or near frequented highways; dragged travellers into their dungeons for the purpose of extorting a heavy ransom; plundered the wagons of the mercantile towns, and bade defiance, from behind their strong walls, to the powerless laws and tribunals. Attempts were made to remedy this state of things, 1. By the secret proceedings of the Fehmgericht (secret tribunal), established by the archbishop of Cologne in Westphalia (Dortmund); 2. By confederations of numerous towns for the purpose of mutual defence. The most important of these confederations were the Hanseatic, in Northern Germany, which included Hamburg, Lubeck, Bremen, Wismar, Rostock, Stralsund, Riga, and many other trading cities; and the confederation of the Rhine, which embraced the towns of Worms, Mayence, Spire, Strasburg, Basle, and numerous others.

2. ORIGIN OF THE POWER OF THE HOUSE OF HAPSBURG AND OF THE HELVETIC CONFEDERATION.

§ 251. During the interregnum, many of the princes and bishops had assumed the rights of sovereignty. To avoid losing what had been obtained, the princes to whom the right of election then chiefly belonged, and who were in consequence called Electors, sought to prevent the elevation of any prince whose lands and vassals rendered him formidable. At the same time, they required an energetic man, who should be able to restrain the prevailing lawlessness, and to break the threatening power of Ottocar, king of Bohemia, Moravia, and Austria. All these qualities were possessed by Count Rudolf of Hapsburg, who was elected emperor by the influence of the archbishop of Mayence, with whom he was then on friendly terms. His moderate hereditary estates, in Alsatia, occasioned no alarm to the princes; his courage, strength, and skill had been long proved and acknowledged; but what contributed especially to his election was his piety, and the inclination he had always displayed to the church and clergy. When, therefore, Rudolf had assured to the pope and the German princes the continuance of the privileges and territories that they had either usurped or acquired by violence, his election was generally recognized, and Alfonso of Castile was induced to abdicate. Ottocar alone refused to do homage, and failed to appear at the appointed diet. Upon this, Rudolf declared war against him, marched into the enemy's territories with the aid of his Switzers and Alsatians, and that of the German princes whom he had connected to his house by marriages with his numerous daughters, and won the glorious victory on the Marchfeld. Ottocar was killed in the fight; nothing but Bohemia and Moravia was left to his son Wenceslaus; the remaining countries of Austria, Styria, and Carniola, Rudolf settled on his sons, and by this means became the founder of the Austrian house of Hapsburg.

Rudolf of Hapsburg, A. D. 1273–1291.

A. D. 1278.

§ 252. As Rudolf of Hapsburg avoided all interference in the affairs of Italy, he was able to turn his undivided energies to Germany. He succeeded, after a succession of campaigns and battles, chiefly in Swabia, against the rapacious Eberhard of Wirtemberg, and in Burgundy, in regaining many of the fiefs, lands, privileges, and revenues, that had been alienated from the empire. But his greatest service was his securing the peace of the country and restoring law and order. He traversed the whole empire, and called the robber nobility to a severe reckoning. In Thuringia alone, he had twenty-nine knights executed, and destroyed sixty castles, and reduced, in a single year, upwards of seventy fortresses in Franconia and on the Rhine. He died at an advanced age, at Gomersheim, during one of these expeditions, and was buried at Spire. His simplicity, virtue, and honesty gained him no less respect than his intelligence; his impartial justice, and his warlike achievements. He was only wanting in the poetical magnanimity of the house of Hohenstaufen.

§ 253. The princes, partly out of fear of the power of the Hapsburgers, and partly from dislike to Rudolf's cruel and avaricious son Albert, were induced, at the instigation of the archbishop of Mayence, to elect

Adolf of Nassau, A. D. 1291–1298.

Count Adolf of Nassau. But he, like Rudolf, attempted to enlarge his own small territories, and made use of the loan he had received from the king of England to assist him in raising German troops, in purchasing Thuringia and Misnia from Albert the Uncourteous (§ 240). This disgraceful transaction involved him in a war with Albert's son, "Frederick with the bitten cheek," and Diezman, whom their degenerate father had attempted to deprive of their patrimony. The public disgust at this dishonest proceeding, and the discontent of the electoral princes of the Rhine (the Palatinate, Mayence, Treves, and Cologne), whom the emperor had deprived of the unjustly-acquired tolls of the river, had aided in forming a party favorable to his opponent Albert. Albert procured the deposition of Adolf and his own election; he then marched with his army upon the Rhine, and was victorious in the battle at Göllheim near the Donnersberg.

A. D. 1298.

Adolf, hurled from his horse by the lance of his rival, found his death in the tumult. His body rests in the cathedral of Spire.

Albert of Austria, A. D. 1298–1308.

Albert of Austria was an energetic but severe man, whose inflexible disposition might be read in his gloomy and one-eyed visage. He was ambitious, and desirous of enlarging his territories; and he therefore not only prosecuted the war against Thuringia, but attempted to gain other lands besides. Feared and hated, Albert was at length murdered at Windisch on the Reuss, by his own nephew, John of Swabia, (Parricida), just as he was making preparations for the subjugation of the free Swiss. John expiated his deed in a cloister; but a fearful revenge was taken by the emperor's wife and daughter upon those who assisted in the assassination (Wart, Balm, and Eschenbach), and upon all their friends and relatives.

§ 254. Albert's severity was the foundation of the Helvetic confederation. Helvetia was a component part of the German empire, and was

under the protection of prefects, who exercised there the highest offices of jurisdiction. This office was at first filled by the rich and powerful dukes of Zähringen, — the founders of Bern and other states. After the extinction of this house, the counts of Savoy in the South, and the Hapsburgs in the North, elevated themselves above the other
A. D. 1218. families by their power and possessions. The latter, to whom the landgravate of Aargau belonged, exercised, in the name of the empire, the functions of protectors over the original cantons on the lake of Lucerne, Schwyz, Uri, and Unterwalden, where they held possessions.

When the Hapsburgs ascended the imperial throne, they attempted to bring these cantons under the sovereignty of Austria. In furtherance of this purpose, Albert gave permission to the governors (Vögte), who ruled the lands of Hapsburg, to exercise the laws of the empire over the free communities and peasants, and to abuse their position by the oppression of the simple, warlike, and freedom-loving mountaineers. Upon this, the three oldest cantons, under the guidance of Walther Furst, Werner Stauffacher, and Arnold Melchtal, concluded an alliance on the Rutli for the protection of their liberties, the results of which were, that the fortresses were stormed and the governors expelled, after William Tell (as the legend goes) had killed Gesler, the most tyrannical of their number, with an arrow, because he had compelled him, for some trifling disobedience, to shoot an apple from the head of his son. Albert's assassination saved the Swiss from the effects of his anger, but his plans were taken up by his son Leopold. He marched against the forest cantons with an army, but suffered a severe overthrow in the narrow
A. D. 1315. pass of Morgarten. The power of the Hapsburgs declined from this period in Switzerland. By the accession of the Austrian town of Lucerne, in 1332, the whole of the shore of the lake of the four cantons fell into the power of the confederation, which was soon
A. D. 1339. joined by Bern, Zurich, Zug, and many other towns. In the
A. D. 1386. battle of Sempach (§ 261), the allies (like the Athenian democracy at Marathon), underwent a fiery trial against the Austrian and German chivalry, and proved themselves worthy of their freedom.

3. PHILIP THE FAIR OF FRANCE, AND THE EMPEROR LOUIS THE BAVARIAN.

§ 255. The ambitious Boniface VIII., in whose person the papacy attained its highest glory, was the origin of its downfall. He assumed the office of umpire in a war between Philip IV. the Fair of France, and Edward I. of England; and when Philip declined his interference, he forbade the levying of taxes upon the French ecclesiastics. Upon this, Philip prohibited the exportation of silver and gold from his kingdom, and by this means prevented the receipt of the papal revenue. The quarrel to which these proceedings gave rise, during which Boniface declared every man a heretic who did not believe that the king was subject to the pope in spiritual as well as temporal matters, and Philip by his deputies solemnly asserted the independence of the throne, ended by an excommunication. Upon this, Nogaret, the chancellor of France, entered Italy, and having hired some troops, seized the pope in his native city Anagni, and held him prisoner. It is true that Boniface was rescued by the country people, who rushed to his assistance, and that he hastened to Rome; but the impression made by the disgrace upon the proud and violent man was so powerful that he went mad and died. A. D. 1303. The French party now succeeded, not only in getting the excommunication withdrawn, but in inducing the new pope, Clement V. (hitherto bishop of Bordeaux), to take up his residence at Avignon in the south of France, and thus to put the papacy under the influence of the French court. This separation of the head of the church A. D. 1305. from Rome, which was mourned over as a second Babylonian captivity, lasted for nearly seventy years.

§ 256. The dissolution of the Order of the Temple (227 b) was the first consequence of the alliance between the pope and the French king. Dark reports of the blasphemous practices, of the secret crimes and vices, of the infidelity and voluptuousness, of which the Order had rendered itself guilty, gave Philip the Fair a pretext for suddenly seizing upon the persons of the Templars, and confiscating their vast possessions. By an unjust prosecution of six years, and by the tortures of the rack, a confession was at length obtained from the prisoners, which appeared to prove the crimes laid to their charge; and when fifty-four of their number retracted the confession extorted from them by torture, as untrue, they were condemned as apostates to a lingering death by fire. A. D. 1310. It was in vain that Jacob of Molay, the grand-master, protested against the proceedings, and offered to disprove the whole of the accusations. He himself died on the funeral pile, after he A. D. 1312. had summoned the king and the pope to a higher judgment-seat. The people reverenced him as a martyr, and recognized the judgment of God in the death of the two princes which shortly followed. The French king appropriated the largest share of the estates and treasures of the Templars.

Henry VII. § 257. During these events, Henry VII., of Luxemburg, A. D. 1308–1313. was governing Germany, not without renown. After adopting vigorous measures for the preservation of the internal peace of the empire, he took advantage of a contest for the crown of Bohemia to add this kingdom to the possessions of his own house, with the consent of the Bohemian estates, by marrying his son John to the sister of the last king, who was childless. Scarcely had he brought this affair, which was the foundation of the vast power of the house of Luxemburg, to a happy conclusion, than he turned his eyes to the long-forgotten

and disunited Italy, and undertook an expedition to Rome. The advent
A. D. 1310. of the emperor was greeted with joy by the oppressed Ghibellines; and the great poet Dante, of Florence (§ 249), celebrated his appearance by a Latin essay on monarchy, and by songs that were soon in the mouths of everybody. Henry received the crown of Lombardy in Milan, collected with rigor the taxes that were due in the towns of Upper Italy, and experienced an honorable reception in the Ghibelline city of Pisa. But despite all his efforts to assume the character of an establisher of peace, the Guelfs and the haughty Florence, with the king of Naples at their head, rose against him with reason. The pope himself opposed him, so that his coronation at Rome only took place after a lengthened contest. Upon marching into Tuscany for the purpose of humbling Florence, Henry died suddenly in the flower of his age, near the Arno. The joy displayed upon his death by the Guelfs, gave rise to the belief that he had been poisoned by a Dominican monk. The sorrowing Pisans buried him in the churchyard (Campo Santo) of their town.

§ 258. The death of Henry VII. again produced a contest for the crown in Germany; for, of the seven princes who now usually exercised the right of election (Palatinate, Mayence, Treves, Cologne, Bohemia, Saxony, Brandenburg), some chose Louis of Bavaria, the others, Frederick the Fair of Austria. The consequence of this division was an eight years' war, which was carried on with particular vigor by Frederick's brother, Leopold. Despite the superior strength of the Austrian party, Louis, who was an excellent general, maintained his cause with success, especially after Leopold's force had been weakened at Morgarten (§ 254).
A. D. 1322. It was not, however, till the battle of Mühldorf (or Amfing), where Frederick was defeated and taken prisoner by the skill of the Nuremberg general, Seyfried Schwepperman, that Louis attained a decided superiority. Leopold, however, would not submit to a peace. Supported by the pope, John XXII., who pronounced an excommunication and an interdict against Louis for having aided the Ghibellines in Milan, and by several princes of the empire, Leopold continued the war, and attempted a new election of emperor. Upon this, Louis set at liberty his rival, who was imprisoned in the castle of Trausnitz, upon condition that he should renounce the imperial dignity, and persuade his party to a peace. But when neither the pope nor Leopold would listen to the proposal, Frederick, true to his word, returned to captivity, a conduct which so moved his chivalrous opponent, that he lived with him henceforth in the closest friendship, and would even have shared
A. D. 1326. the empire with him, had not the Electors prevented it. Leopold died shortly afterwards, but the impetuous pope retained his animosity against Louis, which induced the latter to appoint Frederick regent of the empire, and undertake an expedition into Italy

§ 259. Louis was at first successful in Italy. Supported by the Ghibellines and the Minorites, he made brilliant progress, and succeeded in getting an anti-pope elected; but when, for the purpose of satisfying his mercenary troops, he exacted heavy levies of money from the Italian towns, matters were quickly altered. His retreat to Germany, where Frederick had in the mean time died, completed the triumph of the papal party. On the other hand, the obstinacy with which John XXII. and his successor Benedict XII. retained the excommunication pronounced against Louis, and rejected all attempts at reconciliation, irritated the German princes to such a degree, that, at an electoral Diet held at Rense, they uttered the declaration, "that henceforth every election of emperor by the princes was valid, without the confirmation of the pope." The ecclesiastics who obeyed the interdict were treated as disturbers of the public peace, and deprived of their offices. The notorious influence exercised by the French court upon all the proceedings of the pope, and the avarice and sensuality of the head of the Church and of the cardinals in Avignon, diminished the authority of the court of Rome. But Louis himself very soon forfeited the confidence and affection of the German princes, by allowing his avarice and desire of enlarging his territories to lead him into unjust and violent measures. Thence it was that the French and papal party succeeded in gaining over a part of the electoral
A. D. 1346. princes, and getting a rival emperor chosen from the house of Luxemburg. But the greater part of the German people, and particularly the imperial towns, sided with Louis, so that the new emperor, Charles IV. (son of King John of Bohemia), was not generally recognized, until the robust Louis lost his life in a bear-hunt, near
A. D. 1349. Munich, and his successor, Günter of Schwarzburg, elected by the Bavarian party, had sunk into an early grave at Frankfort.

4. THE EMPERORS OF THE HOUSE OF LUXEMBURG.

Charles IV. A. D. 1346-1378. § 260. Charles IV. was a sagacious prince, who was intent upon his own interests and the increase of the power of his house, and in whose mind money and property held a higher place than honor or renown. It was through him that the imperial power lost all respect in Italy, where he permitted the imperial privileges to be purchased by the towns and princes. The contests between Guelf and Ghibelline ceased from this time, but they only gave place to contentions between the princes and free towns concerning the enlargement of their territories; mercenary troops were now employed (as formerly in Greece) instead of the earlier militia, and the enterprising leaders of these bands (Condottieri) not unfrequently held the fate of states in their hands, and succeeded in getting possession of their government. The efforts of Charles in Germany, also, were chiefly directed to the gratification of his avarice and lust of territory. He sold the liberties and privileges of the imperial towns; he granted letters of nobility for money; he added Brandenburg and other territories to his patrimonial possessions. His agency was most beneficially felt in Bohemia, which attained by his means to greater prosperity. Artists and artisans were summoned from Germany and Italy, towns (Carlsbad) and villages were built, agriculture and trade encouraged, roads and bridges planned, and heaths and forests brought into cultivation. Charles, with the consent of the pope and the coöperation of the poet Petrarch, erected the first German

A. D. 1348. university in Prague (§ 249), which soon numbered from 5000 to 7000 students. From Charles IV. emanated the first imperial code of laws, known by the name of the Golden Bull, which referred the choosing of emperors exclusively to the seven Electors, and determined the precedence of the princes.

§ 261. The imperial authority was much decayed, and confusion and lawlessness prevailed all over Germany. The laws respecting disturbance of the public peace were little regarded; club-law (faustrecht), the only law attended to, called upon every man to take care of himself, and alliances were formed to do this more effectually. This state of disorder became particularly prevalent under Charles's son and succes-

Wenceslaus, sor, Wenceslaus, a rude, hot-headed man, devoted to drink.

A. D. 1378–1400. For whilst the emperor was leading a dissolute life in Bohemia, devoting himself to hunting, quarrelling with his nobles and the clergy, and rendering himself hateful and contemptible by his cruelty, and barbarous conduct to the vicar Nepomuk, whom he ordered to be thrown from the bridge of Prague into the Moldau, the German empire, with its battles and its miseries, was left to its fate. The towns in Swabia, in Franconia, and on the Rhine, united themselves in an alliance to preserve the peace of the country, and for defence against the rapacious nobles. The knights, who gained their living by plunder and highway robbery, and who were threatened by this alliance, followed the example of their enemies, and strengthened themselves by confederations of knights (called the Schlegler, and the Löwen and Hornerbund). The two confederations were perpetually engaged in war with each other, till at length, the murder of the bishop of Salzburg by a Bavarian duke occasioned the great cities' war, which produced extreme

A. D. 1388. distress in the south of Germany. The citizens were victorious in Bavaria; in Franconia, the fortune of war was rendered dubious by the courage of the Nuremburgers; but in Swabia, where the valiant enemy of the towns, Eberhard the Grumbler, of Wirtemberg, stood at the head of the nobility, the burghers suffered great loss near Döffingen, and at Worms and Frankfort, succumbed to the iron ranks of the knights of Hesse and the Palatinate. About the same time, the Swiss confederation was contending with far greater success against the

nobles of southern Germany. Duke Leopold of Austria invaded the freedom-loving mountaineers, with a host of armed nobles, who reverenced him as the flower of chivalry. But in the battle of
A. D. 1386. Sempach, where the heroic Arnold Winkelried of Unterwalden "made a path" for his countrymen into the iron-clad ranks of the knights, by embracing a number of their lances and burying the points in his bosom, the proud duke, with 656 of his nobles, fell beneath the maces of the Swiss peasants.

§ 262. The inability of the emperor to remedy the prevailing confusion at length induced the Electors, in a diet at Lahnstein,
A. D. 1400. to pronounce Wenceslaus's deposition, "because he had not aided the peace of the Church, had sold the title of duke to the rich and crafty Visconti in Milan, had not maintained the public peace, and had governed tyranically and with cruelty in Bohemia." Rupert of the Pa-
Rupert, A. D. 1400-1410. latinate was elected in his place; he was the grandson of that Rupert who, in the year of the battle of Sempach, had founded the university of Heidelberg. But even he, despite many good qualities, was not equal to the difficulties of the times. He was compelled to grant the princes and estates the right of forming confederations, and of maintaining the public peace in their own way; and when he attempted to restore Milan to the empire, he suffered a defeat from the Italian Condottieri (§ 260), who had discovered a more scientific system of tactics. He was equally unsuccessful in his attempts to restore tranquillity to the Church, an object that was first accomplished with unspeakable difficulty by his successor, Sigismond, the brother of Wences-
Sigismund, A. D. 1410-1437. laus. The great council of the Church, that was held by Sigismond for this purpose, exhausted the treasury to that degree, that the emperor was obliged at first to pledge the March of Brandenburg, and the electoral dignity, to Frederick of Hohenzollern, and afterwards to surrender them to him as his private and hereditary property.

5. THE DIVISION IN THE CHURCH AND THE GREAT COUNCILS.

§ 263. It had long been wished that the papal chair should be removed from Avignon to Rome; but the cardinals who were in the French interest, and who felt themselves better and more independent under the mild and beautiful sky of southern France, prevented the measure. This, at length, induced the Italian party to elect a pope of their own. By this means, the Church got two popes, one in Avignon, the other in Rome, each of whom declared himself the rightfully elected head of the Church, and fulminated anathemas against his rival and his adherents. The whole of western Christendom was divided, consciences perplexed, and the Church rent asunder. It was in vain that the synod of Pisa attempted to heal the evil by deposing one pope and electing another; — the

former two maintained their claims, so that the Church was now triply divided. A general discontent spread through the Christian world, and engendered a loud demand for a reformation of the Church, both in its head and members. Whilst the moderate party, and in particular, the learned theologians of the university of Paris (Sorbonne), wished to bring about this reformation by a general council, which should be superior to the pope, the disciples and adherents of the Oxford profes-
A. D. 1384. sor, John Wickliff, aimed at a thorough change both in the doctrine and constitution of the Church. Wickliff had not only declared the papacy to be an unchristian institution, and preached zealously against absolution, monachism, the worship of saints, and similar matters, but had stood forward as a reformer, by translating the Bible into English, and rejecting many articles of faith, such as auricular confession, celibacy, and transubstantiation. The most celebrated of his followers was John Huss, professor in Prague, a man distinguished for his learning, and moral life, as well as by Christian gentleness. He preached against the abuses of the papacy; against the wealth and secular power of the clergy; against monachism and absolution: and although the pope excommunicated him and condemned his writings, the number of his adherents, among whom a Bohemian nobleman, Jerome of Faulfisch, distinguished himself by his zeal, increased every day. The Germans in the university of Prague were curtailed of their privileges for showing an inclination to the new doctrines of Huss, for which reason 5000 students and professors quitted the place, and thus brought about the foundation of other universities, that of Leipsic among the first.

§ 264. When at length, Pope John XXIII., importuned by the Emperor Sigismond, called the Council of Constance, troops of temporal and spiritual dignitaries of all nations poured into the town, where the splendor of the whole West was at once united. 150,000 men are said to have assembled there.

Council of Constance, A. D. 1414-1418.

The unity and reformation of the Church was the lofty aim of the synod. In the first place, therefore, the three popes were either deposed or persuaded to resign; and when John XXIII. seized the opportunity afforded by a tournament to escape in disguise, by the aid of Frederick of Austria, and recalled his abdication, the council declared itself independent and superior to the pope, and united with the emperor in punishing the refractory. Frederick of Austria was outlawed, and deprived of Aargau and other possessions by the Swiss, and John was for a long time held prisoner in the castle of Heidelberg. But the efforts of the French and Germans, who wished in the first place to reform the Church, and then to elect a new pope, were frustrated by the Italians (Ultramontani), who insisted before all things upon an election of pope. Their opinion prevailed, and Martin V., was raised to the papal chair. He was a moderate man, who contrived, by abolishing a few abuses, and by skilfully conducted negotiations, to divide the votes and baffle the efforts of the council. In this way, the hopes and wishes of the people were disappointed; the pope retained his power, and the Church was left in her corruption. But the Council of Constance has enriched history with one deed of horror, — the burning of Huss and Jerome of Prague. The council proceeded at its commencement to an examination of doctrines deviating from those of the Church, and had condemned Wickliff's writings to the flames, and summoned Huss to answer for his opinions. Huss proceeded to Constance, provided with an imperial passport, by which he was assured of a safe return to his home, but was imprisoned as soon as he arrived there, and accused of disseminating heresy. It was in vain that he defended himself with dignity against the charges — his judges were his accusers; it was in vain that his friends appealed to the imperial safe-conduct, — the synod laid down the principle, that no faith was to be kept with heretics, and demanded an unconditional abjuration. When Huss refused to do this, he was condemned to

A. D. 1415. suffer death by fire as an obstinate teacher of heresy; a doom which he underwent with the firmness and composure of a martyr. A year later, Jerome also endured the agonies of the burning pile with the courage of a stoic.

§ 265. The intelligence of this horrible event at Constance incited the Hussites to a furious religious war. The cup, which, according to the views of Huss, was not to be withheld from the laity, was borne before their armies as the symbol of their cause (hence Utraquists and Calixtines); and a heavy vengeance was exacted from the priests who refused to administer it. It was in vain that the pope fulminated an interdict against the adherents of Huss, their numbers increased daily; they stormed the town-house of Prague, and murdered the counsellors, which so enraged the old Emperor Wenceslaus, that he died

A. D. 1419. of apoplexy. Sigismond ought now to have become king of Bohemia also; but the whole nation flew to arms, to prevent the faithless emperor from taking possession of the country. John Ziska, a general expert in war, valiant, and endowed with a wonderful talent of governing the masses, placed himself at its head. It was in vain that Sigismond led three imperial armies against the Hussites; his troops recoiled in dismay before the wild fury of the enraged people. The Hussites burnt down the Bohemian churches and convents, and carried their ravages into the neighboring countries. The name of Ziska, the blind general, was a terror to the nations. After his death, the moderate party (Calixtines) separated themselves from the radicals (Taborites). The latter, under the conduct of Procopius the Great and the Little, continued their incendiary course, ravaged Saxony, and extorted tribute from Brandenburg and Bavaria, whilst the Calixtines consented to a peace. when the Council of Basle consented to the use of the cup in the Lord's

Supper, and to preaching in the vernacular tongue. It was only when the Taborites suffered a defeat near Prague, and the two

A. D. 1433. Procopiuses were killed, that the emperor, by the dexterity of his chancellor Schlick, succeeded in bringing them to a peace; whereupon Sigismond was acknowledged king. But the glory of Bohemia was humbled to the dust. A few decades later, a small party of the former Hussites separated from the Church and formed a separate sect, since known as the Bohemian and Moravian Brethren, "poor, scripture-proof, and peaceful."

Council of Basle, A. D. 1431-1449.

§ 266. In the council of Basle, to the summoning of which, Martin V., predecessor of Eugenius IV., had, after long hesitation, consented, the reformation of the Church, which had been interrupted in that of Constance, was to be concluded, and the Hussite controversy arranged. But the proceedings here soon took a course that seemed to endanger the papal power. The assembly, which consisted in part of the lower order of clergy, diminished the money charges that the court of Rome imposed upon the provincial churches, and interdicted the incroachments of the pope in the filling up of bishoprics and benefices. Eugenius was rendered so anxious by these and other similar resolutions, that he seized the first pretext for removing the council to Ferrara, and afterwards to Florence. But many of the clergy would not attend; they chose another pope, and again asserted the former principle, that a synod of the Church was superior to the pope, and that the former and not the latter was infallible. Upon this, Eugenius, encouraged by the fears, entertained both by princes and people, of another division in the Church, anathematized the refractory members of the council, and rejected their decisions; and for the purpose of overcoming more surely the opposition of the Germans, gained over the crafty Italian, Æneas Sylvius (afterwards Pius II.), who was private secretary to the emperor Frederick III. By the aid of this shrewd man, who is also known as an author, the pope succeeded in winning over the weak emperor to the Aschaffenburg concordat, by means of which, the Church remained in its former state, and all the abuses and extortions, with a few trifling exceptions, were continued. It was in vain that the patriotically-minded Gregory of Heimburg advocated the liberties of the Church and the rights of Germany with intelligence and eloquence; abandoned by the emperor and most of the princes, the council, after a little hesitation, recognized Eugenius's successor, Nicholas V., as lawful pope, and then dissolved itself. In this way, the papacy came forth, for the second time, victorious from the fight, but less by the inherent power of truth than by unecclesiastical expedients.

6. GERMANY UNDER FREDERICK III. AND MAXIMILIAN I.

§ 267. When the male line of the house of Luxemburg expired with Albert II. of Austria, A. D. 1437 - 1439. Sigismond, his son-in-law, Albert II. of Austria, ascended the imperial throne of Germany, which from this time remained in possession of the Hapsburg-Austrian family. Albert was a well-disposed and energetic man; but as Bohemia and Hungary engaged the whole of his exertions, he could effect nothing of importance during the short period of his government. His nephew, Frederick III., A. D. 1440 - 1493. Frederick III., was his successor in the empire, a prince endowed with domestic virtues, but possessing slender talents for government, and who opposed nothing to the troubles of his lengthened reign but a dull and passive indifference. He looked quietly on while the Turks took possession of Constantinople, and carried their ravages into the hereditary territories of Austria, when Hungary and Bohemia elected native kings, when Charles the Bold of Burgundy extended his dominions to the banks of the Rhine (§ 293), when Milan and Lombardy were separated from the German empire (§ 261). In Germany, the imperial authority fell into utter contempt, the princes made themselves independent, and exercised the privilege of private warfare without hesitation. The Swabian alliance was engaged in a furious war with Albert (Achilles or Ulysses), the valiant margrave of the Brandenburg territories in Franconia (Bayreuth), a war in which nine battles were fought and 200 villages reduced to ashes. The neighborhood of the Rhine and the Neckar was desolated by the war of A. D. 1461. the Palatinate, during which, the palgrave, Frederick the Victorious, gained a glorious victory near Seckenheim, and made prisoners of his enemies, Ulrick of Wurtemburg, the margrave of Baden, and the bishop of Metz; but was unable to prevent the deposi- A. D. 1462. tion of his ally, the banished archbishop, Dieter of Mayence, in whose defence he had taken up arms.

§ 268. This state of disorder and self-redress increased the desire for a fresh constitution of the empire. But as the princes refused to sacrifice any of their real or pretended rights, every proposal that seemed likely to increase the power of the emperor, or diminish that of the princes, encoun- Maximilian I., A. D. 1493 - 1519. tered a resolute opposition. At length, Maximilian I. agreed with the Electors, the secular and spiritual nobles, and the representatives of the free towns, at the imperial diet at A. D. 1495. Worms, to form a constitution which restrained the right of private warfare, but completely undermined the authority of the emperor. At this diet, the eternal Land-peace was established, and every act of self-redress by arms forbidden, under pain of ban and outlawry. An imperial chamber was at once established to compose all quarrels among the members of the empire, and a short time afterwards,

the empire was divided into ten circles. 1. The Austrian. 2. The Bavarian. 3. The Swabian. 4. The Franconian. 5. The Rhenish Electorate. 6. The Upper Rhenish. 7. The Lower Rhenish Westphalian. 8. Upper Saxony. 9. Lower Saxony; and 10. The Burgundian. By this alteration, the power of the princes was raised to a still greater height, so that at last they could act in their own territories as absolute rulers. The Swiss confederates, who were at that time in alliance with France, refused to recognize the imperial chamber, and denied the contingent of troops. Hereupon, Maximilian attempted to compel them by force of arms, but was worsted in the contest, and obliged
A. D. 1499. to forego his demands in the peace of Basle, and to admit the independence of the Swiss of Germany.

§ 269. Maximilian's reign forms the transition period between the middle age and the modern time. He himself, with his stately aspect, his bold and dangerous huntings, his valiant deeds in battle and tournament, may well be looked upon as the "last knight" on the imperial throne of Germany; his love of the decaying chivalrous poetry, his marriage with Mary of Burgundy, his wars in the Netherlands and in Italy, are all stamped with the character of the middle age. On the other hand, it was at this time that the commencements of a more refined political science, and of a greater intercourse among nations, displayed themselves, which, combined with new discoveries and inventions, brought about the modern period.

VI. HISTORY OF THE REMAINING EUROPEAN NATIONS DURING THE MIDDLE AGE.

1. FRANCE.

a. FRANCE UNDER THE HOUSE OF CAPET.

§ 270. The first successors of Hugh Capet (§ 205) possessed but little power and a narrow territory. The dukes and counts of the different provinces looked upon the king, who, properly, was only lord of France, as their equal, and only allowed him the first rank among themselves, in so far as they were obliged to recognize him as their feudal superior. The nobles dared not weaken the rights that appertained to him in this capacity, lest they should afford an example of breach of faith to their own subjects, and encourage them to similar behavior towards themselves. For the rest, the possessions of the great vassals were independent counties and principalities, which had no closer connection with the French throne than the western territories on the Seine, Loire, and Garonne, which belonged to the king of England; or the eastern (Burgundian) lands on

the Rhone and the Jura, which were portions of the German empire. But in the attempt to increase the kingly power, the house of Capet were not less aided by their good fortune than by their wisdom. It was fortunate, that, owing to the lengthened lives of most of their kings, the throne was seldom vacant, that there was almost always a son of age to succeed his father, and that, consequently, there was never an interregnum. But it was wisdom in the first kings to have their eldest sons crowned during their lives, and to make them their partners in the government, so that, on the death of the father, little or no change was suffered. The
Louis VII., A. D. 1137-1180.
most important kings after Hugh Capet were Louis VII., who undertook the second crusade, and during his absence intrusted the government in France to the politic Abbot
Philip Augustus II., A. D. 1180-1223.
Suger of St. Denis; Philip Augustus II., who wrested Normandy and the other territories in the west from the English king, John Lackland; and Louis VIII., who enlarged his
Louis VIII., A. D. 1223-1226.
dominions on the south by the war against the Albigenses (§ 228). But the reigns which had the greatest influence
St. Louis, A. D. 1226-1270.
upon the history of France were those of St. Louis and Philip the Fair. The former improved the laws, and caused the royal courts of justice to be looked upon as the highest in the land, and the disputes of the nobles among themselves or with their vassals to be brought before them for decision: the latter, on the other hand,
Philip the Fair, A. D. 1285-1314.
increased the consequence of the towns by granting various privileges and liberties to the citizens, and by being the first who summoned the representatives of the towns to the diet during his contest with the pope. (§ 255). After the death of Philip's
A. D. 1328.
three sons, who reigned one after the other, but left no male heirs, the French throne passed to the house of Valois.

b. FRANCE UNDER THE HOUSE OF VALOIS (A. D. 1328-1589).

§ 271. Philip VI. of Valois, brother's son of Philip the Fair, in-
Philip VI., A. D. 1328-1347.
herited the French throne. But Edward III. of England also asserted his claims, as son of a daughter of Philip the Fair. Without regard to the Salic law, which prohibited the succession of females, he assumed the title of king of
A. D. 1346.
France, and made war upon Philip. After a bloody contest of a few years, the battle of Crecy was fought, in which the English were the victors, and the flower of the French chivalry, together with John, the blind king of Bohemia, fell on the field. The possession of the important town of Calais was the fruit of the vic-
John the Good, A. D. 1347-1364.
tory. Philip died in the following year, and his son, John the Good, succeeded to the contested crown. Eager to obliterate the memory of Crecy, he attacked the English army, which was under the command of Edward III.'s heroic son, the Black Prince,

but suffered a decisive defeat at Poictiers, and was obliged to proceed as a captive to the capital of England. Whilst he was absent,
A. D. 1356. the kingdom was governed by the crown prince (Dauphin).
During his rule, an insurrection broke out in Paris and over the whole land, which was attended with great devastations and outrages,
A. D. 1358. until the imperfectly-armed citizens and peasants were subdued by the French knights, and visited with severe punishment. Shortly after this, a peace was established between France and
A. D. 1360. England, by which Calais and the south-west of France was surrendered to the English, and a heavy ransom promised for John, whilst Edward, on the other hand, renounced his pretensions to the French throne. But when the collection of the ransom money was
A. D. 1364. delayed, John voluntarily returned into captivity, and died in London.

Charles V., A. D. 1364–1380. § 272. John's son, Charles V. (the Wise), healed the wounds of his country. He quieted men's minds by his good and gentle government, and by prudence and valor, recovered the lands that had been lost on the Loire and the Garonne; so that,
A. D. 1377. when the Black Prince fell a victim to a wasting disease, and Edward III. shortly after followed him into the grave, nothing remained to the English of all their conquests but Calais. But under his successor, Charles VI., who became insane shortly after coming
Charles VI., A. D. 1380–1422. of age, France again fell into a state of confusion and lawlessness. Two powerful court parties, headed by the uncle of the king (the duke of Burgundy), and the king's brother (the duke of Orleans), contended for the government; whilst the burghers rebelled against the heavy imposts, and demanded an increase of their privileges. About the same time in which the towns were waging war against the knights in Germany (§ 261), the Swiss peasants were contending against the nobility, and a dangerous popular insurrection, under Wat Tyler and others, was making rapid progress in England, the citizen and peasant class rose against the court and the nobility in Flanders and
A. D. 1383. France also. But want of union among the insurgents gave the latter the victory, and the outbreak was followed by a diminution of the privileges of the people. The Burgundian party favored the citizens, the Orleans party the nobility.

§ 273. The chivalrous king, Henry V. of England, took advantage of these circumstances to renew the war with France. He demanded the former possessions back again; and when this was refused, he entered
A. D. 1415. France by Calais, and renewed at Agincourt, on the Somme, the days of Crecy and Poictiers. The French army, four times the number of its opponents, was overthrown, and the flower of the French chivalry either fell in the field, or were taken prisoners by the enemy; nothing stood between the victor and Paris, where party violence

had just now attained its highest point, and murders and insurrections were matters of daily occurrence. The Orleans party joined the Dauphin, whilst the Burgundian party, with the queen Isabella, united themselves with the English, and acknowledged Henry V. and his descendants as the heirs of the French crown. The whole of the country to the north
A. D. 1422. of the Loire was soon in the hands of the English. But Henry V. was snatched away by death in the midst of his heroic course, in the same year in which the crazy Charles VI. sank into the grave, and the Dauphin took possession of the throne under the title
Charles VII., of Charles VII. But this made little difference to France.
A. D. The English and their allies proclaimed Henry VI., who was
1422 - 1461. scarcely a year old, the rightful ruler of the country, and retained their superiority in the field, so that they already held Orleans in siege.

A. D. 1429. § 274. In this necessity, the Maid of Orleans, a peasant girl of Dom Remy in Lorraine, who gave out that she had been summoned to the redemption of France by a heavenly vision, aroused the sinking courage of Charles and his soldiers. Under her banner, the town of Orleans was delivered, the king conducted to Rheims to be crowned, and the greater part of their conquests wrested from the English. The faith in her heavenly mission inspired the French with courage and self-confidence, and filled the English with fear and despair.
A. D. 1431. This effect remained after Joan of Arc had fallen into the hands of the latter, and had been given up to the flames on a pretended charge of blasphemy and sorcery. The English lost one province after another; and when Philip the Good of Burgundy recon-
A. D. 1435. ciled himself with the king, Calais soon became their last and only possession in the land of France. Paris opened
A. D. 1436. its gates and received Charles with acclamations. He reigned over France in peace for twenty-five years; but he was a weak man, who suffered himself to be guided by women and favorites. He was followed
Louis XI., by Louis XI., a crafty but politic prince, who, by cunning,
A. D. violence, and unexampled tyranny, rendered the power of
1461 - 1483. the throne absolute, and enlarged and consolidated his empire. He robbed the nobility of all their choicest privileges, and gradually united all the great fiefs with the crown. He then, by the assistance of the Swiss (whose hardy youth he and his successor engaged as mercenaries), overthrew Charles the Bold, and made himself master of the
Charles VIII., dukedom of Burgundy. The stings of conscience and the
A. D. 1483 - fear of men tortured him in the lonely castles where he
1498. spent the last years of his life. His two successors, Charles
Louis XII., A. D. 1498 - VIII. and Louis XII., conquered Brittany, but dissipated
1515. the strength of the kingdom in their expeditions to Italy.

2. ENGLAND.

Henry II., A. D. 1154–1189. § 275. With Henry II., of Anjou, the great-grandson of William the Conqueror (§ 207), the renowned race of Plantagenet ascended the English throne. They possessed much land on the Loire and the Garonne, and as Normandy also belonged to the English, the whole of the west of France was in the power of the kings of England. Many quarrels and battles arose from this state of things, for the kings of France laid claim to the rights of feudal supremacy over these western lands, which rights the English kings refused to render. Henry II., a contemporary of Frederick Barbarossa, was a powerful and intelligent sovereign, who acquired especial renown by his improvement in the administration of the laws. In furtherance of this object, he attempted, by the Constitutions of Clarendon, so to limit the ecclesiastical jurisdiction, that the clergy should be subject to the royal tribunals in temporal matters, without any appeal to the pope. Upon this point, Henry had a violent contest with the archbishop of Canterbury, Thomas à Becket. Becket rejected the Constitutions of Clarendon, and dismissed every priest that submitted to them; and when he was threatened with legal proceedings, he quitted England and anathematized Henry. But an arrangement was brought about, for a short time, by the intervention of the pope. But scarcely was Becket returned to Canterbury, when he resumed all his former severity against the clergy who received the Constitutions of Clarendon. The king, who was just then in arms against France, suffered an exclamation of discontent against Becket to escape him, which induced four of his servants to hasten to England, and to slaughter the archbishop on the steps of the altar. A. D. 1170. This sacrilegious deed occasioned universal horror, and procured the pope a complete triumph in England. The murderers were punished, the Constitutions of Clarendon abolished, and Thomas à Becket canonized. Thousands made pilgrimages to his altar; and the king, a few years afterwards, gave a memorable example of his penitence, by suffering the monks to scourge his bare shoulders at the grave of the martyr.

§ 276. Two of Henry's sons survived their father; Richard Lionheart (§ 223), and John Lackland. Richard Lionheart, A. D. 1189–1199. Much as the former distinguished himself by his courage and chivalrous daring, his reign was not advantageous to England. The latter was worsted in every contest in which he engaged. John Lackland, A. D. 1199–1216. In the first place, he lost Normandy, and all the hereditary possessions of his house on the Loire and the Garonne, to the shrewd and enterprising Philip Augustus of France; and when he got involved in a quarrel with the pope, about the appointment to the chair of the archbishopric of Canterbury, in consequence of which the holy father pronounced an anathema and interdict upon England, released his subjects from their oath of allegiance, and summoned the king of France to take possession of the land, John humbled himself, surrendered the throne of England by a solemn act to the pope, and received it back again from the hands of the legate as a papal fief, in return for a yearly tribute of 1000 marks. John was now released from the interdict, and the French king forbidden to prosecute the expedition against him. Enraged at this disgraceful transaction of a king, who, by his severity, arbitrariness, and cruelty, had embittered every class against himself, the nobles of England seized their arms and compelled John, by the grant of the great charter (Magna Charta), in a meadow near Windsor (Runnymede), to lay the foundation of the free constitution of England. The long reign of John's son, Henry III., was favorable to the growth of liberty, melancholy as, on the whole, the condition of the land under him was. His extravagant profuseness to favorites, and the exactions of the papal legates and the Italian clergy, inflicted grievous wounds on the prosperity of the country, and at length drove the people to rebel and seize upon the king and his family, till the abuses were removed, and fresh liberties granted.

A. D. 1215.

Henry III., A. D. 1216–1272.

§ 277. Henry III. was succeeded by his chivalrous son, Edward I., whose reign is rendered memorable by a succession of bloody wars. He added the hitherto independent Wales to his dominions, introduced there the laws and constitution of England, and was the first who gave the title of Prince of Wales to the heir to the throne. Upon a quarrel for the crown breaking out shortly after in Scotland, between Robert Bruce and John Baliol, in which he was chosen umpire, Edward took advantage of the opportunity to establish the much contested feudal superiority of the English kings over Scotland, and decided in favor of Baliol, who was ready to do him homage. This irritated the Scotch, who were proud of their independence. They seized the sword, and under the conduct of heroic knights like Wallace, fought many battles for their liberties which are renowned in song and legend. Furious contests drenched the plains of the south of Scotland with the blood of heroes; Wallace was taken prisoner, and put to death by the hangman. The coronation stone of the Scottish kings at Scone was brought to London, were it still ornaments Westminster Abbey; Edward's victorious host marched through the whole of Scotland as far as the Highlands, and yet the Scots still maintained their independence. Robert Bruce, the grandson of the before-mentioned candidate for the throne, after many changes of fortune, obtained possession of the crown, which became hereditary in his family, and passed at length to the kindred house of Stuart.

Edward I., A. D. 1272–1307.

A. D. 1283.

Edward's son of the same name was a weak prince, who could neither make conquests abroad, nor preserve peace and order at home. The nobles repeatedly took up arms against him, killed his favorites, and at last looked quietly on, whilst the queen and her paramour, Mortimer, thrust the unfortunate monarch from the throne, and had him put to a cruel death in prison. But when his energetic son, Edward III., came of age, he punished the atrocious deed by executing Mortimer, and banishing the queen to a solitary fortress.

Edward II., A. D. 1307–1327.

Edward III., A. D. 1327–1377.

§ 278. Edward III. governed with vigor and renown. He took measures for checking the encroachments of the pope upon the English Church, in which he was actively supported by the Oxford professor, Wicliff, and granted to many towns the privilege of sending representatives to parliament, as his predecessors had before done. By this means, the number of representatives increased to such an extent that they were divided, and from this time, the nobles and bishops formed the Upper House (House of Peers), and the members for the towns and counties the Lower House (House of Commons), of Parliament. No tax could be imposed without their consent. The wars of succession which Edward III. and his son, the Black Prince, waged with France, were to the advantage of the English (§ 271). But the government of his grandson and successor, Richard II., was disturbed by domestic troubles; a dangerous insurrection of the people was only suppressed with difficulty by the ready courage of the king; and when Richard at length banished his cousin, Henry of Lancaster, who was the originator of the disturbances, from the kingdom, Henry formed a party, had the king deposed from the throne by an act of parliament, and then assumed himself the royal title. Richard died of starvation in a remote castle, whilst Henry IV., in whose person the house of Lancaster ascended the English throne, was securing to himself and his posterity, by his prudence and valor, the crown he had so flagitiously obtained. An insurrection of the English nobles under the duke of Northumberland and his heroic son Percy, surnamed Hotspur, ended with the defeat of the insurgents. The followers of Wicliff, called Lollards, were persecuted for the sake of propitiating the clergy in favor of the royal house. Henry IV. was succeeded by his more valiant son, Henry V., whose youthful follies, as well as his nobleness of soul and heroic greatness, have been portrayed in so masterly a way by the great British poet, Shakspeare. He conducted successful wars with France, but all that he gained by his fortune and courage was again lost in the reign of his infant son, Henry VI.

Richard II., A. D. 1377–1399.

House of Lancaster.

Henry IV., A. D. 1399–1413.

Henry V., A. D. 1413–1422.

§ 279. This sixth Henry was the most unfortunate prince that ever sat on a throne. The crown of France, which he had received when a child of one year old (§ 274), was wrested from him by the Maid of Orleans, and he was deprived of his English possessions, also, by the wars of the Red and the White Roses. Richard, duke of York, great-grandson of king Edward III., deemed that he had better pretensions to the crown of England than Henry VI. He formed a powerful party, unfurled the banner of rebellion, and commenced the bloody civil war which, from the cognizance borne by the chiefs of the parties, was called the War of the Red (Lancaster) and White (York) Rose. It is true that Richard was defeated in a furious battle by the forces of the queen, who ornamented his head with a paper crown, and placed it upon the battlements of York. But Richard's eldest son, the chivalrous Edward, revenged the insults offered to his father. He got possession of the throne, and, despite the many changes of fortune he met with during his reign, he finally maintained himself upon it, after Henry of Lancaster, who had four times exchanged the crown for a prison, had ended his miserable existence in the Tower, and his son had been put to death. But the blood-stained throne brought no blessing to the house of York. Edward first got rid of his brother Clarence by assassination; and when he himself died, leaving behind him two infant princes, his younger brother, Richard (III.), had these put to death in the Tower, and took possession of the throne, upon which he in vain hoped to secure himself by fresh crimes. Henry Tudor, a descendant of the royal house of Lancaster, who had saved himself from the general ruin of his family by flying to France, landed on the coast of England, and won crown and victory in the field of Bosworth, where Richard was slain. Upon this, Henry VII., with whom the house of Tudor rose to the throne, brought about a reconciliation between the Roses by marrying the daughter of Edward IV. The history of the world scarcely relates another war in which so many atrocities were committed as in the contest between the Red and the White Rose. Eighty members of royal families, and the ornaments of the nobility, fell by the sword. Owing to this, the politic and hard-hearted Henry VII. could give greater power to the crown than it had possessed under the Plantagenets.

Henry VI., A. D. 1422–1461.

House of York.

Edward IV., A. D. 1461–1483.

Richard III., A. D. 1483–1485.

A. D. 1485.

House of Tudor.

Henry VII., A. D. 1485–1509.

3. SPAIN.

§ 280. For several centuries, the two kingdoms of Aragon and Castile (§ 194) stood side by side in separate independence. The former attempted to extend itself towards the east, and gained possession, not only of the coast lands of Catalonia, Valentia, and Murcia, and the Spanish islands, Majorca and Minorca, but subjected, at different times, Sardinia and Sicily, and in the reign of Alfonso V.,

Alfonso V., A. D. 1416–1456.

even conquered Naples. Castile, on the other hand, enlarged itself on the south, and by successful wars against the Moors, gained possession of Cordova, Seville, and Cadiz. These contests had the greatest influence on the history and character of the Spanish nation. First, They produced a love of war and a chivalrous turn of mind, and were the occasion that the Spanish nation took delight in contests and arms, in tournaments and knightly exercises, and in romantic poetry and minstrelsy. Secondly, They preserved the zeal for religion, and were the foundation of that predominance of the clergy which has always been a characteristic of Spain. Thirdly, They aroused a feeling of liberty and self-reliance among the people,—hence the Spanish Estates, which assembled regularly in the Cortes, and claimed and exercised privileges which were to be met with in no other monarchy. The Estates of Aragon not only possessed the right of legislating and of consenting to the levying of taxes, but the king was obliged to consult them in the choice of his council. Quarrels between the Estates and the king were decided by an independent chief justice (Justitia).

§ 281. The chivalrous Peter III., the conqueror of Sicily (§ 240), is the best known of the Aragonian kings, and Alfonso X., the Wise, of the Castilian. The latter occupied himself with astronomy and astrology, with music and poetry, enlarged the university of Salamanca, encouraged the development of the national language, and had works prepared on history and jurisprudence; but he was wanting in the practical wisdom of life. To gain the shadow of the imperial Roman throne, and to gratify his taste for magnificence and pleasure, he oppressed his people with taxes, and plunged his land into confusion by extravagance, and by debasing the coinage. Alfonso XI. overcame the Moors on the river Salado, and took the strong town, Algeciras, in Andalusia. To defray the expenses of the war, the Estates introduced the tax, alcavala, which was levied upon all movable and immovable property as often as it was sold or exchanged, and which proved extremely detrimental to trade and commerce. This impost has continued to exist in Spain ever since. Alfonso's son, Peter the Cruel, outraged his wives, his brothers and relatives, the nobles and the people, so long, that at length his half-brother, with the assistance of some French troops, overcame and killed him, and then assumed his place. The marriage of queen Isabella of Castile, with Ferdinand the Catholic of Aragon, led to the union of the two kingdoms, and consequently to a new epoch for Spain, towards the conclusion of the fifteenth century.

Alfonso X., A. D. 1252-1284.

Alfonso XI., A. D. 1324-1340.

A. D. 1340.

Peter the Cruel, A. D. 1350-1369.

Isabella, A. D. 1474-1504.

Ferdinand, A. D. 1479-1516.

§ 282. Ferdinand and Isabella, directed by the counsels of the shrewd cardinal Ximenes, strove for a common object;—they sought to diminish the power of the nobility and clergy, and exalt the of the crown. For this purpose, Ferdinand obtained from the pope the grand mastership of the three wealthy orders of Castilian knights, and the privilege of filling up the Spanish bishoprics. He next deprived the nobility of the administration of justice, that he might transfer it to the royal courts, and established the armed Hermandad (police), to preserve the peace of the land, and to abolish robbery and private warfare. But the most important means of raising the power of the throne was the court of Inquisition, in which the king had the appointment of the grand inquisitor and all the judges. This royal court of faith, provided with spiritual weapons, was not only the terror of heretics and secret Mohammedans and Jews, but held the nobility and clergy in awe, and imposed heavy chains upon the free activity of the mind. The slightest suspicion, the false testimony of an enemy, might lead to the frightful dungeons of the Inquisition, where the most dreadful tortures of the rack were employed to force a confession of guilt, and wiles, equivocations, and insnaring questions were made use of to entrap the resolute. Numberless victims were given up to the flames in the midst of pomp and magnificence (auto de fé), or pined away their lives in mouldering dungeons, whilst the treasury of the state was enriched with their property. Never were the throne and altar united in a bond so dangerous to the liberties of the people, as in Spain since the establishment of the Inquisition.

§ 283. The banishment of the Moors is one of the most melancholy phenomena in Spanish history. When the Moorish kingdom of Granada, after a war of ten years, fell before the arms of Ferdinand and Isabella, the Mohammedans were allowed no alternative but to leave their country or embrace Christianity; hereupon, many of them quitted their native land, others, with inward repugnance, adopted the doctrines of the Gospel, but were driven, by the cruelty of the Inquisition and the oppression of the government, to repeated rebellions, by which their condition was always rendered worse than before. But their lot was most deplorable under the fanatical Philip II. and his successor of the same name. A command was first given that they should renounce their language, their national dress, and their peculiar customs; and as if even this tyrannical order were not sufficient to destroy the last traces of their Arabian origin and their foreign faith, they were mercilessly driven away from the Spanish territory. 800,000 Moors, men and women, old men and children, left the land of their birth, their blooming fields, and the houses their own hands had built. The flourishing plains of the south soon became a desert, agriculture decayed, and trade stagnated; prosperous villages were reduced to ruins, towns once animated by commerce became depopulated, poverty, dirt, and sloth, took possession of the once rich and happy country, the departed splendor of which is still attested by magnificent ruins. A similar fate attended the Jews; priests and courtiers divided the possessions and treasures of the banished.

The destruction of the privileges of the Estates and of the liberties of the people, were also consequences of this mischievous union between the crown and the altar.

4. ITALY.

a. UPPER ITALY.

§ 284. In Upper Italy, the two republics of Venice and Genoa raised themselves by their trade and navigation, to a prosperity that recals the memory of the most flourishing period of ancient Greece. Venice directed her view to the Adriatic and Ægean seas, and sought to make conquests on their coasts for the purpose of obtaining suitable havens, marts, and magazines; as those in Dalmatia, Greece, the Archipelago, Constantinople, and many other places. This remarkable city, which had originated from the union of several islands, became rich and powerful by her oriental traffic. Magnificent churches (the cathedral of St. Mark), gorgeous palaces (that of the doge), splendid squares (the place of St. Mark), boldly constructed bridges (that of the Rialto), made Venice a wonder of the world. But magnificence, wealth, and pleasures, could not make amends for the want of freedom. The original democratic constitution was changed, during the thirteenth and fourteenth centuries, into an oppressive hereditary aristocracy. An elected doge, with limited authority, stood at the head of the state; but the whole power rested in the high council, to which only a limited number of noble families (nobili), whose names were written in the golden book, had admission. For the purpose of preventing any alteration in the constitution of the state, a council of ten persons was furnished with dictatorial power, and provided with a state police of spies and informers, and a state Inquisition with subterraneous dungeons, racks, and leaden roofs. Every motion was watched, every word listened to, every movement of the people observed.

In the fourteenth and fifteenth centuries, Venice attempted to extend her rule on the Italian continent, and obtained possession, by the help of skilful generals, of Verona, Padua, Brescia, and many other cities and territories of Upper Italy. By this means, however, she came into hostile contact with other European states, and was not unfrequently threatened with destruction, particularly in the beginning of the

A. D. 1508. sixteenth century, by the league of Cambray, in which, the emperor Maximilian, Louis XII. of France, Ferdinand the Catholic of Aragon, and pope Julius II., united together for the purpose of dividing the Venetian territory. The French were already threatening the wealthy city, when the Venetian council succeeded in dividing the league, and gaining over the pope and Ferdinand. In this manner, Venice was saved, and the French driven out of Italy. But the wounds which Venice received in her eastern possessions by the establishment of the

Ottoman empire, and in her trade by the discovery of a sea passage to the East Indies, were incurable. Since then, the allegorical marriage of the doge with the Adriatic in the state vessel, the Bucentaur, has been a ceremony without a meaning.

§ 285. Genoa was the proud rival of Venice. The mutual jealousy of the two republics respecting the trade with the East was the occasion of many wars and many bloody naval engagements, in which, however, Venice was generally the victor. Genoa's splendid marble palaces, her havens covered with a forest of masts, and her exchange, bore witness to her wealth. But quarrels between democrats and aristocrats, between Guelfs (Fieschi and Grimaldi) and Ghibellines (Spinŏla and Doria), weakened her internal strength. Incapable of governing herself, she sought for foreign rulers, till at length she fell alternately under the power of the
A. D. 1528. French and Milanese. The excellent constitution which the naval hero, Andreas Doria, planned in the sixteenth century for his native city, after he had overthrown the French government there, and brought back the republican forms, restored the state to its outward independence, but by no means to its internal tranquillity.
A. D. 1547. Twenty years later, the handsome, rich, and accomplished Fiesco attempted to deprive the house of Doria of the office of doge; but the enterprise was frustrated by the unexpected death of the daring conspirator.

§ 286. Milan came gradually under the government of the wealthy family of Visconti, who obtained the ducal title from the emperor, and conquered the greater part of Lombardy by the aid of condottieri and mercenary troops. When the male line of the Visconti became extinct
A. D. 1450. in the middle of the fifteenth century, the Milanese transferred the sovereignty of their beautiful land, which was aimed at both by the French and Spaniards, to Francisco Sforza, the
A. D. 1500. most able of these condottieri. The conquest of the country by Louis XII. of France was facilitated by quarrels in Sforza's family. Louis carried away the duke (Louis Moro) prisoner, and suffered him to pine for ten years in a subterranean dungeon. The French were indeed driven out of Italy a few years later, and the son of the captive Moro raised to the dukedom of Milan; but the first war-
A. D. 1515. like action of the chivalrous Francis I. was the "battle of giants" of Marignano, in which the duke and his Swiss were defeated, and Milan again joined to the French kingdom. Ten years afterwards, the dukedom fell into the hands of the Spaniards, who remained in possession of it for nearly two hundred years.

§ 287. The western states of Upper Italy fell, for the most part, under the power of the counts of Savoy, who, by prudence, good fortune, and force of arms, gradually enlarged their originally narrow territory to a dukedom, which extended northward over the south of Switzerland to

Jura (Geneva, Vaud, Valais), and included on the south, Piedmont, with Turin, the county of Nice, and other territories. But when the warlike Swiss confederates on the north, and on the west, France, which was now united into a powerful kingdom, became the neighbors of Savoy's frontiers, its circumference began gradually to lessen. The Valais was lost in the Burgundian war (§ 293), Geneva freed itself during the contests of the Reformation, and in the wars which Francis I. carried on with Charles V., for the possession of Milan, duke Charles III. of Savoy, the ally of the latter, lost the greater part of his hereditary estates, which his son again received, with some loss, at the peace of Cam-
A. D. 1559. bresis. But his successors, by taking advantage of favorable opportunities, amply repaid themselves for their losses by conquests in other quarters (Sardinia, Genoa), and at length obtained possession of the kingly power.

b. MIDDLE AND LOWER ITALY.

§ 288. The trading town of Pisa was the first to flourish in Tuscany. When this city had fallen before the army of the Genoese, Florence raised itself above the other towns, and at length reduced Pisa itself to subjection. Florence was at first governed by the nobility; but when this class had been weakened by the party contentions of the Guelfs (Black) and Ghibellines (White), the government was obtained by the people, who were divided into guilds, and who consisted, for the most part, of masters of manufactories and workers in wool. But scarcely was a complete democracy established in Florence, when a new quarrel for supremacy sprang up between the rich merchants and the poorer artisans, the result of which was, that the state was governed alternately by a money aristocracy and by the democratic guilds. Love of freedom, patriotism, and refinement were developed in the midst of these contests, so that Florence might be compared to the ancient Athens. At length, the wealthy family of the Medici succeeded in so completely winning to themselves the affections of the poor by their kindness and benevolence, and those of the illustrious by their friendly affability, that
Cosmo de Medici, A. D. 1428-1464. Cosmo de Medici, a man of lofty mind and patriotic spirit, without assuming either rank or title, governed the Florentine state with almost unlimited power, and rendered it flourishing and powerful by successful wars abroad, and by encouragement of the arts and sciences at home. To him belongs by right the surname of "Father of his Country."

Lorenzo the Magnificent, 1472-1492. § 289. Cosmo's grandson, Lorenzo the Magnificent, trod in the path of his ancestors, and rendered Florence the seat of every art and science, and a seminary for all Europe. His court was ornamented with artists, poets, and writers; learned men from Byzantium, who were flying from the sword of the Turks, taught

the Greek language and literature in Florence. Under his rule, the
arts of sculpture, painting, and music began to unfold their choicest
blossoms. After Lorenzo's death, the animated discourses of the Dominican, Savonărŏla, induced the Florentines to drive out the Medici, and
to restore the democratic republic. But when the pope excommunicated
the bold "prophet of Florence," and the priests, against whose wealth
and luxurious lives his zeal had been chiefly directed, rose against him,
his enemies succeeded in effecting his overthrow; upon which, he was
condemned to be burnt as a disturber of the Church and a corrupter of
the people. The Medici soon returned; and when a demo-
A. D. 1498. cratic spirit, after some time, again awoke, and a second banishment followed, the emperor, Charles V., having an understanding with
the Medician pope, Clement VII., marched upon Florence, compelled it to
surrender after a close siege, and placed the cruel Alexander
A. D. 1530. de Medici as duke over the humbled republic. Alexander,
after many years' tyranny, was killed by the people, but the government,
nevertheless, remained in the hands of the Medici. Among the many
artists and writers that lived about this time in Florence,
Michael Angelo, A. D. Michael Angelo, who was equally distinguished as an archi-
1474–1563. tect, sculptor, and painter; and the clever statesman, Mac-
Macchiavelli, chiavelli, author of "The Prince," the "History of Flo-
A. D. 1527. rence," and "Discourses on Titus Livius," are the most
distinguished names.

§ 290. During the residence of the popes in Avignon (§ 255), violence
and lawlessness, occasioned by the bloody family quarrels of the Colonna
and Orsini, had reigned in the ecclesiastical state of Rome. This inspired
Cola di Rienzi, a man filled with enthusiasm for ancient Rome, with the
project of bringing back peace and the ancient greatness to the state by
the restoration of the republican constitution. His fiery eloquence transported the Romans. They established a new republican
A. D. 1347. Rome, raised the popular orator to the office of tribune, and
drove the nobles from their walls. But Rienzi's splendid part was soon
played out. Pride and vanity blinded him; oppressive taxes deprived
him of the favor of the people; so that his enemies succeeded in procuring his overthrow, and compelled him to fly. He returned, indeed, a few
years after, but it was only to meet with his death in a popu-
A. D. 1354. lar commotion. After arranging the division in the Church
(§ 263), a few distinguished popes made an attempt to heal the wounds
of the state and the Church. Among these, may be particularly men-
A. D. tioned Nicholas V., the founder of the Vatican library, and
1450–1460. Pius II. (Æneas Silvius, § 266), known as a clever and versatile writer,—both of them patrons of cultivation and science. On
the other hand, Alexander VI. (Borgia) was the scandal of all Christendom by his abandoned life, and his family (Cæsar and Lucretia Bor-

gia, in particular) were guilty of frightful crimes. Alexander's successor, Julius II., possessed a magnanimous disposition, but his pas-
A. D. 1503. sion for war suited ill with his spiritual office. He marched into the field himself, and enlarged the possessions of the Church by the addition of Bologna, Ancona, Ferrara, and other towns and territories. Leo X., the highly accomplished son of Lorenzo de Medici, united in the Vatican all the splendor of art and refinement as an inheritance of his house. But in studying the productions of Greek and Roman paganism, he lost sight of the doctrine of the Church and of reverence for the Gospel; yet he taxed the religious faith of the people by the sale of
Raphael, indulgences, that he might be able to support the expense of
A. D. building the magnificent church of St. Peter, and to reward
1483 - 1520. artists with a liberal hand. The "divine" painter, Raphael, was the ornament of his court.

In Ferrara, during the fifteenth century, reigned the younger branch of the house of Este, which was not less distinguished for refinement and encouragement of the arts and sciences than the Medici. Ariosto, the writer of "Orlando Furioso," and Torquato Tasso, the poet of "Jerusalem Delivered," were the ornaments of the ducal court of Ferrara.

§ 291. The descendants of Charles of Anjou reigned in Naples, which, since the fall of the house of Hohenstaufen (§ 239, 240), had become a papal fief. The Guelfic party found in them as zealous defenders, as the Ghibelline in the kings of Sicily of the princely house of Aragon. Two wicked queens, Joanna I. and Joanna II., filled the kingdom
Joanna I. A. D. 1343 - with acts of cruelty, war, and confusion. The latter, before
1382. her childless departure, named, first, an Aragonian, and after-
Joanna II., wards a French prince, for her heir, and by this means pro-
A. D. 1414— duced two parties, a French and an Aragonian, that con-
1435. tended till the end of the fifteenth century, with great bitterness and various success, for the possession of Naples, till Frederick the Catholic of Aragon at length gained possession of it by craft
A. D. 1504. and the success of his arms, and again united it with Sicily. The kingdom of Naples and Sicily remained subject to the Spanish sceptre for two hundred years, and was governed by a vice-king. Increase of taxation, and the destruction of the privileges of the Estates, gradually produced poverty and loss of freedom.

5. THE NEW BURGUNDIAN TERRITORY.

Philip the § 292. Philip the Bold had received the dukedom of Bur-
Bold, A. D. gundy from his father, king John of France, in fief. He
1363 - 1404. united to this, by inheritance and marriage, the Burgundian
John sans Franche Comtè, formerly an appanage of the German em-
Peur, A. D. pire, and the rich lands of Flanders, together with Artois,
1404 - 1419. Mechlin, Antwerp, and some other towns. His son, John

sans Peur, and his grandson, Philip the Good, extended their possessions still farther over the other states of the Netherlands, and established a kingdom that, in civilization, industry, and prosperity, could vie with Italy. Philip the Good was one of the most powerful and richest princes of his time, and his Netherland chivalry were distinguished by their splendor, adroitness, and polished manners. The wealthy trading and manufacturing towns of Ghent, Brussels, Antwerp, Bruges, Louvain, &c., possessed great privileges and liberties, and a warlike militia.

Philip the Good, A. D. 1419–1467.

§ 293. Philip's son, Charles the Bold, enlarged the dukedom and raised the splendor of the chivalrous court to the highest point. He was a man of vigor, courage, and warlike spirit; but ambition and violent passions rendered him rash, insolent, and obstinate. His efforts were directed to the enlargement of his dukedom into a Gallo-Burgundian kingdom, with the Rhine for its eastern boundary. But his undertakings were frustrated by the crafty and faithless Louis XI. of France. For when Charles the Bold threatened the duke of Lorraine (whose lands and chief city, Nancy, he was longing for), with war, Louis brought about an alliance between Lorraine and the Swiss. Hereupon, Charles, with a stately and splendidly equipped army, marched across the Jura against the Swiss, but suffered such a defeat in the battle of Granson, that the survivors were dispersed in disorderly flight; and the admirable artillery, together with a magnificent camp, filled with costly stuffs, gold, silver, and precious stones, fell into the hands of an enemy who did not know their value. Maddened by this disgrace, Charles, a few months afterwards, marched with a fresh army against the confederates. But the battle of Murten ended in the same way: the victors were again enriched with an enormous booty; Berne wrested the Valais from the ducal house of Savoy, which was in alliance with Burgundy, and the duke of Lorraine again gained possession of his lands, which had been seized upon by Charles. Misfortune confused the mind of the Burgundian duke: blind with rage, and meditating nothing but vengeance, he rejected every proposal of accommodation, and marched for the third time against the enemy, who were prepared for the encounter. But in January, 1477, his army suffered a third frightful overthrow in the frozen fields before Nancy, partly by the swords of the brave Swiss, Alsacians, and Lorrainers, and partly by the treachery of his Italian condottieri. Charles himself was killed in a frozen morass during the flight.

Charles the Bold, A. D. 1467—1477.

A. D. 1476.

§ 294. After the death of Charles, Louis XI. seized upon the proper dukedom of Burgundy (Bourgogne), as a vacant fief of the French crown, and attempted to get possession of the other lands. At this juncture, Charles's daughter, Mary, was married to the chivalrous Maximilian of Austria, who overcame the French

A. D. 1479.

and compelled them to relinquish their purpose. Mary died shortly afterwards by a fall from her horse, whilst hawking. The French king again renewed his treacherous intrigues for the purpose of exciting the towns of the Netherlands against Maximilian, who had been appointed guardian of his infant son, Philip of Burgundy. Ghent fell off; the guilds of Bruges kept him for some time a prisoner; Brabant wavered; but nevertheless, Maximilian, by his courage and conduct, brought the whole of the Netherlands to acknowledge his rights of guardianship. Philip's son, Charles (V.), who was born to him by the Spanish Joanna, and who was born in the beginning of the century at Ghent, inheri-
A. D. 1500. ted all the lands of his parents and grandparents. Yet his heart was with the rich, cultivated, and industrious Netherlands, which he had united into a whole by the acquisition of Utrecht, Gueldres, and some other towns, and added to the German empire, under the title of the Burgundian Circle.

6. SCANDINAVIA.

§ 295. After the daring sea expeditions and wanderings of the Normans and Danes (§ 204, 206) had ceased, an enterprising prince was here and there successful in raising himself above the other heads of tribes (fylken kings), and in founding a kingdom by uniting several tribes (fylken) together. This was effected in Norway by Harald Fair-
A. D. 875. hair; in Denmark, by Gorm the Old; and in Sweden, by
A. D. 900. the Ynglians. But it was with reluctance that the warlike Norman chiefs bowed beneath the authority of a supreme king, and many of the discontented renewed the expeditions by sea, and sought for a new home abroad. Thus, Rollo (Robert) in Normandy (§ 205). The contests of the kings with the chiefs of the tribes lasted for many centuries, and impeded the rapid and effectual introduction of Christianity into the Scandinavian kingdoms. For although the Gospel had been preached in the three kingdoms as early as the ninth century, by Ansgar, the "Apostle of the North," and single kings, as Harald Bluetooth in Denmark, and Olaf Skotkonung in Sweden, had been converted to it as early as the tenth century, yet the pagan worship of Odin still wrestled with Christianity for the mastership, for more than a hundred years. In Denmark, Harald's grandson, Canute the
A. D. 1025. Great (§ 207), and in Norway, Olaf the Saint, gave the victory to the doctrine of a crucified Saviour; but this did not take place in Sweden till the middle of the twelfth century, in the reign of Eric the Pious, and not till even later than this among the half-savage Fins. Christianity produced the most beneficial effects in the Scandinavian kingdoms. The Benedictine monks not only laid the germ of spiritual development, but they also improved the manner of living, and made the people acquainted with the advantages of civilization. They introduced

the art of writing, and banished the rude and defective Runic characters by the Latin alphabet; they encouraged agriculture and planted new kinds of corn; they built mills, opened mines, and accustomed the warlike people to the arts of peace, to trade and agriculture. Christianity diminished the vast gulf that had hitherto existed between freemen and slaves, by awakening in every breast the sentiments of the dignity of human nature, and the equality of all men in the sight of God. The clergy, moreover, obtained great wealth, privileges, and possessions, so that they could place themselves on terms of equality by the side of the freeholders of land. But the peasant class, on the other hand, remained in a state of dependence, and the towns arrived at neither prosperity nor importance.

§ 296. Denmark, to which Norway was united, acquired a great extent in the eleventh and twelfth centuries, under a few warlike kings. Waldemar II., the Conqueror, prosecuted the conquests of his father and grandfather on the coasts of the Baltic with such success, that he at last united all the Slavic lands on the south and east coasts of the Baltic, from Holstein to Esthonia, — Lauenburg, Mecklenburg, Pomerania, a part of Prussia, the coast land of Courland, Livonia, and Esthonia, with his other possessions, and could call himself king of the Danes and Slavi, and lord of Nordalbingia (Sleswick-Holstein). But his severity engendered hate and bitterness; so that when, whilst engaged in the chase, he fell into the power of count Henry of Schwerin, whom he had deeply injured, and was kept prisoner by him for more than two years in the strong castle of Danneberg; the princes who were his vassals revolted from him and maintained their independence with the sword; so that, in a short time, the proud fabric of Waldemar fell to the ground. Hamburg and Lübeck became free imperial towns; the present republic of the Ditmarsens regained its independence, and the German provinces returned to the government of the emperor. After Waldemar II.'s death, there occurred a time of internal confusion, which was taken advantage of by the aristocracy of nobles to increase their privileges. In addition to their freedom from taxes, the holders of land now obtained a jurisdiction peculiar to themselves. Waldemar III. again governed with a firm hand: his daughter, Margareta, united the three Scandinavian kingdoms under one sceptre, by the Union of Calmar.

Waldemar II., A. D. 1202–1241.

A. D. 1227.

Waldemar III., A. D. 1340–1375.

A. D. 1397.

§ 297. In Sweden also, the power of the kings had been much diminished, and that of the chivalrous nobility increased, by the protracted contests for the crown. Even the powerful family of the Folkungs, which had ascended the throne about the middle of the thirteenth century, succumbed in a few generations to the strokes of fate which smote all the princely houses of Sweden. Of the seven kings of this royal house, five were dethroned, and died either in prison or banishment.

A. D. 1363. After the deposition of the last Folkung, Magnus II., the Swedish throne descended upon his sister's son, Albert of Mecklenburg, who, however, after a few years, was conquered and robbed of his kingdom by the Danish Margareta; whereupon Sweden concluded the Union of Calmar with Denmark. A. D. 1397.

This Union of Calmar proved a blessing to neither of the three kingdoms. In Denmark and Norway, under the weak kings who succeeded Margareta, the power of the state fell more and more into the hands of the rich nobles, whilst Sweden was treated and governed by the Danish kings almost as though it were a conquered country. Dissension soon loosened the bonds of the Union of Calmar, without, however, tearing them completely asunder. The Hanseates, who sought to prevent a firm union of the three kingdoms by every possible method, encouraged these divisions from interested motives. The house of Oldenburg assumed the government of Denmark, in the person of Christian I. Sweden, also, at the same time, obtained a sagacious and valiant ruler in Steno Sture. This prince curbed the insolence of the nobles, elevated the peasant and burgher classes, founded the university of Upsala, and invited men of learning and printers from foreign lands into the country. Steno Sture governed the kingdom with almost absolute power; but when his second successor, Steno Sture the younger, quarrelled with the archbishop of Upsala, the tyrannical Christian II. succeeded, by the aid of the latter, in establishing anew the supremacy of Denmark over Sweden. Steno Sture was overcome in the field and mortally wounded, whereupon Christian II. commanded ninety-four of the most influential and powerful persons to be beheaded in Stockholm. But this cruelty, after a few years, dissolved forever the bonds between Denmark and Sweden.

Christian I., A. D. 1448–1481.

Steno Sture, A. D. 1471–1504.

A. D. 1520.

7. HUNGARY.

A. D. 973. § 298. Shortly after Otho's victory on the Lechfeld (§ 210) had put an end to the incursions of the Hungarians, Geisa became a convert to Christianity, and ordered the doctrines of the Gospel to be taught to his own people by German missionaries. What he began was brought to a conclusion by his son, Stephen the Pious, who received the kingly dignity from the pope. He provided for the diffusion of Christianity, (to which the Maggyars, partly from inherent barbarism, and partly from dislike of the Germans, were averse,) by founding monasteries, and calling the Benedictine monks into the country; he reduced the state to order by dividing the kingdom into comitates (shires), and by intrusting the management of the affairs of the army, the government, and the administration of

Stephen the Pious, A. D. 1000.

justice, to intendants appointed by himself: he became a legislator, inasmuch as he accustomed his subjects to civil order, agriculture, and industry. But the warlike character of the Magyars, and their repugnance to the Christian worship of the West, which brought servitude, soccage duties, and the troublesome labors of agriculture with it, in place of the old wild freedom, occasioned desolating wars and fresh confusion after the death of Stephen.

Geisa II., A. D. 1150.

Under Geisa II., troops of Flemish and Low-German settlers established themselves in Transylvania, who, under the name of Saxons, retain to this day the manners, customs, and institutions of their fatherland. By patience and industry, they have converted the land from a desert into a blooming region, with rich towns and prosperous villages, and have vigorously defended their liberties against all attacks. In the thirteenth century, the Hungarian nobles (magnates) wrested a charter ("the golden privilege") from the king, Andreas II., which secured important privileges to the clergy and nobility, and, like the Magna Charta of England (§ 276), formed the foundation of the free constitution of Hungary. An infringement of the "golden privilege" by the king justified the nobles in an armed opposition.

A. D. 1234.

§ 299. When the royal house of Arpad was extinguished by the death of Andreas III., Hungary became an elective kingdom. Hereupon, Louis the Great, of the royal Neapolitan house of Anjou, was raised to the throne. Under this distinguished king, Hungary reached the highest point of its external power and domestic prosperity. He obtained the crown of Poland, extended the frontiers of Hungary to the Lower Danube, and made the Venetians his tributaries. The hills around Tokay were planted with vines, the administration of justice was improved, the citizens and peasants were secured against oppression and arbitrary treatment; schools for education were established. After the death of Louis, who conducted many wars in Italy, long and violent contests were carried on for the throne, at the termination of which, the German emperor, Sigismond, united the Hungarian crown with his others, and arranged the representation of the kingdom by means of Estates. Under the weak successors of his daughter, Hungary would have fallen a prey to the Ottoman Turks, had not the heroic Huniades saved the land by his valor and military skill. The nation, out of gratitude, conferred the throne of Hungary upon his energetic son, Matthias Corvinus, who occupied it for thirty-two years, as the worthy successor of Stephen the Pious and Louis the Great. Matthias shone in the arts of peace as well as in those of war. He held the power of the Ottomans in check, enlarged his territories towards Austria and Germany, and improved the affairs of the army. A new university was founded by him in Buda,

Louis the Great, A. D. 1342-1382.

Matthias Corvinus, A. D. 1458-1490.

a library established, and the civilization of the people promoted by the introduction from all quarters of men of learning and artists, printers and architects, gardeners, persons skilled in agriculture, and artificers. These advantages were again lost under his successors. The Turks carried their victorious arms over Belgrade, the western acquisitions were surrendered by treaties of peace; at the same time, the royal power was so curtailed, that henceforth, not only the levying of taxes, but even war and peace were dependent upon the National Diet, and at length, the magnates took possession of the whole authority for themselves. The fall of Louis II. at Mohacs (§ 307) occasioned a contest for the crown, the result of which was, that the country was divided into two halves: Transylvania and East Hungary, as far as the Theiss, which was under the dominion of the Turks; and West Hungary, which Ferdinand of Austria incorporated for some time with his other dominions, till the whole fell into the hands of his successors.

A. D. 1526.

8. POLAND.

§ 300. The vast plains of the Vistula and the lands on the Oder and the Wartha were inhabited by Slavonic tribes, who were sometimes governed by a single chief, and sometimes divided into several principalities. From the time of the conversion of duke Miesco (Mieceslav) to Christianity by German missionaries, Poland was looked upon as a fief of the German empire, but was very slightly connected with it, and in the time of Frederick II. rendered itself entirely independent. The kingdom of Poland was torn and weakened by many divisions, so that, in the twelfth century, the Silesian principality on the Oder was entirely dissevered from it, and united with Germany. Poland first rose to importance in the fourteenth century, when Vladislaus IV. permanently united the principalities on the Wartha (Posen, &c.), as Great Poland, with the lands on the Vistula (Little Poland); had himself crowned in Cracow, and transmitted the title of king to his posterity. His son, Casimir the Great, who extended his domains over Gallicia and Red Russia, and built a university in Cracow, also deserved well of Poland by his merits as a legislator. But despite his efforts to diminish the power of the nobility and to increase that of the cities, no free burgher class could flourish in a nation so addicted to war and so deficient in civilization. The dominion that rested on the sword still remained with the nobles,—money, retail traffic, and trade, with the Jews; the peasant led a wretched life as a serf, and won but a miserable support from the fertile corn-fields of the Vistula.

Vladislaus IV., A. D. 1320.

Casimir the Great, A. D. 1333-1370.

§ 301. With Casimir, the male line of the Piasti became extinct; whereupon, the Poles transferred the crown to his sister's son, Louis the Great of Hungary. From this time forth, Poland became an elective kingdom; the nation, nevertheless, adhered for two hundred years to the race of the Jagellons, which, however, was obliged to grant the nobles an immunity from taxes and other great privileges in return for its election. Under the first king of this race, Jagello (Vladislaus), Lithuania was added to the Polish empire, after Christianity had been established and the idols overthrown there. The woolen garments that were distributed during baptism attracted thousands of half-willing Lithuanians to the new faith. Jagello's second successor, Casimir IV., induced the German orders to relinquish Culm, Elbing, and Marienwerder, and to recognize the suzerainship of Poland; in doing which, he was obliged to purchase by fresh concessions the aid of the nobles, who, in the Polish diet, alone possessed the privilege of consenting to the raising of taxes and the levying of troops. That every noble might not always be obliged to appear personally at the Diet, it was arranged that a certain number of authorized deputies should be sent from all the Voiwodeschafts, to whom the king added besides a few representatives of the clergy and of the higher officials. Without the consent of this assembly, to which the burgher class was not admitted, the king could adopt no measure, either of taxation or legislation, nor take any important step in the government or in the conduct of war. The nobles were regarded as the only true citizens of the state: and the principle that they were all exactly on an equality, raised their power in the same proportion that frequent changes of the throne and wars of succession depressed that of the king.

Louis the Great, A. D. 1370 - 1382.

The Jagellons, A. D. 1386 - 1572.

Casimir IV. A. D. 1447 - 1492.

In the century of the Reformation, king Sigismond established the suzerainship of Poland over the dukedom of Prussia, which had been recently founded by the grand master of the German Order, Albert of Brandenburg, who was a convert to Lutheranism, and enfeoffed Gotthard Keltler, chief commander of the Order of the Sword, who had also gone over to Protestantism, with Courland: but owing to the selfishness of the nobles and internal dissensions, the Polish kingdom was unable, for a permanency, to afford any sufficient opposition to the advance of the Turks and Russians.

9. THE RUSSIAN EMPIRE.

§ 302. When the great grandson of the Varangian chief, Ruric (§ 206), Vladimir the Great, who held his residence in Kiow, introduced the Greek Christian Church into his dominions, the latter extended from the Dnieper to the lake of Ladoga and to the banks of the Dwina. But they suffered so much in their union and strength under his successors, by divisions among heirs and internal wars, that the Lithuanians, Poles, and Brethren of the Sword, &c., in the West, gained possession of large portions of terri-

Vladimir the Great, A. D. 1000.

A. D. 1237.

tory, and at length, the Moguls conquered all the land from the Dnieper to the Vistula, and made Russia tributary. The great khan of the Golden Horde of Kaptschak, whose residence, and fixed quarters were on the east bank of the Volga, exacted, during two hundred years, an oppressive tribute from the Russian princes and their subjects. It was not until the power of the Golden Horde had been broken by dissension, that the chief prince, Ivan Vasilyevitsch the Great of Moscow, succeeded in freeing his kingdom from tribute, and in extending it in all directions by successful wars. The rich city of Novogorod, which belonged to the Hanseatic confederation, and which had possessed, for centuries, a republican constitution, and had known how to defend its liberties by a stout militia, was subjected and robbed of its privileges, and a number of its chief citizens were removed to other towns. Ivan was not only a conqueror, but a legislator and politician, although in mind and manners he remained a rude and cruel barbarian. He adopted measures respecting the succession of the throne, to the end that the kingdom might not be farther divided; and he invited masons and mechanics from Germany and Italy, to plant the seeds of civilization among his barbarous people. He built the Kremlin (citadel) for the defence of his chief city, Moscow.

Ivan Vasilyevitsch, A. D. 1462-1505.

Since the destruction of Constantinople by the Turks, the Russian metropolitan (afterwards called Patriarch) had been elected by the native bishops, and thus the independence of the church maintained. Ivan's grandson, Ivan Vasilyevitsch, who first assumed the title of Tzar, or ruler of all the Russians, conquered Kasan and Astracan, extended his kingdom to the Caucasus, and made preparations for the discovery and subjection of Siberia. He laid the foundation of a standing army by the establishment of the brigade of arquebusiers (Strelitzes). The male line of Ruric became extinct with Ivan's son, Feodor.

Ivan Vasilyevitsch II., A. D. 1533-1588.

A. D. 1598.

10. MOGULS AND TURKS.

Zengis-Khan, A. D. 1227.

§ 303. In the beginning of the thirteenth century, Zengis-Khan (Temudschin), the chief of a warlike nomadic horde, marched forth to conquest from the elevated plains of Middle Asia. He scaled the Chinese wall and subdued the "celestial empire." Neither Hindostan, nor the vast empire of the Carismans on the Caspian Sea and in Persia, could withstand the savage strength of this advancing pastoral tribe. Bochara, Samarcand, and Balch, with all their treasures of art and science, perished in the flames. Zengis-Khan's sons and grandsons pursued his conquests. Batu subdued the lands to the north of the Black Sea, made Russia tributary, burnt Cracow, and filled Poland and Hungary with slaughter and desolation. At length, the Moguls (who are also called Tatars) crossed the Oder; Breslau was reduced to ashes, duke Henry of Lower Silesia fell, with the flower of his Christian warriors, on the field of battle near Leignitz, beneath the blows of the pagan nomads; the people took refuge in the mountains; the whole West trembled; the pope and the emperor, engaged in a furious quarrel (§ 236), did nothing towards aiding Christendom. Happily the enemy proceeded no farther. The bravery of the European warriors and the strength of their castles scared them away. They turned back from a land where there were no riches to attract them, and carried their arms against the luxurious khalifate of Bagdad, for which they prepared a bloody end. After the last khalif, with 200,000 Moslems had fallen, and the ancient seat of the empire of the Abassides had been plundered for forty days, the Tatars pressed forward upon Syria, where they destroyed the magnificent Haleb (Aleppo) and Damascus, and trampled the Christian and Arabian culture under the hoofs of their horses. In a few generations, the empire of the Moguls separated into a number of independent states. But the Russians on the east of the Volga still bore for more than two centuries the yoke of the "Golden Horde," and Hungary and Poland recovered but slowly from their devastations.

§ 304. Towards the end of the thirteenth century, the Ottomans, pressed upon by the Moguls, left the region they had hitherto occupied, on the east coast of the Caspian Sea, and descended upon Asia Minor. They were a warlike, nomadic race, professing the Mahommedan religion, and incited by their priests (dervishes) to make war upon the Christians. Othman marched into Bithynia, chose Prusa

A. D. 1299.

(Bursa) for the seat of his empire, and maintained his conquests against the indolent Greeks and their western mercenaries. His successors improved their army by forming the strongest and handsomest youths, whom they selected from their Christian captives, into an effective infantry (janissaries), by means of a military education.

Amurath I., A. D. 1361-1389.

After Amurath I. had reduced the whole of Asia Minor under his yoke, he passed into Europe, and subjected, in a few campaigns, the whole country between the Hellespont and the Hæmus. Adrianople was taken, embellished with splendid mosques, and selected for the seat of Amurath's government. His son, the energetic but cruel Bajazet, continued the victorious course of his predecessor with such success, that he was called the "lightning." He con-

Bajazet, A. D. 1389-1403.

quered Macedonia and Thessaly, penetrated through Thermopylæ into the desolated Greece and Peloponnesus, took Argos by storm, and allowed his swift horsemen to wander to the southernmost point of the ancient Laconia. At length, the West armed itself against this terrible enemy. Sigismond of Hungary, John of Burgundy, the flower of the French chivalry, and many German and Bohemian nobles, together more than 100,000 strong, marched to the Lower Danube. But in the bloody battle of Nicopolis, the Christians, despite their valor, suffered a great defeat. Many counts and knights fell into the hands of the Turks, and only obtained their liberty by a heavy ransom. 10,000 prisoners of inferior rank were put to death by the order of Bajazet.

§ 305. The victorious course of this mighty prince was checked by an enemy who trod a more vast and bloodier path than himself. This enemy was the Mogul ruler, Timour the Lame (Tamerlane), a descendant of Zengis-Khan, whose dilapidated kingdom he determined to restore. He left Samarcand, the charmingly situated seat of his empire, at the head of his warlike pastoral tribes, for the purpose of subjceting every nation between the wall of China and the Mediterranean, by the edge of the sword. After he had marched triumphantly through India and Persia, and destroyed Bagdad and Damascus, he filled Asia Minor with desolation and terror. Smoke, ruins, and hills of slain marked his victorious path. At this point, Bajazet relinquished the siege of Constantinople, and marched against the conqueror of the world. A fearful

A. D. 1402.

battle was fought near Angora (Ancyra), which, despite the valor and conduct of the Turks, terminated to the advantage of the Moguls. Bajazet was taken prisoner, and died the following year of grief. Timour's empire fell to pieces as rapidly as it had been formed.

Amurath II., A. D. 1421-1451.

§ 306. Bajazet's grandson, Amurath II., restored the shattered Ottoman kingdom to its ancient strength and former compass in Asia and Europe. He reduced the Byzantine empire to the strong chief city and a few neighboring places, and made it tributary. At this juncture, John VII. (Palæologus), determined to gain the aid of the West, by uniting the Eastern church with the Roman. With this object, he proceeded to Italy, accompanied by the Patriarch and a few bishops, where, after a long and vehement dispute upon certain religious and ecclesiastical questions, an ambiguous union was effected, which, however, was rejected by the zealous confessors of both churches, and the division made greater than before. Nevertheless, the composition was attended with this result, that the pope, by his legate, Julian, united the Christian princes in a campaign against the Turks, and in the mean while, attempted to persuade the Hungarians and Poles to an attack upon the Ottoman empire. Ladislaus, king of Hungary and Poland, and the heroic Huniades of Transylvania, crossed the Danube, but were totally defeated in the bloody battle of Warna.

A. D. 1444.

The young king was one of the slain; his head was carried about on a spear; the legate, Julian, was overtaken by death during the flight.

§ 307. The last hour of the Byzantine empire was approaching, when, upon the death of Amurath II., his energetic but bloodthirsty son, Mohammed II., became sultan of the Ottomans. Resolved upon making Constantinople the seat of his government, he advanced to the siege of the city, and harrassed it for fifty

Mohammed II., A. D. 1451-1481.

days by repeated assaults to such a degree, that, despite a gallant defence, it could hold out no longer. When the walls were scaled, the last emperor, Constantine, who still possessed some feeling for the old Roman greatness — for freedom, for religion, and for his country, — joined in the combat, and fell bravely fighting on the walls of his capital. The ancient seat of Byzantine magnificence became the residence of the sultan. The church of St. Sophia was turned into a mosque, and the half-moon of Islam was planted on the ruins of Christian civilization. Many learned men fled in terror to the West, and were instrumental in diffusing the Greek language and literature. The fall of Constantinople was followed by the conquest of Greece and the Morea (Peloponnesus), and the subjection of the countries on the Danube; it was only in the mountainous regions of Albania and Epirus, that the warlike hero, Alexander Castriota

A. D. 1467. (Scanderbeg), maintained an independent authority till his death, whilst the independence of Hungary was secured by the victory of Huniadès at Belgrade. But under Solyman

Solyman the Magnificent, A. D. 1520-1566. the Magnificent, who wrested the island of Rhodes (§ 227) from the knights of St. John, after a most gallant resistance, the half of Hungary, together with Buda, fell, after the terrible battle of

A. D. 1529. Mohacs, into the hands of the Ottomans, who now extended their ravages to the walls of Vienna, and alarmed the whole West. It was under Solyman that the Turkish empire attained its most extended limits and its greatest internal strength. In Asia, it embraced Syria and the whole country as far as the Tigris; in Africa, Egypt, with the sea-coast, and the piratical states of Algiers, Tunis, and Tripolis.

A. D. 1566. After Solyman, who died at an advanced age before Sigeth, in Hungary, (in defence of which the magnanimous Zriny met with the death of a hero), the warlike power of the Turks gradually decayed under the exhausting influence of debauchery and sensual indulgence.

BOOK THIRD.

THE MODERN EPOCH.

I. THE FORERUNNERS OF THE MODERN EPOCH.

1. THE SEA PASSAGE TO THE EAST INDIES, AND THE DISCOVERY OF AMERICA.

§ 308. In the fourteenth and fifteenth centuries, many great inventions began to be applied, by which the condition of the middle ages experienced a complete revolution. An Italian, Flavio Gioja, prepared a compass by means of the magnetic needle, by which a mighty impulse was given to navigation; gunpowder, which, according to some, was the invention of a German monk, Berthold Schwarz, and in the opinion of others, had been known at a remote period by the Chinese and Arabians, came into use in the middle of the fourteenth century, and prepared the downfall of chivalry. But the invention which was most
A. D. 1440. fertile in results, was the art of printing, which was called into existence by John Guttenburg of Mayence. His assistants in the work, who alone derived any advantage from the discovery, were Fust or Faust, a goldsmith of Mayence, and Peter Schœffer, a writer of books. The latter introduced types of metal in place of the wooden ones which Guttenburg had employed. At first, the art was kept secret; but it was carried by German workmen into all the countries of civilized Europe. By this means, books, which had hitherto been only attainable by the rich, came into the hands of the people, inasmuch as their cost was materially lessened by the ease with which they were multiplied.

§ 309. By the use of the compass, it became possible to extend navigation, which had hitherto been confined to the coast and the Mediterranean, over the ocean. This was first done by the Portuguese. The discovery of the islands of Porto Santo and Madeira, where the culture of the vine and sugar-cane succeeded admirably, was soon followed by the possession of the Azores and by the discovery of the Cape de Verd and the coast of Upper Guinea, rich in gold dust, ivory, gum, and Negro slaves. Lower Guinea (Congo) was also discovered in the reign of king John II. It was from this point that the daring Bartholomew Dias reached the southern extremity of Africa, the original name of which, "the Cape of Storms," was soon changed by the sanguine king into that of "the Cape of Good Hope." Eleven years afterwards (1497), the enterprising Vasco da Gama discovered from this point, in the reign of Emmanuel the Great, the sea passage to the East Indies, when he sailed from the east coast of Africa over the Indian Ocean to the coast of Malabar, and entered the haven of Calicut. It was here that the Portuguese, after some sharp encounters with the natives, established the first European commercial colony, — an undertaking which they completed with perseverance and courage.

A. D. 1486.

After Vasco da Gama and Cabral (who discovered Brazil during the passage, [A. D. 1500], and took possession of it for Portugal), came the gallant Almeida, who reduced many of the Indian princes to pay tribute and compelled them to submit to the establishment of factories in their chief cities. After he had been killed by the wild Hottentots on his return, Albuquerque, in whom heroic courage was united with wisdom, received the governorship of India. He conquered Goa, and made it the capital of the Indian colony; he stormed Malacca, the emporium of the trade of Father India, reduced the ruler of Ormuz in the Gulf of Persia to subjection, and caused the name of Emmanuel to be feared and respected. But the latter rewarded his faithful servant with ingratitude; and grief at this broke the hero's heart. During the next ten years, the Portuguese established colonies and factories on the island of Ceylon, and the coast of Coromandel, and subjected the spice-bearing Molucca and Sunda islands. Lisbon became the seat of the commerce of the world; but avarice and selfishness soon stifled the nobler emotions in the hearts of the Portuguese.

A. D. 1510.

A. D. 1515.

§ 310. The zeal for discovery, which was awakened by the enterprises of the Portuguese, inspired the bold Genoese, Christopher Columbus (Colon), with the thought of discovering a new way to the vaunted Indies, by a western passage. He imparted his project to his native city, Genoa, and begged for support; but there, as well as by the Portuguese and English, he was refused. At length, Isabella of Castile, in the joy of her heart at the fortunate conquest of Granada, allowed herself to be persuaded to fit out three vessels, and to intrust them to the bold voyager. The title of Great Admiral and Viceroy of all the lands and islands that should be discovered, and a tenth part of the revenue that might be expected to be received from them, were promised to himself and his posterity, as the reward of his success. On the 3d of August, **1492**, the little fleet left the Andalusian harbor of Palos, and passed the

Canary islands, sailing constantly to the westward. The fear and anxiety of the seamen increased with the distance they traversed, and at length broke into murmuring and open mutiny. The crew were already threatening their magnanimous leader with death unless he returned, when the discovery of the island Guanahani (since then called St. Salvador), on the 12th of October, saved him. They found a beautiful and fruitful country, with naked copper-colored savages, who looked on without the slightest suspicion, whilst their land was taken possession of in the names of the royal pair of Spain, and who exchanged their goods for toys and spangles; but the anticipated treasures in gold, precious stones, and pearls, were not met with in the abundance that was hoped for, either here or on the two larger islands of Cuba and Hayti (Hispaniola, St. Domingo), which were shortly afterwards discovered. After Columbus had established a colony on Hispaniola, he returned to Spain, and after a dangerous voyage, brought back to astonished Europe the intelligence of a new world, which, in consequence of the original error, received the name of the West Indies. In the course of his three following voyages, Columbus discovered more islands (for example, Jamaica), and at length, also, the north-east coast of South America, not far from the mouth of the Oronoco. But this new portion of the world did not bear the name of its discoverer, but that of its describer, the Florentine, Amerigo Vespucci. Columbus shared the lot of many other great men; he was not permitted to enjoy the fruits of his labors. The colony that had been left behind in Hispaniola had fallen into confusion, in consequence of quarrels among themselves and with the natives. When Columbus, for the purpose of restoring order, wished to punish some of the most licentious disturbers of peace, the latter made an accusation against him at the Spanish court. Hereupon, king Ferdinand sent a narrow-minded official to make inquiries, who commenced his undertaking by depriving Columbus of his governorship, and ordering him to be carried in fetters to Spain. Here he was indeed released from his chains, but nothing was thought about the fulfilment of the stipulated contract. Columbus, deprived of his offices and dignities, died,
A. D. 1506. shortly after another and unfortunate voyage, in Valladolid, whence his dead body was afterwards carried to Cuba. The fetters in which he had been brought bound to Spain, were placed with him in his grave, by his son Diego.

§ 311. A new spirit of heroism had been awakened by Columbus; all courageous men who were acquainted with the sea went forth to make discoveries. Who could wish to remain idle when so rich a field for gold, renown, and ambition stood open? The hardy and enterprising Balboa surmounted the rocky isthmus of Panama under in-
A. D. 1514. credible difficulties, and discovered the Pacific Ocean. The Portuguese Magelhaens, sailed through the straits, named after him, into

the Pacific, reached the East India islands, after enduring the extremities of famine, and thus made the first voyage round the world. Both died violent deaths, the former by order of Davila, governor of Darien, the latter by the hand of an assassin on the Philippines.

A. D. 1520. The most remarkable event, however, was the discovery and conquest of Mexico by Ferdinand Cortez. The contest
A. D. 1521. here carried on was not with savages, but with a people who dwelt in towns, exercised arts and trade, clothed themselves in cotton stuffs, and lived under a regular system of government, with a king, a rich nobility, and a powerful priesthood. With 500 valiant Spaniards, who were accompanied by a few native tribes (the Tlascalans) as allies, Cortez subjected a populous nation, who were deficient neither in warlike spirit nor patriotism, took their king, Montezuma, prisoner in his own palace, and conquered the chief city, Mexico. The frightful effects of the thundering ordnance, the stately cavalry, the splendor of the European military accoutrements, engendered a notion among the natives, that the Spaniards must be a higher order of beings, whom it was impossible for them, with their feeble strength and miserable weapons (iron was unknown to them), to withstand. Within two years, Cortez conquered the land, and put an end to the horrible idol-worship, in which thousands of men were every year offered in sacrifice; but he was prevented by the suspicious government from establishing a new and regulated system. He was recalled, and died forgotten in Spain, A. D. 1547.

A. D. 1529–1535. With still smaller means than Cortez, Pizarro and Almagro, men of great courage and enterprise, but without cultivation, and governed by selfishness and the coarser passions, effected the conquest of the golden land of Peru. The Peruvians, ruled over by the rich royal race of Incas, were a civilized nation of mild character, unstained by the frightful idolatry of the Mexicans, but also devoid of their military virtue. A contest for the throne among the royal family facilitated the conquest of the land by the Spaniards. After the cruel Pizarro had made himself master of the king, and, despite his promise to set him free in return for an enormous mass of gold, ordered him to be executed, he subjected the beautiful land which abounded in the precious metals,
A. D. 1535–1538. and founded the new capital, Lima. Francis Pizarro and his brother soon quarrelled with Almagro (who in the mean time had discovered Chili), and they turned their arms against each other. Almagro was overcome and beheaded, but his son avenged the death of his father on Francis Pizarro. The land was reduced to the brink of destruction by the wild rage of the discoverers. At this crisis, Charles V. sent a wise and prudent priest, Gasca, as governor to Peru: Gasca
A. D. 1548. subdued the rebellious troops, had the last Pizarro hung on the gallows, and then arranged the state anew.

§ 312. Much as we may admire the heroic courage and the enterprising spirit displayed by Europeans in the conquest of the New World, we must equally deplore the severity and avarice which impelled them to the most cruel ill-usage of the natives. Those who escaped from the sword, the destructive effects of gunpowder, and the multiplied diseases, were mercilessly destroyed by severe labors. They were compelled to take care of the plantations which the conquerors made on their property, to dig in the gold and silver mines which were opened in their country, and to carry burdens for which their feeble bodies were not fitted. It was in vain that well-meaning priests, who attempted as missionaries to bring Christianity to the savages, preached kindness and humanity, — selfishness hardened the hearts of the Europeans and rendered them insensible to the teaching of the Gospel; and when at length the noble priest Las Casas, with the purpose of lightening the lot of the Indians, recommended the more robust African negro for the severe labors of the plantations, this gave occasion to the horrible slave-trade, which was a curse upon the black population, without preventing the gradual extinction of the copper-colored native. The discovery of the New World and the introduction of American productions were attended with vast results on the European manners and mode of living. Have not colonial wares, coffee, sugar, tobacco, &c., since they have been in general use, become indispensable necessaries? Do not potatoes, which we received from thence, form the most important part of the food of the people? What influence has not the increased quantity of the precious metals, which the mines of Peru have yielded, exercised upon all the relations of life and upon the value of property? The natural sciences and geography have been so enriched, that since then they have had an entirely different aspect. Trade also took a different direction: — as formerly the Italian trading towns, so now the western states, Portugal, Spain, the Netherlands, and, somewhat later, England, became the centre of commerce and the seat of wealth. But as both the former fettered their trade from its very commencement, and excluded other nations from their colonies, the season of their prosperity was but transient.

2. THE REVIVAL OF THE ARTS AND SCIENCES.

§ 313. In the fifteenth century, Italy was the central point of Western civilization; many splendid courts and opulent cities contended for the glory of becoming patrons of the arts and sciences. The Medici in Florence (§ 288, 289), and several popes, caused manuscripts to be purchased, and founded libraries and academies; the printing establishments which arose in all quarters came to the assistance of their efforts. At first, attention was exclusively directed to the Latin language and literature; but when, after the taking of Constantinople by the Turks, many of the learned men of Byzantium took refuge in Italy Greek also came into fashion. Dictionaries and grammars were compiled; the comprehension of the ancient authors was facilitated by commentaries and translations, and a classical Latin style became the distinguishing mark of an educated man. The next consequence of the revival of classical studies was the establishment of fresh seminaries of education, first, in Italy, and afterwards, in the other countries of Europe. Many universities, gymnasiums, and educational establishments of all sorts arose, especially in Germany, which had long maintained a close intercourse with Italy; and many learned men, as John Reuchlin from Pforzheim (A. D. 1521), Erasmus of Rotterdam (A. D. 1536), and Ulrick of Hutten (A. D. 1523), rivalled the great Italians in the knowledge of the Greek and Latin languages and of science. The friends of the new culture were called Humanists; their opponents, the supporters of the scholastic wisdom of the middle ages, and above all others, the Dominicans, were named Obscurantists. The Humanists of all countries were connected with one another. Latin, then the universal language of all learned and educated men, and a rapid interchange of letters, which supplied the place of newspapers, facilitated this intercourse. The contest between the new culture and the Obscurantists, with their barbarous Latin, reached its highest point in the dispute which was conducted by Reuchlin with the Dominicans of Cologne. The latter wished to burn all the Hebrew books, because they were supposed to contain blasphemies against Jesus Christ. Reuchlin, who was appointed umpire in the matter by the emperor, declared the charge to be untrue, and opposed himself to the design. This so enraged the monks, that they accused Reuchlin of heresy, openly burnt one of his works, and condemned the study of the Greek and Hebrew languages. This produced a literary war, in which all the friends of education took the part of Reuchlin, and the cause of the Humanists obtained a complete triumph. The pope at length put an end to the contest: the Dominicans were condemned to pay the costs of the process; and when they delayed to do this, they were forced to discharge their obligations by Francis Sickingen. From the crowd that assembled itself around Reuchlin, proceeded the *Epistolæ obscurorum virorum*, which are said to have been chiefly the production of Ulrick von Hutten. In these letters, the proceedings and stupid insolence of the monks are faithfully but satirically displayed in their own barbarous Latin. Hutten, one of the boldest and most powerful advocates of Germany's freedom and independence, died, persecuted and a fugitive, on the island of Ufnau in the lake of Zurich, in the 36th year of his life. Erasmus of Rotterdam, an elegant scholar in ancient literature, fought, with all the weapons of wit and intellect, against schoolmen and monks. Among his numerous works, the most important are The Praise of Folly,—a satirical composition, and an edition of the New Testament in the original Greek text, with a Latin translation and paraphrase. At first, a friend of Luther

and Hutten, he afterwards turned from them and opposed them in vehement controversial writings.

II. THE TIME OF THE REFORMATION.

1. THE GERMAN REFORMATION.

a. DR. MARTIN LUTHER.

§ 314. The cry that passed through Europe in the fifteenth century, for a reformation of the Church both in its head and members, had remained unheeded by the popes; and the great ecclesiastical synods (§ 264, 266) had been followed by no results. The Church had refused the voluntary self-purification that had been required of her, and turned a deaf ear to the voice of the people. Since then, the abuses had not been diminished. The court of Rome derived a vast revenue from the churches of other countries; the lower clergy were lazy, immoral, and ignorant, and took little or no interest in the new culture and the impulse that had been produced by it; the higher clergy led an entirely worldly life, found their enjoyment in sensual indulgences and princely magnificence, and in the study of works of art and literature, and of the philosophy of heathen antiquity, frequently lost sight of the doctrines of the Gospel. Nothing but an impulse was wanting to unite the dissatisfied members of the Church in a mighty opposition. This impulse was given by Pope Leo X. For the purpose of defraying the expenses of the erection of the church of St. Peter, and of other works of art, Leo offered an indulgence for sale, through the Elector, Albert of Mayence, in which forgiveness of sins, reattainment of God's grace, and remission from the punishments of purgatory, were assured to the purchaser. Albert, who received one half of the profits, employed in Saxony the Dominican monk Tetzel, in the sale, who went so audaciously to work, that the Augustine monk, Dr. Martin Luther, who saw that real penitence and respect for the confessional were thereby endangered, felt himself compelled to affix ninety-five theses to the castle church at Wittenberg, on the eve of All-Saints, with the offer to defend them against any one. In these, he contested the efficacy of absolution without repentance, and denied the power of the pope to grant remission of sins to any except the penitent.

§ 315. Martin Luther was born on the 10th of November, 1483. Destined to study by his father, a respectable miner, he had devoted himself to jurisprudence, for four years, in Erfurt, when anxiety for the salvation of his soul, and the sudden death of a friend during a heavy thunder-storm, determined him to enter a cloister. He once more entertained himself among his friends with cheerful singing, music, and wine, and then shut himself up in the silent cell of an Augustine monastery at Erfurt. He here submitted himself to all the duties and servile offices of a mendicant monk, but without thereby obtaining alleviation of his melancholy, or of the sufferings of his soul. It was not until he arrived at the conviction that man can only be saved, not by his own works, but by the mercy of God in Christ, that his heart found repose. By the recommendation of the chief of the order, Staupitz, Luther was summoned to Wittenberg, in 1508, to give lectures in the University newly established by Frederick the Wise. He had attended with great diligence to his duties as teacher, preacher, and pastor of souls, when he was now called by Providence to a more extended sphere of exertion.

§ 316. This bold stepping forward of Luther, in whom a deep religious earnestness was not to be mistaken, found great sympathy in the whole of Germany. A summons was soon issued to him to come and defend himself in Rome; but upon the intercession of the Elector of Saxony, who was favorably disposed to the reformer, the papal nuncio, Cajetanus, undertook the examination in Augsburg. Luther, provided with a safe conduct, appeared in a poor plight at Augsburg: the proud Dominican thought to refute the humble monk by his theological learning; but Luther displayed more depth and reading than the former had given him credit for. After a short disputation, Cajetan commanded him to be gone, and not to appear again before him till he (Cajetan) should call him. After drawing up an appeal to the pope *better informed*, Luther fled hastily from Augsburg during the night. It was in vain that Cajetan required the Elector either to send the audacious preacher to Rome, or at least to banish him from his states. Frederick replied, that Luther's wish to be brought before an impartial tribunal appeared to him to be reasonable. This protection of the Elector was of the more importance to Luther, as the former, since the death of the emperor Maximilian, was conducting the government, until the princes could agree respecting a fresh election. For as the pope wished to exercise an influence on the election of emperor, he attempted to gain over the Electors to his own side. He sent his chamberlain, Miltitz, an adroit Saxon nobleman, with a golden rose, to Wittenberg. He was commissioned at the same time to dissuade Luther from farther proceedings against the Church. Luther promised to let the contest drop if the trade in indulgences was put a stop to, and silence imposed upon his adversaries as well as on himself; and to prove his sincerity, he required, in one of his writings, every man to give respect and obedience to the Roman Church, and assured the pope, in a humble letter, that it had never been his intention to attack the privileges of the Roman chair.

§ 317. But the wished-for reconciliation did not take place. John von

Eck (Eckius), professor in Ingolstadt, a learned man and skilful in argument, had a disputation with Luther in Leipsic. Here
June, 1519.
Luther, in the heat of controversy, maintained that the bishop of Rome had become the head of the Church, not by the ordination of Jesus, but by human arrangements made centuries later, and threw doubts upon the infallibility of popes and councils. Irritated at this audacity, Eckius at once composed a learned book, in which he attempted to prove that the papacy was derived from Christ himself through Peter, and that, consequently, it must be a Divine institution. Eckius hastened to Rome with this book, and procured a
June 16, 1520.
Bull, in which a succession of Luther's doctrines were condemned as heretical, his writings sentenced to be burnt, and he himself threatened with excommunication unless he recanted within sixty days. This proceeding of the Roman court, which condemned the German reformer upon the accusation of an opponent, without so much as hearing his defence, was disapproved of by all Germany. The Bull of excommunication, which was made known by Eckius, produced, therefore, very little effect; it was only in Cologne, Mayence, and Louvain, that the order for burning Luther's writings was carried into effect; the Bull was not even admitted into Saxony. By so much the greater was the effect of some vigorous pamphlets of Luther, "To the Christian Nobles of the German nation," and "On the Babylonian Captivity and Christian Freedom," in which he exposed without reserve the abuses and failings of the existing Church, and demanded their removal. Encouraged by the enthusiasm with which these writings were received, and the cry for freedom that resounded through the German nation, Luther now ventured to take a step that separated him by an impenetrable gulf from the Romish Church. He proceeded, at the head of all the students, to
December 10, 1520.
the Elster gate of Wittenberg, and there cast the Bull of excommunication, together with the canons and decretals of the Church, into the flames.

§ 318. In the mean time, Maximilian's grandson, Charles V. of Spain and Burgundy (§ 294), was elected emperor of Germany, and his first undertaking was to be an arrangement of the contentions of the Church. He appointed a diet at Worms, and ordered Luther, under the assurance of a safe conduct, to appear. Full of courage and confidence in God, but not without fear of experiencing the fate of Huss (§ 264), Luther arrived at Worms in the midst of the sympathizing crowd that was streaming thither. The splendid assembly, in which, besides the emperor and the papal ambassador (Alexander), there were present many princes, nobles, prelates, and deputies from the states, at first disconcerted him. When called upon to recant, he begged till the following day for consideration. At his second appearance, he had recovered the whole of his strength and resolution. He declared himself, freely and openly, to be the author of the writings that were produced before him; rejected the invitation to recant, with the words "That so long as he should not be convinced out of the Holy Scriptures that he was in error, he could not and would not retract, for that his conscience was imprisoned in God's Word;" and concluded with the exclamation, "Here I stand, I can take no other course; God help me. Amen." All attempts to induce him to soften this declaration failed; yet no violent proceeding was ventured upon. Luther departed in safety; many princes and members of the diet did the same; then, the ban of the empire was first uttered against Luther and his adherents, and his writings condemned to the flames. Charles V., at this time in more close alliance with the pope, was determined to exterminate heresy. But Luther was already secure. During his return home, the Elector Frederick had him seized upon, and carried as a prisoner to the castle of Wartburg, under the title of *Ritter George*. He lived here nearly a year; at first, he was lamented by his friends, till some bold fugitive pieces, and an angry letter against Albert of Mayence, who was again practising the sale of indulgences, convinced them that he was still alive and active. Albert repented, and discontinued the traffic.

§ 319. Whilst Luther, although troubled by sickness and melancholy, was leading an active life at the Wartburg, proceedings calculated to disturb tranquillity arose in Wittenberg, which were not repressed with sufficient earnestness by the pious and peace-loving Elector. Dr. Carlstadt, a man of confused mind and unsettled in his principles, abolished the mass, extended the cup to the laity, and exercised his zeal against images and ceremonies. He was soon joined by the so-called Zurickhauer prophets,—men without education, and under the dominion of fanatical feelings,—who declaimed against the baptism of infants, insisted upon the rebaptism of adults (hence called Anabaptists), and believed in immediate inspirations from God. Images, and the garments used in the celebration of the mass, were destroyed in some churches, monks fled from their cloisters, and confusion took possession of men's minds. Luther was no longer at peace in the castle of Wartburg. He hastened to Wittenberg, preached daily for a week against the overhasty and uncharitable innovations, dismissed the Zurickhauer fanatics, and won men's minds to a peaceable development of the Reformation. Wittenberg now became the centre of German culture. It was here that Philip Melancthon of Bretten, who, when a youth of twenty, had already fathomed the depths of learning, and by whose means the Saxon schools and church attained a high degree of prosperity, labored by the side of Luther. Luther's impetuous and boisterous energy was well fitted to pluck down, whilst Melancthon's mild and yielding nature was adapted to the work of restoration; and, as Melancthon, the great adept in, and promoter of, humane studies, sought, by his learned Latin

March, 1522.

writings to establish the new Church doctrines on a scientific basis, so Luther won the hearts of the people by his German writings and songs, and especially by his translation of the Bible. This Lutheran Bible, which was begun in the castle of Wartburg and finished in Wittenberg, after careful consultation with his friends, appeared completed in 1534, a master-piece of the German language and of the German spirit.

§ 320. The new doctrine soon spread beyond the limits of Saxony. Besides the Elector of Saxony, the energetic landgrave, Philip of Hesse, the founder of the university of Marburg, was, in particular, a zealous promoter of the Gospel. But it was the educated burghers of the imperial cities who distinguished themselves beyond all others by their zeal. The assembled people would often, of their own accord, set up a psalm or a hymn, and by this means gave an impulse to the abolishing of the mass. Where the church was denied to the evangelically-minded people, they held their devotions in the open air, in fields and meadows; and where religious motives were not sufficiently powerful, there the view of the Church property and worldly advantages helped out what was wanting. The whole of Germany appeared to be hurried away in this church movement, and a national Church, independent of Rome, to spring up from it. But the pope won over Ferdinand of
A. D. 1524. Austria, the duke of Bavaria, and several South-German bishops, to the alliance of Regensburg, in which they vowed mutually to support each other, and to exclude the innovations of Wittenberg from their dominions. Thus were the seeds of an unhappy division spread abroad in Germany at the very moment when the freedom and independence of the nation was the aspiration of her noblest spirits.

b. THE PEASANT WAR.

§ 321. The general call to freedom and independence, that, since Luther's appearance, had resounded through all Germany, filled the peasants with the hope of alleviating their condition by their own exertions. In this way originated the peasant war. At first, patriotically disposed men, like Sickingen and Hutten, appeared to wish to place themselves at the head of the movement, and to carry through the renovation of Germany, both in state and Church, by the sword. But Sickingen's early death during the siege of his castle of Landstuhl, and Hutten's flight, delayed the outbreak, and robbed it of plan and proportion. The fanatical discourses of the fickle Anabaptist, Thomas Münzer, who talked of abolishing temporal and spiritual power, and of setting up a heavenly kingdom where all men should be equal, and every distinction between rich and poor, noble and base, should disappear, confused the understandings of the excited peasants. It was not long before the people, from the Boden Lake to Dreisam, assembled themselves around Hans Müller of Bulgenbach, who had formerly been a soldier. He marched in a red mantle and cap from village to village, at the head of his followers. The chief banner was borne behind him on a carriage decorated with boughs and ribbons. They carried twelve articles with them, the importance of which they were ready to maintain with their swords. By these articles, they demanded the liberty of hunting, fishing, cutting wood, &c.; the abolition of serfdom, soccage duties, and tithes; the right of choosing their own ministers; and the free preaching of the Gospel. Their example was soon followed by the peasants in the Odenwald, and by those on the Neckar and in Franconia, under the conduct of the audacious publican, George Metzler. They compelled the counts of Hohenlohe, Lowenstein, Wertheim, Gemmingen, the superiors of the German Order in Mergentheim, and others to accept the articles, and to concede the privileges demanded, to their subjects; whoever dared to resist them, as count Helfenstein von Weinsberg, was put to a cruel death. They marched through the land burning and devastating; they destroyed the monasteries and castles, and took a bloody revenge on their oppressors and adversaries. Under the conduct of brave knights, like Florian Geier and Götz von Berlichingen of the Iron Hand, they penetrated into Wurzburg, whilst other bands ravaged the lands of Baden. The insurrection soon extended itself over the whole of Swabia, Franconia, Alsacia, and the lands of the Rhine. The spiritual and temporal princes became alarmed, and conceded a part of the demands of the irritated peasants. In Thuringia and the Harz, the revolt assumed more of a religious character. In Muhlhausen, Thomas Münzer had acquired great respect and the reputation of a prophet. He rejected Luther's moderate views, girded himself with the sword of Gideon, and wished to establish a Divine kingdom, the members of which should be all free and equal. The people, excited by his preaching, destroyed castles, monasteries, and the memorials of antiquity, in their barbarous fury.

§ 322. In the commencement, before the insurrection had yet assumed so formidable an aspect, Luther attempted to restore peace: he represented to the nobles and princes that they had been guilty of acts of violence; and at the same time, exhorted the peasants to refrain from rebellion. But when the danger increased, when temporal and spiritual things were mingled together, he published a forcible tract "against the plundering and bloodthirsty peasants," in which he called upon the magistrates to attack them with the sword, and to show them no sort of mercy. Upon this, the nobles and knights assembled themselves from all quarters against the rebels. The elector John of Saxony, the landgrave Philip of Hesse, and others, marched into Thuringia and won an easy victory, by means of their artillery, over Thomas Münzer and his half-armed peasants. A place of execution was set up before Muhlhausen, on which the Thuringian "prophet" was put to a bloody death after undergoing frightful tortures.

Truchsess of Waldburg, captain of the Swabian league, restored peace in Swabia, and then marched, in conjunction with the Elector of the Palatinate and the warlike archbishop of Treves, against the bands of Franconia, who were besieging the strong castle of Wurzburg. Here, again, superior military skill and better arms triumphed over the disorderly crowd. The insurgents, after a short defence, betook themselves to a headlong flight, in which most of them were killed; the prisoners were put to death, and a severe punishment inflicted on the citizens of the Franconian towns, who had sided with the rebels. The axe of the executioner was long busy in Wurzburg. The same was the case in Alsacia, and the Middle Rhine-land, and also the Black Forest, and at the sources of the Danube, where the insurrection had lasted longest. At length, Truchsess of Waldburg and the renowned condottiere, George of Frendsberg, succeeded, by dint of severity, in restoring order. In the majority of places, the peasants were again oppressed with all their former burdens, and in many spots the cry was loudly echoed, "If they have formerly been chastised with rods, they shall now be scourged with scorpions."

c. THE PROTESTATION AND THE CONFESSION OF AUGSBURG.

§ 323. The new Church grew stronger and stronger in the midst of battles and disturbances, and Luther's energy increased with opposition. He left the cloister of the Augustines in 1524, and, in the following year, married Catherine of Bora, who had been formerly a nun. Surrounded by a circle of sincere friends, and by his brothers in office, he now led the life of domestic happiness which was so well suited to his disposition. His energy and cheerful confidence in God were neither broken nor disturbed by his poverty, or the repeated attacks of illness he experienced. By his two Catechisms he laid the foundation of a uniform confession of faith, and of a better religious education. Melancthon, upon whom the Elector, about this time, devolved the troublesome task of holding a general visitation of the churches all over Saxony, was not less active. The Reformation made such advances by the united efforts of these two men, that the Catholic princes, both temporal and spiritual, became alarmed. They therefore passed a resolution at the diet of Spire, that no farther innovations should be made in religion, that the new doctrines should not be farther disseminated, and that no impediment should be given to the celebration of the mass. It was against this decree of the Diet, by which the Reformation would have been condemned to a fatal pause, that a *Protest* was entered by many of the princes and imperial towns. It was for this reason that they, in common with all those who rejected the authority of the pope and the doctrines of the Roman Catholic Church, received the name of PROTESTANTS. As the emperor would not receive the protestation, which was

A. D. 1529.

brought to him in Italy, the protesting princes and towns would at once have arranged a confederacy for their mutual defence, had not Luther and the evangelical theologians, with "a magnanimous scrupulousness," rejected every defence of the Word of God by worldly weapons.

§ 324. In the following spring, the emperor opened the splendid Diet of Augsburg. It was here that the *protesting* Estates presented their Confession, which had been drawn up by Melancthon both in the German and Latin languages, and approved of by Luther. In this Confession, they endeavored to show that they had no wish to establish a new Church, but only to purify and restore the old one. This Confession of faith, which was composed with great temperance and clearness, embraced, in the first part, the doctrines of the Reformers, laid down in as close accordance as was possible with the faith of the Catholic Church; and in the second part, the abuses against which the Reformers were contending. After the reading of the AUGSBURG CONFESSION, the assembly embraced the resolution of justifying the doctrines and usages of the Catholic Church by a refutation, and then seeing if it would not be possible to bring about a composition by a conference between men of moderate tempers selected from both parties. But the "Refutation," drawn up by Eckius, Cochlæus, and some others, produced but little effect, owing to the weakness of its arguments, and was entirely overthrown by Melancthon's "Apology;" the conference also led to nothing, since both the pope and Luther, who, during the Diet, had remained at Coburg, were averse to any further concessions. It seemed that the unity of the Church could be only restored by the sword. The protesting princes and the principal imperial towns rejected the decision of the Diet, by which they were prohibited from extending their doctrine and were proscribed as a sect, and quitted Augsburg. The resolution of the Diet that was determined on after their departure, in which the new sect was threatened with a rapid extirpation, and the sentence of excommunication denounced against all those who, within a certain space, should not renounce their arbitrary innovations, alarmed neither the princes, the peace of whose consciences was a matter of higher importance to them than the favor of the emperor, nor the reformer of Wittenberg, whose confidence and cheerful trust in God was at that time at its height, as is testified by the immortal hymn, "The Lord is a strong castle," which was composed during the storms of those days.

d. ULRIC ZWINGLE.

§ 325. The Protestant Church of Germany was unhappily, even at this time, divided into the Lutheran and Zwinglian. Ulric Zwingle (born 1484), a classically-educated, liberally-minded priest of republican principles, exerted himself zealously as canon of Zurich against the sale of indulgences by the Franciscan monk, Samson; against ecclesiastical abuses of all kinds; and against the custom of the Swiss, of engaging themselves as mercenaries in foreign services. Zwingle, a man of practical understanding, without the religious depth of mind or the disposition of Luther, did not busy himself with the reformation of doctrine and articles of faith, but with the improvement of life and morals. He set about the work also with far less ceremony, inasmuch as he wished to restore primitive Christianity in its simplest form. Having a good understanding with the chief council of Zurich, he undertook a complete revolution of ecclesiastical doctrine and practice, banished all images, crosses, candles, altars, and organs, from the churches, and administered the Lord's Supper, in which he recognized nothing but a token of remembrance and fellowship, after the manner of the early Christian love-feasts; that is, the communicants received the consecrated elements whilst sitting. This latter proceeding entangled Zwingle in a fatal controversy with Luther. Luther would not receive the words employed in instituting the sacrament, "this is my body," in the sense of "this represents my body," as Zwingle explained them, but asserted the bodily presence of Christ in the Lord's Supper. It was in vain that Philip of Hesse attempted to prevent this dangerous division by a disputation at Marburg. Luther saw a denial of Christ in the doctrine maintained by his opponent, and thrust back the brotherly hand that Zwingle offered him with tears. He also opposed himself to any union with the towns of Upper Germany which had adopted Zwingle's views, so that these presented their own confession of faith to the Augsburg Diet.

§ 326. The same disturbances succeeded the appearance of Zwingle in Switzerland as had followed that of Luther in Germany. In Zurich, Basle, Berne, in Schaffhausen, the Rhinethal, and other cantons, the Church was reformed according to the principles of Zwingle; in Appenzell, the Grisons, St. Gall, Glarus, and other places, the adherents of the old Church contended with those of the new; but in the four forest cantons (Schwitz, Uri, Unterwalden, and Lucerne), and in Zug, the Catholic faith remained predominant. This was occasioned, in addition to the influence exercised on the simple inhabitants of these original cantons by the monks and clergy, by the circumstance that the engaging in foreign military services, a custom opposed by the Reformers, here formed one of the principal means of support. These five places concluded an alliance with Austria, and suppressed every innovation with a strong hand; whilst Berne and Zurich, on the other hand, afforded their assistance with uncharitable zeal and violence in the frontier towns of the Reformation. In this excited state of men's minds, a war was inevitable, particularly as Zwingle entertained the project of effecting such a political revolution in Switzerland as would give the supremacy to the two most powerful cantons, Berne and Zurich. Mutual revilings of the clergy, which remained unpunished, increased the irritation and provoked hostilities

Zurich and Berne blocked up the public roads, and prevented the transport of goods and of the necessaries of life. This proceeding enraged the Catholic cantons. They made preparations in secret, and fell upon the people of Zurich. The latter, surprised, irresolute, and forsaken by the Bernese, marched with a troop of 2,000 men against an enemy of four times their number, but sustained a bloody defeat in the

A. D. 1531. battle of Kappel. The courageous Zwingle, who had marched with them as field preacher, fell beside the banner of the city, and with him fell the staunchest friends of the Reformation. His dead body, after being exposed to the insults of the enraged multitude, was at length burnt and the ashes scattered to the winds. This event restored the old Church in many places that were favorably disposed to the Reformation, and was the occasion of the religious divisions that since that time have prevailed in Switzerland.

2. THE WARS OF THE HOUSE OF HAPSBURG WITH FRANCE.

Charles V., A. D. 1500-1558.

§ 327. Charles V. reigned over an empire such as had not existed since the days of Charlemagne. Before arriving at years of maturity, he was already lord of the rich Netherlands, which had devolved upon him as his maternal inheritance; when a youth (after the death of his paternal grandfather, Ferdinand the Catholic), he obtained possession of the united Spanish empire, with the beautiful kingdoms of Naples and Sicily, and the newly-discovered territories in America in the West Indies; he inherited in early manhood the Hapsburgo-Austrian States (which he relinquished to his brother Ferdinand), and became the successor of his grandfather, Maximilian, on the imperial throne of Germany, by the choice of the Electors. He might say with truth, that the sun never set in his dominions. He was a man of rare sagacity and indefatigable activity; great in the cabinet, as director of the affairs of state, and brave in the field, as leader of the ranks of war. His antagonist and rival was Francis I. of France, who was as much renowned for his love of the arts and sciences, and for his chivalrous conduct in the field, as he was infamous for his tyranny, his luxury, and love of pleasure, and his devotion to his mistresses. An unextinguishable jealousy subsisted between Francis and Charles. Each wished to be the first prince in Europe; and each eagerly contested the possession of the imperial throne of Germany, which could alone procure him this supremacy. Charles triumphed, and from that moment Francis became his decided enemy, and sought every means of weakening his power. Four wars arose out of this contention, which were principally occasioned by Milan. This beautiful dukedom had remained in the hands of the French since the battle of Marignano (§ 286); but Charles claimed it as a fief of the German empire, and led a vast army, composed chiefly of German peasants, under the conduct of the valiant condottieri, Frundsberg,

Schartlin, and others, against the French and their allies, the Swiss. At that time, war was carried on with mercenary troops exclusively; no nation could venture to oppose themselves to the Helvetians and Germans; the knightly tactics of an earlier period had fallen before their matchlocks, as the castles before their heavy artillery. The French were conquered. They lost Milan and Genoa, after several bloody encounters, and were forced to retreat over the Alps. It was during the retreat, that the gallant Bayard, "the knight without fear and without reproach," fell by a ball from a German arquebusier. The imperial army, conducted by the Constable of Bourbon, the richest and the most powerful of the French nobles, who had entered into Charles's service for the purpose of revenging his injuries and wrongs upon the French court, marched into the south of France, but soon found itself compelled to retreat by the gallant resistance of the burghers of Marseilles.

§ 328. Francis I. himself now marched into Italy, at the head of a stately and well-appointed army, for the purpose of wiping off the disgrace of the defeat, and winning back that which had been lost. But being detained for a long time before the walls of Pavia, the active Bourbon succeeded in collecting a fresh army of peasants, and uniting himself with the Spanish general, Pescara. But want of money and the necessaries of life soon reduced the united forces to the greatest distress, whilst the wealthy camp of the French was abundantly supplied with every thing needful. Bourbon and Frundsberg took advantage of this circumstance to excite the peasants to attempt the storm of the French camp.

A. D. 1525. The bloody fight of Pavia, in which the French were defeated, originated in a nocturnal attack. Francis I. himself, after a chivalrous defence, was compelled to surrender, and to proceed as a prisoner to Madrid. 10,000 gallant warriors found their deaths on the field of battle, or in the waters of the Ticino. After a year's captivity, Francis, with inward reluctance, consented to the Peace of Madrid, in which he swore to renounce his claims upon Milan, and to surrender the dukedom of Burgundy.

Scarcely, however, had Francis, after giving up his two sons as hostages, regained his own kingdom, than the pope released him from his oath, and concluded a holy alliance with him, the king of England, and some Italian princes, for the purpose of delivering Italy from the Spanish yoke. The flames of war burst forth anew in Italy; the beat of the drum was again heard in the German states to summon the peasants to the standard. As this was an expedition against the pope, the Lutherans came forward in crowds, so that the brave Frundsberg was soon enabled to lead a gallant army across the Alps, and to unite himself with Bourbon. But money was soon wanting to pay the troops; a rebellion in the army gave such a shock to Frundsberg that he was deprived of speech by an attack of apoplexy, and shortly after lost his life. The troops demanded to be led to Rome, and Bourbon yielded to their wishes. It was on the 6th of May, 1527, that the Spanish and German soldiers scaled the walls of Rome. Bourbon was one of the first who fell. The licentious bands, unchecked by the presence of a leader, dispersed themselves through the city and committed every sort of outrage. The rich palaces and dwelling-houses were plundered, the churches robbed of their vessels and ornaments; the Germans insulted the pope and cardinals by ridiculous processions and mummeries. Clement was obliged to purchase his freedom under harsh conditions, and made use of the first opportunity to escape. The emperor affected a display of grief and displeasure at the injuries suffered by the head of the Church, though inwardly pleased at his humiliation.

In the meanwhile, the French had made some conquests in upper Italy, and then marched into Naples, for the purpose of wresting this kingdom from the Spaniards. But their army suffering severely from pestilence, and the troops of the emperor being reduced one half by their excesses in Rome, both parties became desirous of peace. The contending kings arranged their differences by the interposition of the mother of Francis and the aunt of Charles, in what was called the Ladies' Peace of Cambray; in virtue of which, Francis relinquished his pretensions to Milan, and paid two million crowns for the ransom of his two sons, but retained possession of Burgundy. The pope also, and the Italian princes, soon made their peace. Charles was invested with the Roman and Lombard crowns by Clement, who lived with him in Bologna under the same roof, and promised, in return, to exterminate heresy, and to bring back the expelled Medici to Florence. The latter project was accomplished; Florence was conquered and deprived of its republican constitution (§ 289). But the restoration of the unity of the Church was no longer in the power of man. The Diet of Augsburg, that was appointed for this purpose, did not conduce to the desired result (§ 324).

A. D. 1529.

§ 329. Francis, however, did not relinquish the thought of again recovering the dukedom of Milan, and even entered into an alliance with the Turks a short time after, for the purpose of attaining this object. In the same year in which Charles took Tunis by a gallant attack, put an end to the piracies of the Mohammedan prince, Hayraddin Barbarossa, and set 20,000 Christian captives at liberty, Francis made a sudden campaign into upper Italy, and took possession, as a preliminary step, of Savoy and Piedmont, the duke of which was a relative and ally of Charles. But in the following year, Charles marched with a stately army into Provence, for the purpose of carrying the war into his enemy's own territory; but was compelled to retreat with loss, in consequence of the French general, the Constable Montmorenci, reducing the whole of the level country between the Rhone and

A. D. 1535.

the passes of the Alps to a desert, and thus producing scarcity and disease in the emperor's army. But as the whole of Christendom was indignant at the alliance between Francis and the Ottomans, who committed horrible devastations in lower Italy and the Greek islands, Pope Paul III. interposed as a mediator, and brought about the
A. D. 1538. conclusion of the third war by the ten years' truce of Nice, which allowed every one to retain that of which he was then in possession. A personal interview between the two monarchs was to have obliterated all their differences forever; and Charles was so
A. D. 1539. convinced of the knightly faith of his rival, that, in the following year, when an insurrection in Ghent required his immediate presence in the Netherlands, he took his road thither through Paris. But this friendship was not of long duration. In the year 1541, Charles undertook
A. D. 1541. a second African expedition, for the purpose of completely destroying the corsairs, who rendered the Mediterranean insecure from Algiers, as they had formerly done from Tunis. But this time, the attack was frustrated by the storms and rains of the later autumn, and by the attacks of the enemy, which were rendered particularly dangerous by the swampy character of the ground. The emperor, who magnanimously shared all the dangers and sufferings of the meanest of his followers, was obliged to retreat without effecting his object, after suffering a considerable loss in ships and troops. This termination of the enterprise may have filled the French king with the hope that he might at length be able to overpower his adversary. He, therefore, after effecting
A. D. an alliance with the sultan, commenced a fourth war against
1542-1544. the emperor. But when the latter marched with a vast army out of Germany into Champagne, and approached within two days' march of the terrified capital, Francis hastened to conclude
A. D. 1544. the peace of Crespy. From this time, the supremacy of the house of Hapsburg in Italy remained undisputed. Francis I. died three years afterwards, but his son and successor, Henry II.,
Henry II., A. D. 1547-1559. followed the same path. During the war of religion in Germany, he entered into an alliance with the Protestant princes (§ 337), whilst in his own dominions he suppressed the new doctrines by bloody persecutions. When Charles V. at length quitted the world's stage, the war was still continued for a few years between his son, Philip II., and the French king, till at length the peace of Chateau-
A. D. 1559. Cambresis put an end to the open contest between the two monarchs, without, however, extinguishing the hereditary animosity between the royal houses of France and Hapsburg.

3. THE WAR OF RELIGION IN GERMANY.

§ 330. This war, and the apprehensions that were entertained of the Turks, who led army after army into the Austrian territories, prevented

the emperor from putting into effect the resolution of the Diet of Augsburg against the German Protestants, and compelling them by force to return to the bosom of the Catholic Church. When, in consequence of this order, the imperial chamber began to proceed against the evangelical states on account of their confiscation of ecclesiastical property, the Lutheran princes and cities, under the conduct of the Elector of Saxony and the landgrave of Hesse, formed themselves into a league at
A. D. 1531. Smalcald, in the Thuringian forest, for their mutual defence in case any of them should be attacked for the word of God's sake. In the following year, the emperor concluded the peace of Nuremberg with this league, in which both parties promised to refrain from hostilities till a Council of the Church, the calling of which was vehemently urged upon Clement VII. by the emperor, should be assembled. The law proceedings were, in the mean time, to cease. This treaty bound the hands of the Protestants, without giving them any assurance for the future; but afforded great facilities for the diffusion of the Gospel over the whole of Germany. The introduction of the Lutheran form of worship into Wirtemberg was an event of the greatest importance. Duke Ulrick, a hasty-tempered and cruel man, who, from motives of jealousy, had slain a knight of his court (Hans von Hutten) with his own hand, had compelled his wife to take flight by his bad treatment, had oppressed his subjects and conquered the imperial city of Reutlingen, was at length outlawed for disturbing the peace of the country, and driven from his land and vassals by the Swabian league. For fourteen years, Ulrick was compelled to lead a wandering life abroad, and to shun his dukedom, which, in the mean time, was placed under the government of Austria, when the landgrave Philip of Hesse embraced the resolution of restoring to Wirtemberg the duke, who was then living at his court. He marched into Swabia with a well-appointed army, defeated the Austrian governor at Laufen on the Neckar, and reëstablished the lawful ruler. Ulrick was received with joy by his people, who had forgotten his former tyranny, and who were easily induced to receive the evangelical doctrines which Ulrick had adopted in his misfortunes, and which he now had disseminated by Brenz and Schnepf. The Church in Wirtemberg soon became Lutheran, and Tübingen was one of the most distinguished seminaries of evangelical learning.

§ 331. But the new Church was not wanting in spurious growths. The doctrine of the Anabaptists, who mistook their own passions for divine inspirations, had not been suppressed by the death of Thomas Münzer. (§ 322.) Notwithstanding the opposition of the Reformers and the discouragement given by every lawful magistrate, it would re-appear here and there, in places where it had been secretly carried by fugitives. The doctrines of these Anabaptists displayed themselves in their most frightful shape in Munster. It was in this place that the Reformation had made violent way for itself, and had compelled the bishop and canons to take flight. But it soon became evident that Rottman, the most influential of its preachers, entertained Anabaptist notions. When two vagabond prophets from the Netherlands, Jan Matthys and his countryman and disciple, the tailor, John Bockhold (called John of Leyden,) joined themselves to him, the Anabaptist party in a short time attained so complete a supremacy, that they got possession of all the city offices, drove all the inhabitants who were not of their own way of thinking out of the town in the midst of winter, and divided their property among themselves. They now established a religious commonwealth, in which Matthys possessed unlimited power, introduced community of goods, and conducted the defence of the city against the besieging army of the bishop of Munster. The fanaticism rose to its height when Matthys was killed in a sally against the enemy, and Bockold was placed at the head of the commonwealth. This man transferred the government of the city to twelve elders, whom he selected from the most violent of the fanatics, and among whom, Knipperdoling, who was burgomaster and executioner, played the most distinguished part. He then introduced the practice of polygamy, and mercilessly put to death those who indignantly denounced this outrage to Christian morality. When this crazy fanaticism had reached its highest pitch, the prophet assumed the title (from Divine inspiration) of "King of the New Israel." This "tailor king," ornamented with the insignia of his rank (a crown and a globe suspended by a golden chain), and magnificently clothed, held his sittings for the administration of justice in the market-place of Munster, where the "chair of David" was set up, and introduced a government of mixed tyranny and fanaticism, in which spiritual pride and carnal lust were most repulsively associated.

For a long time, the Anabaptists resisted the attacks of their imperfectly armed enemies with courage and success; when the besieging army had been reinforced by the empire, and the closely pressed town began to suffer the horrors of famine, they still resolutely maintained their defence; and even when the enemy were within their walls, they still resisted with the courage of desperation. Rottman fell fighting; John of Leyden and Knipperdoling were put to death by torture, and their dead bodies suspended in iron cages on the tower; the others were either executed or expelled the city. The bishop, the canons, and the nobility, returned and introduced Catholicism again in all its rigor, which since that time has retained its preëminence in Munster.

After a few decenniums, the Anabaptists experienced a wholesome reformation of their doctrines and discipline from Menno, in which they have continued to the present day, under the name of Mennonites. They are still distinguished by simplicity of dress and manner of living, by their rejection of a separate priesthood, of infant baptism, of oaths, of military service, &c.; but they have given up those principles of an earlier period which were dangerous to morality and the state. They lead a quiet life as tenant farmers and peasants.

§ 332. Shortly after this, the Reformed doctrines gained admission into the duchy of Saxony and the electorate of Brandenburg, by the death of two princes who had hitherto clung resolutely to the Roman Catholic creed. Duke George of Saxony was followed by his brother
A. D. 1539. Henry, who, like his son Maurice, was devoted to the Reformation, and ordered the Reformed worship to be established in Leipsic, Meissen, and Dresden. In the same year, Joachim II. received the Lord's Supper under both forms in Spandau, upon which the country embraced the Protestant doctrine. The conversion of Saxony and Brandenburg was decisive for the whole north of Germany. Henry of Brunswick-Wolfenbüttel, a cruel and profligate man, alone adhered to the ancient Church, less from conviction than from animosity to the landgrave of Hesse, the former friend of his youth. But the Gospel triumphed even in Wolfenbüttel, when, after a furious controversy, injurious alike to the dignity of princes and human nature, Henry was overpowered by Hessian and Saxon troops and carried into captivity. Otho Heinrich ordered the Lutheran doctrines to be taught in the Upper Palatinate, by the Nuremburger preacher, Osiander; and a few weeks before Luther's death, the Eucharist was administered in both forms in the Palatinate of the Rhine, after the congregation which assembled on the 3d of January to hear mass, in the Church of the Holy Ghost, had set up the evangelical hymn, "Salvation hath visited us." Baden Durlach also acknowledged the Reformed confession; and when the Elector, Hermann of Cologne, proposed a moderate plan of reformation to his Estates, and the duke of Cleves appeared inclined to join the league of Smalcald, it seemed that the Catholic Church of Germany must succumb, unless a stop were put to the progress of the Reformation by force. The emperor was convinced that neither Diets nor religious discussions could heal the division in the Church; his hopes rested entirely on the general Council, which Pope Paul III. had summoned at Trent. But the Protestants, who foresaw that their doctrines would be condemned in a Council that was thus held under the authority of the pope, rejected it, as being neither free nor impartial, and demanded a general Synod of the Church of Germany. This destroyed the emperor's last hope of an amicable arrangement, and determined him to attempt the restoration of
Luther dies, the Church by force of arms. One year after Luther's
Feb. 18th, death, at his native city of Eisleben, whither he had been
1546. summoned to compose a difference, the war of Smalcald broke out between Charles V. and the Protestant princes and cities of Germany.

§ 333. When the emperor had determined upon war, he entered into a secret alliance with the pope, who promised him subsidies of money, with the spiritual Electors, and with the duke of Bavaria; but he found the most important of his allies in the Protestant duke, Maurice of Saxony. This young, shrewd, and military prince, who, since 1541, had been the ruler of Albertine Saxony, had long separated himself from the league of Smalcald and joined the emperor, out of envy and hatred to his cousin, John Frederick, although Philip of Hesse was his father-in-law. This alliance was again renewed. Maurice promised obedience and devotion to the emperor, and submission to the resolutions of the Tridentine Council, provided it gave its sanction to the three chief points in the Protestant view,—justification by faith, the cup, and the marriage of the clergy. Charles, in return, held out the prospect of an increase of his territories and the electorship of Saxony. The Protestants had so little suspicion of this arrangement, that when the Smalcald forces marched into the field, the Elector, during his absence with the army, made over the government of Courland to his cousin Maurice. The brave Schärtlin, whom the Upper German cities had chosen general, wished to bring matters to a conclusion, by making a rapid advance upon Regensburg, where the emperor was posted with a handful of troops; but the council of war, fearful of doing injury to Bavaria, forbade the enterprise. Upon this, Schärtlin turned towards Tyrol, with the purpose of cutting off the advance of the Italian troops, or of dispersing the Council of Trent;—but this undertaking was also disapproved of, lest Ferdinand should be offended. In this manner, Charles, who had already pronounced the ban against the Elector and Landgrave for treason against the emperor and the empire, gained time to draw his auxiliaries from Italy, and to occupy a strong position at Ingolstadt. Here, also, the Protestants threw away the time in trifling and useless encounters, till the troops of the Netherlands having united themselves to the imperial army, Charles was in a position to assume the offensive. He marched into Swabia, whither he was followed by the army of Smalcald. The damp and cold weather occasioned sickness among the Spanish and Italian troops, and afforded the Protestants a hope of effecting a favorable composition, when the intelligence that Maurice and his friends and companions in the faith had proved traitors, and had marched an hostile army into Courland, changed the whole face of affairs. John Frederick at once hastened back to his states; the landgrave and the other leaders soon returned, and in a short time the whole army of Smalcald was dissolved.

§ 334. South Germany now stood open to the emperor. Well-intentioned advisers endeavored to persuade him to allow free toleration to religious opinions, and by this means to bring back his estates to their former obedience and devotion. But Charles was bent upon bringing back the unity of the Church, and, at the same time, on restoring the imperial authority to its ancient dignity. With this object, he required the princes and cities of southern Germany to submit themselves, and to renounce the league of Smalcald. The terrified imperial cities soon yielded obedience to the demand. Ulm surrendered her artillery, and purchased the favor of the emperor by large sums of money; Heilbron, Esslingen, Reutlingen, and many others, did the same. Augsburg was so well provided with artillery and provisions, that Schärtlin offered the magistrates to defend it for a year and a day, till Protestant Germany should have recovered itself and be prepared for fresh encounters; but the pusillanimous council of traders (Fugger, in particular) gained the victory. The emperor took possession of the town, and with it, the admirable artillery and a large sum of money. Frankfort and Strasburg soon followed. The old duke of Wirtemberg humbled himself, paid his contributions to the war, and surrendered his most important fortresses to the imperial troops. The old Elector of Cologne, anathematized by the pope, threatened by the Spanish troops, and at last abandoned by his estates, renounced his office in favor of a follower of the old creed, who soon thrust aside by the mass the German worship of God. By the spring of 1547, the whole of southern Germany was reduced to obedience without a blow being struck.

§ 335. In the mean time, John Frederick had repulsed the troops of Maurice, taken possession of his own territories with but little trouble, and conquered the greater part of Albertine Saxony, as far as Dresden and Leipsic. Wherever he went, he was received with acclamations by the Protestant part of the population, and it would not have been difficult for him to collect a considerable force, and to bid defiance to the enemies of the evangelical doctrines; but John Frederick was not an enterprising man, and despite the ban, respect for the emperor was not yet extinguished in his pious heart; — he rejected the proffered aid. Maurice in his need invoked the assistance of the emperor. The latter hastened with his army into Bavaria, in defiance of the gout, and, uniting his forces with those of Maurice and Ferdinand, marched against his enemy, who was posted on the Elbe with 6000 men. Upon the approach of the emperor, John Frederick wished to fall back upon the strong town of Wittemberg, until he could collect the scattered divisions of his army; but the imperial force, 27,000 strong, crossed the Elbe under the guidance of a peasant, surprised the cavalry, who were engaged in a retreat, on a Sunday morning, when the Elector was attending Divine worship, and won an easy victory in the battle of Mühlberg. John Frederick, a heavy man, was wounded in the face and taken prisoner after a brave defence. In prison, he displayed the serenity of soul which is the fruit of a good conscience and a firm trust in God. He heard the sentence of death that was pronounced upon him by the emperor with the greatest composure, and without even interrupting the game of chess in which he was engaged. But Charles did not venture to carry the sentence into execution. He proposed to change the punishment of death into that of imprisonment for life, upon condition that John Frederick should give up his fortresses to the emperor, and surrender his territories, together with the electoral dignity, to Maurice. In this manner, the electorship of Saxony passed from the line of Ernest to that of Albert.

It was now the turn of the landgrave of Hesse to be punished. Maurice and Joachim of Brandenburg interceded for him, and obtained the assurance, "that if he would make an unconditional surrender, apologize for his proceedings, and deliver up his castles, he should be punished neither with death nor with perpetual imprisonment." These conditions were afterwards modified during a personal interview, and the two princes assured the landgrave of the safety of his person and possessions. In reliance on this assurance, Philip, provided with a safe conduct, presented himself at Halle, where the imperial camp was posted. It was here that, after having asked pardon on his knees in the midst of a magnificent assembly, he was invited to supper by the duke of Alba, and on going to the castle, was retained prisoner in spite of all objections. The emperor could not deny himself the triumph of having his two greatest opponents in his power. He shortly afterwards left Saxony, and took his prisoners with him. This proceeding was the first occasion of a coolness between Maurice and the emperor.

§ 336. In the meanwhile, the Council of Trent, which was opened on the 13th of December, 1545, had held its first deliberations. But as the proceedings were carried on under the guidance of the papal legates, and the chief part of the assembly consisted of the regular clergy and the uncompromising adherents of the pope, the resolutions assumed such a shape that the Protestants saw in them rather a widening of the previous divisions, than any approach to a reconciliation. This course was highly displeasing to the emperor, who hoped now to have brought about that unity of faith which had so long been wished for; he remonstrated, and wished the resolutions to be kept secret, as he had just brought the Protestant Estates to promise that they would submit themselves to the Council, if the points already determined upon might be reconsidered. But Paul III., who saw clearly that the emperor cherished the wish of limiting the power of the pope, and of introducing such reforms into the Catholic Church that the Protestants should no longer hesitate to join her communion, not only allowed the resolutions to become known, but removed the Council to Bologna. The emperor was extremely irritated at this; he forbade the clergy to leave Trent, but could only retain the smaller number, and for the purpose of paving the way to a reunion of the Church in Germany, he proclaimed an edict, which set forth how matters should be conducted until the termination of the Council. This was done by the Augsburg Interim; which, at first designed for both religious parties, was afterwards restricted to the Protestants. By this instrument, the use of the cup and the marriage of priests were permitted to the confessors of the evangelical Church; an attempt was made to approach their opinions on the doctrines of justification, the mass, &c., by the use of indefinite modes of expression; but in the celebration of Divine worship and in the ceremonies, the old usages were retained. This Interim met with great opposition, less from the Protestant princes, than from the towns and preachers. The latter could not be prevailed upon to receive a religion that was offensive to their consciences, either by deprivation of their offices or by loss of their property or freedom. Driven from their posts, they left their homes and household hearths to fly by secret paths to the north of Germany, where the Interim was utterly rejected. Nearly 400 preachers became exiles; Magdeburg, which was under the ban, afforded an asylum to the greater number. In Saxony, also, the cradle of the Reformation, many preachers fled, from dislike to the Leipsic Interim, by the composition of which Melancthon incurred the charge of weakness and want of courage. A multitude of pamphlets, satires, satirical poems, and wood-cuts, proceeded from Magdeburg, which were intended to bring down hatred and contempt upon the Interim and its originators.

§ 337. At the moment when the emperor believed himself to be on the point of attaining the object of his wishes; when the Council had been again removed to Trent, and even attended by some of the Protestant Estates; when every circumstance seemed to combine to raise him to the position of temporal head of Christendom, in the sense in which the term was understood in the middle ages; when he already cherished the thought of having his son elected as his successor, and thus rendering the imperial throne hereditary in his family,—he suddenly found an unexpected opponent in the man to whom he had been hitherto indebted for his triumphs,—in Maurice of Saxony. This sagacious prince saw plainly in what a perilous position the civil and religious liberties of Germany would stand, if Charles should conduct his plans to a successful issue; he saw clearly that he had incurred the hate of all Protestants by his treachery to the common cause, since he had undertaken, in the name of the emperor, to prosecute the ban against Magdeburg, and had already commenced the siege of the city, where alone the pure word of the Gospel had found an asylum. He could only restore his lost reputation by a great and daring action. He concluded a secret alliance with several German princes, and assured himself of the aid of the French king, Henry II., by a treaty, in virtue of which the latter was permitted to occupy the towns of Metz, Toul, and Verdun, without infringement of the rights of the empire. The chivalrous margrave, Albert of Brandenburg Culnbach, conducted the negotiation. Upon this,

Maurice granted pardon and the free exercise of religion to Magdeburg, which immediately submitted. Warnings were sent to the emperor, who was at that time in Innsbruck; but Maurice, who was a master in the art of deception, knew how to dissipate all suspicions as they arose in his mind, and Charles, who was practised in the intrigues of Spain and Italy, thought it impossible that he should be outwitted by a German. Maurice suddenly advanced with three divisions of his army into the south, took possession of Augsburg, and marched into the Tyrol. He was already approaching Innsbruck with the purpose of making the emperor prisoner, when a mutiny among the German peasants afforded the latter an opportunity for escape. The Tridentine Council was broken up in confusion, and Charles, after setting the imprisoned Elector, John Frederick, at liberty, fled during the night, ill with the gout and disheartened, over the snow-covered mountains of the Tyrol into Carinthia; leaving to his brother Ferdinand the difficult task of establishing peace. Ferdinand immediately concluded the treaty of Passau with the Protestant princes, by which unconditional religious liberty was granted to the adherents of the Augsburg Confession, the Interim was abolished, the Protestants were declared independent of the Council of Trent, and the landgrave of Hesse was set at liberty. A permanent peace and amnesty was at the same time decided upon.

March, 1552.

§ 338. The treaty of Passau was the last work of Maurice. When his former confederate, Albert of Brandenburg, refused to accede to it, and continued his wars and robberies in Lower Saxony, Maurice marched against him to compel him to peace. A battle was fought near Sivershausen. The active Maurice was victorious, but he received a gun-shot wound in the wild confusion of the battle, of which he died two days after, in the flower of his manly strength. He was a man of rare qualities, "prudent and secret, enterprising and energetic." Two years after his death, the Religious Peace of Augsburg was concluded, by which the Protestant Estates who followed the Augsburg Confession were not only assured of full liberty of conscience and religion, but also of political rights equal to those enjoyed by the Catholics, and the continued possession of the confiscated ecclesiastical property. A free right of departure was permitted to subjects who did not follow the religion of the Electors; and a free toleration for those that remained. The demand made by the adherents of the ancient faith, that, in future, those of the clergy who should join the new Church should lose their incomes and offices, occasioned the most vehement disputes. As it was impossible to come to an agreement, the point was left undecided, and admitted as a spiritual reservation into the laws of peace — "a seed of bloody contests."

A. D. 1553.

§ 339. This religious peace frustrated the most zealous attempts of the emperor to restore the unity of the Church, and deprived him of the interest he had hitherto taken in the affairs of the world. Oppressed with discontent and bodily suffering, he embraced the resolution of renouncing his government, and of passing the remainder of his days in quiet retirement and monastic penance. With this object, he made over to his son Philip, at a solemn assembly at Brussels, first, the Netherlands, and a short time after, the kingdoms of Spain and Naples, together with the New World; he committed the government of the Austrian states and the affairs of Germany, however, to his brother Ferdinand. After this, he retired to the west of Spain, where he had had a residence built near the convent of Juste, on the pleasant declivity of a hill, surrounded by plantations of trees. He lived here for two years in quiet retirement, busied with the practices of religion and with pious contemplation. In the mean time, Ferdinand I. received the imperial throne of Germany by the election of the princes, after he had pledged himself to observe the Peace of Religion,— an engagement he honestly fulfilled.

4. PROGRESS OF THE REFORMATION THROUGH EUROPE.

a. LUTHERANISM AND CALVINISM.

§ 340. The greatest divisions arose in Germany, where the movements in the Church had taken their origin, in consequence of the Reformation. The Lutheran form of worship strove long with the Catholic for the mastery. The former extended itself gradually from Saxony and Hesse over the neighboring countries, acquired the supremacy in northern Germany, made triumphant progress in Swabia and Franconia, and opened itself a path from Strasburg into Alsacia and Lorraine. The doctrines of Luther had penetrated at an early period to the Vistula and the shores of the Baltic, where the Grand Master of the German Order (§ 227), Albert of Brandenburg, pressed upon by the Poles and deserted by the emperor and empire, had joined the evangelical Church, converted Prussia into an hereditary dukedom, and acknowledged the suzerainship of Poland. The same thing happened in Courland and Livonia, with the Head of the Order of the Sword. The Catholic form of worship found its most zealous partisans in the dukes of Bavaria, in the royal house of Austria, in the spiritual Electors, and in the prince-bishops. Ingolstadt was an active seminary for the ancient faith. Nevertheless, as the two emperors, Ferdinand I. and Maximilian II., both disdained to do violence to the consciences of their subjects, the evangelical doctrines soon obtained numerous adherents in the hereditary possessions of Austria. The Protestants obtained religious toleration for themselves, and built several churches in the archduchy of Austria, in Carinthia, and Styria. In Hungary and Transylvania, the Reformation made such progress that the evangelical party outnumbered their opponents, and obtained religious freedom and equal political rights with the Catholics. In Bohemia, the old Hussites (Utraquists) mostly embraced the Lutheran doctrines. But numerous as were the treaties that guaranteed the rights of Protestants in the Austrian dominions, they were disregarded by later rulers, who restored the Catholic State Church to the preëminence.

The Reformed Church that originated in Switzerland, also found its way into Germany at an early period. It is true that the doctrines of Zwingle were only received and maintained by a few towns in the south of Germany; but when Calvin, in Geneva, seized upon the principles of Zwingle, and fashioned them into a complete system of doctrine by uniting them with his own views, the reformed Church in Germany gained a constant succession of adherents. Frederick III. introduced this system into his own land from the Palatinate, and ordered Ursinus and Olevianus to draw up the Heidelberg Catechism, a widely
A. D. 1559. extended compendium of Calvin's doctrine; the same thing happened in Hesse, Bremen, and Brandenburg. Even Melancthon and his disciples (Philippists, and Cryptocalvinists) were convinced in their hearts of the truth of Calvin's views. The former so embittered the evening of his life by promulgating these opinions, that he sank into his grave calumniated and full of sorrow, and his disciples brought
A. D. 1560. persecution and imprisonment upon themselves in Saxony. The Form of Concord, a confession of faith that was subscribed, about 1580, by ninety-six of the Lutheran Estates of the empire, was intended to restore harmony among the German Protestants; but it merely confirmed the division between the Calvinists and Lutherans, and increased the unhappy animosity of one party against the other.

§ 341. Switzerland also received evangelical confessions of faith, as well as the Catholic doctrines; only the system of Zwingle, that was received in the greater German cantons (§ 326), differed less from the doctrine of Calvin which was predominant in French Switzerland, than it did from that of Luther. John Calvin, a learned refugee from France, introduced the Reformation and the confederation into Geneva, a town delightfully situated on the frontiers of Savoy and
Geneva. France, and then, like the lawgivers of antiquity, he exercised the greatest influence on the government, the religion, the manners, and the education of the city, till his death in 1564. Calvin was a man of great intellect and moral power; severe to others and to himself, and hostile to all worldly enjoyments, — he acquired a command over men by the reverence that was due to his strong and pure will. The doctrine of Calvin is impressed with the character of its originator, — severity and simplicity. In matters of faith, he adheres to Zwingle only so far as the latter embraces the severe views of Augustine (§ 174), and holds that men are incapable of doing good by their own wills. Calvin, like Zwingle, goes back to the primitive apostolic times, and commands the greatest simplicity in ceremonies and forms of worship. Images, ornaments,

organs, candles, crucifixes, all are banished from the churches; the service consists in prayer, preaching, and the singing of psalms, which Calvin's faithful fellow-minister, Theodore Beza, had translated into French; there is no church feast except the rigorously observed Sunday (Sabbath). The constitution of the Calvinistic Church is a republican synodial government. The congregation, represented by freely elected elders (presbytery), exercises the power of the Church, chooses the ministers, watches over morals by means of the elders, administers the discipline and punishments of the Church, and the distribution of alms. The ministers and a portion of the elders constitute the synod, whence the country churches receive their laws. Their severity of morals occasionally induced the Calvinists to wage war against lawful amusements, such as the theatre, dancing, and the more refined pleasures of society; for this reason, their doctrines found less acceptance among the higher than in the middle classes.

France.

§ 342. The Calvinistic doctrines extended themselves from Geneva over the flourishing towns of southern France, where they soon numbered so many adherents that they were able to wage war for many years with the dominant Church. The French court was for some time hesitating which form of religion it should adopt; political motives swayed the decision in favor of the Catholic Church. Commands were now issued against "the so-called reformed religion," Calvinistic ministers were given over to the flames, and an attempt was made to prevent the diffusion of their doctrine by persecution and punishment.

Netherlands.

Calvinism penetrated into the Netherlands from France and Switzerland, where, after many struggles, it became victorious in the northern provinces (Holland). At the synod of Dort (A. D. 1618), the views of the Arminians, who wished to give a milder form to Calvin's severe doctrine of predestination, were condemned, and the Augustine doctrine of election maintained. The chiefs of the Arminians, particularly the deserving statesman, (Van Olden Barnveldt), and the distinguished historian, Hugo Grotius, were punished, the one by death, the other by imprisonment (§ 360).

Scotland.

In Scotland, the evangelical doctrines were long suppressed by the court and the clergy, and many courageous confessors perished in the flames. The regent, Mary of Guise, sprung from a French family, which was zealously devoted to the Romish Church, in conjunction with Cardinal Beaton, suppressed the innovators by severity. But when the cardinal had fallen in his own house beneath the blows of a troop of conspirators, and the regent had died after a three years' contest with the people who were striving for the Gospel, the rude preacher, John Knox, who had known Calvin in Geneva, succeeded in rendering the Reformed doctrines triumphant. The doctrines, the form of worship, and the synodial constitution of the Calvinistic Church, were introduced into Scotland by a resolution of the parliament, the mass forbidden as idolatrous, under penalty of fine and death, and the goods of the Church confiscated. Monasteries, cathedrals, and treasures of art were destroyed with a blind fury. At a later period, the Scottish Church received the name of Presbyterian, from its assemblies. In England, similar principles, entertained by the Puritans, succumbed to the power of the High Church; but they were diffused by numerous sects, and received their fullest development on the free shores of North America.

b. ESTABLISHMENT OF THE ANGLICAN CHURCH.

§ 343. In England, the disciples of Luther were at first bloodily persecuted, and King Henry VIII. obtained such favor with the court of Rome, by a learned controversial work against Luther on the subject of the seven sacraments, that it conferred upon him the title of Defender of the Faith. But Henry's attachment to the pope was converted into hatred when Clement VII. refused to separate him from his Spanish wife, Catherine, an aunt of the emperor Charles V. Some internal scruples respecting the validity of his marriage with Catherine, who had been the wife of his departed brother, and a wish to unite himself to the lovely Anne Boleyn, at length induced Henry to attempt the desired separation by a rupture with Rome. Supported by the opinions of native and foreign universities, and of many learned bodies, as to the invalidity of his marriage, he had had himself divorced from Catherine, and married to Anne, by Thomas Cranmer, the new bishop of Canterbury; he then compelled the clergy to acknowledge him as the head of the English Church, and had a number of acts passed by the parliament, by which the pope's authority and influence were destroyed in England. The king then set about effecting such alterations in the Church as appeared to him to be useful, or which suited his caprice, with unexampled severity and arbitrariness. The numerous monasteries were violently dissolved, the monks and nuns scarcely protected from hunger, and the conventual property either united to the crown or bestowed upon courtiers. The tomb of Becket with its rich altar was desecrated and plundered, and the memory of the ancient saint (§ 275) turned to ridicule, by a ludicrous ceremony. The flames, by which Lutherans as well as papists were consumed, were lighted by the wooden images of the saints. On the other hand, he left the remaining institutions of the Catholic Church untouched, and commanded, by the statute of the Six bloody Articles, the observance, under penalty of death, of celibacy, auricular confession, monastic vows, low mass, transubstantiation, and the withholding of the cup. The venerable Bishop Fisher and the intellectual chancellor, Thomas More, the author of the "Utopia," died upon the scaffold, because they did not approve the innovations in the Church. Enraged at this, the pope at length fulminated a violent

Henry VIII., A. D. 1509-1547.

anathema against Henry and his adherents, at the moment when the discontent at the dissolution of the cloisters had produced an insurrection among the peasantry in the north of the kingdom, in which monks marched at the head of the bands. Upon this, Henry condemned the friends and relations of Cardinal Pole, who had prepared the anathema, to die upon the scaffold or gallows, and delivered over abbots and monks in the dress of their order to the executioner.

§ 344. But the despotism and sensuality of the king were most clearly displayed in his treatment of his wives. Scarcely had the divorced Catherine died, far from the court, a victim to her sorrows and her wrongs, before her rival, Anne Boleyn, was beheaded by the command of her jealous husband. His third wife, the young and gentle Jane Seymour, died a few days after giving birth to the delicate Edward; upon which, Henry suffered himself to be seduced by the advice of his chancellor, and by a portrait of Holbein's, into suing for the hand of a German princess, Anne of Cleves. But neither her figure nor her disposition suited the amorous king, who accordingly procured another divorce upon grounds altogether frivolous. Catherine Howard, Henry's fifth wife, retained her affection for a former lover after her elevation, and expiated her want of faith upon the scaffold; and Catherine Parr, the last of his queens, had only her own shrewdness to thank that she did not fall a victim to her zeal for the Reformation. Since the days of Nero and Domitian, there had hardly been a monarch who had surrendered himself so completely to the promptings of a despotic nature, a passion for blood, and a tyrannical will. Even on his death-bed, he issued orders for executions.

Edward VI., A. D. 1547 - 1553.

§ 345. At the time of his father's death, Edward VI. numbered but six years; Henry had, in consequence, appointed a council, to conduct the government during his son's minority. In this council, Edward's maternal uncle — the duke of Somerset, and the Archbishop Cranmer, attained the greatest authority. The former, raised to the office of Protector of England, gradually got the whole power of the state into his own hands, and favored the establishment of an Anglican Church, which had been undertaken with prudence and moderation by his friend Cranmer. This consists of a mixture of Catholic and Protestant elements. Public worship was accommodated to the Book of Common Prayer, in the English language, which was compiled from the ancient Mass books; the Communion was administered in both kinds; the abolishing of celibacy, and the confession of faith in the Thirty-nine Articles, is in conformity with other Protestant Churches; on the other hand, the episcopal constitution, the continuance in the use of colored robes during divine worship, and a few ecclesiastical statutes, call the Roman Catholic system to mind; only, instead of the pope, the king is the head of the Church, and the bishops and archbishops are appointed by him.

Somerset made many enemies by his ambition, who first procured his fall, and at length his execution. Dudley, earl of Northumberland, the ambitious chief of the opposite party, stepped into his place, and exercised the same unlimited authority over the young king and the country as his predecessor had done. For the purpose of prolonging his sway, he persuaded the dying Edward to alter the will of his father, and appoint, as his successor, Jane Gray, a grand-niece of Henry VIII., who favored the evangelical doctrines, instead of Edward's Catholic sister, Mary. But hatred to the ambitious Northumberland, whose son, Guilford, was the husband of Jane Gray, and the hereditary reverence for the legitimate inheritor, operated in favor of Mary. She brought the people over to her side by the assurance that nobody should be disturbed on account of his religion, and succeeded in gaining the throne. Northumberland died on the scaffold. Dudley and the classically accomplished Jane Gray, who was not less versed in the writings of Plato than in the Bible, after pining for some time in prison, were the victims of a similar fate.

Mary Tudor, A. D. 1553 - 1558.

§ 346. Mary did not remain true to her promise. Bred up in the Catholic faith, for which her mother, Catherine, had suffered, she looked upon the restoration of papacy and the ancient Church forms as the most important of her duties as a ruler. She had the Church Reform of Edward VI. abolished by act of Parliament, and adopted measures, in conjunction with Cardinal Pole, whom she raised to the archiepiscopal chair of Canterbury, for the extirpation of heresy and the restoration of the old system. The refractory bishops were deposed; Cranmer and two of his most zealous coadjutors given over to the flames, and the fires of martyrdom lighted all over the kingdom. To neglect attending mass was to put life in peril. Crowds of refugees fled over the seas, to seek for refuge in Germany and Switzerland. When Mary gave her hand to the fanatical Philip of Spain, the persecution waxed hotter. But grief at the evident dislike of her husband, melancholy, and misanthropy shortened her days. She died at the moment when she was deceiving herself with the idle hope, that she was about to present a Catholic successor to the nation.

Her half-sister, Elizabeth, the daughter of the unfortunate Anne Boleyn, exchanged the residence she had hitherto occupied in the Tower, where she had passed a troublous youth in the midst of sorrow and danger, for the royal palace, and restored, by the Act of Uniformity, the Reformation that had been established under Edward VI. The Book of Common Prayer and the Thirty-nine Articles again resumed their authority; and Elizabeth exercised the influence which she possessed as the spiritual head of the Church, in establishing the Court of High Commission. It was in vain that the exiles, on their return home, hoped to induce the queen to undertake a thorough Reformation, on the model of the Calvinistic Church. Elizabeth's lofty spirit, and her love for religious ceremonial and ecclesiastical pomp, despised the simplicity and popular equality of the Calvinists, who, from their insisting upon the purification of the Church, were called Puritans. When these men found there was no hope for the reception of their doctrines into the Anglican Church, they separated themselves as nonconformists, and established a religious system of their own, with presbyteries and synods, a religious service from which art and poetry were banished, and a system of Church discipline in which every earthly pleasure was a sin. Persecution was soon let loose against the Puritans, under which they became still more gloomy and morose, and at length increased to a dangerous party.

c. THE REFORMATION IN THE THREE SCANDINAVIAN KINGDOMS.

§ 347. In the sixteenth century, a complete revolution in the state of affairs took place in the three Scandinavian kingdoms. Christian II., the last king of the united empire (§ 296), irritated the nobility to such an extent by his severity and cruelty, that insurrections broke out at the same time both in Denmark and Sweden, in consequence of which the union of Calmar was dissolved, and the evangelical Church obtained the supremacy. Gustavus Vasa, a courageous youth, endowed with the valor and wisdom of the Stures, who were his relations, was the originator of this ecclesiastical and political revolution in Sweden, and the founder of a vigorous race of monarchs. He was carried into Denmark as a hostage by Christian II. From this place, however, he soon found an opportunity to escape into Lubeck, where he was not only protected but provided with money, and encouraged with promises of the liberation of his native country. In the same year in which the slaughter

A. D. 1520.

of Stockholm produced a universal horror of the Danish government, Gustavus landed on his native shores. In the midst of a thousand dangers and adventures, he escaped the pursuits of Christian's emissaries, who were perpetually at his heels, by his own courage and the fidelity of his countrymen, till at length he found aid and protection from the rude inhabitants of Northern Dalecarlia. With a band of hardy peasants he conquered Falun, repulsed the troops of the Danes and their allies, and took Upsala. The fame of his name and the attractive call of liberty soon resounded through all lands, and attracted many warriors to his side. Supported by the Lubeckers with troops, money, and artillery, he compelled the Danish garrison to retreat, and then, after having been elected king by the Diet of Strengnas, he held his entry into

June, 1523.

Stockholm. At first, the new kingdom of Sweden remained an elective monarchy, till, twenty years later, the crown was declared by the diet to be hereditary in the male line of Vasa. But as

A. D. 1544.

the possessions of the throne had been so dilapidated by

neglect as not to be sufficient to support the expenditure, the new kingly dignity could not be supported with honor except by an augmentation of the kingly revenue. For this, the Reformation afforded a welcome opportunity. The people, instructed in the Lutheran doctrines by the brothers Olaus and Laurentius Petri, willingly accepted the new faith, and the Diet placed the possessions of the clergy, who during the war had sided with the Danes, and shown no interest in the independence of their country, at the disposal of the king. Gustavus, supported by this resolution, gradually introduced the Reformation into the whole country, and deprived the Church of the greater part of its possessions, for the purpose of attaching them to the crown. The nobility, who were enriched by the proceeding, supported the undertaking. The bishops, who, after a long resistance, submitted to the new system, remained Estates of the empire and heads of the Church, but were dependent upon the king, and held in check by the consistories.

A. D. 1527.

§ 348. A similar revolution had, in the mean time, taken place in Denmark. Frederick I., acknowledged as king by the nobility and people, sought, by supporting the evangelical doctrine, to strengthen himself against his rival, Christian II., who, although at first favorable to the Reformation, had afterwards united himself to the emperor and the pope for the purpose of regaining possession of his states. In the same time in which Frederick admitted Protestants to equal civil rights with Catholics at the Diet of Odensee, and established the Danish Church's independence of Rome, Christian II. made an attack upon Denmark from Norway; but was taken prisoner, and compelled to pine for sixteen years in a gloomy tower, with no other companion than a Norwegian dwarf. Under Christian III., the son of Frederick I., the Lutheran form of worship attained a complete triumph in Denmark also. The clergy lost the greater part of their possessions to the crown and the nobility, and the bishops, whose titles were retained in the Scandinavian kingdoms, fell into complete dependence upon the government. In Norway, the new Church was quietly established by the peasantry; but in Iceland, the Episcopal party fell with the sword in their hands. The Swedish and Danish nobility gained great wealth, power, and privileges by the Reformation.

Christian III., A. D. 1534-1559.

§ 349. Gustavus Vasa had attempted to establish Sweden's prosperity by wholesome laws, and by the encouragement of trade and industry; but evil times came upon the land under the government of his sons. Erich XIV. was of so passionate a disposition that he at length became insane. Whilst in this state, he murdered with his own hand several members of the family of Sture, and caused all the nobles to tremble in anticipation of a similar fate; which induced his brothers to place him in confinement, and at length to send him out of the world by poison. His brother, John III., a weak

Erich XIV., A. D. 1560-1568.

minded prince of unstable character, succeeded to the government. Led astray by his wife, a rigid Catholic and the daughter of a Polish prince, and by a Jesuit who lived secretly in Stockholm as an ambassador, John attempted again to introduce the ancient form of religion into his kingdom, and consented that his son Sigismond, who was to be king both of Sweden and Poland, should be brought up as a Catholic. His scheme proved abortive from the resistance of the Swedish people to the Catholic ceremonies; he himself afterwards repented of his attempt, when his second wife exerted herself in favor of the evangelical doctrine. But the attachment to the Catholic Church proved of great detriment to his son, the Polish king, Sigismond III. For when he refused compliance with the resolution of the Diet, that the evangelical-Lutheran religion should be solely predominant and alone tolerated in Sweden, his uncle, Charles of Sudermania, was named regent. It was in vain that Sigismond attempted to defend his rights by force of arms, he was defeated by his uncle; whereupon the Diet required him either to renounce popery, and to govern his hereditary kingdom in person; or to send his son to Sweden, that he might be brought up in the religion of the country. When Sigismond refused compliance with this demand, Charles IX. received the crown he had long been striving for, and a new law of succession secured it to his family.

John III., A. D. 1568 - 1592.

A. D. 1598.

§ 350. At this time, a war arose between Sweden and Poland. This war, which, after Charles's death, was inherited by his son, Gustavus Adolphus, terminated to the advantage of Sweden, who soon united Livonia and a part of Prussia to Finland and Esthonia, her other provinces on the Baltic.

Charles IX., A. D. 1600 - 1611.

From this time, the power of Poland gradually decayed. An attempt at a reformation of the Church, which would have been attended by a renovation of the state, and a more intimate connection with neighboring countries, was suppressed by a selfish nobility, who thought of nothing but increasing their own power and privileges. It was only a few persecuted and fugitive teachers of the new doctrines that found protection and toleration in Poland. They were opposed to the Catholic Poles under the comprehensive term of *Dissidents*, and succeeded, after many struggles, in obtaining toleration for their religion, and an equality of civil rights; possessions in which they were afterwards seriously disturbed. Several opinions found toleration in Poland that had been rejected by the Reformers as unorthodox. Among these may be mentioned those entertained by the sect of Socinians (Unitarians) founded by the Italian Socinus, who denied the Divine nature of Christ and the doctrine of the Trinity.

d. THE CATHOLIC CHURCH.

§ 351. Traces of the Reformation displayed themselves both in Spain and Italy, but were prevented from extending partly by the character of the people, and partly by the severity of the Inquisition; the suspected died in frightful dungeons, or at the stake. Among the confessors of the new doctrine were found the most illustrious authors and men of learning, who, for the most part, took refuge abroad. Some adopted principles that were rejected as heretical even by the Reformers; for example, the two Italian brothers, Socinus;* and the Spaniard, Servetus, who was burnt to death at Geneva, at the suggestion of Calvin, for holding unorthodox opinions on the subject of the Trinity (A. D. 1553.)

The heads and leaders of the Catholic Church did not give up the thought of suppressing the new doctrines: wherever it was in their power, they sought to attain this object by persecution and violence; and when this was not practicable, they opposed and impeded their diffusion in every possible way. Almost all the popes, even those who, like Adrian VI. and Paul III., were convinced of the prevailing abuses of the Church, and meditated plans for their removal, displayed great severity against the Protestants. Thus Paul IV., an octogenarian and a gloomy monk, provoked the people to such a degree, that, on the day of his death, they mutilated his statues, and burnt down the house of the Inquisition. His successor, Pius IV., brought to a termination the twice interrupted Council of Trent, the third assembling of which commenced with the January of 1562. The resolutions of this Council (in which the Catholics see their own Reformation), form the foundation of the Catholic Church. The religious doctrines that had hitherto been regarded as orthodox were here recognized as infallible, and embodied in expressions as indefinite as possible; a purer code of morals was established, the Church discipline improved, and a more rigorous supervision of the clergy established. The Council of Trent, which was gradually received in all Catholic countries, is the final conclusion of Catholic doctrine; from this time, no more synods have been held. In this manner, every attempt at innovation was prevented, and the character of stability impressed upon Catholicism; whilst, on the contrary, the essence of Protestantism is development and progress.

Adrian VI., A. D. 1522, 1523.

Paul III., A. D. 1534–1549.

Paul IV., A. D. 1555–1559.

Pius IV., A. D. 1559–1565.

Gregory XIII., A. D. 1572–1585.

Gregory XIII., who gave the calendar, which had fallen into confusion, its present improved arrangement, by passing at once from the 18th of February to the 1st of March,

* This is a mistake. Lælius Socinus and Faustus Socinus were not brothers, but uncle and nephew. The title of the Bibliotheca *Fratrum Polonorum*, a collection of the works of the Socinian theologians, may have led Dr. Weber into this error. *Am. Ed*

ordered a Te Deum to be sung for the extirpation of the enemies of Christ when he heard the intelligence of the massacre of St. Bartholomew (§ 363). The most remarkable prince of the Church, during the whole century, was Sixtus V., who, from the condition of a poor shepherd boy, had risen to be a Franciscan, inquisitor, cardinal, and at length, pope. He was a man of a strong and imperious nature, who maintained the discipline of the Church with inexorable severity, erected several remarkable buildings, drew forth the gigantic works of antiquity from their rubbish, and attempted to restore the ancient splendor to the papal chair.

Sixtus V., A. D. 1585-1590.

§ 352. The attempts of the popes to suppress the Reformation, or at least to prevent its diffusion, found their chief support in the Order of Jesuits, which was founded by Ignatius Loyola, a Spanish nobleman of excitable imagination and enthusiastic temperament. Affected by the histories of the saints, which he read during the healing of a wound, Ignatius renounced the profession of soldier, to which he had hitherto belonged, and accomplished a toilsome pilgrimage, with prayers and penance, to the Holy Sepulchre. After his return, he acquired, with incredible perseverance, the education in which he was deficient, in Salamanca and Paris; and then, together with six associates, swore upon the host not only to be true to the three monastic vows of poverty, chastity, and obedience, but to allow the object of their efforts to be determined on by the pope, and then to submit themselves to his decision with unconditional compliance. A short time after, they prostrated themselves at the feet of the Roman pontiff, and obtained a confirmation of the new Order, which received the name of the Society of Jesus. Ignatius became the first general of the Order; but it is not to him, but to his successor, the Spaniard, Lainez, that the Society of Jesus is indebted for its artfully designed constitution.

A. D. 1540.

This constitution was military-monarchical. The superintendents of the provinces (the provincials), were subject to the general in Rome, and under these again were a multitude of heads in various steps and gradations. Obedience and rigid subordination were the soul of the alliance. All the members were most heedfully watched over, and were compelled to tear asunder all the bands that connected them with the world. Postulants were required to pass through a long period of probation, during which, the talents and disposition of every individual were minutely scrutinized, so that he might be devoted to his most appropriate sphere of action. The Jesuits, who were endowed with great privileges, soon attained a vast and multifarious activity. The chief aim of the Order was to oppose Protestantism, and to suppress the freedom of inquiry that had been awakened by the Reformation. They attempted these objects by a variety of ways; they endeavored to lead back the adherents of the new faith into the bosom of the ancient Church by persuasion and seducement; the confessional was made use of to induce princes and men in authority to oppose the Reformation, and to put limits to the freedom of belief; and by the education of youth, which they had known how to get into their own hands, they sought to bring up the young in their own principles. The Order was enriched by presents and legacies, and this wealth facilitated the erection of Jesuitical seminaries, which, plentifully provided with every thing that was requisite, imparted instruction gratuitously, and thus attracted many of the necessitous. Moreover, the object aimed at by the instruction given by the Jesuits was not a free development of the mind, but only the acquirement of knowledge that might be serviceable in life. It might rather be called training than education. Sciences were presented in a certain contracted form, and free speculation was prevented. Readiness in the Latin language, and an acquaintance with a few sciences that were of practical utility, were the aim of the Jesuitical education; the means — severe discipline and the excitement of ambition: philosophy, on the other hand, history, and every thing that directs men's minds to more elevated or comprehensive views, were either banished or taught with restrictions. But what drew down the curses of the people on the Jesuitical order was, that by its dangerous morality it became the destroyer of truth and faith, and the disseminator of malicious and false principles. The revolting doctrine that the end sanctifies the means, and that words and oaths might be rendered invalid by a mental reservation, were brought into use by the Jesuits in a most audacious manner.

5. THE TIMES OF PHILIP II. (A. D. 1556 — 1598) AND ELIZABETH (A. D. 1558 — 1603).

§ 353. Philip II. of Spain was a gloomy and misanthropical prince, who proposed three objects to himself as the aims of his existence, — the increase of his power, the extirpation of Protestantism, and the annihilation of liberty and popular rights. In the attainment of these ends, he sacrificed the happiness of his people, the prosperity of his kingdom, and the affection of his subjects and nearest relations. His chivalrous half-brother, Don Juan, who defeated the Turks in the sea-
A. D. 1571. engagement at Lepanto, was surrounded by the suspicious king with such a web of falsehood, intrigue, and espionage, and so fettered in all his undertakings, that grief and vexation plunged him into an early grave. Philip's son, the impetuous and passionate Don Carlos, died in the dungeons of the Inquisition, — that mighty spiritual court, which, under Philip, became the terror and horror of the people. By means of this horrible Inquisition, and the dreadful *autos da fé*, he was indeed successful in destroying every trace of heresy in Spain and Naples, and in depriving the people of their freedom; but he at the same time annihilated the prosperity, the wealth, and the national greatness of

these countries; and when he attempted to bend the Netherlands under the same yoke, that memorable contest burst forth, out of which liberty came forth triumphant. After a reign of forty-two years, which proved the grave of Spain's greatness, and burdened the once rich land with an oppressive national debt, Philip fell a victim to a dreadful disease. He had a cruel executor of his tyrannical commands in Duke Alba. The curse of the people rests on the names of both.

a. PORTUGAL UNITED WITH SPAIN.

§ 354. Portugal had a similar fate with Spain. In both countries, a powerful priesthood supported by an absolute king, suppressed the spiritual movements of the people, and paralyzed their powers. Freedom and rights were lost, and the ancient heroism, the bloom and the prosperity of an earlier period, disappeared beneath sloth and slavery. This was particularly the case when Portugal, by a gloomy fatality, was united to Spain.

King Sebastian, a young man, and who had been educated by the priests in rigid faith and obedience to the Church and pope, undertook an expedition against the infidel Moors in northern Africa, with the purpose of gratifying at once both his zeal for proselytism and his love of conquest. He commenced an impetuous attack, during the burning heat of an August day, upon the superior force of the enemy, in the plain of Alcassar, and suffered a dreadful defeat.

A. D. 1578.

12,000 Christian warriors covered the field of battle. Sebastian himself was among those who were missing, but his body could be nowhere discovered. The crown of Portugal descended to an ancient relative; and when he died, two years afterwards, without children, Philip II. of Spain made pretensions to the kingdom, and sent Duke Alba with an army against the Portuguese, who, out of national hatred and neighborly jealousy, favored the pretensions of a rival claimant, Antonio. But the latter was not in a position to contest his pretended hereditary claims against the superior power of Spain. He was defeated and compelled to fly, upon which Lisbon and the whole country submitted to the Spaniards. Antonio, after a few unsuccessful attempts, died, poor and harassed by perpetual plots, in Paris; and the false Sebastians that arose from time to time, and endeavored to stir up the Portuguese against their detested neighbors, did not meet with the necessary support. The fourth Sebastian, who by many was regarded as the true one, ended his days in a Spanish prison. The pernicious domination of Spain over Portugal endured for sixty years. At the end of this period, the illustrious duke of Braganza succeeded in bringing the crown into his own family. But in the meanwhile, the navy of Portugal had fallen into decay, and her foreign possessions passed into other hands.

A. D. 1580–1640.

21

b. THE STRUGGLE FOR LIBERTY IN THE NETHERLANDS.

§ 355. The Netherlands, from time immemorial, had possessed chartered rights and liberties, among which, consent to taxation by the Estates of the country, an independent judicature, and the exclusion of Spanish troops and officials, occupied the most prominent place. These rights had been already occasionally infringed during the time of Charles V.; but the love of the emperor for the Netherlanders, among whom he had been born, and for whose manners and customs he retained an affection, prevented any greater hostilities. Philip, on the contrary, was a haughty Spaniard, who looked upon the Netherlands as a conquered country, and who perpetually violated their hereditary privileges. He appointed his half-sister, Margaret of Parma, a woman of masculine spirit, his viceregent in Brussels; but placed a state council at her side, in which a foreigner, Cardinal Granvella, was president, and sent a Spanish garrison into the country. But the Netherlanders, many of whom were inclined to the evangelical doctrines, felt themselves most aggrieved, when the king, for the purpose of maintaining the pure faith and the discipline of the Church, ordered the laws against heresy to be rendered more stringent, and appointed fourteen new bishops in addition to the four already existing. These regulations were intended to facilitate the gradual introduction of the Spanish Inquisition; and the Cardinal Granvella, who, as archbishop of Mechlin, had all the other bishoprics under him, already assumed the title of Grand-Inquisitor. All attempts of the patriotic party, at the head of which stood William of Orange and Count Egmont, to induce the king by petitions to respect the institutions of the country, to mitigate the laws against heresy, and to allow freedom of belief, were ineffectual. Philip replied, "that he would rather die a thousand times, than suffer the slightest change in religion."

§ 356. It was among the burgher class alone that any disciples of the new Church were to be met with; the nobility for the most part adhered to the ancient faith, but were resolute in opposing the Inquisition with all

November, 1565.

their power. With this object, about 400 nobles subscribed the so-called Compromise, and drew up a petition for the repeal of the laws against heresy, and the discontinuance of the proceedings of the Inquisition. When they presented themselves with this before the palace of the vice-regent, she fell into a state of agitation. One of the council who was standing beside her exclaimed, that she should not be alarmed by these beggars (gueux), a word that was communicated to the confederates, and made use of by them as the sign of their alliance. They named themselves Gueses, and from this time wore a medal with the effigy of the king, and the inscription, "True even to the beggar's wallet." The petition remained without result. Heretics were punished in their freedom, property and lives. Despite all this, the new doctrines made more and more progress; psalms were sung, the preachings of the evangelical clergy, which were often held in the open air, were attended by thousands; monks, images of the Virgin, and holy objects were turned to ridicule. At length, the long restrained wrath of the people at the religious persecution burst its bounds in Antwerp, Brussels, and the whole of Brabant. A mob, consisting of the lowest class of the people, mutilated the crucifixes and images of the saints which were standing in the roads; but the increasing multitude soon attacked the churches and cloisters, and perpetrated every kind of sacrilegious atrocity. These occurrences produced a division. The moderate party joined the regent, and assisted her in punishing the guilty. Order was in a short time restored, and Margaret recommended gentleness and moderation as the only means by which the tranquillity of the country could be permanently established. But her representations found no acceptance in Madrid. It was determined to send the cruel Alba with a Spanish army to the Netherlands, and to reduce the people by force and severity.

Alba, A. D. 1567-1573. § 357. The intelligence of Alba's arrival caused the Netherlanders to take flight in crowds. William of Orange, a prudent and circumspect man, in the full vigor of life, resolute, energetic, and taciturn, yielded to the storm and retreated to Holland. He parted in tears from Egmont, whom he vainly attempted to persuade to follow the same course. Egmont's happy nature could not give credit to the Spanish treachery, against which Orange warned him. He trusted to his former services to the royal family of Spain, and remained. But Alba had hardly arrived at Brussels, with unlimited powers, before he placed the unsuspecting Egmont and the gallant Horn under arrest, and caused them, with eighteen others of the nobility, to be executed as traitors. He then established a council of rebellion, called by the Netherlanders The Bloody Council, which punished with unexampled severity not only the disciples of the evangelical doctrine, but the resolute defenders of their country's rights and institutions. The regent, disgusted with these horrors, resigned her office and retired to Italy. Her memory was held in honor. Alba, however, erected a citadel in Antwerp, and for six years (A. D. 1567 – 1573) exercised an oppressive tyranny that threatened the greatest danger to liberty and prosperity. Without regard to the laws of the land, which required that the taxes should be allowed by the Estates of every district, and collected in a manner the best suited to their object, Alba imposed a fixed tax upon the country, and levied it in a manner extremely unfavorable to trade and commerce, inasmuch as, in addition to a property tax, he introduced a high tariff. The discontent and irritation of the people at these oppressive imposts at length produced such a fermentation in the country, that Alba's recall was decided upon in Madrid. The intelligence that a band of exiles,

A. D. 1568.

called Water-Gueses, had stormed the sea-port, Briel, and that the northern states, Holland, Zealand, Utrecht, and Friesland, had united together and recognized William of Orange as their Stadtholder, A. D. 1572. might have convinced the Spanish court that Alba's proceedings were not leading to the desired result. Shortly after the Duke's departure from the Netherlands, the northern states, in the synod of Dort, raised Calvinism to be the religion of the state, received the Heidelberg Catechism, and erected a Protestant university in the town of Leyden, as a reward for the heroic defence of the citizens against the beleaguering Spanish army.

Zuniga, A. D. 1573-1576. § 358. Alba's successor, Louis of Zuniga and Requesens, abolished the Bloody Council, and attempted by milder measures again to confirm the tottering power of Spain in the Netherlands; but the hatred of the people against the foreign troops, whose licentiousness every day increased, prevented a reconciliation. Even his victory on the Mokerheath, where two of the brothers of Orange died as became heroes, failed in producing the expected results. Zuniga died two years afterwards. Before his successor, Don Juan, Philip's gallant half-brother, could enter upon his difficult office, the insolence of Don Juan, A. D. 1576-1578. the savage and unpaid soldiery attained its highest pitch. They filled the wealthy cities of Maestricht and Antwerp with murder, plunder, and desolation. At this crisis, the shrewd Orange was successful in uniting the whole of the states, by the A. D. 1576. alliance of Ghent, in the resolution of mutually assisting each other, with life and property, in driving out the Spanish troops; and Don Juan was not in a position, during the brief period of his exertions in the Netherlands, to reëstablish firmly the shattered power of Spain. Alexander Farnese, A. D. 1578-1592. But Don Juan, as well as his more experienced successor, Alexander Farnese of Parma, son of the regent, Margaret, was intent upon fostering the jealousy and hereditary envy between the northern and southern states, and on maintaining the rights of the Catholic Church in the latter, that the dominion of Spain might be preserved in the southern states at least. This scheme was seen through by Orange, who, being convinced that even the weak were strengthened by union, united the northern states, (Holland, Zealand, Gelders, A. D. 1579. Utrecht, Friesland), into a closer confederacy for the purpose of mutual coöperation, by the Union of Utrecht. This alliance was the foundation of the United States of the Protestant Netherlands. On the other hand, matters in the south became every day more confused and divided by the intermeddling of foreign princes and nobles, so that the energetic Parma was enabled in many places to suppress the insurrection, and to bring back many of the towns to obedience. Philip's wrath was now directed against Orange. He had already outlawed him, and promised a title of nobility and a vast reward to whosoever should

deliver him up either alive or dead. This tempting promise, and the activity of fanatical priests, were followed by several attempts at assassination. Orange escaped one of these, but the bullet of the fanatic, Gerhard of Franche-Comté, laid him dead at the door of the
A. D. 1581. royal banqueting-hall of Delft. The murderer was however seized and put to a cruel death. In the place of Orange, the northern states elected his gallant son, Maurice, as Stadtholder and general.

§ 359. About this time, the religious animosity between Catholics and Protestants was greater than ever in the west of Europe; and whilst the former placed all their hopes upon Philip of Spain, the latter received assistance either private or open from Elizabeth of England. She sent her favorite, Leicester, with an army into the Netherlands, to prevent Parma's complete triumph; she assisted the Huguenots against Philip's allies, the Leaguists and Jesuits (§ 362, 364), and consented to the execution of Mary Stuart, when she found that her
A. D. 1587. own life was threatened by the daggers of fanatics (§ 368). Upon this, Philip determined to annihilate all the enemies of the Catholic Church by a mighty blow, and above all, to chastise heretical England and her excommunicated queen. With this view, he fitted out the Armada or "Invincible Fleet," consisting of 130 large ships of war, and sent them into the Channel, under the command of Medina
A. D. 1588. Sidonia, to the end that, supported by Parma's land force, they might subject, at the same time, England, France, and the Netherlands. But the undertaking ended in the shame and ruin of Spain. The "Invincible Fleet" was destroyed by storms, and the skill and courage of the English; the greater part of that which escaped the fire-ships, the rocks, and the enemy, in the Channel, was wrecked upon the Hebrides and Shetland islands, when Sidonia attempted to return to Spain by sailing round Scotland. It was a fatal blow. Philip admitted this, when he composed the fears of the trembling admiral with the words, "I sent you against men, not against rocks and storms." This event destroyed Spain's supremacy at sea, and secured the independence of the Netherlands. The war, indeed, continued for twenty years longer; but the Spaniards, despite the bravery of their troops and the skill of their commanders, were not in a condition to subject the whole of the country. The northern states, who possessed an admirable leader in Maurice of Orange, maintained the struggle for freedom and independence. A short time before his death, Philip presented the Netherlands to his daughter, Clara Eugenia, on her marriage with the archduke, Albert of Austria, as a fief, under the condition, that the land should revert to Spain in the event of her dying without children. The United States of Holland, however, would not consent to this scheme. They still continued the war after the death of Philip II., till at length, by the inter-
A. D. 1609. mediation of Henry IV. of France, a truce was arranged,

by which their independence, religious freedom, and trade with the East Indies were secured to them. But it was not till the peace of Westphalia that the independence of the United States of Holland was formally acknowledged. The southern provinces (Belgium), on the other hand, remained for a whole century subject to Spain, and then fell into the hands of Austria.

§ 360. TRADE. — GOVERNMENT. — SYNOD OF DORT. — Holland came forth from the struggle flourishing and powerful. Navigation and commerce received a vast impulse, after the Hollanders (particularly the East India Company, established in 1602) entered into direct commercial relations with India, and deprived the Portuguese of many of their colonies. Batavia, in the island of Java, was the centre of their lucrative traffic. The Constitution of the United States, which was mainly the work of the great statesman, Van Olden Barnveldt, was republican. The States General, which were formed by deputies from the seven provinces, possessed the power of legislation; the High Council, with the stadtholder at its head, conducted the government; the affairs of war, however, and the supreme command over the sea and land forces, belonged to the stadtholder alone. The arts and sciences at the same time flourished prosperously; the study of antiquity, in particular, met with unusual attention in the Dutch universities.

But even Protestant Holland did not remain free from the mischievous wars of religion. A dispute respecting the Calvinistic doctrine of predestination divided the country into two parties, — a severe party (Gomarists), to which Maurice of Orange and his adherents attached themselves, and a moderate party (Arminians), whose supporters were Van Olden Barnveldt and Hugo Grotius. The synod of Dort (§ 342) decided in favor of the former; upon which, Van Olden Barnveldt, who had deserved so highly, and was then in his seventy-second year, perished on the scaffold; and Hugo Grotius, the learned historian of the struggles of the Netherlands for liberty, and the founder of civil and international law according to the principles of the ancients, was confined in prison till rescued by the cunning and fidelity of his wife.

c. FRANCE DURING THE WAR OF RELIGION.

§ 361. During this period, furious religious wars were raging in France also. Henry II., a determined enemy of the Huguenots (§ 342), died in consequence of a wound he received during a tournament. His feeble and delicate son, Francis II., was his successor. This prince was married to the fascinating Mary Stuart of Scotland, whose uncles, the Guises, in consequence, enjoyed great influence at the French court. The Guises, as zealous adherents of the Catholic Church and the papacy, made use of their lofty position to suppress the reformed party; but by doing this, gave their opponents, and

Francis II., A. D. 1559 - 1560.

in especial, the Prince Condé, of the family of Bourbon, and the Admiral Coligni, the opportunity of strengthening themselves by joining the Huguenots. The schism increased daily; the one party strove to overthrow the other, and to secure the victory to their own side by the assistance of the king. The day on which the Estates assembled at Orleans was selected by both parties as a befitting time for the execution of this project. The Guises gained the advantage. The chiefs of the Huguenots already found themselves in prison, when a turn was given to affairs by the sudden death of the king. The queen-mother, Catherine of Medicis, placed herself at the head of affairs during the minority of the new king, Charles IX., and the Bourbons assumed a position suited to their birth. The Guises, irritated at the neglect they experienced, retired with their niece, Mary Stuart, into Lorraine, whence the latter, shortly after, departed with sorrow and mourning into Scotland.

Charles IX., A. D. 1560–1574.

§ 362. The removal of the Guises from the court was of advantage to the reformed party. They obtained toleration. Enraged at this concession, the duke of Guise concluded an alliance with some other powerful nobles for the preservation of the ancient faith in France, and returned to Paris. During this return, a horrible slaughter was perpetrated by the Guises and their attendants upon some Calvinists of the town of Vassy, who were assembled together in a barn, for the celebration of Divine worship. This proved the signal for a religious war. The outrage given to the conceded liberty of conscience by this bloody act of violence cried for vengeance. France was soon divided into two hostile camps, that attacked each other with bitter animosity and religious rage. The most horrible atrocities were committed, and the kingdom disturbed to its inmost depths. The Catholics obtained aid from Rome and Spain, the Protestants were assisted by England; Germany and Switzerland supplied soldiers. After the undecisive battle of Dreux, and the murder of the Duke Francis of Guise, at the siege of Orleans, peace was for a short time restored, and the Calvinists again assured of religious toleration — a promise that met with but little attention. The two parties were soon again arrayed in arms against each other. But despite the bravery of the Huguenots in the battle of St. Denis, where the elder Montmorenci lost his life, the superiority remained on the side of the Catholics; particularly when Catherine de Medicis, who had hitherto sided with neither party, embraced the interests of the latter. The sight of crucifixes and sacred objects broken to pieces, during a journey undertaken by the queen and her son, and the advice of the duke of Alba, with whom she had an interview in Bayonne, had produced this alteration in her opinions. After several bloody engagements in the vicinity of La Rochelle, which the Huguenots had selected as their battlefield, and after their gallant leader, Condé, had been basely

A. D 1568.

assassinated during one of them, the peace of St. Germain was arranged, by which the Calvinists were again assured of the free exercise of
A. D. 1570. their religion. Condé's nephew, Henry of Bearn, who had been bred up in the doctrine of Calvin by his mother, Joanna d' Albret, now placed himself at the head of the Huguenots; but the soul of the party was the brave Coligni, who stood by the side of the prince as his guide and adviser.

§ 363. Coligni possessed great influence at the court after the peace. The young king respected him, and favored him with his confidence. For the purpose of bringing about a permanent reconciliation between the religious parties, the king now urged a marriage between his sister, Margaret of Valois, and the Bourbon, Henry of Bearn. This offended the Guises, who believed that Coligni had procured the assassination of Francis of Guise, and they resolved upon his destruction. Coligni was fired at one evening, as he was returning to his own house from the Louvre. The ball, however, only shattered his arm, and it was necessary to devise a fresh plan of destruction. The Guises, in conjunction with Catherine of Medicis, now entertained the horrible project of taking advantage of the approaching marriage, for the solemnization of which many illustrious Calvinists had hastened to the capital, to destroy the chiefs of the Huguenot party. Thus originated the Bloody Nuptials of Paris, in the night of St. Bartholomew, August 24th, 1572. When the alarm bell of St. Germain l'Auxerrois gave the signal at midnight, bands of armed ruffians fell upon the defenceless Calvinists. The grey-headed hero, Coligni, was the first victim that the Guises sacrificed to their hate; the murderous bands then marched through all parts of the city, filled the streets and houses with blood and corpses, and laughed to scorn every sentiment of humanity and justice. The butchery lasted for three days, and was imitated in other towns, so that, at the lowest computation, 25,000 Huguenots must have perished. The king, to whom the plan was communicated a short time before its execution, listened to the voice of his passions, and himself fired upon the fugitives. After the deed had been accomplished, and the Guises had been fixed upon by the public voice as its instigators, and called upon to answer for their conduct, Charles took the whole affair upon himself, and excused the crime by a pretended conspiracy. Many of the French quitted their homes in horror, and sought for security in Switzerland, Germany, and the Netherlands. Henry of Bearn saved his life by a compulsatory abjuration, but returned to his old faith as soon as he found himself in security.

A. D. 1574. § 364. Charles IX. died two years after the night of St. Bartholomew, troubled with evil dreams. His brother
Henry III., A. D. 1574-1589. Henry, who had been for a twelvemonth the elected king of Poland, fled secretly from the rude shores of the Vistula to take possession of the fairer crown of France. Henry III.

was a weak and luxurious prince, without either assiduity or energy. Shut up with his favorites and pet dogs in the inmost apartments of the palace, he forgot his kingdom with its disturbances and miseries; and when remorse at his sinful life, which was passed in lust and debauchery, seized upon him, he sought consolation in superstitious devotion, in pilgrimages and processions, and in penance and flagellations. To bring the Huguenots to peace, so that he might be able to devote himself to the undisturbed enjoyment of the pleasures of his capital, Henry, immediately upon his accession, granted them freedom of conscience, and equal civil rights with the Catholics. Enraged at these concessions, which destroyed all the fruits of their previous exertions, the zealous Catholics, under the guidance of Henry of Guise, and with the cognizance of Philip II. of Spain, concluded the Holy League for the preservation of the Church in all its ancient rights. Many members were won to this alliance by the insinuations of the priests and monks, and by the intrigues of the Jesuits The fickle and faithless king, disturbed by this movement, united himself with the Catholic zealots, declared himself the head of the League, and curtailed the religious peace. The duke of Anjou, Henry's younger brother, died a few years after this; and as he, like the king, was without children, the Bourbon, Henry of Navarre (Bearn), became the nearest heir to the throne. This prospect of a Protestant king (A. D. 1584.) alarmed the Catholic part of France, and gave fresh vigor to the League. The weak king was obliged to recall all treaties with the Huguenots, to announce the extirpation of heresy, and to approve the arrangements of the League. Henry of Guise, at first, only entertained the notion of putting aside the Protestant successor to the throne, who had been excommunicated by the pope; but his courage rose with his increasing power; he soon made attempts upon the crown himself, whilst, as a pretended descendant of the Carlovingi, he asserted the superiority of his claims to those of the reigning family. A conspiracy was formed in Paris (where the citizens were kept in a state of perpetual agitation by fanatical popular orators) against the freedom or life of the king; and when Henry III. attempted to defend himself by calling in Swiss troops, the agitation burst into rebellion. The people assembled themselves around the Guises, who, against the king's commands, were entering the capital, barricaded the streets and bridges, and commenced (May 12, 1588.) a furious contest with single divisions of the troops. The trembling king fled with his favorites to Chartres, and left his capital in the hands of his rival. Henry of Guise now possessed the same power that had belonged to the mayors of the palace in the time of the Merovingi (§ 184). (September, 1588.) But even this position did not satisfy the ambitious party leader. An assembly of Estates, convoked at Blois, where the adherents of the Guises were the strongest party, proposed not only to deprive the Bourbons of their right to the throne and to exterminate Calvinism, but to change the government, and to place the whole power in the hands of the Guises. At this crisis, Henry hazarded a bold stroke; he had the duke of Guise and his brother, the Cardinal Louis, assassinated, and imprisoned the most influential leaders of their party. This proceeding produced a fearful commotion in the whole nation: in Paris, allegiance was renounced to the God-forsaken king, who had overthrown the pillar of Catholicism; the pope fulminated an excommunication at him; revolutionary movements took place in many quarters. Despised and forsaken, Henry III. saw no other way to safety open to him than an alliance with Henry of Navarre and the Huguenots. A frightful civil war burst out afresh, but fortune was hostile to the League. Henry had already laid siege to Paris, and threatened to reduce the faithless town to a heap of ruins, when the knife of a fanatical monk put an end to his life. Henry III., the last Valois, died on the 1st of August, 1589, after appointing Henry of Navarre and Bearn his successor.

§ 365. Henry IV. had still a long struggle to sustain before his head was ornamented by the crown of France. Mayenne, the brother of the murdered Guise, placed himself at the head of the League, and offered a vehement resistance to the Calvinistic claimant of the throne. Philip II. sought to turn the confusion to his own advantage, and commanded his able general, Alexander of Parma, to march his forces from the Netherlands into France. Henry tried for a long time to get possession of his inheritance by the sword: he laid siege to Paris, and caused
A. D. 1590. the citizens to feel all the horrors of famine; but he at length became convinced that he never could gain peaceable possession of the French throne by battles and victories. He thought the crown of France was worth a mass, and went over to the Catholic Church in
July, 1593. the cathedral of St. Denis, and by this means destroyed the power of the League. Paris now threw open its gates, and welcomed the bringer of peace with acclamations. The pope recalled the anathema; the heads of the League concluded a treaty with him, and Philip II., a short time before his death, consented to the peace of Vervins. After foreign and domestic tranquillity had been thus restored to
A. D. 1598. France, the king, by the Edict of Nantes, conferred upon the Calvinists liberty of conscience, the full rights of citizenship, and many other privileges; such as separate chambers in the courts of justice, several castles, with all their warlike munitions (La Rochelle, Montauban, Nismes, &c.,) and freedom from episcopal jurisdiction. He next sought to heal the wounds that had been inflicted on the land by the war, by encouraging agriculture, trade, and commerce; and had the economy of the state and the taxation admirably arranged by his friend and minister, Sully. He won for himself the warmest affections of his people by his genuine French character, and by his cordial and cheerful disposition.

His solitary failing, his too great love for women, was a merit in the eyes of the French. But fanaticism was only slumbering. Henry's tolerant disposition towards heretics awakened it. As he was meditating the vast plan (with the approval of the Dutch Union and other European powers) of founding a Christian community with equal privileges for the three Confessions, and by this means destroying the supremacy of the royal house of Hapsburg, he fell beneath the knife of Ravaillac.

A. D. 1610.

d. ELIZABETH AND MARY STUART.

Elizabeth, A. D. 1558-1603.

§ 366. Whilst France was being torn to pieces by the war of religion, England, under Elizabeth, was making mighty advances in trade and commerce, in navigation, agriculture, and literature. Elizabeth was a despotic ruler, who suppressed the ecclesiastical freedom of the people, and who would suffer no opposition to her will in parliament; but she possessed great talents for government, a mind invigorated by severe studies, and an understanding that enabled her invariably to recognize and select that which was most profitable for the country. She surrounded herself by sage councillors, among whom, Cecil (Lord Burleigh) held the first rank, and maintained order and economy in the management of the state; but the dissimulation she had been accustomed to practise during her perilous youth, rendered the crooked path of falsehood, and the subterfuges of a disingenuous policy agreeable to her. She displayed the latter more especially, in her conduct towards Mary Stuart, queen of Scotland, who, in character, personal qualities, and history, formed a contrast to her neighboring rival. Whilst Elizabeth, from the misfortunes of her youth, had carried with her into life a dowry of unamiability, severity, falsehood, and envy, the beautiful Mary, after a youth passed in joy and happiness, had brought to the Scottish throne a cheerful and engaging nature, an open heart, and a joyous disposition; and whilst the English queen was closely bound to Protestantism, and united in one Church with her people, Mary held fast to the Catholic faith and the papacy, in the midst of a rude nation, who, with their own hands, had raised the Presbyterian Church to be the Church of the kingdom, and who detested the mass as idolatry. Her private chapel was attacked, and the stern reformer, Knox, pronounced severe discourses against her from the pulpit of the palace, as the prophets had once done against the idolatrous kings of Israel.

A. D. 1565.

§ 367. Mary united herself in a second marriage with Darnley, a Scotch nobleman, who had been brought up in England. The union, however, proved unfortunate. The vain, unthinking husband, abandoned to the counsels of insincere friends, found pleasure in nothing but hunting and feasting; and was indignant at finding

that the queen neglected him, and bestowed her confidence on the singer, Rizzio, from Turin, who conducted her correspondence with the Guises and the pope. Darnley, urged on by jealousy, and a feeling of injured honor, and irritated by malicious friends, formed a conspiracy with some nobles,—and Mary's favorite, pierced by many daggers, fell
A. D. 1566. lifeless before the eyes of his mistress, in her own chamber. This horrible deed filled the heart of the queen with bitterness against her husband, of whose guilt, despite his denial, she felt convinced. She separated herself more and more from him, entertained thoughts of a divorce, and turned her favor upon Bothwell, another Scottish nobleman. It was not till Darnley fell ill that she appeared to lay aside her displeasure. She attended upon him with the greatest assiduity, in a remote
February 10, 1567. garden house. But the inhabitants of Edinburgh were awakened one night, during Mary's absence, by a dreadful explosion. The garden house was found shattered to pieces, and Darnley's body, at some distance, apparently suffocated. The public voice pointed out Bothwell as the perpetrator of the deed; and three months after, he was Mary's husband. Was it at all wonderful that she was accused of being an accomplice in the murder? Irritated at this criminal marriage, the Scottish nobility took up arms. Bothwell fled before the battle was fought, and led the life of a freebooter near the Hebrides, but was taken by the Danes, and died in prison, insane. Mary was led in triumph to Edinburgh, amidst the execrations of her people, and then imprisoned in a solitary castle on the island of Lochleven, where she was compelled to abdicate her crown, and to transfer the government to her half-brother, Murray, during the minority of her son, James. Mary, indeed, escaped, and found assistance from the powerful family of Hamilton; but having been overcome in a battle, she would have fallen a second time into the hands of her enemies, had she not fled
A. D. 1568. with the greatest haste into England, to seek protection from Elizabeth.

§ 368. The queen of England declined every interview with Mary until the latter should have cleared herself from the charge of having murdered her husband; and since Mary, as an independent sovereign, would not submit herself to an English tribunal, it was considered necessary to retain her in England. But her presence soon endangered Elizabeth's safety. The duke of Norfolk attempted to gain Mary's hand, but lost first his freedom and afterwards his life. The ancient Church still numbered many adherents in the northern counties; the earls of Northumberland and Westmoreland raised the standard of rebellion, with the purpose of setting Mary at liberty, and restoring the Catholic Church. Their undertaking failed. Northumberland, given up by the
A. D. 1569. Scots as a fugitive, died upon the scaffold. Mary was suspected as an accomplice; she was removed from that neighborhood and

more closely watched. All the efforts of foreign courts to procure her liberation were fruitless. The disturbed state of Scotland, where the rage of party was leading to assassination and civil war, and the religious contests on the continent, seemed to render her continued imprisonment necessary. At this juncture, Babington, with a few companions, embraced the project of murdering Elizabeth, and placing Mary, by the aid of Spanish troops, upon the English throne. Their purpose was discovered. The conspirators died upon the scaffold, and when it appeared, upon examination, that Mary was privy to the plot, the court pronounced her guilty, and Elizabeth was requested by the parliament, for the preservation of religion and the peace of the country, and for the security of her own person, to let justice take its course. She wished for the death of her enemy, but she feared the consequences. At length, the struggle ended. Elizabeth signed the death-warrant, and Burleigh had it hastily executed Mary's head fell on the 7th of February, 1587, in the nineteenth year of her imprisonment and the forty-fifth of her life. She died with firmness, and true to her faith. Elizabeth, however, complained that her minister had ordered the execution against her commands, and punished her secretary, Davison, by fine and imprisonment, for having let the warrant go out of his hands.

§ 369. The pope and Philip II. heard of the deed with horror. The former outlawed the heretical queen, and summoned the Catholic powers to vengeance; the latter fitted out the vast Armada (§ 359), for the purpose of subjecting England and the Netherlands at one blow, and of afterwards founding a Catholic empire in the west of Europe, under the supremacy of Spain. But the destruction of the "Invincible Fleet" raised the renown of England and its queen, and laid the foundation of Britain's empire of the sea and of the greatness of her commerce. From this time, her trade, her navigation, and her colonies, received a vast impulse. Drake, the celebrated circumnavigator of the globe, and other maritime heroes, had discovered the element on which the power and glory of England were to be raised.

It was only in Ireland that Elizabeth's undertakings were unsuccessful. This island, which for centuries had been conquered, but never taken possession of, had been raised into a kingdom by Henry VIII., and subjected to the religious laws of England. But it was only a small proportion of the population, namely, the British colonists, who received the Reformation; the native Irish remained true to their ancient faith and clergy. Elizabeth attempted to bring about a closer political and ecclesiastical union between the island and England. The earl of Tyrone, one of the military chiefs, opposed himself to this project, and obtained help from Spain and Rome. Upon this, the chivalrous earl of Essex, to whom the queen had transferred the favor she had so long bestowed upon his unworthy father-in-law, the earl of Leicester, received the go-

22

vernorship of Ireland. But instead of subduing Tyrone, he concluded a disadvantageous treaty with him. Essex, by this means, incurred the displeasure of the queen; and when, instead of waiting quietly for a more favorable time, he formed a plot with James of Scotland, and attempted to compel Elizabeth by an insurrection to appoint James her successor, he was seized, tried, and beheaded in the Tower, at the age of thirty-three. Grief and remorse at the death of her favorite, and the consciousness that the affections of her people had much cooled towards her, embittered the last years of the queen's life to such a degree, that she passed days and nights in tears on the cushions with which the floors were covered, till her death, at the age of seventy years, put an end to her sorrows. On her death bed, she appointed Mary's son, James of Scotland, her successor.

e. CULTURE AND LITERATURE IN THE CENTURY OF THE REFORMATION.

§ 370. Civilization received a mighty impulse during the sixteenth century in all countries. Schools were improved and universities multiplied; art and literature were fostered and supported. The works of the ancients, which were everywhere translated and explained, awakened new views and cultivated the taste; and the mental energy that had been called into existence by the disputes respecting religion and the Church, furthered the general cultivation and enlightenment, and exalted literary activity. The interest in intellectual gifts produced marvellous creations in the regions of art and science. Germany and Italy were considered the chief seminaries of civilization.

1. The science of antiquity was more especially cultivated and developed in the numerous universities of Germany, and those learned seminaries that rested upon the study of the ancient classical literature were established by the efforts of Melancthon, which extended themselves over all countries. It was in Germany that Nicholas Copernicus, the great astronomer of Thorn, showed that the Ptolemaic system of the universe, the truth of which had remained unquestioned for fifteen hundred years, was founded on incorrect data; that the sun remained stationary in the midst of the planetary system, but that the earth, like the other planets, in addition to the revolution on its axis, had besides an extremely regular motion around the sun. And Kepler, one of the greatest thinkers of any age, sought, in the spirit of Plato, for the laws that govern the eternal order of the world, with the inspiration of a prophet, and the creative power of a poet. Unappreciated, however, and persecuted by religious zealots, he led a melancholy life, in the

Copernicus, A. D. 1473–1543.

Kepler, A. D 1571–1630.

Galileo, A. D. 1565–1631.

midst of oppressive anxieties for the means of living. It fared no better with his great contemporary, Galileo of Pisa, who, because he shared the astronomical opinions of Copernicus, was summoned before the tribunal of the Inquisition, and compelled to renounce his opinions on his knees. He was obliged after this to linger for some years in the dungeons of the Inquisition, where he contracted an affection of the eyes, which afterwards terminated in blindness.

Hans Sachs, A. D. 1494–1576. Brandt, A. D. 1458–1521. Fischart, A. D. 1591.

In the mean time, the "Meistersong," a kind of burgher poetry in which Hans Sachs, a shoemaker of Nuremberg, particularly distinguished himself, was flourishing in the German towns; and Sebastian Brandt of Strasburg (author of the "Ship of Fools"), and John Fischart of Mayence, raised satirical didactic poetry to high perfection. Luther, however, was the creator of German prose by his translation of the Bible, and the founder of German sacred poetry by his spiritual hymns.

The Germans were also distinguished at this time in the fine arts. The pictures of Albert Durer (A. D. 1548), Hans Holbein (A. D. 1563), and Lucas Cranach (A. D. 1553), are still much esteemed, although they do not rival those of their great Italian contemporaries, Michael Angelo (A. D. 1563), Raphael (A. D. 1520), Titian (A. D. 1576), Leonardo da Vinci (A. D. 1519), or Correggio (A. D. 1543).

Macchiavelli, A. D. 1527.

2. In Italy, the flourishing period of art and literature, which had commenced in the fifteenth century, continued throughout the whole of the sixteenth. In Florence, Macchiavelli, one of the acutest of thinkers and most politic of statesmen, composed his remarkable works, "Discourses on Titus Livius," "History of Florence," "The Prince," which still excite universal admiration. In the much talked-of book "The Prince," Macchiavelli presents the picture of a ruler who, without regard to virtue, morality, or religion, knows how to establish his own absolute power, and to make his own will the law. Freedom and national prosperity are as little regarded in this book as truth and justice; intellect alone is held in any estimation. For this reason, a faithless system of policy is distinguished by the epithet, Macchiavellian. In Ferrara, Ariosto wrote the fascinating and sportive heroic poem of "Orlando Furioso;" and the melancholy Torquato Tasso celebrated the first crusade in beautiful language in his "Jerusalem Delivered."

Ariosto, A. D. 1474–1533. Torquato Tasso, A. D. 1595.

Cervantes, A. D. 1547–1616.

3. The sixteenth century was the golden age of art and literature in Spain and Portugal also. Cervantes, in his comico-satirical romance of "Don Quixote," has represented, with such art, a man who completely mistakes the misty creations of a world of dreams for actual existences, and fights for an object that exists nowhere but in his own imagination, that the name of his hero has be-

Lope de Vega, A. D. 1552–1635. come proverbial. The dramatic poetry of Spain reached its culminating point in Lope de Vega and Calderon. The Portuguese poet, Camoens, has ennobled the great epoch of the discovery of India in his poem of the "Lusiad." During a passage home from the East Indies, he lost his property by a shipwreck, and saved nothing but his poem, that he held fast with his teeth as he swam. In Portugal, he gradually fell into such poverty that he had bread collected by an Indian servant to prevent his dying of hunger.

Calderon, A. D. 1600–1687.

Camoens, A. D. 1524–1569.

4. In England, William Shakspeare, one of the greatest poets of any age, gave its full perfection to dramatic poetry, whether tragedy or comedy. His great dramas are founded either upon historical events ("Henry IV.," "Richard III."), or upon the ordinary events of human life ("Macbeth," "Lear," "Romeo and Juliet," "Othello"); the best known of his comedies are, "Midsummer Night's Dream," and "The Merry Wives of Windsor;" in the latter, the fat Falstaff, the companion of Henry V., and the type of a comic character, plays the chief part.

Shakspeare, A. D. 1564–1616.

III. THE SEVENTEENTH CENTURY.

1. THE THIRTY YEARS' WAR (A. D. 1618–1648).

a. BOHEMIA, PALATINATE, LOWER GERMANY, TILLY. APPEARANCE OF WALLENSTEIN.

§ 371. Whilst the dark fanaticism of Philip II. was plunging the West of Europe into a bloody religious war, arms were at rest in Germany under the gentle government of Ferdinand I. and Maximilian II. Both these princes upheld the Peace of Religion with impartiality and justice (§ 340). But when, after the premature death of Maximilian II., his son, Rudolf II., who had been brought up in Spain, came to the throne, complaints arose of the infringement of the law, and of violation of liberty of conscience. Rudolf, a prince zealously devoted to the Catholic Church, but possessed of slender talents for government, neglected the affairs of his kingdom for the study of astronomy, painting, and antiquities, and trusted to the advice of the Jesuits, who strewed with busy hands the seeds of religious discord, and called forth strife, party-spirit, and confusion, both in the German empire and in the hereditary states of Austria. When the archbishop, Gebhard of

Ferdinand I., A. D. 1556–1564.

Maximilian, II., A. D. 1564–1576.

Rudolf II., A. D. 1576–1612.

Cologne, went over to the evangelical Church, that he might marry the beautiful countess of Mansfeld, he was deprived of his dignity; a proceeding that was declared by the evangelical States to be an infringement of the "spiritual proviso." The archduke, Ferdinand, bred up and guided by the Jesuits, refused the numerous Protestants in Styria, Carinthia, and Carniola, the religious liberties they had hitherto enjoyed; had the evangelical churches and schools pulled down, and the Bibles burnt, and drove out of the country, without mercy, all those who refused to attend the mass. The imperial city of Donauworth, which was chiefly Protestant, was placed under the ban for disturbing a procession, taken possession of by the impatient duke, Maximilian I. of Bavaria, and deprived of its Protestant worship. It was in vain that the evangelical Estates presented complaints; the weak and indifferent emperor gave no redress. It was on this account that a number of evangelical princes and imperial cities concluded a Protestant Union, at the instigation of the Elector of the Palatinate, for mutual assistance against aggression and violence. This Union was opposed by the Catholic League, formed by Maximilian of Bavaria and the spiritual Electors (Mayence, Treves, and Cologne), and some bishops (Wurzburg, Augsburg, &c.). In this manner, Germany was again divided: the League united itself with Spain; the Union secured the aid of Henry of France and the Dutch. The death of the childless duke of Cleves and Berg, which occasioned a quarrel for his inheritance between the palgrave of Neuburg, who had gone over to the Catholic Church, and the evangelical Elector of Brandenburg, gave the first occasion for hostilities between the two religious parties. After a long and destructive war, a division was agreed upon, by which Cleves was allotted to Brandenburg, and Berg with Dusseldorf to the Palatinate.

A. D. 1608.

A. D. 1609.

§ 372. The incompetence and carelessness of Rudolf threatened to destroy all respect for the royal house of Hapsburg. His relatives, therefore, compelled him to surrender Austria and Hungary to his brother, Matthias. Rudolf, who was extremely favorable to the Bohemians, whose capital, Prague, he had chosen for a residence, maintained them for some time in their allegiance by the granting of letters patent, which gave to the Utraquists and Lutherans freedom of conscience, equality with the Catholics, and their own defenders. But he was obliged at length to relinquish this kingdom also, with its surrounding territories, to Matthias, so that, when death put an end to his inglorious life, he was in possession of nothing but the powerless imperial throne.

A. D. 1611.

Matthias, A. D. 1612-1619.

But Matthias had just as little energy or talents for government as Rudolf; and being old and childless, he appointed his cousin, Ferdinand of Carinthia, his successor in Austria, Hungary, and Bohemia. The elevation of this rigid Catholic filled the

Protestants (Utraquists, Lutherans) in Bohemia with alarm for their religious liberties. This alarm increased, when, upon the building of two Protestant churches on the territories of the abbot of Brunau and of the monastery of Grab, near Toplitz, a decision was given, that no evangelical church should be erected upon ecclesiastical property; and in consequence of this prohibition, one church was shut up and the other destroyed. The defenders, who saw in this an infringement of the letters patent, held a meeting, and proposed a remonstrance to the emperor, who was then absent in Hungary. The reply confirmed the prohibition, and contained a severe reproof to the complainers. Irritated at this, the defenders, under the guidance of the Count von Thurn, marched in arms to the council-house, for the purpose of calling to account the imperial council, to whom they attributed the offensive writing. After a short dispute, the irritated Protestants seized upon two of the councillors who were present, Martinitz and Slawata, who were particularly offensive to them as zealous Catholics, and threw them, together with the secretary, Fabricius, out of the castle window. But notwithstanding the height, and the shots that were fired after them, they all escaped with their lives. Upon this, the evangelical Estates established a new government, expelled the Jesuits, and fitted out an army under the command of Thurn. The intelligence of these proceedings hastened the death of Matthias, who was already ailing. He died at the moment in which Thurn, supported by the brave general, Ernest von Mansfeld, defeated the imperial troops who had marched into Bohemia, and appeared with his army before the gates of Vienna. The oppressed Protestants of Austria entered into an alliance with Thurn, their ambassadors forced their way into the imperial palace, and demanded from Ferdinand, with threats, religious toleration and an equality of their rights with those of the Catholics. The danger was pressing; but Ferdinand resolutely refused every concession, till the arrival of Dampierre's dragoons freed him from constraint. Unfavorable weather and a deficiency in provisions compelled Thurn to retreat.

May 20, 1619.

June.

§ 373. Shortly after this, Ferdinand II. was elected emperor of Germany in Frankfort; but before his coronation took place, the Estates of Bohemia and Moravia fell off from the house of Austria, and chose for king the Elector, Frederick V., of the Palatinate, the head of the Protestant Union. It was in vain that well-disposed friends warned him of the dangerous gift;—the voice of his haughty wife, a daughter of James I. of England, the exhortations of his Calvinistic court preacher, Scultetus, and his own ambition, determined the result. The vain and weak man assumed the Bohemian throne, and hastened to receive homage and be invested with the crown at Prague, where he squandered the time in idle shows, gave himself up to luxurious living, and offended the Utraquists and Lutherans in Bohemia by his zeal for

November, 1619.

Calvinism. Ferdinand's conduct was altogether different. He concluded an alliance with the shrewd Maximilian of Bavaria, who had been educated by the Jesuits, and who was the head of the well-provided League; and who soon ordered his able general, Tilly, the Netherlander, to march

November 7, 1620.

with his army into Bohemia. The battle at the White Hill was soon fought, in which Frederick's exhausted troops were defeated by the superior force of the enemy, and sought their safety in headlong flight. A single hour decided the fate of Bohemia. Frederick lost courage and discretion so completely, that he fled with the greatest haste across Silesia to the Netherlands, pursued by the imperial sentence of outlawry, which deprived him of his hereditary possessions of the Palatinate. Bohemia and Moravia were again in a few months subjected to Austria. Ferdinand cut the letters patent to pieces with his own hand; twenty-seven of the most illustrious nobles died on the scaffold; hundreds expiated their offences by the forfeiture of their goods; and the confiscated property was bestowed upon the Jesuits and other religious orders. Tyranny, oppression, and seduction, gave a complete triumph to the Catholic religion in a few decades, after upwards of 30,000 families had left the country. Shortly after this, the Union, which had looked quietly on during these proceedings, was dissolved in the midst of universal contempt.

§ 374. After the subjugation of Bohemia, Tilly marched against the Palatinate of the Rhine. Three courageous men ventured to take the field in the cause of the outlawed Elector and endangered Protestantism: Christian of Brunswick, administrator of the bishopric of Halberstadt, a rude soldier, who presented himself as the defender of the electoress Elizabeth, and who, having collected a troop of soldiers, marched plundering through Westphalia towards the Maine; Ernest von Mansfeld, a knightly adventurer, who maintained his troops by plunder and levying contributions, and treated the bishoprics and monasteries on the Maine and Rhine with great severity; and the margrave, George Frederick of

April, 1622.

Baden-Durlach. The two latter united gained a victory over Tilly at Wiesloch (Mingolsheim). But when the victors shortly after separated themselves, George Frederick,

May 6th.

the following month, lost the battle of Wimpfen, and would have himself fallen into the hands of the enemy, had not 400 of the citizens of Pforzheim covered his retreat by an heroic death. A few

June 20th.

months later, Christian of Brunswick also suffered a defeat near Höchst, from Tilly's veteran troops, and marched in conjunction with Mansfeld into the Netherlands, to obtain help from England, whilst the League general stormed Heidelberg, Manheim, and Frankenthal, sent the Heidelberg library to Rome, and filled every place with blood and plunder. In the following year, Maximilian of Bavaria received the electorship of the Palatinate, as a reward from the Diet of Ratisbon.

§ 375. Ferdinand, not content with the defeat of his enemies, wished to make use of his superiority to restore the Catholic Church and to suppress Protestantism. This occasioned anxiety, and procured the enemies of the emperor the assistance of England, Holland, and Denmark. Mansfeld, Christian of Brunswick, and the Margrave of Baden, appeared again in the field, provided with troops and money, and were supported by Christian IV. of Denmark, who was induced to assume arms, partly by religious zeal, and partly by the hope of increasing his territories. A new storm burst forth. Upon this, the emperor, to whom the dependence upon the League and the great authority of Maximilian appeared dangerous, determined to raise an army of his own. In this undertaking, Albert of Wallenstein, a Bohemian nobleman, offered him his assistance. In possession of a vast property that he had gained by marriage, Wallenstein presented himself before Ferdinand with the offer of supporting an army of 50,000 men at his own expense, if he were allowed the unlimited command of them, and the privilege of indemnifying himself from the conquered lands. After some hesitation, Ferdinand acceded to the proposal of the bold adventurer, and granted him the governorship of Friedland, on the northern frontier of Bohemia, raised him to the office of Elector of the empire, and afterwards conferred upon him the dignity of duke. The war now extended itself into the North of Germany. But when Wallenstein with his wild bands took possession of the shores of the Elbe, and effected a junction with Tilly, the army of the League and emperor soon obtained the advantage. Mansfeld suffered a defeat from the Friedlanders at the bridge of Dessau, and was overtaken by death in Bosnia, as he was conducting the remains of his army by a difficult march through Hungary into the Netherlands. Christian of Brunswick sunk into the grave in the same year, and Christian IV. was defeated by Tilly at Lutter, near the Barenberg, and compelled to retreat into Denmark. His ally, the duke of Mecklenburg, was obliged to leave his territories, of which, from that time, Wallenstein, with the emperor's permission, took possession; Holstein, Schleswic, and Jutland soon fell into the hands of the imperialists in the midst of horrible devastations; Pomerania and Brandenburg were compelled to receive imperial garrisons; the whole north laid subdued at the feet of the emperor, and the Protestant princes and cities awaited with fear and trembling the destiny that it should please Austria and Bavaria to award them. In this strait, Stralsund gave an ennobling example of patriotism and heroic courage. The citizens resolutely refused to admit an imperial garrison within their walls. Hereupon, Wallenstein advanced upon the town with his formidable army, and swore that he would take it if it were bound to heaven with chains. But all his attacks were frustrated by the strength of the place and the heroism of the citizens. After he had encamped for ten weeks before

A. D. 1626.

August 27.

the city, and sacrificed 12,000 men, he gave up the attempt. This result checked Wallenstein's plans of conquest, and brought the war to a more rapid termination. Christian IV. recovered his devastated
A. D. 1629. lands by the peace of Lübeck, but was obliged to promise that he would refrain from any farther interference in the affairs of Germany.

§ 376. Austria was again victorious; and the more decisive her victory, the greater was to be the triumph of the Catholic Church. The Protestant worship was suppressed by violence in all the conquered and occupied lands, and the supremacy of Catholicism gradually prepared for. With this object, the emperor, at the instigation of the spiritual Electors, published the Edict of Restitution, by virtue of
March, 1629. which, all foundations and ecclesiastical property that had been confiscated since the treaty of Passau (§ 337), were to be restored to the Catholic Church, the Calvinists were excluded from the religious peace, and the Catholic Estates were not to be interfered with in their attempts to convert their subjects. This arrangement, which threatened to wrest a great number of bishoprics, and almost all the foundations and abbeys of northern Germany, from the hands of their present proprietors, filled the whole of the Protestant part of the country with terror and alarm, and prolonged the destructive civil war. Many princes and cities refused compliance, and the emperor found himself obliged to retain his army under arms to give effect to the execution of the Edict But this army was no longer under the command of Wallenstein. For when the princes made a general complaint, at the Diet of Regensburg of the frightful ravages and barbarous method of warfare pursued by the duke of Friedland, and Maximilian imperatively demanded the removal of his presuming and overbearing rival, Ferdinand, who wished to produce a favorable disposition towards the contemplated election of his son, found himself compelled to pronounce Wallenstein's deposition. The general was informed of the resolution whilst busied with his astrological studies. He retired to his Bohemian estates, where, in proud repose, and in the enjoyment of kingly wealth, he awaited the time when his presence would be again required. Tilly assumed the command over the assembled host, and marched against Magdeburg, which had opposed the execution of the Edict of Restitution. But whilst the Protestant Estates of Germany, helpless and overawed, bent before the superior power of Austria, and looked forward in melancholy expectation for the postponed execution of the Edict of Restitution, a fresh hero made his appearance on the soil of Germany — the Swedish king, Gustavus Adolphus.

b. INTERFERENCE OF SWEDEN. GUSTAVUS ADOLPHUS AND WALLENSTEIN.

§ 377. Gustavus Adolphus, the grandson of Gustavus Vasa (§ 349), determined to interfere in the war of Germany, partly to defend Protestantism, and partly to increase the power of Sweden. He was supported by the shrewd Cardinal Richelieu (§ 400), who at that time governed France, and who looked with jealousy upon the increasing power of the house of Hapsburg. As soon as Gustavus Adolphus had effected a landing on the coast of Pomerania, the old duke June 24, 1630. of the country surrendered his lands, which had been frightfully ravaged by the imperial troops, to Sweden. The piety of Gustavus, and the strict discipline of his soldiers, who assembled themselves twice a day around their field preachers, formed a striking contrast to the desolating mode of warfare pursued by Tilly and Wallenstein, so that the people everywhere greeted the Swedes and their high-minded king as rescuers and deliverers. Not so the princes, who, from fear of the emperor's vengeance, rejected the alliance that was offered February, 1631. them, and at the Diet of Leipsic, embraced the resolution of observing a neutral position. The Electors of Brandenburg and Saxony refused permission to the Swedes to march through their territories; and whilst Gustavus Adolphus was delayed by negotiations on May 16, 1631. this subject, Magdeburg, after repeated assaults, was taken and destroyed by Pappenheim and Tilly. The barbarous troops, urged on by a desire for vengeance, and a love of plunder, burst into the luckless town, which was surrendered to them for three days' plunder, and which now became the scene of the most revolting horrors, till a conflagration, which extended itself on all sides, converted it at length into a heap of ashes. Two churches and a few fishermen's huts, were the sole remains of this flourishing imperial city.

§ 378. The destroyer of Magdeburg now turned a threatening aspect towards Saxony. The Elector, in the anguish of his heart, concluded an alliance with Gustavus Adolphus, that he might be able, by the help of Sweden, to prevent the entrance of Tilly's incendiary troops into his territories. The battle of Leipsic and Breitenfeld was soon September 7, 1631. fought, where the imperial army was completely defeated. Tilly, who was himself in danger of his life, was obliged, after a great loss, to retreat rapidly into the south, whilst the Swedes turned towards the Rhine and the Maine. Before the winter was over, the bishopric of Wurzburg, and the greater part of the Lower Palatinate, were in the hands of the Swedes; and the towns of the Rhine also fell into the power of Gustavus, after he had accomplished the passage of the Rhine at Oppenheim and driven back the Spaniards. In the spring, he marched upon Nuremburg-on-the-Lech, where Tilly had occupied a strong position. The Swedes forced a passage across the vigorously defended river. During the storming of the intrenchments, Tilly was so severely wounded by a cannon-ball that he died fourteen days after, at Ingolstadt, his mind busied with military affairs in the very hour of death. War filled the entire soul of this hero. Simple and moderate in his mode of living, he despised wealth and possessions, as well as titles and dignities. Sensual enjoyments were as unknown to him, as high cultivation or nobility of mind.

After the occupation of Augsburg, where the evangelical form of worship was again restored, Gustavus Adolphus marched into Bavaria, and took possession, as an indulgent conqueror, of Munich, which had been deserted by the court. A fine, and carrying off 140 concealed cannons, was the only punishment inflicted by the king upon the trembling Bavarians.

§ 379. In the mean time, the emperor, in his necessity, had again had recourse to Wallenstein, and prevailed upon him by prayers and great concessions, to raise a fresh army and to take the supreme command. After a successful campaign against the Saxons in Bohemia, Wallenstein, in conjunction with the Bavarians, marched into Franconia, where the Swedes had occupied a strong position near Nuremburg. Here the hostile armies lay encamped opposite each other for months, without coming to an engagement, till at length, all the land for seven miles around the spot was wasted, and even the abundant stores of Nuremburg began to fail. Hereupon, Gustavus resolved to attack the strong camp of Wallenstein, but the gallant assailers were driven back by the tremendous discharge of artillery. The attempt, after a severe loss, was obliged to be relinquished, upon which the Wallensteiners marched into Saxony. The

November 16, 1632. Swedes soon followed them hither, and the eventful battle of Lutzen, where the Swedes triumphed, but their king found the death of a hero in the tumult of the fight, took place upon a foggy day in November. Pappenheim, the gallant leader of cavalry, was also borne from the field of battle mortally wounded; and Wallenstein found himself compelled to leave the field to the enemy, and to retreat into Bohemia with his defeated army. The Swedes dragged the body of their heroic king, plundered and defaced by the hoofs of horses, from beneath the dead, and had it committed to the earth in his native land.

§ 380. After the death of Gustavus Adolphus, the Swedish chancellor, Axel Oxenstiern, a prudent and energetic statesman, undertook the conduct of the war in Germany, after he had prevailed upon a number of the evangelical princes and cities, by the alliance of Heilborn, to continue steadfast in the treaty they had entered into with the

A. D. 1633. king of Sweden. Bernhard of Weimar and the Swedish general, Horn, stood by his side as the chief military leaders. France

gave supplies of money. Thus this mischievous war continued to rage. Bavaria was severely visited by the Swedes, who, since the death of their king, had not been a whit behind their opponents in the destructive way of carrying on the war; and the Friedlanders behaved in such a way in Silesia, that the prosperity of the land was for a long time destroyed. But Wallenstein's course was approaching its termination. His dilatory way of conducting the war, and his unintelligible lingering in Bohemia, were made use of by his numerous enemies and enviers to his destruction. He was accused of entertaining the project of entering into an alliance with Sweden, and of placing the crown of Bohemia upon his own head; it was for this reason that he had set at liberty the captive Count Thurn, the hereditary enemy of Austria; and the contract that had been entered into, by the mediation of Illo, between Wallenstein and the leaders of the different divisions for mutual adherence, pointed to revolt and treachery. The emperor, guided by the friends of Maximilian, by monks and Jesuits, who hated the duke on account of the freedom of his religious views, determined upon the destruction of his too powerful general. After the most influential leaders, Gallas, Piccolomini, and Altringer, had been secured, Ferdinand pronounced Wallenstein's deposition; and when the latter marched towards Eger, with the most devoted of his troops, to be nearer a juncture with the Swedes, he was assassinated, together with his most trusty adherents, Illo, Terska,
February 25, and Kinsky, by the Irishman, Butler, and a few confederates.
1634. The vast possessions of the duke and his friends were confiscated, and presented to his betrayers and murderers. Honors, dignities, and wealth were the rewards of the criminals. Thus died Wallenstein, the terror of the people, and the idol of the soldiery. He possessed an audacious and enterprising spirit, a commanding character, that was exalted by the taciturnity of his disposition and the gloomy severity of his aspect, and a boundless pride and ambition. When his lofty figure, enveloped in a scarlet mantle, and with a red feather in the hat, was seen pacing through the camp, a strange horror took possession of the soldiers.

c. TERMINATION OF THE WAR. PEACE OF WESTPHALIA.

§ 381. After the death of Wallenstein, the imperial army marched into Bavaria, and defeated Bernhard of Weimar in the battle of Nord-
September 6, lingen. Several German princes took occasion from this to
1634. conclude the peace of Prague with the emperor. But the
May, 1635. frightful war was not yet terminated. Richelieu, who was not willing that the favorable moment for diminishing the power of the Hapsburgs, and extending the territories of France, should escape unimproved, promised efficient assistance, both in money and troops, to the

A. D. 1636. Swedes, and supported Bernhard of Weimar in his undertakings on the Upper Rhine. The Swedish general, Banèr, conquered Saxony and Thuringia, and converted the fertile country into a depopulated desert. Unspeakable calamities were press-
Feb. 15th, 1637. ing upon the German nation, when the emperor, Ferdinand
Ferdinand III., A. D. 1637–1657. II., sank into the grave, and was succeeded by his son of the same name. The warlike actions of Bernhard of Weimar were crowned with success. He conquered Rheinfelden, Freiburg, and Breisach, and entertained the project of establishing an independent principality on either side of the Rhine. But Bernhard
July 18, 1639. died suddenly in the flower of life, not without suspicion of poisoning; and the French took advantage of the circumstance to take his army into their own pay, and make themselves masters of Alsace. They soon crossed the Rhine and carried the war into the south of Germany, whilst the gallant Banèr again visited the unfortunate Bohemia with the most frightful calamities. Banèr's audacious plan of breaking suddenly from his winter quarters, and seizing upon the Electors and emperor at the Diet in Regensburg, had not the expected result. The breaking up of the frost and the arrival of the enemy compelled the Swedish general to a retreat, during which he died from the effects of his exertions and of an intemperate life.

§ 382. Torstenson was Banèr's successor; he was the most talented disciple of the school of Gustavus Adolphus. On account of his sufferings from the gout, he was usually carried about in a litter; nevertheless, the rapidity of his movements was the astonishment of the world. He overthrew the imperial army near Leipsic, and at the hill Tabor; pene-
A. D. 1642. trated repeatedly into the heart of the Austrian states, and made the emperor tremble in his capital; he then appeared unexpectedly on the Lower Elbe, took possession of Holstein and Schleswic, and compelled the Danish king to a disadvantageous peace. At length, exhausted by illness, he laid down the leading staff, which was obtained by the gallant Wrangel. Wrangel, in conjunction with the
A. D. 1647. French general, Turenne, carried the war into Bavaria, compelled Maximilian to fly, and to conclude a truce, and was about to unite himself with the Swedish general, Königsmark, in Bohemia, when the news of the conclusion of the peace of Westphalia put an end to military operations. The war ended in Prague, where it had also taken its origin.

§ 383. After five years of negotiations in Münster and Osnaburg, the peace of Westphalia, which the people who were wearied out by the war demanded in despair, was at last concluded. France received the Austrian portion of Alsace, Sundgau, and Briesach; but was obliged to secure to the imperial cities both their former privileges, and their relations to the German empire. Sweden received Upper Pomerania, the island of Rugen, and the towns of Stettin, Wismar, &c., the bishoprics of Bremen and Verden, and an indemnification in money. Brandenburg obtained the eastern part of Lower Pomerania, with the bishoprics of Magdeburg, Halberstadt, Minden, &c. Saxony was indemnified by Lusatia; other princes with other cities, foundations, and bishoprics. Bavaria remained in possession of the Upper Palatinate and of the Electoral dignity; and the Palatinate of the Rhine, with the eighth Electoral dignity, was restored to Charles Louis, the son of Frederick V., who died in the year 1632. The remaining princes and Estates retained their former possessions; and Switzerland and the Low Countries were acknowledged as independent states.

With regard to the affairs of the Church, it was arranged, after long disputes, that the treaty of Passau, and the religious peace of Augsburg, should be confirmed to the Protestants, the "spiritual proviso" abolished, and the peace extended to the Calvinists. In regard to the possession of ecclesiastical property, and the right of free exercise of religion, the year 1624 was taken as the standard. Everything was to remain, or to become, what it had been at that time. At the same time, the privilege of reformation possessed by the princes ceased, and a free exercise of religion and equal civil rights were assured to the three Christian confessions.

The farther consequences of the Thirty Years' War were:—1. An increase of the power of the princes, which was the occasion of expensive courts, standing armies, a multitude of officials, and a high and regularly levied taxation. 2. A purity of faith in the Church, which was not founded upon mere warmth of religious feeling, but upon an unalterable veneration for the literal meaning of the Symbolical Books. 3. A decay of trade, of industry, and of profitable commerce. Though agriculture revived again, and the plough and the mattock restored its former aspect to the desolated country, the aforetime prosperity of Germany never returned. Many of the trading towns sunk into poverty; the imperial towns were gradually overtaken by the princely residences; and trade, industry, and wealth established their seats in Holland and England. German art and literature decayed; everything native was neglected, and fashions, language, and poetry, borrowed from the French. From this period, the old German nationality succumbed to the influence of foreigners.

d. SWEDEN UNDER CHRISTINA AND CHARLES X. CHANGE IN THE CONSTITUTION OF DENMARK.

§ 384. After the premature death of Gustavus Adolphus, the crown devolved upon his daughter Christina, during whose minority the government was conducted by a senate, and the opportunity made use of to increase the privileges and property of the noble families.
A. D. 1644. When the queen herself assumed the government, she assem-

bled around her a brilliant court, summoned artists and learned men out of all the countries of Europe to Stockholm, and displayed a masculine spirit and character in everything. Her taste for art and her love of science found little support in the Protestant north, and she consequently never felt herself at home there. It was on this account, that, after a reign of ten years, Christina abdicated the throne of Sweden

A. D. 1354. in favor of her cousin, Charles Gustavus of Pfalz-Zweibrücken, reserved an annuity for herself, and quitted the land of her fathers. She was solemnly admitted into the Roman Catholic Church at Innsbruck; she then travelled through the Netherlands, France, and Italy, and at length established her permanent residence in a city filled with all the splendor of art — Rome. She died there in 1689.

Charles X., A. D. 1654–1660. § 385. Christina's successor, Charles (X.) Gustavus, was a great warrior. He undertook a campaign for the conquest of Poland, and made himself master of the western territories of that country, in conjunction with the great Elector, Frederick William of Brandenburg, to whom, in return, he promised the liberation of Prussia from the suzerainship of Poland. He would have gained possession of the whole country after the three days' battle of

July, 1656. Warsaw, had not an inroad of the Danes into the territory of Sweden called him to a different scene. He left Poland, and marched with restless haste to the lower Elbe. The Danish army opposed no resistance, so that, before the commencement of the winter, Sleswic and Jutland, with the exception of the fortress of Fredericia, were in the hands of the Swedes. This fortress also was stormed, in the midst of winter, by so daring an enterprise that the king became jealous, and attempted to eclipse the exploit of his general by one still more venturous. He crossed with his army on foot, over the frozen channel of the Little Belt, in January, into Funen, and a few days after, he passed the Great Belt into Zealand, in which passage two companies were drowned before his eyes. Here such confusion was occasioned by the sudden appearance of the enemy, that defence was scarcely thought of, and proposals for peace were at once entered into. But great as were the sacrifices that the hardly-pressed Danish king offered to make, they were rejected by Charles, who hoped to bring the three Scandinavian kingdoms under his own sceptre. But the gallant attitude of the citizens of Copenhagen, who, for a whole twelvemonth, bade defiance to the besieging Swedes, and the assistance of the Dutch, prolonged the war till the sudden death of the king gave a turn to affairs. The Swedish Diet, that conducted the government during the minority of Charles XI., concluded the peace of Oliva with the Poles, and that of Copenhagen

A. D. 1660. with the Danes. So great at that time was the respect for the military skill of the Swedes, that Sweden obtained large territories and important advantages by both these peaces. Prussia's independence of Poland was acknowledged. This war, in which the Danish nobility, who were in possession of great privileges and revenues, made an open display of their cowardice and selfishness, was made use of by the court to overthrow the existing constitution. The elective monarchy was converted into an hereditary one, and unlimited power conferred upon the king by the royal law. The nobility lost their former power and independent position, and were bound to the throne by titles and orders. In Sweden also, the vast power of the nobility was broken by the politic and severe Charles XI., who rigidly demanded back the alienated possessions of the crown; the ancient institutions, however, he allowed to remain.

Charles XI., A. D. 1660–1697.

2. THE REVOLUTION IN ENGLAND AND THE EXPULSION OF THE STUARTS.

a. THE FIRST TWO STUARTS (JAMES I. 1603–1625, CHARLES I. 1625–1649.)

James I., A. D. 1603–1625.

§ 386. Mary's son, James I., was a weak and pedantic prince, of narrow mind and perverted mental constitution. Bred up amidst the contentions of Presbyterian preachers, he was especially furnished with theological learning, and willingly engaged in controversies respecting disputed points of divinity. He was extremely desirous of gaining the reputation of a deeply learned man, both by his writing and conversation, and composed many books; but he was utterly wanting in the penetration and shrewdness necessary in a ruler. A lover of peace from timidity, he sacrificed the honor of his country to its external quiet, and he was so prodigal of his favor as frequently to give himself up entirely to the guidance of unworthy favorites. Among these, George Villiers, duke of Buckingham, distinguished by the symmetry of his figure, exercised the greatest influence upon him. James entertained the most extravagant notions respecting the kingly power. He was firmly persuaded that it was derived immediately from God, and that it was unlimited; and he sought for proofs of this in the Old Testament. It was on this account that he hated the Presbyterian Church of Scotland, where the king was nothing more than an ordinary member of the congregation; but he was devoted to the Episcopal Church of England, in which the king was regarded as the head and source of all spiritual power. "No bishop, no king" became therefore the motto of all the Stuarts, and the introduction of the Episcopal Church into Scotland, and the suppression of the Puritans in England, was, henceforth, the great object of the whole family.

§ 387. There are three points particularly worthy of notice in the reign of James; the gunpowder plot, the nuptial expedition of the prince

of Wales, and the increasing opposition in parliament. 1. James had promised toleration to the English Catholics, for the purpose of rendering them favorable to his ascension of the throne. Scarcely, however, was the crown firmly settled upon his head, before he, like Elizabeth, levied a heavy capitation tax upon the Catholic non-conformists, that he might enrich his favorites, and defray the expenses of his court festivals. The deluded Catholics were exasperated. A conspiracy was formed for blowing up the king and all the members of the Upper and Lower House at the opening of parliament, by means of a mine of gunpowder to be formed in the cellar of the parliament-house, and then for changing the government. The plot was discovered and frustrated a short time before its execution, by a warning in writing received by a Catholic peer. The chief conspirator (Guy Fawkes) was seized and executed; the other participators in the plot fled, and excited an insurrection, in which most of them perished. The English Catholics were then compelled to pay a heavy fine, and to take a particular oath of fidelity to the king. 2. James, in his conceit, thought that no one but the daughter of a king of the first rank was a fit spouse for his son, and accordingly made proposals for the hand of one of the Spanish princesses. This project excited great discontent among the English, both because they were unwilling to have a Catholic queen, and because the lengthened negotiations with Spain that were occasioned by it prevented the king from giving any assistance to his exiled Protestant son-in-law, Frederick V. of the Palatinate (§ 373). At length, the pope and the Spanish court gave their consent, and there appeared to be nothing more to prevent the union. At this point, the frivolous Buckingham persuaded prince Charles to make a voyage to Madrid, and the king, who in his youth had surprised his Danish bride in a similar manner, favored the undertaking. They arrived at Madrid under assumed names, and were treated when recognized with great distinction. But Buckingham's loose and insolent behavior gave offence. He made enemies of the Spanish court and prevented the marriage. Henrietta of France became the wife of Charles. 3. Elizabeth had given but little liberty to the parliament; but the greatness of her talents for government, and her frugal administration, had afforded the people a compensation. But when James, in the conviction of his kingly perfection, pursued the same path, abridged more and more the privileges of the parliament, and burthened the importation and exportation of every kind of goods with arbitrary taxes, a vehement opposition arose. It was in vain the king threatened, repeatedly dissolved the parliament, and placed the boldest speakers under arrest; every fresh assembly held the same language; and when James at length declared that their supposed rights were nothing but privileges for which they were indebted to the royal grace, the members of the Lower House registered a protest,
A. D. 1621. by which they declared that the making of laws, the consent-

ing to taxes, and the other befitting rights and privileges of parliament, were the undoubted native rights and inheritance of every Englishman. Enraged at this audacity, the king tore the leaf with his own hand from the record, dissolved the parliament, and ordered a few deputies to be imprisoned; but the spirit of resistance remained alive among the people, and displayed itself still more violently, when Charles I., a proud and obstinate ruler, took possession of the throne.

Charles I., A. D. 1625–1649. § 388. The government of Charles I. began with so violent a quarrel with the parliament, that the latter was twice dissolved during the first two years of his reign. The support afforded to the German Protestants, and a war with France occasioned by the fickle Buckingham, occasioned great expenses. The king was consequently extremely indignant that the parliament was sparing in voting supplies, and had not once, during his whole government, consented to the levying of tonnage and poundage upon exports and imports, as had hitherto been the custom. But when the French war took a disastrous termination, and the blood and honor of England were ignominiously sacrificed, the third parliament threatened Buckingham with an impeachment. (A. D. 1628.) The king, to save his favorite, was obliged to recognize the validity of the Petition of Right presented by both houses, and by this means to grant its ancient privileges to the parliament, and liberty of speech and security of person and property to its members. (A. D. 1629.) Buckingham was shortly after assassinated, upon which the king removed Thomas Wentworth, an eloquent member of the opposition, from parliament into the privy council, made him earl of Strafford and governor of Ireland, and followed his advice in everything. Wentworth, an ambitious and energetic man, now exerted his most zealous efforts to strengthen the power of the throne, and with this object, advised the king to govern for some time without a parliament. For the purpose of raising money for the current expenses, the government levied the usual imposts without the consent of the parliament, laid heavy indirect taxes upon light wines, salt, soap, and similar articles, and revived ancient and obsolete claims of the throne, such as ship-money, which in former times had replenished the royal treasury. Charles, at the same time, endeavored to establish the Anglican Church on a firmer foundation, and to suppress the Puritans and Presbyterians, whose democratic opinions were every day extending among the people. In this undertaking, he made use of the services of Bishop Laud of London, whom he appointed to the archbishopric of Canterbury. Laud had the cathedral of St. Paul's consecrated afresh, enriched the churches with images and ornaments, and the worship of God with ceremonies, removed the Puritan preachers from their offices, and had heavy and degrading punishments pronounced by the courts (the High Commission and the judges of the Star Chamber) against all those who opposed the existing institutions. Thus Prynne, a Puritan writer, was condemned to be exposed in the pillory, to lose both his ears, and to be imprisoned for life, because, in a bulky volume he had written, he had condemned dancing, masks, and theatrical amusements, matters in which the court delighted.

§ 389. These measures, which threatened to annihilate the civil and religious liberties of England, excited a great commotion over the whole country. John Hampden, a man of considerate and resolute character, refused payment of the ship-money, and conducted his defence before a court of justice so successfully, that the injustice of the government became most apparent. The deposed Puritan ministers wandered about the country, representing the proceedings of Laud as the commencement of the restoration of Catholicism, and, by their passionate exhortations, strewed the seeds of hatred against the court and the clergy. But the king retained his resolution; and, unwarned by the discontent openly expressed in England, he even attempted to introduce the Episcopal Church and the Anglican form of worship into Scotland, a country ever zealous for its faith. When the first attempt at celebrating divine service under the new form was made in the cathedral church of Edinburgh, a tumult arose against the performance of the "worship of Baal." The crowd shouted "Pope!" "Antichrist!" "Stone him!" hurled seats at the priest, and drove him from the building. The old Covenant "for the protection of the pure religion and the Church against the errors and corruptions of Popery" was renewed amidst fasting and prayer. The bishops were driven away, the Presbyterian form of worship restored, and the people called to arms. Upon this, Charles determined to put down resistance by force; but his troops gave way powerless before the zealous Scots, who marched into the field with prayer and psalmody; the hostile squadrons crossed the English borders, and nothing was left to the king but to call together the parliament, after an interval of eleven years, and to ask the assistance of the nation.

July, 1637.

A. D. 1640.

§ 390. The parliament now summoned is known in history under the name of the Long Parliament. The most influential members and speakers, as Hampden, Hollis, Hazelrig, Cromwell, &c., were opposed to absolute monarchical power and Episcopal Church government; they wanted security for the ancient privileges of the Estates, and for religious liberty. But during their contest against the absolute power of kings and bishops, they separated from each other: the more violent gradually acquired the democratical views of the Puritans; and whilst they mingled civil and religious freedom together, they aimed at an object that was only attainable in a free republican commonwealth. The new parliament immediately assumed a hostile attitude against the court and government. Instead of at once voting supplies against the Scottish rebels, the parliament entered into a secret alliance with them, and was the cause that they maintained their position on the frontiers. It then commenced its attack upon the arbitrary proceedings in Church and State. Strafford, "the great apostate," and Archbishop Laud, were impeached. It was in vain that the king, for the purpose of saving them, yielded to all the demands of the House; it was in vain that Strafford defended himself for seventeen days with dignity and presence of mind, and proved, in the most convincing manner, that the charges brought against him could not be regarded as high treason; — the Lower House declared that he must be considered as convicted of an attempt to destroy the liberties of the country; the Upper House embraced the same opinion, and the king had the weakness to confirm the sentence, and to sacrifice the most faithful of his servants to the rage of the people. Strafford died upon the scaffold with great composure. Laud, his companion in misfortune, was retained three years in confinement, before his life also was put an end to by the axe of the executioner. The abolition of the spiritual courts, and the exclusion of the bishops from the Upper House, were the forerunners of the fall of the Episcopal High Church.

May 11, 1641.

§ 391. Shortly after this, intelligence got abroad that the Protestant settlers in Ireland had been set upon and murdered by the Catholic inhabitants. This event was laid to the charge of the court, and especially of the queen, and made use of as a proof that Papists, bishops, and courtiers had united in a conspiracy for the destruction of religion and liberty. From this point, the struggle assumed more and more of a religious character; and as the parliament now overstepped the limits of a monarchical constitution in their demands, inasmuch as they interfered with the prerogatives of government, and required that the appointment of the higher officers of state, and of the commanders of the army, together with the management of the land and sea forces, should be dependent upon their approval, the two parties became more decidedly adverse. The people called the adherents of the king, who were mostly noblemen and officers, "Cavaliers;" they distinguished their opponents, however, by the nickname of Roundheads, from the cut of their hair. The attempt of the king to arrest five of the most violent leaders of the opposition during a debate failed. They fled, but were brought back the next day to the parliament-house in triumph by the people. Enraged at this Charles retired to York and declared war. The queen fled to Holland to claim foreign assistance; but as the whole military force of the Continent was engaged in the Thirty Years' War, no help could be obtained. The war commenced with unequal means for the contest. For whilst the king was unprovided with money, and his army suffered from every kind of want, the parliament was in possession not only of all the public revenue, but was amply sup-

Civil War, A. D. 1642–1646.

ported by private contributions. At the first summons, families brought their plate, women their ornaments; and every tax and impost, that had been obstinately contested with the king, were cheerfully surrendered to the parliament. Charles's small but practised army was, nevertheless, at first successful against the parliamentary forces, that were led into the field by the earl of Essex. In two encounters, the royal cavalry, which was commanded by Charles's nephew, Rupert of the Palatinate, gained the advantage. In the commencement of the second year, the parliament also experienced losses, among which, the death of the upright and gallant Hampden was the most severely felt. But when Oliver Cromwell, a zealous Puritan, formed a resolute band of cavalry from amongst his devout friends, which, in the cause of God, rushed blindly into the fight, matters assumed a different aspect. In the battle of Marston Moor, Rupert, by his impetuosity, lost the victory to Cromwell's gloomy squadrons. From this time, the name of Cromwell stood uppermost in the army, and the Puritans took advantage of the favorable opportunity to banish the Book of Common Prayer from Divine worship, and to thrust aside Episcopacy by the Calvinistic discipline and the synodial form of Church government. Images, ornaments, organs, and so forth, disappeared from the churches, painted windows were broken, monuments destroyed, and festivals forbidden.

July 3, 1644.

§ 392. But divisions soon arose in the camp of the conquerors. The Independents, the boldest and most energetic of the Puritans, were discontented with the synodial constitution of the Presbyterians; they demanded the entire independence, in religious matters, of every individual congregation, and refused to recognize the decisions of the synods as laws universally valid. Violent contests took place between the moderate Puritans (Presbyterians), and the Radicals (Independents). The latter passed the Self-denying Ordinance through the parliament, in virtue of which, no member of either house could fill any place of command or official situation. Essex was, by this means, compelled to lay down his military office, and Fairfax, a talented officer, entirely under the influence of Cromwell, was placed at the head of the army. Cromwell, the head of the Independents, had been one of the most zealous advocates of the Self-denying Ordinance. He repaired to the army to resign his command into the hands of Fairfax; but the latter at once gave the parliament to understand that Cromwell was indispensable — it was only he who could lead the cavalry; for where he fought, in the name of God, along with his pious squadron, there the victory was sure to be. Parliament consented, and the civil war burst forth afresh with redoubled violence. But the battle of Naseby destroyed the last hopes of Charles: he retreated with the remains of his army to Oxford. When Cromwell and Fairfax prepared to besiege him there, he embraced a desperate resolution; disguised as a servant,

February, 1645.

June 14, 1645.

he escaped with two attendants to the Scottish camp on the northern frontier, in the hope of finding truth and attachment among his own countrymen. But all sympathy for fallen greatness was extinguished in the bosom of the Scots, who were guided entirely by their austere clergy. They watched him narrowly, and compelled him to attend the lengthened discourses of their ministers, whose usual text was the misdeeds of himself and his ancestors; and when they found that it was impossible to prevail upon him to accept the Presbyterian faith, or to subscribe the Covenant, they sold their king for a small price. For the moderate sum of £400,000, Charles was delivered up to the commissioners of parliament, who confined him in a strong castle.

May, 1646.

§ 393. In the mean time, the division between the Presbyterians, who were the superior party in the parliament, and the Independents, who prevailed in the army, became every day greater. Cromwell was on the side of the latter; but he knew well how to conceal the falsehood of his heart by an outward appearance of sanctimony.* Whilst he was playing the part of a mediator, the captive Charles was carried off by a zealous tailor, with a troop of horse, and delivered up into the power of the army. Upon this, Cromwell marched upon the capital for the purpose of giving the Independents the superiority in parliament also. In the meanwhile, the king escaped to the Isle of Wight; and both Presbyterians and Independents sought, for some time, to gain him over to their own side, and to make their peace with him in return for certain concessions. But Charles, who relied upon foreign assistance, conducted himself in a deceitful and ambiguous manner, and thus deprived himself of the last chance of a peaceful release. Cromwell now resolved upon his destruction. The army, acting under his secret directions, made itself master of the king's person, and conducted him to a solitary castle on the sea-coast. Colonel Pride then surrounded the parliament-house with his troops, and commanded eighty-one of the Presbyterian members to be excluded by force. After this proceeding, which was known by the name of "Pride's Purge," Cromwell took possession of the royal apartments in Whitehall, — for he was now lord and ruler, and the so-called Rump Parliament, which consisted of Independents, was a mere passive tool in his hand. It was determined to accuse the king of treason before an extraordinary court, for having made war against the parliament. "Charles Stuart" was four times put upon his trial, and condemned to death as a traitor, murderer, and enemy of his country. He was allowed three days to prepare himself, and to take leave of his children. He

June, 1647.

November, 1648.

December, 1648.

* The character given by Weber in the text to Cromwell cannot be regarded as an impartial one. Cromwell's behavior was certainly not always distinguished by perfect candor, but his worst enemies will scarcely deny that his religious professions were, in a great measure, sincere.— *Translator.*

was then led forth upon a scaffold constructed in front of Whitehall, and covered with black, where the sentence was carried into execution by two masked executioners. January 30, 1649. An innumerable multitude gazed in silence upon the frightful scene. It was only when the executioner seized the blood-dropping head by the hair, and exclaimed, "This is the head of a traitor!" that the assembled people relieved their oppressed bosoms by a hollow groan.

b. OLIVER CROMWELL (A. D. 1649 – 1658).

§ 394. The intelligence of the king's death excited a fearful sensation in Ireland and Scotland. The Prince of Wales, who was living in Holland, was recalled to Scotland and acknowledged as Charles II., but was obliged, beforehand, to sign the Covenant and enter the Presbyterian Church. A. D. 1650. Ireland also acknowledged the new king, and flew to arms. Upon this, Cromwell, after arranging a republican government in England, in which Milton, the blind composer of "Paradise Lost," occupied a post, marched against the disobedient island. His path to victory lay over blood and corpses; and when he himself left the country to carry the sword into Scotland, other republican generals pursued the same course. In three years, the threatening rebellion was quelled; but Ireland became a depopulated country of lawless beggars, where the avenger of blood established his fearful dwelling. The arms of the republic were triumphant in Scotland also. The Scottish army had occupied a strong position, which Cromwell could not reach. Hunger and sickness soon diminished the number of his troops, so that he was already meditating a retreat. At this juncture, the preachers who accompanied the Scottish army, and who were annoyed by the cheerful military life and the hilarity of the king and his associates, advised the commanders to make an attack. When Cromwell beheld the movement in the Presbyterian army, he exclaimed, "They are coming down, the Lord has delivered them into our hands!" The battle of Dunbar, fought upon Cromwell's birthday, September 3rd, terminated in the defeat of the Scots. A. D. 1650. Cromwell took Edinburgh, and penetrated into the heart of the country. The Lord of Hosts, who was invoked both by Presbyterians and Independents with fasting and prayer and hypocritical lip-service, was with the bold and strong. Charles suddenly hazarded a daring undertaking. He marched with his troops across the English border, and called upon the adherents of royalty for support. Few joined him, and thus it happened that the royal army suffered a complete overthrow at Worcester, exactly a twelvemonth after the battle of Dunbar. September 3, 1651. This battle made Charles a houseless fugitive, for whose capture the parliament offered a large reward. After a thousand dangers and adventures, he escaped in disguise to France. Scotland was compelled to submit to

the republican government by General Monk. The free state of Eng land was also involved in a war with Holland. During this, the republicans showed that they were not only victorious on land, but powerful at sea. Greatly as the maritime heroes of Holland, Tromp and Ruyter, distinguished themselves by their courage and ability, Admiral Blake, a man of the old republican stamp, and of rude virtues, and General Monk, who was equally experienced in land and naval warfare, succeeded at length in carrying off the victory. The Dutch were obliged to consent to a disgraceful peace, whilst the Navigation Act, which was proclaimed
October, 1651. in England during the war, and which prohibited foreigners from bringing any thing but their own productions to England in their own ships, gave a fresh impulse to commerce.

§ 395. During these proceedings, Cromwell had fallen out with the Lower House, and for this reason he resolved upon dissolving the Long (Rump) parliament. After surrounding the house with troops, he entered
April, 1653. the apartment in his dark puritanical dress, delivered a discourse which was filled with invectives, and then, with the help of the soldiers who had entered, drove forth those who were present, exclaiming to one, "You are a drunkard;" to another, "You are an adulterer;" to a third, "You are a blasphemer of God!" A state council, under the presidentship of Cromwell, then undertook the formation of a new parliament. For this purpose, lists of all the God-fearing people were made out in every quarter, and from these "saints" the representatives of the kingdom were chosen. This assembly (named in mockery, Barebones' parliament, from the leather-seller, Praise-God Barebones), gave evidence of its disposition and religious views by the Biblical names of the greater number of its members (Habakkuk, Ezekiel, Stand-fast-in-the-Faith, &c.). But Cromwell was not able to manage these strange men so easily as he had hoped; and as they wished to introduce several vigorous measures, which would have produced great changes, he took advantage of the openly-displayed discontent to effect a
December, 1653. violent dissolution by means of his soldiers. After this, a new constitution, projected by General Lambert, came into existence, in which a parliament of 400 members composed the legislative body, and Cromwell, as Lord Protector, possessed the executive power and the command of the land and sea forces. As Protector, Cromwell governed energetically and gloriously. His talents for government and his strength of will procured him respect and authority abroad, and his respectable household, and his frugal and citizen-like mode of life, awakened esteem and confidence at home. But honorably as he filled the lofty situation in which fate had placed him, he nevertheless found many enviers and opponents, both among the republicans and royalists, who embittered the evening of his life, and never suffered him to attain to a quiet possession of the government. Rendered gloomy by

suspicion, and in constant fear of assassination, Cromwell died on his
September 3, 1658. birthday, a day that he had always regarded as particularly fortunate.

§ 396. Cromwell's weak son, Richard, inherited the dignity of Lord Protector, which, however, he did not know how to maintain. Three powers were soon arrayed in hostile opposition, the protector, the parliament, and the army, commanded by Monk, Lambert, and others. The military power was victorious; the parliament was dissolved, and the old Rump parliament again summoned; Richard Cromwell, who was neither a soldier nor a preacher, was obliged to abdicate, and to seek for
April, 1659. safety in a foreign land. But the Rump parliament was also obliged to yield in a short time to the power of the army; upon which the direction of affairs was undertaken by a committee of safety, under the presidentship of Lambert. During all these constitutional struggles, the opinion gradually gained ground that nothing but the return of the royal family, and the reëstablishment of monarchy, could effect the permanent reëstablishment of order. For this purpose, General Monk entered into an alliance with Charles Stuart, who was living in the Netherlands, but concealed his plans and opinions most carefully. He obtained the arrest of Lambert, the dissolution of the committee of safety, and the assembly of a new parliament. With this assembly, which consisted for the most part of royalists, Monk hastened to effect the restoration of the Stuarts. An amnesty, and liberty of conscience, were all that Charles had to promise before his solemn entrance into Lon-
May, 29, 1660. don, where he was received by an exulting people. But even these conditions were not observed. Sentence of death was pronounced upon all those who had sat in judgment upon Charles I., and ten of them were actually executed as regicides. The triumph of the royalists at the destruction of their enemies was much diminished by the resolution displayed by the Puritans in their last moments. Cromwell's body was torn from the grave and suspended on the gallows. The Episcopal Church was restored, and the Presbyterian clergy again deprived of their places.

c. THE LAST TWO STUARTS (CHARLES II. 1660–1685, AND JAMES II. 1685–1688.)

§ 397. The government of the fickle, characterless, and voluptuous Charles was fatal to England. Neither the fate of his father, nor the melancholy passages in his own life, served him either for instruction or warning. Severely as the land was visited by the plague, and by a frightful conflagration that destroyed two thirds of London, no interruption was given to the splendid and joyous life that was led by the royal court; and when extravagant expenditure had produced debts and want of money, and the parliament was not so free in its grants as the king desired, Charles sold the honor and interests of his country to the French king, Louis XIV. At that time especially, it was looked upon as a mark of refinement in France if a man left the Protestant Church for the Catholic. This way of thinking found some imitation in England. The duke of York, the brother of the king, openly embraced Catholicism, and Charles was a Catholic in heart, although he outwardly conformed to the English Church, and only betrayed his real convictions when on his death-bed, by receiving the Catholic sacraments. The more, however, the Stuarts favored Catholicism, the more sturdily did the people adhere to the faith of their fathers. The fire of London was attributed by them to the Papists, and this belief was perpetuated by a monument; and that the public offices should not be made use of as rewards for these changes of religion, the parliament, after a long contest, carried the Test Act, which enacted that none but members of the English Church, and confessors of the Protestant doctrine, should be capable of admission into parliament, or of holding offices or military posts. As long as Clarendon, the historian of the English "Rebellion," remained at the head of the ministry, the king was in some degree restrained within the bounds of moderation and legality; but when the former fell into disgrace, and was compelled to end his days as an outlaw in a foreign country, Charles allowed himself to commit acts of all kinds of violence, tyranny, and lawlessness. A ministry that was formed of talented but unprincipled statesmen, and distinguished by the people as the "Cabal" ministry from the initials of its members, now conducted the government according to the wishes of the king, without regard to the privileges and honor of the people. Corruption and venality were no longer regarded as disgraceful among the higher classes, since the king himself drew a yearly stipend from Louis XIV. for supporting the French in their war against the Dutch. A new contest at this time sprang up between the king and the parliament. For, the more openly the former strove for absolute power, the more did the latter endeavor to protect the privileges of the people and the religion of the country. The parliament, anxious lest the English Church should be exposed to danger under a Catholic king, demanded the exclusion of the duke of York from the throne; and Charles found himself so far obliged to yield, that he sent his brother out of the country for some time, and formed a new ministry, in which the ingenious earl of Shaftesbury, who had gone over from the king's council to the popular party, was the president. It was under his administration that the Habeas

A. D. 1679. Corpus Act, that sacred law for the freedom of person, came into existence. According to this act, no one could be imprisoned, without a written order of the court stating the grounds of the imprisonment; and within three days, the prisoner was to be brought before the ordinary judges, and cause was to be shown why he should not be released. In the midst of these parliamentary struggles, two parties sprang up, the

Whigs and the Tories, that exist to the present day. The Whigs regarded the constitution of the state as a mutual compact between the king and the nation, and attributed to the latter the right of active resistance in case of any infringement of the compact; the Tories, on the other hand, rejected the principle that the royal power proceeded from the people, and demanded passive obedience from the subject. The Tories gained the upper hand during the latter years of Charles II.'s reign, inasmuch as the court took advantage of a conspiracy contrived by some worthless men against the lives of the king and his brother, to ruin the heads of the Whig party. Lord Russell and Algernon Sidney, two of the noblest and most respected of men, died upon the scaffold; Shaftesbury fled to Holland; the duke of York again regained his rights and offices; and when Charles died a few years afterwards without legitimate offspring, the Duke ascended the English throne, under the title of James II.

A. D. 1685.

James II., A. D. 1685–1688.

§ 398. A few weeks after James's ascension of the throne, Monmouth, a natural son of Charles II., attempted, by the aid of the Whigs, to deprive his uncle of the crown. The insurrection failed of success. Monmouth died on the scaffold, and the frightful cruelty that James displayed against all the supporters and abettors of the enterprise destroyed the last sparks of attachment in the hearts of the people. The name of the chief judge, Jeffreys, who passed through the counties with the axe of justice and a crew of executioners, is written with letters of blood in the annals of English history. The victory which he had gained so easily, and the terror of the people, induced the king to hope, that by cunning and severity he might gradually restore the Catholic religion to its former supremacy in England. With this object, he made the detested Jeffreys chancellor, presented many offices and military appointments to the Catholics and those who had gone over to the Roman Church, and aimed at neutralizing the Test Act by the introduction of an edict of toleration. But as the parliament, despite the bribery used in the elections, could not be brought to accept this edict, James attempted to destroy the Test Act by another plan; he declared that the throne possessed the power of granting a dispensation from this law; a privilege by which the power and operation of all laws would have been paralyzed. The English people looked on quietly for some time at these proceedings, although with inward repugnance, inasmuch as the king being old and having no male descendants, and his two daughters having been brought up in the English Church and married to Protestant princes, the elder, Mary, to William of Orange (§ 403), and the younger, Anne, to a Danish prince, they hoped for a speedy deliverance. But when the intelligence of the birth of a prince of Wales put an end to all hope of a release from the yoke of popery, they began to entertain the purpose of freeing themselves by their own

efforts, with the assistance of William of Orange. The genuineness of the young prince was called in question; crowds of discontented Britons streamed towards the Hague; the Whigs united themselves with William of Orange, and promised him the support of the Protestant part of the nation. James did not perceive the storm that was gathering around his head, until William had landed with a Dutch force on the shores of England, with the avowed purpose of defending the Protestant religion and the liberties of the country. It was in vain that the king now turned himself to the army and the people, and promised the removal of every measure repugnant to the Constitution; the ground on which he stood had been rendered insecure by the treachery, hypocrisy, and perjury with which the Stuarts had rendered the nation familiar. When a part of the army went over to William, and the general voice declared itself against the king, James sent his wife and son to France, threw the great seal into the Thames, and then fled himself in despair from the land of
December, his fathers, of whose fair crown he had deprived himself and
1688. his Catholic offspring. He lived from this time forth at St. Germain, a pensioner of Louis XIV.

§ 399. After the flight of James, the representatives of the English people declared the throne forsaken, and agreed that the Catholic line of the house of Stuart should be excluded from the government, and that this should be placed in the hands of the royal pair, William and Mary. Instructed however by the past, they secured the liberties of the nation against any future arbitrary acts by the Bill of Rights, without at the same time weakening overmuch the power of the king. The Scots acknowledged the new government, and regained their Presbyterian Church; but the Catholic Irish, supported by France, and led into the
July 1, 1690. field by James II. himself, were first compelled to submission by the bloody battle of the Boyne, and again curtailed of their privileges and property. From this time, England, by her naval power, her trade, industry, and prosperity, took the lead of all other na-
A. D. 1701. tions. When a premature death carried the sickly William
Anne, A. D. childless to the grave, he was succeeded by Anne, the
1702-1714. younger daughter of James II., during whose reign the union
A. D. 1707. between Scotland and England was completed, so that, from this time, the Scottish representatives gave their voices in the English parliament. Anne also survived the whole of her children, so that the English crown devolved upon the Elector, George of Hanover, the grandson of Elizabeth, Palgravine and Queen of Bohemia. Two attempts of the Stuarts, [A. D. 1715 and 1745], to expel the house of Hanover by violence, and to repossess themselves of the English crown, terminated unsuccessfully.

3. THE AGE OF LOUIS XIV.

a. RICHELIEU AND MAZARIN.

Louis XIII. A. D. 1610–1643. § 400. The first part of the reign of the weak Louis XIII., who only numbered nine years at the time of his father's murder (§ 365), was full of mischief for France. During the time the queen-mother, Mary of Medicis, conducted the government, Italian favorites exerted a great influence upon affairs, enriched themselves at the expense of the French, and irritated the pride of the nation by their insolence. Enraged at this, the nobility took up arms, and filled the country with rebellion and the tumult of war. When at length Louis XIII. himself, upon coming of age, assumed the government, he indeed consented that the foreign favorites should be removed by murder and execution, and banished his mother from the court; but the people gained little by it. The new favorites in whom the king, who possessed no self-reliance, reposed his confidence, were not distinguished from the former either by virtue or talents; for this reason, both the nobles of the kingdom and the Huguenots, who felt themselves injured in their rights, again rose against the government, and threw the land into fresh confusion. This melancholy condition of affairs was only put an end to when Cardinal Richelieu was admitted into the state council, and
A. D. 1624. introduced a complete change of system. This great statesman maintained an almost absolute sway in the court and in the kingdom for nearly eighteen years, though the king never loved him, the queen and the nobility were constantly attempting his overthrow, and a succession of cabals and conspiracies were plotted against him. The greatness of his mind triumphed over all obstacles. Richelieu's efforts were directed towards the extension and rounding of the French territory without, and the increasing and strengthening of the royal power within. In furtherance of the former of these objects, he sought to weaken the house of Hapsburg, and for this purpose entered into alliances with the enemies of the emperor not only in Germany, in the time of the Thirty Years' War, but in Italy and other places; and, to attain his aims in regard to the latter project, he neglected to call together the estates of the kingdom, broke the power of the nobility and of the independent officials and judges in the parliament, and attacked the Huguenots, who had formed an almost independent alliance in the south and west of France, with their own fortresses, an effective militia, and great privileges. After conquering the most important of the Huguenot towns (Nismes, Montauban, Montpellier), and destroying their fortifications, in three wars, and when he had at length taken Rochelle, the bulwark of the Calvinists, after a siege of fourteen months, he proceeded to deprive the Protestants of their political privileges and of their independent position,

but granted them, by the Edict of Nismes, liberty of conscience and equal rights with Catholic subjects. The turbulent nobles had been deprived of their greatest support by the disarming of the Huguenots, and the war could now be prosecuted against them with success. The most daring were got rid of by banishment and the executioner. Even the queen-mother and her second son, the duke of Orleans, who had attempted to procure the fall of Richelieu, were compelled to leave the country, and the confidential friend of the latter, Henry, duke of Montmorency, a scion of one of the most renowned families of France, died at Toulouse by the hand of the executioner. A similar fate
A. D. 1632. awaited the count of Cinq-Mars and his friend, De Thou, a few years later, when, in conjunction with the queen and some of the nobles, they formed a conspiracy against the mighty cardinal. The parliament, the upper tax-offices and courts of justice, which, like the king, claimed an independent authority on account of their offices being hereditary, were weakened by the establishment of extraordinary courts and higher officers, who were dependent upon the minister.

§ 401. In the year 1642, died Richelieu, hated and feared by the nobility and the people, but admired by contemporaries and posterity; Louis XIII., a prince without either great virtues or great vices, and dependent upon every one who could either acquire his favor or render himself formidable to him, soon followed him. His widow, Anne of Austria, the proud and ambitious sister of the king of Spain, undertook
Louis XIV. the government during the minority of his son. But as she
A. D. 1643–1715. reposed the whole of her confidence on the Italian, Mazarin, the inheritor of the office and the principles of Richelieu, she met with vehement opposers among the nobility and in the parliament, who attempted to regain their former power and position. The people, in the hope of being relieved of some of their heavy taxes, and guided by the clever and dexterous Cardinal Retz, embraced their cause, with the intent of compelling the court to remove Mazarin, and to adopt a different
A. D. 1648–1653. plan of government. This gave occasion to a furious civil war, which is known in history as "the War of the Fronde." Mazarin was obliged to leave the country for a short time, but so immovable were the favor and confidence of the queen, that he governed France from Cologne as he had formerly done in Paris. But his banishment did not last long. When Louis XIV. had attained the years of kingly majority, and Turenne, the commander of the royal troops, had conquered his rival, the great Condé, the general of the insurgents, in the suburb of St. Antoine, Mazarin returned in triumph.
A. D. 1653. His solemn entry into Paris was a sign that absolute power had gained the victory, and that henceforth the will of the monarch was to be law. Mazarin enjoyed for six years longer the greatest respect in France and Europe; Cardinal Retz, the ingenious composer of the Me-

moirs of this war, was obliged to leave his country, after he had previously expiated his turbulent conduct in the prison of Vincennes; Condé, poor and unhappy, wandered among the Spaniards, till the grace of his master allowed him to return and take possession of his estates; Mazarin's nieces, Italian females without name or position, were endowed with the wealth of France, and sought for as brides by the greatest nobles; and the members of parliament adapted themselves without opposition to the directions they received from above, after Louis had appeared before them in his boots and riding whip, and demanded their obedience with threats. Louis now gave effect to his principle, "I am the state" (*l'état,*
A. D. 1659. *c'est moi*). The peace of the Pyrenees with Spain was the last work of Mazarin. He died shortly after, leaving enor-
March 9, mous wealth behind him. His death took place at the mo-
1661. ment when Louis began to grow weary of him, and was longing to seize the reins of government in his own powerful grasp.

b. GOVERNMENT AND CONQUESTS OF LOUIS XIV.

§ 402. After the death of Mazarin, Louis XIV., in whom kingly absolutism attained its highest point, appointed no prime minister, but surrounded himself with men who merely executed his will, and whose highest aim was to increase and spread abroad the renown, glory, and honor of the king. In the choice of these men, Louis displayed judgment and the talents of a ruler. His ministers, especially Colbert, the great promoter of French industry, manufactures, and trades, as well as his generals, Turenne, Condé, Luxemburg, and the engineer, Vauban, as much surpassed, in talent, acquirements, and dexterity, the statesmen and soldiers of all other countries, as Louis XIV. himself was preëminent among the princes of his age, in the greatness of his power, in commanding presence, and kingly dignity. He rendered the age of Louis XIV. the most illustrious in the French annals, and caused the Court of Versailles (the seat of the royal residence) to be everywhere praised and admired as the model of taste, of refinement, and of a distinguished mode of living. But as he sought nothing but the gratification of his own selfishness, of his own love of pleasure, of his pride, and of his desire for renown and splendor, his reign became the grave of freedom, of morals, of firmness of character, and of manly sentiments. Court favor was the end of every effort, and flattery the surest road to arrive at it; virtue and merit met with little acknowledgment.

§ 403. Louis XIV. wished to enlarge his empire, and to render his name illustrious by military renown. He took advantage, therefore, of the death of the Spanish king, Philip IV., to make pretensions to his
Spanish War, inheritance as the husband of Philip's daughter, and to march
A. D. an army into the Spanish Netherlands. By the triple alliance
1667-1668. of England, Holland, and Sweden, he was indeed compelled,

by the peace of Aix, to surrender, after a short campaign, the greater part of his conquests; but many of the frontier towns of Flanders remained with France, and were converted by Vauban into impregnable fortresses. As Holland had been the chief instrument in checking the victorious course of the haughty king, so she did not fail to experience the vengeance of the French potentate. He won Sweden to his side, purchased the favor of the English king by annuities and mistresses (§ 397), and concluded an alliance with the Elector of Cologne and the bishop of Munster. Thus prepared and protected on every side, Louis began a second war, which at first was directed against Holland alone, but in which almost all the European states were involved during the seven years of its continuance. After the celebrated passage of the Rhine at Tolhuis, the French army pursued its rapid course of victories into the territories of the States General. Holland was now in extremities. The republicans, who had hitherto conducted the affairs of the State with great credit, had been more solicitous about improving the navy than upon maintaining or increasing the land forces; how could they resist the stately armies of France, conducted, as they were, by the most celebrated generals? Liege, Utrecht, and Upper Issel, fell into the hands of the enemy; French dragoons already made incursions into the province of Holland, and approached to within two miles of the capital; — the terrified republicans implored peace, but were not listened to. But whilst the French army was wasting time in the siege of the Dutch fortresses, the republicans, to whom the whole of the mischief was ascribed, were overthrown by the Orange party, their chiefs, John and Cornelius de Witt, murdered in the streets of the capital, and the government then placed in the hands of the shrewd and warlike stadtholder, William III. of Orange. This celebrated general aroused the courage and patriotic enthusiasm of the Hollanders; they cut through their dykes, and rendered the inundated country inapproachable by the French; the walls of Groningen defied all the efforts of the enemy, and the marshal of Luxemburg's daring march against Amsterdam, over the frozen waters, was frustrated by a sudden thaw. These and other circumstances saved Holland. For as the great Elector of Brandenburg, Frederick William, now came to the assistance of the Dutch, and also induced the emperor Leopold to take an interest in the war, the French were obliged to divide their power, and to send their chief force to the Rhine. Spain, also, and the German empire, soon entered into the war against France.

May, 1668.

Dutch War, A. D. 1672-1679.

A. D. 1674.

§ 404. The military power of France increased with the number of her enemies. Turenne crossed the Rhine, after having barbarously ravaged the lands of the Palatinate, and pressed forwards, burning and ravaging, into Franconia. The German princes were divided; the imperial minister of war was in the pay of Louis, and betrayed the military plans to the enemy; the Austrian generals were either incompetent, or, like Montecuculi, engaged in Hungary. The triumph of France would have been complete, had not the great Elector saved the military reputation of Germany. Louis XIV., for the purpose of compelling the latter to separate himself from the army of the Rhine, had induced his allies, the Swedes, to attack the march of Brandenburg. But the energetic Frederick William appeared in his own territories before the enemy entertained the slightest suspicion of his approach, and gave the surprised Swedes a complete overthrow in the battle of Fehrbellin. This battle was the foundation of Prussia's greatness. A month later, Turenne, the greatest general of his age, was killed by a cannon-ball, near Sasbach, and the enemy compelled to retreat across the Rhine. But the war nevertheless continued for three years longer, and was particularly destructive to the lands on the Mosel and the Saar, where the French committed frightful ravages. It was not until the English parliament demanded, with menaces, that the government should dissolve the alliance with France and support the Dutch, that Louis resolved to put an end to the war. By the peace of Nimeguen, the Dutch, who in the mean time had made the office of stadtholder hereditary in the male line of the gallant William of Orange, received back the whole of their lost towns and territories. On the other hand, the Spaniards were obliged to relinquish Franche-Comté, and the whole of the fortified places in the line of Valenciennes and Maubeuge, to France, and the German empire lost not only the town of Freiburg in the Breisgau, but was obliged to submit to the greatest humiliations. The dukedom of Lorraine, which belonged to Germany, and of which the French had taken possession at the commencement of the war, was given back to the duke, who was engaged in the Austrian service, under such degrading conditions, that the latter preferred to allow it to remain still in the hands of the enemy; and the great Elector saw himself compelled to give up to the Swedes the lands and towns he had conquered with so much difficulty in Pomerania.

June 28, 1675.

A. D. 1679.

§ 405. The timorous acquiescence of the German princes inflamed the insolence and ambition of Louis XIV. He asserted that a number of districts and portions of territory, which, at an earlier period, had belonged to the towns and provinces which had fallen to France in the Peaces of Westphalia and Nimeguen, were included in the cession. To arrange this matter, he established the so-called chambers of reunion in Metz and Breisach, and, supported by their decisions, took possession of a number of cities, towns, boroughs, villages, mills, nay, even whole provinces, on the left bank of the Rhine. Success only increased the audacity of the French king, so that, at length, in the midst of peace, he wrested the free town of Strasburg from the German empire. The traitorous bishop, Francis Egon, of Furstenburg, assisted in the

September 1681.

surprise and occupation of the place. The once free burghers were compelled, after being disarmed, to take the oath of subjection to the foreign potentate upon their knees. The ornaments of German architecture were restored to the Catholic worship, and the arsenal was emptied. Instead of chastising this insolence with their united forces, Austria, Spain,
August 15, and the German empire concluded a truce for twenty years
1684. with the tyrannical king, at Regensburg, by which all the annexed and plundered provinces were given up to Louis, with the single condition, that he should be satisfied with what he had got, and should put an end to his annexations.

AUSTRIA'S DISTRESS AND TRIUMPH.

§ 406. During this time, the emperor Leopold was engaged in the eastern portion of his dominions. In Hungary, the oppression exercised by the government upon the Protestants, the burdensome quartering of troops, and some acts of violence against certain magnates, had produced a formidable rebellion at the moment when the Turks were renewing their former plans of conquest, and some active chief viziers were awakning the warlike spirit of the janisaries. The Austrian government hoped to suppress the insurrection by severity. It condemned the leaders to death upon the scaffold, and outraged the chartered rights of the nation. But these acts of violence excited the love of free-
A. D. 1671. dom and the military spirit of the Hungarians. Emmerick Tokeli, an active noble, whose property had been confiscated, unfurled the banner of rebellion. In a short time, he had a consider-
A. D. 1674. able army at his command, with which he drove the Austrian forces out of Hungary. Louis XIV. afforded him assistance, and the Porte, which recognized him as tributary king of Hun-
A. D. 1681. gary, despatched a powerful army for his defence. The Turks marched, plundering and devastating, to the walls of Vienna. The court fled to Lintz, and the capital of Austria seemed lost. But the courage of the citizens and of their leader, Rudiger von Staremberg, together with the Ottoman's want of skill in conducting sieges, preserved Vienna for sixty days, in spite of all attacks, till at length the imperial army, commanded by Charles of Lorraine, and in conjunction with a Polish force under the heroic king, John Sobieski, came to the help of
September, the hardly-pressed town. A bloody engagement under the
1683. walls of Vienna terminated to the disadvantage of the Turks. They made a hasty retreat, and left an enormous booty in the hands of the victors. From this time, the fortune of the war remained with the Austrians. Hungary was conquered, Tokeli compelled to fly, and Buda, which had been in possession of the Turks for 146 years, was wrested from their hands. After the criminal court of Eperies had deprived the Hungarian nobility of their most enterprising leaders, and spread ter-

ror through the whole nation, the emperor Leopold was enabled, at the Diet at Presburg, to abolish elective monarchy, and to banish certain privileges from the constitution that interfered with the royal power, without any opposition. In this way, Hungary became the inheritance of the house of Hapsburg. The Turks made great efforts to regain that which had been lost, and streams of Turkish and Christian blood were shed around the walls of Belgrade; but those great heroes, Charles of Lorraine, prince Eugene, and Louis of Baden, held victory firmly to the Austrian banners. By the peace of Carlowitz, Transylvania, and the whole of the land between the Danube and the Theiss, were ceded to the Austrians.

A. D. 1699.

d. THE WAR OF ORLEANS.

§ 407. For the purpose of creating a diversion in favor of the Turks against the superior power of Austria, Louis XIV. took advantage of affairs relating to the inheritance of the Palatinate and the election of the archbishop of Cologne, to engage in the third war, called the war of Orleans. When the elector Charles died without male issue, and the land fell into the collateral Catholic line of Pfalz Neuberg, Louis XIV. claimed not only the movable property, but also the immovable estate, as the inheritance of Elizabeth Charlotte, the sister of the deceased Elector, and the wife of Louis's brother, the duke of Orleans; and when this claim was not admitted, he marched an army upon the Rhine. For the purpose of rendering it impossible for the enemy to penetrate into France, Louvois, the hard-hearted minister of war, gave command for creating a desert between the two kingdoms by devastating the banks of the Rhine. Hereupon, the wild troops fell like incendiaries upon the flourishing villages of the Bergstrasse, the rich cities on the Rhine, and the blooming districts of the southern Palatinate, and reduced them to heaps of ashes. The shattered tower of the castle of Heidelberg is yet a silent witness of the barbarity with which Melac and other leaders executed the commands of a merciless government. Towns and villages, vineyards and orchards, were in flames from Haardtgebirge to Nahe; in Manheim, the inhabitants themselves were obliged to assist in destroying their own buildings and fortifications; a great part of Heidelberg was consumed by fire, after the bridge of the Neckar had been blown up; in Worms, the cathedral with many of the dwelling-houses became the prey of the flames; and in Spire, the French drove out the citizens, set fire to the plundered city and the venerable cathedral, and desecrated the bones of the ancient emperors.

War of Orleans, A. D. 1689-1697.

June, 1689.

The second occasion of the war, in which, beside the German empire and the emperor, the Netherlands, Spain, and the dukes of Savoy and Piedmont became involved, was the appointment to the spiritual elector-

ship in Cologne, where Louis XIV., by dint of bribery, had secured the election of William von Furstenburg, a man in the interests of France; but both pope and emperor refused confirmation. In this war, also, which lasted for eight years, the French army, which was conducted by the most distinguished generals, maintained its supremacy over the far superior force of the enemy. In Italy, in the Netherlands, in heavily afflicted Germany, in the north of Spain, the French had generally the advantage; even at sea they maintained their honor, although
A. D. 1692. the battle of La Hogue went against them. It was a cause of much surprise that Louis should consent to the universally desired termination of the war, and should show himself far more mo-
A. D. 1697. derate in the peace of Ryswick (between Hague and Delft) than in that of Nimeguen. The German empire was the only loser, inasmuch as it was obliged to leave Strasburg and all the annexed provinces to France. Louis's reason for concluding the peace so hastily was, that he wished to have his hands free at the approaching vacancy of the Spanish crown.

e. LIFE AT THE COURT. LITERATURE. CHURCH.

§ 408. It was during the last three decades of the seventeenth century that France stood at the culminating point of her power abroad and of her prosperity at home, so that the flattering chronicles of those days described the age of Louis XIV. as the golden age of France. Trade and industry received a prodigious development by the care of Colbert; the woollen and silk manufactories, the stocking and cloth weaving, which flourished in the southern towns, brought prosperity, the maritime force increased, colonies were planted, and the productions of France were carried by trading companies to all quarters of the globe.

The court of France displayed a magnificence that had never before been witnessed. The palace of Versailles, and the gardens which were adorned with statues, fountains, and alleys of trees, were a model of taste for all Europe; fêtes of all kinds, jovial parties, ballets, fireworks, the opera and the theatre, in the service of which the first intellects in France employed their talents, followed upon each other in attractive succession; poets, artists, men of learning, all were eager to do honor to a prince who rewarded with a liberal hand every kind of talent that conduced either to his amusement or to his glory. Sumptuous buildings, as the Hospital of Invalides, costly libraries, magnificent productions of the press, vast establishments for the natural sciences, academies, and similar institutions, exalted the glory and renown of the great Louis. The refined air of society, the polished tone, the easy manners of the nobility and courtiers, subdued Europe more permanently and extensively than the weapons of the army. The French fashions, language, and literature, bore sway from this time in all circles of the higher classes.

The consequences of the establishment of the French Academy by Richelieu were a development of the language, style, and literary composition, that was extremely favorable to the diffusion of the literature. The language, so particularly adapted for social intercourse, for conversation, and for epistolary writing, remained from henceforth the language of diplomacy, of courts, and of the higher classes; and although the literary productions are wanting in strength, elevation, and nature,—the polish of the form, and the ease and felicity of the style, gave French taste the supremacy in Europe, and strengthened the French people in the agreeable delusion that they were the most civilized of nations. In the time of Louis, dramatic poetry reached its highest excellence in Peter Corneille (1684), whose "Cid" is regarded as the foundation and commencement of classical stage poetry; in J. Racine (1699), who, in his Iphigenia and Phædra ventured to emulate Euripides, and in the talented writer of comedies, Moliere (1673), whose Tartuffe, L'Avare, Le Misanthrope, &c. evince a profound knowledge of human nature in its aberrations. Boileau (Despreaux) (1711), a dexterous versifier, was admired as the French Horace on account of his odes and satires; Lafontaine's (1694) fables and stories are still familiar in all families as school and children's books, and the adventures of Telemachus by Bishop Fenelon (1715) are translated into all European languages, and have an immense circulation. At the same time, the eloquence of the pulpit was cultivated by Bossuet (1704) and other spiritual orators; the philosophy of scepticism, by the Huguenot, Bayle; and the literature of polemics by the religious party of the Jansenists, in its contests against the Jesuits and their dangerous morality. In this latter class, the Provincial Letters of Pascal occupy the first rank.

§ 409. But however flatterers may sing the praises of the age of Louis XIV., one spot of shame remains ineradicable—the persecution of the Huguenots. The French king believed that the unity of the Church was inseparable from a perfect monarchy. For this reason he oppressed the Jansenists, a Catholic party, which first contended against the Jesuits, and afterwards against the head of the Church himself; and he compelled the Calvinists, by the most severe persecutions, either to fly, or to return into the bosom of the Catholic Church. Colbert, who esteemed the Huguenots as active and industrious citizens, prevented for some time these violent measures; but the suggestions of the royal confessor, La Chaise, the zeal for conversion of the affectedly pious Madame Maintenon, who had been first a tutoress of the court, and afterwards Louis's trusted wife, and the cruelty of Louvois, the minister of war, at length triumphed over the advice of Colbert. A long succession of oppressive proceedings against the Huguenots prepared the way for the great stroke. The number of their churches was restricted, and their worship confined to a few of the principal towns. Louis's paroxysms of repentance and devotion were always the sources of fresh oppressions to the Calvinistic heretics, by whose conversion he thought to expiate his own crimes. They were gradually excluded from office and dignities; converts were favored; in this way, the ambitious were enticed, the poor were won by money, which flowed from the king's conversion chest, and from the liberal gifts of the pious illustrious; a wide field was opened to the zeal for proselytism by the enactment that the conversion of children under age was valid. Families were divided, children were torn from their parents and brought up as Catholics. Court and clergy, the heartless and eloquent bishop Bossuet at their head, set all means in motion to establish the ecclesiastical unity of France. When all other means of conversion failed, came the dragonades. At the command of Louvois, the cavalry took possession of the southern provinces, and established their quarters in the dwellings of the Huguenots. The prosperity of the industrious citizens, whose substance was devoured by the dragoons, soon disappeared. The bad treatment by these booted missionaries, who quitted the houses of the apostates to fall in doubled numbers upon those who remained stedfast, operated more effectually than all the enticements of the court or the seductions of the priests. Thousands fled abroad that they

October, 1685. might preserve their faith upon a foreign soil. At last came the revocation of the Edict of Nantes. The religious worship of the Calvinists was now forbidden, their churches were torn down, their schools closed, their preachers banished from the land; when the emigration increased to a formidable degree, this was forbidden, under punishment of the galleys and forfeiture of goods. But despite all threats and prohibitions, upwards of 500,000 French Calvinists carried their industry, their faith, and their courage to Protestant lands. Switzerland, the Palatinate of the Rhine, Brandenburg, Holland, and England, offered an asylum to the persecuted. The silk manufacture and stocking-weaving were carried abroad by the fugitive Huguenots. Flatterers extolled the king as the exterminator of heresy, but the courage of the peasants in Cevennes, and the number of Huguenots who contented themselves with private devotion, show how little religious oppression conduced to the desired end. For when the persecution was carried into the distant valleys of the Cevennes, where Waldenses and Calvinists lived, according to ancient custom, in the simplicity of the faith, the oppressors met with an obstinate resistance. Persecution called forth the courage of its victims, oppression urged zeal into fanaticism. Led on by a young mechanic, the Camisards, clad in a linen frock, rushed "with naked breast against the marshals." A frightful civil war filled the peaceful valleys of Cevennes; fugitive priests, in the gloom of the forest, exhorted the evangelical brethren to a desperate defence, till, at length, the persecutors grew weary. Nearly two millions of the Huguenots remained without rights and without religious worship.

IV. THE COLONIZATION OF NORTH AMERICA.

[A. D. 1606 – 1732.]

§ 410. North America, with the exception of Mexico, was not colonized by Europeans so early as the southern part of the Continent. The discoveries of Cabot had given England a valid claim to the
A. D. 1497. whole coast from Labrador to Florida; but the country presented none of the allurements that had incited and rewarded the Spanish adventurers. Fertile and well-wooded, indeed, intersected by noble rivers, and inclosing safe and capacious harbors and bays, it seemed a promising region for permanent settlements and agricultural industry, but offered only a faint prospect of wealth to be obtained from gold and silver mines, or from plundering the native inhabitants. There was little chance of glory or gain in subduing feeble and destitute tribes, who had hardly risen above the lowest stage of savage life. Buccaneering Englishmen, like Drake, Frobisher, and Hawkins, thirsting for adventure and gold, contemptuously overlooked the North American Indians, preferring to attack and rob the wealthy settlements already formed by the Spaniards at the south. A party of French Huguenots attempted to colonize Florida; but the Spaniards, who claimed the country, surprised the infant settlement, and massacred nearly all its inhabitants, not sparing even the women and children. This slaughter was soon
A. D. 1564. avenged by a Frenchman, Dominique de Gourges, who captured Fort Carolina, where the victors had established themselves, and hanged all his prisoners; but he made no attempt to form another colony, and did not even disturb the little Spanish city of St. Augustine, which remained, but did not flourish, as the only permanent settlement of Europeans on the coast north of the Gulf of Mexico during the sixteenth century.

The English, under the direction of Sir Walter Raleigh and his half-brother, Sir Humphrey Gilbert, attempted to create a settlement on
A. D. the coast of what was subsequently called North Carolina.
1583 – 1587. Three parties of colonists were sent thither, but they were few in number, and ill provided with necessaries; one returned, and the other two perished, either from starvation or the hostility of the natives. Early in the seventeenth century, the French, under De Monts and Champlain, explored the country around the Bay of Fundy and that bordering on the St. Lawrence, laying claim to Acadie (Nova Scotia) and Canada, which together were called New France. De Monts founded Port Royal (Annapolis), on the eastern shore of the Bay of Fundy, in 1606; and two years afterwards, Champlain established on the St. Lawrence the post of Quebec. In 1609, the Dutch sent out Henry Hudson, who explored the American coast for a considerable distance, entered

New York harbor, and sailed up the river which now bears his name. Stimulated by a feeling of rivalry with the French, the English renewed their attempts at colonization on a larger scale. James I. granted the whole country, from Cape Fear to Passamaquoddy Bay, to two companies of merchants and adventurers. The southern portion, from the thirty-fourth to the forty-first degree of latitude was given to the London Company; and the northern part, from the thirty-eighth to the forty-fifth degree, was to be colonized by the Plymouth Company. Neither was to commence a settlement within one hundred miles of a spot already occupied by the other. Such associations, looking only to the profits of trade, and intended to remain as commercial corporations within the limits of England, were but ill fitted for the great enterprise of founding and nourishing colonies on a distant coast. All their undertakings resulted in disappointment and loss; and they were finally dissolved while the settlements which they had created were still in the weakness of infancy.

§ 411. VIRGINIA. The first band of colonists sent out by the London Company established themselves on a spot which they called Jamestown, on the James river, about fifty miles above its entrance into Chesapeake Bay. The situation was an unhealthy one, and most of the adventurers were poor gentlemen or broken down tradesmen, unused to toil, and "fitter to breed a riot than to found a colony." The direction of affairs had been given to a council, consisting of seven persons, nominated by the Company in England. John Smith, a military adventurer of great courage, enterprise, and sagacity, was one of them; and the incompetency of his colleagues soon becoming manifest, he gradually assumed the lead, and several times rescued the feeble settlements from the imminent perils of savage warfare and famine. Half of the emigrants perished during the first six months; and if the colony had not been fed by frequent supplies of food and additional settlers from England, the enterprise must soon have been abandoned. In spite of Smith's remonstrances, the settlers wasted their time in seeking for gold and silver, instead of cultivating the ground; and they actually sent a vessel to England laden with dirt in which glittering specks had been discovered, which they mistook for gold. Smith explored the country, and coasted the bay in an open boat, entering the principal rivers and inlets, and thus obtaining the requisite information for the construction of a chart, which was transmitted to England and published. In one of these expeditions, he fell into the hands of the savages, and was on the point of being put to death, when he was rescued by the chieftain's daughter, Pocahontas, and after an imprisonment of a few weeks, was sent back to Jamestown. But the colony was soon deprived of his invaluable services; in 1609, he was severely injured by the accidental explosion of his powder bag, and was compelled to return to England for surgical aid. After his departure, the affairs of the colony again declined, and the settlers more than once

A. D. 1607.

determined to abandon the undertaking, and return home. But they were prevented by the seasonable arrival of ships, bringing fresh supplies and a reinforcement of men, whose broken fortunes in their native land made them eager to brave the perils of a desperate enterprise. Thus often rescued from the brink of ruin, the colony struggled on, till its members at last became inured to their novel situation, and acquired the habits of life which alone could meet its exigencies. Novel recruits were sent out from time to time to keep up their numbers. In 1619, ninety young women arrived, of irreproachable character, who were sold at the price of their passage, to become wives to the planters. Many cargoes of vagrants, thieves, and jailbirds also came, to serve as indented servants for a term of years, and afterwards to become free colonists. Then a more lasting impression was made on the future character and fortunes of the settlement by the introduction of twenty negro slaves, who were brought by a Dutch trading vessel, and readily purchased by the settlers. Tobacco had now become the staple product of the colony, and slaves were profitably employed in its cultivation.

§ 412. The London Company obtained a new charter in 1609, which gave them the power of enacting all necessary laws for the Colony, and appointing a governor and other officers to see that the laws were executed. Whatever discontent may have been excited among the emigrants by this measure, which gave the whole control of their affairs to a council resident in England, they welcomed the appointment of Lord De la War to be their first governor, as the good abilities and amiable but resolute character of this nobleman seemed to promise a successful administration. Unfortunately he remained in office but a short time, owing to the failure of his health; and his successors, Dale, Gates, and Argal, governed with a rigor and severity which occasioned loud complaints. But they had many dissolute and turbulent subjects to rule; and the order and discipline which they preserved were favorable to the prosperity of the settlement. Hitherto the land had been held in common, and the products of all labor were thrown into a common stock. But experience having shown that this policy placed the idle and the dissolute on a par with the virtuous and the industrious, besides discouraging the latter, each settler now received an allotment of land as his own, and was allowed to work on his own account. The savages had occasionally given much trouble, and in 1622, they were nearly successful in a plot which they had formed for the entire destruction of the settlements. In one day, they killed three hundred and forty-seven of the whites. A furious war succeeded, in which the Indians, indeed, were defeated and driven back with great slaughter, so that they never became formidable again. But the colony had received a fearful blow, from which it recovered with slowness and difficulty. The number of settlements was reduced from eighty to eight, and a famine ensued that destroyed many lives. The first colonial assembly was called by Gov. Yeardley in 1619, and two years afterwards, a special ordinance confirmed the right of holding such a local legislature.

The proceedings of the Company in England had now awakened the jealousy of the crown; and these misfortunes gave King James the pretext that he wanted for depriving them of their charter, and taking the government into his own hands. Of course, it was administered on the arbitrary principles which were then in favor at court. Complete legislative and executive power was given to a governor and a council of twelve persons, all nominated by the crown; and this power was tyrannically exercised. Yet the General Assembly, though not formally authorized, was still permitted to meet, though it was much restricted in the exercise of its functions. At one time, the patience of the settlers gave way, and they seized their governor, Sir John Harvey,
A. D. 1635.
and sent him a prisoner to England to answer for his misconduct. With the native obstinacy of his character, Charles I. resented this act as savoring of audacity and rebellion, and sent back the obnoxious governor, with a fresh commission, under which he ruled more tyrannically than ever. Still, the prevailing sentiment in the colony was eminently loyal, and during the English Civil War, they took sides, as long as they durst, with the king, against the Parliament. Many of the settlers, as has been said, were decayed gentlemen and unportioned sons of noble families, in whose minds the prejudices of rank were rather heightened than diminished by the want of fortune. The Church of England was established by law, regular stipends being allotted to its ministers in every parish, and the preachers of any other persuasion were not allowed to exercise their functions. The English law of primogeniture and entail regulated the descent of property; and the wealthier colonists, directing the labor of many indented servants and slaves, lived apart on their plantations, affecting something of the state of a landed aristocracy. After the ruin of the king's cause at home, in 1645, many of the disbanded cavaliers found refuge in Virginia, bringing with them their sentiment of chivalrous attachment to Church and King.

§ 413. In 1671, Gov. Berkeley estimated the population of the colony at 40,000, including 2,000 negro slaves, and 6,000 indented white servants. The character of his administration may be inferred from a communication made by him, this year, to the English Privy Council. "I thank God," he wrote, "there are no free schools or printing, and I hope we shall not have any these hundred years; for learning has brought disobedience, and heresy, and sects into the world, and printing has divulged them, and libels against the best government. God keep us from both!" Yet a few years afterwards, discontent had become so general that a rebellion broke out, and for a few months the insurgents had entire control of the government. Nathaniel Bacon, a young lawyer, distinguished for his talents and activity, was the popular leader in this movement. The people wished to commence hostilities with the Indians, whose conduct had been such as to occasion great excitement and fears of a general conspiracy against the whites. But it is probable that other grievances, some of which were of long standing, were the true causes of the outbreak, and that the Indian war was only a pretext.

A. D. 1676. Six hundred volunteers were collected, Bacon was chosen their leader, and Gov. Berkeley was asked to give him a commission to act against the savages. The governor not only refused, but commanded the men to disperse under pain of being considered as traitors; and summoning those who were faithful to his standard, he set out in pursuit of them. But while he was gone, the counties near Jamestown broke out in insurrection, seized the capital, and took possession of the government. Berkeley was compelled to yield, to dissolve the old Assembly, which had been long in session and had become unpopular, and to issue writs for a new election. Bacon and a large majority of his friends were returned to the new Assembly. Among them were many persons of wealth and influence. A commission to act against the Indians was still refused him, and fearing treachery, he left the city, called together his adherents, returned at the head of 500 men, and dictated his own terms to the enraged but powerless Berkeley. Bacon was appointed general, was authorized to raise an army of a thousand men, and to prosecute the war vigorously. The Assembly then turned its attention to the redress of grievances. The right of choosing members of the Assembly and of voting in parish matters was restored to the freemen, some unjust exemptions from taxes were taken away, tippling houses were regulated, and an act was passed of oblivion and indemnity for those who had been engaged in the recent disturbances. But the governor's spirit was not yet subdued. After the Assembly was dissolved, he again denounced Bacon as a rebel, retired for a time to Accomac to muster his friends, and then returned with an armed force, and took possession of the capital. But the insurgents besieged him there, and he was again obliged to leave, while the town was set on fire and wholly consumed. But in the midst of these successes, Bacon was suddenly taken sick and died; and no proper person being found to take his place, the army was dispersed, and the insurrection abandoned. Berkeley returned in triumph, and punished the rebels with great rigor, some of their leaders being condemned and executed, and others were sentenced to pay heavy fines. He then went to England, where, instead of the praise and rewards that he expected, he was severely censured for his cruelty. He died a few months afterwards, as it was reported, of chagrin. An act of general pardon and oblivion was sent out from England, and other mild and popular measures soon wiped out the memory of Bacon's rebellion. Needy and covetous governors still provoked occasional discontent; but the spirit of the people was eminently loyal, so that they were tardy and reluctant to acknowledge the revolution of 1688, and only after repeated commands was a proclamation issued announcing the succession of William and Mary to the English throne.

§ 414. PLYMOUTH. Far different was the character of the emigrants who founded the New England Colonies, under grants from the Plymouth Company. These were Puritans of the straitest sect, Independents in their notions of Church government, and now fast verging towards republicanism, in consequence of their long continued opposition to the constituted authorities of Church and State at home. The intolerant spirit of the English hierarchy and the arbitrary proceedings of the court made their residence in England uncomfortable, if not perilous; and they looked to voluntary exile for deliverance. A company of them, under the Rev. John Robinson as pastor, and William Brewster as ruling elder, embarked for Holland in 1608, carrying their wives, children, and little property along with them. They were kindly received by the Dutch, who were Protestants, and they remained over ten years in peace at Leyden. But Puritans as they were, they were still Englishmen; they disliked the sound of a foreign language, and the prospect that their children would intermarry with the Dutch, and forget their English parentage and the customs of their forefathers. The greater part of them, therefore, determined to emigrate to America, and for this purpose, returned first to England, where they easily procured the promise of a grant of land from the London Company, as they intended to establish themselves within what were then the limits of Virginia. They sailed from Plymouth in the ship Mayflower, and after a tedious and stormy voyage of over two months, arrived at Cape Cod, nearly two degrees north of the place which they had aimed at. The lateness of the season, however, the fatigues of the voyage, and the perils of coasting along a shore which had been but imperfectly explored, prevented them from putting to sea again, and they sought a spot for their settlement in that neighborhood. But as they were then without the limits of the Virginia Company, and the Crown had refused to grant them a charter, they deemed it necessary, before leaving the vessel, to sign an agreement, promising to submit to whatever "just and equal laws and ordinances might be thought convenient for the general good." They selected Plymouth, which offered a tolerably good harbor in the southwestern part of Massachusetts Bay, as a suitable place for the commencement of a colony; and on the 22d of December, 1620, the PILGRIMS, as they might now well be termed, landed there, numbering only one hundred and one, including the women and children. John Carver was chosen their first governor, and Miles Standish their military leader, as they had some apprehensions of the savages. Divided into nineteen families, they immediately began to fell trees and construct houses, in which to find shelter against the rigors of the winter. But their exposure was necessarily great, and they had but a slender stock of provisions and other necessaries. Sickness came upon them, and during the first five months, they lost more than half of their number.

One of their associates, who had been left behind in England, obtained for them a grant of land from the Company which was now incorporated, under a new charter, as "The Council established at Plymouth, in the County of Devon, (England,) for the Planting, Ruling, Ordering, and Governing of New England in America." This grant authorized the colonists to choose a Governor, Council, and General Court, for the enactment and execution of laws. Strictly speaking, however, the Company had no right to give them any thing more than the property of the soil. A charter from the Crown was necessary to complete their political organization; and this they never obtained. But the necessity of the case compelled them to act as if they had received full powers; and their remoteness and insignificance prevented the authorities at home from questioning their right. The agreement which they had signed on board the Mayflower was the basis of their legislation; and for some time, all the settlers came together in a general assembly, to enact the necessary laws. Thus, in its origin, the colony was the purest democracy on earth. Time showed the inconveniences of such an arrangement, and the legislative power was then delegated to an Assembly, composed of representatives from the several towns. Land and other property were at first held in common, the Company in England being entitled to a specified share of the total profits. But this experiment turned out like the similar one in Virginia; finding that industry was discouraged by it, the Colonists succeeded in purchasing, on credit, the share of the London partners. A division was then made of the land and movable property, and henceforth each one reaped the fruits of his own toil. The people were united in religious faith, and wished not to be disturbed by theological controversies; so, when one Lyford, a clergyman of the Church of England, was sent out to them as a suitable pastor, in place of Robinson, who had died at Leyden, they refused to receive him, and exercised their undoubted right of ownership of the soil, by expelling him, and two who adhered to him, Oldham and Conant, from their territory. These banished persons established themselves at Nantasket, just beyond the limits of the Plymouth colonists. The soil around Plymouth was thin and poor, and the people had brought but few worldly goods along with them; thus, the progress of the settlement was slow. Some of their old companions, who had been left behind in Holland, now came out to join them; and a few others, attracted by similarity of worship, and by the prospect of driving a little traffic in fish and peltry, were added to their number. But ten years after the landing at Plymouth, the population numbered only three hundred. Their territory, indeed, was but small, being bounded on the land side by a line drawn northerly from the mouth of Narraganset river, till it met one carried westerly from Cohasset rivulet, "at the uttermost limits of a place called Pocanoket."

§ 415. Massachusetts. But encouraged by the growth of this colony, feeble as it was, the Council of New England proceeded to make lavish grants of their remaining lands, and to send out other bands of emigrants, taking little care to define the boundaries of the new grants, or to avoid ceding to one company or individual the very tract already bestowed upon another. This negligence was the cause of much subsequent dispute and difficulty. A few persons also established themselves at various points along the coast, who had no formal title to any land, but who were afterwards generally admitted to have an imperfect right, founded on occupancy and prescription. Some few fishing settlements were thus established; but their inhabitants had not the disposition to toil, the habits of order and self-denial, or the indomitable perseverance which characterized the Puritans. All their establishments were subsequently absorbed by the Massachusetts colony, which became the chief agent in the settlement of New England.

The persecution of all who would not conform to the Established Church still continuing in England, and king Charles having avowed his purpose to govern without a Parliament, many of the wealthier class of Puritans now determined to emigrate to America. A company was formed at the instigation of Mr. White, a clergyman of Dorchester; among its members were John Humphrey and Isaac Johnson, two brothers-in-law of the Earl of Lincoln, John Winthrop, a gentleman of landed property in Suffolk, Sir Richard Saltonstall, John Endicott, Thomas Dudley, William Coddington, Richard Bellingham, Matthew Cradock, and other merchants and lawyers of wealth and influence in London and some of the northern and midland counties. They obtained from the Council for New England a grant of a tract of land, bounded by two parallel lines running westward to the Pacific Ocean, one drawn three miles north of any part of the Merrimac river, and the other, three miles south of any portion of the Charles. Soon afterwards, their organization was completed by a charter from the Crown, which incorporated them under the title of the "Governor and Company of Massachusetts Bay in New England," with power to admit what new members or freemen they might choose. They were supposed to be a private trading corporation, resident in England, where they were to make laws and regulations for the government of their colony in America. A governor, deputy-governor, and eighteen assistants were to have the management of their affairs; and these officers were to be chosen, and all important laws enacted, at a "Great and General Court" of all the freemen, to be held quarterly. A company of sixty or seventy persons, under John Endicott, were sent out in 1628, who commenced a settlement at Salem;

and these were followed, the next year, by six ships, bringing about two hundred colonists, of whom many were indented servants, together with a stock of cattle and other necessaries. It was soon manifest, however, that a colony, to be prosperous, must have the management of its own affairs, without being obliged to wait for orders from a distance. John Winthrop and many other leading stockholders offered to emigrate, if they were allowed to carry the charter and the government along with them. The legality of such a measure was at least doubtful; but the urgency of the case removed all scruple, and the colonists probably hoped that the remoteness of their new home would screen their proceedings from public notice. New officers were therefore chosen from those who were disposed to emigrate; and in April, 1630, a fleet of fifteen ships, equipped at an expense of £20,000, sailed from the Isle of Wight, having on board Winthrop and Dudley as governor and deputy-governor, together with most of the assistants, and a company of about one thousand persons. They began a settlement at Charlestown, but soon removed to the neighboring peninsula of Trimountain, which they named Boston, after the English town whence some of the chief emigrants came. The hardships of the first winter, which was a severe one, caused disease to break out among them, and over two hundred died, among whom were Isaac Johnson, and his wife, the lady Arabella. But after this period, the order and industry which prevailed in the colony, the commencement of trade with Virginia and the Dutch at Manhattan (New York), and the rapid influx of settlers, driven away from England by the religious and political persecution which still raged there, laid the foundations of steady growth and permanent prosperity. During the first ten years after the settlement of Massachusetts, about twenty-five thousand persons left their native land to find a home in New England.

§ 416. The government of the colony was theocratic in many of its features, modified at first by an aristocratic or patriarchal element, which was soon eliminated, however, by the force of circumstances, that set strongly towards republican institutions. The few men of wealth and consideration, who were the leaders of the emigration, naturally strove to retain the chief power and influence in their own hands, and to govern according to their notions of what religion and the word of God required; and in this attempt, they were strongly seconded by the ministers of the churches. At first, the people, with the instinctive respect of Englishmen for rank and station, gave way to them, and conferred the whole power of legislation on the governor and the assistants, who were familiarly known as "the magistrates." Even a council for life at one time was instituted, but it continued only for a few years, and the freemen also resumed the power of enacting laws. Still, they were moderate in the exercise of their functions; aud persons once chosen to the board of magistrates were usually reappointed, no one being left out but for some extraordinary cause. Purity of faith and worship was the chief motive for establishing the colony. The people wished to be free, not only from persecution, but from the presence of other sects and from theological controversies. Only such persons were to be admitted to be freemen, or voters, as those who were already freemen should designate; and this privilege was soon confined by law to those who were members of the churches. But as there was little difference among them in point of religious opinion, and as most of the adult males, or at least, nearly all the heads of families, were church members, this exclusive privilege created no general discontent. The magistrates exercised their large powers resolutely to keep out heretics and schismatics, and to maintain religious worship and practice in all their purity. Those who did not agree with them were required to go elsewhere, and establish a colony for themselves. Roger Williams, and some followers of Mrs. Hutchinson, did so, and founded a new settlement in Rhode Island. Others took refuge in New Hampshire; but Massachusetts claimed the land there as a part of her own territory, and from 1640 to 1680, the claim was made good. A few Quakers gave great annoyance by their fanatical and outrageous conduct; they were once and again dismissed, with threats in case they returned. They did come again, and then three of them were hanged. The magistrates, on this occasion, published a defence of their conduct, dwelling especially on the case of Mary Dyer, who was a third comer, and had been once reprieved when already on the gallows, as a proof that they desired, not the death, but the absence, of the Quakers. Some adherents of the Church of England, who had come out without invitation to join them, were summarily sent back to the mother country. Two hundred years ago, the principles of religious toleration were but little understood; yet as the Company owned the territory, and had emigrated for the avowed purpose of forming a religious community by themselves, it is perhaps harsh in us to charge them with intolerance. They had a right to expel intruders.

§ 417. Of course, great severity of manners and punctiliousness of religious observances were enjoined. Various sumptuary laws were enacted; the Sabbath was observed with Jewish strictness; blasphemy, witchcraft, and adultery, were punished with death; slanderers were whipt, cropped, and banished. But except in these particulars, and a few others of no great importance, the Mosaic law was not established in the colony. The people had good sense enough to see that it was not adapted to the circumstances and the times. No restriction was imposed upon them except that contained in the Charter, that no laws should be made repugnant to the laws of England; and this was construed very liberally, to mean that no part of the English law was in force there till it was expressly reënacted. At first, the magistrates governed without any other rule than their own sense of right and their interpretation of the law of God. But the people becoming jealous of so large a discretion, a code, or "Body of Liberties," was established, consisting of one hundred articles, drawn up with singular brevity and clearness, embracing many of the best and most liberal provisions of the English Common Law, and, in some respects, in advance both of English and American law at the present day. This code became the basis of legislation, not only in Massachusetts, but throughout New England, the other colonies adopting many of its most important provisions. In one important respect, the Mosaic rule was followed in preference to the English law; the estates of persons dying without a will were divided equally among the children, except that the eldest son received a double share. This law, favoring the distribution rather than the aggregation of property, made the establishment of a territorial aristocracy impossible, kept up the idea of equality among the people, and tended strongly to the development of republican sentiments.

A. D. 1641.

Another circumstance, which silently fostered the democratic spirit of the people, was the great extent of their territory in comparison with their numbers, and the disposition that has characterized them from that day to this, to spread themselves over the face of the country, instead of remaining together on one spot. When as yet they were only a few hundred in number, instead of seeking protection against the savages and other perils of the wilderness by union and concentration, they colonized a dozen or twenty distinct townships, the extremes of which were some thirty miles apart. Eight townships were represented in a General Court held only two years after Winthrop landed; and before the colony was ten years old, or contained in all more than 15,000 settlers, at least twenty distinct settlements were formed. But the most remarkable instance of this tendency to segregation took place as early as 1634, when Mr. Hooker and his whole church at Newtown petitioned for leave to remove to Connecticut, the avowed reason for this step being the want of pasturage for their cattle; and "it was alleged by Mr. Hooker as a fundamental error, that the towns were set so near to each other." The settlements being thus scattered, and the colony as a whole being imperfectly organized, each town was obliged from the first to direct its own expenditures and manage its own affairs. The inhabitants held town-meetings, levied taxes to provide for their common wants, chose executive officers, afterwards termed "selectmen," and in fact created a little republic nearly complete in organization. It is now generally admitted, that the tone of American politics and the general character of American institutions have been more controlled by the influences of the township-system of New England than by all other causes united.

In the main, also, there was great equality among the colonists in point of fortune and social position. Many English gentlemen and wealthy merchants, as we have seen, favored the emigration, and some embarked

26

in it. But the happy and the powerful do not often go into exile, and the perils and hardships of a home in the wilderness prevented many persons of wealth from joining in the enterprise, and caused others to leave it after a brief sojourn in New England. Humphrey, Saltonstall, Vane, and Vassall returned to their native land after a short stay, and the Johnsons died. The great bulk of the colonists were of the middling and lower classes of English society; very few were wealthy, nearly all were dependent on the labor of their hands. Equality of social claims was the natural basis of equality of political rights. There was a germ of republicanism in the colony from the outset,—a natural tendency towards universal eligibility and universal suffrage.

§ 418. The first care of the settlers of Massachusetts was to provide for universal education and universal worship. The several townships that were organized were so many distinct churches, which admitted their own members, chose their own pastors, and managed their own affairs. Each town, either by levying a tax or by voluntary contributions, provided buildings for public worship and salaries for their ministers. When Boston was but six years old, the General Court passed an order, appropriating a sum, equal to the amount raised by a year's taxation to defray all the public expenditures of the colony, for the establishment of a college at Newtown; and two years afterwards, John Harvard, a clergyman of Charlestown, bequeathing half of his estate for the same object, Harvard College was founded. Free schools were established in several of the towns; and in 1649, a general system of popular education was established throughout the colony, each township being required to maintain a free school for reading and writing, and every town of a hundred householders a grammar school, "to fit youths for the university." The preamble of this law declares that the motive for passing it was to provide "that learning may not be buried in the grave of our fathers,"—"it being one chief project of that old deluder, Sathan, to keep men from the knowledge of the Scriptures, as in former times keeping them in an unknown tongue, so in these latter times by persuading men from the use of tongues." The grim Puritan of those days believed his child's soul would be in danger if he were not enabled to read the Bible for himself; and thus care for general education naturally grew out of care for the interests of religion. As the democratic spirit spread among the people, they reclaimed the legislative authority for themselves; and a body of representatives, consisting of two or three delegates from each
A. D. 1634. town, were united with "the magistrates" for the purpose of enacting laws. At first, the representatives sat and voted in the same chamber with the assistants; but in 1644, a division was made, and the two classes afterwards formed separate houses of legislation.

§ 419. During the first few years in the history of the settlement, the Indians had given no cause for alarm. Just before the arrival of the whites, a contagious disease had raged among the native tribes, nearly exterminating some of them, so that the territory seemed providentially left vacant for occupation by the English. But as the white settlements increased in number, the jealousy of the Indians was aroused; and in 1637, the Pequods, a tribe dwelling on the banks of what is now called the Thames river, in Connecticut, began hostilities. But as they were yet very imperfectly provided with fire-arms, they formed but a contemptible enemy. A band of eighty men, under Captain Mason, were sent against them, who, with the aid of a few friendly Indians, attacked their palisadoed village in the grey of the morning, forced their way into it, set fire to the wigwams, and killed about six hundred of the savages. The next month, another band attacked the remainder of the tribe, who had taken refuge in a swamp, killed many of them, and took about two hundred prisoners, who were afterwards kept as slaves, a portion being sent to the West Indies to be sold. The few who escaped found a home among the Narraganset and Mohegan Indians, and the Pequod tribe ceased to exist.

To guard against the dangers apprehended not only from the Indians, but from the Dutch and the French, a confederacy was formed in 1643, between the four colonies of Massachusetts, Plymouth, Connecticut, and New Haven, to form rules for regulating intercourse with the savages, and to render mutual aid if a war should break out. In consequence of this union, the whites became more respected and feared by the native tribes, several of whom sought their alliance and protection. But in 1675, Philip of Mount Hope, a chief of the Wampanoags in Rhode Island, began hostilities, in which he was soon joined by nearly all the native tribes in New England. The Indians were now well supplied with fire-arms, and were expert in the arts of ambush and forest warfare, in which as yet the whites were very deficient. A fearful contest ensued, which brought all the white settlements to the verge of destruction. It lasted nearly a year, in the course of which, upwards of two thousand Indians were killed or taken, and some of the New England tribes were exterminated. The whites suffered terribly; twelve or thirteen of their towns were entirely ruined, six hundred houses had been burned, and about six hundred men had fallen in battle. No assistance was received from England, and the expenses of the war burdened Massachusetts with a heavy debt. But henceforward, no great danger was apprehended from the Indians, except when they acted as allies of the French.

§ 420. Frequent complaints were made to the Privy Council in England, that the acts of trade were generally disregarded by Massachusetts, and that the conduct and laws of the colony in many other respects were in violation of the charter and subversive of the authority of the crown. Commissioners were sent out to make inquiries respecting these subjects of complaint. But the breach was only widened by this measure, as the commissioners were captious and insolent in their language and conduct, and the General Court was obstinate and not over respectful. Charles II., who had just triumphed after a long contest with the popular party at home, had taken away the franchises of the city of London, and confiscated the charters of nearly all the boroughs in the realm, was in no humor to be bearded by a few daring sectaries in New England. Legal proceedings were instituted, and before Massachusetts could engage counsel in her defence, judgment was entered by default, and the charter declared to be forfeited. The government of the colony was thus thrown entirely into the hands of the king; and James II., who had now come to the throne, appointed Sir Edmund Andros to be governor of all New England, the charters of the other colonies being either forfeited or in abeyance. The popular legislative assemblies were dissolved, and Sir Edmund, with authority to appoint and remove the members of his council at pleasure, enacted laws and governed as he saw fit. For more than two years, his yoke was heavy upon the necks of the people. Then came a rumor that a revolution had taken place in England, and that the Prince of Orange already was, or would soon be, on the throne, in place of the deposed James II.; and without waiting to learn whether it was any thing more than a rumor, the inhabitants of Boston seized their arms, imprisoned Andros and his chief adherents, and reinstated their beloved charter government, with the venerable Simon Bradstreet at its head. Then ensued a negotiation with the government of William and Mary, for the restoration of the old charter. But the king and his ministers were determined to strengthen the royal prerogative, and they would only offer a new charter, far less liberal in its provisions than the old one, with the significant intimation that the colony might take that or none. Finding that they would otherwise be governed at the royal pleasure, the people very reluctantly accepted the new instrument, by which Plymouth and Maine were united to Massachusetts, and the appointment of the governor, secretary, and all admiralty officers was reserved to the crown. The governor might convoke and adjourn the General Court at pleasure; he had a negative upon the election of councillors and the enactment of laws, and a right to nominate all judges and military officers. The laws were to be transmitted to England, even after he had sanctioned them; and if disapproved by the king within three years from the time of their enactment, they became void. The right of suffrage was no longer confined to church members, but was given to all who had 40 shillings income from freehold property, or 40 pounds of personal estate.

April, A. D. 1689.

§ 421. The first royal governor appointed was Sir William Phips, whose administration was distinguished only by the unhappy popular delusion, usually called the Salem Witchcraft. Some children were, or pretended to be, thrown into convulsions; and they

A. D. 1692.

accused certain persons of bewitching them. The mania spread; others declared that they were afflicted, pinched, and bruised, and when the witnesses and the accused were confronted in open court, the former seemed to be thrown into an agony, and charged the latter with tormenting them by diabolical means. Every one against whom they "cried out" was arrested, and the prisons were soon filled. Some weak-minded persons among the prisoners were persuaded or terrified into a confession of guilt, and then bore witness against others; and upon this accumulation of evidence, many were convicted. Twenty persons were hanged, among whom was Mr. Burroughs, a clergyman; and one old man, aged eighty years, was pressed to death. Many others were cried out against, and fled for their lives. At last, the extravagance of the evil began to work its cure. The witnesses accused some persons who stood so high in character and station, that the belief even of the credulous mob was shocked. A reaction took place, juries refused to convict, the jails were emptied, and some of the judges and those who had been active in the prosecutions made a public profession of their errors and their penitence.

§ 422. OTHER NEW ENGLAND COLONIES. Having sketched the history of Virginia, Plymouth, and Massachusetts, during the seventeenth century, a few words must suffice for the other Colonies. Roger Williams and some other religious exiles from Massachusetts colonized RHODE ISLAND in 1638, having purchased the land of the Narraganset Indians. They obtained a patent from the Long Parliament six years afterwards, and in 1663, Charles II. granted them a very liberal charter, under which they chose their own officers and enacted their own laws with almost as much freedom as if they had been an independent republic. By the influence of Williams, perfect religious toleration was established in this Colony, men being held responsible for their religious opinions and practice only to their God. The territory of CONNECTICUT was granted, in 1630, to the Earl of Warwick, who soon assigned his right to Lord Say and Seale, Lord Brook, and others. Several settlements were formed on the Connecticut river, in 1635 – 6, by Mr. Hooker and other emigrants from Massachusetts, who at first acknowledged the authority of the Colony they had just left, but soon established a government for themselves, modelled on that of Massachusetts. Hartford was their chief town. About the same time, Lord Say and Seale with his associates sent over John Winthrop the younger, with instructions to build a fort at the mouth of the Connecticut, and erect buildings to accommodate such settlers as might come thither. This was the origin of Saybrook. In 1637, Mr. Davenport, with a company of emigrants, some of them men of wealth, arrived in New England, and after some hesitation as to the choice of a place, they founded a settlement at New Haven. They were rigid Puritans, who wished to establish a community conforming in all things to their peculiar principles. They admitted only church members to be freemen, and resolved that the Word of God should be the only rule in their administration. The Dutch laid claim to the whole country, and the dispute between them and the English settlers was more than once on the verge of breaking out into open war. Charles II., soon after his restoration, granted to Connecticut a charter quite as liberal as that given to Rhode Island; but as this instrument brought together the two distinct settlements of Hartford and New Haven, the people of the latter place were very reluctant to accept it, and only yielded, after some years' delay, to the fear that a general governor might be sent out from England to rule them. From the period of this union, 1665, the progress of the Colony was steady and prosperous. The territory of NEW HAMPSHIRE was granted by the Plymouth Company to Capt. John Mason, in 1629. But few settlements were formed under his management, principally by fishermen and exiles from Massachusetts, who remained for some time without any government but such as they established for themselves. Exeter, Dover, and Portsmouth, then called Strawberry Bank, were the only towns that contained many inhabitants. In 1641, they voluntarily placed themselves under the protection of Massachusetts, who had always claimed the land, and who continued to govern them till 1679, when, by a decree of the king in council, New Hampshire was made a separate province, to be governed by a President and Council, appointed by the king, and a House of Representatives elected by the people. Frequent disputes ensued, both with their rulers, and with Mason and his heirs respecting the titles to their lands. But after the Revolution of 1688, most of these controversies were quieted, and excepting frequent hostilities with the Indians, the people prospered. MAINE was originally granted to Sir Ferdinando Gorges, and was purchased of his heirs, in 1677, by Massachusetts, for £1,200, it having been governed by that Colony for many years previous, under a disputed title. The controversy ending with this purchase, Maine remained a part of Massachusetts till a very recent period.

§ 423. NEW YORK. The Dutch, founding on the explorations of Henry Hudson a claim to the Hudson river and an indefinite extent of territory through which it flows, built some fortified trading posts near its mouth as early as 1613. They also explored the northern coast of Long Island Sound, and both shores of Delaware Bay; and on the strength of these discoveries, an Amsterdam company obtained from the States General an exclusive grant to trade along the coast between the 40th and 45th degrees of latitude, a region by them called New Netherland. The English never allowed their claim, which only became important when, in 1621, it passed into the hands of the Dutch West India Company, a wealthy association with large privileges, and capable of conducting extensive operations. Under their direction, Fort Orange was built where Albany now stands; and in 1626, the island of Manhattan was purchased of the Indians, and Fort Amsterdam erected at its southern extremity. As yet, traffic with the savages in peltry was the only object of these establishments; but in 1629, a scheme was matured for forming Dutch settlements in the country. Extensive grants of land were offered to any member of the Company, who, under the name of Patroon, should establish a colony of at least fifty persons upon it; and as much land as they could cultivate was offered to any free settlers who should remove thither at their own expense. Under these offers, some of the most inviting lands were taken up; but the progress of colonization was slow, agriculture being made secondary to trade with the Indians. A port was established on the Connecticut, near Hartford, which soon led to a sharp dispute with the English settlers in that region. The Swedes also came into collision with the Dutch, by attempting, under the sanction of the renowned Gustavus Adolphus, to found a settlement and trading post on the west shore of Delaware Bay, a region claimed by the Hollanders. The Swedes bought some land of the Indians, and built a fort called Christina, — the germ of the Colony of New Sweden, now the State of DELAWARE. The infant settlement was prudently managed, and might in a few years have become prosperous, if the Dutch had not attacked it, in 1655, with a force of six hundred men, who captured all the Swedish posts, and the region was again absorbed into New Netherland.

A destructive Indian war was added to the other embarrassments of the Dutch. The latter showed themselves as great savages as their red opponents, who nearly overmatched them, and destroyed many of their most flourishing "boweries," or plantations. The people were harshly governed, being allowed no voice in the administration, and they complained that "under a king they could not be worse treated." The English were determined to monopolize the coast, and in 1664, Charles II. granted to his brother a large region, including New Netherland, to be called, in future, in honor of the Duke, NEW YORK. An expedition of six hundred men, under Sir Robert Nicholls, was fitted out to take possession; and so many English were now settled in the Colony, the Dutch also being lukewarm towards their own government, that no opposition was offered. Liberal terms of capitulation were granted, and the territory was annexed without a blow to the domain of England. No popular representation in the government was allowed till 1684, the Duke of York appointing a governor who ruled arbitrarily; and even after that period, the administration continued to be distasteful to the people. When the news of the revolution of 1688 arrived, the inhabitants of New York rose in arms, like their brethren of Boston, and under the guidance of Jacob Leisler, a wealthy German merchant, deposed the former authorities of the place, and instituted a government of their own. The colony remained under Leisler's rule till March, 1691, when Col. Sloughter arrived, with a commission as governor, and his agent demanded peremptorily the surrender of the fort. Leisler hesitated and delayed, and when at last he did obey, he was seized, together with his son-in-law, Milbourne, tried for rebellion, and executed. This proceeding was a harsh and hasty one; and the king subsequently restored their confiscated estates to their heirs, and allowed their bodies to be taken up and reinterred with pomp, while the people cherished their memory with affection and respect.

§ 424. MARYLAND. George Calvert, Lord Baltimore, a Roman Catholic by religion, obtained from Charles I., in 1630, a grant of the then uninhabited shores of Chesapeake Bay, as an asylum for the persecuted Papists. The charter, which secured liberty of conscience, and equal privileges to the members of all Christian sects, was not issued till after this lord's death, and was then given to Cecil, his eldest son and heir.

A. D. 1633. He sent out his brother, Leonard Calvert, as governor, with about two hundred emigrants, mostly Roman Catholics, and a settlement was formed at St. Mary's, the new colony being called MARYLAND, in honor of Queen Henrietta Maria. The proprietary had full power to enact all necessary laws, not repugnant to the laws of England, and not without the advice and approbation of the freemen of the province or their representatives; — this being the first provision in any colonial charter for giving a legislative power to the people. The province was wisely and moderately governed, liberal grants of land being offered to all comers, to be held by the payment of a quit rent to the proprietor. Baltimore did not wish to shut out heretics from his colony; Puritans and Church of England men were invited to come, under a promise of enjoying equal privileges with the Catholics; thus Maryland became a general asylum for the persecuted of all sects. We are not surprised to learn, therefore, that, before Lord Baltimore's death in 1676, he was in receipt of a considerable income from the province, which then contained about sixteen thousand inhabitants, most of whom were Protestants. The people wisely sought support from agriculture rather than mining and trade. Yet they did not pass through the time of the Civil War and the domination of the Long Parliament without annoyances and contests. During this period, of course, Lord Baltimore's principles were not in favor, and his colony was regarded with a jealous eye. William Clayborne had obtained a royal license to trade in all those parts, and he and his associates denied the legality of the Maryland grant. The Parliament sent out commissioners who displaced the officers of the proprietary, and put the government into the hands of the Puritans, who soon passed an act that excluded papists and prelatists from the benefit of the act of toleration. A civil war at one time raged in the colony, Roundheads and Cavaliers being opposed to each other, as in the mother land. But with the restoration of Charles II., these troubles ceased, and the prosperity of the settlement for a long period suffered but little interruption. Yet an order was passed in 1681, for intrusting all offices to Protestants, so that the Catholics were disfranchised a second time in the colony they had founded.

§ 425. THE CAROLINAS. The territory on the coast south of Virginia, extending nominally as far south as St. Augustine, was granted, in 1663, to the great Lord Clarendon, the Earl of Shaftesbury, and six other eminent individuals. The whole region was to constitute one province, under the name of Carolina, the proprietors receiving, together with the grant of the land, ample powers of government. But a settlement had already been formed near Albemarle Sound by some religious exiles from Virginia, and another one, near the mouth of Cape Fear river, by some adventurers from New England, afterwards reinforced by a band of emigrants from Barbadoes. In 1670, three ships were fitted out with colonists from England, under the command of William Sayle, who formed a settlement at Port Royal, which he soon removed to the peninsula at the mouth of the Ashley and the Cooper rivers, giving to the town that he founded there the name of Charleston. As this place was remote fron Albemarle, it obtained a separate government, and thus were created the two colonies of North and South Carolina. The proprietors gave public assurance that the settlers should enjoy unrestricted religious liberty, and that their representatives should have a voice in the enactment of laws. Unluckily they employed the celebrated philosopher, John Locke, to devise a scheme of government for the colony; and he gave them, under the name of the "Grand Model," the most complicated and fanciful system that the wit of man ever contrived, and which was a perpetual source of trouble and confusion for the quarter of a century during which it was in partial operation. It established two orders of nobility, landgraves, and caciques; it assigned two fifths of the land for seignories, baronies, and manors, to be cultivated by a race of tenants attached to the soil, and the remaining three fifths were allotted to private freeholders; and it erected a formidable bureaucracy, with officers and titles enough for a populous kingdom of the Old World. This rickety system could never be put into full operation, and in 1693, it was entirely abrogated. The motley population was swelled by two ship-loads of Dutch emigrants from New York, and by a cargo of slaves from Barbadoes. After the revocation of the Edict of Nantes, many Huguenots came to South Carolina, and settled along the Santee; they had been preceded by some Presbyterian settlers from the north of Ireland, and by a Scotch colony led by Lord Cardross. Religious toleration and the prospect of obtaining land on easy terms were the lures which drew so many different classes of immigrants. The population thus formed did not show themselves very tractable. They persisted in keeping up an illegal traffic with New England, they grumbled at paying quit rent to the proprietaries, and they quarrelled with the arbitrary and rapacious governors who were sent to rule over them. But in spite of these interruptions, the two colonies prospered, advancing steadily, though not rapidly, both in population and wealth.

§ 426. New Jersey. The territory between the Delaware and Hudson rivers, being included in the surrender by the Dutch to the English in 1664, was granted by the Duke of York, under the name of New Jersey, to Lord Berkeley and Sir George Carteret. They sent over Philip Carteret as governor, with a liberal constitution for

A. D. 1665. the new colony, and bountiful offers of land to all settlers who would come thither. Lord Berkeley sold his right, after he had held it ten years, to a company of Quakers, who, wishing to govern separately a region which might be an asylum for the persecuted of their sect, made an agreement with Carteret for the partition of the territory. The western portion was assigned to them, the eastern to Carteret. A large company, consisting principally of Quakers, then came from England, and settled in Burlington and its neighborhood, ample privileges being secured to them by a new constitution. A dispute ensued with the Duke of York respecting the title to their lands, as he pretended that, under a new patent which he had obtained from the crown, his original rights were restored. But the commissioners in England, to whom the matter was referred, adjudged his claim to be invalid, and new settlers continuing to arrive, the colony became very prosperous. East Jersey, also, in 1682, was sold by the heirs of Carteret to William Penn and twenty-three associates, mostly Quakers, who appointed Robert Barclay governor, and endeavored to attract emigrants thither. Many of the Scottish Covenanters, now suffering a deplorable persecution under Lauderdale and Claverhouse, fled from their native land, and found a pleasant and safe asylum in East Jersey. The numerous proprietors, weary of quarrelling with each other and with the people, surrendered their rights to the crown in 1702; and the two divisions were then united under one government.

§ 427. Pennsylvania. Another Quaker colony was established, on a larger scale, by the celebrated William Penn, a man of great ability and integrity, resolute in purpose and energetic in conduct, a keen controversialist, and one who displayed on many occasions more shrewdness, knowledge of the world, and practical talent than are often found united with a fervor and sincerity of religious belief which had the appearance of an unruly fanaticism. The Quakers, indeed, while preserving with great steadfastness most of their inoffensive external peculiarities, had quietly undergone a considerable change in the manner and spirit of their proceedings, — a change attributable in some degree to the influence of Penn himself. They were no longer the wild and extravagant sectaries, whose outrageous conduct, twenty years before, had troubled the peace of Massachusetts. Their manners had become quiet and discreet, and though they remained fearless of persecution, they no longer courted it. In consideration of the services of his father, a distinguished admiral, Penn obtained from Charles II. a grant of the territory on the west bank of the river Delaware, extending five degrees in longitude, and bounded by the 40th and 43d parallels of latitude; and the king insisted on naming it PENNSYLVANIA. The charter gave him the absolute property of the soil and ample powers of government, but required the advice and consent of the freemen of the province for the enactment of laws. The sturdy and independent spirit of the New England colonies having taught the crown lawyers a lesson of caution in drawing up colonial charters, it was stipulated in this case that the king might negative any enactment of the assembly, that parliament might levy taxes, and that an appeal might be made to the crown from the decisions of the courts of justice.

A. D. 1681.

Acting under this charter, Penn drew up a very liberal "Frame of Government," and also published a body of laws, that had been examined and approved by a company of proposed emigrants in England. He also advertised the lands for sale, asking forty shillings, besides a perpetual quitrent of one shilling, for every hundred acres. Unlimited freedom of conscience, and the right to be governed by laws enacted by themselves, were secured to the people. As the terms were liberal, and the advantages of the territory, in respect to climate, situation, fertility of the soil, and the friendly disposition of the neighboring Indians, were considerable, a crowd of emigrants presented themselves, comprising many Quakers and a number from Holland and Germany. The Duke of York, afterwards James II., with whom Penn was high in favor, made over to him all his own right to the three lower counties on the Delaware, first peopled by the Swedes, which had lately been governed as an appendage to the Duke's province of New York. These counties belonged geographically rather to Pennsylvania than New York, and possession of them was important for the new colony, as they already contained about 3,000 inhabitants, Swedes, Finns, and Dutch, steady and industrious in their habits, and inured to their situation. Besides these, a number of Swedish, Dutch, and English settlers were already established in other portions of the territory, by whom the new government was favorably received. William Markham, one of Penn's kinsmen, was sent out in 1681, with three ships and about three hundred emigrants, bearing a plan of the city which was to be founded at the confluence of the Schuylkill with the Delaware, and a very friendly message to the Indians, whose good will the new proprietor was anxious to conciliate. Penn himself came out the next year, in the course of which twenty-three vessels arrived laden with goods and emigrants. He held a friendly conference with the savages, under a large elm at Kensington, which afterwards became an object of much curiosity and respect, as marking the site of this famous interview. A treaty was made by which the Indians sold their lands on terms satisfactory to them, and stipulated to maintain peace and friendship, which promise was long religiously observed. The savages named him Onas, and though they gave the same title to the subsequent governors of the colony, they always referred to him as the great and good Onas. After laying out the new city of Philadelphia, so called from the spirit of brotherly love which was to animate its inhabitants, and holding a conference with Lord Baltimore about the disputed boundary between Delaware and Pennsylvania, Penn returned, in 1684, to England. He did not visit America again till 1699, and then made but a short stay. The progress of the new province was as rapid as its commencement had been auspicious. In 1684, it contained twenty settled townships and seven thousand inhabitants; and not many years afterwards, the population was estimated at thirty thousand. Some of the laws proposed by Penn and adopted by the Assembly bore the imprint of his quaint and benevolent disposition. To prevent lawsuits, three arbitrators were to be appointed by the county courts, to hear and determine small controversies; children were to be taught some useful trade, to the end that none might be idle; agents who wronged their employers should make restitution and one third over; and the property of intestates was to be divided equally among the children, except that the eldest son should receive a double share. And yet Penn reaped little but disappointment and vexation from his connection with the colony. His great mistake seems to have consisted in reserving a quitrent, instead of making over the land absolutely to the settlers. Though the annual payment was but small, and was justly due to him, as in no other manner could he be remunerated for his actual outlay, the demand of it was a fruitful source of annoyance and discontent. Penn had great difficulty in collecting it, became impoverished, and was at one time imprisoned for debt. The impossibility of satisfying all the demands of the people while their uneasiness really proceeded from this annual exaction, and the boundary controversy with Lord Baltimore, embittered all the latter part of his life. He founded a prosperous colony, but he sacrificed his own interests and his peace of mind in the undertaking. The lower counties on the Delaware, complaining that their peculiar interests were not attended to, were allowed to dissolve the legislative union with Pennsylvania, but remained subject to the same governor.

§ 428. GEORGIA was founded in 1732, under a plan formed by General Oglethorpe and some other benevolent gentlemen, in order to establish a place of refuge for poor debtors and other indigent persons from

Great Britain, and for persecuted Protestants from all nations. A grant was obtained from the king of the unoccupied territory on the right bank of the Savannah river, the land to be apportioned gratuitously among the settlers, charitable donations being made to defray the expense of transporting them across the Atlantic, and supporting them during the first season. Funds were freely contributed for this generous purpose, under the hope that the measure would reduce the poor rates in England, and empty the workhouses and debtors' jails. But the class of persons thus sent out were very unfit for the work of creating a new settlement and subduing the wilderness. They were chiefly broken-down tradesmen and impoverished debauchees; while sailors, agriculturists, and laborers from the country were needed. A company of persecuted Lutherans from Salzburg, and one of Scotch Highlanders, who settled respectively the towns of Ebenezer and New Inverness, formed industrious and thriving colonists. Oglethorpe brought over the first band of emigrants, and founded the city of Savannah. The colony being regarded as in a state of pupilage, its affairs were administered, for the first twenty years, by a board of trustees, nominated in the charter, who were to appoint their associates and successors, and had the exclusive right of legislation. The generous motto on their official seal, *non sibi, sed aliis* (not for themselves, but for others,) showed the benevolent purposes with which they acted. Some of their measures were wise, others were preposterous. They strictly forbade the introduction of negro slaves; the use of rum was prohibited; no grant of land was to exceed five hundred acres; the land was not to be sold or devised by the holders, but was to descend to male children only, and in case of the failure of such heirs, was to revert to the trustees. But these laws did not long remain in force; slavery was introduced from the neighboring province of Carolina; females were allowed to inherit, and the land became subject to the same regulations as other property. So long as the colony was managed by trustees, and considered as an object of charity, it languished, and large sums were expended upon it in vain. At last, the government was abandoned to the crown, its institutions were assimilated to those of the other colonies, and it then had a steady and prosperous growth. The Methodists and Moravians were numerous in Georgia, the two renowned preachers of the former denomination, Wesley and Whitefield, residing in it for several years.

§ 429. It is apparent from this review, that the English colonies in North America, with the exception of Virginia and New York, were founded and peopled chiefly by religious exiles. The English Puritans were most numerous in New England, the Quakers in New Jersey and Pennsylvania, the Roman Catholics in Maryland, Scotch Presbyterians, French Huguenots, and Methodists in the south, and German Lutherans in Pennsylvania and elsewhere. Earnestness, sobriety, an independent spirit, and a determined hatred of oppression thus characterized the people from the beginning. Whatever emigrants came out solely in quest of wealth were soon disabused of their error, and either returned to the Old World, or learned to labor and to endure in their new home. Property was very evenly distributed, and there were no marked inequalities of rank or social position. Protected by their feebleness and insignificance in the outset, and by their distance from the mother country, the colonists were, in the main, allowed to enact their own laws, and manage their own affairs. Without any marked purpose of deviating from the policy, or shaking off the yoke, of England, they were, from the commencement, semi-republican and semi-independent. Disciplined by privation, exile, and peril, thrown on their own resources, governing themselves, their situation developed in them the elements of a thoughtful, vigorous, and resolute character. After they had overcome the first difficulties and obstructions in the way of founding a new home in the wilderness, their habits of endurance, industry, and frugality soon gave prosperity to their undertakings. Agriculture and commerce flourished, and they increased rapidly in population and wealth. They were no longer the feeble dependencies of a remote power; they could boast that they had laid the foundations of a great empire.

V. THE EIGHTEENTH CENTURY.

1. THE SPANISH WAR OF SUCCESSION (1702–1714).

§ 430. When the childless Charles II., the last of the house of Hapsburg in Spain, was near his end, he suffered himself, from a feeling of irritation towards the European powers who had arranged a partition of his lands during his life, to be persuaded by the French ambassadors to make a secret will, by which the second grandson of Louis XIV., duke Philip of Anjou, was named heir to the whole Spanish monarchy, to the exclusion of Austria, which, according to an earlier family compact, had the nearest claim upon the vacant throne. Charles II. died at the commencement of the new century, and Louis XIV., guided by his council and his second wife, Madame Maintenon, a woman of inferior birth, determined, after some hesitation, to adopt the will, much as his exhausted kingdom required repose. This resolution was followed by the most desperate war that had hitherto taken place. The emperor Leopold took up arms for the purpose of securing the inheritance of the Hapsburgs for his second son, Charles, by force. On the side of Austria were ranged, not only the

A. D. 1700.

Leopold, A. D. 1657–1705.

greater part of the princes of Germany, particularly the Elector, Frederick of Brandenburg, who for this assistance was adorned with the title of king of Prussia, and Hanover, for which a ninth Electorate had recently been made, but the maritime powers, England and Holland; the latter, out of fear of the threatening superiority of France, the former, from anger that the French king had recognized the Pretender, James (III.) Stuart, on the death of his father, as king of England. The Elector of Bavaria and his brother, the Elector of Cologne, were the only princes that sided with France. Spain was divided. The eastern provinces, Aragon, Catalonia, Valencia, were for the Austrian claimant of the throne; Castile, on the other hand, and the rest of the kingdom, took up arms to defend the Bourbon king, Philip V., who was descended on his mother's side from the Hapsburgs, and whose character bore the impress of Spain.

§ 431. The reason that the fortune of the war remained this time so closely bound to the banners of Austria and England, was, that their armies were conducted by the two greatest generals of the age, prince Eugene of Savoy, and the duke of Marlborough. The former at once increased the renown he had already acquired in the war against the Turks by a masterly campaign in Italy, where he drove back the gallant General Catinat and brought over the duke of Savoy and A. D. 1701. Piedmont to the side of Austria; while Marlborough, who was the chief of the Whigs, (who since Anne's coming to the government had guided the political helm,) and consequently, endowed with almost unlimited power, was distinguished both as a warrior and statesman, but stained his glory by avarice and love of gain. The duke of Savoy brought the calamities of war upon his own land by his alliance with Austria. Vendome, a skilful general, subdued Piedmont and the fertile plains of Lombardy, and thought to unite himself with the Elector of Bavaria who had marched into the Tyrol; but the daring rise of the gallant Tyrolese, who, from their inaccessi- A. D. 1703. ble mountain heights and the crevices of their valleys, attacked the Bavarians with their rifles, and prevented their advance by a well-managed guerilla warfare, prevented this plan. The Elector was compelled, after severe loss, to evacuate the Tyrol; whereupon he joined the French army, which had marched through the Kinzigthal in Swabia, under the command of the marshals Villars and Tallard. It was here that Eugene, and Louis of Baden, the commander of the imperial forces, opposed themselves to the enemy. Marlborough, after a masterly march on the Rhine and the Mosel, soon joined the other two, upon which, Eugene and Marlborough despatched the old and cautious Louis to the siege of Ingoldstadt, and then defeated the French and Bavarian army August 13, at the battle of Hochstädt, (or, as the English call it, the 1704. battle of Blenheim). Tallard, and a great part of his force were made prisoners; the whole of the munitions of war fell into the hands of the enemy. The Elector of Bavaria was obliged to follow the French over the Rhine, and expose his territories to the Austrians, who exercised the most frightful oppression there; so that, at length, the people, driven to despair, made an insurrection, which, however, had only the effect of increasing the measure of their sufferings. For the purpose of chastising the unpatriotic sentiments of the princely house of Bavaria, Joseph I., A. D. 1705-1711. the new emperor, Joseph I., who trod the same path his father had done, pronounced the ban against Max Emmanuel, and his brother, the Elector of Cologne.

§ 432. Fortune was also adverse to the French both in the Netherlands May 23, 1706. and in Italy. In the former country, Marlborough gained the splendid victory of Ramillies from the incompetent marshal Villeroi, the favorite of Madame Maintenon; upon which, the Spanish Netherlands acknowledged the Austrian competitor for the September 7, 1706. throne: and in Italy, prince Eugene defeated the superior force of the French at Turin; whereupon, Milan and Lombardy, together with Lower Italy and Sicily, fell into the hands of the victors. The glory of Eugene spread far and wide, and his name became henceforth familiar in the mouths of the people, who celebrated his deeds in their songs. It was in Spain only that Philip of Anjou maintained himself against the English and Austrian army. It is true, that the provinces of the ancient kingdom of Aragon, out of national hatred to Castile, sided, for the most part, with the Austrian claimant of the throne, when the latter landed in Catalonia. Barcelona, Valencia, and A. D. 1704. all the cities of importance united themselves to him, whilst the English fleet took Gibraltar. Philip V. nevertheless maintained his supremacy by the adherence of the Castilians, and visited the revolted provinces with a severe chastisement after the victory of April 25, 1707. Almanza. The beautiful plains of Valencia were ravaged, the resolute inhabitants, who were prepared to undergo the worst extremities rather than submit themselves to the detested Castilians, suffered death in all its forms; and, to avoid the insults of their enemies, they even set fire to their own houses, and perished, like the citizens of Saguntum and Numantia, beneath the ruins. When at length resistance was broken by the capture of Saragossa and Lerida, and the heads of the boldest had fallen beneath the axe of the executioner, the three provinces of Valencia, Catalonia, and Aragon lost the last remains of their rights, and were governed henceforth by the laws of Castile. Barcelona, however, maintained a gallant resistance to the end of the war.

§ 433. In the year 1708, the two great generals, Eugene and Marl- July 11, 1708. borough, increased their military renown by the victory of Oudenarde on the Scheldt. At this point, Louis XIV. began to despair of the successful termination of the war; and, taking the exhausted condition of his kingdom into consideration, he now wished for peace. But, by the influence of Eugene and Marlborough, who wished to take advantage of their success for the humiliation of France, conditions of great severity were demanded of him. It was not only required that the French king should renounce all pretensions to the collective empire of Spain, but that he should surrender Alsace and Strasburg; and, hard as this abasement must have appeared to the proud potentate, he would have accepted the conditions, had not his enemies added the degrading demand, that Louis should himself assist in driving his own grandson out of Spain. This appeared too severe to the French court, and the war continued. But in the murderous battle of Malplaquet, France lost more troops than in any previous engagement, and would have been compelled to accept peace under any conditions, had not Divine Providence now wished to chastise the insolence of others, that men might learn moderation.

September 11, 1709.

§ 434. A quarrel between the proud and ambitious wife of Marlborough and queen Anne, and the intrigues that sprung from it, had occasioned the exclusion of the duchess from the court, and the expulsion of the Whig ministry by the Tories. The latter, with the celebrated statesman and writer Bolingbroke at their head, now wished for the termination of the war, in order that Marlborough, who was at the head of the opposite party, might be no longer indispensable; and with this object, entered into negotiations for peace with France, which were brought to a more rapid termination by the death of the emperor Joseph I. without male heirs, in the following year, and by the succession of his brother, Charles, who was the intended inheritor of the Spanish monarchy. It could now be no longer the interest of the foreign powers to add the territories of Spain to those of Austria, and thus to establish the supremacy of the house of Hapsburg in Europe. A truce between England and Spain, after the conclusion of which Marlborough lost all his offices, and was accused in parliament of embezzlement, was the forerunner of the peace of Utrecht. By this, the Spanish and American possessions were left to the Bourbon king, Philip V., under the condition that the crowns of France and Spain were never to be united; England received Nova Scotia and other possessions in North America from France, and Gibraltar, and certain commercial advantages from Spain; the duke of Savoy received the island of Sardinia and the title of king.

A. D. 1710.

Charles VI., A. D. 1711-1740.

May 11, 1713.

The emperor and the German empire did not join in the peace of Utrecht, and continued the war for some time longer. But the emperor quickly became convinced that he was unequal to conduct the war by himself for any lengthened period, and gave his consent to the peace of

27 *

Rastadt, to which also the German empire acceded at Baden in the
March 7, Aargau. By this, Austria obtained the Spanish Nether-
1714. lands, and Milan, Naples, and Sicily, in Italy; the Elect-
September, ors of Bavaria and Cologne were again restored to their
1714. lands and titles, and the royalty of Prussia generally acknowledged.

September 1, § 435. FRANCE. Louis XIV. died in the following year,
1714. weary of life, and borne down by severe strokes of fate.
Within two years, he had lost his son, his grandson, and his intellectual
Louis XV., wife, and his eldest great-grandchild, so that his youngest
A. D. great-grandchild, then five years of age, succeeded to the
1715-1774. throne, under the title of Louis XV. During his minority,
Orleans, the government was conducted by Philip duke of Orleans.
Regent, A. D. This prince, like his former preceptor, cardinal Dubois,
1715-1723. whom he raised to the ministry, was a man of intellect and talent, but of most profligate morals, who despised religion and virtue, and by his dissolute and voluptuous life outraged decency and morality, and squandered the revenues of the state. The Mississippi scheme, which was established by the Scotchman, Law, and which not only promised a high rate of interest, but held out hopes of vast profits in America, produced an incredible intoxication of mind throughout all France, which the unprincipled regent and his companion well knew how to take advantage of. Almost all the gold coin flowed into the bank, and was exchanged for paper money, till at length a bankruptcy took place, which deprived thousands of their property, whilst the greedy magnates were enriched by the spoils.

§ 436. SPAIN. The Spanish king, Philip V., was a weak prince, who was governed by women, and who at length fell entirely into melancholy, and surrendered the government of his empire to his ambitious second wife, Elizabeth of Parma, and the intriguing Italian, Alberoni. These two contrived, by dint of war and intrigue, that Elizabeth's eldest son, Charles, should receive the kingdom of Naples and Sicily; and her second son, Philip, the dukedom of Parma, with Piacenza and Guastalla. In this way, these states received Bourbon rulers. When Philip V.
Ferdinand VI., sank, full of trouble, into the grave, he was succeeded by
A. D. his son, Ferdinand VI., who inherited his father's hypo-
1746-1759. chondria, and at length sunk into an incurable melancholy, which, like that of Saul, could only be relieved by singing and playing on the harp; hence the singer Farinelli obtained great influence at the court.

§ 437. ENGLAND. The free constitution of England obtained such
George I., stability during the reigns of the kings of the house of Hano-
A. D. ver, George I., II., and III., that the personal character of
1714-1727. the monarch exercised but little influence upon the course of

events. The government, which was responsible to parliament, had
George II., more regard to the prosperity of the kingdom and to the
A. D. 1727-1760. greatness of the nation, than to the wishes of the court. It
George III., was for this reason that trade, industry, navigation, and pros-
A. D. perity received an immense development. Under George I.,
1760-1820. who restored the Whigs to his confidence, James (III.) Stu-
A. D. 1715-17. art attempted, with the aid of the discontented Tories (Jacobites), to regain the English throne; but his undertaking failed, and involved his adherents in heavy penalties. The same thing took place in a second attempt, which was hazarded by James's son, Charles Edward, in
the reign of George II. Aided by France, he landed in Scot-
August, 1745. land, where he found numerous adherents among the gallant Highlanders. His first successes encouraged him to march upon
England. But fortune soon forsook him, and the battle
April 27, 1746. of Culloden destroyed the hopes of the Stuarts for ever. Charles Edward, upon whose head the English government had set a price, was saved, as once Charles II. had been, by the friends and adherents of his house, in a wonderful and romantic manner. His abettors were proceeded against with frightful severity; there was no end to executions and confiscations of property; the prisons were filled with Jacobites from Edinburgh to London.

2. CHARLES XII. OF SWEDEN AND PETER THE GREAT OF RUSSIA IN THE NORTHERN WAR (1700-1718).

§ 438. SWEDEN AND RUSSIA. At the commencement of the eighteenth century, Sweden stood at the highest point of her power. The possessions of the crown had been increased, and the treasury filled, by the prudence and frugality of Charles XI.; the fleet and army were in good condition; the coast lands of the Baltic, with the rich towns of Wismar, Stralsund, Stettin, Riga, and Revel, and the effluxes of the Weser, Oder, Dwina, and Neva, were included in the Swedish territory, the site now occupied by St. Petersburg being a swampy hollow on Swedish land. In courage and military spirit the Swedes were inferior to none.
Imperial house But a powerful neighbor had arisen in the East, since the
of Romanof, Russians had united and strengthened themselves under the
A. D. 1613. rule of the house of Romanof; and they now began to extend their frontiers in every direction. This was especially the case under
Alexis Romanof and his two sons, Feodor and Peter. Alexis
Alexis, A. D. conquered Smolensk and the Ukraine, compelled the warlike
1645-1676. and well-mounted Cossacks to acknowledge the supremacy of Russia, and encouraged the civilization and industry of the country;
but it was Feodor who established the absolute power of the
Feodor, A. D. Tzars, by destroying the genealogical registers upon which
1676-1682. the noble families founded their pretensions.

§ 439. PETER THE GREAT. Peter the Great perfected that which his predecessors had commenced. By his extensive travels through the countries of Europe, he made himself acquainted with the customs of civilized nations, and with the advantages of a regular government; by this means he obtained a love for civilization, and directed the whole of his efforts to convert Russia from an Asiatic state, which it had hitherto been, into a European one. With this object, he encouraged the immigration of foreign artisans, mariners, and officers into Russia, without regard to the hatred of foreigners entertained by his countrymen; that he might himself be able to share their labors, he made himself acquainted with the art of ship-building in Holland and England, and inspected the workshops of artists and of the artisans of mills, dams, machinery, &c. An insurrection of the Strelitzes, produced by the exasperation occasioned by these innovations, was suppressed, and taken advantage of by the emperor for reforming the affairs of the army upon the European model. By the frightful punishments inflicted upon the guilty, the hangings, beheadings, and breakings upon the wheel, which continued for weeks, and in which the Tzar himself took a share, Peter showed that civilization had not penetrated his own heart. Despite all his efforts to introduce European refinement into his dominions, and despite his European dress, which he commanded to be worn by all his subjects, he remained, in manners, in mind, and in his mode of governing, a barbarian, devoted to brandy, coarse in his desires, and frantic in his wrath.

Peter the Great, A. D. 1689-1725.

§ 440. POLAND UNDER FREDERICK AUGUSTUS THE STRONG. Whilst Russia was raising and confirming her power, Poland, by her wild and ungoverned freedom, was proceeding towards her downfall. After the death of the military king, John Sobieski, a furious contest arose respecting the election of another sovereign, from which Frederick Augustus, Elector of Saxony, a prince distinguished for his bodily strength, as well as for gallantry and love of magnificence, at length came forth victorious. He was called to the throne of Poland, after having gone over to the Roman Catholic Church. But the Polish nobility, who alone were in possession of any political rights, whilst the peasants pined in serfdom and the citizens were unable to raise themselves from their subordinate position, had already so contracted the royal power, that the state had acquired the form of an aristocratic republic, in which the elected chief was little more than the executor of the resolutions of the Diet.

A. D. 1696.

A. D. 1697.

§ 441. When Charles XII. ascended the throne, at the age of sixteen years, the rulers of Russia, Poland, and Denmark thought the time was arrived for depriving Sweden of the lands she had conquered. The Russian Tzar, Peter the Great, wished to obtain a firm footing on the shores of the Baltic; the elective king of

Charles XII., A. D. 1697-1718.

Poland, Frederick Augustus the Strong, Elector of Saxony, endeavored to get possession of Livonia; and the Danish king, Frederick IV., attempted to wrest Schleswic from the duke of Holstein-Gottorp, a brother-in-law of Charles XII. They accordingly concluded an alliance by the mediation of the Livonian, Patkul, after which, Frederick Augustus marched with a Saxon army to the frontiers of Livonia, and threatened Riga; whilst the Russians attacked Esthonia and besieged Narva; and the Danish king waged war with the duke of Holstein-Gottorp. But to the astonishment of Europe, the young king of Sweden, who had hitherto been looked upon as obtuse and of weak intellect, suddenly displayed a lively and energetic spirit and distinguished military talents. Enraged at the unprincipled attempts of his enemies, he rapidly crossed over to the island of Zealand with his gallant army, commenced at once
A. D. 1700. the siege of Copenhagen, and spread such terror among the Danes, that Frederick IV. renounced the alliance against the Swedes, in the peace of Travendal, and promised to indemnify the duke of Holstein. Hereupon, Charles directed his arms against his other oppo-
A. D. 1701. nents. On the 30th of November, with 8,000 Swedes, he defeated a force of the Russians of ten times that number, before Narva, and captured a number of cannon and a large quantity of ammunition. He then marched across Livonia and Courland into Poland, repeatedly defeated the united armies of Saxony and Poland, and took one town after another. The trembling citizens of Warsaw surren-
A. D. 1702. dered him the keys of their capital, and paid the military levies imposed upon them; Cracow fell into his hands, and the fertile plains of the Vistula, with Thorn, Elbing, and Dantzic, were soon in the power of the Swedes. Charles now demanded of the Poles that they should depose their king, Frederick Augustus, and undertake
A. D. 1703. a new election; and despite the resistance of the nobility, the Swedish king, supported by the Polish party spirit, compelled the required deposition, and obtained the election of Stanislaus Leczinski, voiwode of Posen, a creature of his own, in an elective
July, 1704. assembly which was surrounded by Swedish soldiers.

§ 442. After a few difficult campaigns in the southern provinces of Poland, where the Swedish king, despite the boggy soil and the poverty of the country, drove back the superior forces of the enemy, Charles determined upon seeking his opponent, Frederick Augustus, in his own territories. Without asking permission of the emperor, he marched across Silesia into Lusatia, and was soon in the heart of Saxony, which, notwithstanding the severe military discipline of Charles, was dreadfully desolated by the hostile force. The inhabitants of the plains fled into the towns, the royal family sought refuge in the neighboring state. Augus-
September 24, tus, for the sake of saving his land, gave his consent to the
1706. disgraceful peace of Altranstadt, by which he engaged to

renounce the crown of Poland for himself and his posterity, to dissolve his alliance with the Tzar, and to give up the Livonian, Patkul, to the king of Sweden, who put him to a cruel death upon the wheel. Nevertheless, the hostile army still remained for a whole year in Saxony, to the great detriment of the country, which suffered from the extravagance of the court of Dresden, as well as by the quartering of troops and military levies. Whilst the Estates consented with sighs to the heavy taxes, and the impoverished peasant was almost starving, the Elector gave one magnificent court banquet after the other, and squandered enormous sums upon his country-seats. What did not the entertainment and support of the mistresses and illegitimate children of the gallant prince cost!

Charles XII. was a remarkable contrast to this luxurious and frivolous prince. He possessed the nature of a perfect soldier; his temperance was so great that he refrained from all spirituous liquors, and whilst in the field, contented himself with the slender rations of the army; he wore the same plain dress both in summer and winter—a soldier's long frock, with brass buttons, and horseman's large boots; during a march or in battle, he subjected himself to the greatest toils, privations, and dangers; he avoided the company of women; the only thing that possessed any charms for him was the military life and its dangers; the noise of battle, the whistling of balls, and the neigh of the war-horse were more congenial to him than operas, court-banquets, and concerts.

§ 443. Whilst Charles XII. was lingering in Poland and Saxony, Peter the Great was making preparations for subjecting the possessions of Sweden on the Baltic, and adding them to his own dominions. He built the fortresses of Schlüsselburg and Kronstadt, had the swampy hollows of the Neva drained by serfs after unspeakable exertions, and laid the foundation of the new capital city, St. Petersburg.
A. D. 1708. Nobles, merchants, artisans and their families, from Moscow and other cities, were compelled to settle there, and foreigners were encouraged to emigrate thither. Had Charles XII., when he at length left Saxony to turn his arms against the last and greatest of his foes, chosen the lands of the Baltic for the scene of his military operations, Peter's new plans and creations might easily have been destroyed; but fortunately for him, Charles decided to march upon Moscow, and to penetrate into the heart of the Russian dominions. He captured
A. D. 1708. Grodno and Wilno, crossed the Beresina in June, and pursued his course towards Smolensk. No Russian army opposed the foolhardy king, who, at the head of his gallant forces, waded through streams and marched across pathless morasses. But now came the turning point in the life of Charles. Instead of waiting for his general, Löwenhaupt, who was on his way to join him with fresh troops, and with clothing and provisions for the exhausted army, he suffered himself to be persuaded

by the old Cossack chief, Mazeppa, to undertake a toilsome march in the woody and desert Ukraine. Löwenhaupt, attacked by a superior force of Russians, despite his distinguished military talents, was obliged to sacrifice the whole of his artillery, his baggage, and his provisions, to enable himself, with a small host, to reach the king, who was restlessly hastening forward. The autumnal rains were followed by an unusually severe winter, in the course of which, many hardy warriors perished of cold, and the hands and feet of thousands became frost-bitten. At length, Charles advanced to the siege of the strong city of Pultowa, which, however, was protracted by the want of artillery, till Peter himself approached with a vast army. The battle of Pultowa, which terminated in the total defeat of the Swedish army, was now fought; all the baggage and the rich military chest fell into the hands of the enemy, and the surviving officers and soldiers were made prisoners. Charles XII., the once proud conqueror of three kings, was now a helpless fugitive, who by his utmost exertions barely succeeded in saving himself, with about 2,000 followers, in a foodless and shelterless desert in the dominions of Turkey. Löwenhaupt collected the remainder of the fugitives, but as retreat was impossible from the want of provisions and artillery, he was obliged to surrender himself with 16,000 men. Not one of these brave warriors ever revisited his home; they were dispersed over the vast empire, and some died in the mines of Siberia, others as beggars on the highways. Thus perished this heroic band, as admirable in their endurance as in their triumphs.

A. D. 1708–9.

July 8, 1709.

§ 444. Charles XII. was honorably received and generously treated by the Turks. In his camp before Bender, he lived in royal fashion as the guest of the sultan. But the thought of returning as a vanquished man, without an army, to his kingdom, was unendurable to his haughty soul. He wished to persuade the Turks to a war with Russia, and then to march at their head through the territories of his enemy. Whilst he was wasting his time and energies at Bender in furtherance of this project, and employing every means to gain over the Turks to his plans, his three opponents renewed their former alliance; upon which, Frederick Augustus again made himself master of the throne of Poland, the Tzar Peter extended his conquests to the Baltic, and the king of Denmark again took possession of Schleswic. Prussia and Hanover, also, soon united themselves, and seized upon the Swedish possessions in Germany. At length, the plans of Charles seemed about to succeed. A Turkish army marched into Moldavia, and reduced the Tzar to so critical a position on the Pruth, that he and his whole army were in great danger of becoming prisoners of war. But Peter's wife, Catherine, who, from a slave of the Russian minister, Menzikoff, had become empress of all the Russias,

A. D. 1710.

A. D. 1711.

found means to corrupt the Turkish army, and to bring about the conclusion of a peace. Charles XII. foamed with rage at finding the end he thought so near now farther removed than ever. He however still adhered to his purpose, and even remained at Bender after the Porte had withdrawn its hospitality, discontinued the supplies of money it had hitherto furnished, and commanded him to quit the Turkish territory. He allowed the Porte to supply money for his journey, and nevertheless remained. At length the janisaries stormed his camp, set fire to the house in which he defended himself like a lion, and took him prisoner as he made a furious sally. But he still remained ten months longer in captivity in Turkey, and wasted his strength in childish obstinacy. Was it to be wondered that people at length began to look upon him as deranged? It was not until news was brought him that his possessions in Germany, as far as Stralsund, were in the hands of the enemy, that he suddenly quitted Turkey, after a residence of five years, and arrived
October, 1711. unexpectedly before the gates of Stralsund, after a journey of fourteen days, performed on horseback without the slightest interruption.

§ 445. Stralsund was defended, by dint of the greatest exertions, for
December, 1715. upwards of a year by the brave Swedes; at length, the city was compelled to yield, whereupon Pomerania, with the island of Rugen, fell into the hands of the Prussians. But still the obstinate king would not listen to a peace. By the advice of the intriguing Baron von Görz, he caused paper money to be prepared to defray
A. D. 1716. the expenses of his new preparations for war, and without awaiting the result of the negotiations that Görz had entered into with the Russian emperor, he fell upon Norway with two divisions of his army, for the purpose of chastising the king of Denmark for his breach of the peace. It was here that Charles met with his death before the fortress of Friedrichshall, which he was besieging in the midst of winter. As he was leaning at night upon a breastwork, inspecting the operations in the trenches, he was killed by a bullet, which came, apparently, from the hand of an assassin. The Swedish nobility now assumed
December 11, 1718. all the power to themselves, excluded the rightful heir to the throne (Frederick of Holstein-Gottorp) from the government, and presented it, under great restrictions, to Charles's younger sister, Ulrica Eleonora, and her husband, Frederick of Hesse-Cassel. From this time forth, Sweden was a monarchy in nothing but name; the power was all in the hands of a senate of nobles. The barbarous execu-
A. D. 1719. tion of the count Görz, and the hasty conclusion of a succession of treaties of peace, by which Sweden, in return for an
A. D. 1720. indemnification in money, gave up all her foreign possessions, with the exception of a small portion of Pomerania, was the commencement of the government of a selfish aristocracy, who cared nothing for the honor or well-being of the country.

§ 446. Whilst Sweden, broken and exhausted, was thus escaping from the contest, Russia was rising into European importance. The acquisition of the Swedish provinces of Ingria, Esthonia, and Livonia, to which Courland was also added a few decades later, was the commencement of a new epoch for Russia. As long as Moscow had remained the capital city, the views of the Tzars had been directed towards Asia, to the inhabitants and customs of which the Russians were more assimilated than to those of Europe; but since Petersburg, which lay nearer to the civilization of the west, had become the seat of the government, and risen into importance by the magnificence of its plan and of its buildings, Russia had become a European empire.

The restless activity of the great emperor produced a total revolution. Trade and navigation were encouraged by the formation of roads, canals, and harbors; internal industry, trades, manufactories, and mining met with special encouragement; and even learning and a higher grade of refinement were provided for by the foundation of an academy of sciences. The government and police were also remodelled upon the pattern of other free states, so that the power of the emperor was increased and that of the nobles (Boyards) diminished. One of the innovations of Peter the Great, which was followed by the most important consequences, was the abolition of the dignity of Patriarch, and the creation of the sacred synod as the chief ecclesiastical court, to which the emperor communicated his orders.

§ 447. Whilst Peter was thus reforming his kingdom, he saw, with grief, that his only son, Alexis, was disinclined to the alterations, restricted his intercourse entirely to the friends of the old system, and cherished the intention of again removing his residence to Moscow. It was in vain that the emperor attempted to bend the stubborn and defiant spirit of his son, and to make him a friend to European civilization; Alexis retained his opinions, and at length disappeared from the kingdom. Upon this, Peter, anxious for the permanence of his institutions, ordered his son to be arrested, brought home as a prisoner, and condemned to death. Whether Alexis was put to death, or whether he died before the execution of the sentence, is disputed. An ukase declared the appointment of a successor to the throne to be dependent upon the will of the reigning emperor. After Peter's death, his wife, Catherine I., succeeded him in the government. Under her and her successor, Peter II., Menzikoff, who had risen from the lowest condition to be the favorite of the emperor and an all-powerful minister, exercised the greatest influence upon the government. But he was overthrown at the moment when he imagined that he was about to marry his daughter to the young emperor, and ended his days in exile in Siberia. Anna, the successor of Peter II., reposed her confidence in

A. D. 1722.

Catherine I., A. D. 1725-1727.

Peter II., A. D. 1727-1730.

Anna, A. D. 1730-1740.

two energetic Germans, Ostermann and Münnich, of whom the former was at the head of the cabinet, the latter conducted and arranged the affairs of the army. But these, as well as Anna's favorite, Biron, who was to have managed the government after her death, were banished to Siberia,
Elizabeth, A. D. 1741-1762. when Elizabeth, the youngest daughter of Peter the Great, was raised to the throne by a revolution in the palace. Ivan, a child one year old, whom Anna had named her successor, was thrown into prison, where he grew up like a brute without the slightest education. Elizabeth gave herself up to a voluptuous and profligate life, and relinquished the government to her favorites.

§ 448. Under Frederick Augustus II., the love of magnificence, the luxury and debauchery, that prevailed in Dresden, penetrated into Poland, and destroyed the remaining moral power of the nobles. New vices were associated to the old ones, and proved the more pernicious, inasmuch as the Polish nobility possessed merely the outward polish of European civilization, and that inward barbarism and sensual excitability were united with refinement. Frivolity, arrogance, and religious intolerance were now more prevalent in Poland than ever. The Jesuits suc-
A. D. 1717. ceeded in depriving the Polish Dissidents of their civil and religious privileges by an extraordinary Diet, and when the general hatred broke forth in a popular insurrection in the Protestant town of Thorn against the Jesuitical colleges, the burgomaster was put to death and the town severely punished. After the death of Frederick
A. D. 1733. Augustus II. arose the Polish war of succession. Stanislaus Leczinski (who, flying from Poland after the battle of Pultowa, had wandered in poverty about Alsacia, till he was delivered from want by the marriage of his daughter with Louis XV.) again made claims to the crown, and, trusting to aid from France, travelled in disguise to Warsaw. But Russia and Austria supported the claim of
Frederick Augustus, A. D. 1733-1763. Frederick Augustus III. of Saxony. Stanislaus, although acknowledged by the majority of the Polish nation, was obliged to yield the field to his opponent when the Russian army, under the conduct of Münnich, marched into Poland. He fled in the dress of a peasant to Königsburg, and from thence to
A. D. 1734. France. After some time, however, a peace was concluded which was extremely favorable both to France and Stanis-
A. D. 1737. laus. When the house of Medici was nearly extinct in Florence, the emperor Charles VI. wished his son-in-law, Francis Stephen, to exchange his hereditary dukedom of Lorraine for Tuscany, so that the former might devolve upon Stanislaus, and, after his death, upon France. Charles VI. made this sacrifice to secure the accession of the French king to the Pragmatic Sanction. Stanislaus Leczinski lived for twenty-nine years after this in Nancy, a benefactor of the poor, and a patron of the arts and sciences. But Poland

under the government of the weak and indolent Frederick Augustus III., was approaching every day nearer to its dissolution.

3. RISE OF PRUSSIA.

Frederick William, A. D. 1640-1688.

§ 449. Frederick William, the great Elector of Brandenburg, enlarged his territories on the east and west by successful wars, and secured the lofty position of his state by the formation of a considerable army; he, at the same time, encouraged the internal prosperity and civilization of his dominions, by giving efficient aid to industry and the arts of peace, and by favoring immigration from civilized foreign countries, especially that of the French Huguenots, into his own states. After this energetic and sagacious prince, his splendor-loving son succeeded, Elector Frederick III., to whom the outward magnificence with which Louis XIV. had surrounded the court of Versailles appeared the greatest triumph of earthly majesty. He accordingly attached the highest importance to a splendid court and magnificent feasts. He looked with envy upon the Electors of Hanover and Saxony, who had obtained that, which, in his eyes, was the most inestimable of possessions — a royal crown, the former in England, the latter in Poland; and great was his joy when the emperor Leopold showed himself disposed to confer upon him the title of king of Prussia, in return for his assurances of vigorous support in the war of the Spanish succession. After a solemn coronation in Königsburg, in which the Elector placed the crown upon his own head and upon that of his wife, and after a succession of splendid banquets, the new king, Frederick I., held a magnificent entry into Berlin, which he attempted to render a suitable residence for royalty, by public buildings, pleasure grounds, and monuments of art. The arts and sciences were encouraged. In the country seat of Charlottenberg, where the highly accomplished queen Sophia Charlotte held her gracious rule, there was always an assemblage of distinguished and intellectual people. Societies for the cultivation of the arts and sciences were established in Berlin, under the auspices of the great philosopher Leibnitz; a flourishing university arose in Halle, distinguished by a noble freedom of spirit, and became the scene of the labors of such men as Christopher Thomasius, the powerful advocate of reason, and of the German language and mode of thinking, the pious Hermann Franke, the founder of the orphan asylum, that "trophy of trust in God and love to men," and the philosopher, Christopher Wolf.

Frederick III. as king. Frederick I., A. D. 1688-1713.

A. D. 1700.

§ 450. This expenditure, combined with the support of a considerable army in the service of the emperor, pressed hard upon the impoverished land; the citizen and peasant class were oppressed with heavy taxes; the new splendor of the royal house appeared to be full of evil for the country; fortunately, the extravagant Frederick I. was succeeded by the frugal Frederick William I., who was in every thing the opposite of his predecessor. The jewels and costly furniture that had been collected by the father were sold by the son, who paid the king's debts with the proceeds; every thing in the shape of luxury was banished from the court, the attendants were reduced to those that were absolutely necessary, and every superfluous expense avoided. The king and his court lived like citizens, the meals consisted of household fare, and the queen and her daughter were obliged to occupy themselves in domestic duties. The clothing and furniture were simple. The smoking-club, in which Frederick William and his "good friends" practised coarse jests at the expense of the simple or good-natured, and where every one was obliged to have a pipe in his mouth, usurped the place of the intellectual circle with which Frederick I. and his wife had surrounded themselves; the opera-singers and actors were discharged; French *beaux esprits*, as well as teachers of languages and dancing, were banished; poets, artists, and men of learning were deprived of their pensions in part, or entirely; Wolf, whose philosophy was offensive to the orthodox and pious, received notice to quit Halle within twenty-four hours, "under penalty of the rope." But offensive as this severity and coarseness on the part of the king might be, as well as his contempt for all cultivation, learning, and refinement, it must be confessed that his powerful nature, his sound judgment, and his sparing housekeeping gave strength and firmness to the young state. He relieved the peasants for the purpose of raising agriculture; he encouraged internal industry, and forbade the importation of foreign manufactures; he settled the Protestants, who had been driven from their houses by the bishop of Salzburg, in his own dominions; and although his severity was occasionally exercised at the expense of personal freedom, it also compelled judges and officials to an efficient performance of their duties. The king's own example affords a proof of how much may be effected by frugality and good management; for although he spent enormous sums upon his Potsdam guards, for which he had "tall fellows" enlisted or kidnapped from all the countries of Europe, and although he called many useful institutions into existence, he left, at his death, a sum of money amounting to 8,000,000 thalers, a great treasure in silver plate, a regulated revenue, and a large and admirably organized and disciplined army.

Frederick William I., A. D. 1713 - 1740.

§ 451. His great son, Frederick II. pursued a different path; whilst his father was engaged in his wild hunting parties, or pursuing his coarse amusements with his companions, the talented and intellectual prince was busied with the writers of France, and with his flute, which he passionately loved. The difference of their dispositions rendered them strangers to each other. Frederick was offended

Born January 24, 1712.

by his father's harshness, and the latter was angry with his son for pursuing a different course, and would willingly have forced him from it by severity. This coldness and aversion increased with years; so that Frederick, when his father, out of caprice, refused to sanction his intended marriage with an English princess, embraced the resolution with a few young friends of flying to England. An intercepted letter of Frederick's to his confidant, the lieutenant von Katte, revealed the secret. The king foamed with rage. He commanded the crown prince to be confined in a fortress, and Katte to be executed before the windows; all those who were suspected of being implicated were severely punished by the irritated monarch. It was not until Frederick had penitently implored his father's pardon, that he was released from the fortress, and had his sword and uniform restored to him. Shortly after this, followed the marriage of Frederick with a daughter of the princely house of Brunswick-Bevern. But his spirit found little pleasure in the narrow bounds of domestic life; he seldom visited his wife, especially after his father had relinquished the little town of Rheinsberg to him, where, from this time, he led a cheerful life amidst a circle of intellectual, accomplished, and free-thinking friends, in which wit, jest, and lively conversation alternated with grave and diversified studies. He read the works of the ancients in French translations, and derived from them a noble ambition of emulating the heroes of Greece and Rome in their mighty deeds and their mental cultivation; he admired French literature, and conceived such a veneration for Voltaire, that he addressed the most flattering letters to him, and, at a later period, summoned him to his presence. They were both, however, soon convinced that no personal intercourse could long endure between men of such similarly sarcastic natures, and separated from each other in anger; but they still kept up a correspondence in writing. Frederick displayed his free way of thinking by receiving a number of French authors, who had been banished from France on account of the hostility of their writings to the Church; and, after his ascension of the throne, proved the liberality of his views in regard to religion, by recalling Wolf to Halle, with the well-known expression, "that, in his kingdom, every man might be happy in his own way."

A. D. 1730. A. D. 1734. A. D. 1740.

4. THE TIMES OF FREDERICK II. AND MARIA THERESA.

a. THE AUSTRIAN WAR OF SUCCESSION (A. D. 1740 — 1748).

§ 452. The emperor Charles VI., a good-natured but in no ways distinguished prince, died shortly after the accession of Frederick II., having, however, concluded the disgraceful peace of Belgrade with the Turks previous to his death. As he had

September 18 1739.

no male heirs, it had been his anxious care through his whole reign, to secure the succession of his only daughter, Maria Theresa, wife of Francis Stephen of Lorraine, to the hereditary states of Austria. With this object, he purchased, by great sacrifices, the acknowledgment from all the courts of the domestic law known as the Pragmatic Sanction, by virtue of which, the Austrian hereditary lands remained undivided, and, in the event of the male line becoming extinct, descended upon the female branch. Scarcely had the emperor closed his eyes, before Charles Albert, Elector of Bavaria, who was descended from the eldest daughter of the emperor Ferdinand I., made claims upon the Austrian patrimonial states, not only in right of his descent, but upon some pretended testamentary intentions of the emperor. Charles Albert, who was a weak, narrow-minded man, devoted to superstition and ostentation, would not have been in a position to make his claims valid by the resources of his exhausted land, had not the French court, despite its acknowledgment of the Pragmatic Sanction, supported him with money and troops, in the hope of thereby rendering the emperor and the German nation dependent upon France. In the treaty of Nymphenberg, the Bavarian Elector sold himself to France, as his predecessor, Charles Emmanuel, had done before, for gold for his vanity, and troops for the acquisition of the throne. Frederick II. of Prussia, also, was not willing to let slip the favorable opportunity of urging the established pretensions of his family to the inheritance of the Silesian principalities of Jagendorf, Leignitz, Brieg, and Wohlau; and accordingly supported the Bavarian Elector in his claims upon Austria, Hungary, and Bohemia, and in his suit for the imperial crown. Saxony, also, would not relinquish her share of the expected booty; the indolent and stupid Augustus III., who left his government entirely in the hands of the extravagant and unprincipled count Brühl, raised claims to Moravia, and brought inexpressible misery upon his wretched and heavily oppressed country by his participation in the war.

October 10, 1740. § 453. A few weeks after the death of Charles VI., Frederick II. marched with his admirable army into Silesia. The king himself accompanied his troops, more for the sake of learning the art of war, and of exciting the courage of the soldiers by his presence, than with any purpose of assuming the chief command, which he rather relinquished to the two experienced generals, Schwerin and Leopold of Dessau. (A. D. 1740-1742.) This first Silesian war soon showed that a fresh spirit had come over the Prussians. (April 10, 1741.) After their victory in the battle of Molwitz, they took possession of the greater part of Upper and Lower Silesia.

The French army, under Belleisle, shortly after marched into Germany, and being supported by Bavaria and Saxony, made themselves masters of the territories of Upper Austria and Bohemia. Charles

October, 1741. Albert received homage as archduke in Linz, and was invested with the royal crown of Bohemia at Prague, in the midst of magnificent coronation banquets. He now stood at the summit of his happiness. The election of emperor had terminated in his favor, and he was already making preparations for a splendid coronation in Frankfort.

Charles VII., A. D. 1741-1745.

§ 454. In this distress, Maria Theresa turned towards the Hungarians. At a Diet in Presburg (where, according to a widely-circulated legend, she is said to have appeared with her young son, Joseph, in her arms), she excited such an enthusiasm among the magnates by the description of her distresses, and by gracious promises, that they rose up with an unanimous shout of "Vivat Maria Theresa Rex," and called their warlike countrymen to arms. The Tyrolese, also, in a similar manner, announced their ancient truthfulness to Austria. A gallant force soon marched into the field from the lowlands of Hungary. The warlike tribes of the Theiss and the Marosch, the wild bands of the Croats, Slaves, and Pandours, under the conduct of Khevenhüller and Bärenklau (Pereklo), marched into Austria, drove back the Bavarian and French troops with little difficulty, and pressed forward, plundering and ravaging, into Bavaria. At the very moment at which Charles Albert, by French assistance, and in the midst of splendid banquets, was invested with the much-coveted imperial crown, the enemy entered his capital, Munich, occupied Landshut, and foraged the country as far as the Lech with their wild horsemen. Deprived of his hereditary possessions, the new emperor, Charles VII., was soon reduced to such extremities, that he could only support himself by the assistance of France.

January 24, 1742.

§ 455. At the same time, an Austrian army marched into Bohemia to drive the French out of this country also; and Maria Theresa, to deprive them of the assistance of the Prussians, consented, though with a heavy heart, to the peace of Breslau, by which almost the whole of Upper and Lower Silesia was surrendered to Frederick. In a short time, the greater portion of Bohemia was again in the hands of the Austrians; the capital, where Belleisle lay with a considerable army, was already besieged. At this juncture, Belleisle, by his daring retreat from Prague to Eger, in the midst of winter, showed that the military spirit of the French was not yet extinguished. The road was indeed strewed with dead or torpid bodies, and even those who escaped bore the seeds of death within them.

July 28, 1742.

A. D. 1743. In the following spring, Maria Theresa was crowned in Prague, and at the same time acquired a powerful confederate in George II. of Hanover and England. After the battle of Dettingen (near Aschaffenburg), where the English and Austrian troops bore off the victory, the French retreated over the

June 27, 1743.

Rhine, and Saxony embraced the cause of Austria, and received subsidies from England.

§ 456. The success of the Austrians rendered Frederick II. anxious for the possession of Silesia, and he therefore commenced a second Sile-
A. D. sian war against Maria Theresa. Whilst he was hastily
1744-1745. advancing upon Bohemia, as a confederate of the emperor, with a strong army of imperial auxiliaries, Charles VII. found an opportunity of regaining his hereditary territory of Bavaria, and of returning
January 20, to his capital, Munich, where, however, he shortly after died.
1745. His son, Maximilian Joseph, renounced all claim to the Aus-
April. trian heritage in the treaty of Füssen, and at the election of emperor, gave his voice for the husband of Maria Theresa, whereupon the latter was crowned in Frankfort as Francis I. In the mean while, Frederick II. had lost the greater part of Silesia to the brave Austrian
field-marshal, Traun; but the splendid victory of Hohenfried-
June 4. berg again restored him the superiority. The military renown of the Prussian monarch, and of his generals, Ziethen, Winterfeld, and others, had spread far and wide, and prince Ferdinand of Brunswick gave the first proof of his talents as a general at Sorr. When the old Dessauer conquered the Saxons in the midst of winter, in the bloody field of Kesselsdorf, and Frederick marched into the capital of Dresden,
December 25, which had been deserted by Augustus III., Maria Theresa,
1745. in the peace of Dresden, again consented to the cession of
Francis I., A. D. Silesia; and Frederick, in return, acknowledged her hus-
1745-1765. band as emperor.

§ 457. The war, which was ended in Germany, continued for some time longer in the Netherlands. It was here that the French, under the conduct of the talented and brave, but immoral and dissolute, marshal Saxe,
A. D. a natural son of Frederick Augustus II., gained a succession
1745-1747. of splendid victories in the battles of Fontenoy, Raucoux, and Laffeld, by which the Austrian Netherlands fell almost entirely into
October their power. But as the exhausted states were all longing
18-20, 1748. for a cessation of hostilities, the peace of Aix was at length arranged, by which the Austrian hereditary territories were awarded to Maria Theresa, with the exception of Silesia, which remained with Prussia, and a few possessions in Italy, which she gave up to Sardinia and to the Spanish-Bourbon prince, Philip. The other states resumed their former relations, and France gained nothing by this expensive war but military renown.

b. THE SEVEN YEARS' WAR (A. D. 1756-1763).

§ 458. Maria Theresa could not forget the loss of Silesia. She therefore took advantage of the eight years of peace that followed the conclusion of the Austrian war of succession, to form alliances that produced important consequences. Russia's dissolute empress, Elizabeth, offended by the sarcasms of Frederick, was easily induced by her minister, Bestucheff, to enter into a confederation with Maria Theresa; as was also Augustus III. of Saxony, by count Brühl, who likewise felt himself injured by the scorn with which the great king always spoke of him. But it was a master-stroke of crafty policy that Maria Theresa, by her shrewd and dexterous minister, Kaunitz, induced the court of Versailles to renounce the ancient policy of France, which had always been directed to weakening the house of Hapsburg, and to unite itself with Austria against Prussia. For many years past, Louis XV. had allowed himself to be led into a profligate course of life by the pleasure-seeking and dissolute nobles. In the society of his licentious favorites and shameless mistresses, he gave himself up entirely to his sensual nature, and plunged from one pleasure into another. In the excesses of the table, and the joys of the chase and the bottle, he forgot his kingdom and the welfare of his people. Maria Theresa made use of these circumstances for her own advantage. The proud empress, who stood upon her morality and virtue, descended so far as to write a flattering letter to Louis's all-powerful mistress, madame Pompadour, for the purpose of winning her over to her interest. An alliance was accordingly entered into, by means of the Pompadour and her creatures, by France and Austria, the object of which was to deprive the king of Prussia of his conquests, and to reduce him again to the condition of an Elector of Brandenburg.

September, 1751.

§ 459. Frederick, who received accurate information of all the plots laid against him from a secretary of Brühl's, whom he had corrupted, determined to anticipate his enemies by an unexpected attack. He fell suddenly upon Saxony, took possession of Leipsic, Wittenberg, and Dresden, which had been deserted by the court, and established the Prussian form of government. The taxes and all the public rents were seized, the magazines thrown open to the Prussian army, and the arms and artillery sent to Magdeburg. For the purpose of justifying these proceedings, he published the documents which he had discovered in Dresden, and which contained the plans of his opponents. The Saxon troops, who had taken up a strong position at Pirna, on the Elbe, were blockaded by the Prussians, and compelled by hunger to surrender. 14,000 gallant warriors were made prisoners. Frederick compelled them to enter the Prussian service; but they fled in troops at the first opportunity into Poland, where the Saxon court remained during the whole war. Frederick lingered in Dresden, and exacted heavy contributions in money and recruits from the conquered country, for which, war was declared against him by the German empire, for breach of the Land-peace; and the aristocratic government of Sweden, which only acted according to the instigations of France, also joined the enemies of

A. D. 1756.

Prussia. It was only England and a few German states (Hanover, Brunswick, Hesse-Cassel, Gotha) that adhered to the cause of Frederick.

§ 460. In the spring of the following year, Frederick marched with his chief force towards Bohemia, whilst his allies advanced
A. D. 1757. against the French, who were between the Rhine and the Weser. By the gallant efforts of his troops, and by the heroic courage
May 6, 1757. and heroic death of Schwerin, Frederick won the splendid but dearly bought victory of Prague. But no later than the
June 18. following month, the defeat at Collin, by the brave Austrian field-marshal Daun, deprived the Prussian king of all his advantages. His melancholy, both before and after the day of Collin, gave evidence of the weight of care by which he was oppressed. A short time after, the French also gained a victory over Frederick's allies at Hast-
July. enbeck, on the Weser, and prepared to take up their winter quarters in Saxony along with the German imperial army. The prince of Soubise, a favorite of madame Pompadour, and a confidential associate in the orgies of Louis XV., was already on the Saale with a large army, when Frederick made an unexpected attack, and in the battle
November 5. of Rosbach, gained a most splendid victory. The imperial army fled so hastily at the very commencement of the battle, that it re-received the name of the Runaway Army from the jests of the witty; the French soon followed, abandoning their baggage, which was rich in articles of luxury and fashion. Seydlitz, the leader of the cavalry, had particularly distinguished himself. A month later, the Prus-
December 5. sian king also won a famous victory from Daun, in the battle of Leuthen, and again occupied Silesia. But in the mean time, the miseries of war pressed heavily upon poor Germany; Hanover, Brunswick, and Hesse-Cassel, in particular, were harshly treated by the extravagant and dissolute duke of Richelieu, by exactions and military levies.

§ 461. Since the battle of Rosbach, Frederick had been
A. D. 1758. no less the idol of the people in England, than in France and Germany. The English ministry, in which the elder Pitt (Lord Chatham) possessed the greatest influence, accordingly determined to support the king of Prussia more liberally with troops and money; and to leave the appointment of generals in his hands. He named the circumspect Ferdinand of Brunswick the leader of the allied force, who drove back the French over the Rhine in the commencement
A. D. 1758. of the spring, and secured the north of Germany against their predatory inroads. In the mean while, the Russians, under Bestucheff, had penetrated as far as the Oder; but as this general behaved in a very ambiguous manner during a dangerous illness of the empress Elizabeth, he was banished, and Fermor appointed in his stead. The latter occupied East Prussia, compelled Königsburg to do homage, and advanced with his wild hordes, ravaging and plundering, into Branden-

burg. Hereupon, Frederick executed a masterly march upon the Oder,
August 25. and, in the bloody battle of Zorndorf, gained a victory that was certainly dearly purchased. After this, Frederick wished to march into Saxony to the assistance of his brother Henry; but being surprised in an unfavorable position by the superior force of Daun, he lost the whole of his artillery and many brave soldiers in the attack at
October 14. Hochkirk. He nevertheless effected a juncture with Henry by a dexterous march, and again drove the enemy out of Silesia and Saxony.

A. D. 1759. § 462. Frederick's means of continuing the war began to dwindle. Whilst he was with difficulty filling up the gaps in his ranks by oppressive levies of young and inexperienced recruits, and could only supply his want of money and necessaries by severe war-taxes and imposts, Maria Theresa was constantly receiving fresh supplies of money and men from France and Russia.

For the purpose of preventing the union of the Russians and Austrians, Frederick advanced to the Oder, but was so completely defeated by the
August 12, 1759. Austrians under their skilful general, Laudon, in the bloody engagement of Kunersdorf, after he had already victoriously repulsed the Russians, that he began to despair of a successful termination of the war. Dresden and the greater part of Saxony was lost to the Prussians. But the want of union between the Russians and Austrians prevented the proper advantage being taken of the victory. In the mean time, the allies of Frederick, under Ferdinand of Brunswick, had been more successfully engaged against the French. It is true, that Broglio
April 13, 1759. had obtained the advantage in the battle of Bergen at Frankfort-on-the-Main, but Ferdinand's victory at Minden drove back the French over the Rhine, and saved Westphalia and Hanover.

A. D. 1760. § 463. The war had already so weakened the Prussian army, that the king, contrary to his usual custom, was compelled to remain on the defensive. It is true that Frederick's name, and the dexterity of his recruiting officers, brought troops of soldiers from all quarters to the Prussian standard; but even Frederick's military talents could not entirely replace the loss of expert officers and veteran troops. To defray the expenses of the war, he was obliged to have recourse to the most oppressive taxes and to a debased coinage. Whilst Frederick was in Saxony, the brave Fouquet, the friend of the king, suffered a defeat in Silesia, in consequence of which the Austrians took possession of the whole country. Upon this, Frederick relinquished Saxony, that he
August 15. might again conquer Silesia. He gained this object by the victory over Laudon at Liegnitz on the Katzbach; but he was unable to prevent the Austrian and Russian troops from breaking into Prussia, taking possession of Berlin, and visiting the hereditary lands of the king with plunder and desolation. Daun now occupied a strong position on an

eminence near the Elbe, for the purpose of wintering in Saxony. To prevent this, Frederick hazarded a desperate attack upon Daun's camp, though his brave soldiers fell in crowds before the artillery. By the dearly bought victory of Torgau, which was gained by the November 3. assistance of Ziethen, the Prussian king again regained Saxony, and could make his winter quarters in Leipsic; but 14,000 of his soldiers required no shelter; Daun's camp had been their burial place.

§ 464. (1761 – 1763.) In the year 1761, it appeared that Frederick must succumb before the disasters that were pouring in upon him on all sides; for not only had his numerous enemies taken possession of a great part of his lands, but England, after the accession of George III., had refused all farther assistance. Frederick indeed resisted with vigor the enemies that were pressing upon him; but his melancholy and despondency are betrayed in his letters to his friends, and in his poetry. It appeared that Silesia must fall to Austria, and Prussia to Russia. But in the very extremity of Frederick's distress, the empress Elizabeth died, January 5, and her nephew, who was a great venerator of the Prussian 1762. king, ascended the throne of Russia. This change produced a sudden alteration in the state of affairs. Peter, a good-natured but inconsiderate prince, who acted over hastily, at once concluded a treaty of peace with Frederick, and united his Russian army with the Prussian. This connection, however, did not last long. Peter made enemies of his subjects by imprudent innovations in the Church and State, and by remodelling the army upon the Prussian pattern. A conspiracy was formed against him, with the knowledge of his wife, whom Peter treated harshly on account of her dissolute behavior, in consequence of which, Peter III. was barbarously murdered by some Russian noblemen, and Catherine II. made herself mistress of the government which belonged by July 9, 1762. right to her son, Paul. The empress recalled her army from Prussia, but confirmed the peace that had been concluded with Frederick; and the Russian general, before his departure, assisted the Prussian king in obtaining a victory.

§ 465. The exhausted states were now all anxious for the conclusion of the war. The Germans, whose lands had been ravaged, whose industry had become stagnant, whose agriculture had been ruined, and whose prosperity had been destroyed, demanded peace in despair; this induced the greater number of the princes to withdraw from the alliance against Frederick; and, as the finances of Austria were also deranged, Maria Theresa no longer opposed the peace that was universally desired. February 21, A truce afforded an opportunity for negotiations, which, in 1763. the following February, led to the peace of Hubertsburg. In this, the possession of Silesia was secured to the king of Prussia for ever. The fluctuating land and naval war, that had been carried on between England and France in America, was, at the same time, terminated by the peace of Paris, by which England got possession of Canada. From this time, Prussia assumed her position among the five great powers of Europe.

c. THE GERMAN EMPIRE AND THE AGE OF FREDERICK.

§ 466. The German empire had so entirely lost all respect as a political body, that it was not represented at the peace negotiations at Hubertsburg, and the sentence of outlawry pronounced against Frederick II. was received with scorn and ridicule. The power of the Emperor was sunk to an empty shadow, and his revenue to a few thousand florins. Nearly 350 princes and commonwealths, with the most varied powers and the most unequal extent of territory, ruled in Germany with all the rights of sovereignty, and left nothing to their common chief but the confirmation of mutual compacts, promotions, declarations of majority, and the determination of precedence. During war, the German princes not unfrequently embraced the hostile cause. Bavaria was always in alliance with France. The Diet, which had, for a long time, been held in Regensburg, and which consisted of representatives of the princes and imperial towns, had lost all respect, since it was too much occupied with speeches and debates to come to any decision, or if it came to any, was unable to give it authority. Obsolete rights were contended for with a little-minded jealousy; rank, title, and the right of suffrage, were watched over with the greatest care, and all time and energy devoted to doctrinal disputes without object; whilst foreign nations made Germany the theatre of their wars, and treated the imbecile body politic with insolence and contempt. The state of tribunals of justice was not less melancholy. The imperial chamber of Wetzlar, in which the complaints of Estates of the empire against each other or against their vassals were examined, proceeded with such tediousness and prolixity, that causes were often pending for years before judgment was pronounced, the suitors either died or fell into poverty, and the records increased to an immeasurable extent. The judges were chiefly dependent upon the fees for their remuneration, and in this way a door was thrown open to corruption. An attempt on the part of the emperor, Joseph II., to improve and accelerate
Joseph II., the progress of justice in the imperial chamber, was frustrated
1765-1790. by the selfishness of the interested parties. As regards the lower courts, the great diversity in the laws, the number of small states, and the unlimited power of the judges and officials, rendered it extremely difficult for the humble man to procure justice. The weak were exposed without defence to every injustice of the crafty and the strong. It was the golden age of jurists and advocates.

§ 467. Whilst the German empire was sinking lower and lower, Prussia, under her sagacious and energetic king, rose to ever increasing power and prosperity. Frederick attempted to heal the wounds inflicted by the seven years' war, to the best of his ability, by supporting the decayed land proprietors and the manufacturers in Silesia and the March with money, by remitting their taxes for a few years, and by relieving the lot of the peasants. He encouraged agriculture, planting, and mining; established colonies in the uncultivated portions of his dominions; and fostered industry, trade, and commerce with the greatest care. By these means, the country became prosperous, and he was enabled to increase his taxes without oppressing the people. His own frugality, the simplicity of his court, and the well-regulated economy of the state, were the occasion that the public treasury was every year better replenished. It was not until a later period that he adopted severe and oppressive measures. Among these, his management of the customs and excise may be particularly mentioned. He made the sale of coffee, tobacco, salt, &c., a royal monopoly, and forbade the free trade in these articles. For the purpose of preventing any clandestine traffic, he appointed a number of French excise officers, who, by their insolence, made the regulation, which was otherwise so oppressive to the citizens and peasants, utterly detestable. The affairs of the Church and of education gained the least by the attention of the king. In a small place, the situation of public instructor was frequently a retiring post for a discharged petty officer, whilst the higher institutions were often left to the management of Frenchmen. The free-thinking king took little interest in the affairs of Christianity or the Church; but we must admit that he procured the universal admission of the principle of Christian toleration in his dominions. Frederick devoted great attention to the affairs of justice. The rack and the horrible and degrading punishments of the middle age were abolished, the course of justice simplified, and the laws improved. The new book of laws that was introduced under his successor, Frederick William II., as the Prussian code, was prepared under Frederick. More important, however, than all these laws and arrangements was the fact, that Frederick II. inspected every thing himself, and narrowly inquired, during his journeys, after the administration of justice and the management of affairs, ejected the negligent and chastised the dishonest. By his untiring activity from early morning till late at night, he acquired a comprehensive knowledge of all the affairs of his kingdom, and his commanding character, which scrupled not at corporal punishment, terrified the slothful and the unjust. One peculiarity of the great king has often been blamed with justice—his love for what was foreign, and his neglect, nay contempt, for the things of his own country. It was not only in literature that Frederick gave the preference to the French, so that he wrote his own letters and works in their language; the whole proceedings of this nation were admired, and, as far as possible, imitated by him. French adventurers, by the hundred, found honor and support in Prussia; and as this admiration of foreigners became the mode in other courts, all quarters of Germany swarmed with hare-brained Frenchmen. Parisian barbers, dancing-masters, and boasters were often preferred to the most deserving natives in the appointment to the higher offices of the court and government.

§ 468. Frederick, in his old age, was once more involved in a war with Austria. At the close of the year 1777, the Bavarian line of the house of Wittelsbach became extinct with Maximilian Joseph, and the electorship devolved to the next heir, Charles Theodore of the Palatinate. This licentious, profligate, and bigoted prince, who, despite his many failings and vices, is still affectionately remembered by the people of the Palatinate, and whose love of art is borne witness to by many remarkable erections in Mannheim, Schwetzingen, and Heidelberg, possessed neither legitimate offspring nor love for the land he inherited. He consequently easily allowed himself to be persuaded by the emperor Joseph II. to a treaty, in which he acknowledged the validity of Austria's claims to Lower Bavaria, the upper Palatinate, and the territory of Mindelheim, and declared himself ready to relinquish these lands in return for certain advantages being assured to his natural children. Frederick II., alarmed at this aggrandizement of Austria, attempted to interfere with the project by inducing the future heir, duke Charles of Zweibrucken, to protest against the contract in the Diet; and as this was attended by no results, he ordered an army to march into Bohemia to prevent any change in the existing state of things. This gave occasion to the Bavarian war of suc-
A. D. 1778, cession, which was carried on more with the pen than the
1779. sword, inasmuch as both parties attempted to prove themselves in the right by learned treatises. But as all the states were averse to a general war, Russia and France succeeded in persuading Maria Theresa, who had no liking for the zeal for innovation displayed by her son, to the peace of Teschen, by which Bavaria was secured to the house of the Palatinate, Innviertel with Braunau to Austria, and the succession of the Margravate of Anspach and Bayreuth to Prussia. The emperor, irritated at this, made a second attempt, after the death of Maria Theresa, to possess himself of Bavaria, offering in exchange the
A. D. 1785. Austrian Netherlands (Belgium) as the Burgundian kingdom. Charles Theodore allowed himself to be persuaded to this also. But Frederick II. now attempted to frustrate this project, and to secure the succession in Bavaria to the house of the Palatinate, by establishing an alliance of princes, which was gradually joined by most of the princes of Germany. This princely confederation increased the power and consequence of the king of Prussia, in the same proportion that it entirely undermined the authority of the emperor. Each prince sought for independent and unlimited power; each formed a miniature court, to which, in magnificence and profusion, in morals and fashions, in language, literature, and art, the court of Versailles served as a pattern.

d. THE INTELLECTUAL POPULAR LIFE IN GERMANY.

§ 469. Prejudicial as this division of Germany was to its external power and greatness, it was in an equal degree advantageous to the development of the arts and sciences. Many princes were patrons and encouragers of literature and cultivation; they sought to attract men of celebrity to their capitals and universities, and encouraged poets and men of learning to undertake great works by rewards and distinctions. Thus it happened, that in the second half of the eighteenth century, when Germany's political and military consequence was entirely lost, literature, poetry, science, and the entire spiritual life, received a mighty impulse, and created a degree of refinement such as has scarcely been equalled in
Klopstock, A. D. 1724-1803.
modern history. Poetry especially flourished. Klopstock, by his great epic poem, the "Messiah," and by his odes and war-songs, awakened a warmth of Christian feeling, and a patriotic spirit of liberty; he formed his severe and solemn diction and
Lessing, A. D. 1729-1781.
his rhymless metre upon the model of the ancients. Lessing, the great thinker and critic, in his "Hamburg-Dramaturgy," first exposed the weakness of French dramatic literature, and by his own pieces for the stage ("Minna von Barnhelm," "Emilia Galotti," "Nathan the Wise,") showed the way by which it was possible to attain to genuine dramatic poetry; he at the same time, in his "Laocoon," opened the eyes of thinkers to the essence of poetry and plastic
Winckelmann, A. D. 1717-1768.
art, the understanding of which was revealed during the same period by Winckelmann, in a different way; and in his remarkable controversial writings against the pastor Göze of Hamburg, on the Wolfenbüttel fragments, he displayed a vigor of language and a clearness of argument which are astonishing. Upon his
Herder, A. D. 1744-1803.
shoulders stands the poetical and intellectual Herder, who went back to the original sources of language and poetry, and revealed with fine taste the beauties of the Oriental poetry of nature ("On the Spirit of Hebrew Poetry," "Palm-leaves," &c.), and displayed the deep merit of the artless popular songs of different nations (in the "Cid," 'Voices of the People in Songs"), and gave a mighty impulse to further inquiries by his "Ideas towards a Philosophy of the
Wieland, A. D. 1733-1813.
History of Man." Wieland, the cheerful philosopher of life, in his romances ("Agathon," "The Abderites," "Aristippus"), which are for the most part based upon the ancient Greek manners, with a modern coloring, addressed the sentiments and mode of thinking of the upper classes, which were formed upon the French model, and preached the wise enjoyment of life in loose and waggish language, a doctrine well suited to the higher ranks of society, and introduced German literature into a circle that had hitherto read nothing but French works. He, at the same time, renewed the romantic epic

poetry of the middle age in his "Oberon." German prose received a complete revolution from these three men: Lessing gave it strength, sharpness, and perspicuity; Herder, elevation and richness of imagery; Wieland, fluency and grace. It was on the ground prepared by these men that Goethe, the great genius of the century, brought forward his creations, in which the spiritual life of the nation and the progress of his own culture are reflected. At the genial and energetic age of seventeen, when the youth who was pressing onwards with violence, despised all the rules of art and usage, set no value on any thing but the productions (even when formless) of genius, praised the depths of original and natural poetry, delighted in popular ballads, and gazed in wondering admiration upon Ossian and Shakspeare, "The Sorrows of Werther," a romance in letters, and the drama of "Gotz von Berlichingen," in which these poets served as models, awakened a storm of enthusiasm; when Lessing and Winckelmann had revived the interest for ancient art in Germany, the classical dramas, "Tasso" and "Iphigenia," in the spirit and in the clear and harmonious form of antiquity, appeared in a time adapted for them; and the impressions and feelings that the poet had received during his travels in Italy are reflected in the unsurpassable popular scenes of the tragedy of "Egmont." The idyllic epic, "Hermann and Dorothea," touched upon the mighty period of the French revolution and the sorrows of the emigrants; the romance of "Wilhelm Meister," in which the life of a player is described, and the novel of "Elective Affinities," belong to the new romantic time, which found pleasure in the mysterious, the wonderful, and the fabulous. In "Poetry and Truth," Goethe displays the progress of his own life and mental development; and in the magnificent dramatic poem of "Faust," with which we find him engaged through his whole life, he has left to posterity a picture of the most inward conditions of his soul. In the mean while, the political world had experienced violent convulsions, and the attention of the people was directed towards history and the affairs of state. At this juncture, Schiller, by his historical dramas, that presented before the soul of the nation similar tempestuous periods taken from foreign and domestic history, and by his enthusiasm for freedom, fatherland, and human happiness, struck the chords that found the deepest response in the bosoms of the people. His first three tragedies, "The Robbers," "Love and Intrigue," and "Fiesko," belong to the stormy period of youth; with the drama of "Don Carlos" begins a more refined period; during his residence in Jena as professor of history, he occupied himself with the "Thirty Years' War," with the "Revolt of the Netherlands," and with the trilogy of "Wallenstein;" and in the last years of his life, in Weimar, which were rendered gloomy by sickness and anxieties about the means of subsistence, he composed "Maria Stuart," the "Maid of Orleans," the "Bride of Messina," and the

Goethe, A. D. 1749-1832.

Schiller, A. D. 1759-1805.

magnificent drama of "William Tell." Schiller gained the friendship of Goethe by the purity of his feelings and the truthfulness of his efforts, different as the natures of the two men were. Their united activity marks the culminating point of German poetry.

§ 470. Not poetry alone, but the science of religion, philosophy, history, the affairs of education, in a word, the whole spiritual life, experienced a mighty revolution. Protestant theologians searched through the Bible, and presented systems of Christianity in accordance with the direction of their own minds. Some, like Lavater, the pastor of Zūrich, sought to preserve the world in a rigid faith by means of religious writings, and to establish the conviction that man is brought into immediate union with God by prayer; others, like the Berlin bookseller and author, Nicolai, would admit no other judge in spiritual things than human reason and the power of reflection, and declared that every thing that was opposed to this was superstition. The former class were called Supernaturalists, the latter Rationalists. A third party, which included Hamann, the philosopher, Fr. H. Jacobi, and the poet Fr. Stolberg, like the mystics of the middle ages, made religion a matter of feeling. Lavater was also the inventor of the dubious science of physiognomy, which teaches how to discover men's characters from the contour of the head and features of the countenance, but which was exposed to some severe attacks from the clever humorist and satirist, Lichtenberg of Göttingen. In philosophy, the great thinker, Kant of Königsburg, erected a system that soon penetrated into all the sciences, and excited and swayed the learned world of Germany. Spittler, by his perspicuity and acuteness, and the Swiss, John Müller, by his learning and artistic descriptions, established a new epoch in historical writing; and in the affairs of education, Basedow, by the model seminary of Dessau (Philanthropium), and Campe and Salzmann, by their writings for children, called a new method of instruction into existence, upon which the Swiss, Pestalozzi, founded his system of infant education and of popular schools.

Lavater, A. D. 1741-1801.

Nicolai, A. D. 1783-1811.

Kant, A. D. 1724-1804.

VI. THE PROGRESS OF THE NEW WORLD.

1. CONTEST OF THE ENGLISH WITH THE FRENCH FOR THE POSSESSION OF NORTH AMERICA.

[A. D. 1700-1763.]

§ 471. The French regarded with some uneasiness and alarm the enlargement and prosperity of the English colonies in North America. Their own settlements in Acadie (Nova Scotia), along the shores of the Bay of Fundy, and in Canada, though formed before Jamestown was built or the Pilgrims had landed at Plymouth, seemed to have no element

of life or progress; they were military or missionary posts, rather than agricultural colonies firmly rooted in the soil. Among the French were found excellent pioneers, bold explorers of the wilderness, and devoted and successful missionaries. Fond of rambling and adventure, averse to the prolonged labors of agriculture, and satisfied with moderate gains and much amusement, they pushed their explorations and their alliances with the Indians far beyond the English, but gained no permanent possession of the country. The plastic nature of the Frenchman fitted him to become a friend and ally of the red men; he did not do much towards civilizing the savages, but was in some danger of becoming a savage himself. He joined them in the chase and the dance, built a wigwam in their village for his dusky concubine, and trained his children to become members of the tribe, and to adopt every peculiarity of Indian costume and manners. Still, he did not lose his nationality, but preserved his loyalty and his religious faith, and rendered cheerful obedience to the representative of his monarch, the governor of Canada. The Jesuits and Recollet missionaries braved all the perils of the wilderness in their zeal to Christianize the natives; they made converts of many, — that is, they baptized them, hung crucifixes about their necks, and taught them to repeat the simplest formulas of prayer. While in company with their spiritual guides, the Indians were docile and devout; separated from them, they soon relapsed into all the excesses of barbarism. The French missionaries made many geographical discoveries; they were the first to explore the Great Lakes, the first white men who beheld the great Falls of the Niagara. As early as 1565, Father Allouez reached the outlet of Lake Superior, and, three years afterward, in company with Marquette and Dablon, he visited the tribes on the southern border of this lake, and traversed the country between it and the foot of Lake Michigan. Trading and missionary posts were established by the French in this region, and they became the rallying points of civilization for the country around the upper Lakes. In 1673, Marquette and Joliet discovered the Mississippi, finding their way to it by the Fox and the Wisconsin rivers; they sailed down the great stream to Arkansas, and on their return, passed up the Illinois, and thence found their way back to Green Bay. Nine years afterwards, Robert de la Salle accomplished the work which they had begun, by passing down the river to its entrance into the
April, 1682. Gulf of Mexico, and taking possession of the country on its banks and at its mouth in the name of his king, in whose honor he called it LOUISIANA. Louis XIV. granted him a commission to found a colony there, and an expedition on a liberal scale was fitted out from France for this purpose. The vessels arrived in the Gulf of Mexico, but were not able to find the entrance of the Mississippi, and the company were obliged to land on the coast of Texas, where they formed a temporary settlement. While conducting an expedition by land to discover the great river, La

Salle was murdered by one of his companions, and his associates in Texas were attacked and massacred by the Indians. So disastrous was the failure of this expedition that the French did not renew, for some years, the attempt to colonize Louisiana.

§ 472. But Louis XIV. was anxious to complete the glories of his reign by creating for France a colonial dominion on the banks of the great "Father of Waters," which should rival or eclipse the flourishing colonies of England on the Atlantic coast, that had been planted for her, in their penury and homelessness, by the hard hands and stout hearts of her political and religious exiles. After the peace of Ryswich, therefore, a brave French officer, Iberville, assisted by his two brothers, Sauvolle and Bienville, was sent out in command of four vessels, and a band of about 200 emigrants, to renew the attempt made by La Salle.

A. D. 1699.

Aided by Father Anastasius, who had been one of La Salle's companions, he succeeded in finding the entrance of the Mississippi from the Gulf. But the low and marshy banks of this river appearing an unsuitable position for a settlement, he chose rather the barren and sandy shore of Biloxi bay, at some distance to the eastward from the river's mouth, and there disembarked his companions. As the emigrants thought not at all of agricultnre, but only of mining and trade with the Indians, they readily accepted a spot where no green thing could ever grow, any more than on the desert of Sahara. Expecting to receive their chief supplies from France, their first object was to secure easy communication with the ships. But even this end was imperfectly obtained, for owing to the shallowness of the water, vessels could not come within a league's distance of the shore. The colony was afterwards transferred to an island over against the bay, where also the soil was a fine sand, white and shining as snow. About the same time, Mobile was founded, at the head of the bay of that name. An offer of four hundred Huguenot families, already inured to exile, hardship, and toil, to join the settlement, was rejected by the bigotry of the king and his ministers; and the colony was left to consist of Canadian hunters, vagrant speculators, intent only upon trafficking in furs and hunting for the precious metals, and indolent office-holders who thought of nothing but their salaries. We are not surprised to learn, therefore, that, in 1708, the colonists hardly equalled in number those who first came out with Iberville, though a fresh band of emigrants had joined them almost every year. In 1723, the French government was informed that the inhabitants could not subsist if they did not receive a supply of salt provision. A few years before, an eye-witness says the famine was so great at Biloxi, that over five hundred people died of hunger. The lavish supplies furnished by the mother country alone preserved the colony from extinction. But the government, growing weary of such a burden, sold the settlement, in 1712, to a wealthy merchant, who, in return for the exclusive right of trade and other privileges, undertook to defray its expenses; and five years afterwards, this merchant transferred his right to the famous Mississippi Company, which was projected and managed by John Law. The money lavished upon Louisiana for a few years by this gigantic corporation, and the involuntary or hired emigrants who were sent thither, gave it for a time a gleam of prosperity. New Orleans was founded, and a fort and settlement begun higher up the river, where Natchez now stands.

A. D. 1718.

§ 473. On the possession of this sickly colony, and on the previous explorations which had made known the course of the great river and the country around the great Lakes, the French founded their claim to the whole valley of the Mississippi. But the English always maintained that their possession of the seacoast gave them a valid title to the country in the interior for an indefinite extent to the west; and in conformity with this idea, the charters of several of the Colonies made their territory stretch across the whole breadth of the continent, from sea to sea. The Five Nations, a powerful Indian confederacy, the steadfast friends of the English and enemies of the French, also claimed by right of conquest the whole country of the northwest, lying between the Alleghanies, the Great Lakes, and the Mississippi; and England sought to perfect her title by annexing to it this pretension of the savages. So long as the two countries were at peace with each other, this controversy led only to a series of border disputes, encroachments, and intrigues with the native tribes, neither party being numerous enough to colonize the territory which both coveted. But when England and France were at war, their respective Colonies in America also engaged in a murderous and protracted conflict, which, because the savages were enlisted in it, was fearfully destructive of life and property. The details of this warfare in the wilderness are shocking to humanity. It spared no sex, profession, or age, and through the mutual exasperation that it provoked, both parties in it were guilty of excesses which shamed their pretensions to Christian civilization.

§ 474. The first struggle took place during the war which began with the accession of William of Orange to the English throne, and ended with the peace of Ryswick, in 1697. The weight of it, in America, fell chiefly upon New England and New York, the other Colonies being protected by their distance from the French settlements, and the mother country having too much employment for its arms in Europe, to be able to send much aid to its suffering children in America. At this period, and during the subsequent wars, the people of New England had their own peculiar grounds of quarrel with the French, who were their rivals in the fisheries, who encroached upon their boundaries, endangered their outlying settlements, and stirred up the savages against them, and whom, as Roman Catholics, they feared and hated even more than if they had been pagans. The French in Acadie and Canada, too feeble and few in number to accomplish much by their own efforts, placed their chief dependence upon their Indian allies, the native tribes at the eastward being uniformly on their side. They thus succeeded in desolating the frontier, while Massachusetts retaliated by fitting out regular expeditions, and striking heavy blows against the chief settlements of the French. Dover, in New Hampshire, was burned by the Indians, and its inhabitants were killed or carried off as prisoners; the fort at Pemaquid was taken, and though an attack upon Casco was repulsed, all the settlements further east were desolated. The next year, Schenectady, on the Mohawk river, was attacked at midnight, burned, and most of the people were massacred, while another party of French and Indians destroyed Salmon Falls, in New Hampshire, and a third reduced Casco. Massachusetts, in return, sent out a little fleet, conveying about 700 men, under Sir William Phips, against Acadie; he easily subdued Port Royal, and by ravaging that place and the neighboring settlements, obtained plunder enough to defray all the expenses of the expedition. He then sailed with 32 ships and 2,000 men, to attack Quebec, while a little army of Massachusetts and New York troops, under Fitz John Winthrop, marched against Montreal. Both were unsuccessful, being defeated by the great activity and vigilance of the aged Count Frontenac, then governor of Canada. The expenses of these bootless expeditions proved a heavy burthen to Massachusetts, obliging the General Court to make a considerable issue of paper money. The war then languished, though a sickening contest was kept up by small parties on the frontiers, which caused great misery, and ruined many flourishing settlements. Peace was made in 1697, the treaty stipulating that each party should retain the possessions it had before the war.

A. D. 1689.

§ 475. Four years afterwards, hostilities were renewed by the war of the Spanish Succession, which ended only with the Treaty of Utrecht, in 1713. The Spaniards had a few small settlements in Florida, and as they were now the allies of the French, some of the disasters of the war fell upon the English Colonies at the south. Governor Moore, of South Carolina, led 600 men against the fort and settlement at St. Augustine; but before the fort had surrendered, the appearance of two Spanish men-of-war in the offing induced him to retreat precipitately, leaving behind his vessels and stores. Three years afterwards, he conducted fifty white volunteers and about a thousand friendly Creek Indians against St. Marks, Florida, and the Spanish missionary villages in its vicinity, where a portion of the Appalachian tribe, half civilized and converted to Christianity, were established. The fort could not be taken, but Moore desolated the Indian villages, robbed and burned the churches, and gave up the country to his Creek allies, the Appalachians removing their settlement to the banks of the Altamaha. In retaliation, a French frigate and four Spanish sloops made an attack

A. D. 1702.

upon Charleston; but the governor of South Carolina assembled 900
A. D. 1706. men, captured the French vessel, and beat off the assailants with great loss. At the north, the war was conducted, as before, by small parties of Canadians and Indians, who made daring inroads into the English settlements, plundered and burned one or two towns, massacred half of the inhabitants, and carried off the others into Canada, before a force could be collected to oppose them; while the Colonies, with a little help from England, sent out formidable expeditions against Acadie, Montreal, and Quebec, which were generally unsuccessful, though they sometimes inflicted great suffering upon the enemy, especially upon the Acadians. Deerfield and Haverhill in Massachusetts were thus sacked and burned by a party of French and Indians under De Rouville, and the alarm spread even to the towns in the near vicinity of Boston. The government offered a considerable reward for Indian prisoners or for scalps, — a fearful act, which shows how the atrocities committed during the war had broken down all the feelings of a common humanity. Indeed, after the terrible scenes which had taken place at Schenectady, Deerfield, and Haverhill, the colonists had come to regard the French and Indians as wolves that should be hunted down without pity. Stimulated by these rewards, a class of forest scouts and Indian hunters was gradually formed and trained, who soon rivalled their savage foes in all the arts of bush-fighting and in disregarding the cry for mercy. Massa-
A. D. 1707. chusetts, assisted by Rhode Island and New Hampshire, sent out an expedition of a thousand men, under Colonel March, against Acadie, hoping thus to check the destructive war on the eastern frontier. March did not succeed in capturing Port Royal, but he ravaged all the settlements along the coast, and did much to cripple the enemy's strength in that quarter. Much greater preparations were made two years afterwards, by a combination of the northern Colonies, for an attack on Montreal and Quebec, under the expectation that a British fleet and army would be sent to coöperate with them. But the British ministry did not keep their promise, and after waiting a long time for the appearance of the fleet, the forces were disbanded without attempting anything. At last, in 1711, the Tory ministry of Queen Anne did make an effort against Canada for the relief of the suffering Americans. A powerful fleet under Sir H. Walker, and a large body of troops commanded by General Hill, brother of the celebrated Mrs. Masham, arrived at Boston when nobody was expecting them. But some provisions and Colonial forces were hastily got together, and embarked in the fleet, while a large force was collected at Albany to proceed against Montreal, as soon as they should hear of the fall of Quebec. But the British commanders proved to be wholly incompetent for so important a trust. Through the obstinacy and negligence of Walker, eight or nine of the transports were wrecked in the St. Lawrence, and a thousand men

were drowned. The disheartened admiral immediately turned about and made sail for England, and the troops at Albany were dismissed before they had seen the enemy. The disgraceful failure of this enterprise excited much grief and indignation both in the Colonies and in the English House of Commons, where the whole undertaking, so suddenly begun and lightly abandoned, was denounced as a flagrant political job. The treaty of Utrecht put an end to the war, and afforded a little guaranty for the future, as it ceded the province of Acadie or Nova Scotia to the English, and recognized the Five Nations as subjects of England. But it was long before the northern Colonies recovered from the disasters they had experienced in the murderous and ill-managed conflict.

§ 476. Sir Robert Walpole's ministry maintained peace for about a quarter of a century, a peace broken in America only by a few short and comparatively insignificant contests with the Indians. But this minister was driven against his will into a war with Spain in 1739, and three years afterwards, France also became a party in the contest. Gen. Oglethorpe was appointed military commander in Georgia and the Carolinas; and with about 1,200 men, and a body of Indians, he
A. D. 1740. made an attack upon St. Augustine, but was unsuccessful. All the Colonies were then required to furnish their quotas for a force of about 4,000 men, to aid Admiral Vernon in his unfortunate expedition against Carthagena. They readily complied, furnishing both men and money, and were thus deeply concerned by the failure of that ill-starred enterprise. Then the Spaniards, in their turn, became the assailants, and sent a considerable force against Georgia and Carolina, which was repelled by Oglethorpe without much difficulty. At the north, the chief incident of the war was the capture of the strong French fortress of Louisburg, on Cape Breton, by an army fitted out in great part from Massachusetts, and commanded by an enterprising militia
A. D. 1745. officer, Colonel Pepperell. This place had been so heavily fortified as to be deemed impregnable, and it was called the Dunkirk or Gibraltar of America. In war, it was a source of great annoyance to the New England Colonies, as it gave shelter to the privateers which swarmed upon the coast, destroying their fisheries and breaking up their general commerce. Its unexpected capture, after a siege of six or seven weeks, by a force seemingly very inadequate to make an impression upon it, was about the only gleam of good fortune that illustrated the arms of Great Britain during this inglorious war. Col. Pepperell received a baronetcy as his reward. Again a project was formed to capture Quebec by a fleet and army from England, to be joined at Louisburg by troops from New England, while an army furnished by the other Colonies should proceed against Montreal; and again, after a large Colonial force had been collected, and great expense incurred, the English fleet and army failed to appear, and the enterprise was abandoned. As Mas

sachusetts guarded her frontiers with as much energy as she had shown in acting against Louisburg, she suffered comparatively little from the incursions of the French and Indians. The war was ended in 1748 by the treaty of Aix la Chapelle, which, to the great chagrin of the New Englanders, ceded back Louisburg to the French.

§ 477. The decisive struggle between France and England for the possession of the country on the Mississippi and the Great Lakes began in 1753, though war was not formally declared till three years later. Louisiana had at last gained wealth and strength, and the French missionary and trading establishments on the Lakes had been converted into military posts, formidable not so much from the strength of their garrisons, as from the savage allies by whom they were surrounded, or who could be quickly summoned to their defence. A plan was formed to connect Canada with Louisiana by a line of forts, extending from Lake Erie along the upper waters of the Ohio, and thence by the course of that river to the Mississippi; thus hemming in the British settlements, which occupied a narrow strip of land on the Atlantic coast, and had nowhere passed the Alleghanies. This project soon brought the French into collision with the Ohio Company, an association formed in London and Virginia, which had obtained from the crown a grant of a large tract of land along the Ohio, and had erected trading houses there. The French warned the English traders off, or sent them prisoners to Canada; and complaint was therefore made to the Governor of Virginia, who sent out George Washington, then a young officer in the militia service, on a message to the French commander, requiring him to withdraw his troops from that region. An unsatisfactory answer was returned, and Col. Washington was again despatched, at the head of four hundred men, to drive off the intruders. He captured a scouting party that

A. D. 1754.

was sent against him, but was soon after assailed by a very superior force of French and Indians, and after a brave defence, was obliged to capitulate on honorable terms, and return to the eastward. Preparations for war were now made by both parties, though the contest seemed a very unequal one. The population of the English colonies amounted to a million and a half, while the French scarcely numbered one hundred thousand. But the latter were difficult to be reached, as their forts were remote points in the wilderness, surrounded by a cloud of Indian allies; and from these forest fastnesses, they menaced the whole English frontier. The British army of that day was an unwieldy and cumbrous machine, overburdened with baggage and the munitions of war, led by brave but pedantic officers, and likely to be thrown into inextricable confusion and distress by the difficulties of hewing a path through the forests and over the mountains, in constant danger of surprise by a light-heeled and enterprising foe.

§ 478. General Braddock was sent from England with two regiments, to be joined by some provincial troops from Virginia, and then to march against Fort du Quesne, which the French had lately built

A. D. 1755.

at the head of the Ohio, where Pittsburgh now stands. He crossed the mountains in June, with about two thousand men, Colonel Washington acting as his aid-de-camp. The difficulty of making a road through the wilderness induced him, at Washington's advice, to leave behind his heavy baggage under a rear guard, and press forward rapidly with a band of 1,200 men, to secure the post before French succors could arrive. Neglecting the precautions which he had been urged to take against surprise, when near his journey's end, he fell into an ambuscade formed by only 250 French, with a large party of Indians, and was totally routed, more than half of his troops being killed or wounded. Braddock himself was slain; and the panic being communicated to the rear guard, all the artillery and baggage were abandoned, and the feeble remains of the army fled in great disorder across the mountains, leaving the border settlements defenceless. The other expeditions planned by the British ministry and the Colonies for this year had but little success. Acadie, or Nova Scotia, indeed, was easily reduced, the French inhabitants of this province, notwithstanding its cession to England thirty years before, having assisted the operations of the enemy. For this act, and

September, 1755.

for refusing to take the oath of allegiance, they were now inhumanly punished; seven thousand of them were forcibly put on shipboard, and transported to the English colonies, where they were scattered round, and maintained as paupers. Their villages were burned, their fields devastated, and the few that remained were driven for shelter to the woods and mountains. An army under Sir William Johnson, directed against Crown Point, was encountered, near Lake George, by Baron Dieskau, who had recently arrived with fresh troops from France. An English party that had been sent in advance fell into an ambuscade, and was routed with great loss. But when the French, flushed with this success, advanced to attack Johnson's main body, who had now thrown up a slight entrenchment, they were very warmly received, and, after an obstinate conflict, were driven from the field, and totally dispersed, their commander being wounded and taken prisoner. Satisfied with this victory, Sir William Johnson gave up the movement against Crown Point; and the expedition to Niagara also proved a failure, the troops not being able to reach that place, owing to the lateness of the season.

§ 479. A meeting of delegates from seven of the Colonies had been held at Albany, to secure the friendship of the Indian con-

A. D. 1754.

federacy of the Five Nations, and to take other measures for the common safety. A plan of union between the several Colonies, drawn up by Dr. Franklin, was proposed at this convention, and accepted by the delegates. Had it gone into operation, it would have given greater unity to the efforts of the Colonists in war, and might have led to important consequences by cultivating among them, at this early day, a feeling of nationality and a sense of mutual dependence. But the project fell to the ground, being disliked in England because it gave too much power to the people in the Colonies, and in America, because it conceded too much to the crown.

§ 480. The year 1756 passed away without any thing of consequence being attempted by the English in America; while the French, under the able guidance of the Marquis de Montcalm, now their commander-in-chief, struck one vigorous and important blow. This was directed against Oswego, a strong English post on the southern shore of Lake Ontario, which the French suddenly invested with a large armament, and compelled it to surrender, with a garrison of over a thousand men, and a great quantity of artillery and stores. The western Indians, sustained and guided by the French at Fort Du Quesne, wasted the frontiers of Pennsylvania and Virginia with a pitiless and desolating war, and their scalping parties came within thirty miles of Philadelphia. The next year

A. D. 1757. was marked by equal inactivity and feebleness on the part of the English, and by another successful enterprise of the French. Several of the Colonies showed great energy in raising men and money; but their efforts were paralyzed by the want of concert with each other, by the necessity of waiting for orders from England, and by the pompous and dilatory proceedings of the incompetent generals who were sent over to command them. On the other hand, Montcalm, not obliged to take council with any one, suddenly collected a force of 8,000 men, crossed Lake George, and laid siege to Fort William Henry at its southern extremity. The garrison was 2,000 strong, and General Webb was at Fort Edward, only fourteen miles distant, with 4,000 more. But not a man did Webb send to the relief of the beleagured fort; and after six days' siege, the garrison was compelled to surrender, on condition of being allowed to retire to Fort Edward unmolested. But as soon as they were disarmed, Montcalm's Indian allies fell upon them, massacred a considerable number, and drove the others into the woods, where many perished before reaching the settlements. The capture of this post created great alarm in New England and New York. Pepperell, the captor of Louisburg, was called out from his retirement and made Lieutenant-General of Massachusetts, where 20,000 men were collected in arms. But satisfied with the success already obtained, Montcalm retired to Canada without attempting any thing further.

Thus far, the war had been very disastrous to the English. After three campaigns, the French not only retained possession of every foot of the disputed ground, but had captured Oswego, driven their opponents from Lake George, and, through their savage confederates, had carried the brand and the tomahawk into the heart of the English settlements.

§ 481. To remedy this train of disasters, the elder Pitt was called to the head of the English ministry, and his vigor and determination soon gave a new aspect to the war. Abercrombie, who was called to the command in America, found himself at the head of 50,000 men, of whom about one half were provincial levies.

A. D. 1758.

All the Canadians who could bear arms did not exceed 20,000, and these had been kept so constantly in service that agriculture had been almost entirely neglected, and the horrors of a famine were added to those of war. An attack was first made on Louisburg, which was soon compelled to surrender by a large fleet and an army of 14,000 men, under General Amherst. Forbes marched against Fort Du Quesne with so considerable a force that the garrison, reduced by the desertion of most of their Indian allies to less than 500 men, did not venture to await his approach, but set fire to the works, and retreated down the river. Abercrombie, who advanced with the main body of the army against Ticonderoga, was not so successful. Montcalm had thrown himself into that fortress with a strong garrison, and had so obstructed the approaches to it by an abatis of felled trees, that the place was really impregnable except by the regular operations of a siege. The English rashly attacked at once, and in front, with bulldog courage; but after a gallant struggle, they were beaten off with heavy loss, and compelled to retreat in disorder to Fort William Henry. But Bradstreet, at the head of a provincial force from New England and New York, made amends for this repulse by the capture of Frontenac, which gave the English the command of Lake Ontario, and shut off Montreal and Quebec from the French posts at the west. The Indian tribes along the Ohio and the upper Lakes now sued for peace; and a treaty, formed with them at Easton, once more gave security to the frontiers of Virginia and Pennsylvania.

§ 482. Stimulated by the successes of this year, Pitt resolved to make a great effort, the next campaign, for the conquest of Canada. The Colonies, their former expenditures having been promptly reimbursed by the English government, nobly seconded his endeavor by bringing 20,000 men into the field, and raising a large sum in money for their outfit. The command of the main expedition against Quebec was given to Wolfe, a young general of much gallantry and promise, who appeared in the St. Lawrence in June, with a powerful fleet, and an army of 8,000 regular troops. Two subsidiary expeditions were organized, one, under Amherst, to proceed by way of Lake Champlain against Montreal, and the other, under Prideaux, against Fort Niagara. The want of vessels impeded Amherst's operations; but Ticonderoga and Crown Point fell into his hands without a struggle, the danger of Quebec having caused the garrisons to be withdrawn; and a detachment from his army attacked and burned the Indian village of St.

A. D. 1759.

Francis, whence many of those scalping parties had issued which had desolated the frontiers of New England. Prideaux was killed at the siege of Niagara by the bursting of a gun; but his successor, Sir William Johnson, defeated a force of 1,200 French who advanced to relieve the place, and pressed the siege with so much vigor, that the garrison soon surrendered. He should then have proceeded down the Lake and the St. Lawrence, to coöperate in the attack upon Quebec; but the want of vessels frustrated this part of the project also, and Wolfe was thus left to his original resources. His force, indeed, outnumbered that of the enemy, and was better disciplined; but the latter had the advantage of one of the strongest positions in the world, well fortified, and were commanded by a general who had merited the highest honors in war. As long as Wolfe attacked the French intrenchments below the city, along the banks of the St. Charles, on which side alone he was expected, Montcalm easily frustrated all his efforts. But the British general conceived the bold plan of secretly passing up the river, and scaling by surprise the Heights of Abraham, as the lofty plateau is called on a projecting point of which lies the upper town of Quebec. The project was gallantly executed, though the lofty bank of the river was so precipitous that the men could with difficulty pull themselves up by clinging to projecting roots and stones. Finding that the English had thus got in his rear, where his defences were weak, Montcalm drew out all his troops before the city, and put the fate of Canada upon the arbitrament of a single battle. The issue was not long doubtful; the undisciplined and half famished levies that formed the greater part of the French army, fled hastily after a few vollies, and were pursued with great execution to the gates of the city. Montcalm and Wolfe both fell on the field, mor-
September 18, 1759. tally wounded. Quebec surrendered in less than a week, and the war in North America was virtually at an end, though Montreal was not taken by the English till the following year. A capitulation was then signed by the French governor-general, which surrendered to the English all the remaining posts in western Canada. The
A. D. 1762. peace of Paris soon followed, by which France ceded to England all North America east of the Mississippi, except the island and city of New Orleans, which, with all Louisiana west of the great river, were given to Spain. England also received Florida from Spain, in exchange for the Havana.

§ 483. The war between the Europeans was at an end; but the English Colonies had still to sustain a desperate struggle of the Indians, who could not be easily won to respect the authority of their new masters.
A. D. 1760. The Cherokees had previously broken out into a war, after suffering some gross wrong from the English; had ravaged the frontiers of Virginia and the Carolinas, and defeated a considerable detachment of troops, and were finally driven to sue for peace only by

the presence of an overwhelming force. Hardly had the English taken possession of the posts at the west and around the Lakes, when Pontiac, an Indian chief of much activity and address, was able to unite all the northwestern tribes in a conspiracy against them. The secret

A. D. 1763.

was so well kept that, at the appointed time, the savages took by surprise all the posts at the west, except Detroit and Fort Pitt (Du Quesne), and massacred the garrisons. The border settlements were swept with a more destructive war than they had ever before experienced. Several detachments of troops, that were sent out to relieve the two beleaguered forts, were intercepted and cut to pieces. At last, two considerable expeditions were fitted out, the one to advance through Pennsylvania, and the other to proceed along the Lakes; and after some hard fighting with the former one, the Indians submitted, and made peace

A. D. 1764.

upon the terms that were required of them.

§ 484. The protracted contest with the French and the Indians being brought to a close by the complete triumph of the English, the American Colonies were seemingly in the full tide of prosperity. The great exertions they had made during the last war had taught them the secret of their strength; that war had cost them, it was computed, about 30,000 lives and over sixteen millions of dollars, of which only five millions were repaid by the British ministry. Immigration rapidly increased, and the vast forest in the interior began to be explored by those who were in search of a new home. The Delaware and Hudson rivers were crossed by a thronging multitude, the Alleghanies were surmounted, and white settlements were formed upon the upper tributaries of the Ohio. No longer hemmed in, as with a ring of iron, by the French and the savages, the internal principle of expansion, which has been at work ever since, received its first free development, and carried the limits of civilization every year farther west. Trade flourished on the sea-coast; Boston had long been distinguished for enterprising traffic, and Newport, New York, Philadelphia, and Baltimore were rising rapidly in commercial importance. Printing presses and newspapers, schools and colleges, flourished, though the literature of the Colonies as yet existed only in the humble form of sermons. Yet the metaphysical writings of Jonathan Edwards slowly acquired a European reputation, and the fame of Dr. Franklin was carried, by his brilliant discoveries in electricity, to the bounds of the civilized world.

2. THE WAR OF AMERICAN INDEPENDENCE, AND THE ESTABLISHMENT OF THE AMERICAN CONSTITUTION.

§ 485. But the prosperity of America was now to receive a sudden check, and a contest to begin more important to her, and more momentous in its consequences, than any which the world had ever witnessed. England was oppressed by a heavy debt, which had been more than doubled by the heavy expenses of the late war, and the people were overburdened with taxes. In an evil hour, it occurred to the Chancellor of the Exchequer that this pressure might be lightened, if the American Colonies could be made to contribute to the general expenses of the empire. The war, though not undertaken for their relief or advantage, but to gratify the ambition of the mother country by enlarging the bounds of her colonial dominion, had still, by its successful termination, contributed largely to their prosperity; and it was plausibly urged that they ought to bear a portion of the weight which it had entailed upon the nation. It was forgotten that they had expended blood and treasure during the contest at least as freely, in proportion to their means, as England; that if the war had benefitted them more, it had also cost them more; and that they were already heavily taxed by their assemblies, to pay the interest on their colonial debts and defray the necessary expenses of these provincial governments. Though they had never been taxed by the authority of England, they had made liberal contributions to the king's service when asked to do so, and when they were invited to judge of the exigency of the case, and to determine how the money should be raised. They did not refuse to give, but they insisted that their money should not be given without their consent,—that they should not be taxed without their consent. But the British ministry refused to listen to these considerations; they thought only of the paramount authority of parliament, and of the means of lessening their own unpopularity by alleviating the taxes at home. The late war had thrown new light upon the magnitude of the resources of the Colonies; and to the argument that they had never been taxed before, the minister had no better answer to make than the insolent plea of Dr. Johnson, that "the ox had no reason to complain of the aggravation of the burdens laid upon the calf." They forgot that the horns of the ox had grown; that if the Americans were now more able to pay taxes, they were also more able to defend themselves against unjust impositions. Yet was the step not taken without some hesitation. The plan had been proposed before, to the ministry of Sir Robert Walpole and to that of the Pelhams. But those sagacious statesmen had refused to hazard so dangerous an experiment. Even George Grenville, the author of the present scheme of parliamentary taxation, would not reduce it to practice till he had tried the temper of the people, and ascertained by parliamentary measures how much they were able and willing to bear.

§ 486. The Americans had always admitted, in general terms, that parliament had a right to regulate their trade; but practically, and favored by their insignificance and remoteness, they had always evaded these regulations, and had enjoyed almost as much license in commerce as in the management of their domestic affairs. A large part of the trade maintained by the northern Colonies was known to be contraband, and the occasional endeavors of the government to enforce the Navigation Act and other laws of commerce had no other effect than to harass and irritate the people. A vigorous attempt to enforce these laws to the letter was to be the prelude to direct taxation. Cruisers were stationed on the coast, and enjoined to be vigilant; custom-house officers and informers were stimulated by the offer of rewards; and Writs of Assistance were granted, which empowered an officer to enter any shop or dwelling house, and search for contraband goods. So gross a violation of the principle of English law that every man's house is his castle, could not fail to make a ferment; no name or occasion being specified in the writ, the officer who held it could select any dwelling that he saw fit, and thus, perhaps, gratify some personal grudge. The legality of these writs was denied, and on as good ground, apparently, as that on which the validity of "general warrants" was afterwards questioned in England. When the cause

February, 1761.

which was to determine their legality came on for trial at Boston, James Otis, a lawyer of great ability, high reputation, and an eager and impetuous spirit, resigned his lucrative office of advocate-general for the crown, which would have obliged him to argue in favor of the writs, and appeared as counsel for the petitioners in opposition to them. The speech which he then delivered, for boldness and eloquence in asserting and defending the rights of the Colonies, was a memorable one, and produced a marked effect on public opinion in Massachusetts. John Adams, who was present at its delivery, says, "Every man of an immense crowded audience appeared to me to go away, as I did, ready to take arms against Writs of Assistance. Then and there was the first scene of the first act of opposition to the arbitrary claims of Great Britain. Then and there the child Independence was born. In fifteen years, that is, in 1776, he grew up to manhood, and declared himself free." The court postponed judgment on the case, and never delivered it; but these writs were never afterwards used in the Colony.

§ 487. After this scene, and many others of similar tendency, had created much alarm and awakened a spirit of determined resistance in

February 6, A. D. 1765.

America, Mr. Grenville introduced into parliament his bill for imposing a stamp tax on the American Colonies, and it became a law with little opposition. Stamped papers, upon which a considerable impost was to be paid, were required for all judicial proceedings, clearances at the custom-house, bills of lading, and even the diplomas granted by seminaries of learning. The law was not to take effect for about seven or eight months after its passage. The news that the bill had become a law arrived in Boston early in April; and the effect was as if a cannon had been fired so near the ears of the people that they were all stunned by the explosion. They seemed stupified at first; there was no popular outbreak, no meeting for the passage of violent resolutions. But it was the lull which precedes, and not that which follows the tempest. The General Court assembled in May, and they immediately resolved that the other Colonies should be invited to unite with them in sending delegates to a Congress, to be held in New York in October, to consult together on the present state of affairs and the recent acts of parliament. This was a significant intimation that the Colonies were at last aware of the strength and firmness which they might acquire by concert and union. As this Stamp Act Congress, as it was called, was not to meet till the month before the time appointed for the law to go into operation, the people meanwhile took the affair into their own hands. Newspapers, pamphlets, sermons, and associa tions served to kindle and to manifest their indignant feelings. An agreement not to import any more goods from England till the obnoxious act should be repealed was very generally signed in the commercial towns; and combinations were also formed to encourage American manufactures, to wear American cloth, and to increase the supply of wool by ceasing to eat lamb or mutton. Such a ferment of opinion could not long prevail without leading to acts of violence; though the patriot leaders deplored this result, and exerted themselves to prevent it, foreseeing its injurious effect upon the cause. Mr. Oliver, who had accepted the post of distributor of stamps in Boston, was hung in effigy, a building designed for his office was demolished, his house was assaulted, and he was so much frightened that he consented to appear before the people and publicly resign his commission. A few days afterwards, the mob entered the houses of two officers of the customs, and damaged the furniture, and then proceeded to the residence of Lieut. Governor Hutchinson, which they completely gutted, and burned his furniture in the street. A town meeting was held the next day, at which the citizens expressed their detestation of these outrages, and offered aid to the magistrates in their endeavors to prevent a repetition of them. In the other Colonies, also, the stamp distributors resigned their offices, enough of popular violence being shown to intimidate them. The Virginia Assembly, as soon as the news of the passage of the Stamp Act arrived, passed a series of resolutions, under the influence of Patrick Henry, one of which declared that "the sole right and power to lay taxes was vested in the General Assembly," and could not be transferred to any other persons whatever. But this resolution passed by a majority of only one vote, and the next day, it was reconsidered and expunged from the journals. Delegates from nine of the Colonies assembled at the Congress in New York, and assurances were received from two other Colonies that they would acquiesce in the result. The proceedings of this Congress were singularly moderate, considering the excited temper of the people. They only published a declaration of the Rights and Grievances of the Colonies, and addressed a petition to the king, and memorials to the two houses of parliament; and the tone of these documents,

October 7.

though firm, was mild, argumentative, and respectful. They claimed all the privileges of British subjects, and especially that of not being taxed without their own consent. When these papers were signed, the Congress was dissolved, after a session of little more than a fortnight. The chief advantage derived from it was, that it made the patriot leaders from the different Colonies acquainted with each other, and enabled them to give assurances of mutual support. November came, but the stamps were nowhere used, and the business even of the courts of justice, after a short suspension, was resumed. The act was practically nullified, with the assent, either free or enforced, of the judges and the governors.

§ 488. The cause of the Colonies, which they pleaded with much earnestness and ability, soon found sympathy in the whole of Europe; and in England itself, it was embraced by a powerful party, which opposed the measures of government both in speech and writing. At the head of this opposition stood the great statesman and orator, the elder William Pitt, afterwards Earl of Chatham; and he was actively supported by Conway, Col. Barrè, and Lord Camden, afterwards Lord Chancellor, and, next to Lord Mansfield, the highest legal authority in the realm. This powerful opposition produced a change of ministry in July, 1765, and, after a vehement debate, after Dr. Franklin had undergone a memorable examination before the House of Commons, in which he declared that the Act could never be enforced, the Stamp Act was repealed. But a bill was passed at the same time, declaratory of the power
March, 1766. and right of parliament to bind America in all cases whatsoever. In the Colonies, the news of the repeal was received with great rejoicing, the accompanying act being justly regarded as a mere contrivance to save the honor of government. Lord Camden, indeed, in the House of Lords, had strenuously opposed the declaratory bill as "absolutely illegal." "Taxation and representation," he declared, "are inseparably united; God hath joined them, and no British parliament can put them asunder." Indemnity was demanded from the Colonies for those officers of the crown who had suffered from the late riots; and both New York and Massachusetts granted them full compensation.

§ 489. But the joy of the Americans was of short duration, for in little more than a year, another act was passed by parliament, imposing duties on all tea, paper, glass, paints, and lead, that should be imported into the Colonies. This was an avowed attempt to raise a revenue, though, in form, the bill was like other acts for regulating trade; and it was hoped that, on this account, it would escape censure. But the principle first advanced by James Otis was now generally adopted by the Colonists, that revenue bills under the form of regulations of trade violated their rights quite as much as direct taxation. Thus the flame of opposition was kindled anew, and raged as hotly as ever. Non-importation was an obvious and legal means of escaping these taxes; and ex tensive combinations were therefore formed to refrain from the use, not only of the taxed articles, but, as far as possible, of all other British commodities. Able leaders and defenders of the popular cause were not wanting. Besides James Otis, there were the two Adamses (Samuel and John,) and John Hancock in Massachusetts, John Dickenson in Pennsylvania, (the author of the celebrated "Farmer's Letters," an able plea for Colonial rights,) Patrick Henry and R. H. Lee in Virginia, and Gadsden and Rutledge in South Carolina, besides Dr. Franklin, whose reputation and abilities were of great weight in London, where he resided for many years as agent of several of the Colonies. The profits of British merchants were soon so much diminished by the non-importation agreements, that they petitioned for a repeal of the law; and in deference to their wishes, not to the rights of America, the duties were taken off from all the articles except tea, the impost on that being avowedly retained for the sole purpose of asserting the authority of parliament to pass such a law. This duty was very small, only three pence on the pound; and as a drawback was now allowed, of a shilling on the pound, originally paid on the importation of the article into Great Britain, the Colonists might actually receive their tea at a lower price than they had formerly paid. But the principle was at stake; the Americans saw very well, that if they submitted to this law, all imported commodities would soon be subjected to heavy duties. No tea was imported; and other subjects of controversy also coming up, a furious contest, in speech and print, raged both in England and America. But public sentiment in the former country was generally turned against the Colonies; high notions of government and unfounded opinions in political economy, the pride of national dominion and a disposition to stretch the authority of parliament to the utmost, all served to nourish the fatal error. As Dr. Franklin observed, "every man in England seems to consider himself as a piece of a sovereign over America; seems to jostle himself into the throne with the king, and talks of '*our subjects in the Colonies.*'" George III. also, with the high notions of prerogative that had been instilled into him before he came to the throne, and with the dogged obstinacy of a dull intellect, adhered to the delusion long after the nation, the parliament, and even the ministry, had been cured of it, and wished to retract.

§ 490. The war of pamphlets, newspapers, and speeches, the sharp controversies between colonial assemblies and royal governors, and occasional outbreaks of popular violence continued for four or five years, till the Americans were well nigh weaned from their old affection for the land of their forefathers, and had ceased to glory in the British name. Boston was the head quarters of opposition to the policy of the English ministers, and several regiments of British troops were accordingly sent thither to dragoon the inhabitants into submission. But this measure served only to increase the irritation, and to make the breach irreparable.

An affray soon took place between the mob and the soldiers, in which
March 5, 1770. the latter fired, and killed three of their unarmed assailants, besides dangerously wounding five others. It was late in the evening; the alarm bells rang, the citizens rushed into the streets, and an open battle between the people and the troops was with difficulty prevented. The next day, the irritation of the people was so strongly manifested in a town meeting, that the governor and the military commander consented to remove the troops to an island in the harbor, and quiet was restored. The soldiers who had fired, with their officer, were brought to trial for murder; but Adams and Quincy, two of the most distinguished advocates of popular rights, nobly consented to act as their legal defenders, and made out so clear a case for them, that they had acted under strong provocation, that the jury acquitted them of murder, and only two were convicted of manslaughter and slightly punished. Yet the story of "the Boston Massacre," as it was called, served long to inflame the passions of the multitude against their British oppressors.

§ 491. As yet, no revenue had been received from the duty on tea, because the Americans would not import any of that commodity, the little which they consumed being obtained by smuggling. But the contest was brought to a crisis, in 1773, by the East India Company, which, instigated by the English ministry, sent several cargoes of tea to the Colonies, supposing with good reason that it would be purchased if it could only be landed and offered for sale. But the patriots were on the alert, and immediately formed combinations to prevent the landing of the tea, and to force the consignees to send it back. In New York and Philadelphia, popular vengeance was denounced against any persons who should receive the article, and even against the pilots if they should guide the ships into the harbor; and the vessels were thus obliged to return to England, without even effecting an entry at the custom-house. At Charleston, the tea was landed and stored in damp cellars, where it was quickly spoiled. At Boston, Governor Hutchinson and Admiral Montague succeeded in preventing the vessels from leaving the harbor, in spite of the menaces of the inhabitants; whereupon, about fifty persons disguised themselves as Mohawk Indians, boarded the ships at the wharf, and, in the presence of a great crowd of people, drew up the chests of tea from the holds, and emptied their contents into the water. When the news of this act arrived in England, the indignant ministry resolved to punish the contumacious Bostonians, and for this purpose, introduced three bills into parlia-
March, 1774. ment, one of which shut up the port of Boston, and removed the custom-house to Salem; another virtually abrogated the charter of Massachusetts, by giving to the crown or to the governor the appointment of the Council and of all officers, and even the selection of juries, and by prohibiting town meetings from being held without the governor's consent; and a third provided that persons accused of mur-

der might be sent to England for trial. These bills were strenuously opposed by Fox, Burke, Barré, and Dunning, but were carried by majorities of more than four to one. Another law provided for the quartering of troops in America. Four more regiments were sent to Boston, so that the town was now strongly garrisoned; and Gen. Gage being appointed governor, in place of Hutchinson, the people of the province were virtually placed under military law. The Quebec Act passed at the same session, for the purpose of preventing Canada from taking part with the other Colonies, extended the boundaries of that province to the Ohio and the Mississippi, established the old French law in all judicial proceedings, and secured to the Catholic Church there the enjoyment of all its lands and revenues. A short time before, as if the feelings of the people of Massachusetts had not been sufficiently irritated, their agent in London, Dr. Franklin, was made the object of an indecent and scurrilous invective before the Privy Council by the Solicitor General, Wedderburn, the avowed intention being to insult him and his constituents. He was charged with having transmitted to Massachusetts certain letters, written by some officers of the crown in that province, on public subjects, to their friends in office in England, which letters had been given to Franklin by some person who had obtained them by stratagem or unfair means. But before making this charge, the ministers themselves had repeatedly intercepted the letters of Franklin and other Colonial agents, and read them.

§ 492. The passage of the Boston Port Bill was the virtual commencement of the American Revolution, though a collision with arms did not take place till another year had elapsed. The agreements to import no more British goods, and to abstain from the consumption of them, were renewed with greater solemnity and strictness than before. Another general Congress was called by Massachusetts, to meet at Philadelphia in September; and committees of correspondence were instituted, to render the action of the different Colonies harmonious, and to keep them advised of each other's proceedings. Closing the harbor had deprived the people of Boston of their usual means of livelihood; but Salem and Marblehead generously tendered them the use of their wharves, and subscriptions for the more indigent were obtained all over the country. The Congress met at the appointed time and place, and twelve Colonies were represented in it, only Georgia sending no delegates. Among the members were the two Adamses from Massachusetts, and Washington and Patrick Henry from Virginia. Memorials and addresses were sent forth, as by the former assembly; and the tone of these papers was naturally firmer and more decisive than on the former occasion, though it was still moderate. A dignified and eloquent Address to the People of Great Britain, written by Mr. Jay, was much admired. The Declaration of Colonial Rights was precise and comprehensive, and it included a protest against the employment of a standing army in the Colonies without their consent. Professions were made of perfect loyalty to the king, and of great solicitude for the restoration of former harmony with Great Britain; and, from a majority of the delegates, these professions were undoubtedly sincere. After a session of eight weeks, the delegates separated, having first recommended that another Congress should meet in the ensuing May, if the difficulties with England were not previously adjusted.

§ 493. In Massachusetts, hostilities seemed to be on the point of breaking out. Governor Gage prorogued the General Court before it had come together; but the members met at Salem, in spite of the prorogation, organized themselves into a provincial congress, chose John Hancock for their president, and proceeded to business. In an address to the governor, they protested against the presence of British troops and the erection of the fortifications in Boston. They appointed a committee of safety, to take measures for the defence of the province, and another committee to obtain provisions and military stores. They forbade the payment of any more money to the late treasurer, and ordered all taxes to be collected by an officer whom they had appointed. Three generals were commissioned by them, to take the command of the militia, who were organized and disciplined with much diligence. Gage issued counter orders and proclamations, but no one out of the range of his soldiers' muskets listened to them. His power was limited to Boston, which he held by a considerable military force, and had carefully fortified; but the people throughout Massachusetts rendered strict and cheerful obedience to the provincial congress. Later in the year, 12,000 "minute men" were enrolled, being volunteers from the militia, who pledged themselves to be ready for service at a minute's notice. Minute men were also enrolled in the other New England colonies, where, also, measures were taken to procure artillery and military stores.

§ 494. A striking peculiarity of the early part of the contest was the hearty and spontaneous coöperation of the larger and smaller towns throughout New England. The movement did not begin in a conspiracy first organized in the metropolis, and gradually diffused, by the action of a secret society, throughout the land. In fact, there was no secrecy, no conspiracy, in the case. The opposition to the offensive acts of parliament was open and avowed from the first; it was manifested with as much spirit in little villages—in such places as Hingham, Bedford, Concord, and Danvers—as in Boston. The common people, the farmers and mechanics, of these little communities acted in concert with the only authorities whom they were wont to recognize,—with their own selectmen. They held town meetings, in which they concerted measures of defence, and passed resolutions declaratory of their opinions and their rights, and expressing sympathy with the people of Boston. Having made their rude military preparations, they waited patiently, with arms in their hands, for the first act of aggression on the part of the British. From the commencement of the difficulties, their attitude was strictly a defensive one; they waited till the first blow should be struck by their opponents. They were not entirely unanimous; in most of the towns, there were individuals known to favor the cause of the crown. But these persons were watched with great vigilance, and whenever their movements became suspicious, they were seized and placed in custody. There were some popular outbreaks; but the mob did not seize obnoxious persons, and hang them up to a lamp post, or to the next tree, and then make targets of their bodies. In a few instances, the houses of known Tories were roughly visited, and their furniture was injured or destroyed; but the greatest violence ever done to their persons was to tar and feather them. And even these outrages were discountenanced or sharply reproved by the most influential patriots. The machinery of popular agitation on a large scale had not then been invented. The people consequently manifested but little enthusiasm; but they adhered to their purpose with a cool and dogged determination, and an unflinching fortitude, which bore them triumphantly through the long struggle. Other wars, before and since, have been waged *for* the people, and in the name of the people; but the American revolution was the first war actually waged *by* the people, that is recorded in history. Because town and country acted heartily together, neither absolutely taking the lead, and neither being wholly dependent on the other, the occupation of Boston by the British was no greater detriment to the patriot cause than if the troops had been stationed anywhere else in the province. The object was to get rid of them altogether; and in their measures for obtaining this end, the people were as careful to keep law and justice on their side as to provide for defence against unprovoked aggression. The Port Bill went into operation in June, 1774, and the battle of Lexington was not fought till the following April. During the intervening months, the attitude of the whole people was calm and watchful; they did not collect together in large bodies, they made no menacing demonstrations, but waited patiently till their opponents should commit the first overt act of hostility.

§ 495. It was the firing of the king's troops on Lexington common which rang the alarm bell of the revolution, and the hitherto seemingly quiescent Colony burst at once into a flame. This event took place at four o'clock in the morning; and before noon, the hills and roads were alive with "minute men," hurrying from all quarters to the scene of conflict. General Gage had sent out Colonel Smith, the night before, with 800 men, to destroy some military stores which the patriots had collected at Concord. On arriving at Lexington, Colonel Smith found a company of "minute men" collected on the common, who

April 19, 1775.

were ordered to disperse, and almost at the same moment, were fired upon by the British, who killed or wounded eighteen of them. A few shots were fired in return, and the king's troops then passed on to Concord, where they destroyed a few stores, were attacked by the provincials, and commenced their retreat to Boston about noon. But the minute men were now rapidly coming up from the neighboring towns, and each company, as it arrived, without waiting for orders, or stopping to concert action with those already on the field, took the best position it could find for annoying the enemy, and opened its fire. The woods and stone walls on each side of the road were lined with sharp shooters, who availed themselves of every advantage of the ground as skilfully as if they had been directed by an able general. When the British, on their retreat, had reached Lexington, they were met by a reinforcement of 1,200 men, without which they would probably have been cut off. But as soon as they resumed their march, they were again attacked, and the affair continued as it had begun, each company of the rustic soldiery finding its own station and fighting on its own hook. The action ended only when the harassed king's troops reached Charlestown, where they found safety under the guns of their shipping. They lost about 270 in killed, wounded, and missing, while the American loss was but 93.

§ 496. The manner in which this battle was fought was a type of the whole contest in New England, from the time when the tea was destroyed till Boston was evacuated. It is the most striking, perhaps the only complete, instance which all history affords, of the whole population of a country, self-moved and self-governed, acting together with great unanimity and vigor, yet acting patiently, prudently, and with even a punctilious regard for the laws, while their excitment was intense, and while they were bravely defying a powerful empire, and setting at nought an authority, which, when exercised within the bounds of justice, they and their fathers had always implicitly, and even lovingly, recognized. The first action of the Massachusetts Provincial Congress, after the battle of Lexington, was characteristic of the men and the times. They appointed a committee to take the depositions of those who were present, in order to prove that *the British fired first.* If they had been conducting a lawsuit about the title to a farm, they could not have been more anxious to collect testimony, and show that "the law" was on their side. Most of the resolutions which they passed at this period were accompanied by formidable preambles, in which the justice and legality of the measure proposed were demonstrated at length, though often with more earnestness than logic. The time for action had now arrived, and it soon appeared that the spirit which the people had shown at Lexington was no transient feeling. Within a few days, an army of about 16,000 men had come together, and the siege of Boston was begun. This, again, was a spontaneous and unconcerted movement; they assembled before preparations were made for them, before a commander-in-chief had been appointed, or any plan of action formed. Rhode Island and Connecticut retained the control of their own troops, and the care of providing them with arms and sustenance, merely instructing them to coöperate with the Massachusetts army. But for the excellent spirit of the men, the army would have been merely an armed mob. But the ranks were filled with steady farmers and mechanics, who were brought thither by their attachment to the cause, and who needed little discipline to keep them in order.

§ 497. Ammunition and artillery were yet wanting, though great exertions had been made to obtain military stores. But this want was partially supplied by an enterprise of the "Green Mountain Boys," as the inhabitants of the country which is now the State of Vermont were then called. It was known that the fortresses of Ticonderoga and Crown Point had but slender garrisons and were imperfectly guarded. Ethan Allen and Seth Warner, who commanded some armed volunteers in that region, undertook upon their own responsibility to take these forts by May, 1775. surprise, and they suceeeded. Two hundred pieces of artillery and a considerable supply of powder were thus obtained for the camp near Boston. The British army at that place had been reinforced, and now amounted to 10,000 men, under Generals Howe, Clinton, and Burgoyne. To straiten their quarters, Col. Prescott was sent, with about a thousand men from the American army, to throw up an entrenchment on Bunker's Hill in Charlestown. A small redoubt was constructed there in the night time, on which, as soon as it was discovered June 17. in the morning, the English ships in the harbor opened their fire. This produced but little effect; and the reinforcements sent to Prescott during the forenoon enabled him to throw up an imperfect breastwork, and other slight fortifications outside of the redoubt. Generals Putnam, Pomeroy, and Warren joined him at this time, but did not take the command out of his hands. Three thousand men were sent over at noon from Boston, led by Howe and Pigot, to take the hill by assault. They advanced bravely, but the fire of the Americans was so close and well-sustained, that the British wavered, and fell back in great disorder. Gage then ordered the village of Charlestown, which was near the foot of the hill, to be set on fire, and while the flames were raging, the troops again moved forward. Again, as they approached the redoubt, the murderous fire of the Americans, many of whom were practised marksmen, burst forth, and again the assailants were driven back to the landing place. They formed and advanced a third time, and as the ammunition of the Americans was now nearly spent, they succeeded in getting possession of the hill. But their opponents retired in a body, and were not pursued, though they suffered much from the fire of the shipping in their retreat. The victory of Howe might well be considered a defeat, for he lost over a thousand men in killed and wounded, while the American loss was not half as great. But Gen. Warren was among the slain. The battle was as characteristic as that of Lexington; a Colonel commanded, and three Generals either served under him, or acted independently in directing the troops. The result was very encouraging to the Americans, as it proved that their raw levies were capable of waging a desperate conflict with regular troops.

§ 498. Congress had again assembled at Philadelphia, at the appointed time, and it began to exercise all the functions of a government, though there was no formal union of the Colonies, and the cheerful acquiescence of the people was the only basis of its authority. But the delegates were not yet prepared for a total rupture with England; they voted to send another petition to the king, and an address to the people of Great Britain, in which they declared that they did not intend to throw off their allegiance, and professed an anxious desire for peace. At the same time, they resolved to put the country in a state of defence, and to complete the organization of an army. George Washington, a delegate from Virginia, was chosen commander-in-chief, the members from New England heartily concurring in his nomination, from their wish to secure the coöperation of the southern Colonies. Ward, Lee, Schuyler, and Putnam were commissioned as major-generals, and ten brigadiers were appointed, among whom were Gates, Greene, Montgomery, and Sullivan. Most of these officers had seen service in the French and Indian wars. Bills of credit, or paper money, were issued to the amount of three millions of dollars; a post-office department was organized, and a committee was appointed to secure, if possible, the neutrality of the Indians. Massachusetts asked the advice of Congress, in reference to its form of government; and it was advised to establish a provisional government, that should conform as nearly as possible to the charter. The governors of most of the Colonies had now either abandoned their posts, or were coöperating with the enemies of the country; and the direction of affairs had generally fallen into the hands either of the most numerous representative body under the old organization, or of such an assembly created for the occasion. It may be observed here, by anticipation, that new constitutions of government were established by all the Colonies, except Connecticut and Rhode Island, during the progress of the war. New Hampshire formed such a constitution in 1775; New Jersey, South Carolina, Virginia, Pennsylvania, Delaware, Maryland, and North Carolina, in 1776, — the first three before the Declaration of Independence; Georgia and New York, in 1777; Massachusetts, in 1780. The forms of government thus established were not arbitrary and novel. They supplied omissions, it is true; but they made no unnecessary innovations. They were the old forms of polity, adopted by the first settlers, or created for them by charter, with such modifications only as were rendered necessary by the transition from a state of partial, to one of total, independence. Connecticut and Rhode

May 10.

Island did not find it necessary to make any change; their charters were so liberal that the people, in fact, had always chosen all their own officers, and enacted all their own laws; and under these charters, the government continued to be administered for nearly half a century after the Revolution.

§ 499. Washington assumed the command of the army before Boston about a fortnight after the battle of Bunker Hill, and immediately endeavored to improve its organization and discipline, and to obtain supplies of arms and military stores. The troops at first consisted entirely of volunteers, and so many of these left and went home after a short stay, that it was feared the camp would be deserted. An attempt was now made to enlist soldiers for definite periods, to form them into regiments, and accustom them to discipline and the use of their arms. The most pressing want was that of powder, of which there was not enough to furnish nine rounds to a man, and the whole supply in the country was so inadequate that active operations could not be undertaken for some months. Attempts were made to establish manufactories of saltpetre and to import powder and lead from the West Indies; and a small supply of military stores was obtained from captured vessels. The patience and firmness of the commander-in-chief were severely taxed by the many discouraging circumstances of his position, at the head of a motley collection of troops, with insufficient means of paying them and of providing many necessaries of war. Reserved and dignified in his demeanor, inflexible in purpose, circumspect and yet enterprising in his plans, industrious and methodical in business, he united the highest qualifications for the elevated post which he was called to fill. His equanimity was seldom ruffled, and no failures or disasters could dishearten him or paralyze his energies. A keen judge of character and qualifications, he was generally fortunate in selecting his agents and giving his confidence. Under his direction, and in spite of the most adverse circumstances, the raw levies were gradually converted into disciplined and effective troops, and the efforts of an enemy greatly superior in means and equipment were successfully foiled.

§ 500. Congress had projected an expedition against Canada, in the hope of obtaining the sympathy and aid of the French inhabitants of that province, or perhaps of inducing them to unite with the other Colonies in resistance to the British ministry. Schuyler and Montgomery, at the head of a small body of troops, advanced by way of Lake Champlain against Montreal, whilst Arnold, with about a thousand men, was detached from the camp before Boston, to ascend the Kennebec river, and then make his way through the wilderness to the banks of the St. Lawrence opposite Quebec. Schuyler being prevented by illness from advancing farther than St. John's on the Sorel, the command devolved on Montgomery, who, after a few weeks' siege, captured St. John's, and then advanced against Mon-

August, 1775.

November 3.

treal, which was surrendered to him without resistance. Arnold's troops, after suffering great hardships from exposure and want of food while passing through a wild and uninhabited region, reached the southern bank of the St. Lawrence, where they were joined by Mont-
December 1. gomery, who came down the river to meet them. Their united forces hardly exceeded a thousand men, while Carleton, the British commander, by landing the sailors and organizing the citizens into military companies, had garrisoned Quebec with 1,200. The artillery of the Americans not being sufficient to make any impression on the works, they resolved to attempt to carry the place by assault. Under cover of a snow-storm, the men advanced to the attack with great gal-
December 31. lantry, and forced their way into the lower town; but Montgomery was killed, Arnold's leg was broken by a musket ball, and after some desperate fighting, the party in the streets found themselves surrounded and were obliged to surrender. Arnold, with about 600 men, retreated a few miles up the river, and there kept up the blockade of Quebec through the winter. Reinforcements were sent to him; but after the spring opened, a large body of British troops arrived at Quebec, and the Americans were forced to retire, first to Montreal, and afterwards to St. John's.

§ 501. Howe's army in Boston, having learned caution from the battle of Bunker Hill, made no attempt at offensive operations during the autumn and winter; and the want of cannon and powder in the American camp prevented Washington from attacking them. But through the great exertions of Colonel Knox, over fifty pieces of artillery were dragged on sleds, over the frozen lake and the snow, from Crown Point and Ticonderoga; and active measures were then adopted to drive the British out of the place. On the evening of the 4th of March,
A. D. 1776. the attention of the enemy being drawn by a brisk cannonade to the opposite quarter, a large body of troops secretly took possession of Dorchester heights, and erected a line of fortifications there which commanded the harbor and the town. The English general made immediate preparation to attack these works; but a furious storm of wind and rain, that prevailed for two days, prevented the troops from crossing in boats to Dorchester, and when this had ceased, the intrenchments seemed too strong to be forced. General Howe consequently resolved to evacuate the town; and on the 17th, the fleet sailed, carrying off the whole army, and about one thousand inhabitants of the place and its vicinity who adhered to the king's cause. The recovery of Boston caused great rejoicing throughout the country; the thanks of Congress were voted to the general and his army, and a gold medal was ordered to be struck in commemoration of the event. After a delay of a few days, Washington marched with the main body of the army to New York. The Loyalists, or Tories, as the favorers of the British cause were called, were nume-

rous in that place and its neighborhood, and for this reason, among others, it was supposed that Howe would carry his army thither. In reality, the British troops sailed for Halifax, where they remained inactive till the end of June, and then, after receiving large reinforcements, proceeded to New York.

§ 502. A year had now elapsed since the battle of Lexington; it had been passed in active hostilities, the exasperation of both parties had increased, and there seemed to be no longer any hope of a reconciliation with England. Lord North's ministry, supported by the obstinacy of the king and by a large majority in both houses of Parliament, evinced no disposition to change its policy; on the contrary, treaties had been formed with several of the minor powers of Germany, in virtue of which about 17,000 Hessians, Waldeckers, and Hanoverians were collected by crafty recruiting officers, and hired out to England for the purpose of putting down the rebellion in America. Of course, the news that these mercenaries were to be employed greatly increased the irritation of the Colonies. Thomas Paine, a very coarse but vigorous writer, published his famous pamphlet, called "Common Sense," to prove that a final separation from England was inevitable and ought not to be delayed. Written in an eminently popular style, it had an immense circulation, and was of great service in preparing the minds of the people for independence. A proposition to dissolve all connection with Great Britain was first introduced in Congress by Richard Henry Lee, of Virginia, and was warmly supported by John Adams and other members from New England. But it was not carried without difficulty; New York, Pennsylvania, Maryland, and South Carolina hesitated. Indeed, the legislatures of the two former Colonies had expressly instructed their representatives in Congress to vote against it. But the tide of popular opinion now set strongly towards independence, and the waverers were carried along with it, in spite of their efforts. The recusant Colonies recalled their instructions, and on the 4th of July, 1776, the Declaration of Independence, written by Thomas Jefferson, and revised by a committee, of which John Adams and Dr. Franklin were members, was solemnly adopted in Congress by a vote of the whole Thirteen States. This memorable Declaration asserts in grave and dignified language the right of the people to institute, alter, or abolish any form of government; to justify the exercise of this right at the present time, it enumerates at length the wrongs which had been inflicted on the Colonies by the king of Great Britain, and concludes that he is no longer worthy to be the ruler of a free people; and it ends with the formal assertion, that "these United Colonies are, and of right ought to be, free and independent States, and that they are absolved from all allegiance to the British crown:"—in support of which declaration, the signers of the instrument mutually pledge to each other their lives, their fortunes, and their sacred honor.

§ 503. The progress of the contest had been watched with great attention on the Continent of Europe, where the efforts of the Americans were naturally regarded with favor and sympathy, partly out of jealousy of England, but still more from the enthusiasm which a gallant contest for freedom always awakens in the hearts of the people. Among the French particularly, this feeling was very strong, as the success of the patriots would humiliate and weaken the haughty rival that had recently triumphed over France, and deprived her of nearly all her colonial dominion. Congress had previously appointed a "Committee of Secret Correspondence," to keep up intercourse with the friends of the cause in various parts of Europe; and now that the United States had become an independent power, it seemed proper to extend this intercourse, and to establish diplomatic relations with other governments. Three commissioners, of whom Dr. Franklin was one, were sent to Paris, and Arthur Lee was deputed by them to visit Prussia and Spain. These agents were not formally received at court, for no European power was yet prepared for war with England. But the French ministers treated them with much courtesy, and agreed to furnish the Americans with secret supplies of money, arms, and military stores, to a considerable amount. Many shipments were consequently made, and the aid thus received was very seasonable. The appearance of Dr. Franklin, with his high reputation as a philosopher, his plain garb, and agreeable manners, as an envoy from the combatants for freedom in the New World, created a great sensation among the excitable people of Paris. Honors and attentions of all kinds were lavished upon him. "Men imagined," says Lacretelle, "that they saw in him a sage of antiquity, come back to give austere lessons and generous examples to the moderns. They personified in him the republic of which he was the representative and the legislator." The young and wealthy Marquis of Lafayette, inspired with a noble enthusiasm, crossed the ocean to hazard life and property in the cause of American freedom. Some Germans, also, among whom Kalb and Steuben, were best known, and the gallant Pole, Kosciuzko, with a number of volunteers from other nations, went to the aid of the Americans.

§ 504. The campaign of 1776 was very disastrous to the American arms, and but for the surpassing fortitude and magnanimity of their great military leader, it would have been ruinous to the cause. Washington's army was very weak when it arrived in New York; several regiments had been left behind to garrison Boston, and others were detached to strengthen the northern army, then lying near Montreal. Unfortunately, also, the men had been enlisted for very short periods, owing to the uncertainty how long the war would continue; and now, when their services were most wanted, and they had been trained and disciplined, whole regiments had to be disbanded and sent home, and their places were taken by raw recruits. Frequent drafts were made from the militia, to meet pressing emergencies; but these raw troops could not be depended upon for efficient service. The Continental troops under Washington at New York did not number more than 8,000, while the British army, which Howe led thither in June, including the German mercenaries, amounted to 24,000. Among them were the troops lately employed against Charleston, South Carolina, where they had attempted to land, but the fleet had been driven off by the heavy fire from the forts. The fortifications at New York did not prove so formidable, as the British vessels passed them without damage, and entered the Hudson river. Howe landed most of his troops on Long Island, where the Tories were very numerous, and marched to attack the Americans, who were in an entrenched camp at the western end of the island, opposite New York. A battle followed, in which the British army succeeded in gaining the rear of the Americans by an unguarded road, and totally defeated them, taking over a thousand prisoners. The remainder of the army secretly retreated, on the second night after the battle, from Long Island to New York. Leaving a garrison in the town, Washington placed the body of the troops on Haerlem heights, a strong position at the northward. But the garrison was soon obliged with loss to quit New York, as the place was not tenable except by a large force, and even the troops on the heights behaved so ill that a farther retreat became necessary. Discouragement was now very general; the militia deserted by companies, and the Continentals, as the regular troops were called, began to follow their example. Washington adopted the only system of warfare which was practicable under these gloomy circumstances; he resolved to risk no general engagement, to encamp only in strong positions, to weary out the enemy by frequent marches, and not to meet them except in skirmishes. A partial action was fought at White Plains without any decisive result, and most of the Americans were then withdrawn to the western shore of the Hudson, as an invasion of New Jersey was threatened. A large garrison was left in Fort Washington, on New York island, about ten miles above the city; but the British attacked it before the fortifications were completed, and the commander was obliged to capitulate, giving up the place and stores, and over 2,000 prisoners. The enemy then crossed the Hudson in force, and Washington was obliged to abandon Fort Lee, on the Jersey shore, with a great quantity of baggage and artillery. He then retreated rapidly southward through New Jersey as far as Trenton, where, for safety, the army crossed the Delaware into Pennsylvania. At this gloomy period for the American cause, Sir William Howe issued a proclamation, offering pardon to all who would return to their allegiance within sixty days, and commanding all persons who had taken up arms, and all congresses and associations to desist from their treasonable proceedings and give up their usurped authority. Many individuals, among whom were two former members of Congress, were

October 28.

weak enough to accept the proposal. As the British army approached Philadelphia, Congress adjourned to Baltimore, having first granted to the commander-in-chief almost dictatorial power.

§ 505. Washington perceived that some bold stroke was necessary to revive the spirits of his countrymen. Some reinforcements had joined him, and the English army had gone into winter-quarters, being stationed in detachments at several places in New Jersey. On Christmas night, at the head of 2,500 men, he recrossed the Delaware with great difficulty, as the river was full of floating ice, surprised a body of Hessians in Trenton, took 900 prisoners and then returned to his former position with only a trifling loss. A week afterwards, he reöccupied Trenton with a larger force; but Lord Cornwallis came up to meet him with a large portion of the British army, and it appeared too hazardous either to stand an engagement, or retreat when the enemy were so near. Washington devised a manœuvre which was completely successful. Leaving the watch fires burning in the deserted camp, the troops were led by a circuitous route into the rear of the British, and then conducted to Princeton, where they fell unexpectedly upon three regiments that were stationed there, drove them out of the town with great loss, and took 300 prisoners. Cornwallis heard the firing in his rear, and divining the cause, hurried off in pursuit; but before he could overtake the Americans, they were encamped on unassailable ground at Morristown. These exploits taught Sir William Howe to respect an opponent whom he had begun to contemn; and he therefore withdrew his troops from the greater part of New Jersey, and concentrated them round New York. Washington stationed his army at Morristown, Princeton, and in the Highlands on the Hudson; and the next six months were spent in organizing it anew, and reducing it to discipline. The British had taken possession of the southern part of Rhode Island, and had surprised and captured Gen. Lee. On the other hand, privateers and national cruisers had been fitted out in the ports of Massachusetts, and had captured many valuable British ships, which were carried to the West Indies and the harbors of continental Europe, and sold.

§ 506. The next year was the turning point, or critical period, of the war. It was checkered by good and evil fortune. It was a period of much financial difficulty and great suffering both by the army and the people; but towards its close, the unexpected and great success of the American arms at the north really decided the fate of the contest, and showed that the attempt of Great Britain to reduce the Colonies by force to their former allegiance was a hopeless undertaking. About the end of May, the American army, now much strengthened by recruits, left its winter quarters, and took a strong position at Middletown. Howe manœuvred for some time, in the hope of inducing or compelling it to fight a battle on equal ground. But finding that

A. D. 1777.

Washington was too cautious to run this hazard, he suddenly embarked his army on board the fleet, and carried it round to the head of Chesapeake Bay, where he landed and began his march for Philadelphia. He was obliged to take this route, as the American fortifications on the Delaware made it too hazardous for the fleet to ascend that river. Anxious to save the city which was the seat of Congress and was regarded in some measure as the capital of the country, Washington marched hurriedly southward to intercept him. After passing through Philadelphia, he first attempted to check the progress of the enemy at Brandywine, where a creek, everywhere fordable, guarded the front of the American position. The British passed this stream in two divisions, at considerable distance from each other; and Washington's army being thus attacked in front and on the flank, some regiments broke and fled, and the rest were forced to retreat in some disorder. The Americans again offered battle five days afterwards, but a violent storm interrupted the engagement almost as soon as it began. The hope of saving Philadelphia was then abandoned; Congress adjourned to Lancaster, the magazines and public stores were removed, and Howe entered the city on the 25th, leaving the bulk of his army ten miles off, at Germantown. It was a barren conquest; experience was now teaching the British that they could hold no more ground in America than what they actually occupied with their troops; and these were not to be too much scattered, or they were liable to be cut off in detail. To raise the sinking spirits of his men, Washington planned a surprise of the British army in Germantown. The enterprise seemed successful at first; but the troops got separated from each other, in the darkness of the morning, by the inequalities of the ground, a panic seized upon some, and the whole were then driven to make a disorderly retreat. Rightly deeming that Washington could not soon make another attack after this repulse, Howe resolved to attack the forts on the Delaware, in order to establish communication with his fleet, which had not yet been able to pass up the river. Count Donop, with 1,200 Hessians, assaulted the post at Red Bank, on the Jersey shore, but fell in the attempt, and his men were driven off with great slaughter; and of the ships which assailed Fort Miflen, on an island in the Delaware, a sixty-four was blown up, a frigate was burned, and the others were much injured and compelled to retire. The enemy then erected land-batteries, which kept up so heavy a fire that the fortifications were ruined, and the garrison was withdrawn. Red Bank was also evacuated, and the Delaware was thus opened to the British fleet.

September 11.

October 4.

October 22.

§ 507. But the most important military operations of this year took place at the north. Gen. Burgoyne received the command in Canada, with a finely appointed army of 10,000 men, and was instructed to force his way down Lake Champlain, and then cross to Albany, and descend

the Hudson, to join the British forces in New York. This plan, if executed, would have cut off New England from the other Colonies, and have rendered the subjugation of the Americans extremely probable. And there was great danger for a time that it would be executed. Burgoyne summoned the Indians to his standard, and easily drove the feeble and disorganized army of St. Clair before him, captured Ticonderoga and Skenesborough, and prepared to force his way
July 6. through the wilderness, from the head of the lake to the Hudson. St. Clair had brought a poor remnant of his army to join Schuyler at Fort Edward, on the Hudson; but their united forces did not number 5,000, most of them were militia, and both ammunition and provisions were wanting. The news of the loss of Ticonderoga and the rapid progress of Burgoyne created great consternation; the militia of New England came forward readily, and in considerable numbers, to strengthen the northern army, which also received some detachments from the posts in the Highlands. Schuyler was superseded by Gen. Gates, and under him were placed Arnold, Morgan, Lincoln, and others, who were among the best officers in the army. Burgoyne had succeeded in reaching the Hudson after immense labor and fatigue, but he found that difficulties were now beginning to thicken around him. He had sent out a strong detachment of regular troops, Tories, and Indians, to his right, to turn the alarm to the western frontier of New York, and lay siege to Fort Schuyler at the head of the Mohawk. Arnold was sent against him, and the fear of his approach caused so many of the Indians to desert, that St. Leger was compelled to raise the siege and retire so precipitately
Aug. 22. that most of his stores and baggage fell into the hands of the Americans. Another and stronger detachment was sent out to the left, under Col. Baum, to try the temper of the people and to obtain horses and provisions; this was encountered, at Bennington, by some
Aug. 16. New Hampshire militia and Green Mountain Boys, under Col. Stark, and totally defeated, most of the German soldiers being taken prisoners. Col. Breyman, who had been sent with 500 men to aid Baum, came up two hours after the battle was fought, was himself attacked by the victorious party, and obliged to make the best retreat he could, with the loss of all his baggage and artillery. Thus both of Burgoyne's wings were clipped, and he found himself at Saratoga, on the west side of the Hudson, in the heart of a difficult country, short of provisions, and with an enemy constantly increasing in numbers on all sides of him. He first tried an attack upon Gates' camp, upon Behmus's Heights,
Sept. 19. in his front; and the result was a drawn battle, in which he lost 500 men, and gained not a single advantage. A party of Lincoln's militia had got into his rear, surprised the posts around Lake George, and besieged Ticonderoga, so that his communications were cut off. But he was encouraged to hold out, as a letter reached him from Clinton in New

York, saying that the latter was about to make an expedition up the Hudson, which would operate as a diversion, and might reach Albany, so as to place Gates between two fires. The promise was kept, the passes of the Highlands were forced, and the British had proceeded as far north as Esopus, when they learned that they were too late, and found it prudent to return. Burgoyne offered battle again on the 7th of October, and his troops were defeated and driven back into his camp, his entrenchments in one quarter were forced, and a part of his artillery and ammunition were captured. His position was thus rendered untenable, and he secretly drew back in the night to a rising ground in the rear. Thence he retreated, two days afterwards, to Saratoga, and found that the difficulties of the country and the position of the American parties were such that he could go no further. He held out a week longer; and then, his provisions being exhausted and his camp surrounded and hard
Oct. 16. pressed, he was obliged to capitulate. He had already lost about 4,000 men, and 5,642 others were now surrendered as prisoners of war, all his arms, baggage, and camp equipage also passing into the hands of the victors. The garrison of Ticonderoga, when they heard of this calamity, hastily retreated into Canada, and the Americans again took possession of this renowned fortress.

§ 508. Two days after the news arrived at Paris of the capture of Burgoyne and the battle of Germantown, the French ministry intimated to Dr. Franklin that they were willing to consider the project of a treaty of alliance with the American States. Two treaties were accordingly framed, in one of which France acknowledged the independ-
Feb. 6, 1778. ence of the States, and formed relations of amity and commerce with them; in the other, which was to go into effect if Great Britain should make war upon France, the two contracting parties bound themselves to aid each other as good friends and allies, to maintain the sovereignty and independence of the American States, and not to make a truce or peace except by mutual consent. About the same time, the British ministry caused two laws to be enacted, declaring that no tax should hereafter be imposed by parliament on the Colonies, and appointing commissioners to treat with them on almost any terms short of absolute independence. The concession was ample, but it came too late; Congress refused even to hold a conference with the commissioners before the British armies were withdrawn and the independence of the country acknowledged. England therefore declared war against France, and prepared to keep up in America some years longer a useless, expensive, and murderous conflict, in which she had hardly a hope of ultimate success. The Colonists were indeed compelled to pay a heavy price for their freedom. The public finances were in a deplorable state; recruits could not be obtained except by enormous bounties, and the troops were but half fed and half clothed; and the people generally were suffering from the

interruption of trade and agriculture, and the scarcity of breadstuffs. There was hardly a family in the land to which the war had not already brought privation and bereavement. And yet the spirit of the people continued high; they expected much from the French alliance, and, except among the Tories, hardly a wish was breathed for peace on any terms short of independence. For the army, which had passed the winter in miserable huts at Valley Forge, suffering from cold and disease, and to some extent also from hunger and nakedness, Washington set apart a day for rejoicing when the news of the treaty with France were received. Losses and hardships were then forgotten in the general exultation; "every heart was filled with gratitude to the French king, and every mouth spoke his praise."

§ 509. The quarters of the British army were now found to be too much extended; and it was resolved to evacuate Philadelphia and retreat to New York. The American army, which had been reinforced in the spring, and somewhat trained and disciplined through the great efforts of Baron Steuben, a brave and skilful Prussian officer, hung upon their rear and gave them much trouble. A battle between them was fought at Monmouth, with indecisive results, though the British loss considerably exceeded that of the Americans. Many of the German soldiers, also, took the opportunity to desert. Count D'Estaing soon arrived with a powerful fleet, having 4,000 French soldiers on board, and a scheme for a combined attack on New York having failed because the pilots would not conduct the heavier ships over the bar, an expedition against Newport was agreed upon, that place being held by Gen. Pigot, at the head of 6,000 men. The fleet blockaded the harbor, and forced the English to sink some of their frigates; but the Continental troops and New England militia did not arrive soon enough to coöperate with the ships, which were compelled to put to sea by Lord Howe's fleet, and were also crippled by a storm. The undertaking was abandoned, and Gen. Sullivan had much difficulty in bringing off the American troops, as the British had received a large reinforcement. These were the only military operations on a large scale during the year; though as the war was now prosecuted both by the British and the Tories in a less hopeful and more revengeful spirit, several predatory expeditions were sent out that did much wanton injury, and in some skirmishes no quarter was given, and acts of sickening barbarity were committed. Wyoming, a flourishing settlement in Pennsylvania, was desolated by an incursion of Indians and Tories, the male inhabitants were massacred, the houses burned, and the cattle killed or driven off. Some towns on the coast of Massachusetts were burned, and a heavy contribution was levied on a defenceless island. In New York, Baylor's troop of dragoons were surprised, and the men bayonetted, under Gen. Gray's orders to give no quarter; and the same fate befell the infantry of Pulaski's legion.

June 28.

August.

There was some excuse for the Tories in these proceedings; their property had been very generally confiscated, they often had rough personal treatment, and on slight pretexts, some of them had been hanged.

§ 510. During the next two years, the war was chiefly carried on by the British in the southern States, where the population was more scattered and divided in opinion, and the country offered fewer means of defence. At the close of 1778, Savannah was taken by an expedition from New York, and another body of royal troops coming up from Florida, nearly completed the conquest of Georgia. Gen. Lincoln was sent to take the command in this department, and by great exertions he
A. D. 1779. protected Charleston and South Carolina from the enemy till September, when D'Estaing, with a French fleet and 6,000 men, arrived on the coast, and the two armies in concert laid seige to Savannah. But as the French could remain but a short time, the attack was made prematurely, and the besiegers were beaten off with great loss, the
Oct. 9. gallant Count Pulaski being among the slain. Gen. Matthews was sent from New York, with 2,500 men, on a plundering expedition to Virginia. He took possession of Portsmouth and
May. Norfolk, burned some ships of war and many private vessels, and brought off a large quantity of tobacco, after destroying private property to the amount of two millions of dollars. At the north, Congress took measures to punish the Indians for the atrocities they had committed at Wyoming, and other places. Gen. Sullivan led an expedition of 4,000 men into the heart of their country, in the western part of the State of New York, destroyed their villages, cut down their
September. fruit trees, and so devastated the region, that the miserable savages could attempt nothing more till the close of the war. Some British troops under Gen. Tryon paid a marauding visit to the Connecticut shore, plundered and burned several towns, and destroy-
July. ed a large amount of property. About the only legitimate military exploits of the year, at the north, were the capture by the British of Stony Point and Verplanck's Point on the Hudson, thus rendering the communication between New England and the Middle States more circuitous and difficult, and the recapture of Stony Point in a very gallant manner by the Americans under Gen. Wayne.

§ 511. Spain had now joined the alliance against England, though with no very definite purpose, except the hope that, while the
June, 1779. attention of the British ministry was occupied by so many enemies, she might regain possession of Gibraltar. For a short time, the united French and Spanish fleet swept the British seas; but it was soon compelled to go into harbor. The next year, 1780, added another European power to the list of England's enemies, and brought her assumed empire of the seas into great danger. To check the maritime superiority of the British, who, during the war, had greatly disturbed the neutral

trade at sea, and molested the ships of every country by an oppressive search for contraband goods, Catherine II. of Russia concluded an alliance with the several neutral powers, which should maintain the principle of "free ships, free goods," and thus secure the trade of the neutral states on the coasts and in the harbors of either of the belligerent powers. The confederacy also declared that no blockade of any port should be deemed effectual, so as to exclude neutral vessels from entering it, if there were not an adequate naval force present to maintain the blockade and render it very dangerous for any ship to attempt to enter. This neutral alliance was constituted successively by Russia, Denmark, Sweden, Prussia, Austria, Naples, and Portugal. But Holland, whose adherence was very important from her situation and maritime strength, hesitated so long that England got information of the project, and declared war against the Dutch before they could give in their adhesion at St. Petersburg. Holland thus disappeared from the list of the neutral powers, and the alliance was deprived of her aid towards accomplishing their great purpose.

§ 512. A powerful British armament, under Clinton and Arbuthnot, appeared before Charleston in February, 1780, and laid siege to it, with a view to the ultimate conquest of the whole State. Gen. Lincoln's means of defence were very inadequate, and though he made every effort, he was compelled, after a resistance of 42 days, to surrender the city and give up his whole army as prisoners of war. The enemy then easily overran South Carolina; and many of the inhabitants, to avoid the extremities of war, took "protections" from them, and thereby avowed themselves to be British subjects. Lord Cornwallis was then left to command at the South, while Clinton returned to New York. Congress appointed Gen. Gates to oppose the former, and by great exertions an army of 4,000 men was collected for this purpose, mostly militia, who were ill fed and ill armed, and not at all disciplined. With the rash confidence inspired by his success against Burgoyne, Gates advanced hastily and with little precaution, was attacked under unfavorable circumstances by Cornwallis, near Camden, and his army so completely routed that not a fourth part of them could be again brought together. The southern States were thus rendered almost entirely defenceless, though the British for the present were not able to invade North Carolina from the want of supplies. Sumter and Marion, also, noted partizan officers, gave them great annoyance by collecting bands of irregular troops, and waging a kind of guerilla warfare against their outposts and detachments. One motley collection of such troops, chiefly mounted backwoodsmen with their rifles, under Shelby and Sevier, intercepted Ferguson, an active Loyalist, at the head of about 1,000 Tories, at King's Mountain, and totally defeated him, taking most of his men prisoners, and hanging some of them as traitors. At the end of the year, Gen. Greene was sent to take Gates's place, and a small

August 16.

October 9.

regular army was collected for him, which he led with consummate ability. At the north, a French fleet and army, the latter under Rochambeau, arrived at Newport, but were blockaded there by a superior British fleet, so that they accomplished nothing. Another remarkable incident of the year was the treason of Gen. Arnold, a very brave officer, but dissolute, wayward, and extravagant, who sold himself to the British for £10,000 and a general's commission, covenanting to give into their power, also, West Point and the other American fortresses in the Highlands. The
September. conspiracy was detected just before the time fixed for its execution. Arnold succeeded in making his escape; but Major André, a gallant English officer whom Clinton had sent to negotiate with him, was seized when in disguise within the American lines, and was tried and executed as a spy. The want of pay, and the impossibility of complying with the just demands of the soldiers, caused some Pennsylvania regiments, who were encamped near Morristown, to break out into open revolt. They were invited to join the British, as Arnold had done; but they refused, and after the matter had been compromised by Congress, some of their grievances being redressed, they gave up the emissaries of the enemy, who were hanged as spies. Some New Jersey troops quickly followed this example of insubordination; but their revolt was crushed with a strong hand, and a few of the ringleaders were executed.

§ 513. The comparative ease with which Georgia and South Carolina had been subdued caused great efforts to be made, in 1781, for the conquest of North Carolina and Virginia. In January of this year, the traitor Arnold was sent with 1,600 men, chiefly Tories, to plunder and devastate the country on the Chesapeake and the James river, in order to cripple the resources of the State; and after he had accomplished this service, he was joined by Gen. Phillips, with 2,000 troops from New York. But these marauding expeditions did not help the British cause much; they caused great misery, but they incensed the people so much that they lost all thoughts of acquiescence and submission, and made desperate efforts to repulse the destroyers. The plan was, that Cornwallis should march north, to join Phillips and Arnold, their united forces being deemed sufficient to crush all opposition at the South. But Cornwallis had now an able and determined opponent in Greene, who gave him enough to do in the Carolinas. Half of Greene's force, under Morgan, who had been sent to put down the Tories in the west, encountered the British light troops under Tarleton, at the Cowpens, and gave them a signal defeat, killing or taking prisoners over 600 of them. Cornwallis instantly started off in great haste, to overtake and punish Morgan before he could rejoin his commander. But the activity of the Americans baffled him. Still the British general pushed on; and Greene's whole force being much inferior, he was obliged to make a rapid retreat into
March 15. Virginia. He soon returned, however, with some reinforce-

ments, and offered battle at Guilford Court House, where Cornwallis indeed defeated him, but the victory was equivalent to a defeat. The British loss was greater than the American, and Cornwallis was obliged to retire to Wilmington, near the sea. Greene pursued him for a while, and then took the bold step of marching directly into South Carolina, which had been left in charge of Lord Rawdon with a small force. Finding it impossible to overtake him, Cornwallis imitated his bold policy by marching north, to join the king's troops in Virginia. Greene and Rawdon came in conflict with each other at Hobkirk's Hill, and the former was again defeated, though his loss was no greater than the enemy's, and the advantages of the encounter were all on his side. Lee and Marion, with other partizan officers, encouraged by his presence, roused the inhabitants to arms, nearly all the British posts in the upper country were captured or abandoned, and the larger part of South Carolina was restored to the Americans. Their irritated opponents shot as deserters all whom they captured in arms that had once accepted British protection; among these victims was Colonel Hayne, an eminent citizen of Charleston, whose fate caused much sorrow and indignation. The conflict on both sides had all the aggravated features of a civil war.

April 25.

§ 514. The arrival of a powerful fleet under Count De Grasse having given the French a temporary superiority at sea, the French forces at Newport were released, and an attack upon the British in New York was projected for the combined army of Washington and Rochambeau. But this came to be thought an enterprise beyond their strength, and it was resolved in preference to strike a blow at Cornwallis at Virginia. That enterprising general, after vainly endeavoring to overtake and crush the small American force commanded by Lafayette, had retired to Yorktown, a peninsula at the mouth of York river, where he had strongly intrenched himself at the head of 8,000 men. Here he was blockaded by De Grasse's fleet, and, a fortnight afterwards, was invested by the combined French and American army, 16,000 strong. About the same time, also, the ever active Greene had fought another battle with the British in South Carolina, at Eutaw Springs, the immediate result of which was indecisive, the loss on each side being about 700; but the general consequence was, that the British were thenceforward cooped up in Charleston and the small district between the Cooper and Ashley rivers. Cornwallis was vigorously pressed, his intrenchments being ruined and his guns dismounted by the fire of heavy breaching batteries. He tried a sally without improving his situation; and then, all hope of aid from New York having failed, he was obliged to capitulate and surrender his whole army, still about 7,000 strong, as prisoners of war. This grand stroke was virtually the end of the armed contest in America; having sacrificed two large armies, and protracted the struggle for six years, the British could no longer hope to retain a foothold in the United States, far less to bring them back to their former allegiance.

September.

§ 515. Such now came to be the general opinion even in England, where, indeed, for the last three years, the war had been very unpopular. It had added over one hundred millions sterling to the national debt; it had sullied the military reputation of the kingdom, which had never stood higher than in 1760, and never lower than after the capture of Cornwallis; it had brought France, Spain, and Holland into a league of hostilities against her, and had combined the other, professedly neutral, powers in an alliance hardly less injurious to her interests and her fame. Even the signal victory obtained by the English admiral, Lord Rodney, over De Grasse's fleet in the West Indies, and the equally signal defeat of the Spaniards in their last and desperate attempt to take Gibralter, failed to restore English self-complacency, or to reconcile the nation to that ministry, (Lord North's,) which had brought them into so humiliating a position. These successes were but casual gleams of good fortune that came to lighten the close of a long period of disaster and shame. The phalanx of Lord North's parliamentary supporters was broken, his ministry was driven from office, the king's obstinacy was overcome, and the Whigs, under the guidance of Lord Rockingham, were established in power, with the express understanding that they were to make peace by submitting to the independence of the United States. Negotiations were immediately commenced with the American commissioners at Paris, Franklin, Adams, Laurens, and Jay; they were protracted by points of form, and by the breaking up of the Whig ministry through the death of Rockingham; but provisional articles of peace were signed on the 30th of November, 1782, and the cessation of hostilities was agreed upon in January following. Owing to the necessity of including the Continental powers of Europe in the pacification, the definitive treaty of peace was not concluded till the next September. In this, the independence of the United States was acknowledged, their boundaries adjusted, and a share in the fisheries secured to them; while the claims of the other belligerent powers were adjusted by the surrender or return of the conquered towns and islands.

April 12, 1782.

September.

§ 516. The peace came not too soon for exhausted and bleeding America. The impossibility of satisfying the just demands of the army, the consequent sufferings both of officers and men, and the prospect of being disbanded at the peace and sent home in utter poverty, created a determination among many of them to insist upon the payment of their dues with arms in their hands. Nothing but the moderation, wisdom, and firmness of their great commander-in-chief saved the country from the horrors of military usurpation. Some of the officers so far misjudged Washington as to think that he might be tempted to play the part of Cromwell; but his prompt and stern rebuke put an immediate end to the project. He then exerted himself, and with success, to soothe the passions that had been excited, and to lead the army back to moderate and patriotic counsels. The officers and men were persuaded to accept certificates of debt, with interest, for the arrears that were due to them, and to rely upon the efforts of Congress and the gratitude of the people for their redemption.

A. D. 1783. The troops were quietly disbanded in the course of the summer and autumn, and towards the close of the year, after the British had evacuated every place upon the seaboard, Washington was admitted to a public audience by Congress, when he resigned his commission, and took a final leave, as he supposed, "of all the employments of public life." Universal gratitude and respect, which amounted almost to veneration, attended him to his retirement at Mount Vernon.

§ 517. At the close of the war, the United States were burdened with a heavy debt, of which they had not the means even of paying the interest, the public credit was annihilated, commerce and manufactures were in a torpid condition, and the country was almost without a government. During the greater part of the struggle, Congress had possessed no authority but what was tacitly granted to it from the necessity of the case. The individual States were unwilling to give up any portion of that independence which they were striving to vindicate against a foreign power. They claimed complete sovereignty, and were unwilling to appear only as the members of a confederacy, under the general control of a central government. Besides, it was hard to adjust the terms of such an alliance. Perfect equality was hardly to be expected among states that differed so widely from each other in regard to population, wealth, and extent of territory; yet on no terms short of equality would any one State consent to a union with the others. There were also many unadjusted controversies between them, in respect to boundary, and the ownership of that vast territory beyond the Alleghanies which had been wrested from the French. In 1777, a plan of union had been framed and adopted in Congress, after two years' discussion, not as the best which could be imagined, or as adapted to all exigencies, but as the only one "suited to existing circumstances, or at all likely to be adopted." It was not to go into effect until it was ratified by all the States; and only four of them could be induced at first to adopt it. Slowly and reluctantly the others gave in their adhesion, the consent of New Jersey and Delaware not being obtained till 1779, and that of Maryland not till 1781, when, at last, the final sanction of the articles of Confederation, as they were termed, was joyfully announced by Congress. But the union thus effected was very inadequate for the ends in view. It did not establish a central government; it was only a league of several independent sovereignties. Congress was the only organ of the confederacy; each State had but one vote in this body on the decision of any question; and in respect to many subjects, the consent of nine States was requisite before the measure could go into effect. And after all, Congress had no power but to recommend measures; it could not enforce them. It could "ascertain the sums necessary to be raised for the service of the United States," and determine the quota or proportion which each State ought to pay; but it depended upon the States whether the specified amount should be raised and paid, or the recommendation entirely neglected. The fact generally was, that they refused compliance, or paid no attention to the demand; of the many requisitions of Congress, not one fourth were complied with. Excuses or palliations of such conduct were not wanting; the States were very poor, and had heavy debts of their own to provide for. Again, Congress could not impose duties upon imports, and the circumstances of the case prevented even the individual States from exercising this power. If imported goods were taxed by one, they were admitted free by another, which thus obtained a larger share of domestic and foreign trade, while the ports of its rival were deserted. Treaties with foreign powers could not be negotiated, as there was no power in the country to enforce the provisions made in them, the authority of Congress and that of the separate members of the confederacy just serving to paralyze each other. There was no common tribunal to which the States could appeal for the adjustment of their controversies with each other; and the ill compacted league was therefore liable to be broken by the first serious dispute which might grow out of many conflicting interests. It was obvious that this state of things could not long continue without bringing upon the country all the evils of anarchy and civil war.

§ 518. The condition and temper of the people increased this hazard. The vast exertions they had made during the armed struggle had exhausted their energies, and, to a certain extent, had demoralized them. On the one hand, there was a general feeling of lassitude, an indisposition to make any further sacrifices or efforts, and on the other, a fierce impatience of any act or movement which should even seem to limit their recently acquired, universal freedom. The load of public and private debt was enormous. Of what use was it, that the people had successfully resisted English bayonets, if they were now to be called upon to respect implicitly the orders of the sheriff and the staff of the constable? To what purpose, had they braved the wrath of the crown and the parliament, if creditors were still to distress them, and county courts sentence them to fine and imprisonment? Or why tax themselves millions of hard dollars, when they had just gone through a seven years' war because they would not pay an impost of three pence a pound on tea? It is no cause for wonder that such questions were frequently asked, or even that a majority of the people were inclined to answer them in a way most consonant with their present feelings. It was a period of general anxiety and gloom, — a true crisis in the history of free institutions, not only in this country, but throughout the world. It was now to be determined whether national independence was to prove a blessing or a curse; — whether the people, after throwing off all foreign restraint, would be wise and magnanimous enough to impose laws upon themselves, and to respect them when made, or whether they would follow that course of anarchy, license, and civil war which has subsequently rendered the history of the South American republics and of the ephemeral republican governments of the Old World a warning to mankind.

§ 519. The matter was brought to a crisis in 1786, by the breaking out of a rebellion in Massachusetts, the object of the insurgents being to close by violence the courts of law, thus putting a stop to legal measures for the collection of debts, and to compel the government to issue paper money, in order that all obligations might be discharged in a much depreciated currency. Job Shattuck and Daniel Shays, formerly a captain in the revolutionary army, were the leaders of the disaffected party, and it was at least doubtful whether they did not count a majority of the people among their followers. Job Shattuck, at the head of an armed force, took possession of the court-house at Worcester, and sent a written message to the judges, "that it was the sense of the people that the courts should not sit." At last, by great exertions on the part of the government and the well-affected citizens, an army of 4,000 men, under General Lincoln, was fitted out, and after a very severe campaign in the midst of winter, this dangerous insurrection was suppressed with but little loss of life. An indirect but happy consequence of this rebellion was, that it convinced a majority of the people throughout the United States that a strong central government was indispensable, not merely for their well-being, but for the preservation of society itself from anarchy and ruin. "You talk, my good Sir," wrote Washington from Mount Vernon, "of employing *influence* to appease the present tumults in Massachusetts. I know not where that influence is to be found; and, if attainable, it would not be a proper remedy for these disorders. Influence is not government. Let us have a government, by which our lives, liberties, and properties will be secured, or let us know the worst at once."

§ 520. Accordingly, a Convention of delegates from eleven of the States was held at Philadelphia in May, 1787, to revise the Articles of Confederation, or, in other words, to frame a Constitution of government for the whole country. The delegates from New Hampshire did not appear till the Convention had been two months in session, and Rhode Island was never represented at all. Among the members present were Dr. Franklin, then in his 81st year, and Washington, who was unanimously chosen president of the Convention. After they had been in session four months, with closed doors, strict secrecy being observed as to all their proceedings, they framed and published the present Constitution of the United States, approved by the signatures of all but three of the delegates who were then present, and which was to go into effect after it had been ratified in nine of the States, by conventions that were to be called for the occasion. Not without great difficulty, and many compromises of conflicting opinions and interests, had this great step been taken. The central government established by the Constitution was to consist of three departments, legislative, executive, and judicial. The legislature, called the Congress, was to consist of two branches, the Senate and the House of Representatives. In the former, the representation was equal, each State having two senators; in the latter, the number of representatives was to be proportioned to the population, which was to be ascertained every ten years by adding to the whole number of the freemen three-fifths of the slaves. Two classes of opposing claims were thus adjusted by concessions on both sides. The executive power was vested in a president, chosen for four years, by electors equal in number, for each State, to all its senators and representatives in Congress. The President was allowed a qualified negative on the enactments of the legislature, as a bill to which he refused his consent was to become a law only when approved by two-thirds of the votes in both branches. The judicial power was vested in a Supreme Court, and such inferior courts as Congress might establish; and it extended to all cases arising under the Constitution, the laws of Congress, and treaties made with foreign powers, to all cases of maritime jurisdiction, and all controversies between States, between citizens of different States, and between foreigners and citizens. Congress was not to prevent the importation of slaves till the year 1808, and slaves escaping from one State to another were to be delivered up. Congress received the power to declare war, to raise and support armies, to lay and collect taxes, duties, imposts, and excises, to coin money, to establish post-offices and post-roads, to provide and maintain a navy, and to call forth the militia for the purpose of executing the laws, suppressing insurrections, and repelling invasions. The States were prohibited, generally, from exercising any of the functions that were conferred upon Congress. In general terms, the States retained the power of domestic legislation upon all subjects in regard to which their interests were not likely to conflict, or which could be effectually disposed of without the coöperation of the whole Union; while the Federal government assumed the functions which the States were deprived of, and received whatever other authority was needed to enable it to negotiate effectively with foreign powers as the representative of one nation. Numerous provisions were borrowed from Magna Charta and the more liberal portions of the English Common Law, and incorporated into the Constitution, to protect the liberty and the rights of individuals, and to guard against acts of oppression and injustice on the part either of the Federal or the State government. The instrument was very practical in its character, and far more simple and concise than could reasonably have been expected, considering the complicated subject with which it had to do, and the difficulty of adjusting the relations of the Federal government to the individual States, and of so distributing power between them that they could work together harmoniously and effectively. As a whole, if judged either by the most approved maxims of political science, or by the light reflected upon it from that experience of more than sixty years to which it has been subjected, it may claim a high place among the best models of government that have been devised in ancient or modern times. It has required but few and slight amendments, and it has accomplished the whole work which it was designed to perform.

§ 521. Great difficulties were again experienced in obtaining its ratification by the conventions in the several States to which it was soon submitted. The two parties which were then formed, of its advocates and opponents, divided the people very equally between them, and, with some modifications, these parties have subsisted to the present day. The consent of nine States was necessary; five ratified the instrument soon and with little difficulty. Then the question came up in Massachusetts, where the parties were nearly equal, though the democratic and independent spirit of the people seemed to incline the balance against the Constitution. Every thing was thought to depend upon the decision in this State and Virginia, on account of their great weight in the Union, and the influence which they would respectively exert at the north and the south. Governor Hancock and Samuel Adams, the former being the president of the Convention, and the latter one of its most influential members, wavered. The Convention at last decided to propose certain amendments for adoption in the form prescribed by the Constitution itself; these served as an anodyne for the scruples of the two leading patriots, and the ratification was finally carried, though by a very slender majority. The consent of Maryland, South Carolina, and New Hampshire was then obtained, and next came that of Virginia, though after as warm a struggle as in Massachusetts, the opposition being led with great effect by Patrick Henry. The question was now virtually decided, and New York therefore gave a tardy and reluctant assent, which would probably have been a refusal if the measure could thereby have been defeated. North Carolina would only ratify upon certain conditions, and Rhode Island would not even hold a Convention to consider the subject; but as eleven States had adopted the Constitution, their approval was not absolutely necessary, and it was finally given after the new form of government had been some time in operation. It must be granted, in favor of the opposition, that they showed no factious spirit, but calmly acquiesced in the decision of the majority of their countrymen. Congress appointed the first Wednesday in January, 1789, for the choice of electors, the first Wednesday in February for those electors to choose a president, and the first Wednesday in March for the new government to go into operation. As had been anticipated, George Washington was unanimously elected president; indeed, the certainty that he would be chosen to this office induced many to vote for the Constitution who would otherwise have opposed it. John Adams was elected Vice-President, and senators and representatives were also chosen to form the first Congress. Proceedings were commenced at New York on the 4th of March, 1789; but a quorum of both houses did not come together till April, and on the 30th of this month, President Washington was sworn into office, and the new government went into full operation.

BOOK FOURTH.

THE LATEST PERIOD.

A. THE FORERUNNERS OF THE REVOLUTION.

1. THE LITERATURE OF ILLUMINATION.

§ 522. IN the course of the eighteenth century, a shock was given to all existing ideas by the literature of France. Ingenious, but, in part, mistaken men, opposed religious constitutions and ecclesiastical order, attacked the forms of government, and represented the conditions and shapes of society in the light of antiquated abuses. Whilst, at first, they laid hold of real blemishes and faults as points of attack, in religion and the Church, in politics and law, in civil regulations and social relations, they undermined by degrees all the foundations of human society and convulsed all rules of customary ordinance; whilst they sought to annul immunities, privileges, and class prerogatives, and to give freedom and personal merit their due value, they weakened also the force of old statutes and rights, and the strength of authority; and whilst they assailed superstitious prejudices and worn-out opinions, they perplexed at the same time faith and conscience, destroyed the veneration and esteem for things holy and customary in the hearts of men, and propagated the idea that the happiness of the world could blossom only on the ruins of existing things. This was done especially by Voltaire, Montesquieu, and Rousseau, whose ingenious writings, owing to the charm of beautiful language and powers of description, were read by the whole of educated Europe. The paths were different, but the result the same.

§ 523. Voltaire, a versatile and ingenious author, who had distinguished himself in all kinds of literature, attacked with the arms of wit and a sharp intellect every thing customary and long-established, all dominant opinions and existing regulations, without concerning himself about what should come in their place. In poems, dramatic and epic, ("Mahomet," "The Henriad," "The Maid

Voltaire, A. D. 1694-1778.

of Orleans,") in satires and romances, in historical and philosophical works ("Essay on the Customs and Genius of Nations," "Times of Louis XIV.," "History of Charles XII. of Sweden," &c.) he laid down his views and doubts, his thoughts and criticisms, his investigations and conclusions. Religion and the Church, priesthood and popular belief, experienced the most violent attacks; and if it cannot be denied that Voltaire's sarcasm and wit have destroyed many prejudices, removed many superstitions, and exhibited ecclesiastical exclusiveness in all its nakedness, so also it is to be lamented that he has broken down religious feeling in many a heart, sown doubt and unbelief in many a mind, together with cold, worldly wisdom, and therewith selfishness, and represented self-love and self-interest as the highest motives of human actions.

Montesquieu, A. D. 1689-1755. Montesquieu, a more earnest writer, drew attention to the faultiness and absurdity of the existing state of things, with a view to its improvement and reorganization in accordance with the spirit of the age. In the "Persian Letters," he attacked with the same wanton scorn as Voltaire the faith of the Church, and the whole form and system of government in France, and in the same way, by wit and irony, turned the customs and social position of his contemporaries into ridicule. In his ingenious treatise "On the Causes of the Greatness and the Decline of the Romans," he tried to prove that patriotism and self-reliance rendered a state great, but that despotism brought it to destruction. His third work, "On the Spirit of Laws," presents the constitutional government of England as that best suited to the present race of men.

J. J. Rousseau, A. D. 1712-1772. J. J. Rousseau, the son of a watchmaker of Geneva, combatted existing conditions of society by an alluring description of an opposite state of things. After a youth full of mutations and abounding in necessities and errors, which he has displayed to the world with singular candor in his "Confessions," he arrived, by the solution of a prize question on the influence of the arts and sciences upon manners, at the fundamental doctrine of his whole life and efforts, — namely, the principle, that a high degree of civilization is the occasion of all the misery and all the crimes of mankind; and that, consequently, it is only by a return to a state of nature, full of innocence and simplicity, and by shaking off all the fetters imposed by civilization, education, and custom, that the world can arrive at happiness and safety. This principle forms the central point of all his writings, which are more distinguished by sentiment and attractive descriptions, than by profundity or truthfulness. In the "Nouvelle Heloise," a romance written in poetical language and in the epistolary form, he contrasts the pleasures of a sentimental life of nature with the perverted relations of actual existence and the compulsions of society. In the "Emile," he attempted to establish a rational system of education, founded upon nature and parental affection, and thus expiated the sin he had committed by allowing his own children to be taken to the foundling hospital. The "Confession of Faith of a Savoyard Vicar," which is to be found in this work, and in which he taught and recommended a religion of the heart and feelings in opposition to the predominant Church doctrine, brought banishment and persecution upon him. In the "Social Contract," he represented the equality of all men as the condition of a well-ordered state, and found the most estimable government in a perfect democracy, with legislative popular assemblies. In all these writings, golden truths are contained side by side with many essential errors and seductive fallacies. His words are the expression of a deep inward feeling, and penetrate to the heart because they come from the heart. The effect of his writings was immeasurable, and every spot which his foot had trod, or where he had resided as a persecuted fugitive, was gazed upon with reverence by the rising generation. A feeling for nature, simplicity, and the domestic affections was awakened in France by Rousseau; but at the same time, there was aroused a passionate longing for the lauded state of primitive liberty and equality, which could only be slaked by the destruction of existing arrangements and relations.

§ 524. The influence of these men upon the opinions of all Europe was so much the greater, inasmuch as Paris then gave the fashion in every thing; the French language and literature were alone read or spoken by the higher classes, and these writings excited universal attention by their agreeable form and ingenious descriptions. Princes, like Frederick II., Gustavus III. of Sweden, Charles III. of Spain, Catharine II. of Russia, the greatest statesmen of all countries, and many persons of influence, were in personal or epistolary correspondence with Voltaire and many of his similarly-minded contemporaries. Among these contemporaries, D'Alembert, mathematician and philosopher, and the wanton poet, Diderot, are particularly well known. They were the originators of the Encyclopædic Dictionary, which was a clear, large-minded, and unprejudiced summary of all human science, but hostile to every lofty effort. From this work, they and their coadjutors received the name of Encyclopædists.

The first consequence of this literary activity was the triumph of enlightenment in most of the countries of Europe. This victory shortly displayed itself in religious toleration, in the successful struggle of reason against superstition and prejudice, in the vigorous reforms of many princes and ministers, and, above all, in the abolition of the order of

A. D. 1773. the Jesuits, in the formation of the society of Illuminati, in the Latin work of the suffragan bishop, Hontheim of Treves (who, under the name of Febronius, pointed out the origin of the papal power and attempted to derive a new canon law therefrom), and in the attempts of several German prelates, in the Congress of Ems, to procure for the Ca tholic Church of Germany a free position in regard to the Roman See. A. D. 1758. The Order of the Jesuits, the great effort of which was to hinder this enlightenment, to retain the people in a state of pupilage, and to oppose every reform and innovation, could not long exist at a time when the whole educated world was striving in the contrary direction. Accordingly, when the minister, Pombal, in Portugal, closed the colleges of the Jesuits, and sent the members of the Order to the States of the Church, and when his example was followed in all the countries governed by the house of Bourbon (Spain, Naples, Parma,) Pope Clement XIV., a liberal and sensible prince of the Church, saw himself con- A. D. 1773. strained to abolish the Order. This obliged Maria Theresa, who had long attempted to retain the Order in Austria, to consent to its dissolution, and the papal order was also carried into effect in Bavaria and the other Catholic countries of Germany. But the activity of the members of the Order was not thereby destroyed. Ex-Jesuits prosecuted the objects of the society with undisturbed perseverance, and strove against the spirit of the time. For the purpose of paralyzing their efforts, A. D. 1777. Adam Weishaupt, professor in Ingolstadt, in conjunction with Knigge and others, founded the secret society of Illuminati, whose objects were the enlightenment of the people, and the improvement of humanity. Their contest against the ex-Jesuits, monks, and clergy, was soon checked by the legal prosecutions of the Bavarian government.

§ 525. In the war which the British Colonies of North America had carried on against their mother country, Europe, which was filled with the ideas and dreams of Rousseau, saw the beginning of that great struggle by which mankind were to enter into a state of paradisiacal happiness; a struggle, by the victorious termination of which the inborn rights of humanity and the people were to attain validity. The North American War of Independence was the first contest of young freedom against the ancient prerogatives, forms, and institutions; and for this reason it had a particular interest for Europe.

Holland, where the hereditary Stadtholder, William V., and his former guardian and constant adviser, Ernest of Brunswick, were entirely devoted to the English, whilst the aristocracy, from regard to the interests of commerce, were in alliance with the French, was injured in its trade, in its navigation, and in its colonies, by this war. Besides the irreparable losses incurred by the East and West Indian trading companies, the Dutch possessions in the East Indies suffered a diminution. Holland afterwards entered into more intimate relations with France. Her people, excited by the notions of republicanism and democratic freedom, which, since the American war, had spread over Europe, gave vent to the animosity they felt against their government, which was favorably disposed towards England, by an insurrection. Duke Ernest of Brunswick was

obliged to leave the country, the Stadtholder and his wife were threatened, and armed mobs committed violence in some of the towns.
A. D. 1784. At length, Frederick William II. of Prussia, brother of the
A. D. 1787. Stadtholder's wife, marched troops into Holland, who quickly put an end to the insurrection and restored order.

2. INNOVATIONS OF PRINCES AND MINISTERS.

§ 526. The French illuminative philosophy and the *Parisian* spirit of the age exercised the greatest influence upon the views and measures of princes and governments. Not only were all the productions of French literature eagerly read and admired in the higher circles of Europe, but it also became the fashion for the well-born youth to spend some time in Paris to complete their education, and no man of consequence could reckon upon consideration or regard if he had not been admitted into the intellectual circles of the French capital. All the princes and statesmen of Europe strove for the favor and friendship of the French literati and philosophers. Is it then to be wondered at, that, in the three last decenniums which preceded the French Revolution, many reforms and innovations were undertaken, which had their origin in that spirit of the times which had been formed in France? The endeavor was to apply practically that which, in speech and in writing, was allowed to be the truth. Zealous efforts were accordingly made on all sides to revolutionize ancient forms and institutions, laws and customs, and to adapt them by fresh arrangements to the spirit of the age. In the region of religion and the Church, this spirit first displayed itself in the establishment of the liberal and magnanimous principle of toleration in matters of faith, in the abolition of the Order of the Jesuits and of the Inquisition, and in the moderation of all principles and institutions dangerous to philanthropy or the rights of mankind. This new epoch of humanity exhibited itself most actively and with the best results in the affairs of law, where efforts were everywhere made to establish, as far as possible, the equal administration of justice to every man, and to ameliorate or abolish the statutes and burdens which had descended from the middle ages. In many countries, serfdom was abolished, feudal duties were done away with, oppressive or degrading relations removed; new codes and ordinances respecting the administration of justice annulled the cruel punishments of a stern and gloomy period, such as the rack, wheel, &c., and conferred the privileges of humanity even on the criminal. In regard to the economy of the state, new principles were established in France, which were adopted in many countries. According to these, money is the great lever of state science, and, consequently, the great object is to raise as large a revenue as possible by labor and by making use of natural agents. If this principle, on the one hand, was the occasion of the encouragement of agriculture, mining, and planting, and that trade, industry, and useful inventions were patronized, it led, on the other, to oppressive duties, to the royal right of preëmption, to indirect taxation, and to paper money.

Joseph Emmanuel, A. D. 1750-1777.
A. D. 1759.

§ 527. The first who reörganized the relations of the state upon these principles was Pombal, in Portugal, the all-powerful minister of Joseph Emmanuel. An attempt to murder the king, which was ascribed to the powerful family of Tavora and the instigations of the Jesuits, was made use of to drive the members of this Order out of Portugal, and afterwards to effect the enlightenment of the people by new seminaries of education and by the diffusion of printed books. The pervading activity of this able man was felt in every quarter. He had the affairs of the army and those relating to war placed on a better footing by the German marshal, William of Lippe-Schaumburg; he encouraged agriculture and industry, to draw the people from dirt and indolence; and when a fearful earthquake destroyed 30,000 houses in Lisbon, he was indefatigable in repairing the mischief. Pombal united the severity and arbitrariness of a despot to the courage and the penetrating will of a reformer. All the prisons were filled with those who opposed him. When these regained their liberty under the reign of the weak Maria, they united themselves for the overthrow of the minister, after which, Portugal was again plunged into the same wretched state as before. In Spain, similar attempts were made to reorganize the affairs of Church and State by liberal ministers, like Aranda and others. When the Jesuits opposed these innovations, Aranda ordered 5,000 of them to be arrested in a single night, embarked on board ships, without distinction of age or rank, and carried off like criminals, with great harshness, to the States of the Church. Their property was confiscated and their establishments closed. During the latter years of the reign of Charles III., however, the clergy and Inquisition again acquired great influence and destroyed or disturbed the greater number of the reforms. In France, the minister Choiseul belonged to the promoters of enlightenment and progress; but under the government of a voluptuous king, like Louis XV., no improvement could take place. After the ascension of the throne by Louis XVI., two men were called to the ministry who possessed both the power and the will to heal the shattered constitution of the state by effectual reforms—Turgot and Malesherbes. They proposed that a new mode of taxation should be introduced, that the nobility and clergy should bear their share of the burdens of the state, and that the institutions of the middle ages should be modified so as to suit the present times. Civil equality before the law, without regard to person, rank, or religion, was to be everywhere maintained; but their plans were shipwrecked by the selfishness of the nobles and the clergy, and by the blindness of the court.

November, 1755.

Charles III., A. D. 1759-1788.

France. Choiseul.

Turgot and Malasherbes, A. D. 1776.

§ 528. Similar attempts at reform were made about the same time
Christian, VII., in the North and East of Europe. In Denmark, under the
A. D. imbecile king, Christian VII., the German physician, Struen-
1766-1808. see, arrived at the dignity of count of the empire and prime minister, by the aid of the queen, Caroline Matilda, a daughter of the royal house of England. Furnished with unheard-of powers, so that all orders signed by him and provided with the seal of the cabinet possessed the same validity as if the king himself had subscribed them, Struensee adopted a multitude of arrangements, in the spirit of the age, for the relief of the citizen and peasant classes, for the curtailment of the power of the nobility, and for the improvement of the proceedings of justice. A man without remarkable qualities, without strength of character, without courage or resolution, he soon laid himself open in such a way that his fall was readily accomplished. His confidential relations with the high-minded although imprudent queen received an unfavorable interpretation; he offended the national feeling of the Danes by his use of the German language in all official proclamations; and by the want of courage he displayed on the occasion of a trifling tumult among the military and sailors, he rendered himself contemptible, and inspired his opponents with confidence. Whilst the minister was at a ball, Juliana, Christian's step-mother, pressed into the king's bedchamber with some of her confidants, and, by her description of the dangers that were threatening, induced him to sign a number of orders of arrest that were already prepared. Upon this, Struensee and his friend Brandt were committed to prison, and, after a most iniquitously conducted trial, punished, the one by being beheaded,
August 28, the other by the loss of his right hand. Caroline Matilda,
1772. betrayed by the weakness of Struensee, was separated from
A. D. 1775. the king, and died, after three years of wretchedness, in Celle. After the death of Struensee, Juliana took possession of the government, and ordered, through her favorite Guldberg, all the offensive reforms to be repealed. But when the Crown Prince, Frederick, came of age, he conducted the government in his father's name, and made over the conduct of the ministry to the gallant Bernstorf.

§ 529. In Sweden, the power of the aristocracy attained its full deve-
Adolf Frede- lopment under the reign of the good-natured king, Adolf Fre-
rick, A. D. derick. The council of state, which had the management of
1757-1771. every thing, consisted of men without either honor or patriotism, who sold themselves to foreign powers, and served the interests of those states from which they drew the largest sums of money; the honor and well-being of the country was a point they never considered. Two parties, called "Hats" and "Caps," the former in the pay of France, the latter in that of Russia, hated and persecuted each other even unto bloodshed, and made the Diet the scene of their hostile attacks. The king possessed neither power nor respect. This state of things came to an end.

when, after the death of Adolf Frederick, the adroit and popular Gustavus III. ascended the throne. Brave, chivalrous, and eloquent, he easily gained over the Swedish army and people to his side, and then compelled the state council, after he had surrounded their house of assembly with troops, to consent to alterations in the government. By this bloodless revolution, the executive power was restored to the crown, and the council of state reduced within the bounds of a deliberative assembly. The disposition of the land and sea forces, and the appointment of state and military officers, were in the hands of the king. He was to collect the votes of the Estates before levying a tax, declaring war, or concluding a peace. But after a few years, he freed himself from this restraint also, by an arbitrary exercise of power, and gave absolute authority to the throne. Endowed with many talents and kingly qualities, Gustavus III. took advantage of his lofty position to introduce many reforms in the government and administration of justice, which contributed to the welfare of his people, and were in accordance with the spirit of the times. But many of his proceedings were the result of a love of magnificence, a desire to imitate French fashions, and an attachment to the departed times of chivalry. The founding of an academy upon the French model, the erection of theatres and opera houses, the revival of tournaments and running at the ring, occasioned great expenses to the impoverished country. The king's unseasonable dreams of heroism, and his chivalrous whims, gave a distorted turn to his activity. When he declared that the distillation of brandy was a privilege of royalty, and compelled the Swedes to buy their accustomed beverage, which hitherto almost every family had prepared for itself, for a high price at the royal distilleries, and when he undertook a useless and expensive war, both by sea and land, with Russia, the affection of his people gradually decayed; and when, at length, before the former wounds had ceased to bleed, he meditated a war with France, for the purpose of opposing the Revolution, and saving the crown of Louis XVI., a conspiracy was formed, in consequence of which Gustavus III. was shot at a masked ball by Ankarstrom, a former officer of the guard.

Gustavus III., A. D. 1771-1791.

A. D. 1788.

A. D. 1790.

March 29, 1792.

Austria.

§ 530. In Austria, Maria Theresa, in conjunction with the enlightened minister, Kaunitz, was the first to abolish many abuses, and to introduce many timely reforms. The affairs of the army and of war were reorganized, the administration of justice was in every way improved; new seminaries of education were established, and the economy of the state properly arranged. But she proceeded with prudence and discretion, and treated with forbearance not only the national faith, but the national rights, and the established usages and customs. Not so her son Joseph II. Scarcely had he become the absolute ruler of the vast Austrian empire, before he undertook a series of reforms which offended the clergy and the zealous friends of the Church, prejudiced the privileged nobility, and outraged the national feelings of the subjects of the imperial house. He first introduced religious toleration, and afforded the adherents of the Lutheran, Calvinistic, and Greek Churches the free exercise of their religion, and equal civil and political rights with the Catholics; he then diminished the number of monasteries, and applied the property of the Church which was thus obtained to the improvement of schools, and to the erection of establishments of general utility; he limited pilgrimages and processions, and embarrassed the communication and intercourse of the clergy with Rome. It was in vain that pope Pius VI. endeavored to bring the emperor to a different course by the unexampled proceeding of a journey to Vienna. Joseph received him with the greatest respect, but remained firm to his purpose. Not less fertile of results were his reforms in civil and political matters. He established personal freedom by the abolition of serfdom, and civil legal equality by the introduction of an equitable system of taxation, and of equality in the eye of the law, without regard to rank or person. Joseph II. had the noblest intentions in these innovations; but he proceeded with too great haste, and too little regard to existing relations, customs, and prejudices, and did not allow the seed the necessary time to ripen. He thus placed in the hands of the opponents of progress the means of throwing suspicion upon his actions and efforts, and of depriving his measures, which were calculated for the happiness of mankind, of all their fruits. When he attempted to introduce his reforms into the Austrian Netherlands also, established a new high court of justice in Brussels, and commenced the reorganization of the university of Louvain, which was under the guidance of the clergy, disturbances arose that at length terminated in a universal rebellion. The Netherlanders refused the taxes, drove the Austrian regency, along with the weak garrison, out of the country, and declared in a congress the independence of the Netherlands. This event, which had been brought about by the nobility and clergy, and similar occurrences in Hungary, broke the heart of the irritable emperor, and hastened his death, the seeds of which he had imbibed in the unhealthy lands of the Danube, during the Turkish wars, when he was the ally of Russia. Joseph's indefatigable exertions, and the activity with which he superintended every thing himself, the freedom with which he admitted both high and low to his presence, and his abolition of the tyranny of officials, met with no appreciation; his views were misunderstood and misrepresented, his noblest plans were frustrated, and his name calumniated. But posterity, which can appreciate more justly his intentions and his efforts, will ever bless his memory. His brother and

Joseph II., A. D. 1780-1790.

A. D. 1787.

A. D. 1790.

February 20, 1790.

Leopold II., A. D. 1790-1792.

successor, Leopold II., restored most of the ancient usages, and thus brought back peace in Belgium and Hungary.

Russia. Catherine II., A. D. 1762-1796. § 531. Even uncivilized Russia felt the influence of the spirit of the age, under the long and splendid reign of Catherine II. The empress possessed great talents for government, and a susceptible mind; she maintained a correspondence with Voltaire and others of similar sentiments, invited Diderot to St. Petersburg, and encouraged sciences and arts. She improved the administration of justice, founded schools and academies, and adopted many arrangements that gave an air of civilization to the country, and which were loudly applauded by the French authors. But the greater part was mere illusion; the celebrated journey of the empress to Tauris, during which, artificial villages, shepherds and their flocks driven to the spot, and country festivals along the road, were to produce the belief that the land was blooming and prosperous, is an image of her whole reign. As regards the private life of the empress and her court, the same immorality, dissoluteness, and luxury reigned in St. Petersburg as in Paris. After Gregor Orloff, to whom the voluptuous empress had surrendered both her person and her empire in return for the share he had taken in the murder of her husband, followed a succession of other paramours, who were all loaded with wealth and honors. The situation of the favored lover of the empress was at length disposed of like a court-office. No one, however, enjoyed her favor so long as Potemkin the Taurian. For a space of sixteen years, he conducted the affairs of government and Potemkin, A. D. 1791. the plans of conquest, lived during the whole of the time in a state of magnificence that bordered on the fabulous, and displayed the wealth that was showered upon him by his liberal mistress in a manner truly remarkable. It was only a man with a spirit of enterprise so daring as to spare neither money nor human life, who, in the eyes of the empress, was capable of giving the befitting glory and renown to her government. The rebellion of Pugatscheff, a Don Cossack, who A. D. 1774. called himself Peter III., and who found many adherents in the neighborhood of the Volga, was speedily suppressed. A. D. 1775. Pugatscheff, betrayed by his bosom friend, was beheaded in Moscow, and his body cut to pieces.

3. THE PARTITIONS OF POLAND, AND RUSSIA'S WAR WITH THE TURKS.

§ 532. The kingdom of Poland had long been a rotten structure, which was preserved upright only by the divisions and jealousies of the neighboring states, and not by its own strength. The elective constitution was the misfortune of the country; every vacancy of the throne produced the most violent contests, by which the nation was divided into parties, bribery and corruption became predominant, and the nobles attained such privileges as were inconsistent with any well organized state policy. The throne was powerless; the Diet, from which "Republican Poland" received her laws, became proverbial from the vehement party contests that rendered every debate fruitless; the whole power was placed in the hands of the armed confederation. A kingdom, where it was only the noble who possessed liberty or the privilege of bearing arms, and who, relying upon his sword, despised the law; where enslaved peasants were held in a condition of serfdom; where commerce, which in other lands is carried on by a cultivated class of citizens, was in the hands of sordid and avaricious Jews, must needs have excited the cupidity of ambitious neighbors.

Augustus III., After the death of Augustus III., the Polish empire again
A. D. 1763. became the prey of the old elective tempests, till at length, Stanislaus Poniatowski, one of the former lovers of the empress Catherine II., was chosen king in the plain of Wola, amidst the clash of Rus-
September, 4, sian sabres. Poniatowski was a connoisseur and patron of
1764. literature and the arts, and an amiable and accomplished gen-
Poniatowski, tleman, but without strength of character or power of will.
A. D. Weak, and with no consistency of character, he was a mere
1764–1795. tennis-ball in the hands of the powerful. The Russian ambassador in Warsaw possessed greater power than he did; and, to prevent the possibility of Poland's escape from this state of disorder and feebleness, Russia and Prussia determined upon maintaining the ancient constitution unaltered.

§ 533. It happened at this crisis, that the Polish Dissidents, under which term were included not only the Protestants and Socinians, but also the adherents of the Greek Church, petitioned the Diet for the restoration of the ecclesiastical and civil privileges of which they had been deprived by the Jesuits. Their petition, although supported by Russia, Prussia, and most of the Protestant governments, was rejected at the Diet by the Catholic nobility, at the instigation of the clergy. The Dissidents, in combination with the "discontented," now formed the General Confederation of Radom, called upon Russia for assistance,
July 23, 1767. and extorted the free exercise of religion, admission to offices, and the churches they had before possessed, from the Diet. Surrounded by Russian troops, the representatives subscribed, under the portrait of the empress, the act of toleration, that was greeted by all Europe, and which was the sign of the impotence of Poland. That this impotence might be permanent, it was decided that no change should be made in the existing constitution without the consent of Russia.

These proceedings offended the national feeling of the Polish patriots, and aroused the religious hatred of the Catholic zealots. The ante-con-
February 28, federation of Bar was formed, which was to free the Poles
1768. from Russian supremacy, and to wrest from the Dissidents

the rights that had been conceded them. France supported it with money and officers. A furious war now arose between the two confederations. But the Russian army, which had remained in the country for the protection of the Diet and the Dissidents, carried off the victory. Bar and Cracow, the chief strongholds of the enemy, were stormed, and they were compelled to take refuge in the Turkish dominions. The Russians followed them over the borders, and did not refrain from murdering, plundering, and devastating even on a foreign soil.

§ 534. This infringement of territory induced the Porte, which was urged on by the French ambassadors, to declare hostilities against Russia, whereupon the Turkish war burst forth, which for six years fearfully convulsed the east of Europe both by land and sea.

First Turkish War, A. D. 1768-1774.

Whilst Romanzoff, after two bloody encounters, was conquering Moldavia and Wallachia, and the dreadful storm of Bender was filling all Europe with astonishment, the Morea, where the Greeks, relying upon the assistance of Russia, had risen against the rule of the Turks, was horribly ravaged with fire and sword by the latter, so that whole districts were covered with ruins and corpses; and in the haven of Tschesme, opposite the island of Chios, the whole Turkish fleet was destroyed by fire.

July, 16, A. D. 1771.

At the same time, Moscow and its neighborhood were visited by a desolating pestilence, and, in Poland, the civil war still raged with increasing fury. It was only by a miracle that Poniatowski escaped from some conspirators, who wished to carry him off from Warsaw. On every side the eye encountered plains soaked with blood, villages burnt to the ground, and weeping inhabitants. The impotence and divisions of Poland invited the neighboring powers to attempt a partition of her territory. After a personal interview between Frederick II. and Joseph II. (the rightminded Maria Theresa was hostile to the scheme,) and a visit of prince Henry of Prussia to St. Petersburg, a treaty of partition was arranged between Russia, Austria, and Prussia, in consequence of which each of these states took possession of the portion of Poland which adjoined their own territories.

August 5, 1772.

It was in vain that the Diet opposed itself courageously and resolutely to the execution of this project, and showed that the pretended rights and claims which the powers insisted upon had long been given up by contracts, surrenders, and treaties of peace; it was in vain that it solemnly protested before God and the world against such an abuse of superior power, and against a proceeding which outraged truth and good faith; surrounded and threatened by Russian arms, it at length yielded to force, and consented to the surrender of the country. It was thus that Polish Prussia, together with the district of the Netz, and the fertile lands of the Vistula (Elbing, Marienburg, Culm, &c.) became the property of Prussia; Galicia, with the rich mines of Wielicza, of Austria; and the lands on the Dwina and

Dnieper, of Russia. The establishment of a "perpetual council," that was completely under Russian influence, deprived the king of the last remains of power. From this time forth, the Russian ambassador in Warsaw was the real governor of the Polish republic. Shortly after, Russia, by the peace of Kudschuck Kainardsche with the Porte, obtained the right of passage through the Dardanelles, and the protective government of Moldavia and Wallachia, and the peninsula of the Crimea.

§ 535. Russia's thirst of conquest was not satisfied with this. A few years afterwards, the khan of the Tartars was compelled to lay down his office; upon which, Potemkin conquered the Crimea, after
A. D. 1783. dreadful devastations, and united it, with the other lands on the Black Sea, into one territory, distinguished by the ancient name of Tauris. Colonists were called forth from Germany into the desolate steppes, the trading towns of Cherson and Odessa arose, and deceived the world by the outward appearance of civilization. But the happiness and prosperity of the inhabitants disappeared with freedom; the once splendid city of tents degenerated into a camp of gypsies; and the houses and palaces of stone fell into ruins. The threatening neighborhood of
Second Turkish War, A. D. 1787-1792. Russia was a cause of anxiety to the Porte. Before long, a second furious war broke out, by land and sea, between Russia and Turkey. But this time, also, victory accompanied the Russian army and its dreadful leader. In the midst of winter, Po-
December 17, 1788. temkin stormed the strong city of Oczakow, after he had filled the trenches with blood and dead bodies; and the brave Suwaroff took the fortress of Ismael under circumstances of similar hor-
December 22, 1790. ror. The road to Constantinople now stood open to the Russians, and the name of Catherine's second grandchild, "Constantine," was supposed to indicate the secret intention of the empress to introduce a Christian prince into the Byzantine capital. This love of conquest displayed by Russia occasioned uneasiness to the other states. England and Prussia assumed a threatening aspect; Gustavus III. of Sweden attacked the Russians by sea and land; and Poland thought that the favorable moment had arrived for withdrawing herself from the dictatorial influence of Russia, and for again regaining her political independence. In alliance with Prussia, the Poles dissolved the perpetual
May 3, 1791. council, turned the elective empire into an hereditary monarchy, gave themselves a constitutional government with two chambers, and a stricter separation of the executive, legislative, and judicial powers.

§ 536. This constitution, appropriate to the age, and the work of patriotically-disposed men, was received with applause by the whole of Europe. The king swore to observe it. Frederick William II. expressed his favorable wishes: even Catherine concealed her vexation. A new spirit seemed to have taken possession of the nation. But party-

spirit and selfishness destroyed the good work. Many of the nobles were discontented with the change; a party was formed for the preservation of Polish "liberty," as they, in their delusion, called the ancient system, and they invoked the aid of the empress. The latter had just concluded the peace of Jassy with the Porte, and embraced with avidity the opportunity of marching her army upon the frontiers. Trusting to this assist-
January, 1792. ance, the Russian party formed the confederation of Targowicz, for the restoration of the old constitution. A Russian
May 14, 1792. army soon stood in the heart of Poland. In vain the patriots called upon Prussia for assistance; opinions had changed in Berlin; an alliance with Russia was preferred to the frienship of Poland, more particularly as an imitation of the new French ideas and forms of government was detected in the new constitution. Nevertheless, the Poles did not despair of their righteous cause. Kosciuzko, a brave soldier, who had fought in the cause of freedom under Washington in America, placed himself at the head of the patriots, and encountered the
July 17, 1792. superior force of the Russians at Dubienka. But party-spirit, dissension, treachery, and want of system impeded every undertaking, and paralyzed every power. The king, hitherto an enthusiastic adherent of the new constitution, soon fell into his old irresolution and faint-heartedness, and allowed himself to be so terrified by a threatening letter of the empress, that he joined the alliance of Targowicz, and renounced all further hostilities. The gallant warriors laid down the sword in wrath, and left their homes to escape the scorn of the victors.

But a new act of violence followed the victory. In April, Russia and
A. D. 1793. Prussia declared that it was necessary to inclose Poland within narrower limits, for the purpose of stifling the intoxication of liberty which had penetrated into the republic from France, and of preserving the neighboring states from every taint of democratic Jacobinism. It was in vain that the Diet assembled at Grodno opposed itself to this new treaty of partition. Every opposition gradually ceased, when Russian troops surrounded the house of assembly, and violently carried off the boldest speakers. Thus followed the second division of Poland,
July 22; October 14, 1793. by which Russia obtained the most important of the eastern districts (Lithuania, Little Poland, Volhynia, Podolia, Ukraine); Prussia gained possession of Great Poland, along with Dantzic and Thorn. The republic of Poland retained scarce a third of her former territory.

§ 537. The partitioned land was occupied by Russian and Prussian troops; and Catherine's ambassador, the coarse and brutal Igelstrom, ruled with pride and insolence in Warsaw. The national spirit of Poland was once more aroused. A secret conspiracy was formed, which extended its branches over the whole country. Kosciuzko and the emigrant patriots returned, and placed themselves at the head of the move-

34*

ment, the central point of which was Cracow. It was from this place that Kosciuzko, who had been named the absolute chief of the national force, issued a summons to the people, in which he represented the restoration of the freedom and independence of the country, the reconquest of the separated territories, and the introduction of a constitutional government, as the objects of the struggle. The insurrection quickly extended itself to the capital. The Russian garrison in Warsaw was attacked on Maundy-Thursday, and either cut to pieces or made prisoners. Igelstrom's palace was destroyed by fire; four of the most illustrious adherents of Russia died upon the gallows. The provinces followed the example of the capital; the king approved the revolt of the misused nation; and every thing promised a successful issue. The Prussians, who had marched into the neighborhood of Warsaw, were compelled to a hasty and disastrous retreat by the brave generals Kosciuzko, Dombrowski, and Joseph Poniatowski (the nephew of the king.) But the success of the Poles increased the enemy's desire of vengeance. Catherine, with the consent of Austria and Prussia, sent her most redoubted general, Suwaroff, into Poland. Kosciuzko was obliged to yield to the superior strength of his opponent. After an unsuccessful engagement, he fell, wounded, from his horse, with the exclamation, "the end of Poland!" and was carried off a prisoner. On the 4th of November, the suburb, Praga, was stormed by Suwaroff; 12,000 defenceless people were either slain or drowned in the Vistula. The shrieks of the slaughtered terrified the inhabitants of the capital, and made them willing to surrender. On the 9th of November, Suwaroff made his splendid entry into Warsaw as a conqueror. Poniatowski was obliged to surrender the crown. He lived in St. Petersburg, on an annuity, till his death in 1798, an object of deserved contempt. A few months later, the three powers declared that out of love for peace and the welfare of their subjects, they had decided upon the partition of the whole republic of Poland. Accordingly, the south, with Cracow, went to Austria; the land on the left of the Vistula, with the capital, Warsaw, to Prussia; Russia took possession of all the rest. Thus the once renowned and powerful Poland disappeared from the ranks of independent States, a victim to a weakness for which she was indebted to herself, and a violence that despised the rights of foreign nations. Kosciuzko, after being set at liberty by Paul I., died as a private man in Switzerland (October, 1817). His dead body was conveyed to Cracow.

April 17, 1794.

October 10, 1794.

January, 1795.

B. THE FRENCH REVOLUTION.

1. THE LAST DAYS OF ABSOLUTE MONARCHY.

Louis XV. died 1774.

§ 538. Louis XV. at first possessed the affections of his people to such a degree, that he was named the "Much-beloved;" and when he was attacked by a dangerous illness in Metz, the whole land went into mourning, and his recovery was celebrated by the greatest rejoicings. But this love gradually changed into hatred and contempt when the king gave himself up to the most shameless debaucheries, and surrendered the government of the country, the command of the army, and the decision upon points of law and state policy, to the companions of his orgies and the ministers of his lusts and pleasures; and when mistresses, without morals or decency, ruled the court and the empire. Among these women, none possessed greater or more enduring influence than the Marchioness of Pompadour, who guided the whole policy of France for a period of twenty years, filled the most important offices with her favorites, decided upon peace or war, and disposed of the revenues of the state as she did of her private purse, so that, after a life passed in luxury and splendor, she left millions behind her. She and her creatures encouraged Louis's excesses and love of pleasure, that he might plunge continually deeper in the pool of vice, and leave to them the government of the state. For the rest, the Pompadour used her position and her influence with a certain dignity, and with tact and discretion; but when the countess Du Barry, a woman from the very dregs of the people, occupied her place, the court lost all authority and respect.

§ 539. This reign of lust and extravagance, together with the useless and costly wars in Germany, exhausted the treasury and increased the burden of debts and taxation. And as all these taxes and imposts pressed entirely upon the citizen and peasant class, whilst the wealthy nobility and the clergy enjoyed an exemption, the man of moderate means was very heavily burdened, especially as the government did not superintend their collection, but left it in the hands of the farmers-general of the revenue and of their blood-sucking subordinates. The land and property-tax, the capitation-tax, the house-tax, the tolls and duties upon salt, wrested from the lower classes (who, in addition, had to pay tithes, labor-dues, and other feudal taxes to their landlords), the fruits of their industry, and prevented the rise of a prosperous middle class. It was the custom that all laws and ordinances relating to taxes should be registered in the parliament of Paris; hence it followed, that in default of the States-General, which since 1614 had no more been summoned, the validity of taxes and orders depended upon its sanction; and that it also possessed the right of opposing the laws and edicts relating to taxes by refusing their registration. This produced a violent contest between the parliament and government at every new tax, which was usually terminated by the king holding a "bed of justice," and overpowering resistance. Beside the tax edicts, the arbitrary *lettres de cachet* were another source of contention between the court and the parliament. These terrible letters, which were easily to be obtained by any one possessing any influence at court, were a despotic attack upon the liberty of the person, inasmuch as by their means any one might be arrested and imprisoned without a hearing. For ten years did the parliament struggle against the court and government, till Louis XV., weary of the perpetual opposition, at length gave a new direction to the matter, and ordered the members of the opposition to be arrested. But they again assumed the same attitude under his successor.

A. D. 1771.

§ 540. When Louis XV., in consequence of his excesses, was carried off in the midst of his sins by a frightful distemper, the treasury was exhausted, the country in debt, credit gone, and the people heavily oppressed by their burdens. It was under these melancholy circumstances, that an absolute throne descended to a prince who certainly possessed the best of hearts, but a weak understanding; who was good-natured enough to wish to relieve the condition of the people, but who possessed neither strength nor intellect for efficient measures. This prince was Louis XVI. Weak and indulgent, he allowed the frivolity and extravagance of his brothers, the count of Provence (afterwards Louis XVIII.), and the count of Artois (Charles X.); and permitted his wife, Marie Antoinette, the highly-accomplished daughter of Maria Theresa, to interfere in matters of state, and to exert a considerable influence upon the court and government. The queen, by her pride and haughty bearing, incurred the dislike of the people, so that they ascribed every unpopular measure to her influence, and put a bad construction upon every liberty she allowed herself in private. Even in the celebrated story of the necklace, in which some swindler made use of her name to gain possession of a splendid ornament, many believed her participation in the guilt.

Louis XVI., A. D. 1774-1793.

The prevailing want of money, and the disordered state of the revenue, could only be remedied by including the nobility and clergy in the taxation, by large reforms in the whole system of government, like those proposed by Turgot and Malesherbes, and by order and economy in the expenditure. But Louis XVI. had neither strength nor resolution to carry out such decisive measures; and as for economy, the extravagant court of Versailles would not listen to it. The Genevese banker, Necker, who undertook the management of the finances after Turgot, was as little in a position as his predecessor to reduce the disorder in the state economy; and when, upon the occasion of a loan, he exposed the financial condition of France in a pamphlet,

Necker's first ministry, A. D. 1771-1781.

he drew upon himself the displeasure of the court and the aristocracy to such a degree, that he was obliged to resign his office. This
A. D. 1781. happened at the time when the American war had increased the scarcity of money, and aroused the feeling of liberty and republicanism in France. It was, therefore, a great misfortune for the French monarchy, that just at this critical moment the frivolous and extravagant Calonne undertook the management of the finances. This man departed from the frugal plan of Necker, acceded to the wishes of the queen and the necessities of the princes and courtiers, and deluded the world with high-sounding promises of putting an end to all difficulties. The most splendid festivals were celebrated in Versailles, and the talents of Calonne loudly extolled. But his means, also, were soon exhausted. He was obliged to resolve upon calling an Assembly of Notables, consisting of nobles, clergy, high state officials, parliamentary council-
February, 1787. lors, and a few representatives of the towns. They rejected the proposal of a universal taxation, which should embrace both the nobles and clergy, and threatened the minister of finance with impeachment, who thereupon resigned his situation and proceeded to London.

§ 541. Calonne's successor in the management of the finances, Lomenie de Brienne, was in a difficult position. To cover the deficit in the revenue, he was obliged to have recourse to the usual measures, increasing the taxes and raising a loan, but encountered so violent an opposition from the parliament of Paris, that the government determined, since the worn out method of compulsion — a royal sitting — no longer availed, to arrest the boldest speakers and banish them to Troyes.
August, 1787. This proceeding excited a great commotion among the people, which induced the government to arrange a compromise with the banished members, and to again sanction the assemblies. But the spirit of opposition had become too strong, and had already seized upon the people. They formed a tumultuous meeting around the house of assembly, and saluted the speakers of the opposition with acclamations and the government party with abuse. They burned the detested minister of finance every day in effigy, and in several towns displayed the excited state of their minds by riotous proceedings. The cry for the States-General was heard in the streets as well as in parliament. It was in vain that the ministry attempted to overcome the opposition by converting the parliament into an upper court (*cour plénière*) and several
August, 1788. inferior courts; a new spirit had taken possession of the nation, that was at length to gain the victory. Brienne was
Necker's second ministry, A. D. 1788-1789. compelled to resign at a time when the scarcity of money had become so great that all ready money payments were suspended, and a state bankruptcy appeared inevitable. The popular favorite, Necker, was a second time summoned to the

ministry. He first allayed the irritation by repealing the resolutions against the parliament, and then made preparations for summoning the Estates. Owing to this, there soon arose a division between him and the parliament and Notables, whom he had again consulted. The latter were of opinion that the new assembly should conform itself, both as to the number of representatives and the mode of procedure, to the Estates of 1614, whilst Necker wished to allow a double representation to the third Estate, and that they should vote individually, and not as a class; a view that was supported by some of the ablest writers of the nation in a multitude of pamphlets. (Abbè Sieyes: "What is the third Estate?") Necker's opinion triumphed. An order of the king fixed the number of noble and ecclesiastical members at 300 each, that of the citizens at 600,
December, 1788. and appointed the following May as the time of opening.
Necker was the hero of the day, but he was not the pilot of the ship, he only "drove with the wind."

2. THE PERIOD OF THE NATIONAL ASSEMBLY.

§ 542. In the beginning of May, the deputies of the three Estates, and among them some of the ablest and most accomplished men of France, assembled at Versailles. The third Estate, irritated by the neglect of the court at the opening and during the audience, came to a rupture with the two privileged Estates at the first sitting, when the latter required that the Estates should carry on their debates separately, whilst the former insisted upon a general council and individual votes. After a contest of some weeks, the third Estate, which had chosen the astronomer, Bailli, the freedom-inspired representative of
June 17. Paris, for its President, but which was guided by the superior talents of Sieyes and Mirabeau, declared itself a National Assembly, upon which it was joined by portions of the other Estates. The Assembly at once passed the resolution of allowing the levying of the present taxes only so long as the Estates should remain undissolved. This proceeding disturbed the court, and inspired it with the thought of granting a constitution to the nation, and thus rendering the Estates unnecessary. For this purpose, a royal sitting was appointed, and the hall
June 20. of assembly closed for a few days. Upon the intelligence of this, the deputies proceeded to the empty saloon of the Tennis Court, and raised their hands in a solemn vow not to separate till they had given a new constitution to the nation. When this Court also was closed, the meetings were held in the church of St. Louis. The royal sitting took place on the 23d of June. But neither the speech of the king, nor the sketch of the new constitution, afforded due satisfaction, and they were consequently received with coldness. After the termination of the sitting, Louis dissolved the Assembly. The nobility and clergy obeyed, but the citizen class retained their seats, and when the master of the ceremonies

called upon them to obey, Mirabeau exclaimed, "Tell your master that we sit here by the power of the people, and that we are only to be driven out by the bayonet!" The weak king did not venture to en-
June 27. counter this resolute resistance by force, but rather advised the nobility and clergy to join the citizens.

§ 543. THE STORMING OF THE BASTILLE. — During these proceedings, the fickle populace of Paris were kept in a state of perpetual excitement by journals, pamphlets, and inflammatory harangues. In the open squares, in the coffee-houses, in taverns, and especially in the Palais-Royal, the dwelling of the profligate, ambitious, and wealthy duke of Orleans, violent discourses were held upon popular freedom, the rights of men, and the equality of all classes, by seditious demagogues, and the assembled crowds were excited to obtain these advantages by violence. Among these popular orators, the accomplished advocate, Camille Desmoulins, a fanatic in the cause of liberty, was especially preëminent. The military who were present in the capital were hurried away by the enthusiasm for liberty, and a portion enrolled themselves in the newly-formed National Guard. The government of the city was made over to a democratic municipality, at the head of which stood Bailli, as mayor. The court, alarmed at this increasing ferment, determined upon retiring to Versailles with a few regiments of German and Swiss troops. In this proceeding, the leaders of the movement believed they saw the purpose of some act of violence, and made use of it accordingly to excite fresh irritation. The intelligence was spread abroad in Paris, that Necker had been suddenly dismissed and banished from the country, and a favorite of the queen placed in his office. This was interpreted as the first step in the contemplated outrage, and proved the signal for a general rise. Crowds of the lowest mob, wearing the newly-invented national cockade, (blue, white, and red,) paraded riotously through the streets, the alarm-bell was sounded, the work-shops of the gunsmiths plundered; tumult and confusion reigned every where. On the 14th of July, after the populace had taken 30,000 stand of arms and some cannon from the Hospital of the Invalides, took place the storming of the Bastille, an old castle that served as a state prison. The governor, Delaunay, and seven of the garrison, fell victims to the popular rage; their heads were carried through the streets upon poles; and many men who were hated as aristocrats were put to death. The banished Necker was recalled, and his entrance into the towns and villages of France was celebrated as that of a hero crowned with victory. In this joyous reception of the minister, the people displayed their enthusiasm for liberty and their hatred to the court and the aristocracy. Lafayette, the champion of the liberty of America, was appointed commander of the National Guard, and whilst the king returned to Paris, and exhibited himself to the assembled people from the balcony of the council-house with the cockade in his hat, the count of Artois, and many nobles of the first rank, as Condé, Polignac, left their country in mournful anticipation of coming events.

§ 544. THE NEW SYSTEM. — Since the storming of the Bastille, the laws and magistrates had lost their authority in France, and the power lay in the hands of the populace. The country people no longer paid their tithes, taxes, and feudal dues to the clergy and nobles, but took vengeance for the long oppression they had suffered by destroying the manorial castles. When intelligence of these proceedings spread abroad, it was proposed, in the National Assembly, that the upper classes should prove to the people by their actions, that they were willing to lighten their burdens, and that, with this purpose, they should renounce, of their own free will, all the inherited feudal privileges of the middle ages. This proposal excited a storm of enthusiasm and self-renunciation. None would be behind-hand. Estates, towns, provinces, each strove for the honor of making the greatest sacrifices for the common good. This was the celebrated 4th of August, when, in one feverish and excited session, all tithes, labor-dues, manorial rights, corporate bodies, &c., were abolished, the soil was declared free, and the equality of all citizens of the state before the law and in regard to taxation was decreed. These resolutions, and the necessary laws and arrangements required for their reduction to practice, which were gradually adopted, produced in a short time a complete revolution in all existing conditions. The Church lost her possessions and was subjected to the state; monasteries and religious orders were dissolved, and the clergy paid by the state, the bishoprics newly regulated, and religious freedom established. Priests were required to swear allegiance, like officers of state, to the new constitution; but as the pope forbade it, the greater number refused the oath, which was the occasion of the French clergy being divided into sworn and unsworn priests; the latter lost their offices and were exposed to all kinds of persecutions, but enjoyed the confidence of the faithful among the people. The noble forfeited not only his privileges and the greater part of his income, but he also lost the external distinctions of his rank, by the abolition of all titles, coats of arms, orders, &c. Upon the principle of equality, all Frenchmen were to be addressed as "citizens." For the purpose of annihilating every remnant of the ancient system, France received a new geographical division into departments and *arrondissements;* a new system of judicature with jurymen; equality of weights, measures, and standards; and lastly, a constitutional government, in which the privileges of royalty were limited more than was reasonable, and the legislative power committed to a single chamber, with a universal right of suffrage.

August 4.

§ 545. THE KING AND THE NATIONAL ASSEMBLY AT PARIS. — When the king hesitated to promulgate the resolutions of the Assembly as laws, the report was again propagated of a contemplated stroke of state policy. This report gained strength when the Flemish regiment was ordered to Versailles, and the king was indiscreet enough to show himself, with the queen and dauphin, at a feast given by the body-guard to the newly-arrived officers, and thus to give occasion to imprudent speeches, toasts, and songs, among the assembled troops, who were heated with drinking. This occurrence was soon made known by busy tongues in Paris, and added to the popular excitement, which had besides been increased by a scarcity of bread. Accordingly, on the 5th of October, an immense multitude, chiefly of women, proceeded to Versailles to demand from the king relief from the scarcity of bread, and a return of the court to Paris. The king at first attempted to pacify them by a conciliatory answer. But a wing of the palace was stormed during the night, and the guard put to the sword; the arrival of Lafayette, with the National Guard, prevented any further mischief. Upon the following day, the king was obliged to consent to proceed to Paris with his family, under the escort of this frightful crew, and to take up his residence in the Tuileries, which had for many years remained unoccupied. Shortly after, the National Assembly also followed, for whom the riding-school in the neighborhood of the palace had been prepared. The power now fell more and more into the hands of the lower class, who were kept in perpetual excitement by licentious journalists and popular leaders, and were goaded to hatred against the court and the "aristocrats." The "Friend of the People," of the insolent Marat, a physician from Neufchatel, was distinguished by its violence. The democratic clubs, which increased every day in extent and influence, also aided the revolution. The Jacobin club, in particular, which had branches in all the towns of France, acquired a place in the history of the world. The members, who wore the red cap of the convicts of the galleys as a distinction, aimed at a republic, with freedom and equality for all the "citizens." With these was joined the club of Cordeliers, which numbered some of the most daring men of the revolution, as Danton and Camille Desmoulins, among its members. The Constitutional club, on the other hand, to which Lafayette had joined himself, declined in importance every day.

§ 546. The Ceremony of Federation.—Flight of the King.

July 14, 1790. On the day of the year in which the Bastille was taken, a grand federative festival was arranged in the Champ de Mars. It must have been a moving spectacle, when Talleyrand, at the head of 300 priests, clothed in white, and girded with tri-colored scarfs, performed the consecration of the banner at the altar of the country; when Lafayette, in the name of the National Guard, the president of the National Assembly, and, at length, the king himself, vowed fidelity to the Constitution; when the innumerable multitude raised their hands aloft and repeated after him the oath of citizenship, and the queen herself, carried away by enthusiasm, raised the Dauphin in the air and joined in the acclamations. This was the last day of happiness for the king, whose situation after this grew constantly worse. Necker, no longer equal to the difficulties, left France and retired to Switzerland. Mirabeau, won over by the court, opposed farther encroachments upon the kingly power with the whole of his eloquence, inasmuch as he believed a constitutional monarchy and not a republic to be the best government for France. Unfortunately for the king, this great man died, April 2, 1791. in his forty-second year, of a sickness brought on by his disorderly life and by over-exertion. A splendid funeral ceremony gave evidence of the influence of the man in whom sank the last strong pillar of the throne. Weak and unselfreliant as Louis XVI. was, he now lost all firmness. By his refusal to receive a sworn priest as his confessor, or to declare the emigrants traitors, who were endeavoring from Coblentz to excite the European courts to a crusade against France, he excited a suspicion that he was not honestly a supporter of the constitution he had sworn to maintain, and not altogether ignorant of the efforts of the emigrants. The more this suspicion gained ground with the people, the more perilous became the position of the king. At this crisis, Louis embraced the desperate resolution of secretly flying to the northern frontier of his kingdom. Bouillè, a resolute general in Lorraine, was let into the secret, and promised to support the scheme with his troops. Leaving behind him a letter, in which he protested against all the acts which had been forced from him since October, 1789, the king happily escaped, with his family, from Paris in a large carriage. But the clumsily executed project nevertheless miscarried. June 21, 1791. Louis was recognized in St. Menehould by the postmaster, Drouet, stopped by the militia at Varennes, and led back to Paris at the command of the National Assembly, who sent three of their members, and among them, Pètion, to receive the royal family. The suspension of the royal authority, which had already been pronounced by the Assembly, remained in force, till Louis proclaimed, and swore to observe, the Constitution completed at the end of September.

3. THE LEGISLATIVE ASSEMBLY AND THE FALL OF THE MONARCHY (OCTOBER 1, 1791 — SEPTEMBER 20, 1792.)

§ 547. THE GIRONDISTS. — As the members of the Constituent Assembly had voluntarily excluded themselves from the new Chamber, the èlections to the Legislative Assembly, which were carried on under the influence of the Jacobins, mostly terminated in favor of the republicans. These latter, however, soon divided into a radical-democratic and a moderate party: the former, from its position in the House, was called the Mountain; the latter received the name of Girondists, because many of its speakers were from Bordeaux and the department of the Gironde

Among the latter, who, at the commencement, assembled themselves around the minister, Roland, and his intelligent and high-minded wife, were men of great oratorical talents and exalted civic virtues, as Vergniaud, Lanjuinais, Barbaroux, Brissot, &c. The Girondists formed the majority, and the ministry, consisting of Roland, Dumourier, &c., belonged to this party.

The attention of the government and the Assembly was particularly directed to the priests, who had refused the oath, and to the emigrants. Both were endeavoring to overthrow the existing order of things: the former by exciting hatred and discontent among the French people; the latter by making military preparations at Coblentz, and endeavoring to stir up foreign powers to an armed invasion of France. The Assembly therefore determined upon seeking out and arresting the unsworn priests, and declaring the emigrants traitors and conspirators, and punishing them by the loss of their estates and incomes. The king put his veto upon both these resolutions, and prevented their execution. This refusal was ascribed to the secret hopes, entertained by the court, of assistance from foreign powers and of the triumph of the emigrants, and thus the temper of the people grew continually more hostile. It was also known that the queen was in correspondence with her brother, the emperor of Austria, and that she looked for support and safety to the emigrant nobility. Neither was it any longer doubtful that war must soon break out, since the emperor of Austria and the king of Prussia, after a conference in Pillnitz (August, 1791,) were making preparations, and demanded of the French government not only to make befitting indemnification to the German princes and nobles who had suffered loss by the abolition of tithes and feudal burdens, and to restore the province of Avignon, that had been wrested from the pope, but to arrange the government upon the plan proposed by the king himself in June, 1789. These demands were followed by a declaration of war against Austria and Prussia on the part of the French government, to which the king yielded his consent with tears. For the purpose of securing the capital and the National Assembly against any attack, it was resolved to summon 20,000 of the federates from the southern provinces, under pretence of celebrating the festival of the Bastille, and to commit the defence of Paris to them. But Louis refused his consent to this resolution also. Upon this, the Girondist ministers laid down their offices, after Madame Roland had reproached and reprimanded the king in a letter that was soon in the hands of every body. These proceedings increased the irritation to such an extent that it became easy for the republicans to excite a popular insurrection. On the 20th of June, the anniversary of the meeting in the Tennis Court, the terrible mob, armed with pikes, marched from the suburbs, under the conduct of the brewer, Santerre, and the butcher, Legendre, into the Tuileries, to force the king to con-

April 20, 1792.

firm the decree against the unsworn priests and for the summoning of the National Guard. But here also Louis remained firm. He defied for several hours all threats and dangers, and endured the insolence of the mob, who even placed the red Jacobin cap upon his head and gave him wine to drink, with the courage of a martyr. The rather tardy arrival of Pétion with the National guard at length freed him from his perilous position.

§ 548. These proceedings were the prelude to the eventful TENTH OF AUGUST. War had already commenced, to the great joy of the Prussian officers, who promised themselves great glory and little trouble from the "military promenade," as they called the French campaign. The Prussians marched into Lorraine under the command of duke Ferdinand of Brunswick, who had become known in the Seven Years' war. An Austrian force, under Clerfait, was placed at his command; 12,000 emigrants joined themselves to him, who were burning with eagerness to overthrow the "government of advocates," and to have vengeance upon their enemies. On setting out, the duke published a manifesto, drawn up by one of the emigrants, full of injurious menaces against the National Assembly, the city of Paris, the National Guard, and all the French who favored the new system. The insolent tone of this proclamation made an indescribable impression upon the people, who were enthusiastic for the new order of things, and produced the fiercest rage against the emigrants and their defenders. This feeling was taken advantage of by the Jacobins for the overthrow of the king. Supported by the declaration of the Assembly, "The country is in danger," they summoned from Marseilles, Brest, and other maritime towns, crowds of the lowest refuse of the people, even galley-slaves, to Paris, then formed a committee of insurrection, and prepared the rude and sturdy inhabitants of the suburbs for a decisive blow. The alarm sounded at midnight on the 10th of August. A fearful mob proceeded, in the first place, to the Hôtel de Ville, for the purpose of establishing a new democratic municipality, and then marched to the royal palace, which was defended by 900 Swiss, and the Parisian National Guard under the command of Mandat. The honest Mandat was resolved to check the advancing masses, which were ever assuming a more menacing aspect, by force; his destruction was consequently resolved upon by the democrats. He was commanded to appear at the Hôtel de Ville, and assassinated on his way thither; upon which the National Guard, uncertain what to do, and disgusted by the presence of a number of nobles in the palace, for the most part dispersed. The mob constantly assumed a more threatening aspect; cannon were turned upon the palace, the pikemen pressed forwards upon every entrance, the people loudly demanded the deposition of the king. At this crisis, Louis suffered himself to be persuaded to seek for protection with his family in the hall of the National Assembly, where they passed sixteen hours in a narrow closet. The king had scarcely left the palace, before the tumultuous multitude pressed forward more violently; the Swiss guard maintained a gallant resistance, and defended the entrance. When the report of musketry was heard in the adjoining Assembly, the indignant representatives of the people compelled the intimidated king to give his guard orders to cease firing. By this order, the faithful defenders of monarchy were doomed to destruction. Scarcely had the furious mob observed that the enemy's fire had ceased, before they stormed the palace, slaughtered those they found in it, and destroyed the furniture. Nearly 5,000 men, and among them, 700 Swiss, fell in the struggle, or died afterwards, the victims of the popular fury. In the mean time, the National Assembly, upon the proposal of Vergniaud, embraced the resolution "to suspend the royal authority, to place the king and his family under control, to give the prince a tutor, and to assemble a National Convention." The Temple, a strong fortress erected by the knights templars, soon enclosed the imprisoned royal family.

§ 549. The Days of September. — After the suspension of the king, a new ministry was formed by the National Assembly, in which, by the side of the Girondist, Roland, and others, the terrible Danton held office as minister of justice. This ministry, and the new Common Council of Paris which had appointed itself, and which, after the 10th of August, had strengthened itself by members who might be depended upon as hesitating at no wickedness, now possessed the whole power. The Municipal Council ordered the police of the capital to be conducted by pikemen, and the prisons were quickly filled with the "suspected" and "aristocrats." It was now that the frightful resolution was matured of getting rid of the opponents of the new order of things by a bloody tribunal, and of suppressing all resistance by terror. After the recusant priests had been slaughtered by hundreds in the monasteries and prisons, the dreadful days of September were commenced. From the 2d to the 7th of September, bands of hired murderers and villains were collected round the prisons. Twelve of them acted as jurymen and judge, the others as executioners. The imprisoned, with the exception of a few whose names were marked upon a list, were put to death by this inhuman crew under a semblance of judicial proceedings. Nearly 3,000 human beings were either put to death singly, or slaughtered in masses, by these wretches, who received a daily stipend from the Common Council for their "labors." Among the murdered was the princess Lamballe, the friend of the queen; a troop of pikemen carried her head upon a pole to the Temple, and held it before Maria Antoinette's window. The example of the capital was imitated in many of the departments. The barbarous destruction of all statues, coats of arms, inscriptions, and other memorials of a former period, formed the conclusion of the August and

September days, which were the transition period between the French monarchy and republic. The autumnal equinox was distinguished as the commencement of the reign of liberty and equality under the republican National Convention. September 21.

Lafayette, who was serving with the northern army, and who, after the days of June, had returned to Paris on his own responsibility, for the purpose, if possible, of saving the king, was now summoned before the National Assembly to answer for his conduct. Convinced that the Jacobins were seeking his death, he fled, with some friends who shared his sentiments, to Holland, that he might escape to America; but he fell into the hands of enemies, who treated him like a prisoner of war, and allowed him to live for five years in the dungeons of Olmutz and Magdeburg. Talleyrand repaired to England, and thence to America, where he awaited better times.

4. REPUBLICAN FRANCE UNDER THE GOVERNMENT OF THE NATIONAL CONVENTION (SEPTEMBER, 1792 — OCTOBER, 1795).

§ 550. EXECUTION OF THE KING. — The new Assembly, which, under the influence of the Jacobins, had been elected by universal suffrage, was composed almost exclusively of republicans, but of different dispositions and opinions. The moderates, Girondists, who were aiming at a republican form of government upon the model of antiquity, or upon that of the North Americans, and who abhorred bloodshed as a means, gradually fell before the radicals and democrats, who first overthrew by violence all the existing arrangements, and then sought to found a new system of "liberty and equality" upon the levelled surface. They acted upon the principle, "that he who is not for us is against us," and attempted to bear down all opposition by terror and bloodshed. Strong in the Jacobin clubs and in the wild bands of the numerous defenders of the revolution, who were distinguished by the name of "Sans-Culottes," and who were maintained in a constant state of excitement by songs (Marseillaise, Ca ira), revolution festivals, trees of liberty, and such matters, the destructive party soon obtained the upper hand. The trial of the king, "Louis Capet," was one of the first proceedings of the National Convention. An iron safe had been discovered in a wall of the Tuileries, containing secret letters and documents, from which it was apparent that the French court had not only been in alliance with Austria and the emigrants, and had projected plans for overthrowing the Constitution that had been sworn to by Louis, but that it had also attempted to win over single members of the National Assembly (for example, Mirabeau), by annuities, bribery, and other means. It was upon this that the republicans, who would willingly have been quit of the king, founded a charge of treason and conspiracy against the country and the people. Louis, with the assistance of two advocates, to whom the noble

Malasherbes, of his own free impulse, associated himself, appeared twice before the Convention (11th and 26th December), but despite his own dignified bearing and defence, and despite the efforts of the Girondist party to have the sentence referred to a general assembly of the people, January 17, 1793. Louis was condemned to death in a stormy meeting, by a small majority of five voices. The party of the Mountain, where the advocate, Maximilian Robespierre, the former marquis St. Just, the frightful Danton, the lame Couthon, and the duke of Orleans, who had assumed the name of Citizen Egalité, were the leaders and chiefs, had left no means unattempted to produce this result by terror; they would, nevertheless, have failed in their purpose, had they not carried a resolution beforehand in the Assembly, that a bare majority should be sufficient for a sentence of death, and not, as had heretofore been the custom, that two thirds of the votes should be necessary. The murder was thus veiled by a show of justice. On the 21st of January, the unfortunate king ascended the scaffold in the square of the Revolution. The drums of the National Guard drowned his last words, and "Robespierre's women" greeted his bloody head with the shout of "Vive la République."

§ 551. Dumourier. — In the mean time, the Prussians had marched through Lorraine into Champagne. But the duke of Brunswick, accustomed to the slow and circumspect proceedings of the Seven Years' war, wasted time in the conquest of unimportant fortresses, and entered Champagne in an unfavorable period of the year, when the roads were impassable from the rain, and the army was weakened and destroyed by September 20, 1792. the use of unwholesome provisions and of unripe fruit. After the battle of Valmy, where Dumourier and Kellerman successfully repulsed the attack of the enemy, the Prussian generals relinquished the idea of any farther advance, and concluded a compromise with Dumourier, by which the Prussians were assured of an uninterrupted retreat. The Austrians, who had marched from the Netherlands, November 6. met with no better success. After the battle of Jemappes, Dumourier conquered Belgium and Liege, and threatened the frontiers of Holland, whilst the hussar-general, Custine, made him-October 21, 1792. self master of the towns on the Rhine, and gained the fortress of Mayence, where there were many adherents of the ideas of freedom and equality, for the French republic. The citizens of Mayence, deserted by their elector, their clergy, and the nobility, received the French troops with enthusiasm. George Foster, the circumnavigator of the globe, was the soul of the republican party in Mayence. This success of the French arms inspired the republicans with fresh courage, and the powers of Europe with fresh alarm. Were they to look quietly on, whilst a king was murdered in a revolting manner in Paris, whilst the revolutionists, intoxicated with success, called upon the people everywhere to overthrow their monarchical governments, and promised them the protection of the French nation in establishing their republics? The enthusiasm of the people for the new ideas gave great assistance to the republican arms: not only the thrones of kings and the dominions of princes, but the privileges and possessions of the nobility and clergy, were in peril. Fresh armies from all parts of Europe were therefore marched across the French frontiers, for the purpose of suppressing a revolution which endangered the peace and security of other states. England, where the Tories, under the guidance of the younger Pitt, were in possession of the government, and where the orator, Edmund Burke, once the advocate of the American War of Liberty both in speech and writing, took the field against the Revolution, and solemnly separated himself from his old friend, Fox, the leader of the liberal Whigs, headed the "Coalition" against France. English subsidies soon gave fresh life to the war. An Austrian army appeared in the Netherlands under the prince of Coburg, who was assisted by Clerfait and the Archduke Charles, drove back the French over the Maase, and defeated Dumourier at Neerwinden. This defeat was ascribed by Dumourier principally to the Jacobins, because they had corrupted the army, had neglected the necessary military supplies, and had placed an incompetent coadjutor by his side. In his disgust, he allowed it to appear pretty unequivocally that he meditated the overthrow of the republican constitution, and the reëstablishment of a king (for which office he had selected the duke of Orleans, or his son, Louis Philippe.) The Convention, apprised of this intention, impeached the general, and required his presence in Paris to answer for himself. But instead of obeying the summons, Dumourier ordered the ambassadors of the Convention to be seized and delivered up to the enemy, and then went over with a part of his troops to the Austrians.

March 18, 1793.

About the same time, Mayence, after the most obstinate defence, and after enduring the extremities of famine, fell again into the hands of the Prussians, who once more approached the frontiers of France.

§ 552. Dumourier's treachery was employed by the Jacobins for the overthrow of the Girondists, to which party Dumourier had belonged. The Girondists, enraged at the increasing power of the populace in Paris, and the unbridled acts of violence committed by the mob, entertained the project of converting France into a republican union like North America, and by this means, destroying the supremacy of the capital. The Mountain and the Jacobins, who saw that this scheme would weaken the revolutionary power of France, and endanger the future of the democratic republic, commenced a war of life and death with the Girondists (also called Brissotins) upon this point. They accused them of an understanding with Dumourier, they reproached them with weakening the power of the people, and destroying the republic at a moment when France was threatened with enemies both within and without; and when all these attacks were ignominiously repulsed by the victorious eloquence of the Girondists, the savage Marat, in his "Friend of the People," called upon the populace to rise against the moderate and lukewarm, and thus gave occasion to daily riots and tumults, which disturbed the capital and endangered life and property. All moderate and reputable people were in continual peril. It was in vain that the Girondists succeeded in having Marat brought before a court of justice, he was acquitted by the Jacobins, and carried back to the Convention in triumph by the people; it was in vain that the Girondists procured the appointment of a Commission of Twelve, who were to discover and punish the exciters of the tumult. When the Commission ordered Hebert, who, in his vulgar and libellous journal, "Pére Duchesne," excited the people to tumult and murder, and some of his associates, to be imprisoned, the raging mob compelled their release, and then arranged the great insurrection of the 31st of May and 1st of June. They made the branded Henriot, who had first been a lacquey, then a smuggler, and lastly a spy of the police, commander of the National Guard. Under his guidance, the innumerable multitude of the sans-culottes surrounded the Tuileries, where the Convention was holding its meeting, and demanded with threats the abolition of the Commission of Twelve, and the exclusion of the Girondists and the moderates. It was in vain that the latter employed the whole force of their eloquence to induce the Assembly not to consent to the demands of the people: the mob pressed into the hall and the galleries, and demanded its sacrifice with wild shouts and cries. It was in vain that the majority of the Assembly, the courageous president, Herault, at their head, attempted to leave the apartment where they could no longer debate in freedom; driven back by Henriot, nothing was left to them but to consent to the demands of the people and the party of the Mountain, and to admit the supremacy of the mob. Thirty-four Girondists were immediately thrust out and imprisoned; twenty of them (Pétion, Guadet, and Barbaroux, were of the number) escaped, and summoned the inhabitants of Normandy, Bretagne, and the maritime cities of the south, to take up arms against the Jacobins; the remainder died some time after on the guillotine. The assassination of Marat, by the noble Charlotte Corday, who was inspired by a spirit of genuine liberty, and a frightful civil war, were the first results of this act of violence. Most of the escaped Girondists also died violent deaths, by their own hands or those of others. Thus died Roland, Pétion, Barbaroux, Condorcet, and others. Madame Roland also died on the guillotine. Seventy-three members of the Convention, who had sided with the Girondists, were also expelled, so that the Convention was now entirely ruled by the democrats of the Mountain.

§ 553. THE REIGN OF THE JACOBINS. — The National Convention

acquired greater unanimity by the exclusion of the Girondists and the moderates; so that, from this time, it was enabled to develop a frightful power and activity. For the purpose of better superintending and conducting its multitudinous affairs, it resolved itself into committees, of which the committee of public safety and that of public security acquired a frightful celebrity by the persecution of every one opposed to the new order of things. A revolutionary tribunal, consisting of twelve jurymen and five judges, to which that man of blood, Fouquier Tinville, occupied the office of public accuser, seconded the activity of these committees by a cruel and summary administration of justice. At the head of the committee of public safety stood three men, whose names became the terror and horror of all just men; the envious and malignant Robespierre, the bloodthirsty Couthon, and the fanatic for republican liberty and equality, St. Just. They pursued their bloody object without regard to human life; every thing that ventured to oppose their stormy course was unpityingly hurled down. Thus originated the terrible period of the years '93 and '94, which displayed itself in three different directions — within, by a cruel persecution of all citizens who were known as aristocrats or favorers of royalty, and by a bloody suppression of insurrections in the south and west; without, by a vigorous defensive war against innumerable enemies.

§ 554. — 1. Persecution of Aristocrats. — Since the municipal government in Paris had been in the exclusive possession of Jacobins and democrats of the extreme class, since democratical committees had had the political supervision of all the sections, since, besides the National Guard, a revolutionary army of sans-culottes had stood at the disposal of the republican government, the whole power had been in the hands of the populace and their frantic leaders. The Jacobin clubs in Paris and the provincial cities possessed the government; their orators and presidents executed, with the aid of the people, the most sanguinary outrages upon all who were not of their own party. The most effectual means of destroying all opponents was the frightful law against the suspected, which threatened with death all "enemies of the country," all who manifested any attachment to the former condition of things, or to the priesthood or the nobility. In consequence of this and similar laws, the prisons were filled with thousands of so-called aristocrats; and forty or sixty men were daily dragged to the guillotine. All those who were distinguished from the ruling democracy by rank, wealth, refinement, or nobility of mind, stood in continual peril of their lives. The malicious slander of an enemy, the accusation of a spy, the hatred of a sans-culotte, were sufficient to bring an innocent man to prison, and from prison to the scaffold. The transition was so sudden, that death lost its terrors, and the prison became the scenes of cheerful and refined society, and of intellectual conversation. The most noble and distinguished men of France

were among the victims. The former minister, Malasherbes, the members of the Constituent Assembly, Bailli, Barnave, &c., all who belonged to the old monarchy, and who had not saved themselves by flight, died by the guillotine. Among them was the severely-tried queen, Marie
October 16. Antoinette, who displayed, during her trial and at her execution, a firmness and strength of soul that was worthy of her education and her birth. Her son died beneath the cruel treatment of a Jacobin; her daughter (the duchess of Angoulême) carried a gloomy spirit and an embittered heart with her to the grave. Louis XVI.'s
May 10, 1794. pious sister, Elizabeth, also died on the scaffold; the head of the profligate duke of Orleans, whom even the favor of Danton could not preserve from the envy of Robespierre, had fallen before her own.

§ 555.—2. Outrages in the South.—The bloody rule of the Mountain party displayed itself in its most frightful excess in the suppression of the revolt against the reign of terror. When the inhabitants of Normandy and Bretagne rose in support of the excluded Girondists, the committee of public safety ordered the district between the Seine, the Loire, and the extreme sea-coast, to be visited with blood and slaughter by the terrible Carrier. This monster ordered, at Nantes, his victims to be drowned by hundreds in the Loire, by means of ships with movable bottoms (*noyades*). The proceedings of the Jacobins in the cities of the south, Lyons, Marseilles, and Toulon, were still more barbarous. In the first of these towns, Chalier, who had formerly been a priest, and now was president of the Jacobin club, excited the people by scandalous placards to plunder and destroy the "aristocrats." Irritated at this audacity, the respectable and wealthy citizens of Lyons, who were
July 16, 1793. thus menaced in their lives and property, procured the execution of the demagogue. This deed filled the Parisian terrorists with fury. A republican army appeared before the walls of the town, which, after an obstinate contest, was taken and fearfully punished. Frèron, a companion of Marat, Fouchè, Couthon, and others, caused the inhabitants to be shot down in crowds, because the guillotine was too tedious in its operations; whole streets were either pulled down or blown into the air with gunpowder. The goods of the rich were divided among the populace; Lyons was to be annihilated, reduced to a nameless common. The republicans raged in a similar way in Marseilles and Toulon. The royalists of Toulon had called upon the English for assistance, and surrendered to them their town and harbor. Confident in this assistance, and in the strength of their walls, the citizens of Toulon bade defiance to their republican enemies. But the army of sans-culottes, in which the young Corsican, Napoleon Bonaparte, exhibited the first proofs of his military talents, overcame all obstacles. Toulon was stormed. The English, unable to maintain the town, set fire to the fleet, and

left the unfortunate inhabitants to the frightful vengeance of the Convention. Here also the barbarous Frèron ordered all the wealthy citizens to be shot, and their property to be divided among the sans-culottes. The respectable inhabitants fled, and abandoned the city to the mob and the galley-slaves. Tallien behaved in a similar manner in Bourdeaux; and in the north of France, Lebon marched from place to place with a guillotine.

§ 556. Scenes of blood in La Vendée.—But the fate of La Vendée was the most frightful. This singular country, situated in the west of France, was covered with woods, hedges, and thickets, and intersected by ditches. Here dwelt a contented people, in rural quietude, and in the simplicity of the olden time. The peasants and tenants were attached to their landlords; they loved the king; and clung with reverence to their clergy and their church usages, which had been dear and sacred to them from their youth. When the National Assembly slaughtered or expelled their unsworn priests, when the blood of their king was poured out on the guillotine, when the children of the peasants were called away, by a general summons, to the army—then the enraged people roused themselves to resistance and civil conflict. Under brave leaders, of undistinguished birth, as Charette, Stofflet, Cathelineau, who were joined by a few nobles, Laroche-Jaquelein, D'Elbée, &c., they at first drove back the republican army, conquered Saumur, and threatened Nantes. Upon this, the Convention despatched a revolutionary army to La Vendée, under the command of Westermann and the frantic Jacobins, Ronsin and Rossignol. These fell upon the inhabitants like wild beasts, set fire to towns, villages, farms, and woods, and attempted to overcome the resistance of the "royalists" by terror and outrage. But the courage of the Vendéan peasants remained unsubdued. It was not until general Kleber marched against La Vendée with the brave troops who had returned to their homes after the surrender of Mayence, that this unfortunate people gradually succumbed to the attacks of their enemies, after the land had become a desert, and thousands of the inhabitants had saturated the soil with their blood. La Vendée, however, was only restored to tranquillity when Hoche, who was equally renowned for his courage and philanthropy, assumed the command of the army, offered peace to those who were weary of the contest, and reduced the refractory to submission. Stofflet and Charette were made prisoners of war, and shot.

§ 557. Fall of the Dantonists.—The rage and cruelty of the Jacobins at length excited the disgust of the chiefs of the Cordeliers, Danton and Camille Desmoulins. The former, who was rather a voluptuary than a tyrant, and who was capable of kindly feelings, had grown weary of slaughter, and had retired into the country for a few months with a young wife, to enjoy the wealth and happiness that the revolution had brought him; but Camille Desmoulins, in his much read paper, "The Old Cordelier," applied the passages where the Roman historian, Tacitus, describes the tyranny and cruelty of Tiberius, so appropriately to his own times, that the application to the three chiefs of the committee of safety and their laws against the suspected was not to be mistaken. This enraged the Jacobins; and when, about this time, several friends and adherents of Danton (Fabre d'Eglantine, Chabot, &c.) were guilty of deceit and corruption in connection with the abolition of the East India Company, and others gave offence by their sacrilegious proceedings, the committee of safety made use of the opportunity to destroy the whole party of Danton. For since the Convention had altered the calendar and the names of the months, had made the year commence on the 22nd of September, had abolished the observance of Sunday and the festivals, and introduced in their place the decades and sans-culotte feasts, many Dantonists, like Hebert, Chaumette, Momoro, Cloots, and others, had occasioned great scandal by their animosity to priests and Christianity. They desecrated and plundered the churches, ridiculed the mass vestments and the church utensils, which they carried through the streets in blasphemous processions, raged with the spirit of Vandals against all the monuments of Christianity, and at length carried a resolution through the Convention, that the worship of Reason should be introduced in place of the catholic service of God. A solemn festival, in which Momoro's pretty wife personated the Goddess of Reason in the church of Nôtre Dame, marked the commencement of this new religion. Robespierre, who plumed himself upon his reputation for virtue, because he was not a participator in the excesses or avarice of Danton and his associates, took offence at these proceedings. He determined to destroy their originators, and in their fall to involve the destruction of Desmoulins and Danton, before whose powerful natures his own spirit, which was filled with envy and ambition, stood abashed. Scarcely, therefore, had Danton resumed his seat in the Convention, before St. Just

March, 1794. began the violent struggle by a remarkable proposal, in which he divided the enemies of the republic into three classes, the corrupt, the ultra-revolutionary, and the moderates, and insisted upon their punishment. This proposal resulted in nineteen of the ultra-revolutionaries, and among them Cloots, Momoro, Ronsin, and several members of the Common Council, being led to the guillotine on the 19th of March. On the 31st of April, the corrupt were placed before the Revolutionary Tribunal, and Danton, Camille Desmoulins, Herault de Sechelles, &c. were maliciously distinguished as their partisans and involved in their fate. But Danton and Desmoulins, supported by a raging mob that were devoted to them, demanded with vehemence that their accusers should be confronted with them. For three days, Danton's voice of thunder and the tumult among the populace rendered his condemnation impossible

For the first time, the bloody men of the Revolutionary Tribunal became confused. The Convention at length, by a law of its own, gave the Tribunal the power of condemning the accused who were endeavoring to subvert the existing order of things by an insurrection, without further hearing; upon which the blood-stained heroes of the 10th of August and the days of September, who during their trial had shown that a lofty spirit might dwell even in the bosom of criminals, were led to the guillotine and beheaded, with a crowd of inferior Hebertists. They died with courage and resolution. April 5, 1794.

§ 558.—3. Wars of the Republic. First Coalition.—Whilst these bloody proceedings were going on within, the armies of almost all the nations of Europe were marching upon the frontiers of France. The Dutch, Austrians, and English were in the Netherlands; Dutch, Prussian, and Austrian troops crossed the Rhine; Sardinia threatened the south-east; and Spanish and Portuguese armies occupied the Pyrenees: at the same time, the English government, conducted by Pitt, sought to destroy the naval power of France, to conquer her colonies, and to keep the war alive by large subsidies to the continental powers. At first, the arms of the allies met with some success; Alsace and Flanders fell into their hands, and the way to Paris stood open. But want of union and want of system prevented any brilliant success, although the new method of warfare had not yet been created in France. The republicans wished to gain the victory by terror. General Beauharnois, who arrived too late to relieve Mayence, died on the guillotine; Custine and his son experienced the same fate; Houchard, the victor over the Dutch and Hanoverians at Handschooten, had a similar fate when he was afterwards obliged to retire before the superior force of the enemy; and Hoche expiated in prison the defeat suffered by the Hollanders and Prussians at Kaiserslautern. But the brave and active Carnot now took his seat in the committee of safety, and gave unity and system to the military operations. The whole nation was interested in the war by a general summons; the newly acquired freedom awakened courage and enthusiasm among the troops; fanatical bands were now opposed to the enemy in masses, and no longer in small divisions; and the greatest commanders of the century rose from the ranks. The generals with their antiquated tactics, and with soldiers who fought for pay, and not for liberty or their fatherland, could not maintain their ground. Jourdain compelled the evacuation of Belgium in June, after the battle of Fleurus; and, by the beginning of autumn, the Austrian Netherlands and the frontier fortresses of Holland were in the hands of the French. It thus became practicable for General Pichegru to undertake a daring expedition in December and January across the frozen waters, against the States-General of Holland. Pichegru, with an army that was suffering from a want of

September 8, 1793.

November 28 - 30.

June 26, 1794.

clothing and provisions, made himself master of the rich land, drove the hereditary Stadtholder to England, and brought about the establishment of a Batavian Republic, with democratic rights, with trees of liberty, and popular Clubs. From this time, Holland remained united with France; and not only were the French troops clothed and maintained at the cost of the country, and vast sums sent to Paris to defray the expenses of the war, but the English at the same time seized upon the Dutch ships and colonies, so that the unfortunate country was a sufferer on all hands.

§ 559. THE PEACE OF BASLE.—The French arms were equally successful on the Rhine. The Austrian and Prussian troops retreated across the German river in October, and abandoned the further side to the French. Shortly after, the Prussian government, which was busied with the proceedings in Poland commenced negotiations with France which led to the peace of Basle. By this disgraceful peace, not only was the left bank of the Rhine, together with Holland, abandoned to the enemy, but the northern portion of Germany separated by a line of demarcation from the southern. Whilst the war was carried on in the latter, the former was declared neutral territory. The Austrians, on the other hand, under the conduct of the brave leaders Clerfait and Wurmser, continued the war with greater energy. After Clerfait's victory over Pichegru at Handschuchsheim, the imperialists took Heidelberg, which was in the possession of the French, and, after a frightful bombardment of several days, the strong town of Mannheim, which, with its abundant military provisions, had been disgracefully surrendered to the enemy at the first summons by the governor, Palgrave Oberndorf. A part of the town was in ruins when the Germans again entered it. The archduke Charles, the brother of the emperor, gave splendid proofs of distinguished military talents. He defeated Jourdain at Würzburg, and compelled him to a hasty retreat upon the Rhine. The inhabitants of Spessart and Odenwald, enraged at the oppressions and exactions of the French, rose upon their retreating enemies, and destroyed them wherever they appeared singly. Moreau was more fortunate; he was indeed driven back from Bavaria and Swabia, but he gained the Rhine without any great loss by a masterly retreat through the valleys of the Black Forest. The German governments, far from encouraging the people in this rising against the enemies of the empire, imitated, for the most part, the example of Prussia, and concluded a peace with France.

A. D. 1794.

April 5, 1795.

September 24, 1795.

September 3, 1796.

September 19—October 24, 1796.

§ 560. ROBESPIERRE'S FALL.—Since the fall of Danton, the committee of safety had ruled with wellnigh unlimited sway, and by repeated executions and arrests had brought the reign of terror to its highest point. But its chiefs had lost the confidence of the people and of the Convention. The friends of Danton were on the watch for the favorable moment of attack, and the number of their enemies was increased, when Robespierre, to put an end to the blasphemous proceedings of the adherents of the worship of Reason, had a resolution passed by the Convention in May, "That the existence of a Supreme Being and the immortality of the soul were truths:" and rendered himself at once hateful and ridiculous by his pride at the new festival in honor of the Supreme Being in the Tuileries, at which he officiated as high priest. Among his opponents was Tallien, who at a former period had been guilty of excesses in Bourdeaux, but who had been brought to adopt different principles by the fascinating Fontenay Cabarrus. With him were joined Frèron, Fouché, Vadier, the polished rhetorician Barrère, and others.

July 27, 1794. On the 9th Thermidor, a battle for life or death commenced in the Convention. Robespierre and his adherents were not allowed to speak; their voices were drowned in the cries of their enemies, who carried through a stormy meeting the resolution, "That the three chiefs of the committee of safety, Robespierre, St. Just, Couthon, and their confederate, Henriot, should be denounced, and conveyed as prisoners to the Luxembourg palace." They were liberated by the mob on their way; whereupon the drunken Henriot threatened the Convention with the National Guard, whilst the others betook themselves to the Hôtel de Ville. But the National Assembly was beforehand with them by a hasty resolution. A loudly proclaimed sentence of outlawry suddenly dispersed Henriot's army, whilst the citizens who were opposed to the Jacobins arranged themselves around the Convention. The accused were again secured in the Hôtel de Ville. Henriot crept into a sewer, whence he was dragged forth by hooks. Robespierre attempted to destroy himself by a pistol-shot, but only succeeded in shattering his lower jaw, and was first conveyed, horribly disfigured, amidst the curses and execrations of the people, before the Revolutionary Tribunal, and then guillotined, with twenty-one of his adherents.

July 28. On the two following days, seventy-two Jacobins shared the fate of their leaders.

§ 561. The Last Days of the Convention. — Robespierre's overthrow by the "Thermidorians" was the commencement of a return to moderation and order. The assemblies of the people were gradually limited, the power of the Common Council diminished, and the lower classes deprived of their weapons. Frèron, converted from a republican bloodhound into an aristocrat, assembled the young men, who from their clothing were called the "gilded youth," around him. These, with the heavy stick they usually carried about them, attacked the Jacobins in the streets and in their clubs at every opportunity, and opposed the song of the "Awakening of the People" to the Marseillaise. At length, the club was shut up and the cloister of the Jacobins pulled down. The

Convention strengthened itself by the recall of the expelled members and of such Girondists as were still left, and ordered the worst of the Terrorists, Lebon, Carrier, Fouquier Tinville, &c., to be executed. But when four of the most active members of the committee of safety (Barrère, Vadier, Collot d'Herbois, and Billaud-Varennes) were denounced, the Jacobins collected the last remains of their strength, and drove the people, who were suffering from a scarcity and want of money, to a frightful insurrection. Crowds of grisly wretches surrounded the house
March 31. of assembly, and demanded, with threatening cries, the
April 1, 1795. liberation of the patriots, bread, and the constitution of 1793. Pichegru, who was just at this moment in Paris, came to the assistance of the distressed Convention with soldiers and citizens, and dispersed the crowd. The still more formidable insurrection of the 1st
May 20, 1795. Prairial, in which the mob held the Convention surrounded both within and without, from seven o'clock in the morning till two at night, for the purpose of enforcing a return to the reign of terror, was also suppressed by the courageous president, Boissy d'Anglas. From this time, the power of the Terrorists was no more. Many Jacobins died by their own hands; others were beheaded, imprisoned, or transported. By so much the stronger became the party of the royalists, who wished to have a king again; and when the new government was shortly after determined upon, by which the executive power was to be delivered to a Directory of five persons, the legislative power to a council of Ancients and a council of Five Hundred, the republican members of the Convention feared that in the new election they might be thrust aside by the royalists. They therefore made additions to the original charter of the constitution, wherein it was declared that two-thirds of the two legislative councils must be chosen from members of the Convention. The royalists raised objections against this and some other limitations of the freedom of election; and when these were unattended with success, they occasioned the insurrection of the Sections. Hereupon, the Convention made over to the Corsican, Napoleon Bonaparte, the supression of the insurgent royalists, who were joined by all the enemies of the republic and of the revolution. The victory of the
October 5, 1795. 13th Vendemiaire, which was fought in the streets of Paris, gave the supremacy to the republicans of the Convention, and the command of the Italian army to Napoleon, who was then twenty-six years of age, and who, a short time before, had married Josephine, the widow of General Beauharnois.

5. FRANCE UNDER THE DIRECTORY (OCTOBER, 1795 — NOVEMBER 9TH, 1799).

§ 562. NAPOLEON IN ITALY. — The French army in Savoy and on the frontiers of Italy was in a melancholy condition. The soldiers were in want of every thing. At this crisis, Napoleon appeared as their commander-in-chief, and in a short time contrived so to inspirit the desponding troops and attach them to his person, that under his guidance they cheerfully encountered the greatest dangers. Where the love of glory and the sentiment of honor were not sufficient, there the treasures of wealthy Italy served as a stimulus to valor. In April, Napoleon

A. D. 1796. defeated the octogenarian Austrian general, Beaulieu, at Milesimo and Montenotte, separated, by this victory, the Austrians from the Sardinians, and so terrified the king, Victor Amadeus, that he consented to a disadvantageous peace, by which he surrendered Savoy and Nice to the French, gave up six fortresses to the general, and submitted to the oppressive condition of allowing the French army to march through his land at any time. By these and other oppressive conditions, the country became entirely dependent upon France, so that, upon the king's death, which took place soon after, his son, Charles Emmanuel (1796 — 1802), surrendered Piedmont to the enemy, and settled himself and his family in Sardinia. The course of Napoleon's victories in Upper Italy was equally rapid.

May 10, 1796. After the memorable passage of the bridge of Lodi, he marched into Austrian Milan, subjected the Lombard towns, and so terrified the smaller princes by the success of his arms and his insolence, that they were only too happy to make peace with the victor at any price. Napoleon extorted large sums of money, and valuable pictures, treasures of art and manuscripts, from the dukes of Parma, Modena, Lucca, Tuscany, &c. He behaved as the Roman generals, with whose lives he was acquainted from the descriptions of Plutarch, had once done; he enriched the French capital with the productions of the mind, that he might please the vain and spectacle-loving Parisians. He supported the weak Directory with the extorted supplies of money.

Wurmser now took the place of the old Beaulieu. But he also was

August 5. defeated at Castiglione, and afterwards besieged in Mantua. The army under Alvinzi that was sent to his relief sustained

January, February, 1797. three defeats (at Arcola, Rivoli, La Favorita), by which the whole Austrian force in Italy was destroyed, dispersed, or captured. This compelled the gallant Wurmser to deliver up Mantua to the glorious victor. Bonaparte, respecting the courage of his enemy, permitted a free retreat to the gray-headed marshal, his staff, and a part of the brave garrison. Pope Pius VI., terrified at these

February, 19. rapid successes, hastened to purchase the peace of Tolentino by cessions of territory, sums of money, and works of art.

Archduke Charles now assumed the command of the Austrian army in Italy. But he also was compelled to a disastrous retreat, and was pursued by Bonaparte as far as Klagenfurt, with the view of falling upon Vienna. The emperor Francis, anxious for the fate of his capital, allowed himself to be persuaded by female influence to conclude the disadvantageous preliminary peace of Leoben, at the very moment when, by the non-arrival of the expected reinforcements, and the threatening movements of the Tyrolese, Styrians, and Carinthians, the position of the French army was becoming critical.

April 18, 1797.

About the time this treaty of peace was concluded, a popular insurrection arose in the rear of the French army, in the territory of the republic of Venice, in consequence of which many Frenchmen were murdered in Verona and its neighborhood, and even the sick and wounded in the hospitals were not spared. This was taken advantage of by Napoleon to destroy the Venetian republic. The cowardice of the aristocratic councillors, who, instead of offering a brave resistance and falling with honor, humbly implored the grace of the proud conqueror, and surrendered the government to a democratic council, facilitated the enterprise. As early as May, the French marched into Venice, carried off the ships and the stores of the arsenal, robbed the churches, galleries, and libraries of their choicest ornaments and most valued treasures, and kept possession of the city till the negotiations with Austria were so far advanced, that the peace of Campo Formio, by which Upper Italy fell into the hands of France under the name of the Cisalpine Republic, was concluded. Austria, who by this peace also surrendered Belgium to the French republic, and consented to the cession of the left bank of the Rhine with Mayence, received the territory of Venice, together with Dalmatia, as a recompense for this loss. The princes, prelates, and nobles, who suffered by this abandonment of the farther Rhineland, were to be indemnified on the right bank of the river, and this, as well as all other points relating to Germany, were to be settled at the Congress at Rastadt. Napoleon opened this congress himself, and then returned to Paris where he was received with acclamations.

October 17, 1797.

December, 1797.

§ 563. Gracchus Babœuf. The Royalists. — The reign of the five directors, among whom La Reveillère-Lepeaux (founder of the Society of the Theo-Philanthropists, Friends of God and Men) and Carnot possessed the greatest influence, was detested by the violent republicans as well as by the royalists, and had, consequently, to sustain the attacks of both parties. The first attempt to overthrow it was made by the republicans, under the guidance of Gracchus Babœuf, who, like the Roman tribune whose name he had assumed, wished to establish an equalization of property, and a new division of lands. He was joined by some of the old Jacobins, particularly by Drouet. The conspiracy was discovered. After some legal proceedings, which attracted a great deal of attention, Babœuf and one other were executed, the others were banished. But greater than this was the danger with which the directoral government was threatened by the royalists. When, in accordance

with the charter of the Constitution, at the expiration of the first year, a third part of the council vacated their seats, and were replaced by a fresh election, the royalists, who had founded the club of Clichy, succeeded, almost entirely, in returning people of their own way of thinking to the legislative assembly. Among them was Pichegru, who as commander of the Rhine army, had been connected with the emigrants, and now, as president of the Council of the Five Hundred, was seeking to effect the restoration of the king. This caused anxiety to the republicans in the Directory and in the legislative chamber. They accordingly sought assistance from Bonaparte. The latter despatched a division of his army to Paris, under the conduct of the shrewd Bernadotte and the gallant Augereau, ostensibly to convey thither the conquered standards, but in reality to assist the Directors against the royalists.
September 4, 1797. On the 18th Fructidor, Augereau surrounded the Tuileries with his troops, and ordered the royalist deputies to be arrested; upon which, eleven members of the Council of Ancients, forty-two of the Five Hundred (among them Pichegru), and two Directors, were sentenced to deportation. The royalist elections were then declared invalid, the returned emigrants again banished, and many journals suppressed. The directoral government, however, possessed neither respect nor confidence. Trade, industry, and agriculture fell into decay, and the national finances were in a dilapidated state. At the commencement of the Revolution, the government had ordered paper money to be issued, for the security and guarantee of which they assigned the confiscated property of the Church and of the emigrants. These notes were called assignats. A want of confidence in the stability of the revolutionary government soon produced a depreciation of this paper money, especially as the increasing number of assignats rendered their redemption every day more improbable. During the reign of terror, no one refused an acceptance that was commanded by law, and the assignats had thus a compulsatory circulation. But after the fall of Robespierre, and the decline of terrorism, this paper money sank daily in value; and, despite the efforts made by the directoral government to restore the confidence of the people by discharging the old assignats and issuing fresh bills (mandats, inscriptions), the new notes were soon as worthless as the old ones. The losses were enormous; property had fled from the rich and the illustrious to the lower classes. To defray the expenses of war and other outlays, the Directory established a complete system of plunder in the conquered countries.

§ 564. The Republicans in Italy. Changes in Switzerland. Italy and Switzerland were particularly exposed to the insolence and rapacity of the directoral government. In the winter of 1797, republican commotions took place in Rome and other parts of the States of the Church, which were occasioned by French influence. During the suppression of these by the papal troops, general Duphot, who was present in Rome, lost his life. This afforded the French government an opportunity of ordering Berthier to march with an army into Rome. A tree

February, 1798. of liberty was erected in the midst of the Roman Forum, the Pope was deprived of his temporal power, which was made over to a republican government, consisting of consuls, senators, and tribunes. The French then imposed severe military levies and imposts upon the town, and carried off the most valuable works of art to Paris; and when this proceeding occasioned some popular commotions,

August, 1799. the grey-headed pope, Pius VI., was led away to Paris, where he died in the following year, and the cardinals were subjected to severe persecutions. Lucca and Genoa also received democratical constitutions, and paid for them with their treasures. But the most remarkable occurrences took place in Naples. The hard-hearted and cowardly king Ferdinand governed there, and devoted himself entirely to hunting and fishing, whilst he left the business of the state to his impetuous wife, Caroline, a daughter of Maria Theresa, who, on her side, allowed herself to be entirely guided by the notorious courtezan, Lady Hamilton, the wife of the English ambassador. Filled with deadly hate against France and the regicide republicans, and informed that the European powers had determined upon a fresh campaign, the queen persuaded her husband to allow a Neapolitan army, under the command of the Austrian general Mack, to march into the States of the Church. The French were at first driven out of Rome, and the town taken possession of; but in a few days they again returned, under Championnet, put the Neapolitans to flight, and marched into the territory of their enemy. Confused and helpless, the Neapolitan court fled to Sicily, or-

November, December, 1798. dered its own fleet to be set on fire, and abandoned the capital and the whole country to the conquerors. But the populace of Naples, excited by the monks and clergy, now arose. Troops of ragamuffins (lazzaroni), united with peasants and galley-slaves, took possession of Naples, and spread such alarm, that the viceroy fled to Sicily, and Mack sought protection among the French. Championnet then marched over blood and corpses into the stubbornly defended town,

January 1799. and established the Parthenopeian Republic. All the respectable and educated Neapolitans, who were inspired with any feeling of patriotism, delighted to escape from years of kingly and priestly despotism, attached themselves with enthusiasm to the new order of things.

In the year 1798, Switzerland also experienced a change in her constitution. Bern, and its associate, Vaud, were governed by an aristocratic council, all the members of which belonged to patrician families. The Vaudois, excited by the French republicans, seized their arms for the purpose of freeing themselves from the government of the Bernese. But as they were not a match for their opponents, they claimed the assistance of France; upon which general Brune took possession of Bern, made himself master of the rich treasures and of the arsenal, and extorted large sums from the land by military levies. Supported by the democratic party, with Ochs of Basle and Laharpe of Vaud at their head, the French converted Switzerland into the single and indivisible Helvetic Republic, with a form of policy borrowed from the directoral government of France. It was in vain that the Catholic cantons on the lake of Lucerne, excited by their priests, opposed themselves to this arrangement and took up arms; they were defeated, and compelled to conform to the new system. Geneva was united to France.

§ 565. THE WAR OF THE SECOND COALITION.—These proceedings, and the simultaneous expedition of Napoleon to Egypt and Syria, produced a fresh coalition of the three great European powers, Russia, England, and Austria, against France. Russia had been governed since the year 1796 by Paul, the eldest son of Catherine, a prince with a mind somewhat deranged, who cherished the bitterest hatred against the Revolution; and who, as a great admirer of the Order of Malta, to the Grand Mastership of which he had had himself appointed, saw, in the capture of that island by Napoleon, a cause for war. England feared danger to her foreign possessions from the Egyptian expedition, and scattered money with a liberal hand to raise up fresh enemies against France. Austria was at variance with the directoral government, because the house of the French ambassador in Vienna, Bernadotte, had been broken open, and the tricolor flag torn down and burnt, during a popular festival, without the Austrian government having afforded the required satisfaction.

War was waged, at the same time, in Germany, in Italy, in Switzerland, and in the Netherlands. After the French had been defeated at Stockach by the archduke Charles, and forced over the Rhine, March 25, 1799. the French ambassadors (Roberjot, Bonnier, Jean Debry), who had hitherto conducted the affairs of peace in Rastadt, and rendered themselves universally odious by their pride and insolence, wished to return. But scarcely had they left Rastadt at the commencement of night, before they were attacked, in defiance of all the rights of nations, April 28. by Szekler hussars, robbed of their papers, and treated in such a way that two died immediately, and Jean Debry, who was severely wounded, only saved his life by crawling into a ditch. This deed excited universal disgust, and was taken advantage of by the Directory to excite the people to vengeance. In Italy, also, the French had the disadvantage. The Russians, under Suwarrow, conquered the Cisalpine Republic in a few weeks, after Moreau had been defeated at Cassano, and Macdonald, who had led the French army out of Naples, at Trebia.

famous for the victory of Hannibal. The bloody defeat of the French
June 17—19. in the battle of Novi, where the young general Joubert died the death of a hero, completed the loss of Italy. This change
August 5. in affairs was a death-blow to the Parthenopeian Republic. Scarcely had the French army left Naples, before the barbarous cardinal
June 13. Ruffo stormed the city with bands of Calabrian peasants and exasperated lazzaroni, and the court returned from Sicily. The republicans of Naples were now visited by a frightful punishment. Supported by Admiral Nelson, who lay with his fleet before the city, and who, seduced by the charms of Lady Hamilton, allowed himself to be made the instrument of an ignominious vengeance, the priesthood and the royal government practised deeds, before which the atrocities of the French reign of terror retreat into obscurity. After the murderings and plunderings of the lazzaroni were over, the business of the judge, the executioner, and the gaoler commenced. Every partisan, adherent, or favorer of the republican institutions was persecuted. Upwards of 4,000 of the most respectable and refined men and females died upon the scaffold or in frightful dungeons. For it was precisely the noblest portion of the nation, who wished to redeem the people from their degradation and ignorance, that had joined themselves with patriotic enthusiasm to the new system. The grey-haired prince, Caraccioli, the former confidant of Ferdinand and the friend of Nelson, was hanged at the yard-arm, and his body plunged, loaded with weights, into the waves. The republican government was also dissolved in Rome, whereupon the new pope, Pius VII., again took possession of the Vatican.

After the conquest of Italy, Suwarrow surmounted the pathless icebergs of the Alps, with the purpose of driving the French out of Switzerland. The Russian army had incredible difficulties and dangers to encounter in this expedition. Combats were sustained on the Gothard and at the Devil's Bridge against the enemy and natural difficulties, that may be classed with the most daring feats in the world's history. But despite all their efforts, the Russians, owing to not being sufficiently supported by the Austrians, were defeated by the French in the battle of
September 25, 26, 1799. Zurich. (During the capture of Zurich, which followed, Lavater was mortally wounded.) Suwarrow conducted the remains of his army across the frozen heights of the Grisons to their
May, 1800. home, where he shortly after died. The simultaneous attempt of the English to drive the French out of the Netherlands, and restore the Stadtholder, had a disastrous termination. The unskilful general, the duke of York, purchased the retreat of himself
October, 1799. and his army by a disgraceful convention, without troubling himself about his allies, the Russians. This ignoble and selfish behavior of the English and Austrians exasperated the Russian

emperor, Paul, so much against the allies, that he retired from the coalition.

§ 566. Bonaparte in Egypt and Syria. — During these transactions, Bonaparte found himself in Egypt, at the head of a considerable army. In the June of 1798, he had sailed from the island of Malta, which had been wrested from the knights of St. John by treachery, towards the land of the Nile. The chief inducements to this strange and adventurous undertaking were the wish to inspire the excitable French nation with enthusiasm for himself by extraordinary actions, the desire of glory, and the thought of being able to weaken the maritime power of England, and to threaten her possessions in the East Indies from Egypt. After his disembarkation at Alexandria, the whole of the French fleet at Aboukir, owing to the carelessness of the admiral, was defeated and captured by the English naval hero, Nelson; and Napoleon was in consequence obliged to make arrangements for a longer stay. In July, he marched from Alexandria through the Egyptian desert to Cairo. The distress of the army, unprovided with water or sufficient necessaries, in the burning heat, was very great. In the battle of the

July 21, 1798. Pyramids, "from the tops of which 4,000 years looked down upon the combatants," the Mamalukes, who at that time swayed Egypt under the Turkish government, were defeated; whereupon Bonaparte marched into Cairo, and established a new government, police, and taxation, upon the European pattern, and ordered the curiosities of this wonderful land to be examined, and its monuments and antiquities to be collected and described, by the artists and men of learning who accompanied his army. In the meanwhile, although Bonaparte and his troops treated the religious customs of the Mahommedans with every possible forbearance, and showed all outward respect to their priests, mosques, ceremonies, and customs, fanaticism was, nevertheless, raging in the bosoms of the Mussulmans, and rendered the rule of the Christians detestable to them. This hatred was increased when the French general levied taxes and imposts; and the Porte, which would not allow itself to be deceived by Napoleon's false shows of friendship and devotion, called upon the Mahommedans to fight against the Christians. A dreadful insurrec-

October 21, 1798. tion broke out in Cairo, which could only be suppressed with difficulty by the superiority of European tactics, after nearly 6,000 Mahommedans had been slain. Napoleon made use of the

February, 1799. victory to extort money, and then marched with his Turkish troops against Syria. After the conquest of Jaffa, where he ordered 2,000 Arnauts, whom he had a second time taken prisoners, to be shot as perjured, he proceeded to the siege of Jean d'Acre. It was there that the fortune of Napoleon met with its first rebuff.

March 20. The Turks, provided with artillery by the English admiral, Sir Sidney Smith, repelled the assaults of the enemy, despite their wonderful valor. At the same time, a Turkish army threatened the European soldiers in the interior of the country. The former was, indeed, defeated and dispersed by Junot at Nazareth, and at Mount Tabor by Kleber; nevertheless, upon the plague breaking out among his troops, Napoleon found himself compelled to give up Acre and to commence a retreat. The horses were laden with the sick; the soldiers suffered the most dreadful privations; the dangers and distresses of the war were frightful. Napoleon shared all the fatigues with the meanest of his army; he is even said to have visited a hospital filled with those sick of the plague. He again reached Cairo in June, and in the following month, defeated a Turkish army of three times his number, at Aboukir. A short time after this, he learned the disasters of the French in Italy from some newspapers; and the intelligence produced such an effect upon him, that he determined upon returning to France. He quietly made his preparations for departure with the greatest expedition. After transferring the command of the Egyptian army to Kleber, Napoleon sailed from the harbor of Alexandria with two frigates and a few small transports, and about 500 followers, and, guided by the star of his fortunes, reached the coast of France undiscovered by the English, and landed at Frejus amidst the acclamations of the people.

July 25.

October 9, 1799.

§ 567. The Eighteenth Brumaire. — Upon his arrival in Paris, Napoleon embraced the resolution of overthrowing the directoral government, which had lost all authority and consideration. With this purpose, he made himself secure of the officers and troops that were in Paris, and consulted with Sieyes, one of the directors, and his own brother, Lucien Bonaparte, who had been elected president of the Five Hundred, on the means of carrying his plan into execution. Lucien transferred the sittings of the council to St. Cloud, for the purpose of bringing the members within the power of the soldiers. There, Napoleon first attempted to win over the members to his plans by persuasion; when he found that he could not succeed in this, but rather, that he was overwhelmed with threats and reproaches, he commanded his grenadiers to clear the room with levelled bayonets. The republicans, who presented a bold front to the danger, were at length compelled to yield to superior force, and sought their safety through the doors and windows. This done, a commission of fifty persons was appointed to draw up a fresh constitution. Thus ended the violent procedure of the 18th Brumaire, in consequence of which Napoleon Bonaparte took the conduct of affairs into his own strong hands.

November 9, 1799.

C. GOVERNMENT OF NAPOLEON BONAPARTE.

I. THE CONSULATE (1800 – 1804).

§ 568. According to the consular constitution, the power of the state was divided in the following manner:— 1. To the Senate, which consisted of eighty members, belonged the privilege of selecting from the list of names sent in by the departments the members of the legislative power, and the chief officials and judges. 2. The legislative power was divided (*a*) into the Tribunate, which numbered one hundred members, and whose office it was to examine and debate upon the proposals of the government; and (*b*) the legislative bodies, who had only to receive or reject these proposals unconditionally. 3. The government consisted of three Consuls, who were elected for ten years. Of these Consuls, the first, Bonaparte, exercised the powers of government, properly so called; whilst the second and third Consuls (Cambacéres and Lebrun) were merely placed at his side as advisers. Bonaparte, as first Consul, surrounded himself with a state council and a ministry, for which he selected the most talented and experienced men. Talleyrand, the dexterous diplomatist, was minister of the exterior; the astute Fouché superintended the police; Berthier held the staff of general. The Code Napoleon, in the composition of which the most renowned lawyers of France were employed, is an illustrious proof of the sagacity of the state council.

§ 569. MARENGO AND HOHENLINDEN.—After the arrangement of the new constitution, Bonaparte wrote a letter with his own hand to the king of England, in which he made an offer of peace; he did the same to the emperor. But this unusual proceeding found little sympathy. A cold answer, in measured terms, spoke of the restoration of the Bourbons, and of a return to the ancient boundaries. The contrast between the apparent warmth, openness, and magnanimity of Napoleon, and the repulsive coldness of the cabinets of London and Vienna, excited the greatest enthusiasm and military ardor among the fiery French. Napoleon was more successful in his attempts to gain over the czar of Russia to his cause. Paul's love for soldiers, and his disgust at the Austrians and English, who would not exchange the captured Russians, were dexterously made use of by Napoleon. He sent some thousands of these prisoners, fresh armed and clothed, back to their homes, without ransom. By this means he won the heart of the emperor, who, with all his eccentricities, possessed a chivalrous spirit; so that the latter entered into a friendly alliance with Bonaparte, and withdrew himself entirely from his former allies.

The First Consul now assembled a large army, with all secrecy, in

the neighborhood of the Lake of Geneva, and undertook the wonderful
May, 1800. passage of the great St. Bernard with the main body, whilst other divisions penetrated into Italy by the Simplon, St. Gothard, and other passes. This bold undertaking, with its difficulties and dangers, recalls to mind the heroic age of Hannibal. The army marched past the Hospice, placed in the midst of snow and icebergs, down into the valley of the Dora Baltea, where the fortress of Bard, which was occupied by the Austrians, appeared to present insurmountable difficulties. But Napoleon's genius discovered an escape. The troops surmounted the neighboring heights by a sheep-path, whilst the artillery was conveyed secretly under the guns of the fort by an artifice. In this way the French descended, quite unexpectedly, upon Upper Italy, at the very moment when the Austrians had compelled Genoa to surrender, and were in possession of the whole country. But the posi-
June 9. tion of affairs was soon changed. Five days after the fall
June 14. of Genoa, the Austrians received a defeat at Montebello, and a short time after, the battle of Marengo was fought near Alexandria, where the Austrians under Melas were completely routed. The unexpected arrival of the brave Desaix from Egypt produced this change, and snatched the victory that was deemed secure from the hands of the Austrians. Desaix, one of the greatest and most noble men of the time of the Revolution, died the death of a hero at Marengo. Milan and Lombardy were the prize of the day. At the same time, an army under Moreau had forced its way into Swabia and Bavaria, driven back the Austrians in several encounters, and compelled them to a truce; but it was the glorious march of Macdonald and Moncey over
July. the icy Grisons, and Moreau's splendid victory in the bloody
December 3. field of Hohenlinden, that first compelled the Austrians to
February 9. accept, in the peace of Luneville, the conditions that had been entered into at Campo Formio, and to acknowledge the valleys of the Rhine and the Adige as the boundaries of the French empire. The formation of an Italian republic under the presidentship of Bonaparte, and the indemnification of the losses of the German princes and the imperial estates, by the secularized Church property and the abolished imperial cities on the right side of the Rhine, were the most important articles in the peace of Luneville. The arrangement that was made, two years later, in the territories of the German States, by the so-called decree of the Imperial Diet, was the first step
February 25, 1803. towards the dissolution of the German empire, and the establishment of sovereign kingdoms and principalities.

§ 570. The Peace of Amiens. — After the peace of Luneville, England alone retained her arms, and as the Russian emperor, Paul, out of hatred to the selfish and insolent islanders, had only a short time before renewed the alliance with Prussia, Sweden, and Denmark, for an

armed neutrality, and by this means stirred up enemies against the British in the Baltic, the English people also were longing for rest and refreshment. Negotiations for peace were accordingly entered into, but were attended for a long time by no result, inasmuch as the parties could not agree respecting Egypt. For Kleber, angry as he was at Napoleon's retreat, had successfully maintained himself against the Turks and the English, and in the battle near Heliopolis, had defeated an
March 20, 1800. army of six times his numbers. But after he had fallen by the dagger of a fanatical Mussulman, in the garden of his palace at Cairo, on the day of the battle of Marengo, the French army, under the conduct of his incompetent successor, Menou, who had embraced Islamism, fell gradually into such distress, that the English entertained the hope of compelling it to surrender, and consequently delayed the negotiations for peace. It was not until the gallant English general, Aber-
March 21, 1801. crombie, had fallen in the battle of Canopus, that they were convinced that neither their own land force, which was composed of recruits from all nations, nor the undisciplined Turkish squadrons, were in
September, 1801. a condition to overcome the tactics of the French in Egypt. A treaty was concluded, by virtue of which the French army, 24,000 strong, with arms, munitions, and all the treasures of science and art, were conveyed back to France in English vessels. This was the preliminary to the peace of Amiens, by which the English promised to surrender the greater part of their foreign con-
March 27, 1802. quests, and to relinquish the island of Malta, of which they had gained possession, to the knights of St. John. This peace, which was concluded with great precipitation on the part of England, met with violent opposition in the country. The press raised its voice loudly against it, and adopted at the same time a hostile tone towards Napoleon. These attacks irritated the First Consul, who could bear neither censure nor opposition ; he replied in a similar strain by the French government paper (Moniteur). This occasioned a mutual ill-temper, which promised a speedy renewal of hostilities; and the English accordingly delayed the evacuation of Malta, and the execution of the disadvantageous conditions of the peace. The dread of Russia had passed, since Paul had met with a violent death. The cruelty, the arbitrary measures, and the gloomy suspicions of this emperor, had increased to such an extent, that there could be no longer a doubt that his mind was incurably affected. A conspiracy was therefore formed amongst those around him, the threads of which were guided by the powerful count Pahlen. The result of this was, that the emperor Paul was attacked in his bed-chamber by Suboff, Benningsen, and others, and when he refused the required abdication of the throne, he was cruelly strangled, and his son Alexander
May 24, 1801. proclaimed as his successor. Under these circumstances, the
May 18, 1803. peace of Amiens had no permanence. At the expiration of

a year, the English again declared war, and Pitt reëntered the ministry. A short time before, Napoleon had reduced Switzerland to the same state of subjection as Holland and Italy. By the so-called Act of Mediation, he had effected such a change in the constitution
February, 1803. of the Helvetic republic, that the cantons had again become independent, but a Landamman and a Diet represented the confederation as a collective state.

§ 571. THE NEW COURT AND THE CONCORDAT. — Bonaparte was at first engaged in reconciling the old with the new, in combining the results of the Revolution with the forms and manners of the monarchical period. But he very soon made known his preference for the ancient system, by the restoration of all the former arrangements and customs. The times and fashions of a previous period, the forms of the old etiquette, the elegance of the kingly period, were soon to be seen at the court of the First Consul in the Tuileries. An aristocratic demeanor, a dignified bearing, and polished manners, were again held in estimation, as the advantages of good society. The social gifts of his wife, Josephine, the beauty and amiability of his step-children (Eugene and Hortense Beauharnais) and sisters (Pauline, Elise), assisted him in this matter.* The reductions in the emigrant lists brought back many royalists to their homes, and the favor shown to them made them courteous and pliant in the service of the new court. Madame de Stael (daughter of Necker) collected, as in the old time, a circle of accomplished and illustrious men in her saloon. The vanity of the French favored Napoleon's efforts; when he instituted the Order of the Legion of Honor, republicans and royalists grasped eagerly at the new plaything of human weakness.

One of the first cares of the Consul was the restoration of Christian worship in the French churches. After he had abolished the republican festivals (10th August, 21st January), and introduced the
July 15, 1801. observance of the Sabbath, negotiations were opened with the Roman court, which at length led to the conclusion of the Concordat.
April 8. By this Concordat, the French clergy lost their early inde-

* Genealogical Table of the Bonaparte family of Ajaccio, in Corsica.

Charles Bonaparte, = Lætitia née Ramolini, A. D. 1736, at Rome.

1. Joseph B., Count Survilliers, A. D. 1767 - 1844.	2. Napoleon B., A. D. 1769 - 1821.	3. Lucien B., Prince Canino, A. D. 1772 - 1841.	4. Eliza Bacciochi, A. D. 1777 - 1820.
5. Louis B., Duke of St. Leu, A. D. 1778 - 1846.	6. Pauline Borghese, A. D. 1781 - 1825.	7. Caroline Murat, A. D. 1781 - 1839.	8. Jerome B., born 1784, Duke of Monfort.

Napoleon Bonaparte, = Josephine Beauharnais, née Tascher de la Pagerie,
A. D. 1763 - 1814.
A. D. 1837.

Eugene, Duke of Leuchtenberg, A. D. 1781 - 1824.

Hortense, Duchess of St. Leu, = Louis B.
Louis Napoleon,
President of the French Republic.

pendence, and were subjected to the head of the Church as well as to the ruler of the state.

No less attention did Napoleon devote to the affairs of education; but he particularly patronized the establishments for practical science, as the Polytechnic School in Paris. An arbitrary and power-loving man, Napoleon wished to guide and govern every thing himself, and thus became the creator of the pernicious system of centralization, by which the vital circulation was suppressed, and the seeds of death were planted in the whole body of the state.

§ 572. Conspiracies. — Napoleon possessed a despotic nature, that found no pleasure in a life of freedom; he accordingly curtailed the liberty and political rights of the citizens, persecuted the Jacobins and Republicans, whom he called "Ideologists," and reposed his confidence in his guard, and in a vigorous triple police, under the superintendence of the crafty Fouché. Repeated conspiracies against the life of the First Consul, sometimes undertaken by the republicans and sometimes by the royalists, were always followed by fresh restrictions and a more rigorous system of espionage. The most desperate undertaking of this kind was the attempt, by means of the so-called infernal machine, — a cask filled with gunpowder, bullets, and inflammable materials, to blow up Bonaparte on his way to the opera-house, — an attempt which he escaped by the rapidity with which his coachman was driving, but which destroyed many houses and killed several people. In consequence of this atrocious deed, a great number of Jacobins were condemned to deportation, though it afterwards turned out that the plot was undertaken by the royalists. Still more dangerous and extensive were the conspiracies against Napoleon, when the office of Consul was conferred upon him for life by the voice of the people, with the privilege of naming his successor. By this means, the Bourbons were cut off from the last hopes of a return, and the emigrants accordingly left no means untried of destroying him. The desperate George Cadoudal, and Pichegru, who was residing in England, and who was as strong as a giant, allowed themselves to be employed as tools. They conveyed themselves secretly to France, but were discovered and arrested, with about forty confederates. Before their fate was decided, Napoleon allowed himself to be hurried into the commission of a revolting crime. It had been represented to him that the duke d'Enghien, the chivalrous grandson of the prince of Condé, was the soul of all the royalist conspiracies. Accordingly, this young nobleman, who was residing at Ettenheim, a small town of Baden, was seized at Napoleon's command, by a troop of armed men, conducted with the greatest haste through Strasburg to Paris, condemned to death by a hurried court-martial, and, despite a magnanimous defence, shot in the trenches of Vincennes. This deed, which placed Bonaparte on a level

December 24, 1800.

August 2, 1802.

March 21, 1804.

with the men of the reign of terror in 1793, revolted all Europe, and put an end to the praises of his admirers. The poet Chateaubriand, the author of the "Genius of Christianity," resigned the official situation that had been conferred upon him by Bonaparte's sister, Eliza, and retired to Switzerland. The fate of the conspirators was shortly after decided upon. Pichegru had already died a violent death in prison, whether by his own hand or that of another is uncertain. George Cadoudal, with eleven confederates, ascended the guillotine. General Moreau, who was implicated, retired into voluntary banishment in America.

II. NAPOLEON, EMPEROR (A.D. 1804–1814).

1. THE EMPIRE.

§ 573. The royalist conspiracies were made use of by Bonaparte to establish an hereditary monarchy. At the instigation of his adherents, the making over the hereditary dignity of emperor to Napoleon was proposed to the Tribunat, sanctioned by the Senate, and confirmed by the whole people by the subscription of their names. Whilst the minds of men were still painfully excited by the late bloody executions, Napoleon was proclaimed emperor of the French, and at the end of the year, solemnly anointed by the pope in the church of Nôtre Dame. The crown, however, he placed on his own head, as well as on that of his wife, Josephine, who knelt before him. This magnificent coronation appeared to be the conclusion of the Revolution, since the whole ancient system, for the extinction of which thousands of human lives had been sacrificed, gradually returned. The new emperor surrounded his throne with a brilliant court, in which the former titles, orders, and gradations of rank were revived under different names. He himself certainly retained his old military simplicity, but the members of his family were made princes and princesses; his generals became marshals; the devoted servants and promoters of his plans were connected with the throne as the great officers of the crown, or as senators with large incomes. The establishment of a new feudal nobility, with the old titles of princes, dukes, counts, barons, completed the splendid edifice of a magnificent imperial court, which soon outshone the courts of princes. The republican arrangement gradually disappeared. The old calendar was again restored; the new nobility were at liberty to establish the right of primogeniture, the press was placed under a censorship, and civil freedom was more and more restricted. Any opposition was intolerable to the ruler; for this reason, he first reduced the number of Tribunes to fifty, and then abolished the whole Tribunat. Obedience was henceforth the only thing; and France was placed under a tyranny more severe than that of the ancient monarchy. But then the tyrant was a great man, and therefore the people willingly

May 18, 1804.

A. D. 1807.

submitted to him; and hardly as the rigorous conscription, the severe restrictions upon trade, and the heavy taxation might press upon them, the burden was the more lightly borne, inasmuch as the great ends attained by the Revolution—equality before the law, the peasants' right of property in the soil and other possessions, remained untouched. Industry made great progress, civil arts and trades received a vast impulse; and an unaccustomed prosperity made itself everywhere visible. Magnificent roads, like those over the Alps, canals, bridges, and improvements of all kinds, are, to the present day, eloquent memorials of the restless activity of this remarkable man. Splendid palaces, majestic bridges, and noble streets, arose in Paris, every thing great or magnificent that art had produced was united in the Louvre; the capital of France glittered with a splendor that had never before been witnessed. The university was arranged upon a most magnificent footing, and appointed the supreme court of supervision and control over the whole system of schools and education. The glory that was conferred by the emperor upon the nation rendered every yoke light to the latter; she forgot that the voice of freedom was dying away amidst the clash of arms and the clang of trumpets, and that the high-flown tone of bulletins, and the ornate language of the senate and legislative body, were destructive of truth and justice.

2. AUSTERLITZ, PRESBURG. CONFEDERATION OF THE RHINE.

§ 574. The English took advantage of the renewal of the war with France to make an unexpected seizure of Dutch and French ships, and then sought to unite Russia and Austria in a new coalition. Napoleon, on the other hand, ordered his troops to advance upon the Weser, and to occupy the electorate of Hanover, which belonged to the king of England. (May, 1803.) The Hanoverian people and army were resolved to hazard life and property in defence of their country; but the selfish aristocracy and officials preferred a disgraceful capitulation, which surrendered the whole country to the French, to fighting. The gallant army was forced to retreat across the Elbe, and there to disband. Arms, munitions of war, and splendid horses, fell into the hands of the French, who forthwith occupied the country with their troops, and exhausted it by military levies and exactions. The threatening attitude assumed by Napoleon in Hanover against the whole north, as well as his arbitrary proceedings in Holland, Italy, and other countries, were sources of anxiety to other powers. In Italy, not only was the Italian republic changed into the kingdom of Italy, and Eugene Beauharnais, the step-son of the emperor, placed there as viceroy, (March 17, 1805.) but Napoleon also enlarged it by the addition of Parma, and gave Lucca to his sister Eliza, the wife of the Corsican, Bacciochi. In Spain and Germany, also, Napoleon acted in the same imperious and arbitrary manner. These, and other causes, united Russia, Austria, and Sweden with England against France, and renewed the war with greater vigor. In Prussia, also, there was a strong party, headed by the high-spirited queen Louisa and prince Louis Ferdinand, in favor of an alliance with the united powers against Bonaparte; but the three ministers, Haugwitz, Lucchesini, and Lombard, who were inclined to France, and utterly wanting in any feeling of patriotism, still possessed the confidence of the irresolute and peace-loving king. Thus Prussia remained neutral, to its own destruction.

§ 575. Whilst the attention of all Europe was directed to the western coast of France, where Napoleon was fitting out ships of every kind with the greatest diligence, and assembling a vast camp at Boulogne, with the purpose, as was believed, of effecting a landing on the English coast, he was making preparations, in all silence, for the memorable campaign of 1805. Never were Napoleon's talents for command or his military genius displayed in a more brilliant light than in the plan of this campaign. Assured of the assistance of most of the princes of southern Germany, Bonaparte crossed the Rhine in the autumn with seven divisions, commanded by his most experienced marshals, Ney, Lannes, Marmont, Soult, Murat, &c., and marched into Swabia; whilst Bernadotte, disregarding Prussia's neutrality, pressed forward through the Brandenburg Margravate of Anspach-Bayreuth upon the Isar. This violation of his neutral position irritated the king, Frederick William III., to such a degree, that he entered into closer relationship with the allies, and assumed a threatening aspect, without, however, actually declaring war. The Electors of Baden, Wirtemberg, and Bavaria, on the other hand, strengthened with their troops the army of the too-powerful enemy, from whose grace they had as much to hope as they had to fear from his frowns. The dukes of Hesse, Nassau, &c., did the same. After Ney's
October 14. successful engagement at Elchingen, the Austrian general, Mack, was shut up in Ulm, and cut off from the main army. Helpless, and despairing of deliverance, the incompetent commander commenced negotiations with the French, which terminated in the disgrace-
October 20. ful capitulation of Ulm. By this arrangement, 33,000 Austrians, including thirteen generals, became prisoners of war. Covered with shame, the once-brave warriors marched before Napoleon, laid down their arms before the victor, placed forty banners at his feet, and delivered up sixty cannon with their horses. When too late, it was seen in Vienna that Mack was not equal to his lofty position, and he was deprived of his honor, his dignities, and the advantages of his office, by a court-martial. Napoleon's joy at this unexampled good fortune was, however, diminished by the contemporaneous maritime victory of the
October 21. English at Trafalgar, which annihilated the whole French fleet, but which also cost the life of the great naval hero, Nelson.

§ 576. The war-party had gained the upper hand in Prussia since the violation of the neutral territory by Bernadotte. The king renewed the bond of perpetual friendship with the sensitive emperor Alexander, in the church of the garrison at Potsdam, over the coffin of Frederick the Great, at night, and then sent Haugwitz with threatening demands to Napoleon. The French emperor, in the meantime, proceeded along the Danube towards the Austrian states, not without many bloody engagements, of which the battles of Dirnstein and Stein against the Russians under Kutusoff and Bagration were of especial importance. November 11. If the French found brave and circumspect opponents in the Russians in these encounters, they had the easier game in Austria. November 13. Murat took possession of Vienna without the slightest trouble; and the prince of Auersburg, who had orders either to defend the bridge over the Danube, which was fortified and filled with gunpowder, or to blow it into the air, allowed himself to be so completely deceived by the bold cunning of the French general, and by pretended negotiations of peace, that he surrendered it to the enemy uninjured and undefended. The irresolution of the emperor Francis, and the divisions between the Austrians and Russians, facilitated the victory of the French, who, laden with enormous booty, pursued the Austro-Russian army, in the midst of perpetual engagements, into Moravia. In Moravia, the December 2, 1805. battle of Austerlitz, in which three emperors were present, was fought on the day of the year in which the emperor was crowned, and in which the winter sun shone upon the most splendid of Napoleon's victories. The emperor Francis, wishing for the termination of the war, suffered himself to be persuaded to pay a humble visit to Napoleon in the French camp, and then consented to a truce which stipulated for the retreat of the Russians from the Austrian states. Upon December 26. this, negotiations were commenced which terminated in the peace of Presburg.

By this peace, Austria lost the territory of Venice, which was united to the kingdom of Italy; Tyrol, which fell to Bavaria; and a portion of Austria, of which the Briesgau and the lands of the Black Forest were allotted to Baden. Bavaria and Wirtemberg received the rank of kingdoms; Baden, that of an archduchy; and all three were joined to the imperial house of Napoleon by the ties of relationship. The daughter of the new king, Max Joseph of Bavaria, was married to the emperor's adopted son-in-law, Eugene Beauharnois, in Wirtemberg; Catherine, the noble daughter of a princely house, was obliged to consent to a marriage with Napoleon's frivolous brother, Jerome, who had shortly before been separated from his citizen wife; and in Baden, Charles, the grandson of the excellent archduke Frederick, was united to Stephanie Beauharnois, a niece of the empress Josephine, who had been adopted by Napoleon. The lands on the Lower Rhine were united into the arch-

duchy of Cleve-Berg, with the capital, Dusseldorf, and presented to the emperor's brother-in-law, Joachim Murat. Holland also was compelled to exchange her republican constitution for a monarchy, and to beg a creature of Napoleon's for a ruler; upon which, the French emperor named his brother Louis king of Holland. The royal family of Naples experienced the wrath of the potentate beyond all others. During the war, an Anglo-Russian fleet had landed at Naples, and been received by Ferdinand and Caroline with joy. Hereupon, Napoleon, the day after the conclusion of the peace of Presburg at Schönbrunn, subscribed the decree which contained the notorious decision, "The dynasty of the Bourbons has ceased to reign in Naples." Upon this, Joseph
December 27. Bonaparte was named king of Naples, and installed in his new dignity by a French army. The royal family, who vainly strove to avert the loss of the beautiful land, at first by entreaties, and afterwards by stirring up the lazzaroni and Calabrese, fled with their friends and treasures to Sicily, where they lived under the protection of the English till Napoleon's downfall. A number of imperial fiefs, with considerable revenues, were established in the conquered and surrendered provinces of Italy, and conferred upon French marshals and statesmen, together with the title of duke.

After the battle of Austerlitz, the Prussian ambassador, Haugwitz, did not venture to convey the charge of his court to the victorious emperor; without asking permission in Berlin, he allowed himself to be induced, partly by threats, and partly by the engaging affability of Napoleon, to subscribe an unfavorable contract, by which Prussia exchanged the Franconian principality of Anspach, some lands on the Lower Rhine, and the principality of Neuremberg in Switzerland, for Hanover. It was in vain that the king resisted the exchange, which threatened to involve him in hostilities with England; separated from Austria by the hasty conclusion of the peace of Presburg, nothing was left to the king but to submit to the dictation of the victor. The news of the sudden change in affairs produced by the battle of Austerlitz produced such an
A. D 1806. effect upon the English minister, Pitt, that he shortly after died.

§ 577. The constitution of the German empire was already dissolved by the elevation of the Elector of Bavaria and of the duke of Wirtemberg into independent monarchs. Napoleon, in consequence, entertained the project of entirely removing the south and west of Germany from the influence of Austria, and of uniting them to himself by the formation of the Confederation of the Rhine. A prospect of enlarging their territories and increasing their power, and fear of the mighty ruler from whose side victory appeared inseparable, induced a great number of princes and estates of the empire to separate themselves from the German empire and to join France. Self-interest was more powerful than patriot-

ism. On the 12th of July, the treaty was signed in Paris, by virtue of which Napoleon, as protector of the Confederation of the Rhine, recognized the full sovereignty of the individual members, upon condition of their maintaining a certain contingent of troops ready at the emperor's disposal. Bavaria, Wirtemberg, Baden, Hesse-Darmstadt, Nassau, and several others, formed the kernel around which the lesser principalities, as Hohenzollern, Leichtensten, Solms, &c., collected themselves, till at length almost all the German confederate states of the second and third rank gave in their adhesion. The Elector arch-chancellor Dalberg, who had been made prince-primate, and who had received Frankfort, together with Hanau and Fulda as a principality, was chosen Napoleon's representative in the Confederation of the Rhine. By the subjection of many small and formerly independent states of the empire under the government of the great prince, the power of the larger number of the members of the confederation was considerably increased. Francis II. now abdicated the title of emperor of Germany, and called himself Francis I., emperor of Austria, and withdrew the whole of his states from the German Union. By this proceeding, the "Holy Roman empire of the German nation" was dissolved. It had been long since reduced to a shadow by internal dissensions and a powerless supreme government. Its mightiest limbs were now the vassals of a foreign tyrant. The sense of degradation pressed heavily upon many a German breast; but who would dare to utter his thoughts after the bold bookseller, Palm, of Nuremberg, had become the victim of a disgraceful judicial murder, for
August 26. refusing to give up the author of a pamphlet published by him on the abasement of Germany?

3. JENA. TILSIT. ERFURT.

§ 578. The wavering conduct of Prussia had filled Napoleon with the deepest anger, and convinced him that the king would be untrustworthy as a friend, and cowardly and innocuous as an enemy. He accordingly flung aside all respect and forbearance, and purposely inflicted many mortifications upon the Prussian government. The irritation produced by this was soon aggravated into a complete rupture by two causes. 1. The formation of the Confederation of the Rhine appeared to indicate an intention of gradually rendering Germany as dependent upon the French empire as were Italy and Holland. Prussia accordingly attempted to frustrate this plan by the establishment of a northern confederation, to which all the estates of the empire which had not yet joined that of the Rhine might connect themselves; and felt herself deeply aggrieved when Napoleon prevented the execution of the project. 2. It was made known in Berlin that the French emperor, during the renewal of the negotiations for peace with the English government, had offered to restore the Electorate of Hanover, that had been surrendered to Prussia without consulting with the Prussian government on the subject. This intelligence, together with numerous violations of territory, convinced the Prussian government that they had the worst to expect from France. A redress of all grievances was demanded in the so-called Ultimatum, the army was placed upon a war-footing, and all connection with France broken off.

§ 579. Whilst people in Berlin were expecting the final answer of France, the French troops under Napoleon and his experienced marshals were already in the heart of Thuringia and Saxony, the Elector of which had united himself, after some hesitation, to Prussia. The first engagement at Saalfeld, where the gallant prince Louis found his death, went against the Prussians; but the defeat suffered by the army under the command of the old duke of Brunswick, in the great double battle of Jena and Auerstadt, was terrible and fatal. It decided the fate of the countries between the Rhine and the Elbe. The former presumption of the officers and young nobles was suddenly turned into despondency, and the greatest confusion and helplessness took possession of the leaders. Hohenlohe, with 17,000 men, laid down his arms at Prenzlow; the fortresses of Erfurt, Magdeburg, Spondau, Stettin, &c., surrendered within a few days, with such wonderful celerity, that the commandants of many of them were suspected of treachery, so utterly unaccountable did such cowardice and such entire want of self-reliance appear. Blücher alone saved the honor of Prussia by the bloody combat in and around Lubeck, though he could not prevent the horrible storming of this slightly-fortified town; in Colberg, also, Gneisenau and Schill, supported by the brave citizen, Nettlebeck, courageously resisted the superior force of the enemy. Thirteen days after the battle of Jena, Napoleon marched into Berlin, and issued his mandates from thence. The elector of Hesse, who wished to remain neutral, and who had withdrawn his forces from the contest, was obliged to surrender both land and army to the enemy, and to seek for protection as a fugitive in a foreign land. He took up his residence in Prague. The duke of Brunswick, who had been severely wounded, and who was carried into his capital on a litter after the battle of Jena, was compelled to seek for refuge in Denmark to die in peace. Jena and East Friesland were united to Holland; the Hanse towns, as well as Leipsic, were oppressed by the deprivation of all English wares, and by severe military taxes; and treasures of art and science, and the trophies of former victories, were carried away from all quarters. It was only to the Elector of Saxony, whose troops had fought at Jena, that Napoleon showed any favor. He set the Saxon prisoners at liberty, and granted the Elector a favorable peace; upon which the latter, dignified with the title of king, joined the Confederation of the Rhine, like the other Saxon dukes. From this time, Frederick

October 10.

October 14.

October 28.

December.

Augustus, to the misfortune of himself and his people, felt himself bound by the ties of gratitude to the French emperor.

§ 580. The king of Prussia had fled to Königsberg, where he vainly attempted to obtain peace. Napoleon's demands rose with his fortunes. In his necessity, Frederick William turned to his friend Alexander, who immediately despatched a Russian army under Benningsen and others into East Prussia, to prevent the French passing the Vistula. Upon this, Napoleon issued a proclamation to the Poles, pretendedly in the name of Kosciusko, by which these misused people were summoned to fight for liberty and independence. The Poles willingly made the greatest sacrifices, and strengthened the ranks of the French by their brave soldiers under the command of Dombrowski. Napoleon marched into Warsaw amidst the rejoicings of the people; but the Poles discovered, only too soon, that the foreign potentate was more intent upon the gratification of his own ambition and love of power, than upon the restoration of their empire. Murderous battles were now fought on the banks of the Vistula, and torrents of blood shed at Pultusk and Morungen. But the great

February 8, 1807. blow was struck in the battle of Preuss-Eylau, where the martial spirit of the French and Russians gave rise to a contest which in loss of men equals any event of the sort in the world's history. Both parties claimed the victory, and their efforts and exhaustion were so great, that the war suffered an interruption of four months. During this interval, negotiations were again renewed; but much as the king, who was waiting with his family in Memel, might desire the termination of the war, that he might free his subjects from the dreadful exactions of the French, he was too honest to dissever his own cause from that of his ally. But when the Silesian fortresses on the Oder, Glogau, Brieg, Schweidnitz, and Breslau, fell into the hands of the French by the cowardice of their commandants, and even Dantzic was sur-

May 24. rendered to the marshal Lefebvre by the gallant governor Kalkreuth, the king lost all confidence in a successful issue. When, after the recommencement of hostilities, the French gained a brilliant victory over the Russians in the battle of Friedland, on the anniversary of the battle of Marengo, and took possession of Königsberg, the allied monarchs, after a personal interview with Bonaparte on the Niemen, thought it prudent to consent to the peace of Tilsit, oppressive

June 7-9. as were the conditions. By this peace, Frederick William lost half his states; he was compelled to surrender all the lands between the Rhine and the Elbe, to consent to the establishment of a dukedom of Warsaw under the supremacy of the king of Saxony, to the elevation of Dantzic into a free state, and to the payment of the unheard sum of 150 millions to defray the expenses of the war. Napoleon formed the states ceded by Prussia, along with electoral Hesse, Brunswick, and South Hanover, into the new kingdom of Westphalia, with the capital,

Cassel, and placed there his youngest brother Jerome as king, under condition, that, as a member of the Rhine Confederation, he should supply the emperor with Westphalian troops, and make over to him one-half the receipts of his treasury.

§ 581. Austerlitz and Jena had broken the power of Austria and Prussia, so that the destinies of Europe were now guided by France, England, and Russia. These three great powers were unanimous in this, that they paid no regard to right except where there existed the power of self-defence, as was shown by the proceedings in Sweden and Denmark. Gustavus IV. of Sweden would not accede to the peace of Tilsit; but, supported by England, continued the war alone against Napoleon. Although his conduct at first displayed strength of character and magnanimity, his boundless conceit, and his total misapprehension of his position and powers, soon showed that his mind must be in a deranged state. Strongly impressed with the sanctity of the kingly dignity, he refused the title of emperor to the ruler of France, and only addressed him as General Bonaparte; involved in the meshes of religious fanaticism, he believed himself ordained by Providence to re-instate the Bourbons, and to overthrow the "beast of the Revelations" (Napoleon). He carried his hatred against Bonaparte so far as mortally to offend Russia and Prussia by sending back their orders, and banishing their ambassadors from Stockholm, because these powers had concluded a peace with the usurper. The French conquered Stralsund and the island of Rugen, whilst the Russian army penetrated into Finland and made themselves masters of the country. The attempts of the French emperor to destroy the trade of Great Britain by a continental blockade made the Swedish war a matter of importance to the English. They feared lest the French should establish a firm footing on the Baltic, and exclude their ships from its shores by shutting up the Sound. They accordingly made a proposal to Denmark to enter into an alliance with them, and to yield up her noble fleet to their keeping. This proposal was rejected with indignation; whereupon the English fleet appeared in
September 2-5, 1807. the Sound, bombarded Copenhagen, laid a part of the town in ashes, and carried off the whole Danish fleet as their prey. This breach of the rights of nations enraged the king of Denmark to such a degree, that he united himself closely to France, and declared war against the English and their ally, the king of Sweden. At this time, Napoleon and Alexander were allies. They held the celebrated meeting
September 27, 1808. in Erfurt, where the whole splendor of European magnificence was displayed, and where four kings and thirty-four princes were assembled together out of Germany, for the purpose of paying their homage to the mighty potentate. Here the two emperors promised not to interrupt each other in their plans of conquest, so that Napoleon was to be left unfettered in Spain, and Alexander in

Finland, Moldavia, and Wallachia. The kingdom of Sweden was now threatened on all sides. The Russians were already approaching the capital, the Danes, and the Spanish troops, who, under the command of La Romana, were serving Napoleon, were upon the frontiers; the army and military affairs of Sweden were in the most wretched condition; the heavy taxes could not be raised from the exhausted land; and yet the king obstinately refused all proposals of peace. At this crisis, a conspiracy was formed in the army and capital, in consequence of which Gustavus IV. was violently seized in his palace, compelled to abdicate his throne, and then conducted to an old insular castle. Hereupon the Diet declared Gustavus IV. and all his posterity to have
March 13, 1809. forfeited the crown, invited his uncle, Charles XIII., to the throne, and restricted the monarchical power. This revolution was followed by a peace, by which Finland and the Aaland islands remained with Russia. The election of a successor to the throne, which was rendered necessary by the childless old age of the king, fell upon the marshal Bernadotte (Ponte-Corvo), who, by his friendly treatment of the Swedish troops during the Prussian war, had gained many friends among the officers. Bernadotte was, with the unwillingly yielded consent of
August 21, 1810. Napoleon, declared successor to the Swedish throne, and, after his accession to the Lutheran church, adopted by Charles XIII.

4. THE EVENTS IN THE PYRENEAN PENINSULA.

§ 582. Led astray by the success of his arms, Napoleon now proceeded from one enterprise to another. Like Charlemagne, whom he adopted as his model, he wished to unite the Southern and Western states of Europe into a vast empire under the supremacy of France. With this object, he sought to gain possession of the Spanish peninsula, and to make himself master of the provinces still left unconquered in Italy. In the first place, he demanded of the Portuguese government to renounce the alliance with England, and to close their harbors against English vessels. When the court of Lisbon refused to yield submission to this mandate, Napoleon bought over the all-powerful favorite of the royal pair of Spain, the "prince of peace," Godoy, by the prospect of a principality in Portugal, and sent marshal Junot with an army directly through Spain into that country. The dastardly court of Lisbon did not await the
November, 1807. coming of the French, but fled, with all its treasures, in English ships, to the Brazils; upon which Junot, who had been created duke of Abrantes, took possession of the capital and the whole country, and then declared, in the name of his commander, "that the house of Braganza had ceased to reign." Godoy, who, without
February 1, 1808. either virtue, talent, or merit, had become the absolute ruler of Spain by the mere favor of the profligate queen and the

boundless weakness of Charles IV., now delivered up his country into the hands of Napoleon. Spanish troops under La Romana entered into the service of the emperor, and fought on the Danish islands against the Swedes, whilst the soldiers of France were occupying Spain in great numbers. This caused commotions amongst the Spanish people; disturbances broke out in Aranjuez and Madrid, in which the palace of the detested favorite was plundered and destroyed, and he himself roughly handled and threatened with death. Terrified by these occurrences, the March, 1808. weak Charles abdicated his throne in favor of his eldest son Ferdinand, who, as the enemy of Godoy, was loved by the people, but, for the same reason, mortally hated by his parents. But notwithstanding the humility with which Ferdinand attempted to gain Napoleon's consent to this change of the crown, and at the same time became a suitor for the hand of one of his relatives — the French emperor concealed his sentiments, ordered Murat to take possession of Madrid, and then invited the royal pair, along with the "prince of peace" and Ferdinand, to a personal conference with him in Bayonne. Ferdinand did not dare to resist the summons of the potentate, although warned by his friends, and though the people sought to restrain him from undertaking this fatal journey. Once in Bayonne, the royal family of Spain was entangled by Napoleon in the meshes of a false and insidious state policy. Charles was prevailed upon to revoke his abdication, and to transfer the regained crown to Napoleon and his family. Ferdinand, incapable of a vigorous resolution, allowed himself to be induced by the emperor's threats and intrigues to acknowledge this arbitrary act. He resided henceforth in France, in the enjoyment of an annuity, whilst Charles IV. and his family settled in Rome. Napoleon then named his brother June 6, 1808. Joseph king of Spain, and sought to win over the people to the new system by the restoration of the Cortes Constitution, and by improving the affairs of government, and of the administration of justice. But the frightful insurrection in Madrid, by which May 2. 1200 French soldiers of Murat's army were killed, whilst the intrigues in Bayonne were yet pending, showed that the nation would not submit so easily to the foreign yoke as the imbecile royal family.

§ 583. Even before Joseph, after the surrender of the kingdom of Naples to his brother-in-law, Murat, held his solemn entry into Madrid, juntas were formed in several towns, which, as provisional governments, took the regulation of affairs into their own hands, and refused obedience to the new king. Armed bands under daring leaders, served them for defence; and, favored by the ravines and mountain heights of their country, began a guerilla war against the French soldiers. Whilst the educated and enlightened were more attached to the new system, which afforded a life of political freedom, than to the kingly absolutism and

priestly rule of the former period, and were consequently nicknamed "Josephinos," the great mass of the people blindly followed the exhortations of fanatical monks and priests, who held the sacrilegious French in horror. It is true that Napoleon's army possessed sufficient power to maintain the king and his minister in Madrid, but their laws were respected no further than they could be supported by French bayonets. The more remote towns and provinces followed partly the juntas, which had their central point in the grand junta of Seville, and partly their own will, without recognizing any government whatever. But anarchy was the very thing that saved Spain in this stormy period. Europe gazed in astonishment upon a people who courageously faced death for their nationality and independence, for their ancient manners and religious usages, for their superstitions and customary arrangements. The leaders of the bands, with their brave but undisciplined followers, avoided open battles; their strength consisted in unexpected attacks and petty warfare. And whilst the French dissipated their strength in these single encounters, and in the seige of well-defended towns, the English, supported by the natives, began the first successful war by land against Napoleon. At first, the French arms were successful. Bessières drove
July 14, 1808. back the unpractised troops of Spain at Rio Secco, and it seemed as if the assumption of arms by the Spanish people was only to increase the triumph of the military emperor, — when suddenly the report spread abroad of Dupont's capitulation at Baylen, in
July 22. Andalusia, by which 20,000 Frenchmen were made prisoners of war, and perished miserably. This blow filled the nation with enthusiasm and military ardor. Joseph left Madrid, the French army retreated beyond the Ebro, and intelligence was shortly after brought that, in Portugal also, the French were obliged to retreat before the English, under Wellington, Moore, and others, and that they would have experienced a fate similar to that of Dupont's army, if the English,
August 30, 1808. by the over-hasty capitulation of Cintra, had not allowed Junot's troops a free passage to France. The affairs of the French in the Spanish peninsula seemed ruined.

§ 584. Napoleon himself now marched at the head of a mighty army into Spain. The unpractised troops of the insurgents, who opposed themselves without any regular plan to the great winner of battles, were defeated in several engagements, so that the emperor, in four weeks, was
December 4, 1808. able to enter Madrid and to give back the crown to his brother Joseph. Whilst Napoleon was making fresh arrangements in the capital, attempting by kindness and threats to induce the Spaniards to acknowledge Joseph, and inflicting severe punishments upon some of the most refractory, his marshals were sustaining bloody en-
February 20, 1809. counters with the guerilla chiefs and the English. Saragossa was taken after the most desperate resistance, and the gallant

July 28. defender of the city, Palafox, conveyed to France; the brave general Moore was killed whilst embarking his troops at Corunna; and although Wellington obtained the advantage in the
July 26. battle of Talavera, yet the English army restricted itself for some time to the defence of Portugal. Seville, also, and the whole of Andalusia and Granada, fell into the hands of the French. Spain, nevertheless, held herself erect. The national government removed to Cadiz, which bade defiance to every storm; and the Spanish general, La Romana, who, upon the news of his country's rise, had escaped with his troops from Denmark in English ships to his native soil, brought system and order to the guerilla warfare.

When, in the year 1809, the new war with Austria called the emperor from Spain, he left behind him a large army, consisting for the most part of Germans. At the conclusion of the Austrian war, this force was increased to nearly 300,000 men, who, under the command of his most experienced marshals, (Soult, Massena, Suchet, Ney, St. Cyr, Marmont, Macdonald, &c.), traversed the peninsula in every direction, and raised the renown of the French arms. But victories only increased the hatred towards the French; the petty war, under the daring leaders, Ballasteros, Empecinado, Morillo, O'Donnel, Mina, Moreto, assumed a more sanguinary character, and no courage was of avail against the assassinations to which the revengeful Spaniards were driven by rage and fanaticism. The most heroic deeds that were performed by Napoleon's warriors, under the fervid sun of Spain, now in the battle-field, and now in toilsome marches, through mountains and ravines, and again in sieges and storms (Valencia, Gerona), contributed nothing to the quiet possession of the country. In the meanwhile, the Cortes Assembly in Cadiz projected the liberal constitution, which is known as the Constitution of the year '12, and which was to have destroyed absolute monarchy and the power of the priests in Spain for ever. But this Constitution, owing to the hatred of the priests, remained unknown and detested by the people.

§ 585. The Russian campaign of 1812 compelled the emperor to diminish the Spanish army. Wellington took advantage of this to march into Spain with a larger force. Supported by the guerilla bands, the British army soon obtained advantages over their opponents, who were
July 22, 1812. suffering from every kind of want. After Marmont's defeat at Salamanca by Wellington, the English took possession of Madrid and drove out the French king. Suchet, duke of Albufera, and Soult, both alike brave and rapacious, held fortune firm to their standards, and Joseph was once more able to take possession of his tottering throne; but the frightful catastrophe produced by the Russian campaign compelled the French army in the western peninsula also to retreat, and obliged Joseph to quit the Spanish territory. After the victory of

Vittoria, Wellington followed the retreating forces over the Pyrenees, but found a brave opponent in Soult, even on French ground.
June 21, 1813. So late as the 10th of April, 1814, when the allies were encamped on the Elysian fields of Paris, the marshal still resisted the advancing enemy at Toulouse, although compelled to yield the field to the superior enemy.

§ 586. Imprisonment of the Pope.—The hatred against the French, and the fanatical fury of the Spaniards, were the work of the priests. Napoleon might have learned from this what power the religion he denied, and its venerable usages, were capable of exerting upon the minds of believers; but in his pride he refused to recognize any bonds that could limit his ambition. When the pope refused to lay an embargo upon the English ships in the ports of the States of the Church, and to enter into an offensive and defensive alliance with France, Napoleon inflicted upon him a succession of injuries, and united some portions of the ecclesiastical States to the kingdom of Italy. This, however, in no ways subdued the resolution of the inflexible prince of the Church; on the contrary, he was thereby induced, in the second war with Austria, to make common cause with the opponents of the emperor, against the supremacy of France. Hereupon, Napoleon, in a decree
May 27, 1809. published at Schönbrunn, declared that the temporal power of the pope had ceased; and when the holy father, irritated at this, ful-
June 16. minated an excommunication against the emperor, Napoleon ordered him to be carried off from Rome by violence, ba-
July 6. nished the cardinals, and united the States of the Church with the French territory. Pius VII. lived in several towns, till at length a residence was allotted him in Fontainbleau. As he obstinately refused, whilst in a state of captivity and deprived of his council of cardinals, to fill up the vacant bishoprics, or to arrange any ecclesiastical affairs, Napoleon found himself again compelled to arbitrary and despotic measures. The pope, however, at length allowed himself, in an unguarded moment, to be persuaded to an arrangement by which his authority was diminished.

5. THE SECOND AUSTRIAN WAR. HOFER. SCHILL. (1809.)

§ 587. Napoleon's arbitrary proceedings in Italy, and his increasing influence in Germany, awakened the anxiety of Austria. The cabinet of Vienna, therefore, resolved once more to try the fortune of war. The popular war in Spain, in which the French emperor was obliged to employ a considerable portion of his forces, the universal discontent at the restrictions upon commerce, the deep movement in Northern Germany, all this seemed to point out that the favorable moment was arrived for Austria to regain the power she had lost, and to break to pieces the foreign despotism. The landsturm was called out, and an attempt was made, by means of vehement proclamations, full of fine promises, to awaken enthusiasm and patriotic feeling. But the magic of the imperial name was still too powerful. The princes of the Rhine Confederation strengthened the French army with their brave troops, and the soldiers of South Germany poured forth their blood for a foreign despot against the warriors of their own race.

A. D. 1809. In April, Austria ordered its army, which was placed under the command of the archduke Charles, to march into Bavaria and Italy. But the first encounters decided the fate of the war. Napoleon, supported by Wirtemberg and Bavaria, marched down the Danube with a considerable force, drove the enemy over the Inn by a succession April 20—22, 1809. of victorious encounters (Abensberg, Eckmühl), and marched for the second time into the heart of the Austrian dominions. On the 10th of May, the emperor stood before the walls of the capital, which, three days after, he entered as a conqueror. Below Vienna, the north bank of the Danube, which is there crossed by numerous bridges, was defended by the archduke Charles. Upon the French army attempting to cross the river from Lobau, an island in the stream, they met with May 21, 22. such opposition in the two days' combat of Aspern and Eslingen, that they were obliged to relinquish the attempt. This bloody, though indecisive battle, where 12,000 French soldiers, including marshal Lannes, were left upon the field, gave the first shock to the belief in Napoleon's invincibility, and increased the confidence of the oppressed people. It was only when the emperor had received reënforcements, and Eugene Beauharnais had united himself to the grand army, after the victory at Raab, that the French again, and this time with July 5, 6. more success, attempted the passage of the river, and defeated the archduke in the great battle of Wagram. The loss on both sides was tolerably equal, and it was not to be disputed that the French no longer retained their former superiority in the field. Austria, a few July 12. days later, concluded, over hastily, the truce of Znaym, that she might open negotiations for a fresh peace.

§ 588. This truce was fatal to the Tyrolese. The warlike inhabitants of the mountainous region of the Tyrol, who were attached with the truest devotion to Austria, had risen at the commencement of the war to free themselves from the detested government of Bavaria, under which they had been placed by the peace of Presburg. The stimulating exhortations of their priests, who possessed great influence over these simple mountaineers, and the enticements and promises of Austria, produced a general insurrection. Trusting to the assistance of Austria, the Tyrolese seized the familiar rifle, and, like the Spaniards, directed from the mountain heights and gullies the unerring tube against the French and Bavarians, hazarding life and property in defence of the customs of their fathers. At their head stood Andreas Hofer, a publican in the Passeyrthal, a man of great consideration among his countrymen both on account of his bodily strength and courage, as well as his piety, his patriotism, and his honorable character. Shrewder and more far-sighted men, as Hormayr, the historian of the Tyrol and of this war, made use of Hofer's influence with the people to carry the movement through the whole land. By the side of Hofer stood Speckbacher, the soul of the confederation. A frightful war broke out; the Bavarians were compelled to evacuate the German Tyrol, and Hofer took possession of Innspruck as the Austrian commandant. The truce of Znaym produced discouragement and irresolution among the insurgents, without, however, putting an end to the war. But when the conclusion of the peace of Vienna or Schönbrunn, by which Austria again lost 2000 square (German) miles and three millions of subjects, deprived the Tyrolese of all hopes of assistance, and the Bavarians and French, with increased forces, marched into the land from three different quarters, the insurrection was quelled. Innspruck again fell into the hands of the Bavarians. Speckbacher and other leaders sought their safety in flight; but Hofer, who, led astray by bad counsel, had again taken up arms, was discovered in a cave where he had concealed himself for two months with his family, and shot in Mantua. (February 18, 1810.) He died with the courage of a hero, and highly reverenced by his countrymen. Tyrol was divided into three portions.

§ 589. During the second Austrian war, attempts were made in various parts of Germany to shake off the foreign yoke. In Kurhessen, the colonel, Von Dörenberg, attempted to overthrow the king of Westphalia by an insurrection. The failure of this attempt did not deter the brave major Von Schill from hazarding a similar one in Prussia. With a troop of bold volunteers, he hoped to arouse the North of Germany against the foreign despotism. But fear of the great emperor of battles paralyzed the arms of the people. Pursued by the enemy, Schill threw himself into the strong town of Stralsund, in the hope of being able to take ship from thence to England. (May 31, 1809.) But he fell during an assault, together with most of his companions in arms, beneath the sabres of the enemy's cavalry; the rest were made prisoners of war, the officers shot in Wesel and Brunswick, and the privates condemned to the French galleys.

Duke William of Brunswick, the heroic son of the field-marshal, was more fortunate. He had marched to the aid of Austria with his "black band;" but treating the truce of Znaym with contempt, because in it he had only been regarded as an Austrian marshal, and not as an independent prince of the empire, he fought his way with incredible bravery through hostile lands and armies to the North Sea, whence he escaped with his followers to England. (October 12, 1809.) The intense excitement of men's minds was evinced by the attempted assassination of Napoleon by a young man of Hamburg named Staps. Being seized by General Rapp, and confessing his intention, he was lead to death.

If the enterprises of Schill and Dörenberg were foolhardy and inconsiderate, they were nevertheless of importance as proofs of the sentiments prevailing among the people, and of the newly-aroused patriotism. These sentiments were encouraged and fostered chiefly in Prussia. It was here that patriotically disposed men had assumed the conduct of affairs after the disastrous days of Jena and Tilsit, and driven the characterless old Prussian party from the councils of the king. The high-minded baron Von Stein attempted to elevate the citizen and peasant class by introducing a liberal municipal government, rendering the possession of landed property attainable by every one, and limiting the class privileges of the middle ages. Scharnhorst completely revolutionized the affairs of the army: the employment of mercenary troops was superseded by the universal obligation to bear arms, the feelings of honor were excited among the privates by throwing open the rank of officer to all, and by the abolition of degrading punishments. It is true that the king, in a short time, found himself compelled to remove his patriotic advisers, when the mandate of Napoleon outlawed the baron Von Stein, and compelled him to take refuge in Russia. But their works, nevertheless, remained, and formed the groundwork of a system of government which was founded upon the legal equality of the whole of the citizens. Stein's successor, the astute chancellor Von Hardenberg, proceeded, as much as possible, upon the same principles; and the Tugendbund, which was joined by some of the noblest men of the country, aroused and encouraged patriotism and love of freedom among the people and the ardent youth.

§ 590. The French Empire at its height. — Napoleon stood at the summit of his power and greatness after the peace of Vienna. It was only the reflection that he had no heir that occasioned him any disquiet; he accordingly got himself divorced from Josephine, upon the December 15, 1809. ground of some informality in their nuptials, and married Maria Louisa, daughter of the emperor of Austria. It was on the 1st of April, 1810, that he celebrated his nuptials with the "daughter of the Cæsars." Five queens supported the train of the bride, and an unexampled magnificence was displayed. But a fire during the ball that was given by the Austrian ambassador, Schwarzenberg, in honor of the newly-married pair, and in which his sister perished in the flames, was regarded as an omen of evil promise. When a son was born to the emperor in the following year, March 20, 1811. who received the pompous title of king of Rome, Napoleon's fortune seemed to be complete and the future of France secured. But pride and ambition drove him on from one act of violence to another; there was no end of the alliances, separations, and interchanges of lands and territories: what the despot created to-day, he destroyed on the morrow; him whom he made a great man one year he humbled in the following. The blockade of the continent became daily more rigid, to the despair of merchants and traders. When king Louis of Holland resisted this, and permitted his people some relaxation, he was so unkindly and unworthily treated by his imperial brother that he renounced the throne, upon which Napoleon united the kingdom of Holland with France. A few months later, he also added the Hanse towns, Hamburg, Bremen, Lubeck, and, besides these, the dukedom of Oldenburg and the provinces between the Rhine and the Elbe, to the French empire, which now ruled the whole coast of the North Sea, and numbered 130 departments. Hamburg was made the capital of the new territory, and the cruel Davoust placed there as ruler. The slavery within increased with the extension without. A formidable state-police suppressed the last remains of freedom, and threatened every suspected person with persecution and imprisonment. Arbitrariness, passion, and despotism, usurped the place of popular rights; restrictions on trade, oppressive taxation, and military conscriptions were the burdens imposed upon friendly states; the calamities of war, exactions, and the quarterings of troops, were the miseries of the hostile.

6. THE WAR AGAINST RUSSIA.

§ 591. The extension of the empire of France even to the shores of the Baltic, by which means the duke of Oldenburg, a near relation of the imperial family of Russia, was deprived of his lands, completely destroyed the friendship between Alexander and Napoleon, which had already grown cold since the increase of the dukedom of Warsaw by the peace of Vienna. This hostile feeling, which was first displayed in the angry language of diplomatists and in newspaper articles, was increased when the Russian government proclaimed a new tariff unfavorable to the importation of French goods. Both parties prepared themselves for a desperate struggle. The emperor of Russia concluded a peace with the Turks by the mediation of the English, and brought over to his side Bernadotte of Sweden, whom Napoleon had greatly injured; the French emperor, on the other hand, arranged a treaty with Prussia and Austria, by which he obtained a considerable increase of his forces. Alexander's defiant demand, that the French garrisons should at once evacuate Pomerania and Russia, produced a declaration of war.

§ 592. In May, Napoleon, accompanied by his wife, made his appearance in Dresden, where the princes of the Rhine Confederation, the emperor of Austria, and the king of Prussia, were likewise present to pay their homage to the potentate who was now summoning half Europe to arms against Russia. After a residence of ten days among this brilliant assemblage of princes, Napoleon hastened to his army, nearly half a million strong, and which, with more than a thousand cannon and 20,000 baggage waggons, was lying scattered along between the Vistula and the Niemen. The left wing, consisting for the most part of Poles and Prussians, under the command of Macdonald, was placed upon the banks of the Baltic; the right, formed by the Austrian auxiliaries led by Schwarzenberg, with a division of French and Saxons under Regnier, stood on the Lower Bug, opposite the southern army of the Russians; the body, commanded by Napoleon himself, and under him by the most experienced marshals of his school, crossed the Niemen in June and marched into Wilna. The appearance of the French awakened the most sanguine expectations and warlike enthusiasm among the Poles. The diet of Warsaw declared the restoration of the kingdom of Poland, and determined upon the formation of a general confederation. But popular movements were not to Napoleon's taste; he forbade a rise *en masse*, and damped the enthusiasm by declaring, that, out of regard to Austria, he could not consent to the restoration of the Polish republic in its whole extent. Nevertheless, Polish warriors under Poniatowski and others fought with their accustomed valor beneath the eagles of Napoleon, and the Polish people supported, to the best of their power, the foreign troops that were now marching in the midst of dreadful rains from Wilna to Witepsk. Moscow, "the heart of Russia," was Napoleon's aim; but he soon discovered what powerful allies the Russians were possessed of in the nature of their country. The roads were impassable, supplies did not arrive, the poor and badly cultivated soil afforded little means of subsistence; diseases diminished the number of troops and filled the hospitals.

§ 593. The Russian generals, Barclay de Tolly and Bagration, avoided a fixed battle, and lured the emperor onwards deeper into the country.
August 17, 1812. The first battle was fought at Smolensk; but after fighting a whole day without any decisive result, the Russians, in the night, left the town, which was in flames. On the following morning, the French found the site of the town drenched with blood and covered with corpses. A council of war was held in Smolensk, but, despite the number of voices that were raised against the continuance of the campaign, Napoleon insisted upon the conquest of Moscow, where he intended to pass the winter, and to force Alexander to a peace. The Russians murmured at Barclay's mode of conducting the war, as the Romans had once done at the delay of Fabius; for which reason, Alexander appointed General Kutusoff to the command, who, as a native of the country, was nearer to the people, and who was much beloved by the lower class of Russians for his attachment to the religious customs, and to the old Russian manners and usages. Kutusoff dared not allow the holy city of Moscow, with its innumerable towers and golden cupolas, to fall into the hands of the French, unless he wished to forfeit all the affections of the people. He halted his troops, and by this means brought about the
September 7. murderous battle of Borodino, on the Moskwa, in which the French indeed remained in possession of the field, but were obliged to allow the Russians to retire in good order. Upwards of 70,000 bodies covered the field; Ney, "the prince of the Moskwa," was the

hero of the day. On the 14th of September, the French entered Moscow. The nobility and the better class of citizens had left the place. A secret horror fell upon the soldiers as they entered the town, and saw nothing but a few of the rabble creeping about; but who can describe their terror when the four days' conflagration of Moscow, which, in the absence of all means of extinguishing it, soon became a sea of flame, reduced the city, which was built of wood, and the ancient Kremlin, which Napoleon himself had chosen for a residence, to ashes? The governor of Moscow, Rostopschin, had given orders for this horrible deed, without the command of the Tzar, for the purpose of depriving the grand army of its winter quarters, and of compelling it to a disastrous retreat. Forgetful of all order and discipline, the soldiers rushed into the burning houses to gratify their passions and love of plunder.

§ 594. From all this it was apparent that the Russians were waging a war of extermination; and yet Napoleon, from some unaccountable delusion, suffered himself to be decoyed, by the artfully sustained hopes of a peace, into remaining thirty-four days in Moscow without perceiving that Kutusoff was seeking to detain him till the commencement of winter, that during the retreat the cold might destroy the half-clad soldiers, who were suffering from want of the necessaries of life. At length, late in October, was commenced that fatal retreat of the grand army, which has no parallel in the history of the sufferings of war. The plan at first contemplated, of marching upon Kaluga, was given up after
October 24. the dreadful battle of Malo-Jaroslowetz, and the road towards Smolensk over the corpse-covered battle field of Borodino was entered upon. In November, the cold reached 18, and afterwards became 27 degrees below zero. Who can describe all the sufferings, battles, and fatigues, by which the grand army was gradually destroyed in the midst of the stern winter? Hunger, cold, and exhaustion produced greater ravages than the bullets of the Russians or the lances of the Cossacks. It was a horrible sight to see thousands of starved or frozen soldiers lying in the public roads, or on the desolate steppes covered with snow and ice, intermingled with fallen horses, abandoned arms, and rich articles of plunder. Kutusoff, who, in a proclamation, ascribed the burning of Moscow to the French, to inflame the hatred of the people still more against them, never left their flank, and forced them to contest every yard of ground. When Smolensk was reached, about the middle of November, the army still numbered about 40,000 men, fit for service; these were followed by upwards of of 30,000 unarmed stragglers, without discipline, order, or leaders; a picture of wretchedness and horror. And yet it was here that the greatest misery began, inasmuch as, by some error in the orders, the expected supplies of arms, clothes, and necessaries were not forthcoming in the town, and the enemy with increased forces were obstructing the path of march. The hero of the retreat was Ney,

the commander of the rear, the "bravest of the brave." His passage over the frozen but partly thawed Dnieper, during the night, was one of the most daring feats recorded in history. On the 25th of November, the army arrived at the ever-memorable river Beresina. Two bridges were thrown across the stream in the presence of the hostile army, and the small remnant that still preserved its discipline passed over in the midst of innumerable dangers; but nearly 18,000 stragglers, that did not arrive in time, fell into the hands of the enemy. How many were drowned between the masses of ice in the cold waves of the river, or were trampled down and destroyed in the dreadful press, no one can tell. After the passage of the Beresina, Napoleon had still 8,000 soldiers fit for service. Ney was the last man of the rear-guard. According to the official account, 243,600 enemies' bodies were buried in Russia. Half of Europe had cause to mourn. On the 3d of December, Napoleon published the celebrated 29th bulletin, which informed the expectant people, who had been without intelligence for months, that the emperor was safe and the grand army destroyed. Two days afterwards, he made over the command to Murat, and hastened to Paris to arrange fresh armaments.

November 26-29.

D. DISSOLUTION OF THE FRENCH EMPIRE, AND ESTABLISHMENT OF A FRESH SYSTEM.

1. THE GERMAN WAR OF LIBERATION, AND THE FALL OF NAPOLEON.

§ 595. The saying attributed to Talleyrand, that the Russian campaign was "the beginning of the end," soon proved true. No doubt, oppressive conscriptions soon filled up the chasms in the French army, but the faith in Napoleon's invincibility was gone; and fresh armies formed from young and inexperienced men were opposed to an enemy inspired to great actions both by the victory they had attained, and by the newly-awakened feeling of patriotism. So early as the 30th of December, the Prussian general, York, who commanded under Macdonald, on the east coast, had entered into an understanding with the Russian marshal, Diebitsch, and had desisted, together with his troops, from any further hostilities. It is true that this proceeding was publicly censured in Berlin; but the king's journey to Breslau, where many patriotic men assembled themselves around him, was the first step towards the alliance with Russia, which was completed in the following February. The boundless ill-usage experienced by Prussia had excited such a detestation of the foreign despotism, that the king's "Call to his people" to take up arms awakened an incredible ardor for war

February 3, 1813.

The enthusiasm seized upon all ages and conditions. Youths and men withdrew themselves from their wonted occupations, and from the circles of affection, that they might dedicate their strength to the liberation of their fatherland. Students and teachers left the lecture-room, officials left their posts, young nobles the homes of their fathers; they seized the musket and knapsack, and placed themselves in the ranks as common soldiers, along with the mechanic who had come forth from his workshop, and the peasant who had exchanged the ploughshare for the sword.

§ 596. The allied monarchs attempted to win over the king of Saxony to their cause. But Frederick Augustus resisted the invitation. Gratitude for the many proofs of favor and confidence which had been shown him by Napoleon, and fear of the anger of that potentate, bound him fast to his alliance with the French emperor. He placed his lands, his fortresses, and his troops at his disposal, and Saxony accordingly became the seat of the war. In the first battles at Lützen, the French indeed re-
May 2. tained possession of the field, and drove back their opponents as far as the Oder; but the heroism of the young German
May 20. warriors, who fearlessly presented their breasts to the storm of balls, showed the enemy that a different spirit had taken possession of the Prussians from that displayed at Jena. Scharnhorst breathed forth his heroic soul at Lützen. Among the thousands who strewed the field in these two engagements were Bessieres and Duroc. The death of the latter, whom Napoleon loved and esteemed above all others for his amiability, fidelity, and attachment, was a great shock to the French emperor. For the first time, a dark presentiment of the mutabilities of life seemed to take possession of his breast. But pride and presumption hurried him onwards. It was in vain that Austria endeavored, during a short cessation of hostilities, to negotiate a peace at the Congress of Prague;
July, 12. Napoleon insolently refused to surrender any of the conquered countries. This was followed by a breaking up of
August 12. the truce, and by Austria's declaration of war against France.
August 26–27. It is true that Napoleon, in the battle of Dresden, once more chained victory to his eagles, and had the pleasure of sceing his opponent, Moreau, whom Alexander had summoned from America, carried from the field mortally wounded; but the fruits of the Dresden victory were destroyed (1) by Blücher's simultaneous engagement on the
August 26. Katzbach in Silesia, against Macdonald, a battle in which Marshal "Forwards" gained the title of a prince of the battle-field; (2) by the French general, Vandamme, being defeated and made prisoner with his whole army, in the hotly contested battle of Culm, a catastrophe that was brought about by Kleist's daring march
Aug. 29–30. across the heights of Nollendorf, and by the pertinacious courage of the Russian guards under Ostermann; and (3)
August 23. by the splendid feats of the Prusso-Swedish army at Gros-
September 6. Beeren and Dennewitz.

§ 597. By the autumn, the result of this great struggle was scarcely doubtful; the princes of the Confederation of the Rhine gradually fell off from Napoleon, and joined the allies; thus Bavaria, who
October 8. concluded the treaty of Ried with Austria. In October, the armies united themselves together in the broad plain of Leipsic; the Austrians, under prince Schwarzenberg, in whose hands the management of the whole was placed; the Russians, under Barclay, Benningsen, and others; the Prussians, under Blücher; and the Swedes, under Bernadotte. The forces of the allies (300,000 men) were superior to the army conducted by Napoleon himself by 100,000 men. It was in vain that the French emperor, to whom the god of battles had so often been propitious, unfolded his mighty talents; it was in vain that the most distinguished marshals of his school, Ney, Murat, Augereau, Macdonald, the Pole Poniatowski, and many others, exerted their strength to the utmost. The
October 16–18. three days' battle fought in Leipsic and the neighboring villages was the grave of the French empire. After suffering an enormous loss, Napoleon, in the night of the 19th October, quitted the town, which was immediately taken possession of by the allies. The over-hasty destruction of the Elster bridge delivered up 18,000 soldiers fit for battle into the hands of the victors, to say nothing of the sick and the wounded. Poniatowski, who during the battle had been made marshal, found his death in the waters. The French, closely pursued by the enemy, advanced by hasty marches by Erfurt to the Rhine. Their passage was opposed at Hanau by Wrede, with Bavarians and Austrians; but by this he only gave the "dying lion" an opportunity of displaying
October 30, 31. his military skill. The victory that was gained at Hanau over the wounded Wrede opened to the French the passage to the Rhine by the way of Frankfurt. But the unfortunates all carried the germs of mortal disease in their breasts, and half of them died before the end of the year in over-crowded hospitals. The dissolution of the kingdom of Westphalia, the return of the Elector of Hesse, and of the dukes of Brunswick and Oldenberg, to their own dominions, the imprisonment of the king of Saxony, and the breaking up of the Confederation of the Rhine, now followed in quick succession. Dalberg renounced his archdukedom of Frankfurt; Wirtemberg, Baden, Hesse-Darmstadt, concluded treaties with Austria, and arrayed their troops beneath the standard of the allies. It was only in Hamburg that the French maintained themselves, under the cruel Davoust, till the May of 1814, and practised dreadful exactions and oppressions. The king of Denmark was punished for his adherence to Napoleon by the loss of Norway, which was given
January 14, 1814. to Sweden by the peace of Kiel. The same thing happened in Italy. The viceroy, Eugene, left the beautiful lands of the Po to the Austrians, after a gallant defence, and joined his father-in-law in Bavaria. The archduke Ferdinand returned to Tuscany, and the

States of the Church received the severely-tried Pope Pius VII. Naples alone remained for a short time in the hands of the cavalry leader, Murat, who, having quarrelled with his brother-in-law, joined himself to Austria.

§ 598. The allied monarchs held a council with their ministers and generals in Frankfurt, established a provisional government over the conquered lands, and again made the French emperor an offer of peace, if he would content himself with the Rhine as the boundary of France. As, however, the vast preparations that Napoleon was making, by means of a severe conscription, convinced the allied powers that their adversary was going once more to try the chances of battle, it was determined to
January 1, cross the Rhine. It was on new-year's night that Blücher
1814. crossed the German river, at several points between Mannheim and Coblentz, with the Silesian army, whilst Schwarzenberg marched with the main body through Switzerland to the south-east of France, and a second Prussian army, under Bulow, freed Holland, and enabled the Stadtholder to return to his states. In Champagne, the armies of Blücher
February 1. and Schwarzenberg met together, and won the battle of Brienne (la Rothiere). But, as the difficulty of obtaining provisions compelled the two armies again to separate, whilst Schwarzenberg marched along the Seine, and Blücher followed the course of the Marne, the French emperor, whose military talents again blazed forth in their fullest lustre, succeeded in repeatedly defeating the Silesian army (at Montmirail, Chateau-Thierry), and compelling it to retreat. After
February 16. this, he suddenly threw himself upon the main army, and drove this also back upon Troyes by the victory of Montereau. These events made such an impression upon the allies, that it would not have been difficult for the emperor, in the fresh negotiations for peace that were opened at Chatillon, to have secured himself upon the throne of France, if he would only have given up the other conquered countries. But, as he increased his demands with every favorable turn of fortune, only gave limited powers to his ambassador, Caulaincourt, and paralyzed the negotiations by ambiguous and undecisive declarations,
March 7, 9. the decision was delayed until Blücher, Napoleon's most implacable enemy, had gained fresh advantages over the debilitated French army at Craonne and Laon. The negotiations were now broken off, and the dethronement of Bonaparte resolved upon. The
March 20, 21. battle of Arcis on the Aube, convinced the French emperor that his weakened and exhausted army would avail no longer against the iron ranks of the enemy; and this conviction made him irresolute. Whilst the allies were marching upon Paris, and his presence in the capital was imperatively called for, he wasted his time in daring but fruitless marches. The heroic exertions of a few thousand National Guards at Fère-Champenoise was the last display of popular energy. A few days later, the hostile army stormed Montmartre. Upon this, Joseph,

to whom Napoleon had entrusted the defence of the capital, placed his authority in the hands of Mortier and Marmont, and retired with the empress and the regency to Blois. The two marshals were soon compelled to yield to superior force, and to surrender the city by March 31. treaty. Hereupon followed the entrance of the allies into Paris, and the establishment of a provisional government under the presidentship of Talleyrand. This astute diplomatist, a master in every intrigue and artifice, now devoted himself to the interests of the royal family, and attempted, by the employment of the principle of legitimacy, to exclude Napoleon, and to bring about the restoration of the Bourbons.

2. THE RESTORATION AND THE HUNDRED DAYS.

§ 599. In the meanwhile, Napoleon, with his Guard and his friends, the number of which diminished every day, was lingering in Fontainbleau. He changed helplessly from one resolution to another, till, at length, the news of Marmont's defection decided him upon abdicating the throne in favor of his son. But this conditional abdica- April 4. tion was not received by the allied powers; he could not continue the contest, for even his nearest friends, Berthier, Ney, Oudinot, and others, had deserted him, and turned towards the new sun. In this extremity, Napoleon signed the unconditional act of abdica- April 7. tion as dictated by the allies. He received the island of Elba as his property, an income of 2,000,000 francs, and the permission to retain 400 of his faithful guard around his person. His wife, Maria Louisa, obtained the duchy of Parma. On the 20th of April, Napoleon ordered the grenadiers of his guard to be drawn up in the castle-yard of Fontainbleau, and, with a broken heart, took an affecting leave of them, amidst the sobs of the veteran heroes. On the 4th of May, he landed at Elba. Shortly after, to the great joy of the people, who were weary of war, the first Peace of Paris was concluded, by which May 30. France received Louis XVIII. as king, a new constitutional government, and the boundaries of 1792. The foreign armies left the French territories, and the Congress of Vienna was to have placed the new order of things in Europe upon a firm foundation.

§ 600. It was a splendid assembly this Vienna Congress. Emperors and kings, princes and nobles, the most celebrated men of all countries, were there assembled, and rejoicing over their victory. The majesty and civilization of all Europe there displayed themselves in their fullest lustre; and the magnificent festivals, the riotous feasts, splendid balls, and evening assemblies, had no end. But the establishment of the new system was no light task; and, in the midst of all this splendor and rejoicing, violent passions were in motion, which threatened to destroy the work of peace before its completion. The return of the legitimate royal families to their lost thrones, and the most complete destruction that was possible of the republican constitutions, were the two principles on which all parties were soon agreed; but when questions respecting the division of the conquered and vacated lands, and the indemnification of the allies, came to be discussed, envy, selfishness, avarice, and all impure motives were aroused. The court of Berlin demanded the union of Saxony with the Prussian kingdom, and Russia entertained the view of getting entire possession of Poland; both demands met with vehement opposition; the dispute seemed to threaten a renewal of hostilities, and the armies were placed upon a war footing. These appearances, and the proceedings in France, where the constitution granted by Louis XVIII. afforded but little defence against the reaction, awakened new hopes in Napoleon. The Bourbons showed by their proceedings "that they had learned nothing, and forgotten nothing." The memory of the Revolution and of the empire was, as far as possible, destroyed. The tricolored national cockade was thrust aside by the white; the old aristocracy treated the new nobility with insolence and contempt, and drove them from the neighborhood of the court, where the tone was given by the polite count of Artois and the gloomy duchess of Angoulême (daughter of Louis XVI.), whose heart was filled with hatred and venom against the men of the Revolution. The guards were discharged, and their places supplied by well-paid Swiss; the officers of the grand army were dismissed upon half-pay; the Legion of Honor was rendered mean and contemptible by the distribution of innumerable crosses to the unworthy; the compact with the banished emperor himself was not adhered to; the clergy and the emigrants, who met with particular favor in the palace, began to dream of a restoration of their lost estates, tithes, and feudal privileges; great discontent took possession of the nation; the wish for a change again became lively, particularly when nearly 100,000 French soldiers, some who had been prisoners of war, and others from foreign fortresses, returned to their country, and diffused their Bonapartist sentiments over the whole land.

§ 601. When Napoleon heard of these errors of the Bourbons, when he learned that there was a wish to restore their lands to the emigrants because "they kept the straight path," when he was instructed by Fouché, Davoust, Maret, the duchess of St. Leu, and others of his adherents, who kept up a constant correspondence with him, of the disposition of the people, he resolved once more to try his fortune. He landed on the south coast of France with a few hundred men; he soon won all hearts to himself by some shrewdly planned and rapidly diffused proclamations. The tricolor was in a short time again predominant everywhere, the troops that were sent to oppose him deserted to him in crowds; the citizens of Grenoble threw open their gates when he approached their town, and Colonel Labedoyère placed the garrison at his disposal. It was in vain

March 1, 1815.

March 7

that the count of Artois hasted to Lyons, and attempted to gain the soldiers by confidence. The shout of "Vive l'Empereur!" rang everywhere in his ears; and when even Ney, who had sworn to bring the usurper in chains to Paris, went over to his former companion in arms,
March 20. the Bourbons, helpless and confounded, quitted for the second time the land of their home. Louis XVIII., with a few faithful adherents, took up his residence in Ghent, whilst Napoleon once more entered the Tuileries, and formed a new ministry from among his followers. Thus began the reign of the Hundred Days, and Europe was threatened with fresh convulsions. Clubs were again formed, and the songs of the Revolution were again heard. But Napoleon had not yet laid aside his dislike to popular movements; he also had learned nothing and forgotten nothing. The imperial throne, with its splendor and its national nobility, was again to arise. This, however, was resisted by
June 1. the people. The new constitution, which was sworn to at the festival of the Champ de Mai, did not satisfy their demands.

§ 602. These events produced the greatest confusion in the Viennese Congress, and restored the unanimity which had been disturbed. Austria and Russia did not at first appear disinclined to open fresh negotiations with Napoleon, who promised to abide by the conditions of the Peace of Paris and never again to disturb the tranquillity of Europe, and to leave either him or his son in possession of the crown of France. But the activity of Talleyrand and the imprudence of Murat again gave the victory to the principles of legitimacy. Murat had at first joined the allies, and made war on the viceroy of Italy. But he soon felt that this was an unnatural proceeding; such treachery to the common cause revolted his honest military feelings. Napoleon's landing and triumphant course were the signal for his taking up arms. The emperor in vain warned him against over-hasty proceedings. Without waiting to see what course events would take, Murat declared war against Austria, and called the people of Italy to arms to defend the unity and independence
May 23, 1815. of the beautiful land of the Apennines. The battle of Tolentino went against him; his army melted away, and whilst he was flying in haste to the south of France, the Austrians marched into his capital and gave back his crown to its former possessor, Ferdinand. After the battle of Waterloo, Murat wandered for some time around the south coast of France, only carefully concealing himself from the pursuit of the Bourbons. At length he escaped to Corsica, and undertook from thence a voyage to Calabria, for the purpose of exciting the people to revolt against Ferdinand. But he and his few followers were easily overpowered, and Murat paid the penalty of his attempt with his life. On the 15th of October, Joachim Murat, who by his courage and good fortune had been raised from the son of an innkeeper to be the king of the most beautiful of lands, was shot at Pizzo.

§ 603. Napoleon's fate was decided even earlier. The European powers set upwards of half a million of men in motion against the outlawed usurper. Before they had all marched forth, Napoleon, after the opening of the Chambers of Paris, advanced, with the soldiers that flocked to him from all quarters, into the Netherlands, to make head against the armies of Wellington and Blücher. The commencement of the campaign was favorable to the French. At Ligny, the Prussi- June 16. ans were forced back after the most desperate resistance; whilst at Quatre Bras, Ney resisted Wellington's army, composed of English, Dutch, Hanoverians, &c. Blücher was wounded in the former place, and in the latter, the chivalrous duke William of Brunswick found his death. Even on the decisive day, the victory was long doubtful. It was not till the Prussians, at the critical moment, came to the assistance of the hardly-pressed army of Wellington, whilst marshal Grouchy, who had been despatched by Napoleon to follow Blücher, kept aloof from the field, that the French, despite the heroic bravery of the veteran warriors, were totally defeated in the battle of Belle-Alliance or June 18. Waterloo. The struggle on the height of Mount St. Jean, from whence the French name the battle, was terrible; and the words which were afterwards attributed to General Cambronne, "The guard dies, it never surrenders!" were retained by the nation in honorable remembrance; whilst the disgrace which Bourmont incurred by his treachery, and Grouchy by his ambiguous conduct, could be obliterated by no defence. Napoleon, pale and confused, allowed himself to be led out of the battle by Soult, and hastened to Paris. The flight soon became general; the whole of the artillery fell into the hands of the enemy; only a fourth part of the brave army was able to escape.

§ 604. The Chambers of Paris, in which Fouché was exhibiting a wretched display of intrigue and deceit, proposed to the emperor, on his return, that he should renounce the crown. After some resistance, the humbled potentate yielded to the proposal; he laid down the government in favor of his son, Napoleon II., and then fled to June 22. Rochefort, with the purpose of escaping to America, when he saw the victorious enemy a second time approaching the walls of Paris. As the English, however, held the harbor blockaded, Napoleon, trusting to the generosity of the British people, sought shelter in one of their ships (Bellerophon). But the statesmen who then guided the helm had no compassion for fallen greatness. Arrived at the coast of England, Napoleon received the terrible information that he must pass the remainder of his life as a state prisoner on the island of St. Helena. All protestations were useless: on the 18th of October, he landed on the place of his banishment, in the midst of the Atlantic ocean.

Here Napoleon lived, a chained Prometheus, separated from his friends in an unhealthy climate, and under the rigid guardianship of the unfriendly governor, Sir Hudson Lowe. A few friends, among them General Bertrand and his family, Montholon, Las Casas, shared his banishment. Grief at his fall, want of his accustomed activity, and irritation at the unworthy treatment he received, broke his proud and strong spirit before its time. After six years of suffering, he found that quiet in the grave, to which during life he had been a stranger. He died on the 5th of May, 1821. His ashes were afterwards conveyed to Paris (1842), and buried in the Hotel of Invalides.

§ 605. After Napoleon's abdication, a provisional government was established under the direction of Fouché. The latter arranged with Wellington and Blücher that no man was to be punished for his actions or opinions, and then surrendered the capital. A few days later, the Bourbons again entered the Tuileries, under the guard of foreign bayonets. The people were quiet and indifferent. The armies were disbanded, the Chambers dissolved, and by a succession of proscriptions, a number of men, who had hitherto guided the fate of France and of her armies, were either deprived of their offices, thrust into banishment, or, as in the case of Ney and Labedoyère, condemned to death.* The allied monarchs again established their residence in Paris, and assisted the Bourbons in settling the new system. At length, when the Restoration appeared secure, the second Peace of Paris was arranged, by which France was confined to the boundaries of 1790, restored all the plundered treasures of art and science to their former owners, paid 700,000,000 francs for the expenses of war, and was obliged to support an allied army of 150,000 men in the frontier fortresses. These garrison troops remained for three years in the French fortresses.

July 8.

November 20, 1815.

* Labedoyère and Ney were condemned to death by the Court of Peers, and shot. The execution of the renowned marshal of the Moskwa, who, when he was shot, with military spirit gave the word of command himself, was looked upon as an infraction of the treaty arranged with Wellington, and brought great disgrace upon the court of Paris. Lavalette also, who, in his capacity of director of the post, had exerted himself for Napoleon's restoration, was condemned to death, but was delivered from prison by his faithful wife. Among the banished were to be found all the members of Napoleon's family; the marshals and statesmen who had joined him during the hundred days, as Soult, Maret, Thibaudeau, Mouton, &c.; and finally, all the regicides, *i. e.* the members of the Convention who had voted for Louis XVI.'s death; Fouché was one of these, and he was accordingly obliged to relinquish the office of minister of police, which he had at first been allowed by the Bourbons to retain, and to retire abroad. Carnot, Sieyes, Cambacères, and others did the same. **Most of them resided in Brussels.**

E. THE UNITED STATES OF AMERICA,

FROM THE FORMATION OF THE FEDERAL CONSTITUTION, TO THE PEACE OF 1815.

WASHINGTON'S ADMINISTRATION. [1789–1797.] § 606. George Washington, having been unanimously reëlected at the expiration of his first term of office, was President of the United States for eight years,— a period long enough to fix, in many respects, the policy of the government, and to determine the practical character of the new constitution. The country was doubly fortunate in securing his services for so long a period, and at this particular crisis in its affairs. Others may have been equally patriotic and disinterested; but no other person could have brought to the office an equal weight of character and influence, or so happy a combination of calmness of judgment, equanimity in good and ill fortune, impartiality towards individuals, and inflexibility of purpose. The friends and opponents of the Federal Constitution were already arrayed against each other as two political parties, styled respectively the Federalists and the Democrats, between whom the people were very equally divided, and who contended vehemently with each other for the control of affairs, each hoping to imprint its peculiar principles upon the early measures of the administration, and upon the organization of the government. The Federalists were reproached as being anti-republican and even monarchical in their notions and their measures; and they, in return, charged their adversaries with hostility towards any stable form of government or any effective union of the States, with indifference as to the preservation of the public faith and credit, and with carrying their democratic principles so far as to undermine every species of authority and reduce the nation to anarchy. Washington's election to the presidency was not a party triumph; in the opinion even of his opponents, he was without and above all party ties,— the only man in the Union who possessed the confidence of the whole people. He had no personal preferences or prejudices; but politically, he was a strong Federalist, an avowed defender of every thing which tended to give unity and strength to the central government. He deplored the excesses of party spirit, and it was his constant endeavor to moderate or prevent them. Upon this principle, he formed his first cabinet, appointing Jefferson, the Democratic leader, Secretary of State, and Hamilton, the ablest of the Federalists, Secretary of the Treasury. Knox and Randolph, the Secretary of War and the Attorney-General, were also opposed to each other in politics, and strongly contrasted in personal character. But under Washington's firm, dignified, and impartial guidance, these men worked together zealously and efficiently; and through them, the President maintained his influence with parties, and preserved the national and equally balanced character of his administration.

§ 607. To establish a revenue for the maintenance of government, and to provide for the debts contracted during the Revolutionary war, were the first objects that claimed the attention of Congress. Hamilton's financial talents were of the highest order, and the plans which he proposed for the accomplishment of these ends, though vehemently contested, were finally approved and carried into effect with the happiest results. As the government for more than ten years had been bankrupt, the public securities, or evidences of its indebtedness, had passed from hand to hand at prices far below their nominal value; and the Democrats now strenuously maintained that they should be redeemed at no higher rate than their present possessors had paid for them. But Hamilton declared that the public faith must be kept by paying the whole amount which the government had originally promised, and also by assuming the debts which the individual States had contracted in support of the common cause. The aggregate debt was a portion of the price which the whole nation had paid for its freedom; and the burden of it, therefore, ought to be equally borne by the whole people. It was the dictate of sound policy, also, as well as of abstract justice, that all pecuniary obligations should be faithfully discharged; for public credit would thus be maintained for any future exigency, and the government would be strengthened, as the great body of the public creditors, the wealthiest and most influential class in the community, would be directly interested in its support. These views ultimately prevailed by a small majority, — a majority obtained in one case only by an agreement to transfer the seat of government from Philadelphia to the banks of the Potomac, thus conciliating the favor of some members of Congress from the southern States. The whole amount of debt thus consolidated and funded was about eighty millions of dollars. At Hamilton's recommendation, also, a Bank of the United States was chartered, with a capital of ten millions, one-fifth of which was subscribed by government, while individuals, who contributed the remainder, were allowed to pay but one-fourth in cash, and the other three-fourths in public stocks. A revenue act was also passed, imposing duties on goods imported into the United States and on tonnage, due discrimination being made so as to encourage American manufactures and shipping. The effect of these measures upon public confidence and the interests of commerce was almost magical. The large amount of public stocks thus created furnished capital and currency, nearly as available as coin, and far more secure than paper money. The funding system afforded a guaranty of the stability of the Union, and encouraged merchants to undertake the large enterprises, an opening for which was created by the country's release from the shackles of colonial dependence. A trade sprang up with India, China, and the northwest coast of the American continent; and the flag of the new nation was soon displayed in every sea, in friendly competition with that of the great naval power, which threatened, a few years before, almost to monopolize the commerce of the earth. The population continuing to multiply and expand, new States were successively formed and admitted into the Union, and the strength of the chain seemed to increase with every addition to the number of its links. Thus, a long pending controversy between New York, New Hampshire, and the "Green Mountain Boys," respecting the ownership of the territory between the Connecticut river and Lake Champlain, was at length adjusted by the creation of the new State of Vermont; and soon afterwards, Kentucky was admitted into the Union, the first State formed in the great valley of the Mississippi.

A. D. 1791.

§ 608. The progress of the settlements at the west, however, was much retarded by hostilities with the Indian tribes on the banks of the Ohio, the Miami, and the Wabash. These claimed the Ohio river as the boundary of their territory, being encouraged to put forward this claim, and to support it by making war upon the Americans, by the British authorities in Canada and at those military posts on the Lakes and the upper tributaries of the Mississippi, which were still retained as a security for the due performance of certain articles in the treaty of peace. The United States had too hastily disarmed themselves at the close of the Revolutionary struggle; weary of the war, and unable to pay the troops, the whole army, with an insignificant exception, had been disbanded. The only force, therefore, which could now be sent against the savages, was composed almost entirely of militia, who could not be relied upon for the great hazards and exposures of a conflict with the Indians in their forest home. Gen. Harmer was first sent against them, with 1,100 men; but several of his detachments were surprised and defeated, and he returned in disgrace, before he had accomplished any thing. Further attempts to settle the difficulties by negotiation having failed, St. Clair was next sent, with an army of 2,000 men, into the Indian country; but when he had reached the banks of the Wabash, the savages attacked his camp by surprise in the grey of the morning, and after some hard fighting, in which about half of the army were killed or wounded, the others were compelled to make a precipitate flight. Gen. Wayne, an officer of much experience and reputation, was then placed in this difficult command, and great exertions were made to raise an adequate force to support him. One year he spent in unavailing negotiations for peace, limiting his military operations meanwhile to the protection of the frontiers. In August, 1794, he advanced, at the head of more than 3,000 men, totally defeated the Indians in one hard-fought engagement, ravaged their principal settlements, destroyed their stores, and left a fort well garrisoned in the heart of their country.

October, 1790.

November 4, 1791.

This decisive blow effectually cowed the native tribes, who soon consented to a peace, the faithful observance of which for many years left no check to the marvellously rapid growth of the settlements at the west.

§ 609. Another difficulty which the government had to contend with was the disaffection created by the excise taxes that had been imposed to eke out the revenue obtained from duties on imported goods. The tax on distilled spirits, especially, bore hard upon the western counties of Pennsylvania, where the people, from the imperfect means of transportation could not obtain a market for their grain except by distilling it into whiskey; and as they were rude and turbulent backwoodsmen, little accustomed to the restraints of government and civilized life, they could not understand the necessity of paying a heavy excise on the most profitable article which they prepared for sale. They set the law at defiance, attacked the revenue officers, drove back the few soldiers who were sent to defend them, and entered into extensive combinations to resist the government. A proclamation of the President, calling on the magistrates to execute the laws, had no effect; and it was computed that there were over 7,000 insurgents prepared to carry out their purposes by force of arms. Washington then resolved to vindicate the majesty of the laws by employing a force large enough to prevent any show of resistance. The militia of four of the States was called out, to the number of 15,000 men, and Gen. Lee, of Virginia, marched at their head into October, 1794. the disaffected counties, and effectually put down the insurrection without bloodshed. Some leaders of the movement were tried and convicted of treason; but they were all pardoned, and this lenity won back the affections of those who had gone astray, while the vigor and promptitude that had been shown made a great addition to the strength of the government.

§ 610. Mr. Jay, who had been appointed minister to England for the purpose, succeeded at last in forming a treaty with that power, which adjusted many subjects of controversy between the two nations, though it left others still pending. The treaty of peace of 1783 had been very imperfectly observed on both sides. Debts to British subjects, contracted before the war, could not be recovered until the national judiciary had been established under the Federal Constitution, and many of them remained still undischarged, and the Loyalists could not recover their confiscated estates; on the other hand, the British troops, when they evacuated the country, had carried off many slaves, for whom compensation was demanded, and the military posts on the northwestern frontier had not been delivered up. The possession of these forts enabled the British to control the trade with the Indians, and even, as was supposed, to incite them to hostilities against the United States. The breaking out of the war between revolutionary France and England opened the immense profits of a neutral trade to the Americans, but also exposed them to the many annoyances and vexations that resulted from the exercise of belligerent rights against neutrals. American seamen, not being easily distinguishable from Englishmen, were often impressed to serve on British men-of-war, and American ships were overhauled to search for contraband goods. Naval stores, also, were asserted by the English to be contraband of war, though in other treaties they were regarded as free goods. Jay's treaty was the best that could be obtained at the time, though it had many acknowledged deficiencies; but as it removed many subjects of dispute, and averted a renewal of the war between the two countries, which seemed to be imminent if no treaty were framed, the Senate approved it by a very close vote, and it was ratified by the President. A storm of popular indignation immediately burst forth, in which were united all the old feeling of hostility towards England and the ill will that had been nursed by the recent controversies. The discussion of the subject agitated the whole country during the autumn, and it soon appeared, when Congress came together in the winter, that a large number, if not a majority, of the Representatives were fiercely opposed to the execution of the treaty. But the President firmly maintained his ground, against the insane clamor out of doors and the fierce opposition in Congress; and after a vehement debate, the appropriations that were needed to carry out the compact were made by a majority of two, and the treaty went into effect. Its happy results soon proved that Washington's course had been as enlightened and far-sighted, as it unquestionably was dignified and independent.

Aug. 14, 1795.

§ 611. The troubles growing out of the French Revolution were not confined to the European side of the Atlantic. The agitation reached the United States also, and, for a time, the republican institutions of America seemed to reel under that shock which had prostrated so many monarchies in the Old World. New bitterness and violence were added to the former dissension between the two great parties into which the people were divided; the Democrats generally espoused the cause of France, with a pardonable preference for what seemed to be the cause of freedom and enlightenment against the old powers of despotism and darkness; while the Federalists, deploring the excesses into which the revolutionists of France had plunged, and foreseeing the anarchy and final triumph of military usurpation which would be their inevitable result, — animated also by a lingering attachment for the land of their forefathers, their language, and their faith, — by a love which ten years of conflict had failed to extinguish, and which a rapid extension of the commercial ties between the two countries was now kindling anew, — generally looked with favor and hope towards England. Unfortunately, belligerent France and England, in the fury of their contest with each other, both disregarded, or rather designedly trampled upon, the neutral rights of America. There was, perhaps, legitimate cause of war against both countries; but the Democrats clamored for war against England, and were disposed to overlook or excuse all slights and injuries received from her opponent; while the Federalists were hostile to France, and palliated every wrong which Great Britain could commit. Again the firmness, moderation, and wisdom of Washington were the means of saving the people from the disasters and sufferings of another war, and from the effects of their own furious party conflicts and ill regulated passions. He saw no causes of dispute, which had yet arisen, that could not be removed or palliated by patience and amicable negotiation; he saw, also, that the country absolutely needed repose and an opportunity to recruit her energies, before she could engage in another struggle with one of the great powers of Europe, with any hope of success, or even of safety. Jay's treaty had averted for a time the hazard of war with England; and Washington had also issued a memorable proclamation of Neutrality, admonishing the people of their duty to observe the strictest impartiality between the two belligerent powers, and to abstain from every act which could justly give umbrage to either. This naturally gave great offence to the party, which, remembering the obligations of America to France for aid bounteously given in the hour of her necessity, and sympathizing with those who assumed to defend the rights of the people everywhere against the oppression of their hereditary rulers, was eager to defend by arms the cause of the French Revolution. They were insanely desirous of plunging into the vortex of European politics and a foreign war. The French republican government, also, adopted an insolent and overbearing tone in its diplomacy, which added fuel to the flame of excitement in the United States. Citizen Genet, the French envoy to America, was received with a popular ovation in Charleston and other places, which so inflamed his ardent temper and republican zeal, that he authorized privateers to be fitted out to cruise against the enemies of France, and when checked in his outrageous conduct, threatened to appeal from the government to the people. But this was going too far; even his friends resented this insult to their great President, and Washington demanded and obtained his recall. The conduct of his successor, M. Fauchet, though more moderate, was still offensive; and the administration had a difficult task in preventing him from stirring up the people to the commission of acts which would afford England a just pretext for hostilities. But the vast influence and reputation of the President, and the evident interest which the country had in the preservation of peace, moderated the excitement, and the aggressive conduct of the French, in making many captures of American vessels on very slight pretexts, soon weaned the nation from its excessive admiration for their principles. The government had the wisdom and good fortune also,

April, 1793.

after the difficulties with Spain had risen to an alarming height, to form a treaty with that power, which not only secured the continu-
A. D. 1795. ance of peace, but gave to the United States the free navigation of the Mississippi, and the privilege of depositing cargoes at New Orleans.

§ 612. When the close of the second period of his administration was at hand, Washington determined to seek that repose in private life of which he had long been desirous. He prepared and published a Farewell Address to his countrymen, in which he announced to them this resolution, and added wise and affectionate advice respecting their future course, and the evils with which the young republic was menaced. Especially he warned them against foreign influence and interference in the controversies of European nations; against all measures which tended to a separation of the Union, or to array parties against each other by geographical discriminations; against the excesses of party spirit, and the first symptoms of disregard for the authority of the laws. "The very idea of the power and right of the people to establish government, presupposes the duty of every individual to obey the established government." This Address was received and read throughout the Union with sentiments approaching to veneration, and has probably contributed more than any state paper that was ever framed to guide the conduct and control the destiny of a whole people. Washington retired to his estate at Mount Vernon, where he spent the short remaining period of his life in arranging his papers and cultivating an extensive farm. He died on the 14th of December, 1799, leaving a reputation unequalled in the world's history as a patriot leader and statesman, "first in war, first in peace, and first in the hearts of his countrymen."

Adams's Administration, [1797–1801.] § 613. John Adams, the candidate of the Federal party, was elected President for the third term, by a majority of only two votes over Thomas Jefferson, who was supported by the Democrats. His administration was a turbulent and rather unfortunate one. In spite of his eminent services during the Revolutionary period, and his acknowledged abilities and integrity, he did not enjoy so much consideration with his own party as Hamilton, who was an admirable political leader; and his opponents wrongly attributed to him arbitrary and monarchical notions of government. His own views of policy were generally sound; but his quick, vehement, and self-willed disposition seldom allowed him to seek or follow the counsels of others, so that he often suffered more in the estimation of his friends than in that of his opponents. Dissension soon appeared in the ranks of the Federalists, and they lost ground with the people, while the other party every day acquired fresh strength. The relations of the country with France still formed the chief difficulty of the government, and the principal subject of dispute between the two parties. The Directory were now in power at

Paris, and their feeble, but aggressive and rapacious, policy was nowhere more signally manifested than in their conduct towards America. They refused to receive Thomas Pinckney, who had been accredited to them as minister by Washington, and even ordered him to quit the territory of the republic; and this insult was given at the very time when their privateers were capturing scores of American vessels, upon pretexts so slight, that, in several cases, they were compelled to admit that they owed reparation for the wrong. Congress manifested a proper spirit, and immediately adopted measures to vindicate the national honor. Laws were passed to hold 80,000 militia in readiness, to fortify the harbors, to fit out vessels of war, and to put the country generally in a state of defence. Still, to manifest the sincerity of their desire for peace, Pinckney, Marshall, and Gerry, (the last named being a Democrat, and therefore regarded as friendly to France,) were sent out as joint envoys to the French Republic, to seek for a reconciliation. On their arrival at Paris, a reception was denied them; but it was intimated to them unofficially, that, on the payment of a heavy bribe to the individual members of the Directory, and the loan of a considerable sum to the republic, a negotiation might be opened. This proposal excited general disgust and indignation in America. "Millions for defence, but not a cent for tribute," was the almost universal cry; and vigorous preparations were instantly made for war, to which the Democratic party offered hardly any opposition. Large additional grants were made for the increase of the navy, the purchase of arms and ammunition, and the fortification of the harbors; and the President was authorized to raise, when necessary, an army of 10,000 men, besides accepting the services of volunteers. There was a great revulsion of opinion throughout the country, which contributed largely to postpone the decline and fall of the Federalist party. Ships of war were authorized to capture any armed vessels which had committed depredations on American commerce, or which were found cruising near the coast with the apparent purpose of committing such acts. There were many French emigrants in the country, and some of these were suspected of acting as government emissaries or spies; the President was therefore authorized to send out of the country any foreigner whose residence in it he might consider to be dangerous. Another act was passed, to define more precisely the crime of treason, and to define and punish that of sedition, which subjected to fine and imprisonment any person who, by writing, printing, or speaking, should attempt to justify the hostile conduct of the French, or to defame or weaken the government or laws of the United States. These two laws, known as the Alien and the Sedition Acts, passed while the people were in a feverish state from the vehemence of party controversy, and only to be justified by the magnitude of the war then deemed to be imminent, were afterwards the objects of bitter reproach, and contributed largely to the downfall of the Federalists.

§ 614. The authority given to act against French armed vessels, now extended to permission to capture them under any circumstances, did not long remain unexercised. The frigate Constellation, Captain Truxton, captured the French frigate, L' Insurgente, of superior force, after an hour's action. Truxton afterwards engaged a still heavier French frigate, La Vengeance, and nearly disabled her, though she succeeded in escaping in the night. Some other French cruisers were taken, and, under the commissions granted to private armed vessels, over fifty French privateers were captured and brought into port, and many American merchantmen were re-captured. Still, war was not formally declared, and the probability of its occurrence was now much lessened by a sudden and eccentric act on the part of President Adams, who, contrary to the wishes of his party, and without even consulting the members of his cabinet, surprised everybody by nominating another minister to France, to make another attempt at negotiation. This act occasioned an irreparable breach in the Federal party. Hamilton, Pickering, and other leaders of it made hardly any secret of their aversion to the President. Owing to the reverses in war which the French had lately experienced, and to a consequent change in the Directory, assurances were sent that the new mission from the United States would be kindly received. In fact, on their arrival in France, the ministers found that a revolution had taken place, and that Bonaparte was now at the head of affairs, who, not wishing to have another enemy on his hands, was eager to negotiate. Difficulties obstructed the conclusion of a perfect treaty; but a convention was agreed upon, by which all captured property not already condemned was to be restored, the indemnities mutually claimed were referred to future negotiations, and all present hazard of war was averted.

§ 615. The dissensions of the Federalists had already foreshadowed the defeat of their party at the approaching presidential election. Adams and Pinckney, their candidates, received but sixty-five electoral votes, while seventy-three were cast for Jefferson and Burr, the favorites of the Democratic party. As these two had an equal number, it devolved upon the House of Representatives, as the Constitution then stood, to decide which of them should be President, and which, Vice-President. The Federalists, who then had the control of the House, formed the strange and factious project of electing Burr instead of Jefferson to the higher office, in order to spoil the victory of their opponents, and because they entertained a faint hope that the former, owing his unexpected elevation to them, might adopt a policy more favorable to the views of their party. The scheme was indefensible either on moral or political grounds, and most of the people rejoiced when it was frustrated. After remaining in session seven days, and balloting thirty-six times, some of the Federalists gave way, and Jefferson was chosen. The office of Vice-President then devolved of right upon Burr. To prevent the repetition of so discreditable a scene, an amendment of the Constitution was soon effected, which required each elector to vote separately for a President and a Vice-President.

Jefferson's Administration. [1801 – 1809.] § 616. The country was in a very prosperous state when Jefferson's party came into power. The serious difficulties that obstructed the formation of the government had all been removed; the finances and the several departments of the government had been fully organized, and the system was in complete and successful operation. The responsibility of devising the requisite measures for these ends had fallen upon the Federalists, the odium which many of them had occasioned had been spent, and the Democrats now entered upon the enjoyment of their predecessors' labors. The revenue, commerce, and population of the country had increased with unexampled rapidity. The census of 1801 showed that the population amounted to 5,300,000, being an increase of nearly a million and a half in ten years. Within the same period, the exports had risen from *nineteen* to *ninety* millions, the tonnage had doubled, and the revenue was increased from *four* to *twelve* millions. At the same time, also, there was a lull in the storm of European warfare. The peace of Luneville was concluded early in 1801, that of Amiens followed a year afterwards, and hostilities were not recommenced till May, 1803. Thus, all the perplexing and dangerous controversies respecting impressment and neutral rights were temporarily put at rest, and the United States reaped the full benefits of a prosperous and uninterrupted commerce. Even the prospect of a renewal of hostilities operated in one respect to the advantage of the Americans. Louisiana had recently been transferred from Spain to France; and as Bonaparte foresaw that he could not defend so distant a possession against the naval power of England, he listened favorably to a proposal for selling the territory to the United States, who were very anxious to obtain it, as it would secure to them the uninterrupted navigation of the Mississippi. A treaty was concluded in April, 1803, which made over Louisiana to the United States upon the payment of fifteen millions of dollars, one-fourth of this sum being retained to meet the claims for the French spoliations of American commerce. Congress had no power expressly granted in the Constitution to purchase additional territory; and as the Democratic party had always maintained that all powers not specifically enumerated were reserved to the States, it was a little awkward for Jefferson to complete this contract. But as no one doubted the great utility of this vast accession of territory, or that it had been obtained on reasonable terms, he swallowed his scruples, and his adherents did the same.

§ 617. The depredations of the Barbary powers upon the commerce of the United States in the Mediterranean, gave rise, in 1801, to a war with Tripoli. Peace had hitherto been purchased with several of these piratical states by the payment of a heavy annual tribute; but their demands having become inordinate, a considerable naval force, commanded at first by Morris, and afterwards by Preble, was sent out to blockade Tripoli, and to act as occasion might require against the other Barbary powers. Several naval actions took place, in which the officers and crews displayed great gallantry, and which caused the American flag to be highly respected in the Mediterranean; while the blockade kept the piratical cruisers in port, and thus protected the commercial shipping. But the Tripolitans were at length brought to terms through a very hazardous and romantic enterprise, undertaken by a gallant American adventurer, named Eaton. The rightful bashaw of Tripoli had been deprived of his government, and exiled, by a younger brother, some years before. Eaton entered into a compact with him to reconquer his dominions, invading them from the side of Egypt. A few hundred men were collected for this purpose, only one-fourth of them being Christians, and of these but nine were Americans. This insignificant and motley troop crossed the desert, suffering frightful hardships by the way, captured the important Tripolitan port of Derne, maintained it against an attack by a vastly larger force of the enemy, and so frightened the reigning bashaw, that he hastily concluded a peace, conceding all the demands of the Americans. A great, indirect advantage obtained from these operations in the Mediterranean was, that they prevented the American vessels of war from going to decay, or being sold, by the ill-judged economy of Jefferson's administration. The party in power were hostile to the existence of a navy, partly because they wished to diminish the expenditures of the national government, and partly because they were averse or indifferent to the growth and prosperity of the foreign commercial interest of the country, and sought to develope only the agriculture and home trade of the States. Jefferson wished to limit the defensive efforts of the country to some very feeble and absurd attempts to protect the coasts and harbors by gun-boats, which could act only in shallow waters, the idea being probably borrowed from Bonaparte's curious maritime preparations at Boulogne. If merchants asked that their ships might be protected, they were told to keep their ships at home. Had not the insults and depredations of the Barbary pirates roused the national spirit so much that it became necessary to make some effort to punish them, it is probable that, before the close of Jefferson's administration, the United States would not have had a single ship of war afloat.

April, 1805.

§ 618. The renewal of the war in Europe, the constantly increasing aggressions of the belligerent powers upon neutral commerce, and the different schemes proposed by the two rival parties in the country to meet and repel these aggressions, renewed the vehemence of party controversy during the second term of Jefferson's administration, and gave a serious check to the commercial prosperity of the United States. The Democrats retained their old feelings of hostility towards Great Britain, and their predilection for France, though the latter country, under the imperial sway of Napoleon, was now, in truth, governed by despotic power. The strength of the Federal party lay in the commercial States, cities, and towns; and the intimate relations of an extensive foreign trade disposed them to resent but slightly the domineering and aggressive policy of England, while they looked with horror upon the conduct of the emperor of the French. But if war should break out with either of the rival powers, it was very certain, from the administration policy of breaking up the navy, and limiting all efforts to coast and harbor defence, that American commerce would be swept from the ocean. The Federalists, therefore, were bent upon preserving peace at all hazards; the Democrats, who depended chiefly upon agriculture, manufactures, and the home trade, who saw no risk that the country would be invaded, and who, after the acquisition of Louisiana, were eager to gain possession of Canada also, by conquest, believing that the English had too much to do in Europe to be able to defend so distant a colony, were clamorous for war. In these opposite feelings and desires, we find a key to the party controversies and the domestic and foreign policy of the United States down to the general pacification in 1815.

§ 619. In 1806, Monroe and Pinckney succeeded in negotiating a treaty with the English ministry, which, like Jay's in 1794, though it left many subjects of dispute undetermined, still adjusted the most pressing controversies, opened the trade between the United States and the European possessions of Great Britain on a footing of entire reciprocity, and afforded a tolerable assurance that peace might be maintained for many years. This treaty President Jefferson rejected, without even consulting the Senate, because it did not directly prohibit the impressment of seamen from American vessels by the British cruisers, though there was a tacit understanding on the subject, which would have led to the gradual abandonment of the practice. Events soon showed that the rejection of this treaty was an act pregnant with a long series of important and disastrous consequences. France and England, endeavoring to retaliate upon each other, published a succession of decrees, the combined effect of which was almost to annihilate neutral commerce, and to subject every American vessel engaged in foreign trade to capture and confiscation by one or the other party. To comply with the regulations made by one of the belligerents, was to afford grounds for seizure by the other.

November, 1806. The Berlin decree, published by Napoleon, declared the British islands in a state of blockade, and subjected to capture every neutral vessel that attempted to trade with them; this was a retaliatory act, because England had blockaded several Continental

November, 1807. ports which she had not invested by her ships of war. Great Britain now proceeded to decree, that neutrals should not

trade with France or her allies till they had paid her a tribute. The
December, 1807. French emperor retorted by a decree, issued at Milan, subjecting every vessel to confiscation which should pay this tribute, or submit to be visited by a British cruiser. The United States
December, 1807. then engaged in this game of prohibitions, by passing the noted Embargo Act, which closed the American ports to all foreign trade whatever, either by native or foreign vessels; even vessels engaged in the coasting trade were required to give heavy bonds that they would reland their cargo within the limits of the United States. This was punishing one's self a great deal for the sake of punishing an opponent a very little. America renounced the whole of her own foreign trade, for the sake of depriving foreign nations, France and England particularly, of a portion of theirs. But as a great effect had been produced, during the contest which preceded the Revolutionary war, by the Non-Importation agreements, Congress had now a vague impression that Great Britain might quickly be brought to terms by a refusal to buy her manufactures, or to sell American produce. This impression was totally unfounded; the feelings of the people not being enlisted in support of the Embargo, a considerable illicit traffic was kept up, which alleviated the effect of the measure upon England, though the commercial interest of the United States suffered a ruinous depression. Our own unemployed shipping rotted at the wharves, while enormous prices were paid for British goods to smugglers. The pressure upon the country was too great; in New England, even the Democratic party opposed the
February, 1809. law. After it had been in force little over a year, the Embargo was repealed, and a Non-Intercourse Act was substituted for it, prohibiting all trade with Great Britain and France, and their dependencies, up to the end of the next session of Congress.

Madison's Administration, (1809 – 1817.) § 620. While the public mind was agitated by these subjects, the end of Jefferson's second term of office approached, and James Madison, the Democratic candidate, was elected his successor, by 122 out of 176 electoral votes. This event did not materially affect the policy of the country, as the new President generally followed the steps of his predecessor, though he was somewhat more moderate in his political opinions, and if he had not been pushed on by the excited feelings of the younger members of his party, he would probably have averted or postponed a war. As it was, however, the relations between Great Britain and the United States every day assumed a more hostile aspect, and it was evident that peace could not long be maintained between them if the war in Europe should not
April, 1809. cease. A negotiation with Erskine, the British minister at Washington, produced an arrangement of the more pressing subjects of controversy; but it soon appeared that Erskine had exceeded his instructions. The English ministry disavowed his act, and the dispute remained

in a worse condition than ever. The American frigate Chesapeake, two years before, had been attacked and captured by the Leopard, a British ship of superior force, under Admiral Berkley's orders, because her captain refused to surrender some seamen who were alleged to be deserters from the British navy; and though the frigate was returned, and Berkley's orders were disavowed, the terms of reparation for the injury and insult could not be agreed upon, and the affair impeded all subsequent negotiations. It was the main cause of the rejection of Erskine's arrangement.

§ 621. The Non-Intercourse Act expired in May, 1810, when an offer was made that, if either England or France would revoke its edicts against neutral commerce, the act should be renewed and enforced against the other belligerent, till its edicts also were revoked. France had recently given additional provocation, by a decree issued at Rambouillet, confiscating all American vessels and their cargoes then found in ports under the control of the French, and directing that, if any should enter a French harbor in future, it should also be seized and sold. Under this decree, American property valued at eight millions of dollars fell into the hands of the French. But Napoleon now took a conciliatory step; he assured the American minister at Paris that the Berlin and Milan decrees were revoked, though the revocation was not to take effect till the first of November next. Relying on this assurance, Mr. Madison, early in November, issued a proclamation restoring the freedom of commerce with France, and prohibiting all intercourse with Great Britain. The English ministry refused to rescind their Orders in Council, under the pretext that they had no official evidence that the French emperor had kept his promise to rescind the Berlin and Milan decrees. The Orders were enforced more rigorously than ever, English cruisers being stationed along the American coast, which boarded and searched all American merchantmen, impressed many of their seamen, and often confiscated both vessel and cargo, if the former was bound to a French port. One of these cruisers, the Little Belt, of 18 guns, fell in with the American frigate President, and an action commenced between them, both parties alleging that the other fired first. The British vessel was soon reduced almost to a wreck, when her opponent ceased firing, and she was allowed to pursue her voyage. This affair was passed over on both sides, as an unfortunate mistake, and terms of reparation were at length offered for the attack on the Chesapeake, which were accepted.

A. D. 1810.

May 16, 1811.

§ 622. In the autumn of 1811, the Indian tribes round the Upper Lakes showed a hostile disposition, and Governor Harrison was sent against them, with 800 men, to make a treaty, if possible, otherwise to strike a blow which should prevent hostilities in future. When he arrived near Tippecanoe, their principal town, he was met by a deputation of the savages, who said that they desired peace, and agreed to return for an amicable conference the next day. The troops therefore encamped where they were, but took strict precautions against an attack by surprise. It was well that they did so; for just before daybreak, the Indians in considerable numbers made a furious assault upon them, and were repulsed with difficulty, after an hour's fighting. Their town was then burned, and Harrison, being encumbered by his wounded men, retreated to Vincennes. The savages caused greater alarm at this time, as it was believed that the British traders and agents from Canada held secret intercourse with them, and urged them to hostilities.

November 7.

§ 623. As the impressments and captures by the English cruisers continued and even increased in number, Congress was called together early in November, and, at the recommendation of the President, they made active preparations for war. It was hoped that Great Britain, thus seeing that America was in earnest, would be unwilling to increase the number of her enemies, and would recede from her imperious and aggressive position. This hope was fallacious; the English ministry was obstinate, their majority in Parliament was subservient, and the spirit of the nation was high. After waging a stubborn war for many years, at least on equal terms, with the great subverter of monarchies and conquerer of half of Europe, they were not to be driven from their position by the menace of hostilities from a young and feeble nation on the other side of the Atlantic. Congress, after spending the winter and spring in warm debates, and in passing bills for augmenting the army and navy, received a secret message from the President on the 1st of June. It was considered in secret session by both Houses, and on the 18th of June, the doors were thrown open, and it was announced that the United States had declared war against Great Britain.

A. D. 1812.

§ 624. Though it had been voted to raise an army of 35,000 men, the United States had but 10,000 men under arms when the contest began, and with these it was resolved to attempt the conquest of Canada. The coast was not fortified, and the navy consisted only of three or four frigates and a few sloops of war; but the chief reliance was placed upon privateers, as a means of annoying the enemy. This expectation was justified by the event; during the two years and a half that the war continued, over 1,500 British merchantmen were captured by American privateers. The public vessels of war, also, slowly increased in number by a few frigates and smaller ships, though detained in port much of the time by a large blockading force, in a few cruises and encounters at sea were very successful, and acquired just fame by destroying the common belief of British invincibility on the ocean. The American navy fought itself into popularity during this war, and has ever since been regarded with peculiar affection and pride by the people. But the attempt to conquer Canada led only to a series of petty and inglorious conflicts on the frontier, not honorable to either party, leading to no important results, and the details of which are almost beneath the notice of history. The British Orders in Council were revoked June 23d, before the news of the American declaration of war arrived in England; but though an attempt was then made to negotiate, hostilities were finally allowed to continue on the ground of impressment alone. Never was a more meaningless contest; after fighting two years and a half, a treaty of peace was made, leaving this question about impressment precisely where it was before.

§ 625. General Hull, who commanded the northwestern army at De-
June 12, 1812. troit, marched a few miles into Canada, with about 1,800 men, and laid siege to a petty fort at Malden. But before the
August 8. place surrendered, he was obliged to recross the river, and take post at Detroit, where his army was soon invested by a superior force of Canadian militia and Indians. The British had
August 16. hardly opened their fire, before Hull offered to capitulate, and surrendered to them his whole force, thus leaving the Territory of Michigan open to them and the Indians. The absolute want of supplies, the consequent inability to stand a siege, and the distance from all means of succor, were the reasons alleged for this mortifying step. Another American army had been collected on the Niagara River, commanded by Van Rensselaer, who sent over a detachment of about 1,000 men, to
October 16. attack the British village of Queenstown. They effected a landing, and had some success at first; but the militia refused to pass over to their aid, for the constitutional reason that they could be called out only to repel an invasion, not to invade another country. Thus deserted, the party who had crossed the river, after some sharp fighting, were compelled to surrender, the total loss to the Americans being about 1,000 men. Another attempt was made on this frontier, about six weeks afterwards, by General Smythe, which proved so ludicrous a failure that the contriver of it was obliged to
November 29. resign his command, and became an object of general ridicule. The third army, the most numerous and best appointed of all, commanded by General Dearborn, on the frontier near lake Champlain, attempted little and accomplished nothing. The British and Americans vied with each other, during this season, in their efforts to construct a naval force which might obtain the command of the two Lakes, Erie and Ontario; but no action of importance took place between them till the next year.

§ 626. To make up for these disasters and failures on land, the Americans had signal success at sea. Yet so little hope was entertained of the little navy effecting anything against the immense maritime power of England, that the Democratic administration was on the point of ordering all the ships to remain in port, to secure them from inevitable capture; and Captains Bainbridge and Stewart with difficulty obtained leave to put to sea. Hardly two months elapsed before their confidence was justified

by events. The frigate Constitution overtook and captured, after a
August 19. short action, the British frigate Guerriere, of slightly inferior force. Of the English crew, 79 were killed or wounded, and their ship was so much injured that it was set on fire and blown up. The Constitution sustained but little injury, and lost only 14 of her seamen. The American sloop of war Wasp, of 18 guns, Cap-
October 13. tain Jones, captured the English war brig Frolic, of 22 guns, after an action of 45 minutes. The Wasp had but five killed and five wounded, while the loss of the enemy was about 80, only 20 of her crew remaining uninjured. Before the Americans could repair damages, a British 74 came up and captured both vessels. A few days
October 25. later, the frigate United States, Captain Decatur, encountered and captured the British frigate Macedonian, of slightly inferior force, the disparity of loss being quite as great as on former occasions. A fourth victory was obtained on the 29th of December, when the Constitution, then commanded by Captain Bainbridge, made prize of the British frigate Java, after a bloody action of three hours, the killed and wounded in the Java numbering 161, while the loss of the Americans was but 34. The effect of these naval victories was very great; they proved that the English had at last found their match on the ocean, and they wholly overcame the prejudice of the Democratic American party against a navy. Congress forthwith ordered the construction of four seventy-fours, six frigates, six sloops of war, and as many vessels on the Lakes as might be needed.

Congress met early in November, and voted to increase the regular army, and to dispense with the volunteer force, which was found to be both costly and inefficient. Additional pay and bounty were offered, but recruits were still obtained with great difficulty. The finances of the country were already in great confusion, the ordinary revenue being quite insufficient for the expenses of the war, and the loans could not be filled up except at usurious rates. Internal taxes were very unpopular, and Congress naturally hesitated to impose them; but the necessities of the government were so great, that an act was finally passed to raise five millions of dollars in this manner, though the taxes were not to commence till 1814.

§ 627. The military operations of 1813, though a little more honorable to the American arms than those of the year before, were equally destitute of any important results. There were many skirmishes and actions of minor importance, that need not be noticed. At the northwest, General Winchester advanced with a portion of Harrison's army, in the hope of
January 22, 1813. driving the enemy out of Michigan. But he was encountered at Frenchtown by a superior force of British and Indians, under Colonel Proctor, and entirely defeated, most of his troops being obliged to surrender. The wounded prisoners were left behind.

and most of them were butchered the next day by the Indians. About 300 men perished in the battle and massacre, and 600 more were taken prisoners. Harrison then advanced with the rest of the army, but was obliged to stop on the Maumee River, where he garrisoned Fort Meigs, and was besieged in it by the British under Proctor. In May, 1,200 Kentuckians came to his relief, half of whom, after capturing the batteries of the enemy, were surprised and made prisoners, while the others, uniting with Harrison, obliged Proctor to retire to Malden.

On the St. Lawrence frontier, Ogdensburgh was attacked and carried by the British, and a great amount of public and private
February 21. property destroyed or carried off. On the other hand, Commodore Chauncey had succeeded in fitting out a small fleet which gave the Americans the command of Lake Ontario. A party of 1,600 picked men were embarked in this fleet, and transported over the Lake, to attack York, the capital of Upper Canada. This enterprise was successful, a garrison of 800 men being driven out of the place,
April 27. several vessels of war captured or burned, and many naval and military stores destroyed. But the explosion of a magazine killed or wounded 200 of the assailants, among whom was their brave commander, General Pike. Another expedition, fitted out in the
May. same manner, caused the evacuation of all the British posts on the Niagara River, including Fort George and Fort Erie. But when a portion of the Americans advanced in pursuit of the enemy, they were surprised by a night attack, and Generals Chandler and
June 6. Winder, with about 100 men, were made prisoners. Another misfortune followed; Colonel Boerstler, who had been sent with 600 men to attack the British at Beaver Dams, fell into an am-
June 23. buscade, and his whole force was obliged to surrender. The enemy, having launched a new frigate, now recovered the command of the Lake, Chauncey was blockaded, and an attack was made on Sacket's Harbor. General Brown succeeded in repelling this attack, but during the alarm, several ships and many naval stores of the Americans were destroyed. The war then languished in this quarter, a few incursions on both sides leading to no important result. But splendid success awaited the Americans on Lake Erie, where Commodore Perry had succeeded in fitting out a little squadron, composed of two war brigs, the Niagara and the Lawrence, of 20 guns each, and seven smaller vessels. He sailed in August to meet the enemy's squadron, commanded by Captain Barclay, and consisting of two ships, one of 19 and the other of 17 guns, and four smaller vessels, one of which mounted 13, and another 10, guns. The force on both sides was about equal; for though the Americans had in all but 55 guns, while their opponents had 63, the weight of metal was in favor of the former. The two
September 10. squadrons met near the western end of the lake, and after a

furious combat of about three hours, in the course of which Perry's ship, the Lawrence, was disabled, and he shifted his flag to the Niagara, all the enemy's vessels were compelled to surrender. The loss on either side was about 150 killed and wounded. Perry announced his success in a very laconic epistle: — "We have met the enemy, and they are ours." As this victory gave the Americans the command of the Upper Lakes, Harrison's army advanced and crossed the river, by the aid of Perry's fleet, into Canada, where they found that Proctor had hastily evacuated Malden, after dismantling the fort and burning the barracks. Harrison soon marched in pursuit, and found the enemy, who were about 800 in number, with a large body of Indians, posted near the Moravian town on the river Thames. A rapid charge of the Americans

October 5.

broke the British line on both flanks, when the greater part of the enemy threw down their arms and surrendered, though Proctor, with about 200 men, effected his escape. The noted Indian chief, Tecumseh, who was the instigator of the war on the part of the savages, was killed in this battle, which was also the means of gaining back all the ground that had been lost by Hull, and of bringing about a peace with the northwestern tribes. Harrison then embarked, with 1,300 men, for Buffalo, to strengthen the army of the centre, as the one on the Niagara frontier was called. This army was now ordered to advance upon Montreal. On its way, the British, in about equal force,

November 11.

were encountered at Chrystler's Fields, and a severe battle was fought with indecisive results. The troops advanced no farther than St. Regis, where the army from Plattsburg failed to join them, and the expedition was consequently given up.

§ 628. Meanwhile British squadrons were blockading the Delaware and Chesapeake bays, New York, Charleston, and other ports, often landing small parties, which burned several villages and did much wanton injury. The Chesapeake, indeed, was permanently occupied by a powerful fleet of the enemy, which kept up a harassing warfare along the coast, without attempting any enterprise of moment. The bitter fruits were now reaped of that wretched economy on the part of the government, which had so long left an immense line of seacoast almost totally unprovided with fortifications. In spite of the blockading force, a few American ships of war succeeded in getting to sea, eager to rival the naval exploits of the former year. The sloop-of-war Hornet captured and sunk the British brig Peacock, of nearly equal force, in

February 24.

a very short action. But the unlucky Chesapeake frigate, with a discontented and undisciplined crew, having sailed from Boston to accept a challenge from the British frigate Shannon, was captured by her after a short but furious action, — the first instance of

June 1.

the American flag at sea being struck to a force which was not decidedly superior. But again, the Argus sloop-of-war was cap-

August 13. tured by the British brig Pelican, of somewhat superior force, after a severe engagement. The Americans soon had their revenge, however, as the Enterprise, of 12 guns, encountered the British brig Boxer, of 14 guns, and compelled her to strike after a desperate conflict.

§ 629. The only other important operations of this year grew out of a war with the Creek and Cherokee Indians, against whom Gen. Jackson was employed, with a militia force from Georgia, Tennessee, and the present state of Mississippi. He first marched against them in October, and in a two months' campaign, captured many of their villages, and defeated several bands of them with great slaughter. So many of Jackson's men then left him, from weariness of the hard service, that he was reduced to inactivity. The consequence was, that in January, 1814, his troops were thrice attacked, and the savages were repulsed with great difficulty. More militia were then called out, and Jackson, having succeeded in cooping up a large body of the Indians in a peninsula formed by a bend of the Tallapoosa river, forced their breastwork, and made frightful havoc among them. About 600 of the savages were killed or drowned, and 250 taken prisoners. Their spirit was thus effectually broken, and the remainder of the tribe sued for peace on any terms.

§ 630. The campaign of 1814 was, in general, honorable to the American arms, though some great reverses were sustained; the troops were now better disciplined, and were led by more experienced and skilful officers, than in the earlier part of the war. Yet the country labored under great difficulties, and a tone of discouragement was perceptible even in the President's message to Congress. The finances were in great disorder, and the public credit had fallen so low that money could not be obtained on loan except at a ruinous sacrifice. The whole Atlantic coast was now blockaded by the British fleet, the slaves in the southern States were encouraged to desert to the ships, and the only mode of preventing the enemy from being supplied with food and other necessaries from the shore was to pass a law absolutely forbidding all exports. The large cities on the coast were kept in constant apprehension of an attack, and the militia had to be called out in great numbers to defend them. New England had always been opposed to the war, and seemed determined to do little but defend her own borders, and sullenly obey the requisitions of Congress. The cessation of the war in Europe, through the overthrow of Napoleon and the entrance of the allies into Paris, early in the spring of 1814, put the fleets and army of England at liberty, and enabled the British ministers to make large detachments to carry on the war in America. On the part of the Americans, all idea of conquering Canada had to be given up, and the war became entirely defensive in its character. But the spirit of the people rose with their difficulties, an obstinate resistance was made at many points, and the resolution was formed and adhered to, not to submit to peace on disadvantageous terms.

§ 631. The military operations of the year were distributed over so vast a theatre, and comprehended so many petty conflicts, that only the more important events can be noticed. On the Niagara frontier, the American army, after it had been rigidly disciplined for several months by Gen. Brown, who was admirably seconded by Scott, Ripley, Jessup, and other able officers, was led across the river, 3,000 strong, and encountered the enemy, of equal force, under Gen. Riall, at Chippewa. A furious engagement ensued, the first pitched battle of the war; after great loss on both sides, the British gave way, and retreated in disorder to their retrenchments in the rear. The next day, they abandoned these also, and retired to Burlington heights. Large reinforcements from England, under Gen. Drummond, arrived to strengthen Riall's position, and on the 25th, the two armies again met in a pitched battle at Bridgewater, very near Niagara Falls. The conflict lasted from noon till midnight, the ground being obstinately contested on both sides, and the result not very decisive, though the Americans had the advantage. They captured Gen. Riall himself and many other prisoners, took the whole of the British artillery, and retained possession of the battle-field for some time after the enemy retired. The British loss was 878, and the American, 743. The army, not strong enough to advance, and unwilling to retreat across the river, then took shelter in Fort Erie, and Gen. Gaines came to take the command. Drummond advanced with a much larger force, and laid siege to the fort, on which he at length made a furious attack by night. After some hard fighting, he was repulsed with the loss of nearly a thousand men, while the Americans lost but 84. Brown then came to resume the command, and found that the enemy were pushing forwards their works for a regular investment of the place. He resolved to try a sortie, which was completely successful. The guns of the besiegers were spiked, their magazines blown up, and 400 prisoners brought off, the killed and wounded amounting to 600 more. The American loss was not half so great. The desired effect soon followed, as Drummond hastily raised the siege and retired behind the Chippewa. This was the end of active operations on the Niagara frontier, as Izard, who next assumed the command, brought the army back to the American shore.

July 5, 1814.

August 15.

September 17.

§ 632. Events equally honorable to the Americans took place on Lake Champlain. From their camp at Plattsburg, most of the troops had been drawn away to aid the operations on Lake Ontario and the Niagara. Macomb was left in command, with only 3,000 men, many of them invalids, and some militia. Sir George Prevost, the governor of Canada, led an army of 12,000 regular troops over the frontier towards Plattsburg, while the British squadron, under Downie, numbering sixteen vessels, and carrying ninety-five guns and 1,000 seamen, sailed down the

lake to the same point. McDonough, the American Commodore, had moored at Plattsburg his fleet, consisting of four vessels and ten gunboats, carrying in all eighty-six guns and 850 men. Macomb's force was strongly posted behind the river Saranac, a rocky and unfordable stream. The attack by land and water took place simultaneously. In
September 11. two hours and a half, all of Downie's larger vessels were obliged to strike to the Americans, and his gunboats escaped with difficulty. Prevost's attack on land had been a feeble one, and immediately after the capture of his fleet, it was abandoned, and the army retreated that night in great haste, leaving baggage and stores, and even the sick and wounded, behind them. A panic seems to have seized Prevost and his troops, neutralizing their great superiority of force.

§ 633. But this was the end of American success for the year; the rest is a story of disaster, with a gleam of light at the close. In July, the enemy took possession of Eastport, in Maine, and in September, they sailed up the Penobscot, burned the frigate Adams, that had taken refuge there, and "annexed" all the country east of that river to the British dominions. Early in August, the English fleet in the Chesapeake was largely reinforced, a considerable body of English troops having arrived from Europe. Great alarm was caused on shore, and the militia were called out in force for the defence of Washington and Baltimore, there being very few regular troops in that region. Most of the British fleet passed the Potomac, and sailed up the Patuxent to Benedict, where Gen. Ross landed with about 5,000 men, and commenced his
August 19. march for Washington, which was about forty miles distant, the road passing through a thinly populated country. Several bodies of militia fell back before him, and a flotilla of gunboats was blown up, the sailors who had manned them being landed and joined to the troops, for the purpose of serving the artillery. At Bladensburg, the British encountered a motley array of militia and a few regulars,
August 24. under Gen. Winder, assisted by the President and the members of the cabinet, most of whom fled before the first shot reached their ranks. But the artillery, served by the sailors, did good execution, until deserted by the other troops, when the guns were necessarily abandoned. Ross then marched on and occupied Washington, where two new vessels of war and the magazines of stores had already been set on fire and destroyed. The capitol, the President's house, and the public offices were burned by the enemy, who also destroyed some private property. Having effected this wanton injury, and being fearful that troops enough might be collected to impede their retreat, the English hastily returned to their shipping. Three days afterwards, their frigates passed up the Potomac as far as Alexandria, and extorted a heavy ransom from that city. The British fleet next appeared off the Patapsco, and the troops were landed again for an attack on Baltimore. A skirmish ensued with

an advanced body of the militia at North Point, Gen. Ross was killed, September 12. and the Americans were not driven from the ground till several hundred had fallen on either side. The cannonading of the forts by the ships having produced but little effect, and the militia appearing to be strongly intrenched about the city, the enemy concluded to retire without effecting any thing.

§ 634. The next attempt was made upon New Orleans. Jackson, who commanded in that quarter, had been compelled, in October, to storm the fort and seize the city of Pensacola, because the Spaniards there had admitted British troops into the place, who had begun to train the refugee Creek Indians for hostilities against the United States. He heard, soon afterwards, that a powerful expedition was on its way to attack New Orleans, and he marched thither, and took very energetic measures to provide for its defence. The militia were called in, martial law was proclaimed, and all able-bodied persons were compelled to work upon the fortifications or to bear arms. Gen. Pakenham, with 8,000 British regu- December 15. lars, approached the city by way of Lake Borgne, while Jackson had but 5,000 men to oppose him, of whom four fifths were militia. When the enemy had taken post about fifteen miles December 23. below New Orleans, the American general drew out most of his troops to make a night attack upon their camp. He threw them into great confusion, and then made good his retreat, with a loss of 220 in killed and wounded, the British loss being somewhat greater. This check made Pakenham more cautious, and he waited for reinforcements and artillery from the fleet, thus giving the Americans time to strengthen their position. During this interval, also, 2,000 Kentuckians arrived, and Jackson was enabled to throw up fortifications on the other side of the river, fearing an attack in that quarter. On the A. D. 1815. 8th of January, the grand attack was made, the British with true bulldog courage marching up in front to storm a position that had been made almost impregnable. A tremendous fire was opened upon them, Pakenham was killed, two other generals were wounded, one mortally, and at last the enemy were compelled to retire, with a loss of over 2,000 men. The Americans, who fought under shelter, lost but 71. The effect of this blow was decisive, and the enemy, as soon as they could bury their dead, retreated to their shipping.

§ 635. The battle of New Orleans was the closing event of the war. On the 11th of February, a vessel arrived at New York, bringing an unexpected treaty of peace, which had been negotiated at Ghent between the English and American commissioners, and already ratified by the British government. Never were tidings more welcome; bonfires and illuminations were made in the principal cities, and the strifes of opposite factions were forgotten in the general rejoicing. The treaty was a very simple one; nothing was determined in it respecting neutral trade and impressment, the discussion of these subjects having been rendered unnecessary by the general pacification of Europe, and most of the lesser subjects of dispute being referred to subsequent negotiation. The two parties, at the close of the war, remained just as they had been, with respect to each other, at its commencement. Both were exhausted by the prodigious efforts they had made, and were weary both of victories and defeats, of glory, hazard, and suffering. Excepting some petty conflicts with the Indian tribes, the United States, after the conclusion of the treaty of Ghent, remained at peace with all the world for thirty years,— a period long enough for a new generation to arise, which could learn only by hearsay the story of the few triumphs and many disasters of the war of 1812.

F. THE PEOPLE AND STATES OF EUROPE FROM THE HOLY ALLIANCE TO THE PRESENT TIME.

1. THE HOLY ALLIANCE AND THE POSITION OF PARTIES.

§ 636. The upper strata of society, which, in the ordinary course of events, suffer little from the mutations of life, had, through the Revolution and the military despotism of Napoleon, been visited by severe strokes of fortune. A more profound consideration of the revolutionary movement pointed to the supervision of a Higher Power, which brings to nought every impious endeavor, and every presumptuous self-reliance. Religious feeling again returned to the bosoms of men, and gave predominance to piety and Christian faith among the upper classes. Penetrated by this feeling, the three allied monarchs, Alexander of Russia, Francis of Austria, and Frederick William III. of Prussia, before their departure
September 25, from Paris, concluded the Holy Alliance, which was joined
1815. by all the sovereigns of Europe, with the exception of the pope and the king of England. In this holy alliance, which was formed without sincere reference to religious views, the three potentates swore, "That in accordance with the words of Holy Scripture, which commands all men to love each other as brethren, they would remain united in the bands of true and indissoluble brotherly love; that they would mutually help and assist each other; that they would govern their people like fathers of families, and that they would maintain religion, peace, and justice." This alliance, beautiful in theory, was soon made the instrument of a faithless and liberty-endangering policy, which sought, by means of religion, to establish the absolutism of princes, and the omnipotence of governments, and to suppress the doctrine of the sovereignty of the people, and the democratical and constitutional forms of government which are its necessary result. Whilst the Holy Alliance made use of Christi-

anity to establish reactionary principles, it drew upon the whole work the reproach of hypocrisy, and the hatred of the people.

§ 637. Whilst princes and governments were, for the most part, striving after absolute monarchical forms, the wishes of the people were directed to the establishment of constitutional governments. According to the constitution which has grown up on the free soil of Britain, the right of voting taxes, and of having a share in the government and the legislation, belongs to the people, as represented by their members of parliament. As the authority of the king and the rights and liberties of the people are alike discerned in this representative constitution, this form appeared best suited for civilized states. The chief efforts of the European nations were accordingly directed to the establishment or enlargement of this constitutional form of government, and public energy was almost exclusively turned to affairs of state and internal political life. Two powerful parties were formed, the one (called sometimes aristocratic, sometimes conservative, sometimes servile) which wished to grant the people as few, the other (called democratic, liberal, and, when its views were extreme, radical) which wished to grant the people as many, privileges as possible; and whilst the former hindered, as far as it could, the introduction of constitutional forms of state, or, if introduced, attempted to deprive them, by any means, of their democratical elements, the efforts of the latter were directed to the founding and developing of the constitutional life, and to increasing the privileges of the people. Governments were, in general, in the hands of the former; consequently, the liberals formed the opposition. Of the five great European powers, England and France alone possessed constitutional governments; Russia, Austria, and Prussia held fast their monarchical absolutism. In Germany, Italy, and the Pyrenean peninsula, history turns principally upon these constitutional contests, by which now one, and now the other, of these state principles obtained the upper hand.

2. FRANCE.

§ 638. A remarkable revolution in opinions and mode of thinking took place in this much convulsed country after the Restoration. The party of zealous royalists (Ultras, or "White Jacobins," as they were called by their opponents) acquired such predominance, that the king had some difficulty in maintaining the constitutional charter. In the place of the freethinking opinions, and the hostility to the Church, which prevailed at a former period, a fanatical religious credulity made its appearance, which, combined with the most enthusiastic loyalty, called into existence horrors which surpassed the bloodiest deeds of the Revolution. September 15. In Marseilles, Toulon, Nîmes, Toulouse, and other places, a furious and fanatical mob fell upon such inhabitants as were known to be Protestants, Bonapartists, or Republicans, and murdered hun dreds of them (among others, Marshal Brune) in a most barbarous manner. The assassination of the Duc de Berri, that nephew of the king upon whom all the hopes of the Bourbons were placed, by Louvel, a political fanatic, facilitated the efforts of the reactionary party, at the head of which stood the count of Artois and the duke of Angoulême. The king found himself compelled to dismiss the moderate ministry of Decazes, and to consent to a limitation of the freedom of the person, of the press, and of the right of voting. The zeal of the royalists reached its climax under the ministry of Villèle. The Chamber expelled the liberal deputy, Manuel, from their body, and the army, conducted by Angoulême, crossed the Pyrenees at the command of the Holy Alliance, for the purpose of restoring unlimited monarchy in Spain.

February 13, 1820.

March, 1820.

A. D. 1823.

§ 639. On the 16th of September, 1824, Louis XVIII. concluded his varied and severely-tried existence. Stern experience had taught him compassion and moderation; the impetuous violence of the other members of the royal family filled the heart of the dying man with melancholy auguries for the future. His brother, the count of Artois, became king of France as Charles X. By his solemn coronation and anointing in Rheims, he appeared to indicate that he intended to govern after the manner of the old "Most Christian" kings. He accordingly turned his affections towards the nobility and clergy, and surrendered himself entirely to the reactionary party, with the watchword "Throne and altar." The emigrants who had suffered losses during the Revolution received 1,000 million francs from the royal Chambers as an indemnification; and a series of laws in favor of the Church and of the Christian religion announced the intention of the king to erect a mighty barrier against revolutionary notions by the ecclesiastical regeneration of France. Charles X. thought to establish this regeneration by founding rich prelacies, by restoring to the clergy their former influential position, by favoring the system of Orders, and by bringing back that holiness of the Church which is founded upon works, together with the whole of the new Romish pomp. The Jesuits, who had long been re-established by the pope, returned, although not publicly; they founded meetings for pious exercises (congregations), and attempted to get the education of youth into their hands. By these means, the king strengthened the liberal opposition, inasmuch as all men of philosophical education, every friend of light and of enlightenment, turned from a government that favored obscurantism. Whilst the deluded monarch believed that he could impose the old fetters upon the minds of the people by inopportune missions and penitential processions, or by compulsory laws and limitations, the assiduous youth were listening to the liberal discourses and doctrines of the enlightened professors of the University of Paris (Guizot, Villemain, Royer-Collard, &c.,) or reading

May 29, 1825.

the bold and free discussions of the opposition press (*Globe, National, Constitutionnel*), or delighting themselves with Béranger's songs of freedom, and the satires of the Hellenist, Paul Louis Courier; whilst the citizen read the widely-spread works of Voltaire and the Encyclopædists, or the histories and memorials of the Revolution, and of the renowned reign of Napoleon (Thiers, Mignet, &c.)

3. THE CONSTITUTIONAL STRUGGLES IN THE PYRENEAN PENINSULA AND IN ITALY.

§ 640. In Spain and Italy, the new political ideas had made no progress among the people, who were ruled by their priests; they existed in the heads of the educated, and, as it was dangerous to avow them openly, they were disseminated in secret societies. Such political associations were the "Freemasons" in Spain and Portugal, and the "Carbonari" in Italy. Abolition of priestly power, introduction of free constitutional forms, enlightenment of the people, arousing patriotism and a feeling of nationality, were their great objects. Their influence was first attended with results in Spain. Ferdinand, a false and suspicious man, and a master in dissimulation, overthrew, after his return, the Cortes' Constitution in Spain, and brought back the unlimited monarchy of the old time and all its evils. (May 10, 1814.) Nobility and clergy again recovered their exemption from taxes; the monasteries were restored; the Jesuits ventured to make their appearance; the Inquisition reappeared, and with it the rack and all the horrors of a dark age. A frightful persecution now arose, not only against all the adherents of France (Afrancesados), and all who had filled offices under Joseph, or had in any way served him, but against the chiefs and adherents of the Cortes, against the leaders of the bands who had shed their heart's blood for king and country, and who now claimed, as a well-deserved reward, a share in the government and civil freedom. Many of these heroic warriors died by the hand of the executioner, others wandered in foreign countries as outlaws and fugitives; those who remained behind concealed their views and their resentment in the silence of their own bosoms. A camarilla, consisting of the selfish privileged class, fanatical priests, obsequious courtiers, and intriguing women, secured Ferdinand's confidence, and incited him to the most cruel persecution of every liberal. The government and the affairs of justice were in a most deplorable condition, the treasury was exhausted, despite the oppressive taxes, trade was stagnant, the South American colonies renounced allegiance to Spain, and engaged in a war which ended in the independence of the separate states, and the establishment of several republics.

§ 641. At this juncture, it happened that, on the New Year's Day of 1820, a military conspiracy broke out among the regiments assembled at Cadiz for embarkation for South America. The standard of rebellion was raised and the Constitution of the Cortes proclaimed. Colonel Riego was the soul of the undertaking; Quiroga, who had been liberated from prison, undertook the conduct of the whole. The insurrection soon spread to every quarter of Spain; the Constitution of the year '12 was everywhere demanded, and nothing was left to the king but to yield to the demand, to summon the Cortes, and to swear to the constitution. March 7, 1820. This triumph of the Spanish democrats excited their party in Portugal and Italy to imitation. Popular tumults took place in Lisbon and Oporto, and resulted in the removal of Lord Beresford, who governed the country in the name of the king, who was still lingering in Brazil, the summoning of the Estates (Cortes), and the introduction of a constitution on the model of that of Spain. January 26, 1821. John VI. returned to Lisbon, and swore to the new constitution for Portugal and Brazil. The Carbonari excited a military conspiracy in Naples, which soon made such progress, that king Ferdinand found himself compelled to consent to the introduction of the Spanish constitution. William Pepe and Carascosa, the heads of the conspiracy, marched in triumph, at the July 13, 1820. head of the insurgent troops and the Carbonari, who had joined them, into Naples. A revolutionary movement broke out also in Piedmont against the absolute monarchy, supported by the aristocracy and priesthood, in consequence of which Victor Emmanuel March, 1821. abdicated, and the Spanish constitution was introduced into the kingdom of Sardinia also.

§ 642. The chiefs of the Holy Alliance, disturbed by this new revolutionary spirit, that seemed to have seized upon the German youth also, embraced the resolution, at the instigation of Metternich, of suppressing the liberal movement. January, 1821. At the congress of Laybach, at which king Ferdinand of Naples was also present by the invitation of the monarchs, it was determined to overthrow the constitutional government in Naples by violence. Ferdinand approved the proposal. An Austrian army was marched in; the dastardly forces of Pepe and Carascosa were quickly overpowered, and either dispersed or forced to surrender, upon which the king again abolished the constitutional government. From this time, priestly power and absolute monarchy, supported by mercenary troops and a system of police, were united together for the suppression of every movement of freedom by terror and the bondage of the intellect.

This result decided the fate of the Piedmontese constitution. It is true that the enthusiastic liberals, under Santa Rosa, resisted their enemies at Novara not without glory; but their strength was soon broken. April, 1821. Turin and Alessandria were occupied by the Austrians; and unlimited monarchy in its severest form, and with all the horrors of the reaction, was again restored in Sardinia.

§ 643. Not much more splendid was the end of the Spanish Cortes.

When the liberals abused their victory, placed undue restrictions upon the kingly power, and proceeded with great violence against the priesthood, the privileged classes, and the ancient and traditionary privileges and usages, the priests and the adherents of absolute power stirred up the people to resistance. A bloody civil war once more threatened to tear the unhappy country to pieces. At this juncture, the members of
October, 1822. the Holy Alliance at the Congress of Verona required the Cortes in Madrid to alter the constitution, and to give the king greater powers. The Cortes rejected this demand with defiance. A French army, under the command of the duke of Angoulême, now
February, 1823. marched over the Pyrenees. It was in vain that the Cortes summoned the nation to arms; constitutional freedom was a word without meaning for people led by priests and monks, and the new system was opposed to their habits and feelings; the popular war, the old renowned guerilla, on which the Cortes had placed its confidence, did not arise; the people and the camarilla saluted the French as deliverers from the detested rule of the Freemasons. It was in vain that a few leaders, like Mina in Barcelona and Quiroga in Leon, resisted with courage and spirit the foreign army; the soldiers showed little love for fighting, and sought to secure themselves betimes by capitulations. The French marched triumphantly into Madrid, and, as the Cortes and king had fled to the south, they appointed a regency. The strong city of Cadiz was the last place of refuge for the friends of the constitution;
August 5, 1823. the French appeared before the town. The courage of the members of the Cortes sank; instead of burying themselves beneath the ruins of the town, as they had formerly grandiloquently expressed it, they concluded a treaty with the besiegers, by which they consented to their own dissolution and set the king at liberty. Ferdinand VII. was now replaced in the fulness of his power by foreign bayonets; the constitution and all its arrangements fell into desuetude, and the apostolic party let loose all the demons of rage and vengeance
November 7. against its opponents. Riego and many of his confederates died by the hands of the executioner, thousands wandered about in foreign countries as starving and houseless fugitives and outlaws, and an equal number were compelled to expiate in mouldy dungeons the crime of having attempted to rob the people of the institutions to which three hundred years of despotism had accustomed them.

§ 644. The lamentable end of the Cortes government of Spain inspired the queen of Portugal (sister of Ferdinand VII.) and her second son, Don Miguel, with the project of getting rid, at the same time, of their detested constitution by an act of violence. They induced the weak king, John VI., to abolish the Constitution of the Cortes, and to sanction the persecution of the Constitutionalists and the Freemasons. Shortly

after this, Don Miguel excited a rebellion against his own father, with
April, 1824 the purpose of obtaining the regency, but gained instead a sentence of banishment from the country. John VI. died
March 10, 1826. two years afterwards. His eldest son, Don Pedro, who, being constitutional emperor of Brazil, could not at the same time become king of Portugal, made over the government of the mother country to his daughter, Donna Maria da Gloria, who was a minor, and granted the Portuguese a liberal constitution. His brother, Don Miguel, having returned from banishment, succeeded, some time after, in again overthrowing this constitution by the aid of the apostolic party. He
June, 1828. robbed his niece of her right to the throne, had himself proclaimed absolute king, and proceeded by banishment, imprisonment, and death, against the friends and adherents of constitutional order. But his reign was short. Don Pedro, compelled in Brazil to surrender his crown to his son, who was under age, landed in Portugal
A. D. with the soldiers he had raised, and reduced his tyrannical
1832 1834. brother to such extremities in a war of two years' duration, that he at length renounced the crown and retired abroad. Upon this, Pedro again restored the Cortes government, which, after his early death, however, underwent many attacks and alterations.

4. GREAT BRITAIN.

§ 645. England had come forth from the long struggle with France powerful and victorious. She had destroyed the fleets of other nations, and put her own marine on such a footing that her empire of the sea was incontestable; she had increased her colonies in the West Indies, had raised Canada, had planted colonies in the west and south of Africa, and had created an empire in the East Indies, after the conquest of the mighty sultan Tippoo Saib, that far surpassed the mother country in size and population, and was an inexhaustible source of trade and commerce. Distant islands, opened to the view of the astonished world by daring navigators, like Cook and others, bowed themselves beneath the sceptre of the island empress of the sea. The possession of Gibraltar and Malta, the protective government of the Ionian Isles, the free passage through the Dardanelles, secured to her, after the peace of Paris, the dominion of the Mediterranean and intercourse with the Levant. By her firmly-established constitution, with the liberty of the press and of speech, and the narrowly defined limits between the rights of the king and of the people, England excited the envy of other nations. But with all this power and prosperity without, the state was suffering from incurable wounds. 1. Whilst a small proportion of the people had amassed enormous wealth, the larger number of them were sunk in the most oppressive poverty. The expensive land and naval wars, and the enormous subsidies that the government sent to the Continent, had raised the national debt to such a sum that the yearly interest amounted to thirty-four million pounds. This burden of debt, together with an extravagant court and excessive salaries, increased the expenditure of the state to such a degree that the necessary sums could only be obtained by a perpetually increasing taxation of articles of trade, necessaries of life, income (income-tax), houses, and landed property. This occasioned the impoverishment of the small landed proprietors and of tradesmen with moderate capitals. The lands fell into the hands of the rich nobles, who discovered the means of increasing their incomes by raising rents and preventing the importation of foreign corn by the corn-laws. Trade fell into the hands of the rich manufacturers, who, by enlarging their business, outdid men of smaller means; the middle class of citizens decreased, while the number of artisans, who lived from hand to mouth, increased to a formidable amount. Heavy poor-rates imposed upon the public, and occasional contributions by the government, were not sufficient to counteract the evil. The lower orders, excited by want and misery, made repeated attempts to improve their condition by insurrections, but their illegal proceedings invariably resulted in their own injury. The unarmed crowd was easily dispersed by the military; but the sanguinary punishments inflicted upon the insurgents of Manchester brought severe censure upon the government. The lower classes soon began to strive for political influence also. To give themselves a voice in the legislature, they demanded universal suffrage, yearly parliaments, and vote by ballot. They laid down their principles in a people's charter, whence they received the name of Chartists. It is to their exertions that the relaxation of the corn-laws, by which the introduction of foreign corn was facilitated, is to be ascribed. In 1846, the corn-laws were entirely repealed.

A. D. 1819.

A. D. 1842.

§ 646. 2. After the severe contest against Napoleon, there came a period of torpor in England. George IV., a king sunk in vice and pleasure, who in his youth had gone with the opposition, put his confidence in the cold-blooded Tories who had grown grey in the state-wisdom of Pitt, and turned away his eyes and his heart from the people. The latter rewarded him with aversion and hatred, especially when he gave notoriety to the first year of his independent reign by a scandalous action for divorce, before the Upper House, against his wife, Caroline of Brunswick, who was living in unwilling separation from him. When the queen died, in the following year, the sympathy and compassion of the nation followed her to the grave, little as her conduct or morals were deserving of praise. Castlereagh, the old associate of George, and the supporter of a false and faithless policy, died by his own hand during a paroxysm of melancholy. This was a great shock to the king, who was burdened by so many sins of youth, and

Court and Government.

A. D. 1820.

A. D. 1821.

August 12, 1822.

made him shun society. He passed the last years of his life in gloomy retirement, whilst the great statesman, Canning, who approached the principles of the Whigs, restored its former preëminence to the insular empire of England. George IV.'s only daughter, the intelligent and amiable princess Charlotte (wife of Leopold of Coburg, afterwards king of the Belgians), having died young and without children, William IV. the king's brother, a plain, homely man, ascended the throne after
William IV., George's death. Under him, the Whigs got the manage-
A. D. 1830 - ment of affairs into their hands, and the important measure
1837. of parliamentary reform, by which the elections for parliament were arranged afresh according to the number of the population and the right of suffrage was made dependent upon a certain income,
March 1, 1831. was carried after the most violent opposition, and formed the
August, 1835. triumph of the middle class over the aristocracy. Shortly after this, slave emancipation, at which Wilberforce and other philanthropists had been working for years, was carried. England, after vast sums paid in indemnifying the planters, set the slaves at liberty in her colonies, and has since endeavored with all her strength to induce other nations to take a similar step, and to entirely suppress the
June 20, 1837. slave traffic. After William IV., his niece, Victoria, married since (the 10th of February, 1840) to prince Albert of Coburg, received the crown of England. Under her government, the great statesman, Sir Robert Peel, attempted to give a fresh impulse to trade by moderating the import duties. Since then, "free-trade" has been the watchword of the day.

§ 647. Ireland to the present hour is the sore spot in the body politic of England. The maltreatment of former generations has
Ireland. produced a gulf between England and Ireland which never permitted a perfect union between two people different in race, religion, and institutions. Two things especially, produced by an old injustice, excited the hatred of the irritable Irish, — the harsh treatment of the poor peasants by their noble English landlords, and the unnatural condition of the Church, where Anglican priests are in possession of the Irish Church temporalities, whilst the poor Catholic population are obliged to maintain their unpaid clergy from their necessity. The complaints of the Irish were unheard; the insurrections that were attempted were suppressed, and increased the oppression. It was not
A. D. 1826 until admission into the English parliament was granted to Irish Catholics by the Emancipation Act, that the Irish people had an opportunity of demanding an abolition of abuses. Daniel O'Connell, who now entered parliament with a "tail" of more than forty similarly-minded Irishmen, threatened a Repeal of the Union, unless attention was paid to the righteous demands of the Irish people. The increasing poverty which, owing to the failure of the potato crop, produced pestilence and

famine, required stringent remedies for the prevailing abuses. Owing to the irritable and excitable nature of the Irish, it was an easy task for the great popular orator and demagogue, O'Connell, to keep the country in a perpetual ferment, and, by the watchword of "repeal," to direct the whole energy of the people to a single object. Repeal associations were formed in every spot and corner, with a common fund for furthering the aims of O'Connell; the Catholic priesthood, who exercised an unlimited power over the ignorant people, were in his service; his word was law in Ireland. The principal demand of the Irish was the abolition of the tithes, which were paid in Ireland to the English clergy. When their proposals were not received by the English parliament, the tenants refused to pay the tithes, and opposed the distraints; and, when the English had recourse to force, they employed force in return. Bands of armed men marched through the country, marking their course with blood and fire. These things pressingly admonished the government to give its best attention to "starving and revolutionary Ireland, the land of passions and of misery." The country was threatened with a state of warfare by the Irish Coercion Bill, in order to maintain obedience by terror; and an attempt was made by the Irish Church Bill, and the so-called appropriation clause, to abolish or moderate the Church payments of the tenants, and to apply a portion of the Church property to secular purposes, namely, to the improvement of public education. But this project encountered such resistance from the High-Church party and the aristocratic Tories, that it was not till after a parliamentary contest of a twelvemonth that the Tithes Bill was passed, and even then in a mutilated shape. The High-Church opposition formed the so-called Orange clubs, which attempted to frustrate all concessions to the Irish, and kept religious and national hatred in constant activity.

5. GERMANY.

§ 648. Germany, after the Congress of Vienna, was weaker and less united than she had been during the empire. It is true that the number of independent principalities and states had been lessened by more than a hundred, and that the bishoprics, abbacies, and imperial towns had been deprived of their independent position; but, on the other hand, thirty-eight territories which had been included in the German Union received sovereign powers, as far as their internal affairs were concerned. In place of the old imperial Diet appeared the Federative Diet of Frankfort-on-the-Maine, composed of representatives of the different governments, under the presidentship of Austria. But, as this assembly was entirely directed by the wishes of single governments, it had no independent power; and the German Union was an impotent member among European states, dependent upon the influence of the two great powers, Austria and Prussia, which assumed the first rank, in virtue of their German provinces. Even foreign kingdoms sent representatives to the Frankfort Diet, as Denmark for Holstein, and the Netherlands for Luxemburg. This powerless condition of Germany gave as little satisfaction abroad as the internal arrangements sufficed at home. Instead of a strong union, with a united federative government and a popular representation, such as patriotic men had hoped and striven for, the creation of the Viennese Congress was a union formed of a number of sovereign states, in which the governments, but not the people, were represented; and the 13th article of the Union Act, by which a general promise was given of the introduction of a state constitution, without any distinct notice of the time and manner of its accomplishment, did not satisfy the expectations of the people. As Prussia, where the men of the retrograde movement, Haller, Schmalz, and others, soon obtained the upper hand of the patriots of the war of liberty, delayed bringing forward the promised state constitution, and at length, instead of the desired imperial legislature, granted only provincial estates with consulting voices, without either publicity or general interest, the discontent of the German people became every day greater. Austria, under the influence of Metternich, was governed in a spirit of complete absolutism, and kept as far aloof from Germany as possible; and Prussia gave herself up more and more to the same views, and allowed herself to be made the instrument of the execution of most unpopular measures. As there was no general system of management or debate, the constitutions that were gradually introduced into Saxe-Weimar, Baden, Wirtemberg, Bavaria, Hesse, and many other small states, turned out very different from each other, so that, in this respect also, Germany appeared torn and divided. And then the duties between different countries, which acted as a bar to their intercourse! It seemed as though Germany was about to be broken up into its separate races and states!

§ 649. This state of things filled the German people with discontent, and shook their confidence in the patriotism of the governments. The liberal party, which was aiming at a progressive development of state affairs in a democratic direction, and kept alive the idea of German unity, gained ground daily. But, above all, the German youth, who had been filled with an admiration of the middle ages by the new romantic poetry, were dissatisfied with the present. They longed for the empire of the middle age, and for the former unity and greatness of Germany; and sought to give life to the new ideas of popular government under the old German forms and titles. Without clearness of aim, and without knowledge or respect for obstacles, the youths who, in the German high schools, had formed the fraternal alliance of the "General Burschenschaft," strove after an ideal world and state creation upon the old German system. This
October 18, feeling first displayed itself during the festival of the Wart-
1817. burg. On the day of the battle of Leipsic, a festival was

celebrated as an introduction to the 300th anniversary of the Reformation, which is always solemnized with great enthusiasm in Protestant Germany; and at the same time, in remembrance of the struggle for liberty, a number of students held a meeting at the Wartburg, near Eisenach, at which fiery speeches were made by the young men, and at the conclusion, following the example of Luther, certain writings of Kotzebue, Kamptz, Haller, Jarke, and others, which were offensive to their views, together with some symbols of an antiquated and feudal period, such as pigtails, breast-laces, corporals' canes, were, with youthful wantonness, committed to the flames. If an undue importance was attached by the government to this occurrence, yet it is not to be wondered at that the bloody deed of one of these confederates of the Wartburg, George Sand, should be looked upon as the act of a great political conspiracy, and give rise to a series of legal investigations and prosecutions, on account of "demagogic intrigues." Sand, of Wunsiedel, a pious and patriotic youth, but full of fanaticism and governed by vanity, embraced the criminal resolution of killing the Russian councillor, Augustus Von Kotzebue, who was suspected
March 23, of endangering Germany's freedom and politic development
1819. by conveying information to St. Petersburg; he wished to rid the German nation from this "Russian spy," this "traitor to the country." He approached the unsuspecting man in Mannheim with a letter, and pierced him through with a stroke of a dagger as he was reading it. The attempt to kill himself was not successful. Sand, re-
September, covered from his wounds, ended his life on the scaffold. After
1819. this followed the decrees of Carlbad, which restrained the freedom of the press by the censorship, established a court of investigation in Mayence, for the suppression of "demagogic intrigues," interdicted the alliances of the *Burschenschaft* with their gymnasia, placed the universities under the supervision of special government officials, and finally gave unconditional validity to the resolutions of the Diet for all governments. Bounds were at the same time set to the democratical spirit of the south German provinces by the concluding act of Vienna.
May 15, 1820. Prussia, which had been so long the hope and confidence of all German patriots, now took the lead in the reactionary and unpopular measures. Men like Arndt, Jahn, &c., whose voices and example had had such influence in time of need, were now brought to judgment as favorers of demagogic intrigues, deprived of their offices, and watched by the police. From this time, the unity of Germany was looked upon as a dream; he who expressed a wish of the sort made himself suspected of demagogic efforts. Every separate state was regarded as an independent whole, and governed without relation to the general interest of the country; and, although many excellent arrangements were adopted in the government administration of justice, and in the affairs of religion and education, little or nothing was done for arousing the feelings of nationality and patriotism.

6. GREECE'S STRUGGLE FOR LIBERTY.

§ 650. While the public energies of the nations of Europe were held in firm bonds by the Holy Alliance, the news of Greece's rise against the Turks produced great enthusiasm, and aroused a fresh political interest among the torpid people. Alexander Ypsilanti, a Moldavian noble in the military service of Russia, was the first who rose up in his country as a liberator, and published a call to his countrymen, which referred to the protection of Russia, to shake off the Turkish yoke. A society, Hetœria, with widely-spread ramifications, the secret object of which was a separation from Turkey, came to the aid of the project. In a short time, Morea (Peloponnesus), Livadia (Hellas), Thessaly, and the Greek islands, were in arms. But the expected aid of Russia did not arrive.

March, 1821. Willingly as the emperor Alexander would have favored the movement, both from religious sympathy and political interest, the influence of Metternich, who, at the Congress of Laybach, placed the insurrection of the Greeks on a par with the simultaneous democratical movements in Italy and Spain, prevented any support being given to them. The Turks foamed with rage, and took a bloody vengeance. The Patriarch of Constantinople, the supreme head of the Greek Church, was torn from the high altar on Easter-day by the infidel Mahommedans, and hung up along with his bishops at the principal door of his church; the greater number of the Greek families of the capital died by violence, or were obliged to wander forth as beggars into banishment. The sacred band of Greeks, under the conduct of Ypsilanti, succumbed to the

June 19, 1821. superior power of the Turks in Wallachia, and were totally annihilated in the desperate battle of Dragaschan, where they fought with the heroic courage of a Leonidas. Ypsilanti fled to Austria, but was doomed to pine for years in a Hungarian fortress. The fall of these magnanimous warriors showed that they were animated by a different spirit from that of the Spanish and Italian champions of freedom.

§ 651. A frightful national war now broke out in all quarters of Greece. In Morea, the wild and warlike Mainotes of the Taygetus rose up under the conduct of Mauromichali and Kolokotroni, and the other inhabitants of Peloponnesus shortly after followed, restrained to a more systematic plan of warfare by Demetrius Ypsilanti, the brother of Alexander. At the same time, the Greeks in Livadia and the islands fought with glory and success; their valor recalled to recollection the deeds of their ancestors, little of the Hellenic blood as may flow in the veins of the modern Greeks. Europe gazed in sympathy upon this war in the east, and hastened to collect money and troops by means of Philhellenic unions to support the courage of the warriors, who, in the beginning of the year 1822, had united themselves into a republic under Ypsilanti and Mavrokordato. The object was to support civilization and Christianity against savage barbarians. Whilst the princes of the Holy Alliance, from a regard for their ease, were exposing a Christian people to the attacks of infidel bands of murderers, crowds of foreign Philhellenists, under the conduct of Normann and others, marched to the ancient birthplace of Christian civilization. The English poet, Byron, devoted his talents, his wealth, and his energy, to the affairs of Greece, where the climate and exertion occasioned his death.

April 19, 1824.

Despite the dissentions and selfishness of the Greek leaders, their arms were generally successful till the June of 1825. At that period, the Porte obtained a powerful supporter in Mehemet Ali, who, as Pasha of Egypt, had destroyed the power of the Mamalukes, and established an army and government upon the plan of those of Europe, by which means Western civilization and Oriental despotism were placed in horrible conjunction. This man sent his son, Ibrahim, with a considerable army of mingled materials to Peloponnesus, on the business of the sultan. The small and disunited body of Greeks was unable to resist him; one town after another fell into his hands; the march of Ibrahim and his brutal troops proceeded onwards over blood, corpses, and burning houses. Peloponnesus and the coasts of Livadia were frightfully ravaged for two years, from the strong city of Tripolizza, which they had chosen as their point of support, whilst cabinets were in vain endeavoring to restrain the war by diplomatic negotiations. The fall of Missolonghi first produced a change in affairs. When that hardly-pressed town was unable any longer to defend itself, the heroic inhabitants with their wives and children made a sally upon the beleaguring enemy; the third part were slain, Missolonghi disappeared in flames, and all who remained in it perished beneath the ruins. The cry of anger that passed through all Europe at this event, awakened the governments from their lethargy.

April 22, 1826.

December 1, 1825.

§ 652. A short time before this, the emperor Alexander had descended to his grave, and as the elder brother Constantine had already renounced the throne, his brother Nicholas obtained the Russian sceptre, after the bloody suppression of a military conspiracy that was to have changed the government and the succession to the throne. In England, the rudder of state was intrusted to the skilful hands of the high-minded Canning, who, in the maturity of his life, had not forgotten the dreams of his youth or his enthusiasm for the liberation of Greece. In France, the government thought itself obliged to pay some attention to the loud clamors of the Philhellenists, especially as, at this time, the bloody destruction of the Janissaries in Constantinople, by which 15,000 Mahommedans died a violent death, filled civilized Europe with horror at the inhumanity of the Turks. At the proposal of Canning, therefore, the three European powers, Russia, England, and France, concluded an alliance, by which they agreed to employ their common exertions to induce the Porte to allow the Greeks

June, 1826.

their liberty. A combined fleet appeared in the waters of the Morea, and demanded from Ibrahim the evacuation of the peninsula; upon the October 20, 1827. rejection of this demand followed the battle of Navarino, where the Turko-Egyptian fleet was annihilated by the European. This decision came so quickly that the allied powers were astonished at the "unexpected event." The battle of Navarino consequently August 8, 1827. remained without results, and as, after Canning's death, the English, who were anxious about their trade, showed themselves more favorably disposed to the Porte, the resolute sultan Mahmud remained firm to his purpose of not giving the Greeks their liberty, and behaved so insolently to the Russians that they declared war against him. This roused the hopes of the Greeks. Whilst the forces of the Ottomans were marching into the lands of the Danube, Ibrahim was at length compelled by the French fleet to evacuate the Morea, whereupon Capo d'Istria, from Corfu, was appointed president of the Greek state. The July, 1829. daring military achievements of the Russians, who, under September 14, 1829. Diebitsch (Sabalkanski), surmounted the Balkan, at length compelled the Porte, by the peace of Adrianople, to grant the Russians favorable conditions, and to acknowledge the independence of Greece. But as it was long before the question of boundaries could be settled, the war still continued for some time in Greece, during which time the admiral, Miaulis, blew up the Greek fleet rather than allow it to fall into strange hands. At length, the three powers agreed in London to form a constitutional kingdom out of Morea, Livadia, a part of Thessaly, Eubœa, and the Cyclades, over which (as Capo d'Istria had in the meantime been murdered by the brothers Mauromichali) Otho I., of the royal May, 1832. house of Bavaria, was placed as king. Since then, Greece has striven to elevate herself to the position of a civilized state, the forms of which she has assumed, without however being able to free herself entirely from the conditions of barbarism and a life of A. D. 1843. plunder. At a later period, the Greeks, from national jealousy, drove away the German foreigners that had come in the train of the court, and thus deprived themselves, at the same time, of the supports of modern civilization.

7. THE NEW ROMANTIC LITERATURE.

§ 653. The years of the Holy Alliance were the flourishing period of romantic literature and art, the chief creators and supporters of which The Schlegels. were the brothers, Augustus William and Frederick Schlegel, the poet Novalis, Novalis. and Ludwig Tieck. They quitted the path of religious illumination and of political candor, and Ludwig Tieck. escaped to the ideas of the middle age and the religious contemplation of the East. The faith in miracles and the religious mysticism of an early period of Christianity, the love affairs and the sensual religious worship of the departed days of chivalry, the sacred art of the middle ages, the flowery poetry of the East, the popular songs and the meditative world of fable of the distant past, permanently engaged their interest. It was for this reason that their views were directed to the forgotten productions of the literature of romance, whilst, following the example of Herder, they collected and elaborated the legends, traditions, and popular songs of German antiquity, and then sought to introduce the chivalrous poetry of the Italians and Spaniards into Germany by means of translations; and drew the mythology, and the poetry founded upon it, of the East and of the Scandinavian North, within the circle of their activity. The profound Dante, the profuse Shakspeare, the Spanish poet Calderon, Cervantes, and many others, were admirably translated by the romanticists, and naturalized in Germany. The Schlegels, in particular, distinguished themselves by their critical and æsthetical writings, by their intelligent researches in the region of the history of literature, by translations, and by references to the language, literature, and "wisdom" of the Indians. Tieck obtained his greatest fame by his elaboration of old popular legends and tales (Genoveva, Kaiser Octavianus, Fortunatus, &c.); and the prematurely deceased Francis Von Hardenburg (Novalis,) by his melancholy poems and poetical essays ("Blüthenstaub," "Spiritual Songs,"), and the unfinished romance, Henry of Ofterdingen. In the same spirit sang the lyric poets, Matthison, Chamisso, Max Von Schenkendorf, the romance writer Arnim, de la Motte Fouqué, Clemens Brentano, Hoffmann, &c. The orientalist, Hammer-Purgstall, excited by the romanticists, undertook the translation of the Arabian and Persian poets, and the great collective work, "Fundgruben des Orients;" and Fr. Rückert, renowned as a lyric poet ("Harnessed Sonnets," "Eastern Roses,"), brought the art of translation and imitation to perfection ("Nal and Damijanti," "Die Makamen des Hariri"). The brothers Grimm, (Jacob and William), were excited by the romanticists to their successful inquiries into the old German language and literature, and to their collection of popular and domestic tales. At the same time, the romanticists elevated poetry and literature generally to a loftier station, gave it dignity and nobleness, and awakened love and sensibility for the fine arts; on the other hand, they afforded pernicious examples in regard to public morality and decency of life. An unbridled and restless life of wandering and travels, to which most of them gave themselves up without restraint, favored the sensual appetites and passions. Not misled by the romanticists, and treading in the path of Schiller, Theodore Korner, Ludwig Uhland, Moriz Arndt, H. Zschokke, Seume, and others, composed poetry; and the lyric and dramatic writers in the spirit of Aristophanes, like Augustus Von Platen ("The Romantic Œdipus," "The Fatal Fork"), paid homage to the spirit of progress. The party of the liberals and the great mass of the German people took most pleasure in the freer, if less vigorous, poetry of the latter.

8. THE JULY REVOLUTION OF PARIS, AND ITS CONSEQUENCES.

§ 654. Charles X. proceeded in the path of reaction without regard to public opinion. The liberal ministry of Martignac had been obliged since January, 1828, to yield to an ultra royalist one, under the presi-
August 8, 1829. dentship of Polignac; and when the Chambers, in their opening address, expressed their discontent at the policy of the government, they were dissolved and a new election followed. In vain the men of the opposition re-appeared in increased numbers, and confirmed the mistrust of the people in the new ministry. Charles X. would not learn wisdom. He vainly hoped that the military re-
May 16, 1830. nown which the French troops had gained about this time in Africa,—where, to revenge the insults offered by the Dey of Algiers to the ships and consul of France, they had taken possession of his capital, and planted the French banners upon the battlements of the
July 5. old city of robbers,—would produce a favorable feeling in the nation. Scarcely had the "Moniteur" published the three celebrated ordinances, by which the freedom of the press was sus-
July 26. pended, the new Chambers dissolved, and the order of election of the next arbitrarily changed, before the July Revolution broke out, by which the people, after an heroic contest of three days, obtained their release from the royal house of Bourbon, and from the rule of the priests. The deputies who were present in Paris established a provisional government on the 29th July, whilst the contest in the streets was at the hottest, in which the banker Lafitte, Casimir Pèrier, Odillon-Barrot, and others, bore a part, until the constitutional party triumphed over the republican, and Louis Philippe, duke of Orleans, was named regent of the empire. When it was too late, Charles X. offered to recal the obnoxious ordinances, and to summon a popular ministry; but he was obliged for the third time to go into exile with his family, whilst his more sagacious relative, Louis Philippe, after he had sworn to observe the hastily revised charter, ascended the throne as king of the French. The restoration of the national colors, and the reëstablishment of the National Guard, under the command of Lafayette, marked the commencement of the new citizen monarchy established by the people. Charles X. died in the year 1836, at Görz.

§ 655. The revolution of July occasioned the total fall of the Holy Alliance, which had already received a shock by the death of Alexander, and called forth a movement throughout all Europe which produced an important change in affairs. It is true that the government of the "citizen king" soon assumed a pacific attitude in regard to other states, and the liberals who had arrived at power in Paris preferred moderate and conciliatory modes of procedure to waging war, and attempted to win over all the moderate and undecided to the support of the existing system, by establishing the principle of "the *juste milieu;*" but the tumult of the first storm was strong enough to give a severe shock to the artful structure of the Viennese Congress. In Belgium, Germany, Poland, Italy, &c., insurrections broke out that could only be suppressed or composed after a two years' contest; and though the influence of the absolute powers of the east — Russia, Austria, and Prussia — was strong enough to preserve or bring back the old system in most states, free opinions, from this time, acquired greater importance, and public opinion increased to a power that bade defiance to all efforts of "state police" and "bureaucracy." In the west of Europe, owing to the influence of England and France, constitutional government and the civil freedom which is allied to it maintained the preëminence.

§ 656. THE REVOLUTION IN BELGIUM was the first consequence of the Parisian July days. The Congress of Vienna, without regard to religion, language, or national interest, had united the Flemish and Brabant provinces to the States-General of Holland, in one kingdom of the Netherlands. The Hollanders regarded themselves as the rulers; they compelled the Belgians not only to share the great national debt and the high taxes, but attempted to force their own language and laws upon them, and placed the education of the Catholic people under the supervision of Protestant courts. When the press allowed itself to adopt a hostile tone against the government, the writers were proceeded against with fine, imprisonment, and banishment. Upon this, the French liberal party, which was struggling for a free political life, and which was in alliance with the chiefs of the Paris opposition, formed a confederacy with the Catholic ultramontane party, which demanded freedom of education, against the Dutch government, — which the king in his speech from the throne designated as "infamous." The dissatisfaction thus produced had already reached the highest pitch, when the news arrived in Brussels of the July events, and set the whole land in a flame. On the evening of the 25th August, after the representation of the opera, "The Mute of Portici," the mob destroyed the printing-house of a journal favorable to the interests of Holland, the palace of the minister of justice, the dwelling of the director of police, &c. To restrain any farther devastations on the part of the people, a civic guard and committee were formed, till the radical and ultramontane parties united themselves in a National Congress, under the guidance of Potter. The example of the capital was followed, so that, in a short time, the standard of Brabant was waving over the whole of Belgium. An attack of the Dutch upon Brussels was repulsed, and the Belgian insurgents even marched against Antwerp, to deprive their detested neighbors of this town also. Upon this, the Dutch general, Chassé, retired into the strong citadel and fired upon the unfortunate town for seven hours, with 300 cannon, by which a vast amount of goods of great value was destroyed. Irritated at this proceeding, the National Congress now declared the independence of Belgium, November. and the exclusion of the house of Orange from the Belgian throne. During the continuance of the war between Belgium and Holland, the five great powers held a conference in London. It was here resolved, after long diplomatic negotiations, to separate Bel- June, 1831. gium from Holland, and to arrange the boundaries in an equitable manner. In accordance with this, Leopold of Saxe-Coburg, who was related to the royal family of England, and who was shortly after united, by a second marriage, to a daughter of Louis Philippe, received the Belgian throne, and attempted to conciliate the liberals by granting a free representative constitution, and the Catholic clergy by the complete independence of the church of the state. It was in vain that the Hollanders attempted again to subject the rebels by force. Threatened and opposed by the French and English, they were compelled, despite December, 1832. the bravery of their army and the courage of their sailors, to desist from the contest. Belgium, on the other hand, flourished under the influence of free institutions and energetic industry.

§ 657. The successful termination of the French and Belgian revolutions urged the Poles to an insurrection. Raised to a kingdom by the Congress of Vienna, and placed under the government of the emperor of Russia, Poland was in a better position than when subjected to the old anarchy. The constitution, with diets and a national armament, afforded the people a regulated freedom; industry increased, literature flourished, passable roads facilitated intercourse; but all these advantages, which, to say the truth, suffered much prejudice from the despotic character of the viceroy, Constantine, were not sufficient to prevent the Poles from cherishing the thought of again revivifying their divided country; and the hope that the French, after the revolution of July, would not neglect to hasten to the assistance of their old confederates, confirmed them in the belief that the moment for the regeneration of the old Poland was again come. It was six o'clock on the evening of the 20th Novem- A. D 1830. ber, when twenty armed young men of the Cadet school, members of a widely-spread military conspiracy, rushed into the palace of the viceroy for the purpose of dispatching him, whilst other conspirators called the inhabitants of the capital to arms. It was only with difficulty that the prince escaped the fate designed for him. He yielded to the storm, and retired from the country with his Russian soldiers and officials. A provisional government, with Czartoryski, Niemcewicz, General Chlopiki, and others at its head, undertook the conduct of affairs in Poland. Instead, however, of employing the newly-aroused military spirit and the fresh enthusiasm of the people in a spirited attack upon unprepared Russia, the regency, which belonged to the aristocracy of Poland, chose the

path of negotiation, and placed their hopes upon the promises of French diplomatists. It made little difference that Chlopiki was shortly after named dictator, and entrusted with the supreme command of military affairs; and that the diet, which was hastily called together, invested the prince Radzivil with the most unlimited power; the irresolute aristocracy, discontented with the violence of the republican and democratic clubs, kept things in check, and paralysed every undertaking by hesitation and dissensions. Whilst the emperor of Russia ordered an army of 200,000
January 25, men to march into Poland, under the command of field-mar-
1831. shal Diebitsch, the diet pronounced the dethronement of the house of Romanoff in Poland, but rejected, from selfish motives, that which could alone save the country, the liberation of the peasants and the excitement of a popular war. What mattered it that the Polish army again gave the most splendid proofs of courage in the field, that Chlopiki and Skrzynecki fought like heroes, and that Dwernicki, who wished to excite Volhynia to insurrection, astonished the world by his daring retreat upon the Austrian territory? When Diebitsch carried off the victory from the army of Skrzynecki, in the battle of Ostrolenka,
May 26, 1831. Poland, through dissension, party spirit, treachery, and the siren voices of French go-betweens, went rapidly to her downfall. Diebitsch died of the cholera. His successor was the enterprising Paskewitsch (Eriwanski). He crossed the Prussian Vistula and approached the walls of Warsaw. The inhabitants of the capital, believing that the miscarriage of the revolution had been occasioned by treachery, gave the reins to their fury against the aristocrats and friends of the Russians, and slaughtered thirty of these unfortunates. Czartoryski, in whose
August. hands the government had been placed, fled in horror to the camp of Dembinski. Krukowiecki was now named president of the government by the diet, with dictatorial power, and thus the supreme authority was placed in the hands of a man who was either a fool or a traitor. When Paskewitsch approached the capital, the dictator gave evidence of his cowardice and despair by the most contradictory orders and preposterous arrangements. The Polish army made a gallant resistance to the attacks of the enemy at Wola, the ancient place of election of the kings, and the heroic deeds of the fourth regiment have since been
September celebrated in songs; but after a storm of two days, Kruko-
6, 7, 1831. wiecki surrendered Warsaw and Praga by capitulation, whereupon the government and the diet, with the troops that were still left, fled to the Prussian territory. Here the bold warriors were disarmed, and detained till the complete subjection of Poland; they then obtained permission to return, under the assurance of an amnesty. But thousands among them rejected the grace of the emperor, and turned their backs upon their fatherland, preferring to eat the bread of affliction upon free, if foreign ground, rather than to gaze quietly upon the gradual ex-

tinction of the nationality of their country. The sympathy of the German people, who received and entertained the unfortunates in their melancholy journey, was an alleviation of their misery. Severe punishments were inflicted upon the guilty in Poland, Lithuania, Volhynia: the mines of Siberia grew populous with the condemned. Poland then lost her constitution, her diet, and her state council, by the "organic statute," and was attached to the great Muscovite empire, with a separate government and administration of justice. Since then, Paskewitsch reigns as imperial lieutenant, with iron sceptre, in humbled Warsaw. The Poles had once more shown that they were capable of magnanimous, patriotic emotions, and of gallant deeds; but not of a united effort or of noble self-sacrifice. The emigrants, however, in vain attempted, in the sequel, to effect the restoration of their country by conspiracies and insurrections in Cracow, Gallicia, and Posen. Fresh persecutions, and at length, the incorporation of the free state of Cracow with the Austrian empire (1846), were the consequences of their foolhardy attempts.

§ 658. In GERMANY, also, the news of the July revolution called forth a mighty movement. The princes, anxious lest the well-known hankering of the French for the boundary of the Rhine should be the occasion of a new war, saw with uneasiness the existing divisions between subjects and governments, and hastened to allay irritation and prevent a general movement, partly by reasonable concessions, and partly by the hasty recognition of successfully accomplished reforms. The insurrections in the kingdoms of Hanover and Saxony were appeased by granting liberal constitutions, and by abolishing oppressive abuses and restrictions; in Brunswick, where the people destroyed the palace and compelled the tyrannical duke Charles to fly, his brother assumed the government, and conciliated the minds of his subjects by improving the constitution of the country. In Hesse-Cassel, the Elector, William II., was compelled by an insurrection to give the country a free constitution. But
A. D. 1831. the hatred which the people shortly after displayed against the countess Reichenbach (Lessonitz), his wife, a woman of inferior birth, offended the Elector to that degree, that he raised his son, the electoral prince, to the co-regentship, and removed with his wife and treasures from Hesse. The freedom of the press was introduced in Baden, the liberals obtained the upper hand in the Chambers of southern Germany, and insisted upon alterations and reforms in the constitution and government. But their increasing audacity in speech and writing, which was
May 27, 1832. particularly displayed at the Hambacher festival in Rhenish Bavaria, soon brought about a reaction and restriction. The peaceful character of the July monarchy and the fall of Warsaw relieved the German governments from the apprehension that the liberal movements might be supported from abroad; and the incon-
April 3, 1833. siderate attempts of a few young madcaps, students, literary

men, and political refugees, to disperse the Diet, and to produce a violent revolution by the conspiracy of Frankfurt, aided the cause of the retrogressive party. This foolish attempt and its lamentable result gave a deep wound to the cause of liberalism, and brought a severe persecution upon its chiefs and leaders. The guilty and the suspected were visited by numberless arrests and judicial examinations; prisons and fortresses were filled with political offenders; numberless fugitives were wandering in France and Switzerland; the censorship was again employed with the greatest severity; the book trade watched, and the privileges of the Estates circumscribed. Thus again were the efforts of the progressive party frustrated by the violence and indiscreet zeal of some of its champions. The governments obtained the most complete triumph; but by the use they made of it, they outraged the people's sense of justice and insulted public opinion. This was especially the case, when, by the ascension of the throne of England by queen Victoria, the crown of Hanover fell, according to the prerogative of German princes, to her uncle, Ernest Augustus of Cumberland, who abolished the constitution which had been granted by his predecessors to the Estates, and restored the former arrangements. Undeterred by the opposition that was displayed against this arbitrary proceeding from every quarter, the king ordered an oath of obedience and homage to be tendered to all servants of the state; and when seven professors of the Gottingen university, among them, Dahlmann, Gervinus, and the brothers Grimm, would not yield to the demand, they were deprived of their chairs, and some of them banished from the country; when the assembled Estates were incompetent to pass resolutions from a deficiency of numbers, the absentees were replaced by the election of the minority. By these measures, a deep gulf was formed between the people and the government, and a profound dissatisfaction with the "police state" took possession of the nation. The existing government was attacked by means of the press, literature, and poetry, and every opposition to the state officials was saluted by the nation with joy. One single effort was visible in the midst of contests and divisions, and was the "red thread" that ran through the whole public life of the people — the striving after national and political unity; and this effort the Prussian government came forward to assist by establishing the Zollverein, the foundation-stone of German unity.

June, 1837.

July 5.

§ 659. In Italy also, the July revolution occasioned some serious commotions. But the hopes of the patriots found an early grave. The insurrections in Bologna, Modena, and Parma, were soon suppressed by Austrian troops; and the regents, who had been driven from the two latter places, were restored to their governments. In the States of the Church the papal troops, who were reinforced by bandits and convicts, were employed in keeping down the rebellious provinces. These men be-

haved in such a way that it was necessary to call in the forces of Austria to protect the land against its own soldiers. To prevent the Austrians
February, 23, 1832. getting the whole power over Italy into their own hands, the French seized upon Ancona by a *coup de main*, and held it for several years. An attack upon Savoy, from Switzerland, undertaken by a troop of refugees under the command of the Polish general, Ramorino, with the purpose of overthrowing the Sardinian throne, and, in conjunction with "young Italy," of exciting the whole land to a revolution, had a lamentable result.

In Spain, the liberals, after the July revolution, again got the upper hand, not by their own strength, however, but in consequence of a quarrel for the crown. King Ferdinand had allowed himself to be induced by his fourth wife, Maria Christina, to abolish the Salic law which
March 29, 1830. prevails in all Bourbon states, and which excludes females from succeeding to the throne, and thus to secure the in-
October, 1830. heritance of the crown to his daughter, Isabella, who was born in the same year. This alteration displeased the apostolic party, which had placed all its trust on Ferdinand's younger
September 29, 1833. brother, Don Carlos. Scarcely therefore had the king closed his eyes, before the absolutists (Carlists) called Don Carlos to the throne as Charles V., and excited a civil war. They found support in the north, especially among the rude mountaineers of the
October, 1833. Basque provinces. Inflamed by priests and monks, and led by bold and enterprising chiefs (Zumalacarreguy, Cabrera), the warlike Basques drew the sword for an absolute king who sought for refuge among them. For the purpose of resisting them with success, the queen, Maria Christina, who had been appointed to the regency until the majority of her daughter Isabella, sought to win the party of the constitution and the liberals to her cause by again introducing the Cortes constitution, and permitting the fugitives and outlaws to return to their homes. In this manner, the contest for the throne took the shape of a civil war and a struggle of opinions. After many bloody battles,
August 31, 1839. the "Christinos" gained the upper hand. General Espartero compelled the Carlist leader, Maroto, to lay down his arms by the treaty of Pergara, whereupon Don Carlos, with his family and several officers and priests, took refuge in France. In Spain itself, Espartero fell into a quarrel with the queen mother, which produced a fresh crop of party contests, alterations of the constitution, and intrigues of the palace. Espartero, created duke of Vittoria, was
May, 1841. sufficiently powerful to effect the removal of Christina for some time, and to get the government into his own hands. But he was soon overthrown by general Narvaez, an adherent of the queen mother, and compelled to fly to England. After this, Christina, and
July, 1843. her daughter, when she came of age, carried on the government in entire accordance with the wishes of France.

9. OVERTHROW OF THE THRONE OF JULY, AND THE LATEST REVOLUTIONARY TEMPESTS.

a. THE YEARS OF POLITICAL AND SOCIAL AGITATION.

§ 660. FRANCE. — The July monarchy, erected upon the unstable foundation of the sovereignty of the people, was exposed to many attacks. Both the adherents of the Bourbons and of monarchy " by the grace of God" (Legitimists, Carlists), and the republicans, grumbled at the new system, and attempted to overthrow it. It was only the prosperous middle class, which, intent upon gain and the peaceable enjoyment of its earnings, could find its safety and object in a constitutional monarchy, that was content with the government of July; and it was upon this class in especial that Louis Philippe leaned for support. But, as the king neglected to give the less wealthy class of citizens a share of political power by extending the suffrage, the number of his adherents was not great. Neither did the king understand how to win the hearts of the French by greatness of mind and noble actions. In the possession of enormous wealth, he made use of his lofty position for the constant increase of his property, and thereby incurred the reproach of selfishness, avarice, and cupidity. This reproach also attached more or less to his councillors, ministers, and officials, who were accused of covetousness and venality; so that, in the eyes of the people, the stain of " corruption" infected the whole July government. The first hostilities against the citizen throne and the ministry of the "*juste milieu*" proceeded from the legitimists. But the hatred of the people against the Bourbons was
February 15, still too recent for their attempts to be successful. The erec-
1831. tion of the white banner on the anniversary of the death of the duc de Berri excited a disturbance, in consequence of which
November, the archiepiscopal palace was destroyed. Just as little suc-
1832. cess attended the attempt of the duchess of Berri to rouse the faithful Vendéans to arms. When she was arrested and the secret of a private marriage came to light, the romantic magic that had hitherto attached to the royal family gradually melted away. The legitimists, with the grey-haired poet, Chateaubriand, at their head, now gave up the hope of raising to the throne their favorite, the duke of Bordeaux (Chambord), whom they had bedecked with the ostentatious name of Henry V., and retired sullenly into the suburb of St. Germaine.

The undertakings of the republicans were more perilous to the throne
A. D. 1831. of July. After the public insurrections in Lyons and Paris
A. D. 1832. had been suppressed by the military power, and their origi-
A. D. 1834. nators and participators punished, they refrained from any further attempts by open violence, but made constant efforts to increase the

number of their adherents by diffusing their opinions in journals, and by means of secret societies. The "National," conducted by Armand Carrel, and, after his death in a duel, by Marrast, was the much persecuted and much punished organ of their party. But the republicans soon separated in different directions. Whilst the moderate (honest) republicans only sought to attack the existing government, and aimed at revolutionizing the affairs of state, others (like Proudhon) declared property to be robbery, and threatened war to all who were in possession of anything; or (like Louis Blanc) they flattered the self-love and self-respect of the working-classes by an over-estimate of their functions and importance, preached up the equality of capital and labor, and demanded better payment and greater security to the latter from the state. These men sought to revolutionize social relations, and to reduce to practice the systems of Socialism and Communism, devised by a few visionaries and men of perverted intellects. Without any conception of the vast machinery of human intercourse, they applied to society the petty measure of the workshop and the club. Liberty, equality, fraternity, were their watchwords; and hatred to the *bourgeoisie* (shopkeepers, middle class,) the essence of their doctrine. These Communistic and Social ideas spread and increased; shrouded in the veil of the forbidden and the mysterious, they seemed to narrow minds and stunted natures the depth of wisdom, the anchor of salvation from poverty and wretchedness. Influenced by the notion that the French government was only held together by the skill and dexterity of its chief, the members of the secret union sought the life of the king, that they might proclaim a republic in the moment of confusion, and then proceed at once with their social reforms. Eight attempts at assassination were made upon Louis Philippe, from the whole of which he escaped with wonderful good fortune. The most dreadful of these was that made in the Boulevards, on

July 28. the celebration of the July days, 1835, by the Corsican, Fieschi, by means of the so-called infernal machine, by which twenty-one people who were near the king, and, among others, the grey-haired marshal Mortier, lost their lives. Fieschi and his two confederates died by the guillotine; but their death did not deter others from similar attempts. Restrictions of the press, of the privilege of forming unions, and of personal liberty, were the result of each of these designs. It was a hard fate for Louis Philippe that his eldest son, the beloved duke

July 13, 1842. of Orleans, met with his death by a fall from his carriage.

§ 661. In the second half of the fifth decennium, all the States of Europe were powerfully excited by events of varied character. In Italy Pope Pius IX. took the lead of all other princes by his timely reforms, and again made the papacy the political centre of the country. He gave greater freedom to the press, improved the affairs of government and the administration of justice, gave the city of Rome a liberal municipal government, and took preparatory measures for a confederation of the Italian States. A mighty enthusiasm seized upon the excitable Italians, and fresh hopes sprang up in the bosoms of the patriots. Sicily raised

January, 1848. the standard of independence, and commenced a fierce war against its oppressor; the king of Naples sought to appease the threatened insurrection of his subjects by giving them a constitution, and thus obliged the other princes to take a similar step. Archduke Leopold of Tuscany, and Charles Albert of Sardinia, followed his example. The duke of Modena, a zealous defender of the divine right of princes, withdrew himself from the hatred of his people by flight; and

December 18, 1847. in Parma, the throne became vacant by the death of the duchess Maria Louisa, the little-loved and little-respected widow of Napoleon. These events filled the Italians with the hope of national unity and civil freedom. Only two powers, a spiritual and a secular, seemed to stand in the way of this object — the Jesuits and the Austrians. The fiery hate of the Italians was consequently directed against both. Vivas for Gioberti, the enemy of the Jesuits, and "Death to the Germans," against Austria, were mingled with the shouts for Pio Nono.

In Germany, the opposition between the people and the governments had risen to the uttermost. The polite literature of "young Germany;" the stirring poetry of Herwegh, Hoffman Von Fallersleben, and other singers of political freedom; the daring daily press; the freethinking and anti-church writings of young philosophers and theologians; the discourses and doctrines of the "friends of light" in the Protestant Church, and of the "German Catholics" in the Catholic — all these spiritual strivings betrayed the profound discontent of a large portion of the German people with the existing conditions of State and Church, and their aversion to the system retained and defended by the governments. Frederick William IV., who, since 1840, had borne the crown of Prussia, a prince of high accomplishments and active mind, deemed himself obliged to make some concessions to the spirit of the age. He threw open the courts of justice, and permitted oral pleadings; he diminished ecclesiastical

A. D. 1847. restraints by an edict of toleration; and by the patent of the 3d of February, he summoned the "United Estates" to a Diet in Berlin. It was here that, despite all the restrictions contained in the patent, so violent an opposition was displayed, former promises were so emphatically referred to, the righteous claims of a civilized nation to liberty of the press and the other privileges of a free state, were so eloquently urged, that the old system of government appeared no longer tenable. The nation followed with pride the proceedings of an assembly which displayed such splendid powers of oratory and such a fulness of intelligence and judgment. Whilst the educated and wealthy were following with intense interest these inward struggles in the region of Church and State, and looking with anxiety on the disturbances in the trading world, where a succession of bankruptcies had deprived thousands of their property, the cry of famine sounded in the huts of the starving, who, in the increasing dearness of provisions, were unable to supply their necessities. The intelligence of the fearful distress which, in Upper Silesia, had engendered pestilence, and in many trading and manufacturing places had produced scenes of Irish misery, together with the exciting literature in the hands of the lower classes, and the suffering that was everywhere prevalent, produced a vast irritation, which at length burst forth in insurrections in Stuttgardt, Munich, and other towns. It is true that these were suppressed by the military and the police, and the benevolence of the wealthy and an abundant harvest soon put an end to the temporary distress; but the increasing poverty, and the great inequality in property and in the enjoyments of life, were now for the first time revealed in their full extent. Men gazed into the abyss of misery and wretchedness in which the lower classes were found. The irritation and discontent thus excited against the political arrangements, to which the whole of the mischief was ascribed, was increased to the highest pitch by the intelligence that the old king, Louis of Bavaria, had been entangled in the snares of a Spanish dancer, Lola Montez, and had allowed himself to be led by her into acts of folly and enormous extravagance. The ultramontane party, which had ruled the king and the country for years, quarrelled with this courtesan, who had been created countess of Landsfeldt, and suddenly found itself threatened with loss of power. The ministry of Abel and the heads of the ultramontane party in the universities were dismissed. This occasioned a commotion among the Bavarian people; and when the king, indignant that the students attached themselves to the ultramontane party, and did not show the respect he required to the insolent dancer, ordered the university of Munich to be closed, and commanded the students to leave the place, an insurrection broke out, by which Louis found himself obliged to recal the suspension, and to get rid of the countess.

About this time there prevailed a great enmity in SWITZERLAND between the Catholics and Protestants, and the conservatives and radicals. In the Aargau, the radical government had abolished the eight monasteries of the country as "meeting-places of rebellion," and confiscated their property. The protests of the seven Catholic cantons (Schwytz, Uri, Unterwalden, Lucerne, Zug, Freiburg, Valais,) produced no effect at the Diet. The division was increased when the ultramontane government of Lucerne, with the aid of the people of the canton, called in the Jesuits to superintend the education of the youth, and repulsed the radicals, who wished to produce a revolution by means of a volunteer expedition. The contest now resolved itself into a desperate struggle between Jesuitism and radicalism. The seven

March, 1843.

Catholic cantons demanded punishment of the volunteers, and legal protection against similar undertakings, and the restoration of the monasteries of the Aargau; and when their demands were not acceded to, formed a "special confederation" for mutual defence against attacks from within and without. The radicals, who, by means of the "Putsche," had a majority in the Diet at Vaud, Geneva, and other places, procured a resolution which dissolved the special confederation, as incompatible with
July, 1847. the government of the union, and banished the Jesuits. As the members of the special confederation refused submission to the decisions of the Diet, the sword became the arbiter. Contrary to expectation, the struggle was soon over. A confederate army, under
November 4. Dufour, subdued Freiburg and Lucerne with little resistance, whereupon the other cantons freely submitted. They were
December 1. obliged to renounce the Sonderbund, to banish the Jesuits, to alter the cantonal government, and to pay the expenses of the war. When too late, the three great powers, Austria, France, and Prussia, offered their mediation. The French found the Sonderbund already dissolved; and the discovery that the minister, Guizot, took the part of the Jesuits, increased the dissatisfaction in France with the July government. The Swiss took advantage of circumstances to remodel their constitution, and to create a stronger federative government.

b. THE PARIS REVOLUTION OF FEBRUARY AND ITS CONSEQUENCES.

§ 662. About the time that the events in Italy and Switzerland were exciting a strong feeling in France, and the policy of Guizot was giving great offence to the liberals, an action for bribery against General Cubieres and the minister, Teste, and the dreadful murder of the duchess of Praslin in her bed-chamber by her own husband, revealed the total want of morality in the upper classes that were grouped around the throne of July. The feeling that a system of government founded upon such rotten supports could not endure, became more and more prevalent among the nation; and the call for elective reform, by which it hoped to infuse fresh vigor into the Chamber and the government, became the watchword of the day. Reform banquets were arranged in all corners of the land, in which the sins of the existing government were mercilessly exposed in daring speeches and toasts. The government not only prohibited this reform festival, but censure was cast in the speech from the throne on a movement that was excited by blind or hostile passions. Despite the prohibition, the chiefs of the opposition in the Chambers, and some of the leaders of the liberals and moderate republicans, proceeded with their preparations for a reform banquet, and published a programme of the procession and the arrangement of the dinner; when, however, the government adopted military measures to ensure respect to its orders, the greater number of the arrangers of the festival desisted from their purpose, and the members of the Left (opposition) resolved to bring forward a motion in the next session for impeaching the ministry for injuring the constitution.

But the people were already too much excited to be pacified by such a measure as this. Crowds of artisans, men in blouses, students, and the refuse of the streets, paraded through the squares and thoroughfares of the capital, with the cry of "Reform!" and "Down with Guizot!" Their numbers increased from hour to hour; the military acted with forbearance, the police was no match for the multitude; in some streets, barricades were erected and maintained. The contest had continued for two days with increasing bitterness, when the king dismissed
February 22, 23. the ministry of Guizot and promised reform. This news occasioned unspeakable pleasure among the excited populace. The crowds marched through the streets with songs and shouts of joy, the barricades disappeared, and the houses were illuminated. At this point it happened that a troop of people marched through the Boulevards, about ten o'clock, with banners and torches. They halted before the foreign office, and demanded the illumination of the house. At this moment a shot was heard, and occasioned a belief, among the military posted in the building, that they were attacked. A volley was suddenly fired upon the crowd, fifty-two of whom fell to the ground either killed or wounded. An indescribable fury took possession of the people. A bier was covered with dead bodies, and paraded through the streets of the city with torches, in the midst of the cries, "To arms!" "We are slaughtered!" The alarm-bell was sounded at midnight, and by the morning of the 24th of February, the whole of Paris was closed up with barricades. Victory, after a violent contest, inclined to the side of the people. Louis Philippe abdicated in favor of his grandson, the count of Paris, and fled with his wife to England, where the other members of his family also arrived by different ways and after many perils. Hereupon, a republican government was established in Paris, under the presidentship of the old Dupont de l'Eure, and in which the poet Lamartine, Ledru-Rollin, the leader of the Left, Arago, Garnier-Pagès, and the socialist Louis Blanc had a share.

But the new form of government did not bring the anticipated happiness. The intoxication of the republican festival, with its joyous feasts and consecration of banners, and the enthusiasm for the watchwords, "liberty, equality, fraternity," passed away, and sober practical life brought with it many difficulties. As the Revolution was the work of the laboring classes, it was necessary to give some thoughts to their elevation and improvement. National workshops were established, where the unemployed were to find occupation and support. It was now that the utter instability of Socialism became apparent. The expenses of the state rose incredibly, and the number of paupers increased daily. It was soon clear to every one that such a system must, in a short time, lead to the ruin of the state, the impoverishment of those who possessed any thing, and the destruction of civilization. Accordingly, when a constituent National Assembly, elected by the voices of the whole people, met together in May, one of its first measures was to close these shops and to withdraw the assistance of the state from the workmen. Upon this, the workmen attempted a new revolution, for the purpose of giving the supreme power to the fourth estate. This led to the dreadful scenes of June, when the supporters of the "red republic" disgraced themselves by deeds of savage brutality. They murdered general Bréa and the archbishop of Paris, and filled the barricades with the dead bodies of their opponents. Horrified at this barbarity, the National Assembly invested general Cavaignac with dictatorial power. Cavaignac defeated the rebels, had crowds of them arrested and deported, and put Paris under military law. Protected by these measures, the Assembly then completed the republican government with a single Chamber, and a president, who was to be elected every four years. It would willingly have given the majority of votes, also, to general Cavaignac at the election of president; but the people, dazzled by the lustre of the imperial name, chose Louis Bonaparte, the same nephew of Napoleon who had before twice attempted to overthrow the government of Louis Philippe by insurrections, and who had paid the penalty of his folly by long imprisonments.

§ 663. The news of the Paris revolution of February occasioned a violent shock all over Europe. Popular commotions took place in Germany, Hungary, Italy, and other places, which, in extent and violence, far surpassed all previous disturbances. A propaganda, which had its seat and centre in Paris, stirred the revolutionary fire, and diffused republican ideas, with a tincture of Communism and Socialism, as the means of exciting the lower classes. The first effects displayed themselves in Baden. The active political life which has always distinguished the Grand Duchy, appeared to give it the right of marching foremost with the banner of progress and reform. Urgent petitions, tumultuously presented to the Estates of the country just then assembled, demanded freedom of the press, juries, a militia under freely elected leaders, and a German parliament, as a popular house, by the side of the Diet. The Baden government not only granted these demands so far as laid in its power, but even adopted other conciliatory measures. The example of Baden acted upon the other states of Germany. The same demands were gradually made every where, and yielded to, and others joined with them. In Wirtemberg, Saxony, and other states, the heads of the liberal opposition were summoned to the ministry and the reins of government placed in their hands. But the Austrian empire suffered the greatest convulsions. An insurrection in Vienna, occasioned by some students and young rioters, and supported by the rabble, had

March 13.

such unexpected success that prince Metternich laid down his exalted office, and sought refuge as a grey-headed fugitive in England. Upon this the old system was dissolved, and a state of lawlessness took possession of the capital. The freedom of the press soon produced a revolutionary daily literature; the right of assembly was made use of for forming tumultuous mobs and democratic clubs; the great number of unemployed workmen facilitated the schemes of the revolutionary party. Thus it happened, that, by the activity of the democrats, who streamed together into Vienna from all quarters, insurrections and street fights were crowded upon each other. The emperor retired, with his court, to Innspruck; and only returned to his capital when the Diet, which had in the mean time been chosen by universal suffrage, assembled, and required him by pressing messages to resume his seat in Vienna.

May.

July.

Berlin had its March days as well as the imperial city. After long hesitation, the Prussian government at length consented to freedom of the press and other reforms, and held out a prospect of a revolution in the relations of the German confederation. But as hostile encounters had, for several days past, taken place between the military and the people, these concessions did not restore tranquillity; the removal of the troops and the formation of a militia were demanded. Poles and other foreign agitators increased the hatred and excitement by inflammatory discourses. The assemblies in front of the palace increased, and the threats against the soldiery became constantly louder. A division of infantry now marched out of the palace, to drive back the increasing masses. Two shots were fired, by whom or from which party is uncertain. They gave the signal for a desperate street battle of fourteen hours. On the morning of the 19th of March, the contest was yet undecided, although most of the barricades had been taken or destroyed by the courage of the soldiers and by the effects of the grape-shot. The king at length gave command for the retreat of the military, dismissed the ministry, and consented to the formation of a militia for the defence of the city and the guard of the palace. An unconditional amnesty, which was shortly after announced, and which was imitated in the other states of Germany, freed from punishment all those condemned for political crimes or offences, and permitted the return of fugitives; and three days later, the king promised in a proclamation, and during a solemn procession through the city, that he would place himself as constitutional king at the head of a free and united Germany. A constituent National Assembly, elected by universal suffrage, undertook, a few weeks later, the great work of framing a representative constitution for the Prussian monarchy.

March 17.

March 18.

March 21.

§ 664. In the mean time, a mighty revolution had taken place in all the German states. The Diet had experienced an increase of liberal members, and seventeen trustworthy men were commissioned to design a new constitution. March 20. In Bavaria, king Louis gave way before public opinion, and resigned the government to the crown prince, Maximilian: a similar change took place in Hesse-Darmstadt. In Hanover, Hesse-Cassel, and the greater number of states, the often-persecuted leaders of the liberals were now called to the ministry, and reforms were introduced in a democratic spirit and with destructive haste. But the movement soon became so powerful that reforms were no longer sufficient, and, here and there, the path of revolution was entered upon. In some neighborhoods, the peasants drove away the stewards, destroyed the land and tithe registers, and the seats of the landlords. It was not sufficient for the lovers of radical reform that the parliament of Frankfurt-on-the-Main, which assembled by its own authority in the beginning of April, laid down the principle of the sovereignty of the people, and embraced the resolution that a freely elected National Assembly should prepare a new constitution for collective Germany, and that a perpetual committee of fifty should watch over the strict execution of this resolution on the part of the government; a radical party, with Hecker, Struve, and others at its head, called the people to arms in the upper part of Baden, for the purpose of establishing a German republic. The republican arms, however, made little progress. After a few expeditions, in which the union general, Frederick Von Gagern, lost his life, the insurrection was quelled and the leaders obliged to fly.

On the 18th of May, the sittings of the National Assembly, which was to frame a constitution, were opened. The assembly in the church of St. Paul in Frankfurt, distinguished by its talent and eloquence, was a worthy expression of German opinion and civilization. One of the first acts of the Frankfurt parliament was to set aside the Diet, and establish a new central power. After some sharp parliamentary contests, in which the "bold grasp" of the president, Henry Von Gagern, determined the result, it was finally arranged that the National Assembly should choose an irresponsible regent, who was then to surround himself with a responsible ministry. The election, which took place on the 29th of June, was decided in favor of archduke John of Austria, July 11. who, after his entrance into Frankfurt, received from the hands of the president of the Diet the power exercised by that body.

§ 665. Not less violent were the convulsions and mutations produced in Italy by the revolution of February. In Sicily, the war against Naples was continued for upwards of a year with great vigor and perseverance, without, however, the unfortunate island being able to attain its asserted independence. The king of Naples, strong in his mercenary Swiss troops, reduced the Sicilians to submission, and then destroyed by violence the constitutional government in Naples, which he had granted in a moment of necessity.

In Rome, the movement soon became too powerful for the weak Pope, Pius IX., to control. It was in vain that he promised a constitutional government to the Ecclesiastical State, and summoned an assembly of the Estates to the capital. His minister, Rossi, was killed by the thrust of a
November 15, 1848. dagger in the throat on the steps of the House of Assembly, after which the democrats took the whole power into their own hands. The pope, filled with terror, fled in disguise to Gaëta, and
February, 1849. relinquished the eternal city to the populace and the volunteers, who now established the Roman republic and seized upon the property of the church. Mazzini, the energetic chief of Young Italy, and Garibaldi, the daring leader of the volunteers, ruled in Rome. The pope now addressed himself to the protecting powers of the Church, and succeeded so far that a French army, under the command of General Oudinot, marched to the walls of Rome, and demanded the restoration of the former system. When this was refused, the French proceeded to lay siege to the city, but encountered so fierce a resistance, that it was only after weeks of sanguinary attacks and encounters that they got possession
July 3, 1849. of the place. The republicans sought for safety in flight; and the old state of things gradually came back under the protection of bayonets.

In Tuscany, also, the democrats gained the upper hand for a short time, and compelled the Grand Duke to take flight; but the republican government lasted but a few weeks.

The most remarkable revolution in affairs took place in Upper Italy.
March, 1848. In Milan and Venice, the Austrian garrisons were driven out by popular insurrections and street-fights, whereupon the standard of independence was raised throughout the whole of Lombardy. This filled the king, Charles Albert of Sardinia, with the hope of making himself master of the Lombard-Venetian kingdom. He declared war against Austria; and being supported in the first moments of enthusiasm and surprise by numerous Italian volunteers, he drove back the enemy to the northern frontier of Italy. But the state of affairs soon changed. On the 25th of July, field-marshal Radetzky, who was eighty-six years of age, gained a victory at Custozza, which was followed by the reconquest of Milan and the whole of Lombardy. The king of Sardinia fled during the night to his own dominions, and concluded a truce with the victors. Urged on by the democrats, Charles Albert again tried the for-
March 20-24, 1849. tune of arms in the following spring. But the old Radetzky's campaign of four days on the Tessino and near Novara brought the enterprise to a rapid termination, and rendered abortive the hopes of the Italian patriots. Charles Albert, despairing of success, abdicated his throne in favor of his son, Victor Emmanuel, and fled by secret paths from the land of his fathers, till he found a refuge in Portugal, where he shortly after died. The young king then concluded a disadvantageous peace with Austria.

Venice, rendered impregnable by its position, withstood for some months longer the besieging army of Austrians, till dissensions within and sufferings without gave back the renowned city of the
August 25. lagunes to its ancient possessors. Things now everywhere returned to their former state, but the honor of Italy had been redeemed by the struggle.

§ 666. In the mean time, Germany and Hungary experienced still more violent revolutionary storms and convulsions. Whilst the constituent National Assembly was consulting in Frankfurt over the new confederate constitution, a sanguinary national war was going on in Schleswic-Holstein against Denmark. Supported by a good old settlement, according to which the duchies Schleswic-Holstein were to remain united, and to descend as a heritage to the male line of the princely house of Oldenburg only, the sturdy inhabitants of these duchies wished, upon the approaching extinction of the royal family of Denmark, to be united to their German relations under the legitimate and native duke of Augustenburg. This hope the king of Denmark, incited by the strong Danish party, had
July 8, 1846. destroyed by the "public letter," in which he announced the indissoluble connection of Schleswic with Denmark and the undisturbed integrity of the Danish monarchy. When, in consequence of the February revolution, a mighty movement was communicated to all nations, the duchies also thought that they must gain their rights by their own strength. Trusting to the assistance of Germany, which had been promised to them in many addresses, they erected a provisional government till their legitimate position should be secured. The central government of Frankfurt recognized their right, and appointed a lieutenancy. This was the signal for war. The German people interested themselves for the land attacked by the Danes. Volunteers, among whom were many students and promising youths, perilled life and health in the unequal contest; the German confederate troops, under the command of Prussia, cleared Schleswic of the Danes. But the strife was rendered unequal by the want of a German fleet, and the maritime trade of the north suffered much loss and disturbance. This circumstance, and the threatening attitude of Russia and England, operated in favor of the Danes; so that the Prussian government, which had committed the management of the Schleswic-Holstein question to the central authority of Germany, entered into diplomatic negotiations, and concluded the not very creditable truce
August 26, 1848 of Malmö. When this truce, after long and violent opposition, was sanctioned by the National Assembly at Frankfurt, the German republican party, which had long been dissatisfied with the prudent moderation of the parliament, made this decision a pretext for attempting to disperse the assembly in the church of St. Paul by means of an insurrection and street-fight, and then to bring about a revolution and a republic. The project was frustrated by calling in the confederate troops; but the frightful murder of two members of the parliament, Auers

September 18. wald and Lichnowsky, in the Bornheimer wood, by the mob, afforded a fearful proof of the height to which rudeness and barbarism had already risen among the irritated populace.

§ 667. This barbarism shortly afterwards displayed itself in the Austrian empire by two deeds not less horrible. The HUNGARIANS, who had for some time past been excited against Austria by Magyar agitators, strove to obtain national independence. The kingdom of Hungary was to have its own government and a separate political existence, totally independent of the imperial government in Vienna, and to share neither in the military system, the national debt or the finance, tax, or trade legislation of the rest of the empire. These efforts of the Magyars, by which the kingdom of Hungary was to have retained merely a "personal union" with the Austrian empire, were now developed with greater energy, but encountered a vehement resistance, not in Vienna alone, but among the Slavish races, Croats, Slavonians, Servians, &c., which were united with the Magyars in the Hungarian kingdom. Jellachich, Ban of Croatia, took the field against the Magyars; his undertaking met with secret encouragement from the court and ministry. This excited the rage of the Magyars to such a height, that the furious mob put the imperial commissioner, Lamberg, to a frightful death upon the bridge of Buda-Pesth. This deed called forth an imperial war manifesto, in consequence of which a portion of the Austrian army received orders to march upon Hungary. But the Viennese democrats, who saw their own cause in the insurrection in Hungary, prevented the march, and excited a rebellion in the capital that surpassed in violence and importance all that had preceded it. A crowd of people, furious with Latour, the minister of war, who had had communications with Jellachich, forced their way into the war-office and killed the unfortunate man with blows of hammers and thrusts of pikes. This was the commencement of the Vienna October days, the most violent catastrophe of this deeply-moved time. Horrified at the fierce proceedings of the aroused masses, the king again left the capital and retired to Olmütz in Moravia. Thence he issued his commands to prince Windischgrätz, who, a few months before, had displayed his vigor and resolution by the energetic suppression of a Slavish insurrection in Prague, to reduce the insurgent capital to submission. Thus commenced the memorable siege and storm of Vienna. For three weeks, the democrats, who were supported by a licentious press, by clubs, and public speeches, defended themselves against the besieging troops. Volunteers and democratic leaders, united together from all parts in the capital, kept alive the spirit of contest. At length, the military superiority of the army carried off the victory. The town was taken by storm and put under martial law; and the leaders and promoters of the revolutionary movement severely punished. Many found their death from what, in military law, is called "powder and lead." Among these was Robert

October 3, 1848. — October 6. — June.

Blum, a member of the Frankfurt National Assembly, and chief speaker of the "Left." He had taken a share in the struggle; his character as representative of the people could not save him from the iron severity of the general; the German democrats regarded him as the martyr of liberty, and celebrated a general funeral solemnity. The Austrian legislative National Assembly was removed from Vienna to Kremsier in Moravia.

§ 668. These proceedings, and the violent contest that sprang up in Hungary, when Windischgrätz, with the proud consciousness of a victor, led the Austrian army against Pesth, confirmed the majority of the Frankfurt parliament in the persuasion that it would be advantageous, as well for the Germans as the Austrian confederacy, if each were separately to erect its new system of government upon a liberal basis, and then to conclude farther federative relations with a trade and customs legislation common to both. Prussia was to be at the head of the German union. This project found its most decided supporter in the president, Henry Von Gagern, who, for the purpose of carrying out the scheme more effectually, assumed in December the presidentship of the imperial ministry. The plan, however, encountered the greatest opposition from the Austrian delegates, who discovered in it the exclusion of Austria from Germany; from the Catholics, who feared the preponderance of Protestant Prussia; and from the republicans, who saw, in a powerful hereditary monarchy, an insuperable obstacle to the realization of their principles, and who were irritated with the Prussian government on account of the dissolution of the constituent imperial assembly in Berlin. The king of Prussia had long been a witness of the senseless proceedings of the democrats; he had repeatedly changed his ministry in accordance with their wishes, he had offered no impediment to the debates of the Diet where the democratic party was in a majority, he had surrendered the capital to the defence of the militia. But when the presumption of the populace, who were kept in a constant state of fermentation by foreign and native agitators, by placards on the walls, and by public orators, exceeded all bounds; when the popular unions ruled the city; when crowds of noisy rioters surrounded the National Assembly, and exercised an influence upon the course of the debates by intimidation, the king at length resolved to put an end to these proceedings. The new Brandenburg-Manteuffel ministry adjourned the National Assembly, and removed the next sitting to the town of Brandenburg; and when a considerable number of the members refused obedience to the command, and continued their meetings in Berlin, despite the state of war with which the city was threatened, and, at length, when driven out by the military, declared the levying of taxes to be contrary to law, the dissolution took place. At the same time, the government itself proclaimed a constitution upon an extremely liberal basis, which was to be submitted to a new elective assembly with two chambers, for its examination and approval.

November and December, 1848.

§ 669. It was not long before a similar measure followed in Austria. For the purpose of getting a free field, the emperor Ferdinand, who, at the time of the disturbances, had made many promises, had been induced to resign the government as early as December, whereupon his youthful nephew, Francis Joseph, obtained the imperial throne. He dissolved the constituent Diet of Kremsier, in March, 1849, and then proclaimed an "octroyed" * constitution, and a law respecting seignorial rights and the indemnification for feudal dues. Hungary was at the same time to be restrained by fresh exertions of power. But the Austrians encountered a noble resistance from this warlike and hardy equestrian and nomadic people, the Magyars. Excited by the fiery eloquence of Kossuth, and supported by Polish leaders, like Dembinski and Bem, the Hungarians compelled the hostile forces to retreat, captured Buda, and got possession of all the fortresses. Görgey, a brave and able general, was at the head of the forces. The army of the insurgents was strengthened by the native militia (Honveds), and by foreign volunteers; Hungarian bank-notes, prepared by Kossuth, were paid and accepted as money. Full of proud

April 14, 1849.

confidence, the Diet of Debreczin declared Hungary's independence of Austria, and established a provisional government under the direction of Kossuth. It was now discovered in Austria that Windischgrätz had undertaken a task to which he was not equal; he was recalled, and field-marshal Haynau appointed in his place. As the Austrian court was convinced that he could not, with his own forces, suppress the Hungarian insurgents, who were now approaching the frontiers of Austria, it called upon Russia for assistance. The hostile armies now marched into Hungary from three quarters: on the north, Paskewitsch with his Russians; on the west, Haynau with his Austrian troops; and on the south, Jellachich with his Croats. The Hungarian army nevertheless resisted for many months, and Görgey, Klapka, and other brave generals yet gained many a splendid victory. But internal dissensions among the Polish and Magyar leaders, and a division that had arisen between Kossuth and Görgey, paralyzed the strength of the insurgents. Pressed upon on all sides, Görgey, who had been named dictator, laid

August 11, 1849.

down his arms to the Russians at Vilagos, and thus brought about the subjection of the country. Kossuth and many of the insurgent leaders found refuge in Turkey; but who can tell how great was the number of those who died by the sentence of courts martial, or pined away in dungeons, or who served in the baggage and conveyance department of the Austrian army? Görgey has since lived in Carinthia; but the public voice of his nation accuses him of treachery to the cause of his country.

§ 670. Hungary's fall, by the catastrophe of Vilagos, was the close of

* That is, granted by the sovereign, of his own free will, and therefore owing its validity to his authority, instead of being formed and decreed by the people themselves or by their representatives.

the revolutionary movement that had spread over Europe after the Parisian revolution of February. It had reached its termination some time previously in Germany.

In the midst of many contests, the Frankfurt National Assembly had at length accomplished the solution of its task. It had established and made known the "fundamental rights of the German people," and had at last accomplished the formation of an imperial constitution. The Gagern party, which was striving for a German confederacy, with an hereditary emperor, and a legislative assembly divided into a government and popular house, had at last carried their proposal by a small majority, after they had won the support of many members of the Left by accepting a democratic elective law with universal right of suffrage. The new imperial constitution was brought to a conclusion by this

March. "compromise," and the transference of the hereditary dignity of the emperor to the king of Prussia was also carried. A solemn deputation, headed by the worthy president Simson, now conveyed the resolution of the Assembly to the king of Prussia, and made him an offer of the imperial crown, upon condition of his accepting the constitution in all its details. It was a great historical moment when, on the 3d of April, king Frederick William IV. met the deputation in the great hall of his palace in Berlin; the results of this event were looked for with the utmost eagerness by the German nation. But the king first gave an ambiguous answer, and at length decisively rejected the dignity offered him by the people. The deputies of parliament had gone forth, as it were, in triumph; they returned to Frankfurt very like scattered fugitives. When the Prussian Assembly of Estates, which, in the mean time, had been again summoned, voted an address to the throne, in which the acceptance of the imperial office and constitution was recommended as the wish of the nation, the second chamber was dissolved and the first adjourned, and then followed an alteration of the elective

April 27. law, so that, in future, an election arranged upon the three tax-paying classes was to take place of the universal right of suffrage.

§ 671. This rejection of the imperial constitution brought fresh revolutionary storms upon Germany. The democrats, who had hitherto been satisfied neither with the Frankfurt parliament, with the imperial constitution, nor with the "historical sentimentality" of an hereditary emperor, now took advantage of the rejection for again assuming arms. Violent insurrections and sanguinary street-fights took place, for the purpose of "carrying through the imperial constitution;" and even first of all in those states which had opposed its introduction — in Saxony, in the Bavarian Palatinate, and in some parts of Rhenish Prussia. Other states also were soon hurried away by the movement; and when a mutiny broke out among the soldiers in the fortress of Rastadt, in the grand duchy of Baden, where the government had acknowledged the imperial constitution, which extended itself to Carlsruhe, and in consequence of which the grand duke was compelled to take flight, and the government fell into the hands of the democratic and republican party, the revolution had gained a broad foundation. In the Frankfurt National Assembly, also, the Left was constantly gaining power by the opposition of the governments to the work of the constitution; especially when many of the conservative and constitutional party voluntarily resigned their seats, and others yielded obedience to the calls of their governments. In this melancholy position, Germany was saved from ruin by the bravery of the Prussian army. Prussian troops first repressed the isolated outbreaks in Eberfeld, Dusseldorf, and many other places; Prussian troops marched to Dresden, at the call of the Saxon government, and rescued the city, after a barricade-fight of six days, from the hands of the provisional government; lastly, Prussian troops and militia marched into Baden and the Bavarian Palatinate, when the grand duke sought assistance from Berlin, and suppressed the revolution at the moment when it threatened to seize upon the kingdom of Wirtemberg. For whilst these proceedings were taking place, the Frankfurt National Assembly was gradually losing its conservative members, so that, at last, the whole authority devolved upon the men of the Left. These determined to support themselves upon the revolution, and accordingly removed their sittings from Frankfurt to Stuttgart, to be nearer the revolutionary mass. The "Rump Parliament," scarcely a hundred men strong, went over to Wirtemberg, established an "imperial regency" of five members, and gave a weight to the revolutionary movements, till the minister, Römer, a man of firm hand and resolute temper, put a term to their proceedings, and compelled them to leave the kingdom. At the same time, the Prussian soldiers, supported by the imperial forces, marched through the grand duchy of Baden, defeated the revolted troops and volunteers, under the Polish adventurer, Mierolawski, in several engagements, and again restored the old system. Some promoters of the insurrection, and among them the parliamentary member, Trütschler, were shot by the sentence of a court-martial; but the immediate originators and leaders saved themselves by flying to republican countries. Whilst the movement was still raging unsuppressed in the open field, the king of Prussia issued a proclamation to his people, which was calculated to awaken their confidence. He promised to satisfy the longing for German unity by establishing a union with a popular representation; and, shortly after, appeared a new imperial constitution on the basis of the Frankfurt proposal, in the name of the three kingdoms, Prussia, Hanover, and Saxony. The approval with which this proffered gift was received by all the moderate party, and in favor of which a large number of the Frankfurt parliament, assembled in Gotha, (the after parliament), declared themselves, contributed materially to the pacification of the disturbed countries. It was not long, however, before Saxony and Hanover, sup-

June 18.

ported by Austria, retired from the "league of the three kings;" upon which Prussia, who, since swearing to the new constitution on February 6, 1850, has entered into the number of constitutional monarchies, attempted, at the Erfurt Diet, to unite the German States, which still adhered to the league, into a confederacy. But this plan also met with opposition from Austria and the other kingdoms, which required the restoration of the old Diet.

§ 672. Owing to these divisions and parties, affairs in Schleswic-Holstein took a disastrous turn. The contest had begun anew in March, 1849, and the news flew like lightning in the dark night through the country, that German troops had sunk the Danish ship of the line, "Christian VIII.," by means of strand batteries; and that the proud frigate, "Gefion," had been compelled to surrender, after the
April 5. loss of her rudder. The victorious Germans soon marched to Frederica, and laid siege to this frontier fortress. But the activity of the allied troops of Prussia and Germany being paralyzed by the peace negotiations commenced with Denmark, the enemy found an opportunity to reinforce the garrison of Frederica, and afterwards to drive back the German army by an unexpected sally, and to make themselves masters of the trenches and the artillery. A fresh truce was now arranged, in consequence of which, Schleswic was placed
July, 1849. under a neutral government, and garrisoned with German and Swedish troops. This truce became a peace in the following year, by which Schleswic-Holstein was to have resumed its former relations with Denmark. But the lieutenancy, that had been established there during the war by the German central power, would not accede to the peace, and determined, after the retreat of the Prussian garrison, to maintain its right by its own strength, and the voluntary assistance of the German nation.

Conclusion. The revolutionary storms of the years 1848 and 1849 have now reached their termination. These two years were rich in hopes and experiences, in disappointments and griefs. Providence has once more placed the conduct and shaping of affairs in the hands of princes; may they employ this power wisely, and to the benefit of their people, that confidence may be once more restored to the minds of men! For, true as it is, that no political or social arrangement can secure the true happiness of the people, unless a deeper morality and religion, a more active sense of civil and domestic virtue, and a warmer feeling of duty, preëxist in their minds; so true is it also, that states can only prosper and flourish when the public faith between a prince and his people is firmly established, and the confidence in the honest and benevolent intentions of the government is exposed to no disturbance.

CHRONOLOGICAL TABLE.

	B. C.
NIMROD builds Babylon	2100
Ninus builds Nineveh	2000
Abraham flourished	2000
Joseph do.	1800
Sesostris king	1500
Moses flourished	1500
Joshua do.	1450
Trojan war	1184
Samuel flourished	1150
Heraclidæ return to Peloponnesus	1104
Saul flourished	1095
Mœris and Cheops	1080
Codrus, king of Athens, dies	1068
David flourished	1050
Solomon do.	1000
Rehoboam do.	975
Jeroboam do.	971
Sardanapalus destroys himself	888
Lycurgus reforms the Spartan constitution	884
Carthage founded	880
Foundation of Rome	753
Decennial Archons at Athens	752
First Messenian war	743 — 724
Salmaneser flourishes	730
Salmaneser subdues Phœnicia	730
Ten Tribes of Israel removed by Salmaneser (Judah remains 130 years longer.)	722
Sennacherib flourishes	720
Sennacherib besieges Jerusalem, but his army is destroyed	720
Archilochus the poet born at Paros	700
Numa Pompilius king of Rome	700
Second Messenian war	687 — 670
Psammeticus puts down the power of the Egyptian priests by Greek mercenaries	650
Tullus Hostilius king of Rome	650
Ancus Martius do.	625

	B. C.
Draco legislator	624
Nineveh destroyed	605
Nebuchadnezzar begins to reign over Babylon	600
Nebuchadnezzar plunders the temple at Jerusalem, and removes the chief inhabitants	600
Periander reigns in Corinth	600
Sappho the poetess born at Lesbos	600
Alcæus the poet born at Mitylene	600
Tarquinius Priscus king of Rome	600
Nebuchadnezzar's attempt on Tyre fails	590
Judah taken into captivity by Nebuchadnezzar, and remains therein seventy years: Jerusalem destroyed	588
Pythagoras flourishes, born at Samos	584
Astyages the Median king flourished	575
Cyrus the Great do.	560
Pisistratus tyrant of Athens	560
Servius Tullius king of Rome	550
Polycrates tyrant of Samos	550
Babylon taken by the Persians, and Cyrus gives the Jews leave to return home	538
Tarquinius Superbus reigns	from 533 — 509
Cambyses conquers Egypt, and flourishes	from 529 — 521
Hippias and Hipparchus begin to rule at Athens	527
Darius Hystaspes comes to the throne, and reigns	from 521 — 485
The Temple at Jerusalem completed in the reign of Darius	515
Republic established at Athens	510
Abolition of royalty in Rome	509
Oppression of the plebeians by patricians for debt	495
Secession to the Sacred Mount	494
Destruction of Miletus	494
Coriolanus banished from Rome	490
Battle of Marathon } Victories gained by the Greeks over the Persians.	490
Battle at the Pass of Thermopylæ	480
Battle of Salamis	480
Battle of Platæa	479
Banishment of Themistocles for ten years	471
Earthquake at Sparta	465
Ezra and Nehemiah rebuild Jerusalem	460
Cincinnatus taken from the plough to be dictator	458
Ambassadors sent to Græcia Magna and Athens, to collect the laws of Solon and select others	452
Decemvirs appointed	450
Herodotus born	450
Battle of Conorea	447
The peace of Pericles	445
The plebeians obtain a share in the consulate	444
Military tribunals appointed	442
Isocrates flourished	436 — 338

	B. C.
Thucydides born	430
Plato flourished	429 — 348
Death of Pericles by the plague which visited Athens	429
Athenians under Demosthenes capture Pylos	425
The peace of Nicias with Sparta	421
The Athenian expedition against Syracuse	415
Destruction of the Athenian fleet at Ægos Potamos	405
Athens compelled to surrender to the Spartans	404
Xenophon born	400
Socrates dies by poison	399
Antisthenes flourished	396
Veii subdued by Camillus	396
Demosthenes flourished	385 — 332
Peace of Antalcidas (Corinthian War)	387
Death of M. Manlius (Capitolinus)	383
Battle of Leuctra	371
Aristippus flourished	370
Battle of Mantinea	362
Destruction of Sidon	350
War between the Romans and Latins	342
Peace between the Romans and Samnites	340
The Latins are defeated by the patriotism of Decius	338
Battle of Chæronea, liberty of Greece ended	338
Battle of Granicus (Persians defeated)	334
Darius Codomanus defeated at Issus	333
Destruction of Tyre by Alexander	332
Battles of Arbela and Gaugamela	331
Agis II., king of Sparta, defeated at Megalopolis	330
Rupture between the Romans and Samnites	325
Diogenes flourished	324
Alexander the Great dies at Babylon	323
Demosthenes destroys himself	322
Antigonus assumes the chief power after Alexander's death	321
Syracuse besieged by the Carthaginians	317
Antigonus is acknowledged regent of Alexander's empire	316
Æschines flourished	314
The Stoics flourished	312
Battle of Ipsus. Defeat of Antigonus	301
Samnites defeated by the devotion of the younger Decius	295
Samnites acknowledge the supremacy of Rome	290
The Mamentines seize Messina, and devastate Syracuse	289
The translation of the Bible from Hebrew to Greek, called the Septuagint Version	284
Pyrrhus engaged in war with Rome	281
Theocritus the poet flourished	280
Euclid the mathematician flourished in Alexandria	280
Pyrrhus defeated by the Romans at Beneventum	275
Pyrrhus dies before Argos	272

	B. C.
The Romans win their first naval battle at Mylæ	261
The Epicureans flourish	260
Aratus the Sicyon chosen commander-in-chief of the Achæan league	250
The Romans make a successful sally against the Carthaginians from Panormus	242
The Carthaginians, defeated at the Ægatian islands, consent to peace, and give up Sicily	242
Agis III., king of Sparta, flourished	240
Sicily made a Roman province	238
Cleomenes III., king of Sparta, flourished	230
The Cisalpine Gauls make an inroad into Etruria, but are defeated. The Roman province, Gallia Cisalpina, established	222
Defeat of the Spartans by the combined forces of the Achæans and Macedonians at Sellasia	221
Hannibal crosses the Apennines	217
Defeat of the Romans at Cannæ, by Hannibal	216
They successfully engage twice with the Carthaginians	215
Marcellus besieges Syracuse	214
Archimedes the mathematician flourished in Sicily	212
Syracuse, by the aid of Archimedes, holds out three years before it is taken and destroyed	212
The Capuans, deserted by Hannibal, surrender to Rome	211
Hasdrubal crosses the Alps to join Hannibal	208
Philopœmen reduces Sparta and destroys it	207
Hasdrubal is slain, and his army destroyed at the river Metaurus	207
Scipio passes over into Africa	204
Battle of Zama. Defeat of the Carthaginians	202
Philip compelled by the Romans to acknowledge the independence of Greece	197
Perseus defeated at Pydna by Paulus Æmilius	168
Macedonia made a Roman province by Metellus	148
Corinth destroyed by Mummius	146
The Maccabees are governors and high priests of Judea	142 — 135
Numantia taken by the younger Scipio	135
Tib. Gracchus proposes the renewal of the agrarian law	133
His brother, Caius Gracchus, proposes the same after his death	123
The attempts of C. Gracchus utterly defeated	121
The Romans defeated by the Teutones and Cimbri	113
Metellus is sent into Africa against Jugurtha, and retrieves the character of the Roman army	109
C. Marius chosen consul by the people	107
The Teutones are defeated at Aquæ Sextiæ by Marius	102
Marius chosen consul for the sixth time	100
The Social war	90 — 88
Sylla sent against Mithridates (first Mithridatic war)	88
Athens captured. Delphi plundered by Sylla	87
Marius gratifies his revenge: is chosen consul for the seventh time, but dies a few months after	86

	B. C.
The death of Sylla	78
The second Mithridatic war	74 — 65
Pompey puts down the rebels under Sertorius	73
The revolt of the slaves	72
They are defeated by M. Crassus	71
Lucullus defeats Tigranes at Tigranocerta	69
Pompey subdues the Armenians and defeats Mithridates	66
Pompey turns his arms against the pirates in the East	67
The Triumvirate formed (Pompey, Cæsar, Crassus)	60
Cæsar made governor of Gaul	58
Cæsar's wars in Gaul	58 — 50
The last insurrection put down at Alesia, by Cæsar	52
The second civil war at Rome	49, 48
Cæsar advances upon Rome with his army	49
Pompey defeated at Pharsalus: is assassinated in Egypt	48
The hopes of the republicans at Rome and their army destroyed at Thapsus	46
The remnant of Pompey's friends defeated at Munda	45
Cæsar assassinated	44
Second Triumvirate formed (Octavius, Anthony, Lepidus)	43
The republicans defeated at Philippi	42
The victory of Octavius at Actium	31
Egypt becomes a province of the Roman empire	30
Augustus, emperor	B. C. 30 A. D. 14

	A. D.
The Roman legions under Varus defeated by the Germans	9
Augustus dies at Nola	14
Tiberius emperor	14 — 37
Caligula do.	37 — 41
Claudius do.	41 — 54
Nero do.	54 — 68
Galba, Otho, Vitellius, emperors	68 — 70
Vespasian emperor	70 — 79
Jerusalem destroyed by Titus	70
Vespasian succeeded by his son Titus	79 — 81
Domitian emperor	81 — 96
Nerva do.	96 — 98
Trajan do.	98 — 117
Adrian do.	117 — 138
The Jewish nation, as a state, at an end	125
Antoninus Pius emperor	138 — 161
Marcus Aurelius do.	161 — 180
Commodus do.	180 — 192
Pertinax do.	193
Septimius Severus do.	193 — 211
Caracalla do.	211 — 217

	A. D.
Heliogabalus emperor	218 — 222
Alexander Severus do.	222 — 235
Philip the Arab do.	243 — 249
Decius do.	249 — 251
Gallienus do.	259 — 268
Aurelianus do.	270 — 275
Tacitus (descendant of the historian) do.	275, 276
Probus do.	276 — 282
Carus do.	282 — 284
Diocletian do.	284 — 305
Constantine overthrows Maxentius at the Milvian bridge, and takes possession of Rome	312
Constantine becomes sole emperor. He favors the Christians	325
Constantinus emperor	357 — 360
Julian restores the renown of the Roman army in the Netherlands	357
Julian proclaimed emperor Constantius' death	360
Julian reigns as emperor	361 — 363
Jovian do. do.	363, 364
The empire divided { Valens rules over the East	364 — 378
The empire divided { Valentinian I. rules over the West	364 — 395
The Goths devastate Thessaly, Central Greece, and the Peloponnesus: made to retreat by Stilicho	396
Alaric devastates the banks of the Po, but is obliged to retreat	403
Duke Radagais and his barbarous horde defeated by Stilicho	406
Rome besieged, taken, and plundered by Alaric	410
Adolf founds the kingdom of the West Goths in South Gaul	412
Valentinian III. reigned	425 — 455
Clovis defeats the Alemanni at Zulpich	496
Ætius defeats Attila on the Catalaunian plains	451
Attila retreats into Hungary	452
An end is put to the Western Empire of Rome by Odoacer	467
Clovis, king of the Franks, conquers the country between the Seine and Loire	486
Clovis puts to death the chiefs of the Frank tribes	507
Justinian emperor of the Byzantine empire	527 — 565
Amalasanta, Theodoric's daughter, murdered	534
Belisarius defends Rome against the Goths	537
Totila made king of the Goths	540
Tejas made king of the Goths, but slain in a battle with Narses	554
Mohammed flourished	571 — 632
Mohammed's flight from Mecca (Hegira), 16th July	622
Abu Bekir succeeds Mohammed	632 — 634
Omar khalif	634 — 644
Persia becomes subject to the Moslems	634
Alexandria taken by the Mohammedans under Amru	640
Othman succeeds to the khalifate	644 — 656
The Ommiades take the khalifate	660

	A. D.
The Mohammedans carry their arms through Cyprus, Rhodes, Asia Minor, and attack Byzantium	668 — 675
Leo the Isaurian emperor of Byzantium	717 — 741
Charles Martel defeats the Saracens between Tours and Poictiers	732
Constantine Copronymus emperor of Byzantium	741 — 745
The dynasty of the Ommiades overthrown	752
Pepin dies, and divides his kingdom between his sons	768
Charlemagne made sole ruler of the Franks	771
The West Goths overthrown at Xeres de la Frontera by the Arabians	712
Charlemagne takes the fortress of Eresburg, and compels the Saxons to make peace	772
Charles conquers Pavia, and unites Upper Italy to his empire	774
Leo IV. emperor of Byzantium	775 — 780
Charles the second time subdues the Saxons	777
Thassilo, Duke of Bavaria, attempts to throw off the Frank yoke	788
Irene empress of Byzantium	800
Leo the Armenian emperor of Byzantium	813 — 820
Louis the Debonnaire flourished	814 — 840
Egbert abolishes the heptarchy in England	827
The sons of Louis take up arms against him	836
Louis dies near Jugelheim	840
The treaty of partition of Verdun	843
Basilius the Macedonian emperor of Byzantium	867
Alfred the Great flourished	871 — 901
The kingdom in Norway founded by Harold Fairhair; and in Denmark, by Gorm the old	875
Charles the Fat flourished	876 — 887
Arnulf flourished	887 — 898
Charles the Simple flourished	898 — 929
Kingdom formed in Sweden by the Ynglians	900
Conrad I. elected emperor of Germany	911 — 919
Henry the Fowler	916 — 936
He defeats the Hungarians at Merseburg	933
Otho the Great flourished	936 — 973
He puts an end to the depredations of the Hungarians	955
The victory of Otho over the Hungarians on the Lechfield	973
Otho II. emperor of Germany	973 — 983
Otho III. do.	983 — 1002
Hugh Capet king of the Franks	987 — 996
Stephen the Pious king of Hungary	1000
Vladimir the Great emperor of Russia	1000
Canute the Great flourished	1017 — 1035
Conrad II. emperor of Germany	1024 — 1039
Canute the Great of Denmark and Olaf of Norway become Christians	1025
The Moorish dynasty in Spain divided	1038
Henry III. emperor of Germany	1039 — 1056

	A. D.
Edward the Confessor	1041—1066
Robert Guiscard (a Norman noble) becomes master of part of Lower Italy	1060
William the Conqueror overthrows Harold at Hastings . .	1066
Robert Guiscard's son, Bohemond, increases his territory . .	1072
Henry IV. defeats the Saxons at Unstruth	1075
He personally implores the withdrawal of the ban of excommunication at Rome	1077
Gregory deposed, and Clement III. elected Pope	1081
Henry's expedition against pope Gregory	1083
Pope Gregory dies at Salerno	1084
At the Assembly at Clermont, pope Urban II. calls upon Europe to recover Palestine	1085
The first Crusade	1096—1099
A large army under celebrated leaders arrives at Antioch on its way to Jerusalem	1097
They come in sight of Jerusalem	1099
Jerusalem taken by the Crusaders, July 15	1099
The Cid (Campeador) flourished	1099
Henry V. emperor of Germany	1106—1125
Lothaire the Saxon emperor of Germany	1125—1137
Roger II. flourished, and forms the kingdom of Naples and Sicily	1130—1154
Louis VII. king of France	1137—1180
Conrad III. Emperor of Germany	1138—1152
Henry the Proud (House of Guelph) dies	1142
The second Crusade originated by St. Bernard . . .	1149
Grisa II. king of Hungary	1150
Frederick Barbarossa emperor of Germany	1152—1190
Henry II., of Anjou, king of England	1154—1189
Frederick undertakes a second expedition against Milan . .	1158
Death of archbishop Thomas-a-Becket	1170
The Germans, under Frederick, defeated at Legnano . .	1176
Frederick deprives Henry the Lion of his dukedoms . . .	1179
Philip Augustus II. king of France	1180—1223
The Crusaders, defeated at Tiberias, and many towns, together with Jerusalem, taken by Saladin	1187
Richard Lion-heart ascends the English throne	1189, 1190
Henry III. emperor of Germany	1190—1197
The news of the taking of Jerusalem gives rise to the third Crusade	1192
John (Lackland) king of England	1199—1216
Waldemar II., the Conqueror, king of Denmark . . .	1202—1241
The fourth Crusade	1203, 1204
The Cross is preached, by order of the Pope, against Raimond VI. and the Albigenses	1205
Philip of Swabia murdered	1208
Innocent III. renews the war between the Guelphs and Ghibellines	1210

	A. D.
Twenty thousand children leave their homes for the Holy Land	1213
Magna Charta granted	1215
Henry III. king of England	1216—1272
Frederick II. emperor of Germany	1218—1250
The House of Zähringen becomes extinct	1218
Louis VIII. king of France	1223—1226
St. Louis do.	1226—1270
Woldemar, king of Denmark, made prisoner by Henry of Schwerin	1227
Zengis Khan chief of the Moguls, or Tartars	1227
The fifth Crusade undertaken by Frederick II.	1228
Jerusalem and a part of Palestine ceded to him	1229
Charter ("The Golden Bull") obtained by the Hungarians from Andreas II.	1234
Russia made tributary to the Moguls	1237
Pope Gregory IX. dies	1241
The Christians are defeated at Gaza by the Carismians	1244
Henry Raspe, of Thuringia, rival emperor to Frederick II.	1246
Alfonso X. king of Spain	1258—1284
Manfred defeated at Beneventum by treachery	1260
Conradine falls into the hands of Charles of Anjou	1268
Egypt falls into the hands of the Mamelukes	1270
Edward I. king of England	1272—1307
Ottocar, king of Bohemia, defeated at Marchfield	1278
Rudolf of Hapsburg chosen emperor of Germany	1273—1291
The French are slain on the Sicilian vespers Peter of Aragon frees Sicily of Charles of Anjou	1282
Dispute between Bruce and Baliol for the Scottish crown	1283
Philip the Fair king of France	1285—1314
Adolf of Nassau emperor of Germany	1291—1298
The Christians retire from Syria, when the Mamelukes take Antioch	1291
Adolf of Nassau is defeated and slain in the battle at Gollheim	1298
Albert of Austria emperor of Germany	1298—1308
Osman makes Prusa in Bithynia his capital, and carries on war against Greece	1299
Pope Boniface VIII. dies	1303
Pope Clement V. removes his court from Rome to Avignon	1305
Edward II. on the English throne	1307—1327
Henry VII. of Luxemburg emperor of Germany	1308—1313
The persecution of the Templars by Philip the Fair Molay, their Grand Master, tried upon various charges	1310
Henry VII. makes an expedition into Italy	1310
Molay condemned and burnt	1312
Leopold defeated by the Swiss at Morgarten	1315
Vladislaus IV. king of Poland	1320
Frederick the Fair defeated at Mühldorf	1322
Alfonso XI. king of Spain	1324—1340

	A. D.
Death of Leopold, the brother of Frederick the Fair	1326
Edward III. king of England	1327—1377
Philip VI. king of France	1328—1347
Casimir the Great king of Poland	1333—1370
The tax, Alcavala, introduced into Spain	1340
Waldemar III. king of Denmark	1340—1375
Louis the Great (of Anjou) elected king of Hungary	1342—1348
Johanna I. queen of Naples	1343—1382
Louis of Bavaria has a rival for the empire in the son of John of Bohemia	1346
Battle of Cressy (English victorious)	1346
A new republican Rome established	1347
Charles IV. emperor of Germany	1347—1378
John the Good king of France	1347—1364
Charles IV. opened the German University in Prague	1348
Louis of Bavaria lost his life in a bear-hunt near Munich	1349
Peter the Cruel of Spain	1350—1369
The death of Cola di Rienzi, instigator of the rebellion at Rome	1354
Victory of the English at Poictiers	1356
Insurrection in Paris	1358
Calais and the south-west of France ceded to the English	1360
Murad I., chief of the Ottomans, subdues Asia Minor, and passes into Europe	1361—1389
Philip the Bold Duke of Burgundy	1363—1404
Magnus II. deposed from the Swedish throne	1363
John the Good returns to his captivity, and dies	1364
Charles V. king of France	1364—1380
Louis the Great made king of Hungary	1370—1382
Death of the Black Prince } Calais alone left to the English	1377
Richard II. king of England	1377—1399
Wenceslaus emperor of Germany	1378—1400
Charles VI. king of France	1380—1422
Wickliff flourished	1384
Battle of Sempach	1386
The Jagellons retain the crown of Poland	1386—1572
The great cities' war commenced	1388
Bajazet, chief of the Ottomans, continues the victories of his father Murad I.	1389—1403
The three Scandinavian kingdoms under one sceptre by the union of Calmar	1397
Henry IV. (Lancaster) king of England	1399—1413
Zurich, Berne, and Zug join the Swiss Confederation	1399
The electors depose Wenceslaus from the empire of Germany	1400
Rupert of the Palatinate is chosen emperor	1400—1410
The Turks are defeated, and Bajazet made prisoner by the Moguls, under Tamerlane, at Angora	1402

	A. D.
John, Sans Peur, duke of Burgundy	1404—1419
Sigismond emperor of Germany	1410—1437
Henry V. king of England	1413—1422
Council of Constance	1414—1418
Joanna II. queen of Naples	1414—1435
Huss condemned	1415
Victory of the English under Henry V. at Agincourt	1415
Alfonso V. of Spain	1416—1456
Wenceslaus died of apoplexy	1419
Philip the Good, duke of Burgundy	1419—1467
Murad II. restores the Ottoman empire	1421—1451
Death of Henry V. of England, and Charles VI. of France	1422
Henry VI. succeeds to the English throne	1422—1461
Charles VII. to that of France	1422—1461
Cosmo de Medici (Florence)	1428—1464
Joan of Arc delivers Orleans	1429
She is captured by the English and burned	1431
Council of Basle	1431—1449
The Taborites defeated at Prague	1433
Calais remains the only English possession in France	1435
Charles's entry into Paris	1436
Albert II. of Austria, emperor	1437—1439
Frederick III. do.	1440—1493
John Guttenburg of Mayence invents printing	1440
Hungarians and Poles defeated by the Turks at Warna	1444
Casimir IV. on the Polish throne	1447—1492
Christian I. (Oldenburgh) of Denmark	1448—1481
Nicholas V., Pope, founder of the Vatican library	1450—1460
The House of Visconti extinct in Milan	1450
Mohammed II. on the Ottoman throne: he takes Constantinople, and puts an end to the Byzantine empire	1451—1481
Sebastian Brandt, poet of Strasburg, flourished	1458—1521
Matthias Corvinus (son of Huniades) made king	1458—1490
Palgrave Frederick's (the Victorious) victory	1461
Louis XI. on the French throne	1461—1483
Edward IV. (York) king of England	1461—1483
Ivan the Great throws off the Mogul yoke	1462—1505
Alexander Castriota (Scanderbeg) maintains his independence against the Turks	1467
Charles the Bold, duke of Burgundy	1467—1477
Steno Sture, king of Sweden (separated from Denmark)	1471—1504
Lorenzo de' Medici the Magnificent (Florence)	1472—1492
Copernicus, the astronomer, flourished	1473—1543
Isabella queen of Spain	1474—1504
Ariosto the poet flourished	1474—1533
Michael Angelo flourished	1474—1563
Charles of Burgundy defeated at Granson by the Swiss	1476

	A. D.
Maximilian of Austria foiled the attempt of Louis XI. upon the dukedom of Burgundy	1479
Ferdinand king of Spain	1479 — 1516
Raphael the painter flourished	1483 — 1520
Richard III. of England	1483 — 1485
Charles VIII. of France	1483 — 1498
Battle of Bosworth	1485
Henry VII. (House of Tudor) king of England	1485 — 1509
Bartholomew Diaz reaches the Cape of Good Hope	1486
Discovery of America by Columbus	1492
Louis XII. of France	1498 — 1515
Maximilian I. emperor of Germany	1493 — 1519
Hans Sachs, the shoemaker poet, flourished	1494 — 1576
The land-peace established at the Diet of Worms	1495
Cabot explores the coast of North America	1497
The return of the Medici	1498
Maximilian admits the independence of the Swiss	1499
Louis XII. of France conquers Milan	1500
Charles V. of Burgundy	1500
Ferdinand of Aragon gets possession of Naples	1504
Death of Columbus at Valladolid	1506
The League of Cambray, for dividing the Venetian territory	1508
Henry VIII. of England	1509 — 1547
Julius II. the warlike pope	1503
Albuquerque founds a Portuguese colony in India	1510
Balboa discovers the Pacific Ocean	1514
The Portuguese establish colonies and factories in Ceylon and on the Coromandel coast	1515
"Battle of the Giants" of Marignano. Swiss defeated	1515
Luther denies the supremacy of the pope	1519
Leonardo da Vinci flourished	1519
Steno Sture slain; Sweden reunited to Denmark	1520
Soliman the Magnificent on the Ottoman throne	1520 — 1566
Conquest of Mexico by Cortez	1521
Luther's doctrines denounced as heretical, and his writings sentenced to be burned	June 16, 1520
Luther burns the bull of excommunication	Dec. 10, 1520
Slaughter at Stockholm	1520
The Knights of St. John, expelled from Rhodes, receive Malta	1522
Luther establishes peace at Wittemberg	March, 1522
Adrian VI. pope	1522, 1523
Gustavus made king of Sweden by the Diet of Strengnas	1523
Camoens the Portuguese poet	1524 — 1569
The defeat of the French at Pavia	1525
Hungary divided on the death of Louis II. at Mohacs	1526
Macchiavelli, the statesman, flourished	1527
Rome taken by the Spaniards and Germans	May 6, 1527
Gustavus introduced Christianity into his dominions	1527

	A. D.
Andrea Doria frees Genoa of the French	1528
Half of Hungary falls into the power of the Ottomans	1529
Pizarro and Almagro conquer Peru	1529 — 1535
Diet of Spire	1529
The Ladies' peace of Cambray	1529
Charles V. restores the Medici, expelled a second time	1530
The men of Zurich defeated and Zwingle slain	1531
League between the Landgrave of Hesse and Elector of Saxony at Smalcald	1531
Ivan Vasilyevitsch II. the first Czar	1533 — 1588
The Bible completed in German by Luther	1534
Christian III. introduces Christianity into Denmark	1534 — 1539
Contest between Pizarro and Almagro. Discovery of Chili	1535 — 1538
Charles V. captures Tunis	1535
The ten years' truce of Nice	1538
The Reformation established at Leipsic and Dresden	1539
Charles V. sends a second expedition to Africa	1541
Francis I. commences a fourth war against Charles V.	1542 — 1544
The order of the Jesuits founded by Ignatius Loyola	1540
Paul III. pope of Rome	1543 — 1549
Corregio flourished	1543
The peace of Crespy	1544
The crown of Sweden given to the male line of Vasa	1544
Council of Trent opened	Dec. 13, 1545
Death of Luther	Feb. 18, 1546
Fiesco attempts the overthrow of the house of Doria	1547
Henry II. on the French throne	1547 — 1559
Edward VI. of England	1547 — 1553
Cervantes flourished	1547 — 1616
Gasca sent to settle the affairs of Peru	1548
Albert Durer flourished	1548
Maurice of Saxony rises against Charles V.	March, 1552
Lope de Vega, Spanish poet	1552 — 1635
The victory of Maurice over Albert of Brandenburg	1553
Mary Tudor queen of England	1553 — 1558
Lucas Cranach flourished	1553
Paul IV. pope	1555 — 1559
Philip II. of Spain	1556 — 1598
Ferdinand I. emperor of Germany	1556 — 1564
Elizabeth queen of England	1558 — 1603
Peace of Chateau Cambresis	1559
The Heidelberg Catechism drawn up	1559
Pius IV. pope	1559 — 1565
Francis II. on the French throne	1559 — 1560
Death of Melancthon	1560
Erich XIV. king of Sweden	1560 — 1568
Charles IX. king of France	1560 — 1574
Hans Holbein flourished	1563

	A. D.
Shakspeare, the English dramatist	1564—1616
Maximilian II. emperor of Germany	1564—1576
400 nobles petition against the Inquisition in the Netherlands	Nov. 1565
Mary Stuart marries Darnley	1565
Galileo flourished	1565—1631
Death of Soliman at Sigeth (Hungary)	1566
Mary's favourite, Rizzio, murdered	1566
Duke Alba of Spain sent to subdue the Netherlands	1567—1573
Death of Darnley, Mary's husband	Feb. 10, 1567
John III. king of Sweden	1568—1592
Egmont and others put to death in the Netherlands	1568
The Huguenots defeated at St. Denis by the Catholics	1568
Mary Stuart's flight into England	1568
Earls of Northumberland and Westmoreland fail to set Mary at liberty	1569
Henry of Bearn takes the lead of the Huguenots	1570
Kepler flourished	1572—1631
Gregory XIII. pope (arranged the present calendar)	1572—1585
The Northern States of the Netherlands recognize William of Orange as Stadtholder	1572
Louis of Zuniga succeeds Alba in the Netherlands	1573—1576
Henry III. king of France	1574—1589
Don Juan succeeds Zuniga	1576—1578
The Pacification of Ghent	1576
Titian flourished	1576
Rudolf II. emperor of Germany	1576—1612
King Sebastian of Spain defeated by the Moors	1578
Alexander Farnese succeeds Don Juan	1578—1592
The Union of Utrecht	1579
The domination of Spain over Portugal lasts sixty years	1580—1640
William of Orange assassinated	1581
Sixtus V. rose from a shepherd boy to be pope	1585—1590
Execution of Mary Stuart in England	1587
The Invincible Armada sent against England	1588
Henry of Guise creates a rebellion in Paris	May 12, 1588
Henry IV. besieges Paris	1590
John Fischart, poet of Mayence, flourished	1591
Henry IV. becomes a Catholic	1593
Tasso the poet died	1595
Henry allows liberty of conscience to the Calvinists by the Edict of Nantes	1598
First permanent French settlement in America	1607
First settlement of Virginia at Jamestown	1607
Champlain discovers Lake Champlain	1609
Charles IX. king of Sweden	1600—1611
Calderon, Spanish poet	1600—1687
James I. (Stuart) king of England	1603—1625
The Protestant Union in Germany concluded	1608, 1609

	A. D
A truce between the Netherlanders and Spaniards; the independence of the former acknowledged	1609
Henry IV. murdered by Ravaillac	1610
Louis XIII. of France	1610—1643
Matthias on the imperial throne	1612—1619
The Dutch erect some trading posts at the mouth of the Hudson river	1613
Imperial House of Romanoff (Russia)	1613
Death of Matthias	May 20, 1619
Frederick V. of the Palatinate made king of Bohemia	Nov. 1619
First settlement of New England, at Plymouth	Dec. 22, 1620
Ernest of Mansfield defeats Tilly, the imperialist general, at Wiesloch	April, 1622
Richelieu changes the government in France	1624
Charles I. of England	1625—1649
Frederick of Bohemia defeated by Ferdinand II.	Nov. 7, 1625
Ernest of Mansfield and Christian of Brunswick die	1626
Christian IV. defeated by Tilly at Lutter	Aug. 27, 1626
The validity of the Petition of Right acknowledged	1628
Settlement of Salem, in Massachusetts	1628
Duke of Buckingham assassinated	1628
Christian recovers his lands by the peace of Lubeck	1629
The Edict of Restitution published by Ferdinand II.	1629
Pomerania surrendered to Gustavus Adolphus	1630
Settlement of Boston, in Massachusetts	1630
Diet of Leipsic	Feb. 1631
Magdeburg taken by Tilly	May 16, 1631
The imperial army defeated at Leipsic and Breitenfield	Sept. 7, 1631
The victory of the Swedes at Lutzen	Nov. 16, 1632
Alliance of Heilbron (Swedes and Germans)	1633
Settlement of Maryland	1633
Wallenstein, the general of Ferdinand II., murdered	Feb. 25, 1634
The peace of Prague between the German princes and the emperor	1634
Richelieu encourages the Swedes in their undertakings in Germany	1635
Settlement of Hartford, in Connecticut	1636
Saxony and Thuringia conquered by the Swedes	1636
War with the Pequod Indians in Connecticut	1637
Ferdinand III. emperor of Germany	1637—1657
Settlement of New Haven, in Connecticut	1637
Episcopal form of service repelled from Scotland	1637
Rhode Island colonized by Roger Williams	1638
Death of Bernhard of Weimar	1639
Charles I. (Stuart) calls a parliament after eleven years' delay	1640
Formation of the New England Confederacy	1643
Frederick William elector of Brandenburg	1640—1688
Strafford and Laud attainted of high treason	1641

	A. D.
Civil war between Charles and the parliament	1642 — 1646
The Swedes defeat the imperial army at Leipsic	1642
Louis XIV. on the French throne	1643 — 1715
Christina queen of Sweden	1644
Battle of Marston-Moor	July 3, 1644
Contests between the Presbyterians and Independents	Feb. 1645
Charles defeated at Naseby	June 14, 1645
Alexis reduces the Cossacks to subjection	1645 — 1676
Charles delivered prisoner to the parliament	1646
Peace of Westphalia	1647
Cromwell marches upon London to give the Independents the superiority in Parliament	June, 1647
Escape of Charles I.	Nov. 1648
Eighty-one Presbyterians expelled from Parliament	Dec. 1648
War of the Fronde	1648 — 1653
Execution of Charles I.	Jan. 30, 1649
Prince of Wales recalled from Holland, and acknowledged as Charles II. by the Presbyterians	1650
Cromwell's victory over the Scots at Dunbar	1650
The royal army overthrown at Worcester	1651
Navigation act passed in England	1651
Long parliament dissolved by Cromwell	April, 1653
Cromwell dissolves by force his second parliament	Dec. 1653
Mazarin's return to Paris	1653
Christina abdicates in favor of Charles Gustavus	1654
Charles X. of Sweden	1654 — 1660
Battle of Warsaw	July, 1656
Emperor Leopold takes up arms to secure the crown of Spain for his son	1657 — 1705
Cromwell's death	Sept. 3, 1658
Rump parliament restored and dissolved by the army	April, 1659
Charles II. returns as king	May 29, 1660
Casimir, king of the Poles, makes peace with Sweden	1660
Charles XI. of Sweden	1660 — 1697
Death of Mazarin	March 9, 1661
The English wrest New York from the Dutch	1664
Settlement of New Jersey	1665
Spanish war	1667 1668
Louis XIV. compelled to surrender the greater part of his conquests in the Spanish Netherlands	1668
The Austrian government executes the leaders of the insurrection in Hungary	1671
Louis XIV. carries his arms against Holland	1672 — 1679
Marquette and Joliet discover the Mississippi river	1673
Moliere died	1673
Spain and Germany join in the war against France	1674
The Swedes defeated by Frederick William	1675
King Philip's war in New England	1675

	A. D.
Bacon's rebellion ın Virginia	1676
Feodor czar	**1676** — 1682
The peace of Nimeguen	1679
Habeas Corpus act	1679
Strasburg taken from the Germans by Louis XIV.	Sept. 1681
Pennsylvania granted to William Penn	1681
La Salle sails down the Mississippi	1682
The Turks defeated before the walls of Vienna	Sept. 1683
Peter Corneille, French dramatic poet	1684
Peace concluded with France at Regensburg	**Aug. 15,** 1684
James II. ascended the English throne	1685
Revocation of the Edict of Nantes by Louis XIV.	Oct 1685
James II. fled from England	Dec. 1688
Sir Edmund Andros deposed at Boston, Massachusetts	1689
Frederick I. king of Prussia	1688 — 1713
The French take and burn Spire	June, 1689
Montesquieu flourished	1689 — 1755
War of Orleans	1689 — 1697
Peter the Great czar	1689 — 1725
Expeditions fitted out by Massachusetts against Acadie and Quebec	1690
New Charter of Massachusetts	1691
French defeated in the battle of La Hogue	1692
Witches hanged at Salem	1692
Lafontaine died	1694
Voltaire flourished	**1694** — 1778
Death of king John Sobieski of Poland	1696
Frederick Augustus chosen king of Poland	1697
Charles XII. of Sweden	1697 — 1718
Peace of Ryswick	1697
James II. and the Catholic Irish defeated at the Boyne	July, 1690
Peace of Carlowitz	1699
Racine died	1699
Settlement of Louisiana	1699
Death of Charles II. of Spain	1700
Charles of Sweden besieges Copenhagen	1700
Frederick I. solemnly crowned at Königsburg	1700
Anne queen of England	1702 — 1714
General Catinat defeated, and Savoy and Piedmont made allies of Austria by prince Eugene	1701
Charles of Sweden defeats the Prussians near Narva	1701
War of the Spanish succession	1702 — 1714
Surrender of Warsaw to Charles XII.	1702
The revolt of the Tyrolese	1703
Charles XII. deposes Augustus king of Poland	1703
Peter the Great founds St. Petersburg	1703
Bossuet died	1704
Battle of Hochstadt (Blenheim)	**Aug. 13, 1704**

	A. D.
Stanislaus Leczinski elected king of Poland	1704
Capture of Gibraltar by the English	1704
Joseph I. emperor	1705 — 1711
Defeat of the French at Ramilies by Marlborough	May 23, 1706
The French defeated at Turin by prince Eugene	Sept. 7, 1706
Peace of Altranstadt	Sept. 24, 1706
Scottish representatives admitted into parliament	1707
Victory of Almanza	Apr. 25, 1707
Battle of Oudenarde won by Marlborough and prince Eugene	July 11, 1708
Charles XII. makes an expedition against Moscow	1708
Charles's army suffers greatly from the severe winter	1708
The Swedish army defeated at Pultowa	July 8, 1709
Battle of Malplaquet. Defeat of the French	Sept. 11, 1709
Death of Joseph I.	1710
Charles XII. escapes into Turkey	1710
Boileau died	1711
Abortive expedition against Canada, under Walker and Hill	1711
Charles VI. emperor of Germany	1711 — 1740
The army of Peter the Great almost made prisoners on the Pruth by the Turks	1711
Charles XII. arrives before the gates of Stralsund	Oct. 1711
Frederick II. born	Jan. 24, 1712
Rousseau flourished	1712 — 1778
Peace of Utrecht	May 11, 1713
Frederick William I. king of Prussia	1713 — 1740
Peace of Rastadt, between the Germans and French	Mar. 7, 1714
The Spanish Netherlands, Milan, Naples, and Sicily, given to Austria. The electors of Bavaria and Cologne restored to their lands and titles	Sept. 1714
Death of Louis XIV.	Sept. 1, 1714
George I. of England	1714 — 1727
Archbishop Fénélon died	1715
Louis XV. of France	1715 — 1774
Philip of Orleans regent	1715 — 1723
James (III.) Stuart attempts to gain the throne	1715 — 1717
Stralsund surrendered to the Prussians	Dec. 1715
Insurrection in Thorn against the Jesuits	1717
Winkelmann flourished	1717 — 1768
Charles XII. killed before Friederichstadt	Dec. 11, 1718
Execution of Baron de Görz	1719
Sweden surrenders nearly all her foreign possessions	1719, 1720
Alexis condemned to death by Peter the Great, his father	1722
Klopstock the poet	1724 — 1803
Kant the philosopher	1724 — 1804
Catherine I. empress of Russia	1725 — 1727
George II. of England	1727 — 1760
Peter II. emperor of Russia	1727 — 1730
Lessing flourished	1729 — 1781

	A. D.
Anna empress of Russia	1730—1740
Georgia founded by general Oglethorpe	1732
The Polish war of succession	1733
Frederick Augustus III. king of Poland	1733—1763
Wieland lived	1733—1813
Frederick II. marries into the House of Brunswick	1734
Francis Stephen exchanges Lorraine for Tuscany	1737
Charles VI. concludes the peace of Belgrade	Sept. 18, 1739
Frederick II. ascends the Prussian throne	1740
He makes an expedition into Silesia	Oct. 1740
First Silesian war	1740—1742
Battle of Molwitz. Victory of the Prussians	April 10, 1741
Elizabeth empress of Russia	1741—1762
Charles Albert crowned king of Bavaria at Prague	Oct. 1741
He is elected emperor of Germany, and reigns	1741—1745
His capital, Munich, taken by the enemy	Jan. 24, 1742
Peace of Breslaw	July 28, 1742
Maria Theresa crowned at Prague	1743
French defeated at the battle of Dettingen	June 27, 1743
Second Silesian war	1744, 1745
Herder	1744—1803
Death of Charles VII. at Munich	Jan. 20, 1745
Treaty of Füssen	April, 1745
Victory of Frederick II. at Hohenfriedberg	June 4, 1745
Battle of Kesseldorf. Frederick marches to Dresden. Silesia ceded to him in the peace of Dresden	Dec. 25, 1745
Francis I. emperor of Germany	1745—1765
Victories of the French at Fontenoy and Laffeld	1745—1747
Charles Edward the Pretender lands in Scotland	1745
Capture of Louisburg, on Cape Breton, by troops from Massachusetts	1745
Ferdinand VI. king of Spain	1746—1759
Defeat of the Pretender at Culloden	April 16, 1746
Peace of Aix la Chapelle with the French	1748
Goethe flourished	1749—1832
Joseph Emmanuel king of Portugal	1750—1777
Alliance between Maria Theresa and the French king against the king of Prussia	Sept. 1751
Braddock's defeat by the French and Indians	1755
Earthquake in Lisbon	Nov. 1755
The French driven into exile from Acadie	1755
Frederick of Prussia falls suddenly on Saxony	1756
He marches against Bohemia	1757
He is victorious at the battle of Prague	May 6, 1757
He is defeated at Collin	June 18, 1757
The French defeat his allies at Hastenbeck	July, 1757
He gains a splendid victory at Rosbach	Nov. 5, 1757
He defeats Daun at the battle of Beuthen	Dec. 1757

	A. D.
Capture of Fort William Henry by Montcalm	1757
Adolf Frederick of Sweden	1757 — 1771
Unsuccessful attack on Ticonderoga, by Abercrombie	1758
Frederick of Prussia receives support from England	1758
His victory at Zorndorf	Aug. 25, 1758
He is worsted at Hochkirk	Oct. 14, 1758
He is defeated by the Austrians at Kunersdorf	Aug. 12, 1759
Ferdinand defeats the French at Minden	April 13, 1759
Schiller flourished	1759 — 1805
The Jesuits expelled from Portugal	1759
Battle of Quebec and death of Wolfe	1759
Charles III. of Spain	1759 — 1788
Ferdinand defeats Laudon and regains Silesia	Aug. 15, 1760
George III. king of England	1760 — 1820
Ferdinand obtains the dearly-bought victory of Torgau	Nov. 3, 1760
Elizabeth, empress of Russia, dies	Jan. 5, 1762
Peter III., emperor of Russia, murdered	July 9, 1762
Catherine II. of Russia	1762 — 1796
Frederick concludes the peace of Hubertsburg	Feb. 21, 1763
The English obtain Canada by the peace of Paris	1763
Death of Augustus III. of Poland	1763
War with the Indians, usually called Pontiac's war	1764
Poniatowski chosen king of Poland	Sept. 1764 — 1795
Passage of the Stamp Act for taxing America	1765
Joseph II. ascends the imperial throne of Germany	1765 — 1790
Stamp Act Congress at New York	October, 1765
Repeal of the Stamp Act	March, 1766
Christian VII. of Denmark	1766 — 1808
The General Confederation of Radovi formed	July 23, 1767
The Confederation of Bar, in Poland, defeated	Feb. 1768
The war between Russia and Turkey	1768 — 1774
Affray with the soldiers at Boston	March 5, 1770
Gustavus III. comes to the throne of Sweden	1771 — 1791
Moscow visited by pestilence, and civil war in Poland	1771
Louis XV. orders his opponents in the parliament to be arrested	1771
Neckar's first ministry	1771 — 1781
The treaty of partition of Poland between Russia, Austria, and Prussia	Aug. 5, 1772
The abolition of the Order of Jesuits	1773
Destruction of the Tea in Boston harbor	1773
The English increase their forces, and shut up the harbor of Boston	1774
A Congress of the American Colonies meet at Philadelphia	Sept. 17, 1774
Rebellion of Pugatscheff, a Don Cossack	1774
Louis XV. of France dies	1774
Battle of Lexington, in Massachusetts	April 19, 1775
Battle of Bunker's Hill	June 17, 1775
Juliana, stepmother of Christian, directs the Danish government	1775

	A. D.
Montgomery killed in an attack on Quebec	Dec. 31, 1775
Pugatscheff is betrayed and suffers death	1775
The British troops evacuate Boston	March 17, 1776
Turgot and Malasherbes (ministers) reorganize France	1776
The Declaration of Independence adopted by the American Congress	July 4, 1776
Battle of Long Island and defeat of the Americans	Aug. 27, 1776
Battle of Trenton	Dec. 25, 1776
Battle of Bennington	Aug. 16, 1777
Battle of Brandywine	Sept. 11, 1777
Battle of Germantown	Oct. 4, 1777
Burgoyne's army capitulates at Saratoga	Oct. 15, 1777
The Bavarian war of succession	1778 — 1779
The French form an alliance with America	Feb. 6, 1778
Battle of Monmouth	June 28, 1778
Spain forms an alliance with America	June 26, 1779
The French and Americans repulsed at Savannah	Oct. 9, 1779
Gen. Lincoln capitulates at Charleston	May 12, 1780
Gates defeated by Cornwallis at Camden	Aug. 16, 1780
England declares war against Holland	Nov. 1780
Joseph II. of Austria	1780 — 1790
Battle of Guilford Court House	March 15, 1781
Neckar obliged to resign his office	1781
Cornwallis surrenders to the French American army	Oct. 19, 1782
The attempt of the Spaniards to take Gibraltar foiled	Sept. 1782
The independence of America acknowledged by the English in the peace of Versailles	Nov. 30, 1782
Nicolai of Berlin	1783 — 1811
Crimea conquered by Potemkin	1783
A democratic insurrection in Holland	1784
Joseph II. offers the Austrian Netherlands in exchange for Bavaria	1785
Shays's rebellion in Massachusetts	1786
Frederick William II. restores order in Holland	1787
The Netherlanders expel the Austrians	1787
Second Turkish war	1787 — 1792
Calonne calls an Assembly of Notables	Feb. 1787
The boldest speakers against taxation in the parliament of Paris are arrested and banished to Troyes	Aug. 1787
Gustavus III. wages war with Russia	1788
Brienne compelled to resign his ministry	Aug. 1788
Neckar's second ministry	1788, 1789
The Estates summoned	Dec. 1788
Oczakow stormed by Potemkin	Dec. 17, 1788
The Federal Constitution of the United States of America goes into effect	March 4, 1789
George Washington, President of the United States	1789 — 1797
The Third Estate declares itself a National Assembly	June 17, 1789
The Hall of Assembly closed	June 20, 1789

	A. D.
Mirabeau opposes the dissolution of the Assembly	June 27, 1789
Storming of the Bastille	July 14, 1789
The equality of citizens declared	Aug. 4, 1789
Gustavus meditates war with France	1790
The Netherlands declare their independence	1790
Death of Joseph II.	Feb. 20, 1790
Leopold II. of Austria	1790 — 1792
The fortress of Ismail stormed by Suwaroff	Dec. 22, 1790
Feast of the Federation at Paris	July 14, 1790
Prince Potemkin, favorite of Catherine II., died	1791
The death of Mirabeau	Apr. 2, 1791
The Poles reorganize their government	May 3, 1791
Louis attempts to escape from Paris	June 21, 1791
The Russian party in Poland form the Confederation of Targowicz	Jan. 1792
Gustavus is murdered by Ankerström	Mar. 29, 1792
France declares war against Austria and Prussia	April, 1792
A Russian army advances into Poland	May, 1792
Kosciuzko defeated by the Russians	July 17, 1792
The assault on the Hôtel de Ville	Aug. 10, 1792
The Prussians defeated at Valmy	Sept. 20, 1792
Republicanism established in France	Sept. 21, 1792
Custines obtains possession of Mayence	Oct. 21, 1792
Battle of Jemappes	Nov. 6, 1792
New partition of Poland between Russia and Prussia	1793
Condemnation of Louis	Jan. 17, 1793
His execution	Jan. 21, 1793
Dumourier defeated by the Austrians at Neerwinden	Mar. 18, 1793
Chalier, the demagogue, executed at Lyons	July 16, 1793
The Dutch and Hanoverians defeated at Handschooten	Sept. 8, 1793
Trial and execution of Marie Antoinette	Oct. 1793
The French, under Hoche, defeated at Kaiserslautern	Nov. 1793
Insurrection of the Poles under Kosciuzko	Apr. 1794
Execution of Danton and Desmoulins	Apr. 5, 1794
Execution of Elizabeth, sister of Louis XVI.	May 10, 1794
Jourdain compels the evacuation of Belgium	June 26, 1794
The Jacobins denounced in the Convention	July 27, 1794
Execution of Robespierre, St. Just, Couthon, Henriot, and other Jacobins,	July 28, 1794
Defeat of Kosciuzko	Oct. 10, 1794
The French compel the Prussians to retreat	Oct. 1794
Poland divided between Austria, Prussia, and Russia	Jan. 1795
The Convention surrounded by the Mob	Mar. 31, Ap. 1, 1795
Peace of Basle	Apr. 5, 1795
The insurrection of the 1st Prairial	May 20, 1795
The Austrians get possession of Heidelberg	Sept 24, 1795
The Royalist party suppressed	Oct. 5, 1795
Bonaparte defeats Beaulieu at Milesimo and Montenotte	1796

	A. D.
Bonaparte's victory at the Bridge of Lodi	May 10, 1796
Wurmser defeated at Castiglione	Aug. 5, 1796
Jourdain defeated at Wurzburg	Sept. 3, 1796
Retreat of Moreau through the Black Forest	Sept. 19, 1796
Peace concluded between the Germans and French	Oct. 24, 1796
French victories at Arcola, Rivoli, La Favorita	Jan., Feb. 1797
Pope Pius VI. concludes the peace of Tolentino	Feb. 19, 1797
Austria concludes the peace of Leoben with Bonaparte	Apr. 18, 1797
The royalist deputies arrested at the Tuileries	Sept. 4, 1797
The peace of Campo-Formio	Oct. 17, 1797
Bonaparte opens the congress at Rastadt	Dec. 1797
Pius VI. deprived of his temporal power	Feb. 1798
Mamelukes defeated by Bonaparte near the Pyramids	July 21, 1798
Insurrection at Cairo against the French	Oct. 21, 1798
Rome retaken from the Neapolitans	Nov. 1798
The Parthenopeian republic established at Naples	Jan. 1799
Bonaparte marches against Syria	Feb. 1799
He besieges Jean d'Acre, but is repulsed	Mar. 20, 1799
French defeated at Stockach by Archduke Charles	Mar. 25, 1799
The French ambassadors assaulted on leaving Rastadt	Apr. 28, 1799
The Russians conquer the Cisalpine republic	June, 1799
Cardinal Ruffo storms Naples	June 13, 1799
Bonaparte defeats the Turks at Aboukir	July 25, 1799
Pope Pius VI. dies in Paris	Aug. 1799
French defeated at the battle of Novi	Aug. 5, 1799
Russians defeated by the French at Zurich	Sept. 25, 26, 1799
The Duke of York's retreat from the Netherlands	Oct. 1799
Bonaparte returns to France	Oct. 9, 1799
He forms a new constitution in France, and takes the direction of affairs into his own hands	Nov. 9, 1799
Victory of Kleber at Heliopolis	Mar. 20, 1800
Death of Suwaroff	May, 1800
Napoleon's passage of the Great St. Bernard	May, 1800
The Austrians defeated at Montebello	June 9, 1800
The rout of the Austrians at Marengo	June 14, 1800
March of Macdonald and Moncey over the Grisons	July, 1800
Defeat of the Austrians at Hohenlinden	Dec. 3, 1800
Attempt to kill Bonaparte by the infernal machine	Dec. 24, 1800
Peace of Luneville	Feb. 9, 1801
Battle of Canopus in Egypt. Death of Abercrombie	Mar. 21, 1801
The French clergy made subject to the Pope	April 8, 1801
Alexander, son of Paul, declared emperor of Russia	May 24, 1801
The Concordat concluded with Rome	July 15, 1801
The French conveyed by the English from Egypt	Sept. 1801
Peace of Amiens	Mar. 27, 1802
Bonaparte made consul for life	Aug. 2, 1802
The Imperial Diet (Germany)	Feb. 25, 1803
The cantons in Switzerland are made independent	Feb. 1803

47

	A. D.
War declared by the English against the French	May 18, 1803
Bonaparte's troops advance upon Hanover	May, 1803
Execution of the Duke d'Enghien	Mar. 21, 1804
Napoleon proclaimed emperor	May 18, 1804
Republicanism in Italy changed into monarchy	March, 1805
The Austrian general, Mack, shut up in Ulm	Oct. 14, 1805
The capitulation of Ulm	Oct. 20, 1805
Battle of Trafalgar. Death of Nelson	Oct. 21, 1805
Napoleon defeats the Russians at Dirnstein	Nov. 1805
Murat enters Vienna	Nov. 13, 1805
Victory of Napoleon at Austerlitz	Dec. 2, 1805
The peace of Presburg	Dec. 26, 1805
The dynasty of the Bourbons ceases in Naples	Dec. 27, 1805
Death of Pitt	1806
Palm, bookseller of Nuremberg, suffers death	Aug. 26, 1806
The Prussians defeated at Saalfield by the French	Oct. 10, 1806
The double battle of Jena and Auerstadt	Oct. 14, 1806
Hohenlohe and 17,000 men surrender at Prenzlow	Oct. 28, 1806
Napoleon makes peace with the Elector of Saxony	Dec. 1806
Battle of Eylau between the French and Russians	Feb. 8, 1807
Dantzic surrendered to marshal Lefebvre	May 24, 1807
Napoleon abolishes the tribunate	1807
Peace of Tilsit concluded	June 7 – 9, 1807
Bombardment of Copenhagen. Capture of the Danish fleet by the English	Sept. 2 – 5, 1807
The flight of the Lisbon court to the Brazils. Junot takes possession of Lisbon	Nov. 1807
Godoy delivers Spain to Napoleon	Feb. 1, 1808
Charles IV. abdicates the throne of Spain	March, 1808
1,200 French killed in the insurrection at Madrid	May 2, 1808
Napoleon names his brother Joseph king of Spain	June 6, 1808
The Spaniards driven back at Rio Seco by Bessiéres	July 14, 1808
Dupont's capitulation at Baylen, in Andalusia	July 22, 1808
Capitulation of Cintra	Aug. 30, 1808
Meeting at Erfurt of Alexander and Napoleon	Sept. 27, 1808
Napoleon enters Madrid, and restores Joseph	Dec. 4, 1808
Saragossa taken by the French	Feb. 20, 1809
Gustavus IV. deprived of the crown of Sweden	Mar. 13, 1809
Austria sends an army into Bavaria and Italy	1809
It is defeated at Abensberg and Eckmuhl	April 20 – 22, 1809
The two days' combat at Aspern and Eslingen	May 21, 22, 1809
Napoleon destroys the temporal power of the pope	May 27, 1809
Major Von Schill falls during the assault of Stralsund	May 31, 1809
Pope Pius VII. taken from Rome by violence	June 16, 1809
The Austrians defeated at Wagram	July 5, 6, 1809
Napoleon unites the States of the Church to the French territory	July 6, 1809
The Austrians conclude the truce of Znaym	July 12, 1809
The French defeated by Wellington at Talavera	July 26, 1809

	A. D
Death of Sir John Moore at Corunna	July 28, 1809
The attempted assassination of Napoleon by Staps	Oct. 12, 1809
Napoleon divorced from Josephine	Dec. 15, 1809
Hofer, the Tyrolese, shot at Mantua	Feb. 18, 1810
Napoleon annexes Hamburg, Bremen, Lubeck, and the duchy of Oldenburg to the French empire	July 9, 1810
Bernadotte declared successor to the Swedish throne	Aug. 21, 1810
Birth of a son (the king of Rome) to Napoleon	Mar. 20, 1812
The French cross the Niemen, and enter Wilna	July 16, 1812
Wellington defeats Marmont at Salamanca	July 22, 1812
The battle of Smolensk fought	Aug. 17, 1812
The French gain the battle of the Borodino	Sept. 7, 1812
The French army enters Moscow	Sept. 14, 1812
The battle of Malo-Jaroslowetz	Oct. 24, 1812
The passage of the Beresina	Nov. 26 – 29, 1812
Prussia forms an alliance with Russia	Feb. 3, 1813
The French victorious at Lützen and Bautzen	May 2 and 20, 1813
The English gain the battle of Vittoria	June 21, 1813
Austria negotiates at the congress of Prague	July 12, 1813
Austria declares war against France	Aug. 12, 1813
The Prusso-Swedish army victorious in the battles of Gros-Beeren and Dennewitz	Aug. 23 and Sept. 6, 1813
Napoleon wins the battle of Dresden	Aug. 26, 27, 1813
Macdonald defeated on the Katzbach, in Silesia	Aug. 26, 1813
Vandamme and his whole army surrounded and made prisoners at Culm	Aug. 29, 30, 1813
The allied armies unite in the plain of Leipsic	Oct. 8, 1813
The French defeated at the battle of Leipsic	Oct. 16, 18, 1813
Victory gained by the French at Hanau	Oct. 30, 31, 1813
Blucher crosses the Rhine	Jan. 1, 1814
Norway given to Sweden by the peace of Kiel	Jan. 14, 1814
The armies of Blucher and Schwarzenberg meet in Champagne, and gain the battle of Brienne	Feb. 1, 1814
Napoleon obtains the victory of Montereau	Feb. 18, 1814
Blucher gains fresh advantages over the French at Craonne and Laon	Mar. 7 and 9, 1814
Negotiations between the allies and Napoleon broken off, and his dethronement resolved on	Mar. 20, 21, 1814
The allies enter Paris	Mar. 31, 1814
Napoleon resolves to abdicate in favor of his son	April 4, 1814
He signs an unconditional act of abdication	April 7, 1814
Soult defeated by Wellington at Toulouse	April 10, 1814
Napoleon lands at Elba	May 4, 1814
Ferdinand restores unlimited monarchy in Spain	May 10, 1814
First peace of Paris concluded	May 30, 1814
Louis XVIII. placed on the French throne	May 30, 1814
Napoleon lands on the south coast of France	Mar. 1, 1815
Grenoble opens her gates to him	Mar. 20, 1815

	A. D.
Murat defeated in the battle of Tolentino	May 23, 1815
The French compel the Prussians to retreat at Ligny	June 16, 1815
Battle of Waterloo	June 18, 1815
Napoleon resigns in favor of Napoleon II.	June 22, 1815
Paris surrendered to Wellington and Blucher	July 8, 1815
Alexander of Russia, Francis of Austria, and Frederick William III. of Prussia form the Holy Alliance	Sept. 25, 1815
Napoleon arrives at St. Helena	Oct. 18, 1815
Second peace of Paris arranged	Nov. 20, 1815
Democratic display at the festival of the Wartburg	Oct. 18, 1817
James Munroe, President of the United States	1817 — 1825
George Sand assassinates Kotzebue	Mar. 23, 1819
Sand is executed	Sept. 1819
Riots at Manchester suppressed by the military	1819
Insurrection of the soldiers at Cadiz	Jan. 1, 1820
George IV. king of England	1820 —1830
Assassination of the duc de Berri by Louvel	Feb. 13, 1820
Dismission of the moderate ministry of Decaze	March, 1820
Ferdinand of Spain obliged to summon the Cortes and swear to the constitution	Mar. 7, 1820
Pepe and Carascosa, with the insurgents, enter Naples	July 13, 1820
George IV. attempts to divorce his wife	1820
The Holy Alliance suppresses the liberal movement	Jan. 1821
Missouri admitted into the Union by a compromise on the subject of slavery	1821
John VI. returns to Lisbon, and swears to a new constitution for Portugal and Brazil	Jan. 26, 1821
A revolution in Piedmont. Victor Emmanuel abdicates	March, 1821
Greece rises in arms	March, 1821
The Piedmontese liberals resist at Novara	April, 1821
Napoleon Bonaparte died	May 5, 1821
The sacred band of the Greeks destroyed by the Turks in Wallachia	June 19, 1821
Queen Caroline (of England) died	Aug. 7, 1821
Lord Castlereagh committed suicide	Aug. 12, 1822
The Holy Alliance requires the Spanish Cortes to alter the constitution	Oct. 1822
A French army, under the duke of Angoulême, crosses the Pyrenees	Feb. 1823
They appear before Cadiz	Aug. 5, 1823
Ferdinand VII. replaced on the Spanish throne	Nov. 7, 1823
Byron dies in Greece	April 19, 1824
Don Miguel is banished from Portugal	April, 1824
Gen. Lafayette visits the United States	1824
Louis XVIII. dies	Sept. 16, 1824
John Quincy Adams, President of the United States	1825 — 1829
Count of Artois becomes king of France, as Charles X.	May 29, 1825
Emperor Alexander dies	Dec 1, 1825

	A. D.
John VI. of Portugal dies	Mar. 10, 1826
Missolonghi taken	April 22, 1826
The destruction of the Janissaries at Constantinople	June, 1826
Canning, prime minister of England, dies	Aug. 8, 1827
Battle of Navarino	Oct. 20, 1827
Don Miguel is proclaimed king of Portugal	June, 1828
Irish Catholics admitted to parliament	1829
Gen. Andrew Jackson, President of the United States	1829 — 1837
Capo d'Istria appointed President of the Greek States	July, 1829
The French Chambers dissolved	Aug. 8, 1829
The Russians surmount the Balkan	Sept. 14, 1829
William IV. on the English throne	1830 — 1837
Frederick of Spain abolishes the Salic law	Mar. 29, 1830
Algiers taken by the French	July 5, 1830
The Revolution of July broke out	July 26, 1830
Louis Philippe appointed regent	July 29, 1830
Louis Philippe king of the French	1830 — 1847
A conspiracy against Russia breaks out in Poland	1830
Isabella, daughter of Frederick of Spain, born	Oct. 1830
Antwerp bombarded by the Dutch general, Chassé	Nov. 1830
A free constitution given to Hesse Cassel	1831
A Russian army of 200,000 men marches into Poland	Jan. 25, 1831
A disturbance excited in Paris on the day of the duc de Berri's death, by the raising of the white flag	Feb. 15, 1831
The Reform Bill passed	Mar. 1, 1831
Insurrections in Paris and Lyons suppressed	1831, 1832, 1834
Battle of Ostrolenka	May 26, 1831
Belgium separated from Holland	June, 1831
Thirty friends of the Russians murdered at Warsaw. Czartoryski flies to the camp of Dembinski	Aug. 1831
Warsaw and Praga surrender	Sept. 6, 7, 1831
Don Pedro compels Don Miguel to renounce the Portuguese crown, and leave the country	1832 — 1834
The French seize on Ancona, and keep it several years	Feb. 23, 1832
Otho elected king of Greece	May, 1832
The Hambacher Festival, in Rhenish Bavaria	May 27, 1832
The duchess of Berri unsuccessful in raising Vendée	Nov. 1832
South Carolina attempts to nullify a law of the United States	Nov. 19, 1832
Holland desists from the contest with Belgium	Dec. 1832
The German liberals attempt to disperse the diet	April 3, 1833
Frederick VII. of Spain dies	Sept. 29, 1833
The Basques, led by Zumalacarreguy and Cabrera, rise in favor of Don Carlos	Oct. 1833
Twenty-one persons lose their lives by the attempt of Fieschi to murder Louis Philippe	July 28, 1835
Slave Emancipation Bill passed	Aug. 1835
Charles X. dies at Görz	1836
Martin Van Buren. President of the United States	1837 — 1841

	A. D.
Ernest Augustus becomes king of Hanover	1837
Victoria ascends the British throne	June 20, 1837
The old constitution of Hanover restored	July, 1837
The Carlist leader, Maroto, lays down his arms	Aug. 31, 1839
Frederick William IV. king of Prussia	1840
Queen Victoria marries prince Albert of Saxe Coburg,	Feb. 10, 1840
Gen. W. H. Harrison, President of the United States. His death	April 4, 1841
Espartero effects the removal of Christina from Spain	May, 1841
The English corn laws relaxed	1842
Duke of Orleans killed by an accident	July 13, 1842
Treaty of Washington, negotiated by Mr. Webster and Lord Ashburton, settles the north-eastern boundary of the United States	Aug. 1842
The Greeks drive away the Bavarians	1843
Switzerland disturbed by a struggle between Jesuitism and Radicalism	March, 1843
Espartero being overthrown, Christina and her daughter carry on the Spanish government	July, 1843
Annexation of Texas to the United States	March, 1845
James K. Polk, President of the United States	1845 — 1849
War between Mexico and the United States	April, 1846
Gen. Taylor defeats the Mexican army at Palo Alto and Resaca de la Palma	May 8, 9, 1846
The king of Denmark destroys the hope of the Schleswic-Holsteiners of being united to Germany	July 8, 1846
Oregon Treaty with Great Britain settles the northwestern boundary of the United States	July, 1846
Capture of Monterey and defeat of the Mexicans by Gen. Taylor	Sept. 21, 23, 1846
Battle of El Paso; Mexicans defeated by Col. Doniphan	Dec. 25, 1846
Frederick William IV. makes some concessions to the Prussians	1847
Battle of Buena Vista; Santa Anna with 22,000 men defeated by Gen. Taylor with 5,000	Feb. 23, 1847
Battle of Sacramento; Col. Doniphan defeats the Mexicans	Feb. 28, 1847
Vera Cruz surrendered to Gen. Scott	Mar. 29, 1847
Mexicans defeated at Cerro Gordo by Gen. Scott	April 18, 1847
The Swiss radicals dissolve the Sonderbund	July, 1847
Battles of Contreras and Churubusco; Mexican army defeated with great slaughter	Aug. 20, 1847
Bloody battle of Molino del Rey; Mexicans defeated by Gen. Worth	Sept. 8, 1847
Chapultepec stormed and the city of Mexico taken by assault by the American army under Gen. Scott	Sept 12, 14, 1847
A confederate army subdues Freiburg and Lucerne	Nov. 4, 1847
The other cantons obliged to submit	Dec. 1, 1847
Death of the duchess Maria Louisa	Dec. 18, 1847
Sicily revolts from the king of Naples	Jan. 1848

	A. D.
Louis Philippe dismisses Guizot, and promises reform . .	Feb. 22, 23, 1848
Louis Philippe abdicates in favor of the Count of Paris. A republican government formed	Feb. 24, 1848
An insurrection in Vienna causes Metternich to resign . .	Mar. 13, 1848
The Prussian government consents to freedom of the press, and other reforms	Mar. 17, 1848
Disturbances in Berlin	Mar. 18, 1848
King Louis resigns the crown of Bavaria	Mar. 20, 1848
After an undecided street-fight of fourteen hours, the king of Prussia grants an unconditional amnesty . . .	Mar. 21, 1848
The Austrian garrisons in Milan and Venice expelled by popular insurrections	March, 1848
The emperor of Austria and his court retire to Innspruck . .	May, 1848
Treaty of Guadaloupe Hidalgo, making peace between Mexico and the United States	May 30, 1848
The emperor returns on the invitation of the Austrian Diet .	July, 1848
Archduke John of Austria is elected regent of Germany, and enters Frankfurt	July 11, 1848
Radetzky gains a victory at Custozza	July 25, 1848
The truce of Malmö concluded by Prussia	Aug. 26, 1848
The German republicans attempt in vain to disperse the National Assembly, and bring about a revolution and republic . .	Sept. 18, 1848
The Magyar mob, enraged at Jellachich taking the field against Hungary, murder Lamberg at Buda-Pesth	Oct. 3, 1848
Latour murdered at Vienna	Oct. 6, 1848
Rossi, the pope's minister, murdered	Nov. 15, 1848
Francis Joseph becomes emperor of Austria	Dec. 2, 1848
A liberal constitution granted in Prussia	Dec. 5, 1848
The pope flies to Gaëta. A republic is established in Rome .	Feb. 1849
Charles Albert takes up arms for the Italians, but is soon defeated by Radetzky	March 20 – 24, 1849
The dignity of emperor of Germany offered to the king of Prussia	March, 1849
A Danish line-of-battle ship and frigate destroyed by the Germans at Eckernford	April 5, 1849
The Diet declares Hungary to be independent of Austria, and appoints a provisional government	April 14, 1849
The dissolution of the second, and prorogation of the first, chamber of the German Assembly	April 27, 1849
Prince Windischgratz sent to reduce Vienna	June, 1849
The minister, Römer, puts a stop to the revolutionists, and compels them to leave Germany	June 18, 1849
A truce completed between Schleswic and Denmark	July, 1849
The French, after a fierce resistance, enter Rome	July 3, 1849
Görgey surrenders to the Russians at Villagos	Aug. 11, 1849
Venice retaken by the Austrians	Aug. 25, 1849

THE END.

www.ingramcontent.com/pod-product-compliance
Lightning Source LLC
LaVergne TN
LVHW021231110826
845150LV00002B/304